D1258411

TWAYNE'S FILMMAKERS SERIES

Frank Beaver, Editor

INGMAR BERGMAN: THE ART OF CONFESSION

Ingmar Bergman

INGMAR
BERGMAN:
THE ART OF
CONFESSION

Hubert I. Cohen

TWAYNE PUBLISHERS • NEW YORK
MAXWELL MACMILLAN CANADA • TORONTO
MAXWELL MACMILLAN INTERNATIONAL •
NEW YORK • OXFORD • SINGAPORE • SYDNEY

Twayne's Filmmakers Series

Ingmar Bergman: The Art of Confession
Herbert I. Cohen

Twayne Publishers   Maxwell Macmillan Canada, Inc.
Macmillan Publishing Company   1200 Eglinton Avenue East
866 Third Avenue   Suite 200
New York, New York 10022   Don Mills, Ontario M3C 3N1

Library of Congress Cataloging-in-Publication Data
Cohen, Hubert I., 1930–
    Ingmar Bergman : the art of confession / Hubert I. Cohen.
        p.   cm. — (Twayne's filmmakers series)
    Includes bibliographical references (p.), filmography, and index.
    ISBN 0-8057-9312-7. — ISBN 0-8057-9331-3 (pbk.)
    1. Bergman, Ingmar, 1918–   —Criticism and interpretation.
I. Title.   II. Series.
    PN1998.3.B47C64   1993
    791.43'0233'092—dc20   93-9506
                                                                            CIP

The paper used in this publication meets the minimum requirements of American
National Standard for Information Sciences—Permanence of Paper for Printed
Library Materials. ANSI Z3948–1984. ∞™

10 9 8 7 6 5 4 3 2 1 (hc)
10 9 8 7 6 5 4 3 2 1 (pb)

Printed in the United States of America

To My Mother

CONTENTS

FOREWORD

Of all the contemporary arts, the motion picture is particularly timely and diverse as a popular culture enterprise. This lively art form cleverly combines storytelling with photography to achieve what has been a quintessential twentieth-century phenomenon. Individual as well as national and cultural interests have made the medium an unusually varied one for artistic expression and analysis. Films have been exploited for commercial gain, for political purposes, for experimentation, and for self-exploration. The various responses to the motion picture have given rise to different labels for both the fun and the seriousness with which this art form has been received, ranging from "the movies" to "cinema." These labels hint at both the theoretical and sociological parameters of the film medium.

A collective art, the motion picture has nevertheless allowed individual genius to flourish in all its artistic and technical areas: directing, screenwriting, cinematography, acting, editing. The medium also encompasses many genres beyond the narrative film, including documentary, animated, and avant-garde expression. The range and diversity of motion pictures suggest rich opportunities for appreciation and for study.

The Twayne Filmmakers Series examines the full panorama of motion picture history and art. Many studies are auteur-oriented and elucidate the work of individual directors whose ideas and cinematic styles make them authors of their films. Other studies examine film movements and genres or analyze cinema from a national perspective. The series seeks to illuminate all the many aspects of film for the film student, the scholar, and the general reader.

Frank Beaver

PREFACE

FILMS AS CONFESSIONALS

Jean Renoir observed that every film auteur tells and retells essentially one story, his own. Ingmar Bergman is the quintessential auteur-confessor. No other director has so frequently used his own life as the central subject matter of his works. One reason is that his films satisfy his unceasing narcissistic need for attention; he even admits "that reading about myself is a kind of narcissism."[1] Of course, his films are more than just disguised autobiography. At their best they are also compelling, uncompromising stories that illuminate their audience's experience. But confession is the most insistent motivation for what he produces, confession inextricably meshed with his witting need to explore and exploit his past—the source of his stories. Tracing Bergman's use of Bergman, paying special attention to his almost pathological narcissism, will be the primary focus of this study.

Bergman has a reputation for being publicity-shy and almost impossible to interview,[2] but as this book's bibliography reveals, Bergman has talked about himself and his ideas in print or before a camera more than any other filmmaker. Besides feeding his narcissistic needs and advertising his films—consider the effect on box-office and critical response to his announcement beforehand that *Fanny and Alexander* (1982) would be his last film—he seemed early on to sense that there is an advantage in getting critics to focus on the man behind the films. Furthermore—and this intention may have been less than deliberate, though not unconscious—he may have sensed that by making each new film seem partly a chapter in his continuing autobiography, he could perhaps establish the terms on which interviewers would regard and analyze it. He could shape in the public's mind his view of his life, the view he was already dramatizing in his plays and films. Take, for example, this exchange between Bergman and Charles Thomas Samuels, in which Bergman momentarily detours the conversation from the abstract to his own wounded personality. "Isn't it true that whereas you are frequently concerned with the impossibility of attaining corroboration for one's faith, in *Winter Light* [1963] you show that the search for corroboration is itself the cause of harm?" asked Samuels. "All the time that I treated the questions of God and ultimate faith," replied Bergman, "I felt very unhappy. When I left them behind, and also abandoned my desire to make the best film in the world . . . I became unneurotic" (Kaminsky, 106–7). Interviews, in fact, form one whole phase of Bergman's output, supplementing and complementing his films. As just suggested, many of the interviews he has granted were in conjunction with the openings of his plays and films. During his tenure as a theatrical director in some of Sweden's major cities he learned that self-promotion is linked to commercial success. The bibliography also lists the remarkable number of program notes he has written to launch the plays he staged and the films he directed. After 1956, by which time his films had attracted international attention, he continued to make himself available for interviews, cannily exploiting the public's perennial interest in celebrities and their new fascination with how films—whose significance as art his films probably more than any of his contemporaries' were criticial in helping to establish—achieved their effects and meaning. He thus gave his person a currency that few other filmmakers have ever enjoyed.

For fame, profit, and/or catharsis, artists have always exposed the experiences that shaped their personalities and influenced their art. Until very recently, however, directors of film—as much a business as an artistic venture—have considered it unseemly to disclose their most intimate selves. In this regard, as in many others, Bergman is atypical. It is true that before and since Bergman directors such as Eric von Stroheim, Orson Welles, Alfred Hitchcock, Werner Herzog, and Woody Allen have successfully created and tailored images of themselves that vie with their works. But none has seemed as driven as Bergman to talk about the raw details of his family and personal life.

Why, one naturally wonders, is he so willing to talk about himself, and why does he seem to relish divulging his "wounds, . . tensions, . . [and] problems"?[3] Bergman offers two reasons: first, his audience has a legitimate claim on that part of his private life that illuminates the genesis of his art; and second, he hopes "people might recognize [in his films and plays] . . . something of their own [wounds, tensions, and problems]" (Weinraub, 17 October 1976, 15). His friend and colleague Vilgot Sjöman believes that Bergman's motives for candidly exposing his feelings are generally less altruistic.

What Bergman gains from these confessions, says Sjöman, is another "outlet for his egocentricity," another opportunity to feed his self-esteem by showing "that of his own accord he can lay bare his worst traits," and, "to crown it all," to then reap praise "for his honesty."[4] Sjöman also observes that when Bergman speaks or writes he "likes the forceful, the drastic, anything that shows up well." (Sjöman, 157). The truth of what Sjöman says will be demonstrated in this book. Bergman is indeed cunning. On occasion he has refused to talk about those personal matters that bear on his art. In one instance, after first warning his readers that he is going to censor what he tells about himself, he proceeds to seduce them with the impossibility of so limiting himself: "I thought I would take you on a guided tour of my internal studios [his most intimate recesses] where, invisibly, my films take form. . . . The lighting is rather bad in certain spots and on the door of certain rooms you will find the word 'Private' written in large letters. . . . Whatever the case may be, we will open a few doors a crack. . . . Let's open up for a moment the most secret of these rooms."[5]

This is not to say that there are not doors marked "Private" that he keeps closed. Until the publication of his autobiography, *The Magic Lantern* (1987), he usually shied away from discussing his several wives and mistresses. Late in his parents' lives, he tried to be circumspect with regard to their feelings. Vilgot Sjöman said that Bergman asked him to eliminate a line from the manuscript of *L 136* that Bergman feared would pain his father should he read it.[6] And those who watched the television talk-show host Dick Cavett interview Bergman caught Bergman editing his picture of his past. When Cavett asked him if he would "object to being analyzed by a psychiatrist," Bergman answered that he had gone to a psychiatrist sometime around 1956, but that after the third visit the psychiatrist pronounced him "extremely healthy." Later in the show, the actress Bibi Andersson, Bergman's colleague and lover at the time of these visits, joined the interview and pointed out to Bergman that actually the psychiatrist "had said that you were so full of neuroses that if he took them away, you would probably stop making pictures." Bergman responded first with his famous explosive laugh and the denial "I can't remember that," and then, in a slightly more serious tone, with "I think she is lying." Realizing that she had opened much too wide a door she had not noticed was labeled "Private," Andersson attempted to mollify him: "But I didn't say that the psychiatrist was right, I just said that that was what he said."[7] Bergman's being caught by millions of viewers in an act of deception might have come from one of his own films. He delights in exposing "the contradiction between [a character's] mask and [his or her] real face" (Weinraub, 17 October 1976, 15).

In the 1960s some critics attacked Bergman's films as too limited precisely because they focused almost exclusively on his own problems and concerns. In *Visionen i svensk film* (Vision in the Swedish Cinema) (1962), a study that was "instrumental" in shaping Swedish criticism, Bo Widerberg, likening Bergman to "a souvenir peddler selling Nordic brooding, metaphysical angst, and alienation to the world," argued that Bergman should make his films more realistic.[8] As an artist of international stature, some contended, he had a responsibility to deal with social and political issues. Though he defended his choice of subject matter,[9] Bergman seemed to respond by making *Shame* (1968) which deals with an imaginary war fought on Swedish soil. On viewing this film one quickly realizes, however, that the war is just another setting for his characters once again to act out his problems. (Later, he would do the same in *The Serpent's Egg* [1977], which is set in pre-Nazi Germany.) If this realization teaches us anything it is that, in the words of Bergman's friend Harry Schein, "one has to accept [Bergman] for what he is."[10] In my examination of Bergman's films I have tried to do just this.

Before we look at Bergman's life and hear his confessions—his films—a few words about my method of treating the films are in order.

"DESCRIPTION IS REVELATION"

Bergman's having made or scripted over 50 films forces some difficult choices, especially since, as Robin Wood has aptly noted, Bergman's most minor films often tell us a great deal both about what he is trying to say and about himself.[11] Faced with the practical reality of not being able to deal at length with so many films, I have chosen to deal with virtually all the films—and for the most part to do so chronologically—but to treat Bergman's apprentice films differently from his mature films. Chapter 1 is biographical; pertinent biographical material, however, as well as brief accounts of how each film came about, are presented throughout the book. Chapter 2 treats Bergman's apprentice plays and films, synthesizing his developing themes and categorizing the signs of his developing artistry. In chapter 3, which contains discussions of Bergman's mature films, and chapter 4 a different method is employed; with few exceptions, this method is employed in the rest of the book.

What the reader will find full-blown in chapter 4 may at first appear to be no more than scene-by-scene recapitulations of each film. But these recountings are far more than mere plot summaries of each film. They are my interpretations. And into these interpretive narratives I weave other sorts of information. After having identified Bergman's themes, character types, motifs, narrative and structural patterns, and the significant artistic and technical devices he uses and reuses, I trace their development from film to film. In the process I also insert pertinent biographical information and, most important, offer my understanding of the motivation and psychology of Bergman's subtly presented, complex characters. Finally, drawing on over three decades of viewing and teaching these films, I weave into the narrative my own responses and those of audiences to certain moments in the films. My critical method, then, is eclectic, a combination of auteur, "new critical," audience response, and phenomenological approaches.

Besides being able to cover all the elements just mentioned, my narrative approach makes it possible to treat the film narratives as events taking place in time, and thus to call attention to the importance of pacing in our ongoing experience of a film. I try to convey a film's impact as well as the method by which that impact—emotional as well as cognitive—is achieved. In the process of telling the reader what to think and consider, I can try to make the reader see, hear, and feel what the audience in the movie theater is experiencing. By making the critical experience dramatic and immediate, by retaining the context that makes the details important, I hope to more naturally marry interpretation and analysis and to avoid divorcing the evidence for my interpretations from the context of the film's drama. The aim is neither to turn the films into short stories nor to have the descriptive and analytical recapitulations stand in for the filmic experience, but to reproduce and retain as much of each film's richness, and as many of its resonances, as possible, an effect that more abstract, stripped-down types of analysis rarely achieve. For example, to focus merely on a film's themes or reduce its characters to their psychoanalytical core, or Bergman's, without involving the texture, the dramatic, pictorial, aural, and rhythmic techniques by which the themes are presented and the characters developed, is to deprive the reader of many of the riches of the dramatic, narrative experience, riches that I hope to suggest through description. "Description," to paraphrase Wallace Stevens, can be "revelation." But the overriding aim of this approach is—as it has to be—to help the reader to understand what he or she has seen and heard in the movie theater, in Bergman's films.

This analytical-narrative approach offers other advantages. Bergman frequently begins and ends his films with the same settings and with virtually the same shots, a tactic that calls attention to the fact that many of his protagonists undergo nearly imperceptible changes over the course of a film. Take, for example, the first and last, almost identical close-ups of Susanne in *Dreams* (1955). On first viewing, the impact and meaning of the first close-up is one-dimensional. When we encounter almost the same close-up in the last seconds of the film the impact is three-dimensional because we have witnessed the process of Susanne's alienation from the man she loves. The more holistic approach that I am essaying traces and evokes this incremental alteration, whereas a summary statement about the pain and hope that Susanne is hiding behind her masklike face is apt not to recall what we feel after having gone through the experience with her. Nor does it necessarily convey the sense of closure that comes from experiencing the second close-up as part of a framing device. The analytical-narrative approach also makes it easier to call attention to what Bergman is emphasizing when he uses parallel cutting (the climax of *Autumn Sonata* [1978], for instance), and for the audience to experience the dramatic irony he often employs—Antonius Block's unwitting confession to Death in *The Seventh Seal* (1957), for example.

The analytical-narrative method also permits me to weave in the subtle details of lighting, sound, music, cinematography, and composition that create important meaning(s) and emotional impact: the almost invisible tear that Agda sheds as she refuses to take back her husband (*Sawdust and Tinsel* [1953]), or the composition that makes the soon to be cuckolded Fredrik appear to be wearing horns (*Smiles of a Summer Night* [1955]). The analytical-narrative approach also preserves a sense of a film's texture and mode. Consider what is lost when a reader is told only that Antonius Block encounters Death personified. By reducing this visually unforgettable, three-dimensional character to an abstraction, we lose not only the feelings of terror, intrigue, and amusement that he provokes but the three-dimensional character of the allegory that distinguishes *The Seventh Seal*. Or take the wonderful moment in *Smiles of a Summer Night* when old Mrs. Armfeldt's wine, which acts as a truth serum, affects her guests. To merely be told that Mrs. Armfeldt serves her guests a mysterious wine that opens them to the painfulness of love inadequately conveys the mesmerizing, delicious mood—infused with the presence of the supernatural—that we participate in.

Over the years Bergman developed his own symbols, as well as verbal, gestural, and stylistic codes, that interested viewers, even after seeing a film two or three times, may still not note. The analytical-narrative approach permits me to illuminate these signature gestures and words and to meld their meanings into my interpretations. The reader's understanding of the films is also enhanced by being able to hear conversations that convey the characters' (or the director's) ideas. Following extended conversations also permits the reader to sense the chemistry between the characters, as well as to luxuriate in their wit or their viciousness. Furthermore, this approach enables me to point out autobiographical details that are relevant to the action and that clarify meaning, as well as speeches, shots, and techniques that Bergman has borrowed from his other films or from the films, plays, and stories of others. Likewise, this approach makes it possible for me to weave in illuminating comments by Bergman and his colleagues about a film's characters, plot, and artistic technique and to indicate significant differences between the screenplays and the films.

The reader will find that my studies of Bergman's films emphasize explication and interpretation more than judgment. Film criticism is especially difficult because film is such a complex and fast-moving medium. A truism too often ignored is that one must know precisely what happens in a film before interpreting or judging it. Too many reviewers and critics do not get clear on what literally happens in the film they are writing about, and as a result, they miss important elements and distort the film's meaning.[12] To cite a few examples from Bergman's films, critics have claimed that at the end of *Monika* (1953) Harry regards his infant daughter—whom one critic misnames—as a burden he will foist off on others; that in *The Seventh Seal* the silent girl speaks before her climactic one-and-only line in the film; that in *The Virgin Spring* (1960) Töre promises to build God a church "to atone for his negligence toward [his murdered daughter] Karin"; and that in *Autumn Sonata* Eva's spastic sister is catatonic. As the reader will discover, not only are none of these assertions true, but they seriously distort the meaning of these films. Even in the recent *Fanny and Alexander* many critics have failed to recognize or credit the miracles that occur. Remembering that Bergman often influences the terms on which his films are approached, it may be that critics inadvertently accept his emphasis and thus neglect important details. My primary goal is to make clear what actually is said, done, and shown in Bergman's films, and what (I think) Bergman intends. Then readers can judge whether or not they like his films.

I have written this book for several audiences: for those whom Vincent Canby calls the "interested, but uncommitted filmgoer"; for the "indefatigable Bergman cryptologist"; and for those who have sampled a few Bergman films and may want to better understand them and their author. Some may read this book from cover to cover. Others, if for no other reason than that they have not seen—and may never see—a number of the films treated herein, will skip to the films they are studying or are interested in. Some readers, however, may read about the films they have not seen precisely to determine which of them they want to see. Whatever one's reasons for proceeding past this preface, I hope that my analyses will make the Bergman films one sees and reads about, or reads about and then sets out to see, a more complex and rewarding experience. The years I have spent studying this masterful artist's films have done precisely that for me.

ACKNOWLEDGMENTS

Before anyone else I must thank my friend Jonathan Marwil for his unwavering encouragement, his untiring, incisive structural suggestions, and the extraordinary amount of time he took out of his busy schedule to edit my prose. Without his help I am not sure just how this book would have turned out. I also want to thank my wife, Ellen, for her patience during this long project. I am indebted, too, to John Cantú for assisting me in checking the page proofs, and, at Twayne, to Frank Beaver for recommending my book, to my editor Mark Zadrozny for his patience and especially for not letting my oversized study be "emasculated," to managing editor Lesley Poliner for being so careful and responsive, to copy editor Cindy Buck for her exceptionally keen eye, and to Sam Flores for possibly being the world's most erudite and appreciative proofreader.

In some instances to make a point I used material that was in the screenplay but not in the film. Therefore I want to acknowledge the publishers of the following screenplays: Pantheon Books' editions (translated by Alan Blair) of *Autumn Sonata* (1979), *Face to Face* (1976), *Fanny and Alexander* (1982), *From the Life of the Marionettes* (1980), *Scenes from a Marriage* (1974), and *The Serpent's Egg* (1978), Simon and Schuster's *Four Screenplays by Ingmar Bergman* (1960; translated by Lars Malmström and David Kushner); Grossman Publisher's *Persona and Shame* (1972; translated by Keith Bradfield); Orion Press' *A Film Trilogy* (1967; translated by Paul B. Austin); Doubleday/Anchor Press' *Four Stories by Ingmar Bergman* (1977; translated by Alan Blair), and Randolph Goodman and Leif Sjöberg's translation of *Wood Painting: A Morality Play* in the *Tulane Drama Review* (1961). I also want to thank the following for their permission to quote: from *The Magic Lantern* by Ingmar Berman. Copyright © 1988 by Joan Tate. Orig. Copyright © 1987 by Ingmar Bergman. Used by permission of Viking Penguin, a division of Penguin Books USA Inc.; from Vilgot Sjöman's *L 136: Diary with Ingmar Bergman* 1978, Karoma Publishers, Inc.; from *Bergman on Bergman* edited by Stig Björkman, Torsten

CHRONOLOGY

1914	Dag Bergman (brother of Ingmar) born.
1918	Ernst Ingmar Bergman born 14 July in Uppsala, Sweden, to Erik and Karin Bergman.
1922	Margareta Bergman (sister of Ingmar) born.
1934	Spends a summer month in Germany and visits Berlin.
1937	Takes his student examination and matriculates.
1938	After a brief time doing compulsory military service, enters Stockholm University. Stages plays at Mäster-Olofsgården.
1939	Works as production assistant at Stockholm Opera.
1940	Leaves the university. Stages plays at Student Theater, Stockholm.
1941	Stages plays at Stockholm Civic Center.
1942	Stages his own play *Kasper's Death*.
1943	Hired to work in the script department at Svensk Filmindustri (SFI). Marries Else Fisher; daughter Lena is born.
1944	His screenplay *Torment* is filmed by Alf Sjöberg and released. Appointed head of Hälsingborg City Theater.
1945	Divorced from Else Fisher. Marries Ellen Lundström, and daughter Eva is born.
1946	*Crisis* released. Joins Terrafilm. Stages his play *Rakel and the Cinema Doorman* at the Malmö City Theater. Writes the play *Jack among the Actors*. Joins Gothenburg City Theater as a director. *It Rains on Our Love* released. Son Jan is born.
1947	Writes screenplay for *Woman without a Face* (directed by Gustav Molander). His plays *The Day Ends Early*

and *To My Terror* are performed. *Ship to India* released.

1948   *Night Is My Future* released. Twins Anna and Mats are born. Collaborates on screenplay of *Eva* (directed by Molander). *Port of Call* released.

1949   *The Devil's Wanton* released. Goes to Paris with Gun Grut. *Three Strange Loves* released. Contract with Gothenburg City Theater expires.

1950   Writes synopsis for *While the City Sleeps* (directed by Lars-Eric Kjellgren). *To Joy* released. *This Doesn't Happen Here* released. Divorced from Ellen Lundström.

1951   Marries Gun Grut. Son Ingmar is born. Writes screenplay for *Divorced,* directed by Molander, who also directs Bergman's radio play *The City. Summer Interlude* released. During studio shutdown in Sweden, Bergman directs cinema commercials for Bris soap.

1952   Appointed director at Malmö City Theater. Stages his play *Murder at Barjärna. Secrets of Women* released. Relationship with Harriet Andersson begins.

1953   *Monika* and *Sawdust and Tinsel* released. Divorced from Gun Grut.

1954   *A Lesson in Love* released.

1955   Stages Molière's *Don Juan,* and Bengt Ekerot directs his play *Wood Painting.* Relationship with Bibi Andersson begins. *Dreams* released. *Smiles of a Summer Night* released. Writes screenplay for *Last Couple Out* (directed by Alf Sjöberg).

1956   *Smiles of a Summer Night* wins the poetic humor prize at Cannes Film Festival.

1957   *The Seventh Seal* and *Wild Strawberries* released. *The Seventh Seal* wins special jury prize at Cannes.

1958   *Brink of Life*—which will win two prizes at Cannes—and *The Magician* released. *Wild Strawberries* wins Golden Bear at Berlin Festival.

1959   Joins Royal Dramatic Theater, Stockholm. Marries Käbi Laretei.

1960   *The Virgin Spring* and *The Devil's Eye* released.

1961   Appointed artistic adviser at SFI. With Erland Josephson, writes screenplay for *The Pleasure Garden* (directed by Alf Kjellin). *The Virgin Spring* wins Academy Award as Best Foreign Film of 1960. *Through a Glass Darkly* released.

1962   Son Daniel Sebastian is born. *Through a Glass Darkly* wins Academy Award as Best Foreign Film of 1961.

1963   Appointed head of Royal Dramatic Theater. *Winter Light* and *The Silence* released.

1964   *Now about These Women* released.

1965   Ill with viral infection at the start of the year. Relationship with Liv Ullmann begins. With Charles Chaplin, wins Erasmus Prize.

1966   Mother dies. Divorced from Käbi Laretei. Daughter Linn is born. *Persona* released. Resigns as head of Royal Dramatic Theater. Builds house on island of Fårö.

1967   Anthology film *Stimulantia*, for which Bergman provided "Daniel," released.

1968   *Hour of the Wolf* and *Shame* released.

1969   *The Ritual* broadcast on television. *The Passion of Anna* released.

1970   Father dies. *The Fårö Document* broadcast on television. Writes the teleplay "The Lie" which is broadcast in several countries. Relationship with Liv Ullmann ends.

1971   *The Touch* released. Wins Irving Thalberg Memorial Award. Has brief affair with Malin Ek. Marries Ingrid von Rosen.

1972   *Cries and Whispers* released in New York in December and wins four New York Film Critics awards but fails to qualify for any Oscars since the film had not yet opened in Hollywood.

1973   *Scenes from a Marriage* broadcast on Swedish television. *Cries and Whispers* released in Sweden.

1974   Sven Nykvist wins Academy Award for Best Cinematography of 1973 for *Cries and Whispers*.

1975   *The Magic Flute* broadcast on television. Writes screenplay for (still unfilmed) "The Petrified Prince." Receives honorary Ph.D. from Stockholm University.

1976   Arrested for tax fraud during the rehearsal for *The Dance of Death*. Exiles himself from Sweden and settles in Munich, where he is given a contract at the Residenztheater. Wins Goethe Prize. *Face to Face* is broadcast on Swedish television.

1977   *The Serpent's Egg* (filmed in Munich) released.

1978   *Autumn Sonata* (filmed in Oslo) released. Celebrates his sixtieth birthday on Fårö with all his children.

1979   Exonerated in tax affair. *Fårö 1979* released.

1980   *From the Life of the Marionettes* released.

1982   Announces his retirement from filmmaking. *Fanny and Alexander* released.

1983   Films short tribute to his mother, *Karin's Face.*

1984   *After the Rehearsal*, filmed for television, released. *Fanny and Alexander* wins four Academy Awards.

1985   Dag Bergman dies.

1987   His autobiography, *The Magic Lantern*, published in Sweden.

1992   Billie August's *The Best Intentions* (screenplay by Bergman) released. Daniel Bergman's *Sunday's Children* (screenplay by his father Ingmar) released.

1993   Publishes *The Best Intentions* as a novel. *Images: My Life in Film,* Bergman's discussion of his films, published in English.

I

Sunday's Child

In the hospital recovering from the birth on 14 July 1918 of her second child, and from the Spanish flu, Karin Bergman recorded in her diary her fear that, owing to a high temperature and severe diarrhea, her skeletal infant, who still had not opened his eyes, might not live. As a consequence, he hurriedly had been baptized. In addition, because the flu had dried up Karin's milk, her mother, Anna Åkerblom, had taken the infant to her summer house in Dalarna where she employed a wet nurse. If he did not survive, she told Karin, she would take care of Karin's four-year-old son Dag. She also urged Karin to leave her husband Erik, a Lutheran clergyman, and return to her profession of nursing. Karin's mother had never liked her son-in-law, and now she was fed up with his unpredictable—she called them "mad"—outbursts and his inability to cope with his family's "practical problems." In her diary Karin acknowledged that Erik had been "overwrought" all spring, and believed, therefore, that she had no right to leave him.[1] The child, Ernst Ingmar, did survive.

Ingmar's being born on a Sunday made him, according to his grandmother's maid Lalla (and Strindberg), one of those rare individuals "capable of perceiving supernatural phenomena, of divining truth, and of stripping away facades of lies and deceits that other characters encase themselves in."[2] The notion of being a "Sunday's child" would have a significant effect on Bergman's thinking and personality.

Bergman's earliest memories of his childhood include sickliness ("always vomiting" and stomach aches), being caught (but not scolded) comparing his body with that of a girl his age, and, most important, the contentment he experienced when his mother touched him or told him stories. The sudden transferral of this attention when he was four years old to a "fat monstrous creature," his baby sister Margareta, began, as he remembers it, the process that crippled his character. For that matter, Dag's hatred of Ingmar had begun at the latter's birth. But in the matter of Margareta both of these nearly life-long antagonists were of one mind. Dag even instructed the eager Ingmar how to strangle the interloper. The would-be murderer misunderstood, however, and instead of grasping his infant sister's throat, merely pressed down heavily on her chest. Margareta's screams and Ingmar's sudden loss of his footing turned his "acute pleasure . . . into terror" (*ML*, 1–3).

Although in time Ingmar and Margareta "got on quite well," Bergman remembers always being afraid of Dag's "sudden flaring rages" and continuous mistreatment of him. Reciprocally, when Dag was ill with scarlet fever Ingmar hoped his brother would die; another time, provoked by some act of perceived injustice, Ingmar stood on a chair behind a door and smashed his brother over the head with a glass carafe. Later, after Dag had retaliated by knocking out two of Ingmar's front teeth, Ingmar tried to incinerate Dag while he slept. Just before his death in 1985 Dag visited Ingmar on Fårö, Ingmar's island home. Dag was by that time so paralyzed by a hereditary disease that his speech was difficult to understand and he could barely move his head. The brothers discussed their "mutual antipathy," and Dag confessed to never having been able to free himself from their mother's influence (*ML*, 8, 5, 56–58).

When they were children, Ingmar, sensing that his mother "loved my brother more than me,"[3] was jealous of her intercessions on Dag's behalf whenever their stern father prepared to thrash him and, afterwards, of her "bathing Dag's back and behind" (*ML*, 7, 3). Much later Ingmar came to understand that his father's severity with Dag was the result of jealousy. Dag, though he tried to ingratiate himself with his hated father, was in turn jealous of Ingmar for being his father's favorite. (Margareta, who remembers their mother as the more "dominant" and as "much more frightening at times,"[4] rejects Ingmar's portrait of their father as a harsh disciplinarian and of himself as "victim," recollecting that sometimes, when their father arrived to administer a beating, little Ingmar charmed him out of it by proposing they "build a hut out of cushions or some such scheme" [Cowie 1982, 10]). Ingmar also believes that his brother's paralysis (and his attempted suicide when he was about to turn 20) was due to the two "suffocating and incomprehensible" forces that, in fact, deformed all their lives: "Father and Mother" (*ML*, 57).

It is best to raise an issue now that impinges on this brief biography. On several points Margareta dissents from Ingmar's version of their childhood, and other family members and close friends have expressed shock and anger at his picture of his parents. This raises the question, should one use what is largely autobiography—Bergman's version of his life—as the main source of this biography? Ideally his version should be tested against independent sources. This challenge is especially pertinent in Bergman's case: as a youth he took refuge in fantasy because he was unable to cope with what he found to be an overly harsh reality. In fact, Else Fisher, Bergman's first wife, testifies that long after childhood Bergman made up and believed "his own truths" (Gado, 10). Nevertheless, we should neither discount as distorted or self-serving everything Bergman recalls nor accept his version of his past, whether "true" or "false," as not self-serving. (More on this in a moment.) Given that, aside from his sister, the essential sources of insight into his personal life, his parents and brother, are dead, reconstructing Bergman's life is an almost impossible task. It is also a project beyond the needs of this study, the focus of which is not the "real" Bergman but merely the Bergman who made the films we are going to examine. That is, to understand these films we need only to recognize and understand Bergman's vision of his life, because it is that vision that he transforms into his films. *We* may not always believe that vision—indeed, in the preface I caution the reader to view some of Bergman's recollections skeptically—but it is probably true that, for the most part, Bergman himself believes what he says about his past. What is certainly true is that he uses his vision of his past as the source of his films. In this sense the question of the truth of his recollections as opposed to *the* truth—or that of the memories of his sister, friends of the family, or any second party—is irrelevant. His memory, accurate or not, supplemented by his ruthlessly candid descriptions and analyses of his personality, is the fountainhead of his creative enterprise. In fact, it can be said that his verbal pictures of his past are as much works of art as any of those he put on celluloid. He has drawn from that past for almost every story he has adapted or written, and for every film he has *had* to make.

Bergman's father, Erik Bergman, was for a period chaplain at Sophiahemmet, the royal hospital, an appointment he received after the queen heard him preach. Later, in 1934, he fiercely competed for and won the charge of Stockholm's beautiful Hedvig Eleonara church and parish. Distinguishedly handsome, Erik's histrionic talents made him a very popular preacher. Karin loyally performed the duties of a pastor's wife—taking part in conferences, motivating welfare societies, serving at her husband's side on official and social occasions, and sitting in the front pew no matter who preached. It was she, Ingmar remembers, who provided what little warmth and stability there was at home.

In front of his community Pastor Erik Bergman was one man; at home he was another. He suffered from oversensitive hearing; "loud noises enraged" him. He insulated his bedroom-study's walls, but the sounds of the slight traffic outside still irritated him. Depressed and melancholy, he was insecure about his public performances, the quality of his sermons, and his effectiveness as an administrator. At home he might play with his children but become unpredictably, violently upset with them for such trivial matters as whistling or keeping their hands in their pockets. And he could be violent, even with his wife. Bergman recalls watching his father trying to prevent his mother from leaving the house. Erik grabbed her by the coat, but she struck him and broke away. Catching her, he threw her against the wall, bloodying her nose (*ML,* 134, 17–18).

After their mother's death in 1966, the children were astounded by the unhappiness revealed in the diaries she had kept since 1916: "Suddenly we discovered an unknown woman—intelligent, impatient, furious, rebellious—who had lived under this disciplined perfect housewife" (Kaminsky, 111–12). They learned, too, that she had had a passionate love affair with another minister and had planned to leave Erik, who, as a consequence, threatened suicide. Husband and wife were finally persuaded by Erik's superior to stay together "for the sake of the children," and a wealthy aunt sent the pair on a trip to Italy (*ML,* 17–18). For the next few years Erik's severe depressions repeatedly required stays in a nursing home (Gado, 7). The adult Bergman reflects that his parents, married for 52 years, never understood each other: "They were as water and fire."[5] The rebellious Dag and the sickly Ingmar did not make life easier for the pastor and his wife, who were hyperconscious that they and their children were expected to be models; their home, the church apartment across from the church, was by tradition open to the congregation—and to its scrutiny. Perfectionists, Erik and Karin made unreasonable demands on their two sons; in contrast, both parents loved Margareta "very much and possessively" (*ML,* 9).

When Margareta's birth "banished" him from his mother's bed and lost him his father's attention, the puzzled Ingmar responded with tears, rage, and incontinence. Furthermore, his mother's mercurial disposition confused him with inconsistent signals: "Her warmth could emerge in flashes, suddenly and, to me, incomprehensibly. Then I would let myself be filled with it, blinded and stunned by it. Just as quickly, that flash of warmth could turn to ice. Then [I] was completely shut out" (Gado, 13). He irritated his mother with his cloying adoration, his fears of animals, of other boys, of seemingly everything[6]—and with his preference for tranquillity and for dolls. She told him that she did not "like being caressed" and that he behaved "like a girl" (*ML,* 2, 284). But he craved her caresses and felt that being a girl was really "much more pleasant" (Gado, 12). Faced with the fact that both his rage and his gentleness were counterproductive, he pretended illness. In the past his "endless ailments" had always aroused her concern. And his strategem worked: he avoided school until he was six. Forced to attend, he went screaming and, once there, would faint or vomit and as a consequence be sent home. When the nurse Karin saw through his shamming, she punished him. Nevertheless, still troubled, she consulted a famous pediatrician, who prescribed firmness: to indulge the child's pretenses would damage him for life. Ingmar shrewdly reversed his field and tried self-control: with cool aloofness he mimicked his mother's indifference and preoccupation. Though intrigued by his tactic, she responded angrily (*ML,* 3–4).

His relationship with his father remained passionately ambivalent. Ingmar's response to his father's rigid sternness, depressions, and, as with his mother, unpredictable and erratic behavior was complicated by his conviction that his father was less concerned with him than with God and Jesus, and by what a Freudian would term Ingmar's oedipal feelings. Just as with his mother, Ingmar bent with the shifting wind that was his father. "I was very much in love with my mother and learned early on to guess what mood she was in. I adapted to please her. It was the same with my father, whom I was quite afraid of."[7] His fondest memories of his father involve being alone with him on Sundays during the family holidays in the spring and summer. (These experiences form the basis of Bergman's script for *Sunday's Children* [1992], which his son Daniel filmed.) Erik used to bicycle to preach in rural churches near Stockholm and in Dalarna. Bergman tells of sitting on the front carrier of his father's bike while his father named or captivated him with fairy tales about the birds and flowers they passed, of sitting naked between his naked father's knees after the two had stopped to swim in a lake, of their taking refuge from a storm in the shell of a deserted barn and his father wrapping him in his coat to stave off the chill, and of his father's softly singing to himself or his laugh after they recovered from a spill. As at home, anger and violence often spoiled these idyllic moments. There was the time, for instance, they took a ferry across a river and Ingmar sat dangling his feet over the side. Suddenly his father struck him on the head. Ingmar sobbed to himself and planned painful ways to kill his father until the latter explained how frightened he had been that Ingmar might be sucked overboard. The unsettling thing was that the child could never be certain what might happen or when. His father could remain in a good mood all day, or he could suddenly turn taciturn and irritable or become brutal (*ML,* 269–71). "He was a very dangerous man," says Bergman, "because he had a lot inside him" (Meryman, 66). (His father's inner rage never markedly dissipated. Retired and frail, the old man accompanied Ingmar in his search for a church in which to film *Winter Light* [1963]; he became enraged when a clergyman, feeling ill, announced he would abbreviate the service. Pastor Bergman pounded his fist on the pew, got up, stormed into the vestry, and took over the service at the altar.[8]

It was not just his parents' withholding of the love he craved or their bewildering behavior that Bergman believes warped him. The entire adult world—with the exception of his maternal grandmother—failed to provide an empathic environment for his admittedly excessive emotional and ego needs. As with any child, his assertiveness required recognition and praise so that he could develop an image of self that he could respect. Whether it was throwing a ball or learning to swim or sketching, he felt "a very strong need to draw the attention of the grownups to these manifestations of my presence in the world. I felt I never got enough attention."[9]

His grandmother alone saved him, treating him with "harsh tenderness and intuitive understanding" (*ML,* 22). Ingmar was as happy to be packed off to her place, usually her apartment in Uppsala, as his parents were to send him packing. When they went to Italy after avoiding divorce, grandmother's stoic, domestic routine—rising before 7:00 A.M., a rubdown in an icy bath, breakfast followed by prayers and supervised homework, tea and sandwiches at 1:00 P.M., walking over to see what was playing at the movies, dinner at 5:00 P.M., reading aloud, prayers, and bed at 9:00 P.M.—restored "order and the illusion of security" (*ML,* 18). More important, she reassured him that his "vision of life was correct"[10] and kept his fragile person-ality intact by providing him with love and the praise for his achieve-ments for which he hungered, a word that in no way exaggerates what he felt: "Artistic creation has always manifested itself for me like a desire for food" ("Commandments," 14). The two developed a ritual. For about an hour before dinner they would sit and discuss things. She told him "about the World, about Life, but also about Death (which was occupying my thoughts a good deal at the time)," and she asked about and carefully attended to what he thought. She "saw through my fibs or brushed them aside with friendly irony. She al-lowed me to have my say as a real person" (ML, 22).

His grandmother's apartment, "the epitome of security and magic" (ML, 18), could nevertheless unsettle him. Left alone, he often felt like a shrunken Alice intimidated by a wonderland of "enormous" carpets, "massive," self-satisfied pieces of furniture, and a maze com-prising 14 giant rooms and long, dark corridors. His grandmother's throne, the "plush-upholstered toilet" with its dark abyss and odors, intrigued him, and he believed that the clocks, which conversed with the furniture and ticked their secrets from room to room, were spying on him. And then there was the fear and fascination he felt for the flat's inorganic decorations: the waves, pigeons, and people in a paint-ing of Venice, or the statue of the Venus de Milo, came to life, and the painting's sunbeams "had sound"; or he saw Death's "yellow skull and dark gangling figure against the panes of glass in the front door" (ML, 21). "I was terribly frightened and terribly fascinated."[11] (Fear and fascination will remain Siamese emotions for Bergman and his characters. When as a child he watched hospital orderlies at the furnace burning boxes filled with human limbs and organs, "it was traumatic, and I loved it!" [Cowie 1982, 9].) And then an experience "impossible to date": forms on the surface of the blinds in his bedroom at home—"they were neither little men, nor animals, nor heads, nor faces, *but things for which no name exists!*"—freed themselves and moved about the room. "They were pitiless, impassive and terrifying" (Geduld, 186–87). (Some of these remembrances will appear as images in his films, for example, *Secrets of Women* [1952] and *Fanny and Alexander* [1982].) The inanimate becoming animate, reality becoming indistin-guishable from fantasy might be a matter of no great concern—attrib-utable to a child's versatile or overwrought imagination—if it were not that the adult Bergman experienced comparable, unsettling vi-sions. Ingmar began increasingly to live in fantasy because "reality was no longer sufficient" ("Commandments," 14), because he was not getting enough attention, or because he was being treated hostilely, unjustly, or sadistically.

Many of his earliest memories, he says, are of cruel or humiliating punishments: ritualized whippings (Donner 1975),[12] his mother trying to cure his bed-wetting by forcing him out onto the street dressed in his sister's red dress (ML, 8), or, worst of all, his parents not speaking to him, freezing him out until he "broke down completely." (Margareta does not recall these punishments and says she is unwilling to believe that her parents were ever so "mad" and "downright sadistic" [Gado, 10].) And there is that now famous, terrifying punishment he describes in Hour of the Wolf (1968) and Face to Face (1976); his beloved grandmother once locked him in a wardrobe where, he was told, there lived a little creature who devoured the toes of naughty children (Gado, 9). (He traces to this experience his fear of the dark and his claustrophobia, which now impel him to always book two rooms in hotels [Sjöman, 162].) With all these punishments, he explains, his parents were doing what the Dr. Spocks of the time were advocating, the underlying idea being that "you should not let your feelings be involved when you punished children. . . . You should be sober and matter-of-fact. . . . It's a wonder it didn't make me a homosexual or a masochist" (Sjöman, 162–63), he adds, not making explicit what elsewhere he acknowledges—that too often it was his parents' anger, not their love, that fueled punishments and wielded the cane.

When he attended, school seemed just another part of the scheme to crush childhood. He recalls that, besides being punished frequently for arriving late for morning prayers, his teachers and fellow students mocked his abject manner and puny physique.

One way he coped was by withdrawing. "I . . . kept my dream world to myself. A young child wanting human contact and obsessed by his imagination had been hurt and transformed into a cunning and suspicious daydreamer. . . . The need to get people to listen . . . was still there. It became stronger the more I became imprisoned in loneliness" ("Commandments," 15). Increasingly he found it difficult to converse; he even developed a slight stammer (Gado, 17). Part of the problem, he says, was not having the words to express what he thought and felt.[13] Thus the importance to him of his dolls, his toy projector, and his puppet theater—each a medium for a language "that bypassed words" ("Commandments," 15). From the age of five until he was thirteen, he claims that he lived alone in dreams, in a world of his own creation where he could satisfy his appetite for attention and love without fear of either humiliation or rejection, and where *his* commands were law and he could vent his fear and anger, be cruel or brave: "I was very interested in death . . . [and] fairy tales—cruel fairy tales" (Cavett). Although his sister, who helped him build his puppets and the scenery, and now and then his mother were sometimes his audience, shyness and fear kept him from inviting in neighborhood children. After a while he had "no desire for company" (*ML*, 20).

On occasion, however, even *his* world became treacherous. As does the schizophrenic Karin in *Through a Glass Darkly* (1961), he found that living voluntarily or involuntarily "sometimes . . . in one world, sometimes in the other" could be frightening. "Suddenly I didn't know whether I dreamt things or they existed" (Cavett). It was a regressive condition[14] that would persist past middle age: "When I was younger, not much younger, say five, six, ten years ago," he said in 1972, when he was 54, "and back into my childhood, I was haunted by extremely terrible dreams, sometimes daydreams; . . . sometimes my dreams were so real that when I tried to remember something, I didn't know exactly if it had happened in reality or if I had dreamed it. It was very painful. . . . I didn't know exactly what was happening to me, and time didn't exist" (Simon, 28–29). His fantasies and involuntary disorientation compounded his difficulties with his parents; they sometimes would ask him in a strange tone why he had done something, and he did not know why. Then they might charge him with lying; "that was the most difficult thing because I didn't know I had been lying because I mixed up things" (Cavett). Only at his grandmother's, he maintains, did the burdensome "mantle of lies" fall away; only there was he able to become the undisputed "ruler of the stage": "I lived trouble-free from day to day without anxiety or guilty conscience. The world was understandable and I was in control of my dreams as well as my reality. God kept quiet and Jesus did not torment me with his blood and murky invitations" (*ML*, 76, 20). But he still had to cope with threats and punishment elsewhere, so he "created an external person who had very little to do with the real me." Soon, however, he found that he was unable to keep his two selves, the public and private, apart. As we shall see, this disassociation from his feelings "had consequences for [his] life and creativity far into adulthood" (*ML*, 10): "I found . . . that my senses did indeed register the external reality, but the impulses never reached as far as my emotions." He lost the ability to spontaneously link his sensory experiences to his emotion: "Was I frightened, angry, embarrassed, curious or just hysterical? I don't know. . . . There was always a micro-second between my intuitive experience and its emotional expression." It would be 40 years before he was again able to spontaneously synchronize them. He has, he now claims, "more or less recovered" from this "neurosis that so effectively gave the appearance of normality" (ML, 170).

Bergman has often told the story of how he had to trade away his army of tin soldiers to Dag for the movie projector he desperately wanted. The black, tin, hand-operated little machine had a simple system of lenses and a paraffin lamp—the smoke escaped through its chimney—that produced the light; it projected ten-foot-long tinted film loops or, if one inserted them into the lens system, colored slides (BB, 6–8). One of the activities he had loved doing with his grandmother involved one or the other of them drawing a picture and the other developing the action with another picture until, over a period of days, they had produced a visual narrative—a written explanatory text connected the pictures—some 40 to 50 pictures long. Now for a few öre he bought scraps of newsreels and films at toy stores and, concocting a unifying story, spliced them together with ascetic ester. One film, in a box entitled "Frau Holle," offered a "girl in national costume who lay sleeping in a meadow." When he turned the handle, she woke, got up and danced around, and disappeared off to the right. That was it, but "she was moving" (ML, 16).[15] The little sorcerer turned a crank and created life. Controlling complex, unvarying images and action provided a sense of peace, security, and power for the powerless boy attempting to master a transient, unpredictable, and all too often overwhelming world of sensations. The images' immutability also symbolizes Bergman's later deterministic attitude toward character: once a person's character is formed by God, heredity, or events, it remains essentially unalterable. A person may come to understand his behavior and motives and may modify superficial facets of his personality, but he cannot fundamentally change his character. For Bergman this drama of free will versus determinism is at the core of filmmaking, which he describes as "a continuous struggle between choice and necessity, vision and reality" (Cowie 1982, 14).

By the age of 10 or 11 he was "a passionate cinema goer" and did not have to wait for his grandmother, his parents, or his brother to accompany him. To feed his habit he drew on his allowance or pilfered coins from his father's unoccupied coat. At the theater he struck up a friendship with a projectionist—Bergman would later ponder just what the affectionate man's intentions were—and thus saved money by watching films from the booth (*BB,* 7). When he was 12, his father, in exchange for a christening fee, thoughtfully arranged for Ingmar to visit the film studios in the film town of Råsunda (Cowie 1982, 14).

Ingmar was almost 12 when he attended Alf Sjöberg's 1930 production of the Swedish fairy tale *Big Klas and Little Klas* at the Royal Dramatic Theater. The experience inspired the youth to upgrade his puppet theater: "I built . . . revolving stages, traps that rose and fell, and all sorts of refinements. . . . I took [my plays] from the whole of world drama. I put on Strindberg's *Lucky Per's Journey* [1880] and *Master Olof* [1872]—Strindberg featured prominently in the repertoire—even Maeterlinck's *Blue Bird* [1908]. But chiefly they had to be spectacular plays that gave plenty of scope for stage machinery and lighting" (*BB,* 8, 9). Through these dramatizations he acted out his anger, love, wishes, and needs, combated and defeated loneliness, evil, death, and that ubiquitous "emissary of evil and persecution," the Devil. "Anyone who, like myself, was born in the family of a pastor . . . make[s] an early acquaintance with the devil and, like all children, you need to give him a concrete form. Here is where the magic lantern comes in. . . . Among others, there [were slides of] Little Red Riding Hood and the wolf. The wolf was the devil, a devil without horns but with a tail and vivid red mouth, a curiously palpable and yet elusive devil" (Geduld, 187).

The education he was receiving at Palmgren, a private grammar school, further fostered withdrawal. No one there let air and light into his world. He may be exaggerating to make his point—though this is essentially his vision when he dramatizes school life in *Torment* (1944)—but he claims that this comatose condition was not unique to him: "My schoolmates were just as dumb. . . . There was absolutely nothing in our milieu which could wake us up or stimulate us" (*BB,* 11). The teaching consisted of a heavy reliance on reward, punishment, and "the implanting of a guilty conscience" (*ML,* 113).

He did poorly in math and anything else that did not have an "emotional anchoring." Geography's maps also eluded him, but history, religion (especially Old Testament stories), and translating old Latin texts (which required "a combination of detective work and a kind of intuition") he found "fun" (Steene 1972, 44). Like other loners, he found some relief in literary voices that gratifyingly described his own condition. The protagonist of Mikhail Lermontov's *A Hero of Our Times* (1840), a book that appears prominently in two Bergman films, says, "Nobody caressed me, everybody offended me: I became rancorous. I was gloomy—other children were merry and talkative. I felt myself superior to them—but was considered inferior. . . . Fearing mockery, I buried my best feelings at the bottom of my heart. . . . I spoke the truth—I was not believed. I began to deceive."[16] But from his adolescence on it was Sweden's literary giant, August Strindberg, who, Bergman says, "expressed things which I'd experienced and which I couldn't find words for" (Simon, 17; *BB,* 24). (When he was 20, Bergman bought a set of Strindberg's complete works. His father ordered them removed from the house.[17]) Indeed, passages from Strindberg's basically autobiographical novels, *The Red Room* (1879)— "I knew its opening chapter virtually by heart" (*BB,* 23)—and *The Son of a Servant,* give the impression that Bergman appropriated his idol's youth for his own. The description we have been listening to of Bergman's childhood roughly echoes Strindberg's description of *his* autobiographical character Johan:

> [He] remained always afraid of life and of people. . . . [Until he entered college] he was still afraid of the dark, afraid of dogs, horses, and strangers. . . . He was extremely sensitive. He wept so often that he was called a crybaby, felt the least remark keenly and was in perpetual anxiety lest he should do something wrong. . . . He was afraid of failing, of hurting himself, of being in the way. He was afraid of being hit by his brothers, slapped by the maids, scolded by his grandmother, caned by his father and birched by his mother. . . . Above the child loomed a hierarchy of authorities wielding various rights and powers, ranging from the seniority privileges of his brothers to the supreme tribunal of his father.

Johan also "withdrew into himself and became bitter . . . grew reserved and shy . . . dissolved the ties which bound him to the realities of life . . . lived a dream life in foreign lands and in his own thoughts."[18] Downplaying the degree to which he let his idol's picture of his youth shape his own, Bergman emphasizes that it was as an outlet for his suppressed anger and violence that Strindberg best served him: "Strindberg's aggressions—and my own—that's what made the deepest impression on me. As for Strindberg's humor, I didn't even notice it . . . what I felt most strongly were the big angry pieces" (*BB,* 23). As Harry Schein has pointed out, Bergman's self-mocking irony "takes the edge out of the kind of demonic madness" that we sometimes find in Strindberg's plays (Steene 1972, 122).

In high school Bergman also would become acquainted, though not intimately, with Dostoyevsky, Tolstoy, Shakespeare, Defoe, Swift, Dickens, Balzac, Maupassant, Flaubert, Georges Bernanos, the Swedish dramatist and novelist Hjalmar Bergman, and Nietzsche, with whose superman he identified.[19] He also read the novelist Agnes von Krusenstjerna, "whose view of women influenced" him (Cowie 1982, 15). When he was no older than 15 or 16, his father rented, to show to his confirmands, *The Phantom Chariot* (1920), a film by the Swedish master of silent cinema, Victor Sjöström; "it made an extraordinarily powerful impression on me."[20] He loved Hollywood horror films, especially Boris Karloff's *Frankenstein* (1931) and *The Mummy* (1932) (Cowie 1982, 14). He also vividly recalls Olof Molander's production of Strindberg's *A Dream Play* (1901),[21] and films by Marcel Carné, Julien Duvivier, and Gustav Machaty, whose *Ecstasy* (1933) featured Hedy Lamarr's hypnotic, lyrical, and, for Ingmar, shockingly liberating nude scene (*BB,* 138). The members of the Bergman family were concertgoers, but not until he had visited Germany—where he heard more Wagner, for whose music at ten he had developed a preference (Hedlund, 49), and where, surreptitiously and inebriated, he became enraptured by the banned recordings of *The Threepenny Opera* (1928), Louis Armstrong, Fats Waller, and Duke Ellington (*ML,* 126–27)—did Ingmar seem at last to appreciate music's potential for expressing his inexpressible emotions. Often, thereafter, music thundered from the high-strung youth's room.

In Ingmar's parents' world there were two things that "anyone who valued respectability never mentioned" (*BB,* 188)—money and sex. Ingmar's notions about a woman's body came not only from contact with his mother—who dropped some "scornful hints" about sex—naked statues, paintings, and the "guilt-ridden games" he played with his sister, but also from some rather bizarre incidents. When he was eight or nine a widow friend of the family got into his bathtub, put his hand between her thighs, cleaned his penis, and rocked him "firmly between her strong soft thighs" in a "most pleasurable and not in the least frightening" manner. Then, when he was ten and left alone in the mortuary chapel's morgue, he acquiesced to "a violent urge which seared and titillated" and drove him to run his hand over a young girl's corpse: "I could see her sex, which I wanted to touch but did not dare."[22] He also had a chaste, prepubescent love affair with a girl called Märta, to whom he explained that he had learned from Strindberg's *The Pelican* (1907) that "human love was egoism" and lechery. At 14, and ready to enter the gymnasium, he met a "nice," "clever, quick-witted, and kind," but tall, fat, and "ugly" classmate who, he says, kept him from going "out of my mind" (*ML*, 107–18). Anna Lindberg meant so much to him because after his first involuntary, explosive ejaculation, he felt a fear of and guilt about sex simultaneously with an obsessive desire to masturbate. Told by Dag, who said he was having sex with his German tutor, to read about that "sickly filth" in the family medical book, Ingmar did, learning there that the habit would lay waste his entire physical and mental being. He fought its promptings—even turning to Jesus and attending confirmation class a year ahead of schedule—but to no avail. Lying about his thoughts and behavior now became even more of a necessity, and the gulf between his real and secret life widened: "My isolation became hermetic and I thought I was going mad." While he masturbated, everyone else, he was convinced, "screwed." He and Anna consummated their sexual desires on his fifteenth birthday, but Bergman is careful to say that he did not love her; of that he was incapable because "there was no love where I lived and breathed" (*ML*, 116).

Though no longer a virgin sexually, Ingmar still was a "political virgin" (Simon, 38). That too changed, but with far less sanguine results. In 1934, when he was 16, he spent a month as one of some 2,000 exchange students *(Austauschkind)* in Germany. Crammed only with German grammar, he was placed in a small town near Weimar with the family of a boy named Hannes whose father was a pastor and an enthusiastic supporter of the Nazis. National Socialism was not an unfamiliar topic to Ingmar. Germany's National Socialism vis-à-vis Swedish socialism was a popular and often heated topic in Sweden in the 1930s. Even when he was 12 and still "horribly innocent about everything political," he remembers Dag—who would help found Sweden's Fascist party—and his father—who voted several times for the Swedish National Socialists—"making a colossal case against [Swedish] socialism" and Swedish socialists, whom they regarded as "unspeakable asses." His father, brother, and many of his teachers were enthusiastic for the "great things" Hitler seemed to be achieving (Donner 1975). Ingmar was a fertile subject for the idealism and zealousness he encountered in Germany. Like many adolescents, he was looking fervently for ideas and men he could believe in and in whose service he could prove himself trustworthy.[23] Hannes and his brothers were in the Hitler-Jugend, and his sisters in the Bund Deutscher

Madel. In church and at Hannes's school, which Ingmar visited, there was "complete political indoctrination." Hannes's father quoted from *Mein Kampf* (1925–27) for church services, and it also "lay on the desks" at school, where the teacher read from the Nazi party's newspaper *Der Stürmer* about the Jews poisoning German society. Ingmar learned to raise his arm and say "Heil Hitler" and went with the family to Weimar to a rally for the tenth anniversary of the Parteitag. The celebration climaxed with a gigantic procession headed by Hitler in his black car. Then, in a downpour, Hitler made a short speech to the "cheering weeping obsessed crowds," and the sun broke through as he finished. "I had never seen anything like this eruption of immense energy. I shouted like everyone else, howled like everyone else and loved it." The festivities ended that night with a performance of Wagner's *Rienzi* (1850) and fireworks. For Ingmar's birthday, Hannes's family gave him a photograph of Hitler to hang over his bed so that "I would always have the man before my eyes." "I loved him. . . . For many years, I was on Hitler's side, delighted by his successes and saddened by his defeats. . . . I fell headlong into an atmosphere glowing with idealism and hero worship. I was also suddenly exposed to an aggressiveness . . . in harmony with my own" (*ML,* 119–32). He returned with Hannes to Sweden "a little pro-German fanatic" (Donner 1975; Cowie 1982, 16).[24]

But reality again betrayed him; Hitler was no King Arthur, Nazi Germany no Camelot. When pictures from the concentration camps verified the rumors of the Holocaust, he saw the Nazis for what they were and, suffering overwhelming guilt, bitterly turned on his father, brother, and teachers for misleading him (Cowie 1982, 14). Along with his idealism, his nascent self-confidence withered. Disillusioned and wary, he disavowed politics: "For twenty years I never read a political article; I never listened to a political speech; I didn't vote." Years passed before he could even admit that had he been German, or a Swede placed by the Nazis in a role of authority in Sweden, he would have dutifully obeyed their orders. This experience explains his admiration for Klaus Mann's *Mephisto* (1936) and, as he has indicated, inspired him to make *Shame* (1968), a film that asks, "How much of the fascist are you and I harboring inside ourselves? What sort of situation is needed to turn us from good social democrats into active Nazis?" (*BB,* 232; Simon, 38–39). His political idealism having collapsed, the youth turned instead to an activity in which he would safely achieve what Henry James termed a "hungry futurity": "I decided I would have nothing more to do with politics. I am an artist. I belong to the world. That's all I really understand" (Donner 1975).[25]

In the summer of 1937, just after he passed the exams prerequisite to entering the University of Stockholm (Cowie 1982, 16), Bergman became ill; for fun, he decided to devote himself to writing, an activity that he had only recently begun to enjoy. He produced "Marie," a novel about "Summer vacation in the Archipelago and The First Great Love"[26]—a story probably based on the sudden death from polio of a young female cousin (BB, 63)[27]—and "Pressure," a story about a high school student who falls in love with a young woman who dies of mysterious, though natural causes. Under extreme emotional pressure from his parents and one of his teachers, the student becomes ill at the time of his matriculation exams. "Marie" would become the basis for Summer Interlude (1951), and "Pressure," enriched by later experiences, for Torment (Steene 1972, 12).

In 1938, before entering the university, he began his two five-month stints of military service; stomach problems led to his early release, though not before the hearing in his right ear was damaged by cannon practice. He has talked little about this experience, but given his physical and psychological vulnerabilities it is easy to accept his assessment, "I don't think I was a very good soldier" (Cowie 1982, 17).

He remained only two years at the university, but while there he studied art history and literature. He credits his fellow students and his professor of Swedish literature, Martin Lamm—whose lectures annoyed him at first because of their lack of reverence for Strindberg—for making him a more discriminating reader (ML, 138). For appearance' sake, he started a course for which he wrote a study of Strindberg's The Keys of Heaven (1892), but his involvement in student drama and with a student actress and poet by the name of Maria were the real foci of his days and nights. His theatrical abilities were soon recognized, and he was asked by Sven Hansson—whose acquaintance he had made at a bookstore where he was seeking out theater publications—to teach a course in stagecraft for Mäster-Olofsgården, a Christian youth settlement. Maria, in whose one-room apartment he spent many nights, not only turned him into a chain-smoker but spurred him into being more rigorously and dispassionately critical; she also satisfied his sexual hunger, "opening the prison bars and letting out a raving lunatic" (ML, 139).

Feeling like an escaped stallion and beginning to receive the recognition he long had felt deprived of, his appetite swelled. The prison walls he had built as a child to shelter himself from what he experienced as a brutal existence "came down and I drew closer to reality" (Donner 1975). Though he still blamed himself "for everything," his growing self-assurance—he assured someone he would be a "great director" (Cowie 1982, 17)—and years of starving for their affection and appreciation had developed in him an acid eye for his parents' limitations. Why didn't they—and other adults—meet the standards they themselves set? "There was so much talk about truth and honesty. . . . A *mother's* love was always beautiful, and *fathers* were always just and fair. . . . But I was a mistreated, tortured little shit, trying to survive by lying or dodging, or by cheating or trying to ingratiate myself" (Donner 1975). He began to recognize that he hated his father, and that his attitude toward his mother had changed during puberty.[28] He bridled at their attempts to control him: "I wanted to live my own life, and my parents wanted me to do things, to obey, to learn the rules of society" (Cavett). At last, his resentment, anger, and frustration became too much to suppress. The event that triggered their release was his father's rage over discovering that he had been spending his nights with Maria. Knowing that any response to his father's demand for an explanation would be useless, Ingmar simply warned his father not to hit him. Erik did, however, "and I hit him back. He staggered and ended up sitting on the floor while Mother alternately wept and appealed to the remnants of our common sense. I pushed her aside and she screamed loudly. . . . Well, I went to my room and locked myself in. That evening I packed a few things and left [with a sense of relief]" (*ML,* 139, 72). Though he roomed with Sven Hansson and did not see his parents for four years, Ingmar did not object to them; his parents, for their part, did not want the break to be permanent and had a friend provide Ingmar with food and drink and retrieve his dirty clothes for washing once a week (Cowie 1982, 17).

A couple of years later, in 1941, a baffled, somewhat defensive Erik Bergman drew for Margareta a largely recognizable word-picture of his son, one in which he himself appears more feeling and concerned than Ingmar saw him:

Ingmar was a good natured child, cheerful and friendly. It was utterly impossible ever to be stern with him. . . . None of you other children has ever caused us such misery and worry as Ingmar has. He's easily led. When I write these lines I have behind me many depressing experiences of his violent temper and unbalanced temperament. At one moment he can be so frightfully hard and unfeeling. The next, he's soft and sensitive as a little child. I can only leave this inexpressibly beloved child in God's hands. Myself, I can do no more, so worried and tormented am I on his behalf. (Gado, 9)

During these first couple of years away from home, Ingmar sustained himself by accepting almost any artistic work he could get. Amateur theatrical groups welcomed his enthusiasm, talent, and ability to work with tight budgets and schedules (Cowie 1982, 21). He directed and/or acted at the Student Theater at Mäster-Olofsgården and at Brita von Horn's Playwrights' Studio (with professional actors); he started the Stockholm Civic Center, staged fairy tales—at which he was expert—for young audiences under the auspices of the public parks, and directed *The Merchant of Venice* using the pupils of the Norra Real High School, one of whom was Erland Josephson (who remembers Bergman as "absolutely clear about what he wanted"). He also worked backstage, often without pay, at the Stockholm Opera (Cowie 1982, 18; Young, 14). Offered a job by a touring actor to produce Strindberg's *The Father* (1887), he gave up school and Maria. The production, however, closed after the first night. He returned to Maria and lived as a part of ménage à trois until she and his rival turned him out.

In 1942, at the Student Theater, he produced *Kasper's Death,* one of a number of plays he had suddenly written in 1940. This play, says Bergman, was "an audacious plagiarism of *Punch's Shrove Tuesday* [1901] by Strindberg and *The Old Play of Everyman* [c. 1500, Anon.], a fact that did not embarrass me in the slightest" (*ML,* 141). About the production *Svenska Dagbladet*'s drama critic wrote: "No debut in Swedish has given such unambiguous promise" (Cowie 1982, 21). The production was seen by Carl Anders Dymling, who had recently become president of Svensk Filmindustri (SFI), Sweden's largest film company, and by Stina Bergman, the head of his screenplay department (and widow of Hjalmar Bergman). "Here, I thought, was a refreshing young talent," writes Dymling, "a little crazy perhaps, certainly immature, but with a lot of bold and fanciful ideas" (*Four Screenplays,* 7–8). He had Stina contact Ingmar. She interviewed the "shabby, ill-mannered and unshaven" male dervish (who emitted "a derisive laughter . . . [and] unconcerned charm") at her home, and she was so flustered by his forceful conversation that she had "to drink three cups of coffee in order to get back to normal."[29] He accepted her offer to be one of her assistants at 500 crowns a month and spent the whole of 1943 trying, unsuccessfully, to improve rather poor scripts. Then, early in 1944, he submitted a treatment, called *Torment,* of one of his own stories. Dymling read it—"It was a startling experience"— and passed it on to Gustav Molander, who read it and recommended that SFI purchase it. They paid Bergman ten times his monthly salary, 5,000 crowns, and had Alf Sjöberg direct it; *Torment* opened in October 1944.

Four years had passed since Bergman walked out of his parents' home. Now, besides working at SFI, he was directing professionally in southern Sweden at the Hälsingborg City Theater. He felt that what he had accomplished in the world would impress his parents, so he arranged a meeting on his own turf where he could show off: "I had my own office *and* telephone . . . I was established." But his parents failed to show as much joyous pride as he longed for. "We met in a state of cautious neutrality with a decent mutual respect" (Cavett).

Before enlarging on the psychological portrait of Bergman I have been presenting, I want to complete the history of this crucial relationship with his parents. In his thirties he saw them somewhat more frequently, but the relationship remained one of "cautious neutrality." They made polite conversation and "were absolutely strange to each other" (Weinraub, 17 October 1976, 15). (Although his children used the familiar form with their grandparents, he addressed his parents until the very end of their lives with the formal pronoun *du* [Cole, 25 October 1959, 1]). Years later, in publicly paying tribute to their contribution to his success, he circumspectly platitudinized while steering shy of irony; ambiguously referring to its "vital importance," he praised the "atmosphere of hearty wholesomeness" they created for him to rebel against, and their having made virtues of efficiency, punctuality, and financial responsibility (*Four Screenplays,* 19). Considerately reconsidering in midsentence whom to blame for the alienation, he added, "It took about twenty years before we . . . I think I . . . matured" (Cavett); but he then reintroduced his belief that his parents shoulder most of the blame, and he expressed his continuing need for intimacy with his mother: "Gradually I came to think of them not as parents but as people. They no longer frightened or threatened me. They were just ordinary people and I began to feel tenderness toward them; and friendship—where my mother was concerned" (Donner 1975).

His father's illness in the early 1960s was the occasion for this closeness to his mother. "I was sitting in the hospital with her for weeks and we became friends, and I tell you it was the most marvelous feeling you can imagine. Something deep inside happens to yourself when you become friends with one of your parents" (Weinraub, 17 October 1976, 15).[30] Before dying in 1966, Karin Bergman suffered a series of heart attacks. During one hospitalization she and Ingmar candidly exchanged memories, and sobbing, she told him that *her* mother never cared for her. At a later date, after she had been released, she phoned Ingmar to get him to visit his father, who was in the hospital being operated on for a malignant tumor. Ingmar refused, saying that he had "neither time nor desire to do so" and that, besides, he and his father had nothing to say to each other.[31] That night, a Tuesday, she braved a snowstorm to visit him at the theater. Outraged, she said she wanted to hear his insulting refusal face to face. He tried to embrace and kiss her, but she slapped his face and, when he laughed, burst into tears. Giving in, he asked for her forgiveness, and they talked until two in the morning. That Sunday she had two more coronaries and, before he reached her, died (*ML,* 5–6). Liv Ullmann tells of Bergman picking her up at the airport on her return from Norway: "'Mama died today,' he said when we were in the car. . . . 'Now I have no one.'"[32] He confided to Vilgot Sjöman that all his relationships with women had been built on his need for mother love: "I've muddled up [my mother and my wives] for years and years. . . . I suppose that's why for a time I unconsciously sought out younger women: merely in order to get as far away as possible from that tendency to mix things up" (Sjöman, 127–28). Liv, whom Bergman met not long before his mother died, acknowledges, without embarrassment or regret, the role she played for him in part: "He sought the mother. Arms that open to him, warm and without complications" (Ullmann, 109). His present wife, Ingrid, bears a "remarkable resemblance" to his mother, he admits.[33]

Bergman ends his autobiography, *The Magic Lantern,* as he began it, focusing on his mother and himself. The "Sunday's child" imagines himself at the repopulated parsonage on a Sunday. His mother catches sight of him, and he kisses her. She immediately admonishes him for not having visited more frequently and questions why he "never" sees his children. Guilt-ridden, he calms her rising anger by promising not to be recriminatory and asks, first, about the "reality" of her visit to him at Fårö.[34] He is referring to an experience in which, on awakening one morning, he had "a very strong feeling" that she was sitting beside him looking at the sea. So certain was he that he was not dreaming that he thought he could touch her. "I knew Mother was with me in the room, or did I imagine it?" He then tries to get his mother to confirm what he has said publicly about the closeness they achieved before her death: "We became friends, didn't we? The old apportioning roles of mother and son were dissolved? . . . We spoke openly and intimately? Did life become comprehensible? Did I get anywhere near to understanding?" He finds himself facing up to the probability that, in fact, their relationship did not change, "only what was said was rewritten . . . on my conditions." Finally, he reminds her of what he calls the Bergman family motto: "Don't disturb, don't intrude," and asks, "Who got Mother's [and Father's] love? . . . Were we given shame and guilt instead of love and forgiveness? . . . Why did my brother become an invalid? Why was my sister crushed into a scream? Why did I live with a never-healing infected sore that went right through my body? . . . Why was I incapable of normal human relationships for so long?" His hope that he and she could deal quietly and melancholically with these mysteries, and that she would provide satisfying answers, ends, as it always has and must, with his accusing her and with her silence. Even so, the aged son recognizes, "I am calling for Mother as I always have" (*ML,* 283–85).

Bergman's relationship with his father ranged from being as formal as the relationship in *Wild Strawberries* (1957) between Isak and his son Evald—who hates his father because he has never been "able to show love or create an emotional situation in his home" (*BB,* 148, 14)—to being dutifully solicitous. What, of course, Bergman would have liked is summed up in that same film: when Isak, who, like Bergman, is revisiting the parsonage, calls up his past and hears someone say that he, Isak as a boy, is fishing with his father, he "felt a secret and completely inexplicable happiness at this message."[35] Understandably, Pastor Bergman's indifference to the films his son turned out year after year gnawed at the filmmaker's sense of achievement; learning that his father liked *The Seventh Seal* (1957) "very much" (Steene 1972, 13) meant more to him than any movie festival award, as evidenced by the fact that what he remembers about his grant of 2,000 *Sek* from the King's Fund in 1956 was that it "put my shares up at home with mother and father" (*BB,* 127).

Erik was lonely after Karin's death. Ingmar visited him with some frequency—once, as already noted, taking him on the location search for *Winter Light*—and they "talked to each other on friendly terms" (*ML*, 277). During Erik's final hospitalization he especially "appreciated" Ingmar's visits (Cowie 1982, 239). A week before he died in April 1970, in a lucid moment, he took his departing son's hand and called "down God's blessing" on him. Remembering a few Christmas Eves when, from behind the dark, distant, and brutal qualities in his father had emerged kindness, cheerfulness, and an ability to make everyone laugh with imitations of his colleagues, Ingmar now says, "I think in my memory I have often done my father an injustice" (*ML*, 15). (*The Best Intentions* [1992] attempts to rectify this injustice.) In his work journal on the day of his father's death Ingmar, who had rejected his father's religious faith, wrote of his own spiritual condition: "I think of him from a despairing distance, but with tenderness. Things are bad for Bergman this day. . . . The yearning for something at last to touch me, to give me grace. Things are bad this day. Not that I feel ill—on the contrary—but my soul . . ." (*ML*, 278).

Years later, having imagined his return to the parsonage and his interview with his mother's ghost, Bergman seems resigned: "I must think about what I have, not what I have lost or have never had. I will collect my treasures" (*ML*, 289). (In 1980, when he told Peter Cowie [1982, 3] that now when he thinks about it his childhood must have been happy and beautiful, Bergman was being sportively sentimental, willfully discounting that for half a century—and in his recent autobiography—he had been driving home to listeners and viewers the damage caused by his upbringing. To be sure, as we shall see, Bergman mellowed near the end of his career as a film director, but even *Fanny and Alexander,* as deliciously mellow as that film sometimes is, offers us a young surrogate who bitterly criticizes and/or rejects his father and mother, and whose immolating hatred for his stepfather results in inescapable guilt. Recollecting his mother's unhappy life and her sobbing revelation that her mother never loved her, he suddenly connects her influence on him and his siblings to the influence his unhappy grandmother had on both his parents. His grandmother had married a somewhat older man who had three sons about her age, and shortly thereafter they had two more children. "What had *she* [his grandmother] been forced to suppress and destroy?" he wonders. "What I can certainly see is that our family were people of good will but with a disastrous heritage of guilty conscience and too great demands made on them" (*ML*, 289). His own resignation is echoed in the line from his mother's diary with which he concludes his autobiography. Faced on that July day in 1918 with the seemingly doomed newborn infant and with the conflict between her mother and her unstable husband, Karin had written, "One will probably have to manage alone as best one can" (*ML, 290*).

By now it is obvious that insight into Bergman's psychological makeup and behavior is essential for understanding his art. Referring to his behavior 40 years before (during his early years in the theater and at SFI), he claims, a bit disingenuously, that he no longer recognizes the lonely, volcanic fellow who, if attacked, "snapped like a frightened dog . . . trusted no one, loved no one, missed no one," who was so obsessed with sexuality that he was constantly unfaithful, and who was tormented by "desire, fear, anguish and a guilty conscience" (*ML, 146*). At that time mixing or just talking with people was an ordeal for him. A troubled, abrasive misfit, he was known to either hide in the bathroom until visitors left or crush them with an enthusiastic welcome (Sjöman, 208).[36] Besides "brief moments in orgasm and drunkenness," his theatrical work was the chief release for his energies and tensions. (Gunnel Lindblom remembers that in his early days Bergman referred to "anyone who didn't throw furniture around as 'inhibited.'"[37]) He relied for acceptance on his theatrical talents and the tolerance of fellow artists, people who generally allow idiosyncratic behavior a wider latitude. As he put it, he took "refuge in a community of feeling, however illusory" (*BB, 62*). He had "surface charm," could be very persuasive, and possessed powers it would take him a long time to learn how to exercise graciously.

Bergman's rage, which could flare to blistering intensity when he was criticized or opposed, was just one symptom of an unpredictably explosive personality that did not mellow much until very late in life. Liv Ullmann recalls that when they were living together she was once "so frightened of [Bergman] that I locked myself in the bathroom. He stood outside hammering and kicking at the door trying to get in. Suddenly to my horror I saw his whole foot come through" (Ullmann, 127). Vilgot Sjöman, claiming that he, and Swedes generally, "fear outbursts of aggressions," is fascinated with "Ingmar's capacity to strike out, hard and suddenly . . . lightning flashes that he *simply cannot check*" (Sjöman, 155, 101).[38] "Maybe it's not noticeable," says Bergman, "but I'm always in a rage. It's one of my life-problems" (*BB, 251*). (One wag described him as being "as relaxed as any tiger" [Cole, 8 November 1959, 1].) Brutality and cruelty fascinate him so, he says, because they mirror his own character: "It's sort of dynamite inside" (Meryman, 67). This sleepless rage—clinicians would call it "narcissistic rage"—is in part the result of his projection onto the world of his own worst qualities and, consequently, of his view of the world as a place full of envy, hate, and revenge (Kernberg, 228, 233). "I am resentful, and suspicious," he admits. "I *never* forget" (Sjöman, 150).

In addition to being the joyous "game" he plays with his colleagues, filmmaking, in Bergman's view, is a process uniquely suited to ritualizing violence—both as a means of exorcising his ample aggression (*BB,* 84, 107, 61) and as an activity that satisfies his "longing for power, for manipulating other people" (Kakutani, 33). His need for omnipotence, he acknowledges, extends beyond his art and manifests itself in ordering *everyone* about: "It's of course . . . a need for power. I've had to keep a terrific check on that both in my private life and in my professional life" (Sjöman, 173). This need is somewhat less intense now than when he was younger: "When you are twenty-five you think you can rule the world. . . . Your ideas and opinions are perfect. . . . You're the ruler of mankind. You've got the body of a young God, your soul is unspoiled. . . . You're preoccupied with yourself—or the theater. . . . Later in life you find out how complicated it all really is."[39] In spite of this awareness, his overweening, narcissistic need for obedience has been such that he has often regarded as disloyalty or rejection any independent action on the part of a person with whom he is emotionally or professionally involved. "It is easy to confuse this strong bond with other feelings. You may fall in love with actors, you may be jealous, you may require a need to manage them offstage or outside the studio. But . . . if you're going to continue in the profession, it's appropriate to be clear about these impulses. I can't deny that in my younger days I managed to make a fine muddle of things for myself and others" (Lejefors, 40).

Liv Ullmann vividly describes the feelings and behavior of both the insecure, omnipotent master and his insecure, devoted slave: "After a short time I was confronted with his jealousy. Violent and without bounds. I had never experienced such a thing before. Now all doors were closed, barred. Friends and family, even memories, became a threat to our relationship. Terrified, I felt I only had him. . . . On the nights when he couldn't sleep, I would be silent beside him, afraid of what he was thinking. Perhaps . . . I disturbed the harmony he tried to create within himself. . . . My security became living the way he wished. For only then was *he* secure." This control extended to the most inconsequential and normally unthreatening of activities. "At dinner," says Ullmann, "he always ordered for both of [us]. When [I] recently dined at a restaurant with Bergman and his new wife, Ingrid, [I] watched curiously to see if the pattern persisted. Sure enough . . . Ingrid glanced cautiously at the master after ordering each item" (Ullmann, 110, 117). Bergman often expects his talented colleagues to be extensions of himself, to be merely selfless marionettes serving his talent and never opposing him. It is noteworthy that although he repeatedly expresses unbounded admiration for actors, the late Gunnar Björnstrand, who appeared in more Bergman films than any other actor, felt that Bergman had a deep contempt for actors, and that "when you've done a good job, you still don't get the credit for it yourself" (Sjöman, 136, 158).[40] In light of this statement, Bergman's decision in several of his published screenplays not to name the actors who played his characters in the films takes on significance. Even in *The Magic Lantern* the names Max von Sydow, Gunnar Björnstrand, Ingrid Thulin, Bibi Andersson, Harriet Andersson, Liv Ullmann— actors without whom Bergman's masterpieces would not be—are absent except insofar as they relate to his personal life (an exception that applies only to the last three).

Besides the fun and the aggression-venting and power-satisfying functions of filmmaking, it provides Bergman with a means of putting his experience in perspective and as an outlet for his need to control. He is proud that he has kept open the channel to that remote archipelago that was his botched, traumatic youth and early manhood. He has compulsively recast, reshot, and reedited the footage of that past, updating and translating it into adult situations. True, some experiences are too painful to reawaken and transform (*BB*, 147–48), but reworking the others that have been fermenting in that broth of memory and imagination has helped him, he says, to quiet, temporarily at least, his festering anxiety and guilt and to put those experiences in perspective. In fact, for Bergman security is seeing "the past in a new and less romantic light" ("Commandments," 14). With regard to the control that filmmaking provides he says, "I believe that in this feeling of a game we can find a stimulating sense of shaping a universe, shaping people, shaping situations."[41] Although detailing and storyboarding every scene are habits of many directors, Max von Sydow says Bergman does it "in order to avoid every risk of being caught off [guard] by situations—to keep control of everything" (Meryman, 70). Bergman agrees: "As I harbor a constant tumult within me and have to keep watch over it, I also suffer agony when faced with the unforeseen, the unpredictable" (*ML,* 33). His intimate friend Vilgot Sjöman comments: "What a fear he must have of anything blurred and chaotic, of being overwhelmed by emotional chaos in himself" (Sjöman, 17), and Erland Josephson writes that, for Bergman, "everything must be predictable and predicted. The only thing allowed to surprise Bergman and others is Bergman himself" *(Chaplin).* "The exercise of my profession," says Bergman, "thus becomes a pedantic administration of the unspeakable. I act as an intermediary, organizing, ritualizing" (*ML,* 33). Directing a film permits him to control "every little detail" (Kakutani, 33). A large part of what he says fascinated him when, as a youth, he made the projected figure in the Frau Holle film move fast or slow—and "what even today still fascinates me" (Geduld, 187)—has to be that very control.

"Born hysterical" (Simon, 37), Bergman derives both a psychological and a physiological benefit from control: it manages the chaos of his sensations. When he was a child the sound of a violin played in a distant room produced in him gloomy visions and violent weeping (Hedlund, 48). Like his father, he finds unendurable even today a wide variety of sounds that most of us dismiss as merely annoying. Visiting London for the first time, he had to use earplugs because the noise was intolerable (Cole, 8 November 1959, 4). During a rehearsal a faint whisper or someone nearby using an eraser will irritate him.[42] An artist using charcoal to sketch him caused Bergman to stuff his ears with wool. Although cannon firing supposedly damaged the hearing in his right ear, a sound technician from SFI recorded in his diary that during the filming of *The Virgin Spring* (1960) Bergman suddenly sensed that the sound was poor. The technicians were unconvinced. Adamant, Bergman ordered microanalysis of the sound track, and the distortion was discovered (Hedlund, 48–49). Light, too, can be painful to him: bright sunlight makes him claustrophobic, and the sun shining day after day can be maddening (*Time,* 61, 48). His "nightmares are always saturated in sunshine" (*BB,* 78). In *The Ritual* (1969), a television film in which he parceled out among five characters different facets of his own personality, he used part of a letter written to him by a young woman he had met in 1934 in Germany. Bergman puts her description of herself in the mouth of a husband describing his "unusual" actress wife, but the director may well be describing himself: "Many would say she is neurotic. I say she is hypersensitive mentally and physically. . . . [Her] overdeveloped senses [are a trial for her. She] react[s] painfully to violent sounds, strong light or nasty smells."

His distinction between hypersensitivity and neurosis is appropriate, but his neuroses are legend. Liv Ullmann, for example, describes neurotic behavior that obviously still rankles her: Ingmar "is particularly angry at me because Linn [their child] has a cold. He has a deathly fear of germs, and looks at me with a wordless fury I recognize all too well" (Ullmann, 231–32). Bergman suffers from chronic stomach problems—some of which his doctor labels psychosomatic (*ML,* 179)—chronic diarrhea, insomnia, and a bad hip. Until around 1980 he also had "an almost clinical aversion to travel," which he found scary, disorienting, and unbalancing (*Playboy,* 62).[43] New cities are too stimulating; even with ear plugs he found London "unmanageable," and he could not sleep in Paris ("Commandments," 60). Yet once arrived and settled in, he can enjoy traveling: "I am a Dr. Jekyll and Mr. Hyde; I hate to go abroad, and I love to go abroad" (Weinraub, 29 April 1976, 54). Liv Ullmann reveals what traveling with Dr. Jekyll and Mr. Hyde is like: the people and the noise at the Copenhagen airport produce panic, and Bergman "feels a strong urge to return home, back to the security of Fårö. The flight is delayed, and he takes an elevator [one of his fears is being confined in a tiny space] down to the men's room. . . . After a while the elevator door opens and Ingmar comes out. He has his little cap on his head, and there is a faint smile of pride. Here is someone who has overcome his phobia, gone into a strange elevator, into a strange toilet, and made it back all by himself" (Ullmann, 213).

The "technical solution" to his fear of meeting new people and to traveling outside of Sweden is "to regulate my life just so . . . [into a] very orderly . . . ritual. That keeps my tensions in balance, keeps the heavy, difficult thing inside me from starting to roll. . . . I think if I let my routine go, in a few weeks the catastrophe would be complete. I mean some sort of self destruction" (Meryman, 70). (The Åkerblom family had a history of "nervous instability" [Gado, 3]). A perceptive observer has noticed that Bergman "is highly dependent on his observations of others to give him a sense of orderly life" (Kakutani, 28). Routine and ritual also manifest themselves in obsessive-compulsive behavior: if he is going to be ten minutes late for an appointment, he sends off a warning telegram; he always eats "the same lunch" (Meryman, 70–71); and he never changes the style of his shoes, shirts, sweaters, pants, jackets, and slippers ("When the old ones wear out they are replaced by replicas" [Ullmann, 213]). He battled with his wife Käbi when she wanted to get rid of his beret and his leather jacket: "I compromised and sacrificed my beret. But not the leather jacket. It contained my past; she took it. But I'm not letting the Volvo go, I'll hold onto that to my dying day" (Sjöman, 173).

There is also a problematic experience that undermines the stability of his world. The picture he presents of having given up "living in a community" and keeping for himself his "world of phantoms" during youth and adolescence, and his repeated accounts of confusing dream and reality, suggest a more protean psyche than he acknowledges. An early playmate of his recalls, "Ingmar never could distinguish between lie and truth, fantasy and reality" (Gado, 10). Though he denies that he hallucinates, evidence suggests that at times he sees or feels the presence of people, demons, or spirits who seem almost as substantial as himself. He has even learned how to invoke them: in *Fanny and Alexander,* watch Alexander's eyes as, under his grandmother's table, he seems to produce a trance that permits him to experience the in-animate become animate. And these visions, however induced, are not always easily exorcised. Just after *Hour of the Wolf* opened Berg-man confirmed that he had used his dreams and nightmares in it as well as in the earlier *Sawdust and Tinsel* (1953) and *Wild Strawberries.* In writing *Hour of the Wolf*—the dramatization of an artist's mental deterioration under pressure from figures from a demonic realm—had he, inquired the interviewer, consciously returned to deal with the schizophrenia experienced by Karin in *Through a Glass Darkly*? "No, not exactly," Bergman replied. "I have always been interested in those voices inside you—and I think everybody has these voices and forces—and I have always wanted to make them visible." He then described how—the pace and volume of his voice increasing as he imaginatively relived the experience—during the writing of *Hour of the Wolf* the demonic characters came to him:

> They came very, very fast, and suddenly they were there!—all of them, and I had difficulty selecting them. They would come, all of them—about 50, 60. And I wrote, I think, three or four books full of notes with people—[here the interviewer tried to interrupt, but the excited Berg-man refused to let him, saying, "Beg your pardon" and rushed on]. . . .
> It was a very hot summer. I was sitting in a room . . . very quiet, silent, with shadows—I don't want to have the sun in the room when I write. I slept there too. And I had to finish—I couldn't sleep there; after two or three weeks I couldn't sleep there because *they* were there! . . . They wouldn't get out! They woke me in the night and they stood there in the . . . hour of the wolf . . . and they talked to me.

He added, "It was a very, very strange time."[44]

When John Simon later queried him about this encounter, Bergman at first contended that his description had been "just a little joke," but he went on to connect the experience with similar, surprisingly recent ones:

> Yet it's not exactly a joke, because when I was younger, not very much younger, say, five, six [years ago—around 1966, the year of *Persona* and *Hour of the Wolf*], ten years ago [1961—the year of *Through a Glass Darkly*] and back into my childhood, I was haunted by extremely terrible dreams, sometimes daydreams; sometimes things happened to me in a very, very strange, mysterious, and dangerous way, and I was very scared, and sometimes my dreams were so real that when I tried to remember something, I didn't know exactly if it had happened in reality or if I had dreamed it. It was very painful. (Simon, 28–29)

When Johan Borg kills a boy in *Hour of the Wolf*, Bergman says that Johan did not know whether it "was a dream or real. . . . The boundary between dream and reality had been blurred" (*BB,* 220). Initially, in *Winter Light,* Jonas Persson visits Tomas just once; the second appearance was to have been an hallucination: "He is a vision. He has never been there . . . you've experienced that yourself, haven't you? One sits there and experiences something so intensely that it is just as if thinking so hard of what he is to say to the fisherman that he imagines Jonas is there. He asks Märta afterwards if she has seen Jonas. . . . 'Did you see anyone go out here?' 'No . . . when I came into the vestry, I saw you sitting at the table asleep.' [N.B.!]" (Sjöman, 39). In his autobiography Bergman goes into additional detail: "Worst are the 'hours of the wolf' in the small hours between three and five. That is when the demons come: mortification, loathing, fear, and rage. There is no point in trying to suppress them, for that makes it worse. When my eyes tire of reading, there is music. I close my eyes and listen with concentration and give the demons free rein: come on then, I know you, I know how you function, you just carry on until you tire of it. After a while the bottom falls out of them and they become foolish, then disappear, and I sleep for a few hours" (*ML,* 226). Having himself broached these experiences with another interviewer, Bergman concluded, "I live at the edge of a very strange country and I don't know what will happen" (Meryman, 67).

The protean quality of Bergman's ego may even bear on his sexual identity if what he says in the following passage, partly quoted earlier, means what it seems to: "You may fall in love with actors, you may be jealous, you may require a need to manage them offstage or outside the studio. . . . I can't deny that in my younger days I managed to make a fine muddle of things for myself and others. You can fall in love with a male actor just as well as a female one, though perhaps rather a female" (Lejefors, 1).

When he was eight and his grandmother's maid Lalla informed him that because he was a Sunday's child he should be able to see ghosts and fairies, he must have begun to believe that in some way he possessed special powers. Though ready to see these spirits, he says he never saw any, except for "a little grey man with a bright spiteful face; he was holding a girl by the hand, and she was no bigger than my middle finger. I wanted to capture her, but the gnome and his daughter got away" (*ML*, 267). He tells of more recent spiritualistic encounters, but in a playful tone that keeps the reader guessing: he recounts his experiences of 1980 and 1983 when he felt the presence of his deceased mother beside him, and of Strindberg phoning and wanting to meet and talk about Bergman's current production of *A Dream Play*. Bergman then says, "I tell all this as an amusing story, but deep down in my childish heart, naturally I do not consider it as such. Ghosts, demons and other creatures with neither name nor domicile have been around me since childhood . . . good, evil or just annoying, they have blown in my face, pushed me, pricked me with pins, plucked at my jersey. They have spoken, hissed or whispered. Clear voices, not particularly comprehensible but impossible to ignore" (*ML*, 202, 204). Asked if he believes in magic or demonic phenomena, he replies—and his character Eva in *Autumn Sonata* (1978) makes the same point—"Obviously I think there's a great deal that we neither see nor hear normally. I think that, with our intellect, we're able to shed light on an extremely small sector of existence" (Lejefors, 39). These attitudes, his extraordinary hypersensitivity, and his possible hallucinatory tendency bear upon the crucial subject of his belief in God. In the chapters that follow we will trace the path of his altering belief, but in recent years he has insisted that he does not believe in God, or in any life other than the present one. "I am neither able nor willing to imagine another life. . . . From somebody I will become a nobody" (*ML*, 264–65). And he hopes, he says, that "I never get so old I get religious."[45] Nevertheless, he remains deeply superstitious, and the reason is not difficult to fathom: can someone for whom, at times, reality turns protean ever believe with assurance that the supernatural (and its centerpiece, God) does not exist? We should probably regard him as a hopeful rather than an optimistic agnostic.

The evidence is persuasive that Bergman periodically has made involuntary and possibly voluntary sallies across the border of the very strange country at whose edge he lives. On one occasion, in fact, he was forced far across the border, on terms not his own, to suffer a sanity- and life-threatening breakdown: he was unexpectedly arrested for tax evasion on Friday, 30 January 1976, at the Royal Palace Theater in Stockholm while he was in the middle of a rehearsal of *The Dance of Death*. On the way home from police headquarters, he says, he "passed the Life Guards' barracks and great flames were shooting out of the roof into the darkening light. Now, afterwards, I wonder whether I had imagined it. I saw no fire engines or crowds. It was perfectly quiet, snow falling, and the Life Guards' barracks on fire" (*ML*, 89). The breakdown came the following Monday when his wife Ingrid had gone to a meeting of lawyers and he was alone. Still a little drowsy from a sleeping pill (though "perhaps I had taken that short step from the accepted reality of the senses into the other reality"), he saw "in the sharp light, a few meters away, I myself . . . standing looking at myself. The experience was concrete and incontestable. . . . This was the end, there was no return. I could hear myself wailing." Bergman says that once or twice he has toyed with the idea of suicide, and that once, in his youth, he made a feeble attempt, but he loves life too much to ever be serious about it. However, he emphatically insists that he now "got up out of my chair to leave through the window" (*ML*, 91), and that had not Ingrid, who unbeknownst to him had returned, stopped him he would have accomplished the act. What he says at this point in his account about his hallucination is important because it insistently contradicts the impression left by almost everything else he has said about the degree to which he confuses fantasy with reality: "My attitude to life . . . presuppos[es] a proper and continuous control of my relation to reality, imaginings and dreams. When that control did not function—*something which had never happened to me before, not even in my early childhood*—the machinery exploded and my identity was threatened." (Later, he said, "I had a feeling that I had lost my identity completely and *I liked it!*")[46] Subsequently, he spent nearly a month in Karolinska Hospital's psychiatric ward.

Bergman's extraordinary, domineering will has been his chief means of fighting the chaos created by his mental and physical hypresensitivity, his phobias, his narcissistic rage, and his problematic hallucinations. When he was filming *Face to Face* he proclaimed, "I feel I have found equilibrium. Living no longer torments me." "Every time he proclaims this," comments an amused Liv Ullmann, "he believes it, because he always says it on a good day" (Ullmann, 235). Though he openly admits to being plagued by tics and phobias, hating to travel, and fearing the darkness, open doors, and people standing too close behind him (Kakutani, 36), he boasts (obviously on a good day), "I know my neuroses and I can say hello to them and I talk to them and I have them under control. I am extremely healthy. My doctor thinks I will [live to] be one hundred and ten" (Meryman, 66).

Studying Bergman's life and films, however, has led me to give great weight to his statement that, "if Bergman could see through his products and especially himself, he would long ago have discovered his hollow emptiness" (*Chaplin*). Although this charge was launched years ago from behind the protection of a pseudonym—Bergman was writing as the contemptuous critic Ernest Riffe—it is not to be dismissed as purely facetious. In fact, several of Bergman's statements that I have already quoted provide a sense of what he is suggesting about himself. One area I hope my chronological analysis of his films will illuminate is the degree to which this judgment of himself is true. I begin, then, with his early plays and films, inserting the remaining, relevant biographical information along the way.

2

Bergman Learning

To write about Bergman's apprentice years is to tell a story more of stumbling than of success; often enough, his ego and obsessions were the source of the problem. Yet, the stages of his development have real fascination as well as importance, and even his apprentice works show signs of genius. I begin this account of his growth as a film-maker with his major themes—narcissism, marriage, God, and death—several of which necessarily interweave in these films, just as they have done in his life.

THE THEME OF NARCISSISM

The reader will not be surprised to find that Bergman sensed early on that narcissism was not only the engine that drove his creativity but his artistic subject matter. Some of the plays that he chose to direct when he joined Mäster–Olofsgården—Strindberg's *The Pelican, Lucky Per's Journey,* and *The Ghost Sonata,* for example—reflect that concern. The first involves a mother who is "so much in love with herself" that she sacrifices her children's health; the second concerns a youth so imprisoned in his narcissism that even though he learns that "one who loves only himself can never love anyone else," finally, hopelessly, and poignantly he has to admit, "I would free myself from self—if I could."[1] *The Ghost Sonata* (1907), a play that never lost its appeal to Bergman, involves a young man, a "Sunday's child," who can see spirits and becomes involved with a man who controls and humiliates others by stripping them of their facades. Bergman's affinity for stories involving narcissists, often diabolical, who control others, and for characters controlled by authority figures, their own obsessions, or such forces as fate, God, or death, links him to a number of earlier Swedish playwrights and novelists: Strindberg, Pär Lagerkvist, Hjalmar Söderberg, and Hjalmar Bergman (no relation to Ingmar). Hjalmar Bergman, in fact, wrote what he labeled "marionette plays," plays in which characters are often unconsciously directed by circumstance, their own past, a person psychologically stronger than themselves, or by death.[2] This vision of a puppeteer controlling marionettes spoke to something important in Bergman; he adopted it early and never abandoned it. His own two-act play *Kasper's Death* (1940) was a marionette play done in Punch and Judy style. In it the immature, frightened, young Kasper feels trapped by his boring marriage to Kasperina. Superficially brave, Kasper seeks relief in a tavern whose clientele consists of prostitutes and criminals, people who represent free expression of aggressive and libidinal urges. In a scene that presages a scene in *The Seventh Seal,* Kasper is forced by revelers to dance on a table until he collapses and dies. Bergman's play *Jack among the Actors* (1946) is also essentially a marionette play. In it he enlarged Kasper into Jack Kasparsson, a (usually) nonlethal Jack the Ripper–like character who is driven by violent sexual and aggressive urges, yet who is fundamentally as frightened as Kasper. Jack meets an elderly, alcoholic actor, Michael Bro, who fears that his life has no meaning.[3] Bro is part of a theater troupe run by the Director whom no one has ever seen but who provides the roles. The drama they perform, entitled *Trio,* mirrors Bro's real-life situation. It concerns a cuckolded husband (played by Bro), a wife (played by Bro's wife), and her lover. The night Bro brings Jack to the performance, Bro refuses, at his cue, to shoot his rival; instead, he tells the audience that people must pray to God and use their short lives to love and help one another, not to act out their base, selfish instincts. Then he crumbles to the stage, a victim of a stroke. Before dying, he warns Jack against stepping into the role of the doomed lover, but when the actor playing that role takes on Bro's, Jack finds the vacant role irresistible. The puppeteer-marionette metaphor is further developed when, a short time later, Jack finally meets the Director, whom Bro had described as God and the Devil rolled into one. The awesome Janus figure tells Jack that he is tired of "pulling the strings" to make people dance "like puppets for my amusement," and that he is disbanding the troupe. The Director, who considers himself "unusually human," condemns his puppets' pride, baseness, egotism, and cruelty and suggests that their conception of God as kind is a joke; God is criminal and probably does not even exist, otherwise he would have committed suicide seeing the universe He created. The Director, however, encourages our identification of him with Him: "I shall die soon. But I was great while I lived. Great! Powerful! I mastered many. I was their God and their Devil! I was great and I was ugly." The bohemian protagonist of Bergman's play *Rakel and the Cinema Doorman* (1946) writes a novel "portraying mankind as marionettes" (Gado, 106), and in Bergman's play *The Day Ends Early* (1947) a God-like playwright and actual puppeteer, Peter, sells his marionettes when he comes to realize that he too is a puppet who has played hundreds of roles unsuccessfully. Bergman's own puppet theater undoubtedly influenced his fascination with this metaphor, and being a puppeteer may also be the source of the image that later makes its horrifying appearance in *Through a Glass Darkly:* God as a spider. The God-like puppeteer positions himself unseen above his world stage and manipulates his puppets by means of a myriad of almost invisible threads dangling from the crossed sticks he holds; hands, sticks, and strings resemble the spider's body, legs, and threads.

In the first film Bergman directed at SFI, *Crisis* (1946), he added the Jack character to Leck Fischer's radio play, *The Mother Heart* (1944), on which the film was based. (Jack was played by Stig Olin, whose physical resemblance to Bergman partially accounts for Bergman's repeated use of him as his surrogate—for example, in *The Devil's Wanton* [1949], *To Joy* [1950], and *Summer Interlude* [1951].) Seducer, crook, and megalomaniac, alternately "arrogant and maudlin," Jack loves to "see people obeying him." After behaving wildly at a small town annual ball—where he has been trying to seduce 18-year-old Nelly (Inga Landgré) after getting her drunk—he looks down from a hill at the crowd he has thrown into chaos and with devilish delight tells her, "Have you ever seen such crazy marionettes? Do you know who set it all in motion? I did." Jack "can love nobody but himself," but like other Bergman narcissists, his ballooning monomania and dissolving sense of reality compel him to seek out the stabilizing companionship of a strong, well-adjusted woman. He tells Nelly he needs her to be his "anchor in reality." Unbeknownst to Jack or Nelly, Jenny (Marianne Löfgren), Jack's beautiful former mistress and Nelly's mother, is eavesdropping. Revealing herself, she informs Nelly that Jack fed her that same line but also offered to shoot himself. She now dares him to carry out his threat. Jack answers, "People like me don't take their own lives; that would be out of character." Jack leaves and proceeds to act out of character (from unconscious guilt and self-hatred[4]): a shot is heard and he is found in front of the theater, his bloodied head covered with the front page of a newspaper bearing Ingmar Bergman's photograph and a headline announcing the "Death of Local Theater Director."

Narcissism is also at the core of the early films that Bergman wrote and/or directed. The story that became Alf Sjöberg's film *Torment* (1944) was written by Bergman when he was about to enter college. Its protagonist is a normal, adolescent narcissist, and the story is about his struggle for independence from forces—family, school, and hostile social institutions—that seek to prevent his realization of self, that is, his fulfillment of his artistic destiny and satisfaction of his lust and need for love. Ultimately he learns how self-centered, controlling, and destructive his love is. A related pattern also appears here: the young man is drawn to a woman who either is or is thought to be promiscuous. Because he does not opportunely come to her aid, he becomes indirectly responsible for her death. This pattern appears to arise from Bergman's "hypothesis" that "all women want to be martyrs" (Sjöman, 128, 134)—his rationalization for seeing others as existing for his (and his alter egos') self-fulfillment or self-understanding.

Torment's Jan-Erik Widgren (Alf Kjellin) is an incipient artist impatient to graduate from high school ("hell") so he can write, play his violin, and find an innocent girl to love forever. One night part of his "adolescent prayer" is answered when he comes upon the drunk, staggering Berta Olsson (Mai Zetterling). He helps her to her apartment and sleeps with her, though not without warning her that he feels nothing serious for her. At her request, however, he returns repeatedly, and soon they have fallen in love, his presence seemingly having driven off the mysterious man who had coerced her into a relationship and terrified her into alcoholism. Infusions of Jan-Erik's will power help her regain her innocence, and she becomes his ideal woman. (So transformed is she that she talks of marriage, but Jan-Erik knows that his parents and teachers would be outraged at his and Berta's relationship.) Clearly young Bergman understood that when the narcissist makes a lover one's "all" he is actually loving an idealized image of his own creation, and that when the lover's inevitable shortcomings are discovered the narcissist not only feels that his lover is not worthy of his idealistic effort but learns that he is not as powerful in his ability to control the world as he imagined. Invariably he turns the anger that results from these feelings against the once idealized lover. Jan-Erik's disillusionment comes when, exhilarated by having successfully completed his exams for graduation, he rushes to share his accomplishment with Berta only to find her smirkingly drunk and numb to his outrage (her tormentor has gotten to her again). Bergman mocks Jan-Erik by having him foreshadow his parents' reaction to what will be his own painful situation: he shouts at her, "Wasn't it 'fun' being *decently* in love? . . . Why did this have to happen to me? . . . I feel as if I really never knew you. Anyway, you've killed what I felt." Jan-Erik sees Berta twice more before her death: first, when she appears in his nightmare to remind him of their love and her need for protection; and again on the day he returns to school after he has recovered from a nervous breakdown. She pleads with him not to abandon her, but he replies curtly, "I am through; I won't have anything to do with you. That's final!" However, that evening he relents and goes to her apartment, only to find her spread across her bed, dead, and his Latin teacher, a man the students refer to as Caligula, cowering among the coats in the entry.

Named by his students after the mild, generous Roman emperor who, after a severe illness, became a monster who tortured and killed thousands of his subjects, this classroom Caligula (Stig Järrel), who also has been sick, torments anyone over whom he has power.[5] A fearful man driven by satanic urges he can barely repress,[6] Caligula is another of Bergman's autobiographical Jacks. Caligula is also characterized as a vampire who sucks life from others; when Berta cuts her finger, Caligula, Dracula-like, involuntarily is drawn to the bleeding cut. As a consequence, the possibility of vampirism crosses our minds later when Caligula is found hiding in her apartment and she is lying dead on her bed, her head thrown back and her neck exposed.

When Jan-Erik's relationship with Berta is revealed and Caligula lies about the situation, the school's sympathetic headmaster is forced to expel the youth. Typically, and like most of Bergman's young protagonists who are confronted by adult authority figures, Jan-Erik at first is self-defeatingly passive. Then, replaying Bergman's rupture with his parents, a point is reached when the lies and taunts of his antagonist trigger violence: screaming, Jan-Erik knocks Caligula to the floor and flees. That night an interrogation by Jan-Erik's unsympathetic, self-concerned father provokes the lad into leaving home. After watching his schoolmates graduate, and confessing to a friend that he fears for his sanity, he withdraws to Berta's dismal apartment and gives himself over to his depression. The headmaster, however, concerned that Jan-Erik might commit suicide, searches him out and advises him not to withdraw into himself and give up on society but to fight for his future. Before leaving, he takes Jan-Erik affectionately by the shoulders and tells him that some good, though it is not always discernible at the time, often comes of unfortunate situations. Alone, Jan-Erik falls asleep. When he awakens it is to spring sunshine, and we hear bright, airy music on the sound track; he has undergone a metamorphic rebirth. Tucking Berta's sensual, frightened kitten—the symbol of his new appreciation of her—under his jacket, he leaves her apartment, only to find the panicky Caligula sitting on the landing outside her door. Having learned by now that people exist who are so evil that compassion cannot ameliorate their condition, but also having been purged of all recriminatory feelings toward those who have injured him, Jan-Erik responds politely to his teacher's paranoid questions and confessions, then steps out of the darkness into the sunbathed street. Accompanied by the sound of church bells and trumpeting, athletic music, he climbs to the top of a hill overlooking the city. After surveying the scene and smiling at the kitten, he confidently steps out of the frame, leaving us to scan the city and speculate on how he will reengage with the society he never wanted to leave. (Järrel's powerful acting leaves Caligula's final, pathetic cry, like that of some lonely, cornered animal, sounding in our memories long after the forced optimism surrounding Jan-Erik.)

The central concern of *Torment,* as of virtually all of Bergman's early films, is the education of its protagonist, often at the cost of someone else's life. (Berta, we learn, died of natural causes, so Jan-Erik is only indirectly responsible for her death and is conveniently freed from a commitment—marriage—he is not ready to make.) Jan-Erik learns from his relationship with Berta that narcissism is destructive, and that he must not impose on his lover his conception of what she should be. He learns that love means "I want *you* to be."

After directing his first film, *Crisis,* Bergman directed *It Rains on Our Love* (1946), wrote *Woman without a Face* (1947), and directed *Ship to India* (1947). *Woman without a Face* continues the Kasparsson pattern. Martin Grandé (Alf Kjellin) reluctantly marries a woman pregnant with his child and soon finds middle-class existence oppressive. Consequently, he deserts his military service and his wife for a gloriously fevered and violent romance with the femme fatale Rut Kohler (Gunn Wållgren)—a woman "with breasts, hips, arms, legs, but . . . without a face"—and her unconventional friends. Only after a great struggle, which includes his attempted suicide, is Martin able to appreciate what he has almost lost. He finally flees Sweden, but the implication is that he will return to his country and his family.

Ship to India is based on Martin Söderhjelm's play, but Bergman infuses it with his own concerns by stressing the hatred of young, hunchbacked Johannes (Birger Malmsten) for his sadistic, narcissistic father, Captain Blom (Holger Löwenadler) (*BB,* 28, 30).[7] Captain Blom also fits the Kasparsson pattern of a man wanting to escape his torpid marriage and job: a Caligula-like captain of a salvage boat, and going blind, he dreams of sailing away to the South Seas with his young mistress Sally (Gertrud Fridh). Given Sweden's geography, a fair number of Bergman's films involve the sea, sailing, beaches, islands, or the archipelago. In the early films the sea and the archipelago represent escape; in the later films the sea dominates and takes on a more universal, even metaphysical significance—from being the source of life it is transformed into a symbol of the cold, indifferent universe.

Ship to India's central focus is the hypersensitive Johannes, whose deformity is both a source of his feeling of inferiority and the symbol of the crippling effect of the suffocating refusal of his tyrannical father and passive, unloving mother to let him achieve independence, that is, to get his sailor's license. Bergman emphasizes the violent swings in Johannes's moods. When the captain brings Sally to live on board the ship with the family, Johannes tries to rape her; a gentle Johannes soon apologizes and makes love to her. But in confrontations with his father he becomes limply passive: in one instance, after Captain Blom seizes him by the neck and twice slaps his face, Johannes drops his arms to his sides, closes his eyes, and throws his head back, inviting another slap. When, as with Jan-Erik, a surge of hate finally overrides his paralysis and spurs him to grab a knife, a third slap saps his courage; he drops the knife and, crying, falls impotently to the floor. Later the two exchange personalities. On discovering that Johannes has won Sally's affection and made love to her, the captain again slaps his son's face. To everyone's amazement, Johannes returns the blow, and the humiliated father goes limp, his ego and sexual superiority dissolving into childlike feelings of powerlessness and hopelessness. With this slap Johannes—who hikes up his pants, tightens his belt, and announces, "I could do with a good breakfast now!"—is liberated; the mantle of his father's authority, as head of the family, as crew boss, and as Sally's lover, shifts to his shoulders. Henceforth, Johannes's hump is virtually unnoticeable.

Following this humiliation, the captain, like the distraught Jan-Erik, secludes himself in his cabin, emerging only to try to murder Johannes by cutting his air hose while he is diving. His wife Alice (Anna Lindahl), however, thwarts the attempt, and the captain flees to his apartment in the city where, virtually blind and half-insane, he attempts suicide when the police arrive by jumping from an upper-story window. He survives but is paralyzed. Johannes becomes a sailor and, after an interval of seven years, returns to fulfill his promise to marry Sally and take her to sea with him.

Sally articulates, and Alice embodies, an attitude that will be held by numerous Bergman characters, especially his women. They hold that almost any kind of relationship is better than being alone. "No-body," Sally tells Johannes, "should be *all* alone. Everybody *must* have someone to turn to, to care for, or to trust. Otherwise, one might just as well be dead." The pathetic aspect of this position is that even though the characters have someone with whom they can share their lives, they seldom have loving relationships. Bergman's alter egos are incapable of connecting in this way.

Though Alice tries to dissuade her husband from leaving her, she timorously stands by when he brings Sally to live on board, and she shocks Sally by admitting that all she wants is to devote the rest of her years to taking care of him. She knows, she tells Sally, that Sally will leave him when he goes blind, and then he will return to her: "I'll take care of him. We'll have our little cottage, our pension. That thought keeps me going." At the end Alice indeed has him: blind, insane, and paralyzed.

The commercial success of Bergman's *Night Is My Future* (1948), a film I will discuss in connection with his attitude toward God, led to his making *Port of Call* (1948), another story about a young, self-centered escapist, a merchant seaman whose motto had been, "When the ship sinks, jump overboard. . . . Swim anywhere, as long as *you* are not sucked down." After eight years of ports, one-night stands with whores from dance halls, and the safety of transience, 29-year-old Gösta Andersson (Bengt Eklund) returns to Gothenburg ready at last to marry and raise a family. At a dance hall he magically—a term, as will be seen, I use purposely—meets Berit Holm (Nine-Christine Jönsson). After sleeping with her and spending time with her, he is ready to marry her, until she insists on revealing, so that he can never say she has deceived him, her reform school stints and love affairs— all of which, through no fault of her own, turned out so badly she finally attempted suicide. Even though he wants to rise above the doubts about her that her story has provoked, Gösta cannot. Berit is numbed by the silence that follows his question, "Why did you tell me?"

Gösta is encouraged by his best friend to forget Berit ("There is only self!"), but he asks, "Why do we overlook our faults but not other people's?" At last he visits the apartment where she lives with her tyrannical mother (Berta Hall), who, like Captain Blom, is intent on preventing her offspring from achieving independence and happiness. Mrs. Holm's insinuations about Berit's past backfire, however; Gösta sees just what kind of mother she is. But then Berit shows him photographs of her old boyfriends, reigniting his doubts.

One day Berit unexpectedly shows up at his apartment with Gertrud (Mimi Nelson), her promiscuous "friend" from reform school. Hemorrhaging from an abortion, Gertrud dies on his doorstep. Afraid of being "sucked down," Gösta watches from behind the crowd as the ambulance takes Gertrud away and the police arrest Berit. Again a protagonist abandons the woman he loves in her time of need, and again the death of a promiscuous woman, here Berit's alter ego Gertrud, shocks him into facing his narcissism. Afterwards, drunk in a room with a whore, he snarls, "Ever see a monster, a two-legged swine? . . . Anybody ever beg you to stay and you just went? . . . I've no conscience!"

When the police release Berit, she returns home to find Gösta asleep on her stairs. She accepts his heartfelt apology and agrees to his suggestion that they flee Sweden, but after making the arrangements they change their minds. The fighter in Gösta reasserts itself. He promises to help Berit deal with her mother and the authorities; together they can overcome all obstacles to her freedom and their happiness. The music swells, and Berit sings out, "And soon it will be summer!"— the symbol of rebirth and hope in Swedish life and literature. A high, distant shot shows them (à la *The Bicycle Thief* [1949]) walking hand in hand and finally merging with and disappearing into the pedestrian traffic crossing the bridge back into the city. This ending is typical:

Bergman structures almost all of his stories around his characters' return home.[8] It is a pattern that evokes a sense of completion and security, a closure that emanates from something deep inside him.

In 1961 Bergman described a possible plot idea to Vilgot Sjöman: "A story about an egocentric young nobleman. . . . His wife is deeply attached to him, but he casts her aside for all kinds of affairs. He's the man who cannot accept love. . . . Until at last he realizes how hopelessly dependent he is on his wife, and goes back to her. . . . But that story's far too easy for me to write, I've written it many times before'" (Sjöman, 5). *The Devil's Wanton* (1949), the first film Bergman was permitted to direct from his own script, is just such a story.

Bergman should have added to that synopsis that it usually takes a jolt—sometimes the death of a lover—for his protagonists to comprehend their narcissism. In *The Devil's Wanton* Sofi (Eva Henning), the wife of the film's narcissistic protagonist Tomas (Birger Malmsten), says early on that only a shock of some kind can change her husband. Unlike Jan-Erik, whose narcissism appears to be just an adolescent phase, Tomas's seems pathological. Almost 30 and a dilettante, he hates himself and feels a profound emptiness that manifests itself in his lack of convictions and ineffectualness. A journalist, he cannot finish his articles; an incipient alcoholic, he is often cruel to his too tolerant wife. (When a friend half-jokingly suggests he would like to run off with Sofi, Tomas comes up behind her chair, playfully grabs a fistful of her hair, and pulls her head backwards to smirk into her pained, upturned face.) Because he feels others are to be treated as extensions of himself, he decides one night, while drunk and feeling his existence to be especially meaningless, that he *and* Sofi must commit suicide—she from his "firm conviction that [she does not] know what's best for [her]." Wary of what in his ineptness he might actually do, she knocks him out and leaves him. (When he recovers, he temporarily believes that he has murdered her.)

That night Tomas is approached by the beautiful 17-year-old prostitute Birgitta Carolina Söderberg (Doris Svedlund), whom he once interviewed for an article. She has just realized that her lover-pimp Peter has no intention of marrying her. (Peter is played by the Bergman look-alike Stig Olin, and Tomas, who sports a beard like the one Bergman wore at the time, describes him as "interesting . . . intelligent, rather handsome. A little like me.") Birgitta Carolina persuades Tomas to help her escape from Peter, and the two take refuge in the attic of a boardinghouse where as a child Tomas used to visit his aunt.

(In *Through a Glass Darkly* Karin's regressive, schizophrenic fantasies occur in an atticlike room. In fact, in a scene cut from *The Devil's Wanton* Birgitta Carolina has an experience with wallpaper that presages Karin's [*BB*, 162].) This repository of his happy childhood—it still contains his rocking horse and movie projector—puts him in touch with what Sofi refers to as the lost, "essential qualities we had as children." In addition, being with Birgitta Carolina brings out a heretofore unseen tenderness in Tomas. Though we are encouraged to believe that Birgitta Carolina has liberated an authentic love in Tomas, the truth is that his transformation is the result of his total control of this desperate young woman.[9] Birgitta Carolina's first clue to his narcissism comes when she inquires if he loves his wife, and he replies, "Yes, but I love *myself* more." That she understands his fundamental character is fully evidenced in her nightmare, which also forces her to remember what she has repressed about her own past: that she gave tacit approval for Peter and her sister Linnéa (Irma Christenson) to murder her baby.[10] (Peter's insistence that a child would make her less appealing to their customers and that, more important, he eventually will marry her and give her another child, persuaded her to let him take their newborn infant.) In the nightmare she comes upon Tomas weeping and hugging his damaged rocking horse, which has been struck by a car (seen overturned in the background). Birgitta Carolina tries to comfort him and, in so doing, reiterates Bergman's theme that any relationship is preferable to loneliness: "I want to stay with you. . . . You can shout at me or beat me. And I'll never be lonely again." Her efforts are fruitless, however; continuing to hug his wooden horse, he ignores her. Worse, when she raises her head from his shoulder she is horrified to find—as Antonius Block will be when he discovers he has been confessing not to a priest but to Death—that Tomas has metamorphosed into her sadistic client Alf (Curt Masreliez), who had pleasured himself by burning her arms with cigarettes.

Days later, while Tomas is making it brutally clear to the visiting Sofi that because he loves Birgitta Carolina their marriage is finished, Birgitta Carolina, so as not to involve him in the murder of her child, leaves him. Tomas rushes to the apartment Birgitta Carolina shares with Peter and Linnéa, but Bergman has him leave without uttering a single word to win her back. Outside, walking along the dock, Tomas comes upon squares chalked by children for their game of jacks. Imprisoned in the last square is a dead bird—in *Port of Call* Berit is symbolized by a caged bird—which he studies and then nudges with the toe of his shoe over the edge of the dock into the water. His act of abandonment in underscored by an ad for a magazine painted on the hull of a decaying wooden ship: "WHY DID YOU LEAVE?" That night, after Peter brings the sadistic Alf to the apartment and he again tortures her, Birgitta Carolina, sensing that for her life is hopeless, descends to the basement and slits her wrists. A passive, amoral child has grown into a moral, tragic adult. Interestingly, Birgitta Carolina's role originally was minor, but Bergman was persuaded to enlarge it and create her suicide, thus providing another woman who, as he puts it, functions as a "sacrificial lamb" and as the "saint [who] bears your sufferings" (*BB*, 43–44).

Tomas returns to Sofi, who reluctantly agrees to "try to start over again" with one proviso—that for the present he not touch her. Her comment, "It will take time," is a realistic (and perhaps autobiographical) detail that is probably unique in films of this period. They smile warmly at each other but sense that they will live in a kind of hell made bearable by something that is not full, mutual love, though it is not loneliness either. Like Lucky Per, Tomas cannot free himself from self, and further—to apply the film's Swedish title (*Prison*) to his situation as well as to Birgitta Carolina's—he is imprisoned in a marriage to someone he would like to love more and whom he needs (she already is mothering his cough). The tether of hope that Bergman throws his protagonists and his audience is shorter than that in the earlier films; only the insight into self that Tomas has gained—and from his attic experience he may also have learned that for him true happiness exists only in childhood—keeps their story from total bleakness.

With *Three Strange Loves* (1949) Bergman began making the marriage relationship itself more central. Still, even though three of the protagonists in *Three Strange Loves* are women,[11] it is again the male, the repressed Bertil (Birger Malmsten), who is "shocked" into a new understanding of his relationship with his narcissistic, psychically damaged wife Rut (Eva Henning).

When Rut's child died at birth, she was left sterile, a condition Bergman and she make emblematic of her psychological state. Until recently a ballet dancer, Rut's sense of herself is based primarily on her looks and body; she is given to studying herself in mirrors and bragging of having "the most beautiful breasts in Stockholm." As a young dancer all she wanted was "to be admired"; she "had no time for love." When an injured knee ended her career, that and her barrenness left her suddenly feeling worthless, pathologically empty. Pathetically she tries to bribe love from children and to beg or extort love from Bertil ("I want you to think I'm beautiful. Yes, caress my face, teach me my face, wake it up, describe it! Describe it for *me*!") Her inner life is torturous; "afraid of silence," she distracts herself from the ache in the pit of her psyche with meaningless chatter, activity, or emasculating comments. An example of the last is her advice to Bertil on how to cure the noise his adenoids make when he eats: "Why don't you have them clipped out? It's an easy operation for a big boy like you. And *you* have nothing to lose; they don't make you sterile." But the image that both conveys her castrating impulse and symbolizes her insatiable emotional-sexual hunger appears early on when, momentarily alone, she sneaks a salami out of their food hamper and, using Bertil's straight razor, slices off a chunk.

In her fashion Rut loves the fastidious Bertil for his heroic patience with her unpredictable moods and hostility and for his detached, sensitive intelligence. (She is proud of how smart he looks when he reads, though Bergman makes even this escape of Bertil's threatening by placing on the cover of his book a gigantic eye that stares coldly across the aisle at her.) But he is no saint. He is penurious when it comes to spending on others but unhesitatingly lays out money for anything he wants himself—coins, expensive rooms, newspapers. He calls Rut his "spendthrift" and lectures her, as he used to lecture his earlier mistress Viola, on the ill effects of smoking, but both women sense that he is less concerned with their health than with the cigarette money. (Malmsten's stiffness and tepid emotionality lend authentic tension to Bertil's anality.) He is most unlikable in his response to a group of starving Germans—he and Rut are returning to Sweden through war-ravaged Germany in 1946—who appear at their train compartment's window. He (unsuccessfully) tries to discourage Rut from sharing their food with them and, afterward, fatuously claims that he envies those who in their pursuance of survival have "no time for neuroses."

Though he keeps as tight a hold on his emotions as on their funds, he is not totally unspontaneous, as evidenced by his unprovoked hugging of Rut in their hotel room. His love-hate ambivalence toward her is powerfully, if a bit melodramatically, conveyed in two scenes. The first comes after Rut's most affecting scene. Unable to sleep, she cries out, "I'm so full of hate I want to live just to make your life miserable. Raoul hurt me physically, but you hurt my soul. I'll never let you go, till death do us part. . . . Some joke, huh?" Her laugh turns to a sob, and suddenly she becomes nauseous from all the wine she has drunk. She dashes out of their compartment and down the corridor to the restroom. Bertil follows, but she does not respond when he pounds on the door. He waits, listening to the ear-piercing train whistle and watching the ghostly gauntlet of curtains being blown wildly into the corridor by the hot summer air coming through the windows. He chews a toothpick, then notices that the exit door is loose, flapping. The camera pans to his fingers as, unconsciously, they snap the toothpick. Bertil's face—his eyes as if in a trance—is reflected in the window of the unfastened door. Rut does not see him when she comes out of the restroom and presses her face against the loose door's glass. Bertil edges toward her, a low angle shot revealing his sweaty, strained expression. His hand steals up toward the camera (Rut), and just as we imagine he is about to push, he grabs and desperately hugs her. The second instance occurs that evening: Rut has come into the compartment where Bertil is asleep in his bunk, and she begins gargling loudly to awaken him. One of his eyes opens, and we hear a magnified heartbeat combined with an electronic tone that grows steadily louder. Suddenly, he reaches out, picks up a beer bottle from the bedside table, and smashes it on her head. She falls, and his sweat-streaked face declares, "That finishes her Hell as well as mine!" But we have been tricked; Bertil is having a nightmare. (Dreaming that one has murdered someone, often a wife or husband, is a device Bergman uses in several films. Recall that in *The Devil's Wanton* Tomas, knocked unconscious, wakes up wanting to believe that he has murdered Sofi.) His nightmare is the kind of shock that illuminates the situations of many of Bergman's protagonists. The two scenes just described clarify Bertil's feelings about Rut, causing him in the film's final scene to tell her of his homicidal nightmare and to admit how much he needs her. Earlier, while talking about the ancient coin that bore the Rut-like face of Arethusa, he had mocked as silly the myth about the river Alpheus's seemingly impossible accomplishment—digging his way under the sea to join his beloved, the freshwater spring Arethusa. Bertil's impulse to murder Rut, and then his imagined murder of her, have made him realize that love or need can overcome seemingly insuperable obstacles. Passionately embracing her, he declares that living without each other "would be *worse* than [their present] Hell." Arethusa's image is superimposed over the pair and then replaced by the sun breaking through the clouds and waves rolling along a rocky coastline, an ending that, though Bergman does not pull out all the stops à la Hollywood, at least does not damn with faint joy like previous endings.

Bergman confesses that in *Three Strange Loves* he "took extreme delight in ripping to pieces" his "tormented marriage" to dancer Ellen Lundström, whom he had married in 1945, the year he divorced his first wife, the dancer Else Fisher. (He had married Else in 1943; they had a daughter.) His next film, *To Joy* (1950), written while he was vacationing in the South of France, apart from Lundström, is, he says, undisguisedly "about Ellen and me" at a time when they still thought their marriage salvageable (*ML,* 159).[12] In it he also dramatizes his concern over the artistic recognition that still eluded him, revising downward his vision of success.

Bergman portrays his alter ego, Stig Eriksson (Stig Olin), as a "conceited mediocrity" and "faithless, bombastic . . . liar." In contrast, he idealizes the Ellen character, Märta (Maj-Britt Nilsson), that is, before he kills her (and one of their two children), an act that Bergman admits was "wishful thinking" (*ML,* 159). Stig and Märta are violinists newly hired by the Hälsingborg Philharmonic. Stig is a fame-starved, bristlingly angry egoist and misfit. At a party with his colleagues, for example, a few drinks make him pugnaciously drunk, aggressive with the women, and obnoxious in his lament that at 27 he is not yet a celebrity. He calls his colleagues "slovenly, dull-witted, [and] insensitive" and claims that he is the one destined for greatness because great artists are unhappy "and I always am." His wondering aloud why he cannot understand "who I am and why I can't be like other men" is made laughably pathetic.

Märta, divorced and wary of entering a relationship because "lovers always hurt each other," and because she feels everything she has undertaken has been a failure, is oddly attracted to Stig from the start. Bergman obviously believes that Stig's boyish intensity, sexuality, self-involvement, fathomless insecurity—while courting Märta he says, "Your being with me doesn't help. A man is *always* alone"—and his dependence on her strength and patient supportiveness all appeal to Märta's mothering instincts and needs. She deceives herself into thinking she can tutor Stig into maturity, even though at one point she says to him, "I've always known you were neurotic and . . . egocentric." Because of his immaturity, she deceives Stig by informing him only moments before the marriage ceremony that she is pregnant. As she expects, when he finds out he claims that the child is not his, demands that she abort it, complains that they cannot afford a child, insists that he hates children, and maintains that a "defenseless child" should not be brought into this "miserable world," a rationalization we will hear from several Bergman males. With the help of Stig's father figure, the conductor Sönderby (Victor Sjöström), Märta chides Stig into behaving like a "simple, normal man" and going through with the ceremony.

The marriage begins happily. Stig welcomes the birth of their twins, and Märta, having quit the orchestra, more than overcomes her earlier wariness about becoming a housewife involved with petty concerns and "no large issue[s]": she rhapsodizes over being able to cook, clean house, feel Stig beside her in bed. And—the refrain marks her as Bergman's creation—she is happy that she will "never again [be] alone."

Things soon begin to sour, however. When a distinguished soloist suddenly dies and Sönderby gives Stig the chance to publicly prove his ability, Stig humiliates himself by playing off-key in several passages. Afterwards, Stig not only attacks Sönderby—who has tried to comfort him by telling him that he is a "fine" though average violinist, and that a "beehive needs worker bees"—but also blames his failure on Märta for all the distractions at home. Immediately, the familiar Kasparsson pattern emerges. Finding Märta's constancy and maturity an oppressive reproach, he sinks into a slough of self-indulgence and surrenders to the "exciting body" of the "little bit crazy" femme fatale Nelly (Margit Carlqvist), the wife of the procurer Michael Bro (John Ekman). Stig even moves into their filthy apartment, which is also inhabited by another member of the orchestra, the sinister Marcel (Birger Malmsten), who, because Bergman frequently places him right behind Stig, seems to represent the satanic in Stig. Stig stops shaving and washing and exists in a virtual sewer of sexual jealousy, neurotic dependency, and self-loathing.[13] One night he does break away, and after first smashing his hand through a window so that he can never again regard himself as a soloist, he returns to Märta, assuring her that he now knows what a mediocrity he is. Unconvinced of his reformation, she points out that everything he says has to do with "I . . . I . . . I." The bedroom scene that follows could have occurred when Tomas returns to Rut at the end of *The Devil's Wanton*. As she undresses, Märta senses that Stig is comparing her to Nelly and refuses to let him touch her when he tries to make love. Stig rejects her reproaches. Realizing that a reconciliation is impossible,

Märta asks for money to take the children and go stay with her mother, but Stig replies that his money is *his*. Outraged at his immature perversity, she reminds him of the money he has spent on Nelly, and when he retaliates by calling Märta a whore, she goes for the emotional jugular, mocking, among other things, his sexual performance. He responds by repeatedly slapping her face, bloodying her nose. (Possibly based on the memory of his father's fight with his mother, a bloody nose occurs in virtually every fight in Bergman's films.) Finally he says, "Forgive me," Bergman's formulaic phrase that invariably indicates that the person asking forgiveness, though momentarily regretful, will continue the offending behavior. When Märta threatens to go into the street to beg for money, Stig relents and tells her, "It will be a relief not to have to see you anymore!"

He returns to Nelly but begins to miss his family. When, at last, his own depravity is driven home to him by that of Michael and Nelly, he leaves their dark, filthy apartment—to the sound of church bells. Lust eventually makes Bergman's characters feel like helpless marionettes who, as *Persona*'s Elizabet once told her husband, are "governed by forces that we do not entirely control." Infidelity will remain a major element in almost all of Bergman's films, but in only a handful—*While the City Sleeps* (1950), *Hour of the Wolf* (1968), *The Serpent's Egg* (1977), and *From the Life of the Marionettes* (1980)—does his male protagonist again wallow in lust and become involved with a depraved or criminal group.

In letters and voice-over narration, Stig persuades Märta to take him back because he now fully appreciates their love, which, he says, is also based on the pain they have caused each other. They live happily until a few years later, when their cottage's kitchen stove explodes and Märta and their little girl are killed. The final scene, which I shall examine later in detail, finds the "worker bee" Stig, having heard the news of the deaths earlier in the day, contentedly rehearsing with the orchestra. Looking back on Bergman's life now, one cannot help but find amusing this anticipatory surrender to anonymity.

During the filming of *To Joy* Bergman met and fell passionately in love with the journalist Gun Grut, a married woman with two children and a strong, open, unself-conscious personality. In August 1949 they went off for three months to Paris. The rapturous happiness Bergman enjoyed was compounded by revelatory artistic discoveries: the Comédie Française's Molière made that playwright a rival of Strindberg in Bergman's pantheon, and he thrilled to Hector Berlioz's

Damnation of Faust (1846), Maurice Ravel's Concerto for the Left Hand (1931), Jean Racine's *Phèdre* (1677), Georges Méliès's films, Louis Feuillade's *Judex* (1916), Carl Dreyer's *Leaves from Satan's Book* (1920), and the impressionists. Forced back to Sweden and separated from Gun by her husband's threat to take her children from her if she saw Bergman, Bergman holed up and wrote a synopsis of a P. A. Fogelström story that would become *While the City Sleeps* (1950), the screenplay for *Summer Interlude,* and a lost play that centers on a silent filmmaker named Joachim who flees his marriage and goes to Lyon, where he tells the following story about the Eiffel Tower. On Bastille Day (Bergman's birthday) the famous tower, tired of people encroaching on its privacy and of having to live a meaningless "life of duty," breaks loose from its foundation. This causes a handful of people to fall to their deaths. The tower escapes by wading out into the English Channel, but a cardinal packs the five dead into a boat and takes them out to the tower, which they shame into returning.[14]

In Fogelström's *While the City Sleeps,* Jompa, the protagonist, is a "victim of environment." But Bergman made him a Jack figure, driven by unassuageable impulses. Jompa has to be forced to marry a girl he has impregnated, does not appear when she delivers their baby, moves in with his mistress, steals, repeatedly ends up in jail, and unintentionally kills a policeman. *This Doesn't Happen Here* (1950), which was wholly Bergman's idea and which he directed, is a spy thriller based on an embarrassing post–World War II incident: the Swedish government did nothing to stop its own agents from turning over to the Soviets many Estonian, Lithuanian, and Latvian refugees who had reportedly helped the Germans. Bergman's "lighthearted" treatment blunted the story's edge; he now calls the film "disgusting" and "hollow" and claims it is one of his few films of which he does not own a copy. He says that he "only made it for the money," that he prepared it while making *Summer Interlude* because beginning in 1951 the whole Swedish film industry was going to shut down to protest the government's refusal to reduce taxes on admissions and to subsidize the studios. Bergman, who had just divorced Ellen Lundström, with whom he had had two sons and two daughters, married Gun Grut after she finally broke with her husband. She was pregnant with Bergman's sixth child (a boy) when she moved in with him. He needed money to support three families. *This Doesn't Happen Here,* made in both Swedish and English, premiered a whole year before *Summer Interlude* because the studio, uncertain as to the commercial possibilities of the latter and facing the imminent suspension of all activities—the strike lasted a year—did not want to take any chances.

THE THEME OF MARRIAGE

In *Summer Interlude* (1951), which was inspired by a story he had written in the summer of 1937, the same summer he wrote *Torment,* Bergman again tells of a person—this time, however, it is a woman—whose first great love affair ends with the tragic death of her lover. Just as Birgitta Carolina represses the memory of her murdered child, the 28-year-old prima ballerina Marie (Maj-Britt Nilsson) represses the memory of her loss, a process that her total devotion to her career has facilitated. Along with her reluctance to end her career, this repressed loss keeps her from accepting an offer of marriage from the young man she now loves. This conflict between career and family is one that, in the next handful of his films, Bergman's women will experience, with virtually every one of them opting for what Bergman sees as her womanly destiny.

The summer she was 15 Marie, now a prima ballerina with the Stockholm ballet, had a love affair with an insecure, lonely, and idolatrous youth, Henrik (Birger Malmsten). Henrik, who never knew his mother and hated his remarried, rejecting father, lived on the archipelago with his old aunt near the summer home of Marie's uncle. A typical Bergman protagonist, Marie is drawn to the dependent and problem-plagued. She loves mothering "blind kittens . . . babies and people who ordinarily are considered ugly." At summer's end, after superficially resolving the conflict between their relationship and her career, Henrik had a fatal accident. Marie has repressed the memory of this tragic moment in her life until one day in her dressing room—the film's opening—she mysteriously receives in the mail her old diary, in which are recorded her thoughts of that summer. The diary, which she had believed lost, disinters Henrik's memory. Just as in *To Joy,* the shock launches the familiar Bergman plot structure: to understand his or her present dilemma, the character actually and/or through flashbacks revisits and reexperiences his or her past.

Before Marie reluctantly sets out on her journey, however, we meet her boyfriend David (Alf Kjellin), a young journalist who is troubled that she treats her job as more important than his and, worse, as more important than their relationship. When she tries to avoid conflict by being playfully imperious, David mockingly tips his hat and leaves her alone on the street. She soon finds herself aboard the boat that will transport her to the scene of that earlier summer of happiness and tragedy. On board she meets Henrik's aunt's pastor (Gunnar Olsson), the memory of whom she also has repressed. When she disembarks a dwarflike woman with a mustache, dressed in black, carrying a black umbrella and black bag, and muttering to herself, crosses her path and stops momentarily to stare at Marie. It is Henrik's icy, self-centered aunt herself, who the doctors had said would die of cancer three years before Marie first met her over a dozen years before. The ancient woman's mustache and breast cancer suggest her lack of womanly compassion. (Bergman refers to her as "Death" and points out that the atmosphere around the young lovers "darkens" when she first appears [BB, 16].[15]) She also acts as a reminder of Marie's "living dead" existence, a reminder that is prepared for in a flashback in which Bergman connects Marie with the ancient woman by having Marie, full of irrepressible, youthful narcissism, boast, "I'll never die. I'll get very old, but I'll never die."

Stopping first at the cottage on her uncle's estate, Marie recalls in two flashbacks how she, a lovely, giddy 15-year-old thirsting after fame and admiration, met and fell in love with Henrik and how she toyed with the fantasies of her Uncle Erland (Georg Funkquist). Erland had loved her beautiful, talented mother, but when she died he settled for her sister Elizabeth (Renée Björling). Insensitive to her aunt's unvoiced pain, Marie told her uncle, who she knew loved her, "Pretend I'm my mother. We should elope you and I. . . . Someday perhaps you may have to marry me." Then she ran out in midflirt. Soon thereafter she told Henrik that she regarded Erland as an "old fool," but after Henrik's death she became his mistress.

After this flashback, Marie walks up to the house, where she is surprised to find her charming, salaciously solicitous, but burned-out uncle. She learns, too, that it was he who sent the diary. He had not sent it earlier, he says, because she was not ready to benefit from it. Though civil, Marie is disgusted with herself, and with Erland, not only for having been his mistress but for letting him help her build around herself a "protective wall that even the Devil" could not breach. (We learn of this in a flashback during Marie's steamer trip back to Stockholm.) Therefore, she had made her life an autumn, if not a winter experience—from the opening shot on, images of barrenness, decay, and death are inlaid in the film.

For the film's penultimate sequence in Marie's dressing room that evening Bergman combines symbolism with theatrical and filmic expressionism. In the background a semicircular window suggests both a staring eye and a prison window. Close-ups of a dripping water tap (which also makes us hyper-aware of the silence) and the rain that streaks the window and is reflected on her face represent the tears that for so many years Marie has suppressed. These images and her thoughts suggest that crying could put her in touch with the feelings buried behind the "protective wall"—here made palpable by her thick, dark makeup, which makes her face a mask: "We're like painted marionettes," she says, "tears would wash off our paint." Bergman presents her in a giant frontal close-up that is startling and disturbing not least because it leaves half her face outside the frame. She is a woman divided and incomplete.

As she is removing one of her false eyelashes, she becomes aware of the ballet master (Stig Olin) in the shadows. (His image had earlier replaced the batlike shadow of the other puppeteer, Erland, as he followed Marie out of the deceased Henrik's hospital room.) He is dressed for his role as Dr. Coppelius, the puppeteer. (Coppelius believes that he transfused into the life-size doll he has constructed and named Coppelia the life from a drugged young man who had fallen in love with her. What actually animates the doll, however, is the young man's fiancée, who has dressed herself as Coppelia and who, defying Coppelius, dances away with her lover.) Bergman traps Marie's face between the ballet master-Coppelius's grotesquely painted face in the mirrors on her right and left. Aware of her relationship with David, he reminds her of how much she has invested in her career and that she will only be able to dance for another eight years. He incisively sums up her divided feelings: she is afraid to leave the theater, but she wants happiness. Her painted face in the mirror dominates the screen as he commands her to remain committed to her art: "You dance! Period!" As tears edge into her eyes, David enters and stands behind the mirror reflecting the two painted faces. His reality wins; the ballet master gives Marie a kiss and leaves. The volatile David is annoyed, but the ambivalence and fractiousness of Marie's whiny, little-girlish pliancy and declaration that she has missed him overcome his irritation. He becomes tender. When he presses her to commit herself to their relationship, however, she again becomes annoyed and even suggests that they end their relationship, an idea that he rejects with unexpected self-assurance. Then, like Berit, who feels she has to reveal her past to Gösta, the tearful Marie gives David—

whom she mistakenly calls Henrik—her diary to read. Tomorrow, after he has read it, she says, they will have their first real talk. David leaves, and Marie removes her masklike makeup. In voice-over she admits to all the years she has wasted and realizes that she no longer has the urge to cry, that, in fact, she is "actually happy"—she even sticks out her tongue at her mirrored, naked face.

The next day, just before Marie goes onstage, she goes up on her toes to David, who is standing in the wings, kisses him, and then, still *en pointe,* dances onto the stage where she balances on the shoulder of her partner, suggesting her new dependency. The ballet is *Swan Lake,* and the lush melody helps buoy these final moments. The swan will die, but much life remains before the final curtain. Like *Torment's* Berta, Jan-Erik's first love, Henrik is just a "coat hanger," a sacrificial victim to facilitate Marie's development, says Bergman. The death of Henrik caused Marie to withdraw from life, but it eventually leads her to abandon her narcissistic behavior and come to terms not only with life's tragic component but with her own mortality. No longer, presumably, does she believe she will "get old, but never die." In addition, we assume she accepts the God she rejected after Henrik's death. And, like *To Joy's* Märta, *Smiles of a Summer Night's* Désirée, and others, this career woman has decided that the next stage in life is to fulfill her wifely and motherly needs. "In [*Summer*] *Interlude* I start to accept life as a compromise," says Bergman (Kaminsky, 195).

Before moving on I want to point out a serious problem with this film. Bergman does not give David sufficient screen time to permit him to accrue dramatic weight. Bergman's belief that women find insecure, defensive men appealing further undermines David's strength as he deals with the older, strong-willed Marie, whose depression makes her seem monumentally unmovable. The decision to change, it is true, must remain Marie's, but Bergman needed an actor with the self-confident charm of, say, a Clark Gable to break through her concrete ambivalence.

Because of the film stoppage, Bergman did not make a film for almost a year and a half, and his "finances were in shreds" (*BB,* 55). In preparation for the day he would get back to work he wrote *Secrets of Women* (1952). Aside from the fact that he had already melded four stories into one *(Three Strange Loves),* the structure of this film was probably affected by the contemporary popularity of the anthology film: *Quartet* (1949) and its sequel *Trio* (1950); *A Letter to Three Wives* (1949); *Le Plaisir* (1951).

Secrets of Women's theme is marriage, for Bergman that necessary and inevitable condition that a person enters out of a mixture of feelings—love, lust, fear of being alone, and, for the woman, the need to fulfill her mothering instinct even though she knows that her husband's selfishness, neuroses, philandering, or weak character will leave her to do most of the compromising and forgiving. As Bergman increasingly focuses on marriage, women necessarily become more central to his films. Here, they are foregrounded from the opening credits, which are superimposed over an oval, neoclassical wall decoration picturing three women pausing from their labors. The men, by contrast, are lumped under "Also Featuring." Set at the Lobelius family summer home in the Stockholm archipelago, *Secrets of Women* is four stories (three in flashback) told by the Lobelius sisters-in-law as they await the arrival of their husbands, a quartet of Bergman narcissists who, with one important exception (Fredrik), are so cursorily presented they barely exist. The theme of mothering—whether of children or of childlike men—is launched immediately as the panicky mothers burst out of the summer house afraid that their children may have drowned. The theme is underscored when the adolescent Maj (Gerd Andersson) shows a fish she caught to the childless and frigid Rakel (Anita Björk), who chides her for taking "it away from its mother."[16] It is when the children are upstairs that Anita (Aino Taube), the wife of the oldest Lobelius male, Paul (Håkan Westergren), formally introduces the topic of marriage. Reminding us of *Ship to India*'s Alice Blom, she unexpectedly confesses her inability to achieve intimacy with her husband: when they were younger they loved one another, she says, but now there is no "warmth or contact. . . . I almost wish he'd beat me. . . . I can't . . . tear out his eyes to make him blind and dependent on me. I can't even take him in my arms and rock him to sleep when he is sad and suspicious. . . . A woman my age should be resigned . . . find comfort in Jesus or grandchildren." Without hesitation or embarrassment, Rakel also volunteers a picture of her marriage. Her story, an overly severe compression of Bergman's earlier play, *Rakel and the Cinema Doorman,* concerns Rakel's confession to her husband Eugen (Karl-Arne Holmsten) of her afternoon's infidelity with her childhood friend, the strutting ego Kaj (Jarl Kulle). Kaj was the only man with whom she had ever enjoyed sex. In response to her confession, the ineffectual, self-pitying Eugen rushed out with a rifle and threatened suicide but was quickly reconciled to Rakel by his brother Paul, who advised, "An unfaithful wife is better than no wife at all. . . . The most terrible thing is not being deceived, but feeling *alone*."[17] After telling her story, Rakel is asked if things are better now. She answers, "For me at least [things are better]. I've come to see that Eugen is only a child and that it is my duty to look after him. . . . [He] is my life and he says that I am all he lives for . . . we help each other. I'm content."

The third story, Märta's (Maj-Britt Nilsson), is composed of flashbacks within flashbacks and contains only about 50 lines of dialogue. It is an attempt by Bergman "to tell a story in pictures," an experiment certainly influenced by the television commercials he made during the film stoppage.[18] However, like Rakel's story, part of this story's problem is that it tries to compress too much into its short span. Märta recounts her stay in the hospital to give birth to the child fathered by Martin Lobelius (Birger Malmsten) before they were married. She had been a pleasure-loving, rather callous young woman—we see her run out on an American pilot who wanted to marry her—until she met and fell in love with Martin, a struggling, young Swedish artist in Paris. Later, when she learned she was pregnant and went to tell Martin the happy news, she found him hysterically screaming at his visiting brothers and their wives that he would not return to Sweden with them to attend their father's funeral. Nevertheless, faced with having his funds cut off if he did not return, Martin changed his mind. Martin's casual words recall Märta's abandonment of the pilot: "I'm so fickle it almost worries me. But so are you, which is a comfort. Maybe we'll play together again sometime." When he finally asked what she had wanted to tell him, she masked her pain with a smile and answered, "It was nothing." The story returns to Märta in the hospital as labor began, her unexpressed pain from the previous scene merging with her screams. Her story completed, Maj, Märta's young sister, asks Märta why she finally married that "silly" Martin. (We experience the same puzzlement when earlier Rakel explains her reasons for remaining with Eugen.) Another Bergman woman drawn to a narcissist, Märta, who has obviously reconciled herself to her husband's almost pathological self-centeredness, answers that she married him simply because she loved him.

The third story-flashback, Karin's (Eva Dahlbeck), is based on an event in Bergman's life[19] and was inspired by Alfred Hitchcock's "shooting long sequences in difficult and cramped circumstances, weeding out everything irrelevant" (*BB*, 67). Just as the first episode was designed to be "chaste" and the second "highly mobile," this story was to be spicy, with a "slightly burlesque tone" (*BB*, 67). Karin recounts what happened on the way home and at their apartment house after the family celebrated the family firm's centenary. Because Fredrik (Gunnar Björnstrand) had had too much to drink, he asked Karin to drive, a request that put her in the simultaneous roles of servant and master. The repartee and the spatial composition establish the characters of this handsome, middle-aged couple: in front, the self-assured, sophisticated woman piloting her husband while exquisitely pricking his picture of himself as the energetic, brilliant chap who has made the company a worldwide success. Momentarily taking a back-seat is the dapper Fredrik, who is wittily aware of his hyperbole. The scene is shot from an oblique angle from in front of Karin so that we see Fredrik over her shoulder and are able to read her editorializing facial expressions when his remarks wound or amuse her, or to read his expression when she scores with a volley of her own.

In the small elevator that takes them up to their apartment Fredrik continues to be immodest in order to provoke Karin's witty put-downs, though what he says about himself he believes to be funda-mentally true. He preens before the elevator's full-length mirror until, as if some goddess had had her fill of his hubris, it comes to a shaking, swaying, screeching halt between floors. He holds onto Karin who, amused at his loss of composure, pats his cheek reassuringly. When all his efforts to get help fail, she tries her hand at operating the con-trols. This throws the elevator not only into new paroxysms but into darkness. When Fredrik lights a match, Karin and we explode in laughter: his top hat is crushed down on one side of his head, and he is doing his best to maintain a dignified appearance while hiding his helpless outrage. Then they discover that the lights come on when one of them sits on the elevator operator's wooden seat. They make themselves as comfortable as space allows. Karin sits on Fredrik's knee and places his arm around her shoulder with his hand near her breast. "Fifteen years ago, you would have adored this," she brags. "Fifteen years ago, you weighed less," he reminds her. Soon, the the-matic raison d'être of the scene is broached as the trapped pair, in a Lubitsch- or Molander-like scene,[20] probe each other's fidelity. Karin shocks Fredrik with her admission that she has been unfaithful, and he admits to affairs, none of which he regrets. He celebrates the idea that he and she "have [their] own lives"; Karin is not so sanguine. Then, when his leg goes numb, she slides down and massages it, arousing him sexually. As Tomas does with Sofi, he grabs her

58

Secrets of Women. AB Svensk Filmindustri

hair, pulls her head back, and asserts, "I love being massaged by you. . . . You're so strong." Karin likes the compliment but not its corollary, "I've always had respect for you." Fredrik proposes that he get his mother to look after the children and that the two of them go to Belgium: "The trip will be an experiment. We may hate each other before it is over, but let's at least try." Happy beyond expectation, Karin confesses that she made up most of the story about her affairs, and Fredrik remarks, "Your décolletage is most becoming." "Can you see in the dark," she queries. "No, not see," he replies, and the scene fades to black as they begin to make love. After her story is finished, Karin, careful not to sound as if she is gloating, tells the other wives that she now travels with Fredrik to "massage his leg."

Though she threatens to emulate her husband's sexual sallies, Karin accepts that she too will be the one who compromises and forgives, and that it is up to her to stroke her husband's ego if the marriage is to work. To his credit, Fredrik seems willing to reform, not from desperation or fear, but because he chooses to be sensitive to Karin's needs. This ideal picture of marriage, though closer to the outlook of

Bergman directing. Svenska Filminstitutet

The Philadelphia Story (1940) than to Bergman's usual grim view, still deals with Bergman's problems. Only here his recipe eliminates the nastiness while adding pinches of charm, wit, and spicy fun to make the situation delicious.

The film ends with a festive party after the husbands rejoin their wives. While the others are partying, Maj elopes with Paul and Anita's son Henrik (Björn Bjelvenstam), who is upset because his uncles want him to study economics and join the firm whereas he wants to see the world. Refusing to have their lives controlled by others and afraid of relationships like those Maj has been listening to—she missed Karin's story—the lovers escape by motorboat. Märta, Maj's sister, and Paul,

Henrik's father, come outside in time to watch them go. Paul pronounces a benediction that is almost a curse on these youngsters who think they will always love one another as they do this night: "Let them go. . . . Let them think they're doing something forbidden. . . . They'll find out soon enough the wounds, the wisdom of life, the other silly matters. They'll come back soon enough"—presaging the subject of Bergman's next film, *Monika* (1953).

Bergman began *Monika* in August 1952, exactly a week after he finished *Secrets of Women*; its script, which he worked on during the film stoppage with the novel's author, P. A. Fogelström, was approved by SFI only after heated arguments. Some board members resigned, complaining that "such filth" should not be made. The "world's cheapest film" (no sets were needed on location), *Monika* was structured by a favorite theme of Bergman's: "Run [from your problems and responsibilities], but come back" (Donner 1966, 88). Twenty-year-old Harriet Andersson, who radiated, in Bergman's words, an extraordinarily "uninhibited, erotic charm" (*BB,* 75), inspired the film. (Bergman had seen her in the film *Defiance* [1952], and he now began an affair with her.)

Monika is a vulgar, shallow, spirited young woman with an imagination shaped by "true confessions" magazines and Hollywood films. Harry (Lars Ekborg), an atypical Bergman male in that he contains nary an ounce of unprovoked anger, is a shy, amorously inexperienced, responsible young man. He falls in love with Monika from the moment she asks him to light her cigarette. She instinctively senses his warmth, desire, and vulnerability and is charmed by his fumbling courtesy since all the other men she knows try to grab, pinch, or fondle her. Both share a dream of a better life. She maneuvers him into taking her to a grotesquely sentimental Hollywood film, and afterwards, working from a scenario in her head that prescribes how a romantic affair should proceed, she coaches his advances, providing the key dialogue ("I guess we like each other very much!"). When Harry suggests that on their next date they go to his apartment while his father is away, she senses that her scenario is unfolding: "Say, that's a swell idea. It's almost like being married. I've never met a sweet guy like you—like somebody out of a movie."

Fed up with living in a squalid two-room apartment with her overworked mother, her alcoholic and sometimes abusive father, and two noisy little brothers, Monika quits her job at the vegetable market,

leaves home, and plants herself and her suitcases on her hero's doorstep. When Harry arrives, she lies, telling him that her father beat her;
the tenor of her crying slipping easily from seemingly terrorized despair into a whiny simper, she demands that Harry take care of her.
They move into his sick father's small boat and spend their first night
together. The next morning Harry, harassed by his coworkers about
his relationship with Monika, quits his job (but not before artfully
exorcising his anger with a piece of blown glass). After collecting his
belongings, he joins Monika at the boat; the two motor out of noisy
Stockholm and dock that evening in a beautiful, isolated cove in the
archipelago. The carefree and sensual sunny days and romantic nights
that follow arouse our envy.[21]

When Monika realizes she is pregnant, Harry tries to persuade her
to return to Stockholm: they will get married, he will get a job, and
he will begin studying to become an engineer. "We'll always love each
other . . . [and] have a nice place for ourselves and for the one who's
coming." For a moment, in the movie in her head, Monika sees herself
as the glamorous, traditional mother and wife, and she replies excitedly, "And I'll have dinner ready for you [and we'll] take our children
out on Sundays and I'll be looking after them and doll them up in nice
clothes." But she refuses to spoil their summer by returning right
away. Soon, however, the clouds hide the sun, chill winds bend the
long grass, and warm clothes replace their nudity. Their funds de-
pleted, they exist on mushrooms and stolen milk. On a foray into an
orchard for apples Monika is caught stealing a roast from a food cellar
and barely escapes being turned over to the police. Back aboard the
boat, she bawls, in her petulant, little-girl tone of voice, her young,
expressive face and stringy, unwashed hair making her look increasingly urchinlike, that she is tired of everything, including this "baby
business." Harry, his arm around her, articulates reality: "We've done
nothing but dream." Monika gives in; her romantic fantasies need re-
charging: "Maybe we should go back. It's been ages since we saw a
movie."

Harry and Monika marry. He gets a job as a machinist and begins
studying to be an engineer, and she gives birth to June (Monika's only
interest in the child is in naming it in honor of their summer). When
the nurse brings June to the window for Harry to look at, the camera
fixes on his joyous awe. At home the hard truth is that June is almost
entirely Harry's responsibility. Monika refuses to have her night's

sleep interrupted. Exhausted, Harry uncomplainingly accepts the responsibility, even though after being up much of the night with the infant he must get up at dawn to do his schoolwork and then go off to his job. Awake, Monika nags that they live like pigs and cannot even afford a movie. She and Harry now hardly ever appear within the same frame.

Harry arranges for his aunt to take care of June when his job takes him out of town for a few days. Monika's good-bye is not a kiss, but that familiar Bergman pat on the cheek that stands in for affection. When Harry returns earlier than expected,[22] he finds Monika in bed with her old boyfriend Lelle. Harry retreats to the street, sickened. The following scene of his return to the darkened apartment is one of Bergman's best written and acted. It is a situation we often encounter in Bergman's films. Between waves of gentleness two people in a claustrophobic setting verbally claw at each other. Unaccusing, but his anguish evident, Harry tells Monika they must separate. Eyes filled with hate, alternately pouting, whining, or sneering, she shrieks that she is sick of him and *his* brat. Then, softening, she throws herself on her bed, breaks into a semisincere, shallow simper, the cry of a child trying to deflect criticism and avoid punishment; finally, she makes a pathetic plea to be left alone so that she can sleep. In a shot that duplicates one of their happiest summer moments, he caresses her arms, kisses her shoulder, and hugs her; then, outraged that they are on the very sheets where she lay with Lelle, he furiously strips the bed. Monika goes into the bathroom to admire her skin and her breasts in the mirror and returns to tell Harry that she loves Lelle and that this is not the first time she has betrayed Harry with him. Harry slaps her but, nearly in tears, apologizes and slips hopelessly to the floor amid the soiled, tangled sheets. Whimpering, Monika moves to the end of the bed and stares vacantly through the bars that suggest she feels imprisoned by adult expectations [see fig. 3 (Wood, 42)]. At last she gathers her clothes and, after a last glance at herself in the mirror, walks out of the apartment, the marriage ending with the loud snap of the door's latch. Harry sells their possessions (even June's stuffed bear, Bergman's symbol of security and dependence) to the peddler we saw at the film's opening. (A pushcart piled high with furniture—an image we will encounter in *The Silence* [1963], *The Serpent's Egg* [1977], and *Fanny and Alexander* [1982]—suggests the uprooting or dissolution of a family.) Then, holding his beloved June,

Monika. AB Svensk Filmindustri

Harry, in brief flashback images, nostalgically remembers his lost nymph.

Finally, we reenter the café where Monika met Harry when she asked him to light her cigarette. A blond male is offering Monika a cigarette; he lights it, and she lights his with the one between her lips. She smiles when he gives her an affectionate clip on the jaw. Sitting back, she picks a tiny piece of tobacco off her tongue, and after taking another drag and exhaling the smoke through her nose, and with the camera dollying in to create a giant close-up, she slowly turns her head to stare directly at us—unflinchingly, impertinently, brazenly, absolutely indifferent to our opinion of her. Monika is irredeemable, a wanton who foolishly continues to dream that at the next table, at the end of another cigarette, someone, some Gable or Cagney, will turn up to fulfill her dream. Nevertheless, we cannot forget Monika's transfixing, erotic appeal. The film ends as the carefree ragtime clarinet is replaced by two low, dark, foreshadowing chords.

THE THEMES OF GOD AND DEATH

In addition to narcissism and marriage, two other important themes run through Bergman's early plays and films—God and death. A clergyman's child, Bergman immediately found himself suspended in the suffocating aspic of God's omnipresence and expectations. Early on, Bergman says, he struggled against it. A good measure of his skepticism about God's existence was fed by his hostility to his father's preoccupation with God and Jesus rather than with his younger son. And again, Bergman took his soundings from Strindberg: "I was unable to conceal my aversion. I hated God and Jesus, especially Jesus, with his revolting tone of voice, his slushy communion and his blood. God didn't exist. No one could prove he existed. If he existed, then he was evidently a horrid god, petty-minded, unforgiving and biased, they could keep him! Just read the Old Testament and there he is in all his glory. And that's supposed to be the God of Love who loves everyone. The world's a shithole, just as Strindberg says!" (ML, 80). The struggle was ongoing: Bergman would try to deny God's existence for most of his life but would not fundamentally doubt it. When things went badly for him, he might speculate that God had abandoned or was punishing him for his denial or doubts, but he still believed that ultimately "God the Father, with Jesus on his right hand, would see that I was hidden" from punishment (ML, 279). And so it would go: "I have struggled all my life with a tormented and joyless relationship with God. Faith and lack of faith, punishment, grace and rejection, all were real to me, all were imperative. My prayers stank of anguish, entreaty, trust, loathing and despair. God spoke, God said nothing" (ML, 204).

The most important question he asked God was, why is there so much evil in me that I am powerless to do anything about it, and why won't You intervene to fashion my razor personality into a plowshare? Why do You leave me tortured and tormented, torturing and tormenting (Donner 1966, 56)? Though he toyed with the idea of God's nonexistence, he almost never looked elsewhere than to Him for the explanation of why he was who he was—his evil character as well as his marvelous talent. He portrayed the struggle raging inside him as one between God and Satan, the latter Bergman's symbol for the hostility, the brutal, erotic fantasies, the ruthless disregard for others that God had rooted in his character, and for the inability of his relationships to fill his emptiness or end his loneliness. The 24-year-old Bergman, who at times signed letters and articles with "the insignia of a little devil" and who wore a Mephistophelian beard [see fig. 4 (Cowie 1982, 24)], told his fiancée Else Fisher, "You will go to Heaven but I am going to Hell" (Gado, 26). Hence the origin of his diabolical Jack Kasparsson. "Now let's get this Devil business straight," he said years later. "What I believed . . . in for a long time—was the existence of a virulent evil, in no way dependent upon environmental or hereditary factors. Call it original sin or whatever, [inside us are] destructive tendencies, conscious or unconscious, aimed both at ourselves and at the outside world. As a materialization of this virulent, indestructible, and—to us—inexplicable and incomprehensible evil, I manufactured a personage possessing . . . diabolical traits. . . . Unmotivated cruelty is something which never ceases to fascinate me" (*BB,* 164, 40). Bergman's notion that the Christian God is a "destructive and fantastically dangerous" power who brings out "dark destructive forces instead of the opposite" climaxed in the late 1960s.

Bergman manifests his faith in God's personal concern for him by having Him, in one way or another, intervene on behalf of his stymied or despairing protagonists to free them from imprisoning situations and relationships and to help them recognize the narcissism that prevents them from achieving happiness or maturity. God frequently appoints a grandfatherly (usually) or grandmotherly intermediary to facilitate the process. The first play Bergman directed at Mäster-Olofsgården was Sutton Vane's *Outward Bound* (1923), which involves a small party of passengers on an ocean liner who gradually realize they are dead and being piloted to the next world. A steward of God intervenes to save a pair of young lovers. In *Kasper's Death,* Kasper, after dying and being packed up in a coffin by Death, is sitting on the lip of his grave questioning God's existence and nature when he is visited by a kindly judge who intervenes on his behalf.[23] In the second film Bergman directed, *It Rains on Our Love,* an elderly lawyer (Gösta Cederlund)—the film's narrator—defends the ex-con David (Birger Malmsten) and his lover Maggi (Barbro Kollberg) against assault charges. At one point he has "wings pinned on him like the angels of [Alf Sjöberg's film] *The Road to Heaven*" (Young, 45); he carries an umbrella that symbolizes his protective role. (At film's end the acquitted pair walk under it through the rain.) Taking many forms over the years, the elderly emissary has most recently appeared as Isak Jacobi in *Fanny and Alexander,* a character based upon an actual Jewish shopkeeper. Bergman first used this character, giving him magical powers and influences with God, in his play *The Day Ends Early.*

In *Rakel and the Cinema Doorman* Bergman complains, through the narcissistic Kaj, "I began to cry for help. And since I had no one in particular to turn to, I turned to God. Do you know what God did? Well, he took me as I was, with my evil and fear and darkness . . . and threw me into one circumstance after another. I had done many people wrong before. But now I was forced, with wide-open eyes, to torture and torment to the right and left." (Bergman also wrote a story in which a fetus resists entering the world out of fear of doing evil.) In *Jack among the Actors* the mysterious, God-like Director dissolves the company, leaving Jack alone on the dark stage; with thunder and lightning threatening, he cries out, stirring our pity with his childlike and selfish ("me/I") helplessness, "God in Heaven, help me! You must be somewhere . . . you must help me . . . not because I deserve help, not for any reason except that I can't stand it. . . . Don't you see that I am little and afraid and that it is so damned dark."[24]

God is not addressed directly in *Torment,* but during Jan-Erik's emotional-physical breakdown (a skull and death mask ostentatiously decorate his room), a doctor describes him as looking like "one of those [lads] who wants to solve the riddle of existence." The death of Berta (from natural causes) and the intervention of the elderly head-master to prevent his suicide seem designed by a higher power to help Jan-Erik master his narcissism. "When I . . . started to write my pictures . . . [my conception of] God was always present. Even if I didn't write about God or even if I didn't write in a religious way, He was always present in all my pictures" (Jones, 57–58).

Bergman's early protagonists are often more concerned with the seeming unjustness of God's world than with His existence, and even though at some point they may reject Him and His world, most of them finally come to accept both. In *Night Is My Future* (1948), scripted from her own novel by Dagmar Edqvist, the supernatural is made explicit. Young Bengt Vyldeke (Birger Malmsten) is about to marry a shallow woman when he is accidentally shot and blinded while completing his military duties. Though he says he is not religious, he questions the suffering in God's world and is contemptuous of his Aunt Beatrice's (Naima Wifstrand) religious platitudes: "Our suffering is the will of God. . . . Our despair is nothing on the enormous canvas of life." Neither the script nor Bergman treat Beatrice with contempt, however, and later Bengt seems open to her statement that "even old age can have its own special beauty, especially when one has faith and trusts in eternal life." Events testify that suffering *is* part of God's plan. Twice, while the blind, self-pitying Bengt lies in bed, we see shadows form crosses on the floor near him, but much more dramatic are the uncanny communications between himself and Ingrid Olofsdotter (Mai Zetterling). Ingrid is a lower-class local girl who comes to Aunt Beatrice—with whom Bengt now lives and who has taught him to play the piano—to find someone to replace the sick church organist who was scheduled to play at the funeral service for Ingrid's father. Coerced into the job, the insecure Bengt freezes as the service commences. Ingrid is following her father's casket into the church a floor beneath the organ loft but senses Bengt's state, stops, effortlessly concentrates, and smiles. Seized by her spirit, Bengt plays. A similar communication occurs later (and in *Winter Light*).

Soon afterwards Ingrid becomes a maid in Beatrice's house. She falls in love with Bengt but leaves when she overhears him scoff at the idea that he should marry his "maid." Years later Bengt, working as a piano tuner in a school for the blind, meets her and her boyfriend Ebbe (Bengt Eklund), both of whom are students at the university. Bengt soon confesses his love for her, but she is uncertain about whom to commit herself to. Meanwhile, Bengt accepts the invitation of a blind friend to meet his new bride, who is arriving by train. At the station, however, the man is so excited by the reunion that he and his wife leave, forgetting that Bengt is there. Hysterical, Bengt rushes out into the railyard, where he is nearly run over by a locomotive. At this very instant Ingrid, dancing with Ebbe at a ball in the university gymnasium, suddenly senses something: "I thought I heard someone calling," she tells Ebbe. Then, recognizing her communicant, she cries, "Bengt!" and rushes off as if in a trance. (As she runs out of the gymnasium, parallel bars cast converging, railroad track–like shadows across her path. These shadows are strikingly intercut with Bengt's flight along and across a medley of actual railroad tracks.) Miraculously, she finds him standing on a bridge, presumably about to commit suicide, and they embrace.[25]

Suffering apparently is part of God's plan; Bengt's blindness has kept him from marrying a vacuous, narcissistic woman, brought him Ingrid, and permitted him to "see" his narcissism. When the elderly rector (Olof Winnerstrand), another of Bergman's benign emissaries, overcomes his reservations about Bengt marrying Ingrid, the impression is that all is right in God's world.

The Devil's Wanton is framed by a little narrative in which Bergman expresses doubts about God. The film opens with Paul (Anders Henrikson)—a world-weary character based on a mathematics teacher in Bergman's play To My Terror (1947)—visiting, at a film studio, his former pupil Martin (Hasse Ekman), now a film director. Paul has recently been released from a mental institution. He since has channeled his sanity-threatening despair into an idea for a film he wants Martin to make: a story about living in a world without God, afterlife, or hope, and in which "our innermost desires" force us to live purposeless lives. In his scenario life is a "laughing masterpiece, beautiful and ugly, without mercy or meaning." "You must admit," says Paul, his little finger tapping Martin's shoulder, "that this makes life easier to understand." The Devil's Wanton's final scene returns us to the movie studio as the technicians are shutting down for the day. Paul reappears to learn Martin's decision (which, it is implied, has been influenced by Birgitta Carolina's suicide). Martin informs Paul that his idea cannot be filmed because it raises questions about life's meaning that only God, if He exists—and Martin does not believe He does—could answer. The lights are extinguished in the studio, and the film ends as it began, with the faint, brief sound of a small, unimpressive gong: not with a bang, but a whimper. Nevertheless, we recall that Bergman saw Birgitta Carolina as God's "saint," His "sacrificial lamb" offered up to Tomas's development: at the moment of her death a cross is created on the basement wall by the shadow from a window.[26]

In To Joy, when the musician Stig tells his wife Märta that he does not believe life has any meaning, she replies that, if it does not, then people have to "invent a meaning." Given his seeming nihilism, one would expect that after Märta and his daughter have been blown up Stig's despair would be fathomless, but not so. When he returns to work later that afternoon, after visiting the scene of the accident—where he has reflected on his life—he declines the maestro Sönderby's permission to absent himself from rehearsal. With Stig's tragedy an unspoken presence in the hall, Sönderby (functioning as another elderly emissary of God) eloquently explains what he wants from the orchestra and chorus in their performance of the "Ode to Joy" movement of Beethoven's Ninth: "The cellos, basses, and violins should sing out like angels. You see, this music is about joy. Not the kind of joy that finds expression in gaiety, or . . . that says, 'I'm glad.' What I mean is the joy beyond men's comprehension. I want music that will purify . . . that is the voice of God."[27] Then, as orchestra and chorus sing out affirmation, Stig's little boy enters and sits in the front row. Stig acknowledges him with a glance and, while playing, recalls key moments with Märta—the images superimposed on his sheet music.[28] Next, crane shots lift us ceiling(heaven)ward, and Bergman super-imposes the image of waves smashing against a rocky shore. The cam-era then descends to Stig's son sitting alone amid rows of empty seats, his motionless hands interlocked. (Though he is sharing his father's experience, this shot of the vulnerable child, his life in the hands of both the Deity being celebrated and his "matured" father, is subtly disquieting.) The worker bee Stig seems comforted, however; his metaphysical doubts about life's meaning seem no longer to exist. Like Bergman, he is with his "family," his fellow artists who, under the fatherly, inspirational Sönderby, labor at the exalting task of ex-pressing "the voice of God" and Schiller's joyous acceptance of the good and evil in God's creation. (Stig also achieves a measure of im-mortality through his son.) Not until *The Seventh Seal*'s reposeful im-age of Antonius Block sharing milk with the holy family—Jof, Mia, and their son—will Bergman so convincingly convey his "hunger for community."

In Molander's *Eva* (1948), after 12-year-old Bo accidentally kills a little blind girl, he comes to not only fear death but hate God. Later his wife Eva, encountering a dead sailor who has washed up out of the Baltic, comes to believe that God has forsaken mankind and that it is wrong to bring children into the world. When, however, their baby is born during a storm, Bo connects the deaths with the birth and happily proclaims, "Death is part of life . . . no other explanations are necessary." This is the conclusion Marie finally arrives at in *Summer Interlude*. After Henrik's accidental death, she tells Erland that she no longer believes anything has meaning and that if God exists, "I'll hate him until I die. If He were standing in front of me, I would spit in His face." The film's final scene, buoyed and informed by the music and theme of Tchaikovsky's *Swan Lake,* strongly suggests that Marie has come to terms with God's world, its joy and tragedy.

However, Bergman's terror of the "frightening executioner," death, persisted for a long time. Before literally personifying death in *The Seventh Seal*, in *Summer Interlude*, as I have indicated, he made Henrik's ancient aunt a symbol of death, and in a scene in *Secrets of Women*, one based on a childhood experience of his own (*ML*, 21), the pregnant Märta, preparing to leave her parents' apartment for the hospital, sees a dark, blurred human shape on the other side of the front door's hammered glass. It and, later, a crippled man evoke death for her.

Bergman's fear that if there is no God then life is empty of significance connects with the feeling of futility and, just as important, the feeling of psychic and spiritual bankruptcy from which, as I noted, some of his early characters suffer: for example, Tomas in *The Devil's Wanton*, Joachim Naken in his radio play *The City* (1951), Eugen in *Secrets of Women*. Using a classic image from the film *The Invisible Man* (1933), Jenny, in Bergman's play *The Day Ends Early*, perfectly characterizes this feeling of psychic emptiness: "Now I have stripped to the skin before you . . . and the same thing happened to me as to a person I saw in a film. When he undressed and unwound the bandages around his face and hands, there was neither body nor face nor hands. There was nothing!" It is a condition that, beginning with *The Passion of Anna*, Bergman will study in detail.

STYLE AND TECHNIQUES

Such are the major themes of Bergman's early films. Before I analyze his stylistic development and his signature techniques, a quick survey of his progress as theatrical director, apprentice filmmaker, and writer will be useful. I want also to take note of the difference in performances of his work when he was finally commanding actors of superior talent who could make his often witty, subtle, but brutally probing psychological dramas an electric experience.

At the time his script for *Torment* was being filmed Bergman became the head of the Municipal Theater of Hälsingborg, making him the youngest theater director ever in Sweden (*ML*, 142). In his two-year stint, though he had little theoretical training and even less understanding of the Stanislavsky he was reading, he got along by being a "self-taught . . . village genius" (*ML*, 147) and by borrowing shamelessly from the masters he worked under at SFI, Alf Sjöberg and Olof Molander (younger brother of film director Gustav and sometime head of Stockholm's Royal Dramatic Theater). His "unshakeable self-confidence" may have assured him of his talent and brilliance, but his insecurity and pride prevented him from seeking more direct help, even from the director Lars-Eric Kjellgren, whose technical mastery Bergman envied (Sjöman, 208). Fortunately, when Bergman was directing his first assignment (Camus's *Caligula* [1944]) at Gothenburg's City Theater (where he remained for five years), a master—the first of several—took an interest in him. During a rehearsal the 62-year-old director Torsten Hammarén, whose acting company was considered the best in the country, took the stage while Bergman was directing and told him, "You provincial little genius, sit down and shut up, then perhaps you'll learn something!" Humiliated, Bergman raged out and sulked in the restroom. He was told that he would be fired if he did not return to rehearsal on the following day. On his way there he ran into Hammarén, and within moments the two were laughing and reconciled; it was not long before Bergman regarded him not only as "the father-figure I had lacked since God had abandoned me" (*ML*, 151) but as Sweden's greatest director of farce (*BB*, 24–25). Hammarén's emphasis on simplicity and clarity in conveying emotions and intentions to an audience became a goal that for a long time Bergman found elusive, if not antithetical to his nature. His resistance to simplifying also may have been encouraged by his study of Victor Sjöström's films, which, as noted earlier, had strongly impressed the 16-year-old Ingmar. Now at SFI Bergman drew on the studio's archives to study the master's other films. He came to admire their precision, clarity, lack of sentimentality, and genuineness (*BB*, 26). Possibly of more consequence was Sjöström's focus on the human being, especially the human face,[29] and his use of "actors to project several things at once" while "underplay[ing] the whole time" (Forslund, 261).

When Bergman began directing at SFI, he was certain that his first film, *Crisis*, would retire Sjöberg, Molander, and even Carl Dreyer (*ML*, 68), but instead he discovered how ill equipped he was to make films. Day after day, for example, his takes were out of focus and scenes had to be reshot. Sjöström, also at SFI, had been assigned the film's artistic supervisor to work with this "highly sensitive and easily put out" young director. Although not "particularly tactful," Sjöström did not threaten his desperate admirer. Grasping Bergman by the nape of the neck, he walked him about and proffered advice. Bergman remembers that Sjöström "obviously viewed the rushes each day. . . . And since he was the only one who bothered to talk to me, it meant of course an enormous amount to me. . . . I grew calmer, and I felt he was speaking the truth, so he was able to put forward any critical opinions whatsoever. . . . I . . . had had no experience other than in the theater. . . . He was on me immediately concerning anything theatrical, stilted, or uncinematic." In addition, he told Bergman to stop quarreling with everyone and to stop making his scenes so complicated, to "work more simply," to treat minor details as minor (ML, 69).

A "fiasco," Crisis got the 27-year-old Bergman kicked out of SFI. But he was hired by the Sveriges Folkbiographen production company, where he worked under Lorens Marmstedt. In contrast to Sjöström, with whom Bergman had felt safe (BB, 215) and who he believes was motivated by seeing something in him that "ought to be cultivated" (Forslund, 263), and Carl Anders Dymling, "who treated me both paternally and with some condescension" (ML, 67), Marmstedt was more than blunt.[30] After viewing the rushes of It Rains on Our Love, the producer reacted "in a sort of cold fury and called me an incompetent bloody amateur—swore he'd scrub the whole production . . . and if I thought I was some sort of a Marcel Carné, and Birger Malmsten was a Jean Gabin, then I was bloody well mistaken, and we were a couple of idiots . . . we weren't filming at all, we were just 'soul-shaking' . . . acting out our private lives in public. . . . He couldn't stand the sight of me. I was pretentious and nasty. Well, I didn't mince words, either. I told him he was nothing but a vulgar, conceited playboy. He ought to stick to his confounded vices, I said, and not meddle with artistic matters he didn't know the first thing about. That's how we carried on!" (BB, 25–26). Bergman's mature judgment, however, is that it was Marmstedt who taught him how to make films (ML, 154), that his "irritable, enthusiastic [bullying made me learn] to look coldly and objectively at my own rushes . . . to ask myself whether I've realized my intentions" (BB, 26).[31] Bergman acquired another mentor in Herbert Grevenius, the drama critic turned screenwriter who had recommended the young "theater maniac" for the Hälsingborg job. The two worked on screenplays together, and in the process, Grevenius also taught Bergman—who for a time viewed himself as a writer as well as a director—greater "orderliness of thought" (ML, 142, 157). Later in his career Bergman would be forced to admit, "I'm not a writer. [My screenplays are] skeletons awaiting flesh and sinew. Words do not suffice for me to com-

municate my message; images do. My screenplays are not made . . .
to be read. They are directions for my co-workers" (Sorel, 19).

Bergman's subsequent films after *Crisis*—*It Rains on Our Love,*
Woman without a Face, (for which he only wrote the screenplay), and
Ship to India—were also "flops," so he was grateful ("I will lick your
ass if you like; only let me make a picture") when Lorens Marmstedt,
producing at Terrafilm, gave him the sentimental *Night Is My Future,*
which Marmstedt was certain would be the box-office success Bergman sorely needed. Marmstedt also kept a close eye on the production; he visited the set daily, forcing Bergman to reshoot scenes that
were "too difficult" or "incomprehensible" and ordering him to get a
little cat or dog into the story and to beautify his heroine by using
more light on her hair.[32] The picture was "a great success" (Kaminsky,
114–15).

Though Bergman then regarded himself a writer, his prose, like
so many other things, suffered, as Vilgot Sjöman points out, from
his passionate personality. He was better able to "express a lyrical
mood . . . in pictures than in words." Bergman "could not get hold
of a lyrical image without believing that he had a simile in hand; and
then he overdid the metaphor until it creaked at the joints. . . . His
other handicap lies in his bent for the over-strong, for the terrible
words. His emotional experiences are evidently so violent that they
seem meager and scraggly on paper if he doesn't use fierce phraseol-
ogy." Fortunately, Sjöman concludes, "a warning voice inside" Bergman kept "telling him how dangerous" that was (Sjöman, 20).
Nevertheless, Bergman's ability to transfix an audience with "dangerous" and "fierce" words, with cruel or perverse speeches, is not to
be slighted. Take, for example, the description in *Torment* of the
Caligula-phobic cat that plunges all its teeth and claws into the schoolteacher's arm, Paul's scenario in *The Devil's Wanton* for a world ruled
by the Devil, or Rut's hate-drenched harangues in *Three Strange Loves.*
(In *Three Strange Loves* Bergman wisely eschewed energetic camera
movement for intense, claustrophobic stasis and the pyrotechnics of
sadomasochistic speech.[33]) This is not to say that, on occasion, Bergman could not be lyrical or funny. In fact, it was the comic sparring
in *Secrets of Women*'s third story that made that film a box-office success, surprising and delighting even Bergman, who says he had never
before heard people howl with laughter "like that" at anything he had
written (*BB,* 55).

The writing in that sparkling episode is certainly crucial, but it is
Dahlbeck and Björnstrand who *make* Karin and Fredrik subtle, full-

bodied, stylish, funny—in a word, unforgettable. Witty dialogue and imaginative staging would not have produced that success without those virtuosi, whose special chemistry evokes that between William Powell and Myrna Loy, Cary Grant and Katharine Hepburn, or Grant and Rosalind Russell. Furthermore, making into comedy the problems he had dealt with in strictly dramatic terms required that Bergman give more form to his raw emotions, that he make sure that motives and dialogue were clear, that he not cram in too much information or rush the action—comic surprise and jokes require time to develop and time for the audience to laugh. In addition, Gunnar Björnstrand possessed a maturity and multidimensional talent that dwarfed that of the film actors who previously had played Bergman's alter egos. And the fact that he was almost ten years Bergman's senior created a fascinating tension between the underlying Bergman persona and the older man's representation of it. Björnstrand gives the abrasive, unlikeable persona stability and elegance and, thus, a wider appeal. And it is the "incomparable" (Bergman's word) Eva Dahlbeck whose acting ability and star quality make Karin—and Marianne in *A Lesson in Love* (1954), Susanne in *Dreams* (1955), Désirée in *Smiles of a Summer Night* (1955), and Stina in *Brink of Life* (1958)—real and yet larger than life.

Acting is the crucial element in *Monika* as well; how stale, flat, and unconvincing that petulant tease would be without Andersson's youth and erotic vitality. And Lars Ekborg's young Harry, the film's moral center, unburdened as he is by Bergman's self-hatred, rage, and ego, is refreshingly average and entirely credible. To a large extent this film's success is due to the actors perfectly synchronizing with the characters as written. Continually having to use actors who had limited ability or were too old had impeded Bergman's creation of what he was most interested in and best at—convincing psychological portraits. Take *Summer Interlude*'s Nilsson and Malmsten. Bergman's judgment is that Nilsson "was wonderful" and kept the "two roles, the older and younger, quite distinct" (*BB,* 54). I feel that her age invests the 15-year-old with too much adult self-awareness and repose, and that her concept of the older woman's depression—this is also the fault of the script—is too unvaried, too monotonous.[34] Malmsten, likewise, not only is too old to play a teenager but is unable convincingly to evoke innocence. Something unspontaneous, cynical, even shabby always creeps into the characters he plays. (These are the very qualities that make his licentious or sinister characters—such as

Marcel in *To Joy,* or the silent waiter in *The Silence,* or the man who robs Jenny and assists her rapist in *Face to Face*—so convincing.) He should have been cast as "the somewhat world weary and scabby journalist," as Bergman dubs David, rather than as Henrik; the more boyish Alf Kjellin could have played the tragic adolescent. While filming *Secrets of Women* Bergman began to realize how limited Malmsten was. During Martin's (Malmsten) speech to Märta in which he explains why he is leaving her for good to attend his father's funeral, Bergman keeps the camera on Märta almost throughout. Bergman did not use Malmsten again until *The Silence.*[35]

It would be some years before Bergman ceased to regard himself as a "technical half-wit" in his command of the film medium. Working with experienced technicians kept his films from looking excessively clumsy—though in *Port of Call* Gösta throws a flower pot through a closed window and the camera misses most of it. After hours Bergman schooled himself at the movies, "clutching" at any film technique he saw. The unaffected, unembellished, gray quality of Italian neorealistic films (especially Roberto Rossellini's) was a "revelation" to him. He soon sensed that joining his documentary scenes with his studio-shot scenes (as Rossellini had done in *Open City* [1945]) created the same "queer . . . hybrid" (*BB,* 32–33). Nevertheless, that semidocumentary style shows up in scenes at the school for the blind in *Night Is My Future* and in *Port of Call.* The most impressive example from the latter film is an early morning scene on the docks in which a gray mist blurs and makes picturesque the dark, dirty ships and giant cranes, while inside a huge, echoing hall worn-out men play checkers, their meaty, gnarled hands and leathery faces functioning visually as their unimpeachable credentials for the sweaty, back-breaking jobs to which they are waiting to be assigned. Bergman also was influenced by and combined film noir and Carné-Prévert "poetic realism"—a style that, unlike German Expressionism, which visually alters its world, employs highly realistic sets but through various filmic devices is paradoxically able to convey a poetic, even metaphorical atmosphere and world. (Thematically, Carné and Prévert were obsessed with fate and clear-cut struggles of good and evil.[36]) More important, he studied the films of Billy Wilder, Ernst Lubitsch, George Cukor, and his favorites Raoul Walsh and Michael Curtiz, whom he admired for being able to "tell a story quite clearly, simply, and straightforwardly" (*BB,* 29). Had he been able to copy his Hollywood models in this respect he would have achieved success sooner; as his mentors kept pointing out, he was packing too much into each film. That is certainly the case with *The Devil's Wanton* and with *Three Strange Loves,* though to be fair, Herbert Grevenius's clunky melding in the latter of the four Bergit Tengroth short stories by means of flashbacks, cross-cutting, and coincidence lamed the film before Bergman touched it. So also with *Secrets of Women.* In contrast, though it has an unfortunate plot contrivance (Lelle turning up at their island retreat) and pacing problems when the lovers return to Stockholm, *Monika* has a straightforward plot that permits the characters time to naturally unfold. Character, after all, and not physical action is the strength of Bergman's films. It is also noteworthy that the services of Bergman's usual editor, Oscar Rosander, were unavailable for *Monika,* and that, according to Bergman, he did his own editing because the substitute editors were incompetent. As a result, he became further acquainted with the whys, whens, and rhythms of cutting. This knowledge paid immediate dividends. In *Monika* he constructed, by means of montage, an enticing picture—wild and lyrical—of the couple's island escape, and he opened the film by repeating part of its final shot (to which, by the end, we react differently because of the accrued associations). His increased involvement with the editing process also bore dividends in his next film, *Sawdust and Tinsel* (1953), which contains one of cinema's greatest sequences, a flashback scene that depends heavily on audacious editing for its effect.

Indeed, the then faddish flashback was a major obstacle to Bergman's achieving simplicity. Though it was a natural device for his stories, which regularly were structured around a character's review of his past to get a fix on his present dilemma, the flashback fed into Bergman's penchant for stuffed, complicated plots. Moving back and forth from present to past fragmented his films, impeding their narrative flow and depleting their energy. Only *Summer Interlude* is not seriously weakened by their use; its many flashbacks, in conjunction with numerous dissolves and superimpositions, connect events, giving the impression that sharp divisions between past and present do not exist and that memory is a ghost that occupies the present.[37] This effect will be achieved even more successfully in *Wild Strawberries,* the only film after *A Lesson in Love* in which Bergman will again use several flashbacks.

As Bergman learned the ABCs of filmmaking he experimented. Coming as he did from the stage, it is not surprising to find him using a fluid camera to reproduce a complex mise-en-scène. We see this in

Ship to India (along with essays into expressionistic lighting, extreme camera angles, and offscreen space) when the captain demolishes his apartment, and in a pseudodocumentary scene that reveals backstage life at a variety theater. Bergman's most ingenious use of the moving camera is at the start of *Monika,* where he uses it surreptitiously to intertwine Monika's and Harry's lives. The camera looks down the center of a deserted street walled in by drab buildings in a poor back section of Stockholm. Suddenly, a peddler pulling a cart piled with used furniture passes near the lens and moves to the far end of the empty street. From the right another man crosses close to the lens, and the camera tails him as he passes a tobacconist closing his shop. Then, as he steps back into the street, we see deep in the frame that the peddler has been joined by a couple of cronies. The tobacconist comes back into the frame, stopping to check his appearance in the full-length mirror beside the entrance to the glassworks. When he moves out of the frame, we continue staring into the mirror at the image of the men around the cart and, close by, the back of a woman who turns and looks into the mirror: it is Monika. Annoyed that the tube of lipstick she has extracted from her purse is empty, she touches up her hair, pivots, and, the camera in tow, saunters across the street toward the café, pinching and yanking downward the rear of her skirt. The first cut comes after she and the men from around the cart have entered the café. The new shot places us across the street behind a railing leading up from a basement; from there we see Harry arrive and politely greet the tobacconist, and we follow him into the café where he will meet Monika.

Bergman also experiments with—and will continue to employ—treating the frame as a stage onto or picture frame into which characters (or parts of characters) make dramatic entries or out of which they exit. Sjöberg's having Jan-Erik vacate the frame in the final shot of *Torment* may also have attracted Bergman to this dramatic device. *Ship to India* provides some of the earliest examples, notably when Captain Blom is alone in his cabin contemplating murder. He paces out of the frame, leaving it momentarily uninhabited. Subsequently, Bergman reemploys it when Blom leaves his cabin to murder Johannes. The film's theme of suffocation, which includes preventing Johannes from fulfilling himself, is articulated when Alice reminds her husband that they once worked together—"I pumped air so you could breathe down there. . . . It was as if I gave you life every time I pumped"—and it is concretized in an imaginatively photographed and edited scene employing offscreen action: Johannes's diving helmet disappears beneath the water's surface, and we see and hear the rising bubbles and the wheezing of the air pump as the homicidal captain, assisting his son, rhythmically raises and lowers the pump's long handle. His arm rises and falls ever more slowly and then stops altogether. The next shot shows only the shadow on the deck of the captain's hand holding the handle, then letting loose and slowly closing into a fist. Suddenly, the severed ends of the rope and air hose slither over the deck's edge into the water.

In *Three Strange Loves* Bergman uses off-screen action to potently convey the utter privacy and determination of Viola's suicide: the camera dollies with her as she walks unhesitatingly to and along the dock past moored ships. The camera stops, but she continues out of the frame. We search for signs or sounds of her as we study the ship's bow and anchor chain and their reflections in the water in front of us. Then we hear a muffled sound, her resolute entry into the harbor's placid waters, and soon notice the almost imperceptible ripples radiating into the framed space before us. In one instance in *Summer Interlude* Bergman deftly employs offscreen space to evoke Marie and Henrik's lyrically sensual mood the morning after they have finally consummated their love: a low angle shot reveals her seemingly empty room, but we hear her giggling. Then, as she says, "It's exciting to have a sweetheart," her hand and arm rise slowly and sinuously into the frame. Henrik's hand slides caressingly up her arm until he grasps her hand, and their intercoiled arms and hands sway like the necks of mating swans. In a later scene Bergman capitalizes on the need to substitute a real ballet dancer for Maj-Britt Nilsson: the replacement permits him to visually underscore Marie's divided loyalties, while conveying her domination of Henrik, by framing only her bare legs and slippered feet as she steps over to start the phonograph. When Henrik knocks, her severed image moves to open the door. Henrik and his dog Squabble enter. Still at leg level, the camera allows us to see all of Henrik, who seats himself, and Squabble at his feet, on the floor next to the great stove. We feel Marie towering over him as he sits passively backed into a corner out of her way. In *Monika* a scene on the rocky shore contains a shot in which Monika suddenly stands up into the uninhabited frame and removes her sweater and brassiere. (In *Persona* a scene on a rocky beach will similarly open with Elizabet startling us by suddenly rising into the uninhabited frame to take our picture with her still camera.) Later, after panning over the rocky shore, the camera settles on Harry in the distance; unexpectedly, Monika enters the frame extremely close to the lens, creating a giant close-up. (In *The Seventh Seal* Death will make a similar and jarringly chilling entrance into the frame just as Antonius Block, unaware of Death's presence, exits it.)

Of all the techniques Bergman employs, the close-up, of course, especially the ultradramatic, giant close-up, is his most recognizable signature. His sense of its power shows up early. In *Ship to India* he photographs a rascally dwarf looking up the dresses of high-kicking dancers at such close proximity that the image blurs, and as early as *The Devil's Wanton* he uses giant, *Persona*-like close-ups (for example, Tomas's and Birgitta Carolina's silhouetted heads as they begin to make love). In *Summer Interlude* the most memorable images in the film are probably the giant close-ups of Marie's painted face—especially the one that is half out of the frame—in the penultimate scene. And as we are about to see, the expressionistic power of the giant close-up is at the heart of *Sawdust and Tinsel*'s extraordinary impact.

Besides the theatrical or expressionistic lighting Bergman employs in the early films, he uses a very unusual lighting effect in two of them. The impression he creates is that the sun has risen (or set) elliptically, mysteriously: there is a quick, unrealistic increase or diminution of light. In *Secrets of Women,* for example, Märta pulls down all the living room shades and lies down on the couch; suddenly, inexplicably, her face is illuminated. A similar light change occurs in *Monika* when Monika and Harry try to make love in his father's apartment. (Bergman will use this same lighting to great effect in *Persona*.)

Bergman opens *The Devil's Wanton* with an experiment that jells immediately, and that would become a trademark of his: a high-angled shot reveals a man in a dark overcoat descending a barren hill toward us. The high-contrast, almost grainy photography and analectic sound—the selection and amplification of only one or two identifiable sounds from out of the natural ambience—create a mood of eerie hopelessness. Bergman would keep these photographic and sound effects in his repertoire, employing analectic sound far more than the high-contrast visual image. The innovation is twofold: employing the high-contrast look associated with documentaries and neorealism, Bergman creates a nightmarish look we might call psychic neorealism; the analectic sound, the aural counterpart of canted camera angles, makes us strain to hear the expected, but missing, natural sounds, thereby causing us to feel ill at ease. This technique is employed, to cite just a few films, briefly in *Summer Interlude,* when Marie disembarks and crosses paths with Henrik's aunt; in the brilliant flashback that opens *Sawdust and Tinsel;* in *Wild Strawberries'* opening nightmare; in the early forest scenes and in the last shot of *The Magician*; and repeatedly in *Hour of the Wolf.*

Bergman's instinct for what music to use in his films seems almost infallible.[38] Until *The Seventh Seal* he frequently used a harp to segue out of flashbacks and between scenes, and as already noted, he successfully integrated classical music into his films. In *To Joy* he and editor Rosander wedded camera placement, camera movement, and editing to the shifting rhythms of Beethoven's Ninth to make *at least* 15 minutes of orchestra rehearsals engrossing, while *Swan Lake's* romantic, uplifting melody is crucial to countering, if not wholly erasing, in a matter of seconds, the dreariness of *Summer Interlude's* long, dark, concluding sequences. Whenever Bergman injects popular music or jazz into these early films—*Three Strange Loves, Secrets of Women, Monika*—it is like a transfusion of vitality.

Finally, already appearing in these early films are nontechnical devices—structural patterns and mannerisms—that will become so habitual that they too can be regarded as Bergman signatures. Besides the structural patterns already discussed—sacrificing a character to benefit his protagonist, having his protagonist leave and then return to society and/or family—Bergman often begins his stories with an event that causes the protagonist to examine his or her life, and frequently he sends the protagonist on a journey (usually homeward) during which his or her problems climax and are worked out. These journeys also provide Bergman's relatively actionless psychological dramas with some movement. In *Three Strange Loves,* for example, Rut and Bertil are returning to Sweden by train. Because a train's interior is often not unlike that of a room, the train's powerful movement feels arrested. This mode of travel enhances the drama's claustrophobic intensity: the two protagonists are imprisoned by their characters, their marriage, and their compartment, yet simultaneously they are being moved toward a goal.

Though not so large a structuring device as those just mentioned, one that Bergman utilizes in virtually every film—no one in film's history has used it as often—is eavesdropping, be it literal eavesdropping (*The Devil's Wanton,*) confession to the wrong person (*The Seventh Seal*), or reading another character's letters or diaries (*Through a*

Glass Darkly, Persona, Hour of the Wolf). Common to the theater, it is a device that dramatically, economically, and simultaneously reveals a character's private thoughts to another character *and* to us. This staple of Bergman's dramaturgy is undoubtedly connected to his childhood, the way he as a frightened, secretive, withdrawn child gained experience and information. We know of his childhood habit of playing—hidden by tablecloths—under tables and standing "in the dark dining room at home, peeping into the salon through the half-open sliding doors" (*ML,* 37). The frequency with which he uses this device also has to be connected to his obsessive need to share his inner life and his need to get behind others' masks to ferret out information that will give him, the master puppeteer, more control. "Everybody," says Bergman, "carries his mask, but . . . somewhere in your face the mask doesn't fit. . . . And that is beautiful if you can somehow see the contradiction between the mask and the real face" (Weinraub, 17 October 1976, 15). Finally, it is a device that speaks to his paranoid sense that it is impossible to keep even one's private life and thoughts confidential. A moment in *Three Strange Loves* sums up this unsettling feeling: Rut comes into her hotel room from the bathroom to find a strange man there. Apologizing—"A mistake. I'm sorry!"—he leaves. It is as if the intruder—and the police who will later invade their train compartment—represented the ever vigilant superego.

A device that will become a familiar Bergman motif is his use of mirrors and reflections. Bergman believes that women especially like to study themselves in mirrors—in *Three Strange Loves* Rut (like Monika after her) repeatedly takes pleasure in what she sees in her mirror—but that men and women alike turn to mirrors to be reassured that the aging process is in remission or to witness its malignancy. (The most transfixing scene in *From the Life of the Marionettes* involves the latter.) In the process Bergman uses mirrors and reflections to achieve choreographic and compositional effects, that is, to enrich the rhythm of his scenes (for example, in *Secrets of Women* the mirrored movements of the trapped Fredrik and Karin in the elevator add to the comedy) and to compress and heighten dramatic oppositions, many of which are symbolic (in *Three Strange Loves* Rut's face is flanked in her makeup table's mirrors on both sides by the reflected images of the two women who want to control her). He often uses mirrors to symbolize divisions within a character: in *Three Strange Loves,* again, Viola reaches out to a mirror as if to grasp her real self behind the reflection; in *Summer Interlude* the ambivalent Marie's face is doubled-divided by the wings of her makeup table's mirror; and years later, in *Persona*, the image of the conflicted Alma—after reading Elizabet's hurtful letter—will be mirrored in a little lake. The mirror motif, which is also an extension of Bergman's fascination with the close-up, brings this chapter full circle, underscoring as it does Bergman's core theme, narcissism. (A form of mirroring that Bergman would terminate after *A Lesson in Love* was his own Hitchcock-like appearances in his films.)

Bergman says his artistic development as a filmmaker was slowed because he constantly felt frustrated both by the filmmaking apparatus and by the feeling he had to compromise. Everything was more important than his realization of his conceptions. With *The Devil's Wanton,* for example, he complains that, because he had only 17 days to shoot it, he had no time to "recast anything, to transform it artistically . . . as I've done since I've come to know more and have more insight into my motifs" (*BB*, 42). In the theater he had absolute control and "felt free and uninhibited"; in the movie studio, "I was wholly in thrall to the machinery" (*BB*, 34–35). But parts of *The Devil's Wanton, Three Strange Loves* (at that time, his most commercially successful film to date), and *To Joy* (which he felt had "some nice bits") demonstrate, he says, that he was getting a grip on the medium. As for *Summer Interlude,* Bergman credits Herbert Grevenius with both encouraging him to enlarge his story "Marie" for the screen and then with keeping an eye on him to "make sure I didn't branch out or add any new ideas." "This was my first film in which I felt I was functioning independently, with a style . . . [and] appearance of its own which no one could ape. It was like no other film. . . . Suddenly I knew I was putting the camera on the right spot, getting the right results" (*BB*, 51). One scene that shows his surer hand takes place after the jealous, drunk Erland has tried to break in on Marie and Henrik, who are sleeping together for the first time. Unable to get in, Erland returns to his room and passes out. In the morning his wife Elizabeth, who also has been drinking, watches from her bedroom window as the young lovers run off to swim. When they are out of view, she pulls down the shade against the rising sun, opens the doors that separate her room from Erland's, moves to his bed, and slides the pillow, which she picks up off the floor, gently under his head. Her unhappiness is as manifest as her loving sympathy for Erland. As passive as Alice in *Ship to India,* she has gained a momentary victory. Although these scenes violate the point of view—Marie is incapable of imagining Elizabeth's feelings—they are the film's most deftly evocative and touchingly written and directed.

Robin Wood describes *Summer Interlude* as the "earliest [film] in which one feels . . . the presence of a great artist, not merely a precocious, or ambitious one." I would agree that an idiosyncratic and certainly more confident talent is apparent in *Summer Interlude,* but it is one that, for the most part, is still visually and narratively conventional, in spite of some unforgettable images and an almost tactile atmosphere. And one scene in the film, one in which Bergman animates Henrik's and Marie's drawings, is "embarrassing," a sign, as Wood himself indicates, of "an immature artist who can't grasp what works and what doesn't" (32). It is *Sawdust and Tinsel,* though also flawed, that signals the presence of not just a precocious but a "great" artist. It is with that film that I now launch my study of Bergman's major films. First, however, I shall bring the reader up to date on Bergman's personal life and career.

3

The Gun Films:
Black and Bright Comedies

When Bergman told his wife Gun Grut about his affair with Harriet Andersson, his confession ended their already deteriorating relationship. They divorced in 1953, but he remained friends with her—as he would with almost all of the women with whom he had relationships—until her death in a car accident in Yugoslavia in 1971. Gun had been the model for Karin Lobelius in *Secrets of Women,* and she would continue for some time to be the inspiration for major characters in his films: Agda in *Sawdust and Tinsel,* Marianne in *A Lesson in Love,* Susanne in *Dreams,* and Désirée in *Smiles of a Summer Night* (*ML,* 171). Except in *Sawdust and Tinsel,* Eva Dahlbeck, because Bergman felt she shared Gun's "indomitable femininity," continued to be the actress he employed to evoke her.

At this time his theatrical life also underwent an important change. Told "in humiliating terms" by the director of Stockholm's Royal Dramatic Theater that he was not up to their standards, Bergman accepted, in 1952, Malmö City Theater's offer to direct. His subsequent eight years there were the "best of my life so far." He was able to do three plays each winter and a film or two each summer, and he was working with talented actors who recognized the advantages of "performing good theatre in the winter and collaborating in Bergman films in the summer" (*ML,* 177). Harriet Andersson went to Malmö with him, but their love did not long survive his bouts of jealousy and his total commitment to his work.

Meanwhile at Sandrews Production Company, Rune Waldekranz, who was in charge of film production, convinced the company to let

Bergman film his script of *Sawdust and Tinsel* because he believed that Bergman was capable of achieving the kind of international success that Alf Sjöberg had recently had with *Miss Julie* (1951). It was not an easy sell. Most who read the script disliked it. Worse, after it was released the critics judged it to be awful; one even called it "vomit." It was also a box-office catastrophe. People were saying, "Bergman is finished!" Bergman himself, who believed he had "made a good, vital film," was devastated (*BB*, 82). He felt his filmmaking career was in jeopardy and that he had better have a commercial success quickly, if for no other reason than to meet all his support payments (Cowie 1982, 120; Kaminsky, 118). So, with Dahlbeck and Björnstrand in mind to play the leading roles, he wrote a marital comedy out of amusing moments in his and Gun's marriage, modeling it on the successful, screwball comedy sequence he had created in *Secrets of Women*. As soon as SFI's Carl Anders Dymling read it he called Bergman to Stockholm, and the film went immediately into production. On release in Sweden *A Lesson in Love* was a critical and box-office success, thus confirming Dymling's confidence. In addition, it established Bergman as a director with a special understanding of women and their emotional problems.

Dreams followed, but like *Sawdust and Tinsel*, it was a critical and financial failure. (It has a special place in Bergman's memory because it also marked the end of his "Harriet period" [*BB*, 99].) Dymling warned that if his next script were "a serious piece" he could forget "about making a film that summer." Bergman, who wanted to keep his troupe of actors together over the summer, felt he had but two alternatives: "Write *Smiles of a Summer Night*, or kill myself." So he wrote a dance of life, a touching, witty comedy "based on a play by Marivaux, in the classical 18th century manner."[1] His most expensive film to date (*BB*, 66–67), it would be the film in which Dahlbeck, Björnstrand, and Andersson gave "the definitive versions of the personae" they had developed in their previous roles (Wood, 67).

Besides having the Gun–Eva Dahlbeck connection in common, these four films also star Gunnar Björnstrand and Harriet Andersson and continue to concentrate on narcissism and marriage, including infidelity, misalliance, and child-parent relationships. Bergman also continues to use the pattern of the sacrificial victim, and he increasingly employs humiliation as a dramatic device.

As in the earlier films, narcissism is a significant factor in the love and marital relationships depicted in these four films. Each involves a middle-aged or elderly man in a relationship with a young woman, and though the degree and style may differ, each protagonist is a narcissist. The middle-aged men delude themselves that the world shares their flattering vision of themselves, and the young women display simple vanity and selfishness. Except in *Sawdust and Tinsel,* in which the older man is rejected by his wife and age-mate and stays with the younger woman (reflecting Bergman's predilection), these films regard misalliances of age as unnatural. The Björnstrand characters all either end up without a woman or come to realize that they love their age-mate, whom previously they have neglected, betrayed, or abandoned. These Gun-Eva Dahlbeck older women are finally preferred to the energetic, unpredictable, and demanding younger ones because they are patient, forgiving, supportive, and motherly. Never long deluded by their own narcissism or illusions, these women are also never in doubt about whom they love and want to be with. In addition, unlike the men, achieving marriage and family so completely satisfies them that they never itch for an occasional infidelity. Finally, it is characteristic of these relationships that appropriate pairing is not achieved without effort; men and women alike use cunning when they can, but neither gender is above using threats or physical force.

SAWDUST AND TINSEL

Sawdust and Tinsel (1953) was written in "a burst of unusually profound misanthropy" (*ML,* 176); its expressionistic presentation of sometimes brutal events contributes significantly to the film's shocking and haunting quality. Two sources partially account for its expressionism. Its greatest scene (and only flashback) was based on a Bergman nightmare, and the film itself was "a conscious reply" to E. A. Dupont's flamboyantly expressionistic *Variety* (1925), a story of jealousy, betrayal, public humiliation, revenge, and murder. As he wrote the script, Bergman had in mind the beefy, mercurial Åke Grönberg to play Albert, the story's middle-aged, paunchy protagonist. Unlike the elegant and intellectual Björnstrand, Grönberg immediately evokes Emil Jannings's proud, burly trapeze artist in *Variety.* Nevertheless, Albert is still Bergman's surrogate; the knitted cap exactly like Bergman's that Grönberg wears in the film underscores the connection (*BB,* 94–95).[2]

Albert is another Kasper. Three years prior he had left his wife and two little boys for the exotic life of the circus, which he imagined would also make him rich. He is now the circus owner, but his dream has miscarried. Audiences have diminished, and Albert is essentially bankrupt; in the last town he had to sell his performers' costumes. Albert's other major concern is that his beloved, young companion, Anne (Harriet Andersson), may begin to desire a man her own age. As the film opens, the circus is returning to Albert's hometown, where he plans to abandon both the circus and Anne. He is going to ask his wife, who makes a comfortable living with her tobacco shop, to take him back. As he spruces up to visit her, the tender affection he and Anne feel for each other is evident, but panic hangs in the air like dust. Bristling with guilt, he professes his love for her and lies that he is only visiting his wife out of concern for his two boys. Anne can barely restrain her anger, and she asks rhetorically why he is suddenly concerned with *them;* then she impales him with his real fear: "You look to be safe. . . . You're getting old and feeble!" Anne, in turn, is no less fearful about the future—"Perhaps you won't come back. . . . How shall I manage without you?"—and threatens not to be waiting for him when he returns. If his wife takes him back, Anne's threat is meaningless, so Albert smiles and says, "That's up to you." Her sobs after he leaves evidence more than just fear; she is deeply hurt.

Albert's wife, Agda (Annika Tretow), is at first unhappily surprised, then sincerely pleased to see him. Albert's embarrassment at his shabby appearance and his reason for visiting is turned to humiliation when Agda offers to sew on the loose button he keeps worrying. He removes his coat to reveal that he is shirtless; a false shirt front covers his underwear, and false cuffs, like large napkin rings, hang clownlike around his thick wrists. When she offers to loan him money, his irritation spills over, and he retaliates by accusing her of being bitter over his abandonment of her and the boys. The serenity of her answer is unintentionally hurtful: "Don't you realize how glad I am? . . . When you left me I was able to find peace at last. My life is my own. I got away from the circus I loathed and feared: all the shrieking and swearing, your world of flight, insecurity, misery, lice, and sickness." And she disapproved of his training of the boys. She *had* loved him, but when he left her, "all feeling died overnight." The chasm between them is spelled out by Albert who, after surveying the room, remarks on how quiet and unchanged it is. "To me, it's fulfillment," she replies. "To me, it's emptiness," he says softly, with profound certitude. Nevertheless, promising never to disappoint her again, he asks her to let him return, help her with the shop, and watch his boys grow up. She turns away so that he does not see her tears and, tactfully, refuses him.

On the way back to the circus Albert sees Anne leave the town's theater, where earlier that morning she had gone with him to borrow costumes for the evening performance. At that time he had eavesdropped on her and a young actor, Frans (Hasse Ekman), flirting. When Albert left to see Agda, Anne, hedging her bets, returned to the theater and told Frans that she was his if he would take care of her. "You needn't marry me." As suave as he is malevolent—wearing a perpetual, feral grin that leaks his narcissistic contempt for the world, Ekman makes Frans the most frighteningly fascinating Bergman villain since Caligula—he tricks her into having sex with him by giving her a worthless pearl locket whose value he promises will maintain her for a year. Devastated by his discovery of Anne's certain betrayal, and humiliated by Agda's rejection of him, Albert returns to their caravan where, partly to subdue his guilt over betraying her, he forces Anne to confess. A long scene follows in which his pendulumlike emotional changes confuse the viewer. His love and hatred for mankind erupt in waves of restraint, depression, and threatened violence. Grönberg is most at one with Albert when he emits a heavy-hearted, ironic, but despairing laugh. He tearfully repeats to Anne what we have heard repeatedly from other Bergman lovers, that he and she are stuck together in Hell. Then, sounding like Jan-Erik refusing to have anything further to do with the relapsed Berta, he tells Anne that he will never marry her because she can never be respectable.

Frans and the rest of the theater group attend that evening's performance, and in the midst of Anne's bareback riding performance he publicly alludes to their afternoon's affair. Then someone explodes a firecracker that spills her from her horse. Albert defends his own and his woman's honor by whisking Frans's hat from his head with his bullwhip and kicking him into the sawdust when he comes into the ring to retrieve it. To our surprise, the thin, light-footed, almost effeminate actor overmasters the bigger man.[3] Kneeling him in the groin, Frans blinds Albert by throwing sawdust in his face and drops him by repeatedly driving his fist into his defenseless opponent's face. The bull of a man writhes and falls unconscious. Some measure of revenge is achieved, however. As Frans is exiting, Anne claws the grin off his face.

Later, in his van, Albert tries to commit suicide (see Fig. 6). When he fails, he takes out his frustration by shooting and killing the female bear trainer's sick bear. In the film's final scene, as the circus pulls out at dawn, Albert is walking beside the wagons when Anne steps out of the shadows. The young woman and the middle-aged man search each other's faces and manners for a sign of acceptance. Both their faces acknowledge shame for past acts; both feel a need to be reconciled, as well as a new humility and respect for the other. Side by side, a few feet apart, they walk silently through the blackness toward the sliver of dawn on the horizon. Their smiles and the dot of light in their eyes (and on Anne's sensuous lips) cue us to the certainty that their needs, and a few hours of salving routine, will eliminate the distance between them.

A LESSON IN LOVE

Bergman's next film, *A Lesson in Love* (1954), treats comically the idea that relationships are hellish because the couples know each other so utterly. Not long into this story we sense that what we are observing is a battle between marital Siamese twins, between a couple, Marianne (Dahlbeck) and David (Björnstrand) Erneman, whose marriage has been made in Heaven.

The action commences with the philandering, middle-aged Dr. David Erneman, a Stockholm gynecologist, being visited by his 21-year-old mistress Suzanne (Yvonne Lombard), who wants him to divorce his wife of 17 years (from whom he has been separated for a year) and marry her. They have just spent a summer together pleasurefully vegetating, though sometimes there were "bitter words and hurtful acts" between them. Having slowly developed a longing for study and his work, however, and more importantly, having decided that it is his wife he loves, David abruptly breaks off his affair with Suzanne. Driven to the Malmö train by his chauffeur Sam (John Elfström), David reminds him to be sure to meet him that evening outside a harbor bar in Copenhagen.

On board the train, David wagers with a salesman (Helge Hagerman) over who will get to kiss the attractive woman in their compartment who has stepped out briefly. The salesman pursues the lady but returns to the compartment rubbing his cheek. He pays his debt,

Sawdust and Tinsel. Sandrews

Sawdust and Tinsel. Sandrews

gathers his belongings, and moves to another compartment. When the lady returns, David strikes up a conversation and, discreetly pressing his body against hers, removes a particle she says has blown in her eye. In the ensuing conversation they discuss marriage and affairs; he offers his favorite witticism, which, it is clear, he uses to rationalize his lust and vanity: "Marriage needs a shock to wake it up. . . . The marital bed is the death of love." Besides, he continues, "women *adore* being married." "How naive," replies the exasperated lady—though it is clear she appreciates the gentleman's style and wit—"a woman wants to feel she is a woman, not a wife." Unexpectedly, David says to her, "You're beautiful, witty—a perfect example of your sex. I admit my inferiority and can only stammer out, 'I love you, I've always loved you, and always will.'" We delight at what we may have already guessed: that this is his wife Marianne, and David is scheming to win her back.

When David leaves the compartment to buy Marianne cigarettes, he makes another wager with the salesman: he, David, will kiss the lady before the next station. Marianne, in the meantime, is recalling (in flashback) her visit to David's office to discuss their deteriorating relationship. The strain that his numbingly indifferent response to her attempt to resolve their problems puts on the film's comic tone is, fortunately, relieved in the next scene when Marianne, having discovered the time and place of David's tryst with Suzanne, delivers them breakfast in bed in their hotel room.

Returning to the compartment, David pretends surprise upon learning that Marianne is planning to marry their old friend, the sculptor Carl Adam (Åke Grönberg), and that she is on her way to see him. The two actors sparkle as Marianne wittily explains why she and David can never again be happy together, and for us their interaction confirms that these two are hand and glove. David counters her argument by gushing hyperbolic love phrases and begging for a kiss. Then Marianne, who had eavesdropped on his last wager, winks and leads him outside to the window of the salesman's compartment. The man's jaw drops when she passionately kisses David. But Marianne is the one upset. Totally self-possessed until now, she has let her feelings betray her. She pushes David away and rushes back to the compartment. When he joins her, she is still angry, but soon the two are giggling infectiously over the memory (flashback) of the day Marianne had first planned to wed Carl Adam. By the end of that day, and after a somewhat labored, farcical melee—on film Bergman never does seem to master farce—she instead married the man she secretly loved, Carl Adam's best man, David. After this amusing recollection, they talk seriously about why David wants to come back to her. "I'm afraid," he admits . . . "of your selfish solitude," she rightly concludes. She then confesses her need to be thought of as the best lover in the world, "although you know I'm not." The viewer gradually recognizes that this self-deceptively liberated, bourgeois couple are at last accepting not only their own limitations but the limitations of their fantasies. Their new goal: to establish a revitalized status quo.

Both recognize that their divorce will upset David's parents, and they recall (in flashback) a conversation they had during the picnic celebrating his father's seventy-third birthday. While contentedly lying together in an idyllic wood (the camera hovers just above their two faces), Marianne had admitted that even though she was totally satisfied with her life, she would like another child—"Just a tiny one. . . . Sometimes my body aches for a baby." "I'd have no mistress then," replied David. (Earlier, he was shocked when Marianne pointed out to him that he was jealous of the attention she paid their children.) We also learn of the Kasperish David's womblike adventure fantasy: to don a diver's outfit and hunt deep-sea treasure and sharks. "And where should I be?" she inquires. Seeing the error of his honesty, David quickly responds, "Oh, on board helping." That night, while dancing, he kisses her bare shoulder and whispers the promise we heard him make earlier on the train: to love her always.

After this harmonious recollection, the viewer expects Marianne to let David carry the day, but she wants him to pursue her further. She has not reckoned, however, on Carl Adam's meeting them as they detrain in Malmö. This boorish, potentially violent, yet good-hearted man behaves as David expected. He brags about his intelligence and strength, and though he had promised Marianne he would not drink, encouraged by David, he does. He also discloses that he does not think Marianne is so bourgeois as to actually want to get married again. Besides, he adds, "only impotent men are faithful." Just as meeting the slick, unappealing King Westley in *It Happened One Night* (1934) or the affected Cecil in *A Room with a View* (1985) instantly establishes that they are not serious competitors in the love triangle, we now wait to see how Carl Adam will be dispensed with. When David, with Marianne's collusion, insists they have one last drink together before he turns his wife over to his friend, they visit a seashore dive in Copenhagen. Not a complete fool, Carl Adam schemes to have the bartender

A Lesson in Love. AB Svensk Filmindustri

A Lesson in Love. AB Svensk Filmindustri

mix David a "Volcano" and then sends a spicy-looking prostitute, Lise (Birgitte Reimar), to pretend that she and David are familiars. When she throws her arms around David's neck and demands a kiss, Björnstrand, in this classic Cary Grant–like situation, keeps the nonplussed David at first delightfully poised. "Are you one of my patients?" he queries. When the "Volcano" erupts, however, David takes Lise in his arms and kisses her. Marianne attacks, screaming and scratching. The cry "Police!" ends this indifferently staged brawl between the two women and sends the people in the bar for the exits.

Outside, in the one especially imaginative scene of this conventionally photographed movie, the camera dollies along one side of the Nyhavn canal while on the other side Marianne, almost in tears and looking small and overwhelmed by the dockside bars in the background, hurries along berating (in close-up sound) David, who backpedals in front of her, trying wittily, if none too diplomatically, to soften her outrage over his kissing Lise. When she cries that she would like to drown herself, he offers the canal a few feet away. Then, raising his hand as if to slap her, he hugs her. She capitulates utterly. At that moment, Sam drives up. They get in the car, and Sam delivers them to the hotel where David has made reservations. To a buoyant waltz, the hotel staff, bearing luggage and champagne, escort the couple to the bridal suite. "You wretch! Were you so sure?" asks the obviously pleased, outwitted wife. "A strategist must foresee all eventualities," replies David in his cockiest, most charming manner. Sam, the hotel staff, and the camera retreat from the room, leaving David and Marianne sitting on the edge of their bed. As the manager closes the door, he hangs a "Do Not Disturb" sign on the doorknob. A moment of silence follows his departure. Then, from around the corner of the empty hallway, a little diapered boy, wings on his back and carrying a bow and arrow, approaches the door, smiles at us, and enters. When Cupid closes the door (the film's last shot), the sign reads, "Silence: A Lesson in Love."

DREAMS

The underrated *Dreams* (1955), Bergman's next film, presents the stylish, mature Susanne Frank (Eva Dahlbeck) sitting at a table in her photography studio in Stockholm, smoking a cigarette in a holder and staring trancelike into her dream of renewing a relationship she broke off with a married man in Gothenburg. She is surrounded by her employees, among whom are a grotesquely obese fashion director, Magnus (Benkt-Åke Benktsson), an effeminate young man, and a shallow, narcissistic model, Doris (Harriet Andersson). These people seem to represent what happens when sexual energy is frustrated, sublimated, or mischanneled, the underlying assumption being that there is a God-given norm for human development. Made edgy by her own unhappiness, Susanne smashes out her cigarette and lunges for the privacy of the darkroom, where she lights another cigarette, paces, and, standing at the door, eavesdrops as a woman employee tells the others that Susanne is still visiting Gothenburg and hanging around outside the house of a married man with whom she had carried on an affair. Returning to the studio, Susanne dismisses people for the day and tells Doris that she must accompany her that evening to Gothenburg for a photo session on the following afternoon. When Doris's boyfriend Palle (Sven Lindberg) arrives, Doris at first refuses to kiss him, because it will spoil her makeup, then breaks their date, even though that evening they were supposed to celebrate the finish of his exams. When he complains, she grumbles at his lack of respect for her work. Palle gets angry and, before storming out, charges, "You are clothes crazy, career crazy, and luxury crazy. Besides, you are selfish, spiteful . . . [Doris volunteers, "boy crazy"] . . . and infantile!" After he is gone, the frustrated Doris screams, "I don't even know what 'infantile' means," a retort so candid that it is as endearing as it is funny.

On the night train to Gothenburg the extremity of Susanne's love is exposed when she considers throwing herself from the train, and when she hears—as we do, just as in *Persona* we will hear an imagined voice telling Alma to go to bed—her name being called by her lover. Her temptation to suicide is staged as if she were suffering a life-threatening fever that suddenly breaks. She opens the window and thrusts her head out into the rain. When she draws back, her face is drenched in beads of rain, sweat, and tears, and her wet hair sticks to her forehead. "Please God," she prays, "help me to see him. . . . I won't say anything. I won't cry." Few Bergman males love so desperately.

In Gothenburg they check into the hotel where Susanne and her lover, Henrik Lobelius (Ulf Palme), held their trysts. After instructing Doris to meet her for the photo session at one o'clock sharp on the museum steps, Susanne hurries to the woods across the street from

Henrik's house. When she is seen by his wife (Inga Landgré), Susanne hastily retreats to a nearby tearoom to phone Henrik, who, after resisting, agrees to meet her later at the hotel.

Doris, meanwhile, is coveting expensive clothes and jewelry. Her image, reflected in a series of store windows and mirrors, is suddenly joined by that of a bearded, elderly gentleman, Consul Sönderby (Gunnar Björnstrand). (The way he materializes, besides suggesting Mephistopheles, echoes shots in Fritz Lang's M [1931] in which the child molester-murderer played by Peter Lorre appears next to his intended victims as they covet toys displayed in store windows.) The two reflections, meeting as illusions dreaming of what might be, acknowledge each other. With some effort, his charm, diginity, and self-confidence acting like a heady perfume, Consul Sönderby finally allays Doris's fear that he is dangerous or making a fool of her. Doris permits him to buy her an evening gown, shoes, and a pearl necklace. What else "beyond the limits of common sense" does his Cinderella wish for? he inquires. "Infantile" Doris captivates her admirer by requesting chocolate with whipped cream but then realizes that she is late for her photo session. Giving her elderly admirer a kiss on the cheek, she rushes off.

Upset from having been seen by Henrik's wife and from a humiliating experience in the tearoom, Susanne takes it out on Doris for being late. She fires her, leaving her crying on the museum steps. Again, the "great magician" Sönderby materializes. Having broken with Palle, and now out of a job, Doris is receptive to her magician's attentions. He takes her first to an ice cream parlor and then to an amusement park. On the roller coaster the exhilarated Doris laughs and screams at each plummeting, body-wrenching dive while old Sönderby, mouth open and eyes shut and clinging tightly to his hat, fights back dizziness and nausea. As they exit the park on their way to his house, they are seen deep in the frame. Bergman has learned—and he will use this knowledge to great effect in Raval's death in *The Seventh Seal*—that horror and shock are "reinforced in long shot" (*BB,* 109). Suddenly Sönderby staggers and falls. Our amused censoriousness at his deserved discomposure is replaced by pity when, after several moments, he is still unable to get to his feet. At last, he accepts Doris's humiliating assistance. Once up, he pushes her away and walks on ahead.

At the Sönderby mansion Doris bandages his cut hand, which throughout the sequence acts as a reminder of his age and folly. Prominent throughout the following sequence is the portrait of Sönderby's wife, who has spent the last 23 years in a mental institution, and whom Doris resembles. When the clothes and jewelry he ordered earlier for Doris arrive, he adds to the trove a bracelet his mother bequeathed to his daughter. While Cinderella is dressing, Uncle Otto, as she has taken to calling him, breaks out champagne. Doris drinks in the bubbly and with it, in the mirror, her glorious appearance. Her tongue and imagination are soon loosened by both. She asks the "great magician" to pay for a crown for her crooked tooth, to make a movie in which she will star, to buy her a car, a villa, or a bungalow. Sober enough, however, to see that her suitor is becoming disenchanted, Doris clumsily pulls back. Again, her disarming candor and tipsy charm win our affection. (Andersson's performance is successful because she does not show the machinery of Doris's decision about how much of herself she will exchange for what she wants.) "I don't want a thing from you. . . . You're really ugly, but *so* ugly that you're sweet," she informs him, but subsequent references to his eyeglasses and his age, and her reassurance that he won't be making a fool of himself if he joins her on the bearskin rug, further sober his fantasies while adding to his dizziness. Faint, he retires to the bedroom, but no sooner has he lain down—we are shown only his bandaged hand gripping the end of the bed—than the doorbell brings him to his feet. Hastily hiding the signs of their partying, he shuts Doris in the bedroom—the door swings open slightly, so she eavesdrops—and admits his visitor. It is his hate-filled, alienated daughter, Marianne (Kerstin Hedeby), who has come for her bracelet and some of her money. By the end of her visit she has revealed her father's selfish penuriousness, his indifference to her existence, and his abandonment of her psychotic, institutionalized mother. Afraid that she will discover Doris, Sönderby writes Marianne a check. Insisting on having her bracelet, she enters the bedroom and discovers her father's "floozy." "Lust has even overcome your avarice," she says with a loathing that matches her father's, though it is delivered without his charming smile. She takes the bracelet from Doris, slaps her face, and departs. After Doris is back in her own clothes, she approaches Sönderby, who is staring out the window. Sheepishly, she thanks him for being "so nice." He turns and looks her coldly and contemptuously in the eye and tells her to leave. Then he resumes his staring, his unfocused gaze, like Susanne's at the film's start, actually focused inward on his shattered self-image and dream. Frightened by his near catatonia, Doris runs out.

She does stop at the gate to glance back: the camera cranes up toward the zombielike figure framed—like the abandoned, psychotic wife in the portrait—in the second-floor window.

A parallel image opens the next sequence. Susanne is staring out the window of her hotel room waiting to catch sight of Henrik's car. When he finally arrives and enters, everything about him says weakness; he is a man who wants a mother almost as much as a mistress. He immediately unpacks his despair and self-contempt, whimpering that he feels old and a failure. Susanne, nevertheless, drinks in his presence, and using another of the formulaic phrases that Bergman's women use to comfort their weak or self-pitying men—"Poor [Henrik]"—she tells him, "I wish I could take you up in my hands and carry you off in my pocket." His pathetic lowering of his bald head so that it just touches the tips of her fingers, which are extended and pressed together as if in prayer, is affecting. He is about to leave when the phone rings, but ironically, when the caller—his wife—does not respond, their passions are unleashed.

Afterwards, Susanne tells Henrik that she wants a child by him. Though she acknowledges being ashamed of "crawling on all fours, begging and begging," she purrs that he will always be her teddy bear. (Unlike Bergman's men—Albert's request that Agda take him back, for example, almost stuck in his throat—most of his women do not seem to let their shameless professions of love inhibit or, afterwards, humiliate them.) Henrik refuses to father a child by her because he wants to "live and grow up" with his children. Susanne confesses, with quiet equanimity but frightened by the intensity of the feeling, that she wishes his wife and children dead. They have just agreed to meet in Oslo when the phone rings. It is Martha Lobelius calling from the front desk. She's coming up to talk with them.

When the severely dressed but modestly attractive Martha enters, she takes command. Her superior smile accents the sure thrusts of her faultless, probably rehearsed delivery. She is uncannily prescient; it is as if she had been eavesdropping on them. (At first, the camera helps establish her seeming omniscience and omnipotence by not letting Susanne into the frame.) She talks to Susanne about Henrik, who stands behind them slightly out of focus, as if he had no say. Martha surmises that Susanne and Henrik plan to go to Oslo. She acknowledges that Susanne's love for Henrik has given him something wonderful, but that Susanne made a grave mistake when she broke off the relationship. "You thought you would force him to come live with you. Instead, he stayed with me. Not because he loves me more, but because he's tired. . . . When he is with me there are no emotional upheavals; he sleeps in peace. Then there are the children . . . the strongest argument. That's why you want a child with Henrik, as a bond between you, or as a souvenir of past love." Then, the coup de grace: Henrik's business is failing, and he has no money; she provides the material comfort so important to him, and to men in general. Susanne's "I understand" marks her surrender. Martha's victory, achieved by humiliating everyone—though we sense that Henrik's pride will mend when Martha subsequently disguises her iron grip in a velvet glove— is Pyrrhic and hollow. She admits that she likes Susanne and that, in fact, she is not jealous: "When I lost him my jealousy died out." Like Albert's wife Agda (*Sawdust and Tinsel*), she is an intelligent and sensitive woman, but also a disillusioned and erotically dead one who now administers her emotions as placidly and routinely as she does her household. Henrik is a necessary piece of the furniture of her life.

After Martha leaves, Susanne tells Henrik to go, assuring him that they will not meet again. When the door closes behind him, however, her hands fly to her mouth to stifle her involuntary "Henrik! Henrik! Henrik!"

As he exits the hotel, Henrik eyes the pretty young woman who enters. It is Doris, who has come to beg Susanne's forgiveness. She is too upset by her experience with Sönderby to fully perceive the uncomplaining Susanne's low spirits. But Doris has learned that "it's not always easy to be a career woman. Your private life often interferes with your job." She also has come to realize that she must bridle her narcissism and, like *Summer Interlude*'s Marie, subordinate her career to love. (On their return to Stockholm Susanne reconciles Palle with Doris, who, now indifferent to her makeup, assaults him with kisses when he visits.)

The last scene opens with Susanne again in the studio, surrounded by her supportive community of grotesques, though Bergman now clusters them more closely. When a note from Henrik is delivered, she characterizes it as "a letter asking for charity" and rips it up—as, at the film's start, she had ripped up a photograph that was not up to her standards. Emphasizing that even though his characters' emotional journeys may not take them great distances, they have nevertheless learned critical things about themselves and their subsequent choices, Bergman once again bookends his film with similar shots. The music swells and the camera dollies in on Susanne for—as in *Monika*—virtually the same pose she was in when we first met her: she removes the cigarette holder from her mouth, leans her head against her hand, and stares dreamily into space. Her expression makes it clear that in the back of her mind she is revising the scenario for her future. Even though she seems to be staring through smoke into nothingness, she has not abandoned her woman's dream. Henrik has been dropped from the script, and behind those eyes she is recasting.

SMILES OF A SUMMER NIGHT

Smiles of a Summer Night (1955), Bergman's next film and the first in a series of period dramas, takes place in 1901. As in *Dreams,* a woman's break with her lover propels the plot. When the actress Désirée Armfeldt (Eva Dahlbeck) ended her two-year relationship with the lawyer Fredrik Egerman (Gunnar Björnstrand)—an affair that began after his wife died—he married Anne (Ulla Jacobsson), a woman virtually the same age as his 19-year-old son Henrik (Björn Bjelvenstam). Anne has not let their marriage be consummated.[4] Bergman occasionally uses the decor to comment on Fredrik. For example, apropos of his unconsummated marriage, early in the film Bergman shows Fredrik on his way home, his thoughts filled with his beautiful wife, walking briskly past a row of phallic-shaped cannons whose barrels are plugged. (The cannons also foreshadow his final encounter with Count Malcolm.) The film's early scenes function, too, as the benchmark of Fredrik's energy: vigorous at the start, at the end he lies exhausted on a couch.

Fredrik's starchy manner, closely cropped hair, and mincing beard gently mock his conception of himself as a demigod, a man of parts for all seasons, an image that, as he enters his house, is reinforced by his attractive, 18-year-old maid Petra (Harriet Andersson). She, who admits to preferring older men, subtly propositions him. Clearing his throat and his mind, he rejects the temptation while registering the flattery. Next, he pauses outside the doorway to the living room to eavesdrop on his son—Henrik's black garb and white clerical collar indicate that he is a student of the ministry—reading to his attentive young stepmother Martin Luther's injunction to resist temptation. (Like Anne, whom he loves, Henrik is a pre-Freudian character. Thus, they are not fully conscious of their feelings and are confused by the

Smiles of a Summer Night. AB Svensk Filmindustri

Smiles of a Summer Night. AB Svensk Filmindustri

promptings of their sexuality.) Though Fredrik does not take their infatuation seriously, Bergman throws a shadow across Fredrik's face and places the camera in front of him so that the antlers on the wall behind him appear to sprout from his head (see fig. 9).[5] When Fredrik enters the room, his face betrays no sign that he intends to put his rival in his place by displaying his proprietary rights. He produces two tickets for a performance that night of a play featuring Désirée Armfeldt. Excited, the girlish Anne leaps into his lap.

The couple nap before leaving for the theater. Husband and wife, fully clothed, lie stretched out side by side on the bed like carved figures atop a sarcophagus. Fredrik, asleep and dreaming, turns on his side and touches Anne's face. His unthreatening somnambulism emboldens her to press his hand to her breast, move closer, and explore his beard and lips with her own hand. Fredrik kisses her and somniloquizes, "Désirée . . . how I have longed for you." Sitting bolt upright, her eyes glazed with tears, Anne stares at the stranger beside her.

At the theater Désirée has just delivered a witty speech about how women must manage their men when Anne, crying, softly asks Fredrik to take her home. She is upset further when their early return compels Henrik to cover up signs of his attempted wooing of Petra. Anne rushes off to bed. When Fredrik looks in on her to bid her goodnight—he is sneaking back to the theater—she is again teary-eyed. Her questions indicate that her childlike naïveté is beginning to dissolve. Would he, she asks, be jealous if she were attracted to Henrik? And why, when she suggested they marry that summer after his wife died, was a man his age attracted to a 16-year-old? Afraid that he is disappointed with her, she promises that "one day" she will truly be his wife and even bear him a child. He does not press her. The fact is that the narcissistic Fredrik eschews mature relationships. Like Torvald's love for Nora in *A Doll's House* (1879), Fredrik's love for Anne is based in part on being able to regard her as a pet or a child, someone he can attend to when it suits him, someone whose complex or inconvenient emotional demands (like his son's) he does not have to take too seriously. Désirée will explain to him that his concern only for himself was one reason she broke off their relationship. Reassuring Anne that he will patiently wait for her complete love, he pats her cheek—that familiar Bergman gesture—and kisses and places her hands on her chest, as would a parent putting a child to bed. Interrupting his departure, Anne calls to him to slyly observe that Désirée Armfeldt looks "very old."

At the theater Fredrik eavesdrops on Désirée from the wings after her last curtain call as she stands alone behind the lowered curtain and stares into it. Her stare is like Susanne's (*Dreams*); she has become increasingly aware that professional success is not enough. As if her dreamy wish were answered, she turns to find Fredrik. They hug and, like David and Marianne (*A Lesson in Love*), exchange mutually appreciated, barbed witticisms that testify to their perfect compatibility. (During the ensuing conversation in Désirée's dressing room Fredrik is photographed with heart-shaped wall ornaments—in place of antlers—behind his head.) Fredrik tells Désirée of his suspicion that in his sleep he spoke her name to Anne; he confesses that his marriage has not been consummated because he wants Anne to come to him of her own free will. Hidden from Fredrik because she is sitting behind him, Désirée's face reveals the full progression of her emotions: first humor and envy, and then, at the news that the marriage has not been consummated, hope, and then surprise that aging and Anne have actually produced in Fredrik something that resembles real love. She is sadly resigning herself to this situation when Fredrik, watching her bathe, tells her, "The years have given your body the perfection which perfection itself lacks." He adds, "You are my only friend . . . the only human being to whom I've dared show myself in all my appalling nakedness." Fredrik, she realizes, is hers for the getting.

She invites him to her apartment, and as they walk along a puddle-lined street she sings a song that associates her with the film's overseeing force, God as love: "Love is life in eternal rebirth." At the entrance to her building, however, the elegant demigod Fredrik suffers the first of a series of humiliating falls, physical and emotional, that structure this film. Just as Désirée is warning him to watch his step in the flooded entry, he slips. Sitting hip-high in dirty water, he good-naturedly and stylishly ignores the absurdity and ignominiousness of his condition. Like Désirée, we cannot restrain our laughter, and the fun carries over into the next shot, which reveals Fredrik in a night-shirt and pointed nightcap (which belong to Count Malcolm, Désirée's lover). Fredrik is further disconcerted when a four-year-old named Fredrik—"FREDRIK!" Fredrik cries in a high, squeaky voice as the name's significance sinks in—also in a nightgown, marches past to the bathroom. Désirée's coyness about who the boy's father is leads Fredrik to blurt out that she is not fit to raise a child. She slaps his face and angrily points out that he has not changed after all; he is "dead serious" when *his* problems are involved but "cynical and stupid when it comes to others." Fredrik apologizes, and they begin discussing their former relationship. One reason she broke it off, she says, was that he treated her as something to boast about to his bachelor friends. (The collection of antlers we saw earlier also suggests a man who keeps trophies of his exploits.) Her anger returns when he ducks the question of whether he ever really wanted to marry her. "I thought that we were friends," he responds, and she, echoing Karin Lobelius's (*Secrets of Women*) characterization of her Fredrik, asks rhetorically, "You, who never had any other friend but yourself?" Fredrik's narcissism is immediately thrown into relief by that of Count Carl-Magnus Malcolm (Jarl Kulle), who enters to a comic, military fanfare. This caricature of unself-conscious military macho inquires why Fredrik is camped inside his nightshirt and robe. (Malcolm's stiff, dirtied uniform—he too has suffered a fall—is threateningly and comically juxtaposed to Fredrik's dainty nightshirt.) Fredrik's purposeful contempt for his jealous, weapon-minded rival leads him to the edge of disaster, but he avoids it by heeding the amused Désirée's suggestion that retreat is the better part of valor. Divesting himself of Malcolm's robe and adjusting his frilly collar as if it were an elegant cravat, Fredrik bows, soundlessly clicks his slippered heels, pivots, and exits. Afterwards, we learn, Malcolm threatens Désirée with a poker, which she, looking for a convincing means of breaking off their relationship—he was never an object of her affection, only a tool of her vanity and her physical and material needs—subsequently applies to his head.

Désirée visits her ancient, invalided mother (Naima Wifstrand), who lives isolated in a mansion given her by a lover in exchange for her promise to not write her memoirs. Mrs. Armfeldt is sitting on her bed, looking as if she were on an island in a vast, white space. Though she is related to such living-dead figures as Henrik's ageless aunt in *Summer Interlude* and Isak Borg's ancient mother in *Wild Strawberries,* old Mrs. Armfeldt has cast her lot with life. Her wisdom and magic help her in her role as love's midwife. So does her wit. On meeting Fredrik, she notes that his children are lovely, especially the girl; the self-conscious Fredrik corrects her, "That girl is my wife." But all her powers are unable to protect her from melancholy or the ravages of time. Bergman emphasizes the former at the end of Désirée's visit by having Mrs. Armfeldt comment that seeing so much human suffering has exhausted her, and the latter by having Petra view the "magnificently shaped" statue of the young Mrs. Armfeldt and exclaim, "Oh my God . . . what life does to us!" (In *Sawdust and Tinsel* Albert is concerned with aging, and in *Dreams* Consul Sönderby's age is near the heart of his actions. In subsequent films Bergman devotes increasing attention to aging and death.) Fittingly, Mrs. Armfeldt is playing solitaire, a game that, like the film's plot, aligns cards of the same suit. (The game motif runs through the film—for example, marksmanship with knives and guns, croquet, Russian roulette.) As part of her plan to win Fredrik, Désirée gets her mother to invite the Egermans and the Malcolms to her castle.

Returning from the hunt, Count Malcolm's young wife Charlotte (Margit Carlqvist) joins her husband in their indoor shooting gallery. She is an attractive, aggressive woman of masculine independence and habits, but her compulsive love for her unfaithful husband makes her a bridling vassal. Learning of the invitation from Désirée's mother, Charlotte looks forward to meeting her husband's former mistress. Still jealous of Fredrik, Malcolm—the wound from Désirée's blow with the poker almost invisible—assigns Charlotte the job of informing her friend Anne Egerman of what transpired the previous evening. Seeing the request for what it is, Charlotte responds, "Poor Malcolm, are you so jealous?" Heading for the door, the furious Malcolm stops briefly to declare, "I can tolerate my wife's infidelity, but if anyone touches my mistress I become a tiger!" Charlotte raises the pistol she has been firing, with ever more accuracy as Malcolm's conversation has angered her, and pulls the trigger once more, shattering the glass in the door through which he has departed.

Early the following day at the Egermans', Anne inquires of Petra if losing her virginity was "disgusting." Petra, whose refreshingly uninhibited sexuality keeps us cognizant of the artificial sexual games people play, is emphatic that it was exciting and fun, and soon the two have collapsed on the bed in a spasm of audience-infecting giggles. Anne buries Petra under a body-sized pillow and kisses her, an expression not only of girlish high spirits but of her frustrated, overflowing love. Then Anne, who has decided to be a proper manager of her husband's household, sets out to take charge. She quickly discovers, however, that all the duties were performed by the servants before she was even out of bed. Like a child who does not know what to do with herself, she visits Henrik, whose face she ends up slapping for carrying on the previous night with Petra. Wiping away her tears, she leaves the puzzled boy and enters Fredrik's study.[6] Like the lambs in the laps of the ladies in the paintings on the wall, she crawls into his lap. She sets aside his repellant (phallic) cigar and gives him a daughterly kiss. Barely looking up from his ledgers, Fredrik asks distractedly, "Did my little girl want anything in particular?" No, she says, vaguely dis-appointed, and leaves to play with her caged canaries. Charlotte ar-rives and springs the story of Fredrik's departure in his nightshirt from Désirée's. Although we regret that Anne has to relinquish her doe-eyed innocence for duplicity and self-protective cruelty, we enjoy seeing her give as good as she gets. She lacks Désirée's verbal panache, but she acquits herself admirably by innocently observing that the whole town knows of the count's affair with Mademoiselle Armfeldt. The unforeseen and trancelike effect of this on Charlotte is a tight-lipped, whispered liturgy of love and loathing for Malcolm and men in general: "I hate him! Men are beastly! They are arrogant and vain and have hair all over their bodies. . . . In spite of everything I love [and] . . . would do anything for him . . . just so that he'll pat me and say, 'That's a good little dog.'" This aria of ambivalence is accom-panied by low, somber musical chords, and her conviction is intensi-fied when the camera dollies in on her as her passion peaks. No other scene in this film is so totally without mirth and wit. When she fin-ishes, the music disappears, the emotional pitch rises an octave, and the conversation regains its former pace. Fredrik interrupts to inform Anne of their invitation to Mrs. Armfeldt's. He then retires to his study, where he deals out in front of him, as if he too were playing solitaire, photographs of his beautiful wife. As he gazes at them, his glasses steam up and he mutters, "I don't understand."

The invited guests and their servants arrive at Mrs. Armfeldt's. Her middle-aged coachman, the lusty, exuberant Frid (Åke Fridell), and Petra begin a relationship, and Désirée immediately connives with Charlotte to help Charlotte get back Malcolm while Désirée secures Fredrik for herself. The plan is to be put into operation at dinner.

The night of truth begins. The superannuated Mrs. Armfeldt be-comes a fairy godmother, love's midwife, as, with an uncharacteristic feyness, Bergman spins a mood of luxury, mystery, and magic.[7] At dinner the first part of the plan is executed when Charlotte bets Mal-colm she can seduce Fredrik in 15 minutes or less. The second phase is instigated by Mrs. Armfeldt's magic wine, every cask of which has been improved by a drop of milk from the breast of a woman who has given birth to her first child and "a drop of seed from a young stallion." The wine's bewitching power is cued when we hear waves of harp arpeggios, which also act as auditory wipes terminating the previous image in preparation for the camera's repeatedly swooping in for a close-up as each person makes a wish and drinks (Simon, 118). Each major character's close-up is also composed differently. Being framed by sparkling candles and (in the shadows behind her) servants enhances Désirée's glamour and complexity. Malcolm, by contrast, is shot close to the camera and backed by complete blackness. Anne is flanked by a serving girl in a lace apron and an elegantly attired male servant, and a servant stands uncomfortably close to Henrik. We are somewhat distanced from the characters because we know what each is wishing and, thus, cannot help reflecting on his or her character. Fredrik, for instance, wishes to possess Anne fully, but we also see him as "an aging, slightly pathetic loser" (Simon, 130).

The action comes to a climax when the wine causes Henrik to rebel against his father's narcissistic control: "You behave like some kind of demigod who decides what everyone in your house can think and do!" His words cause Anne to place her hand softly on his shoulder. Suddenly, Fredrik's face fills the screen, and discordant, laughably melodramatic (nondiegetic, that is, sound that comes from a source outside the represented space of the story) trumpets blare forth as, at last, he realizes the seriousness of Anne's love for Henrik. Henrik then attacks Malcolm for ridiculing his idealism, but he is intimidated by the military man and defeated by Mrs. Armfeldt's question, "Why is youth so terribly unmerciful?" and Désirée's answer, "They stake all on never growing old." Bergman makes us sympathize with both youth and age. Though the film salutes, even envies youth and shares its aversion to seeing love perverted into puzzling games and artificial rituals, its overall point of view is middle-aged; it looks melancholically at youth's romantic illusions. In a cruciform stance, Henrik asks forgiveness and then rushes out. Afraid that he may harm himself, Anne starts after him but collapses. Fredrik rushes to her, but Petra subtly bumps him aside and leads her out. Smiling, Mrs. Armfeldt announces that coffee is to be served in the pavilion. Before retiring there, however, Charlotte, who describes herself to Fredrik as honest as a rattlesnake, offers herself to him in earnest.

Fear of aging and death is the focus of the pavilion scene. Désirée sings a carpe diem song as each character stares straight ahead, reflecting on his or her own mortality. The candles in the chandelier and candelabra, tall, straight, each tipped with a tiny flame, are eloquent: as each flame burns toward self-extinction, it is increasingly encased in the eroding wax, evoking a tragic sense of the human spirit encased in sagging flesh.

Meanwhile, Henrik's desire to sin bursts as he watches Petra and the satyrlike Frid cavort on the lawn. He veils his head in the gauzy white curtains—this material represents virginity—and prays to lose his virtue. Hating his sinfulness and convinced that the adult world is hostile to his self-fulfillment—a typical Bergman adolescent—he decides to commit suicide. Henrik climbs onto a tile stove, ties his robe's belt to a projecting prong, then steps into space. The prong snaps, and he is propelled across the room and falls against a mechanism that triggers the entry into his room of Anne, asleep in her bed, from the adjoining room. At first unable to believe he is not dead, he finally kisses his sleeping beauty, who confesses that she loves him. So, as in Marivaux, "the forces of life win out over the kind of spirituality which makes one yawn."

In the early hours the young couple, having consummated their love, interrupt love's Sancho Panzas, Petra and Frid, as Frid is explaining the summer night's first smile—it is for that rare love that is both a gift and a punishment (for example, Henrik and Anne's). They have just readied the carriage for Henrik and Anne's elopement when Fredrik happens on the scene. (Again, Bergman employs the stage convention of having the eavesdropper close but invisible to those on whom he is spying. Nowhere is this device, transformed, used more effectively than it will be in *Wild Strawberries*.) Fredrik is speechless. As the lovers ride off Anne releases her long, white veil, the symbol of her virginity. It falls at Fredrik's feet, causing him to stumble and age before our eyes.

The action now turns to the object of the summer night's second smile—those lusty incorrigibles whose enchanted elixir is beer and whose magic bedroom is a haystack beneath a windmill. Having given herself sexually to the rhapsodic and ambitious Frid, Petra, astride his chest, demands that he now keep his promise to marry her.

Meanwhile, having discovered that Charlotte has betrayed her and is trying to seduce Fredrik, Désirée tips off Malcolm. As he takes off in pursuit, he modifies his previous declaration and cries out, "I can tolerate someone dallying with my mistress, but if anyone touches my wife I become a tiger!" He finds the couple in the pavilion and, after sending his wife out, challenges Fredrik to Russian roulette. Our apprehensions for the worst find support in such earlier omens as the dark tone of Charlotte's speech about men, the carpe diem references, and the carved figure of death that unexpectedly emerged from the tower clock's carillon. Björnstrand's portrayal of Fredrik's brave-faced cowardice during his first two successful turns at firing is comic perfection. But when Malcolm reminds him that he has just been betrayed by his wife and son, the comedy vanishes. It is Fredrik's turn to spin and fire, and he welcomes the bullet. Fredrik puts the muzzle to his temple and squeezes the trigger.

The loud report startles Charlotte and Désirée, who are waiting outside. Malcolm comes out of the pavilion, stares gravely into the frightened women's eyes, and then explodes in laughter. Though we do not fully credit his reason—a nobleman does not "risk his life with a shyster"—the cad has tricked Fredrik by using a blank. While Désirée goes to Fredrik, Charlotte, who would have won her wager, demands that Malcolm pay up: he must devote himself to her alone. "Impossible!" he responds; women are all "ridiculous . . . absurd and fickle." He confirms our reading of him as an empty narcissist whose diet of females helps fill an inner void and whose continual need for competition stems from his need to master everyone and everything. But showing more good nature than we imagined he possessed, and contradicting our certainty that no philosophical thought has ever half-stepped through his head, he laughs and, qualifying his contract, gives in. "I can never be at ease, you know that. . . . I'll be faithful to you until the last great yawn separates us; in short, in my fashion." Malcolm kisses Charlotte, his pistol prominently displayed beside her head.

We reenter the pavilion and laugh. Because there was soot in the blank that Malcolm substituted in the gun, Fredrik looks as if he were a member of a minstrel show. He has suffered the last of the falls meant to shatter his energizing illusions. Like Albert (*Sawdust and Tinsel*), he has suffered a symbolic death. We are ready for him to recognize his folly and accept the truth revealed to him in his dreams, but he is not quite there yet. He is studying Anne's photographs, which he has again spread out on the table. Désirée, like a mother attending a child, leans over, wipes off some of the soot with a napkin, and gently tries to mock away his tragic feelings. Then, like a gambler, she sweeps her winnings—Anne's photos—from the table and slips them into her skirt pocket, informing Fredrik, in a double entendre, "I'm putting your love in my big pocket." Dizzy and exhausted, Fredrik lies down on the couch. When she attends him, he puts his hand over hers and asks her not to leave him alone. It is clear that his thoughts are turning toward family because he inquires, "Why did you call your son Fredrik?" Her answer is another double entendre: "Isn't that a good name for a little boy?" Désirée knows he wants a mother and a protector in a wife, and that she will have to nurse his dignity back to health and wait for him to fully accept the mature and independent woman he has been making love to in his dreams. (We recall the speech she gave in the play early in the film.) She is also aware that on occasion Fredrik's eye will wander and that he may never be capable of loving as unselfishly and deeply as she would like, though age has helped increase his insight into himself and made him more considerate. Sitting where he had sat, she confirms victory by lighting up a cigar, the film's symbol of security and authority (and of comfort with the phallus).

This scene's dim lighting and potent mood of enervation and melancholia are replaced—tempered—by animal high spirits. Bergman ends the film by celebrating another relationship between an older man and a younger woman. He displays Frid stretching in the bright rising sun and proclaiming to the skies (echoing *Sawdust and Tinsel's* Albert), "This is the life. There's none better!" The film ends with the barefoot Petra hiking her skirts can-can fashion and high-stepping it through the swaying golden wheat, leading her man back to the castle for breakfast.

Far more successful than the fitfully effective *A Lesson in Love*—which nevertheless beguiles us with a wit, honesty, and charm that time has not dimmed—*Smiles of a Summer Night* balances the comic with the potentially tragic. The statement made by the voice-over at the start of *A Lesson in Love* applies as well to *Smiles of a Summer Night:* "This comedy might have been a tragedy, but the gods were kind." In spite of an occasional lapse of tone, this "incredible confection" of "lyricism, farce, fantasy, satire and naturalism"[8] is so lively and re-strained, displaying so gossamer a lightness—"White is suitable for both laughter and tears," says Anne—that someone viewing the dark, heavy, and claustrophobic *Sawdust and Tinsel,* with its brutal as well as gentle passions and audacious style, could not easily imagine that the later film originated from the same sensibility.

As these films show, Bergman had decided that another troublesome aspect of his marriages, his relationships with his children—several of whom obviously had made their feelings known to him—could be fruitfully dramatized. And to his credit, he approaches the subject from both the children's and the adult's point of view. His feelings toward his own parents naturally feed his complex reaction of love-hate, indifference, and guilt.

In *Sawdust and Tinsel* Albert's claim that he wanted to return to Agda to be with his boys is belied not only by his previous neglect of them but by his discomfort around them. His older son reciprocates.

The nine-year-old seems indifferent to the big man with the greasy face and white gloves, and he reveals undisguised distaste when Albert asks him if he would like to work in the circus. Interestingly, though, when Agda and Albert withdraw behind the closed doors of the parlor, Bergman has the lad eavesdrop, revealing an almost instinctual desire to know more about his father. Apparently Agda has not been able to inoculate their youngest son against the spirit of adventure that the circus represents. He arrives to ask for money from his parents for the organ grinder's monkey.

In *A Lesson in Love* we are able to observe David with one of his two neglected children, his 15-year-old tomboy daughter, Nix (Harriet Andersson). He encounters her as she is running away from her mother's home. He is not surprised by her formality—when he asks whether she would like some ice cream, she replies, "Have you time?"—or her anger toward him for neglecting her and her younger brother and separating from their mother, but he is taken back a bit at her disapproval of his and Marianne's sexual behavior. Disconcerting, too, is her ambivalence about her own gender and sexuality, and her request that her gynecologist father operate and turn her into a man. She is disgusted that women, rather than doing significant things, as men do, are so passive and preoccupied with silly magazines, their appearance, and love. She wants to create with her hands. (A hairline crack in the credibility of the 22-year-old Andersson's portrayal is due to her physical movement and delivery, which suggest a girl older than 15.) Responding to her need for a parent-counselor, David spends the day with her. He takes her to the home of Uncle Axel (Carl Ström), the potter. There father and daughter sit at potter's wheels separately shaping lumps of soft clay into elementary—but symbolic—pots (see fig. 8). When she learns that David is unsure whether he and Marianne will divorce, Nix crushes her pot and rushes out crying, "I never want to love anybody." David pursues her, but the camera stays, dollying in on his pot, slightly lopsided yet still upright.

Sitting with her father on the grass, Nix expresses annoyance with her girlfriend's enjoyment of petting and with her own mother's sexual relationship with Carl Adam. Noticing David's surprise at hearing about the latter, Nix responds, "Mommy naturally has a lover when you have a mistress." David does not find talking intimately with his daughter easy, but he tries to show that he understands what is troubling her by articulating the same idea that will deeply trouble *Perso-*

na's Alma: our ideas about life fail to fit our actions, or, as David puts it, "We try to be ourselves and we find that we're other people too." But this notion and his belief that "life at its best is cooperation," are too abstract for Nix, who is struggling with the disgust she feels for sex (linking her to Anne and Charlotte in *Smiles of a Summer Night* and to Hjördis in the upcoming *Brink of Life*). When David agrees that wallowing in physical love is baboonlike, Nix, thinking of his mistress, asks him if he therefore despises himself. David's candidness is frightening: "Yes I do. Everything leaves me cold." Nix's reaction is natural: "Even what happens to Mommy and me and Pelle?" David rubs her cheek and reassures her, "Not any more. That's *all* I care for." (This satisfies Nix, but it is impossible for viewers familiar with Bergman's pathological narcissists, characters unable to relate deeply, to disregard his "Everything leaves me cold.") David arranges for Nix to be apprenticed to Uncle Axel, and that evening she falls asleep in her father's arms, indicating that loving parents may be, after all, a child's most overriding need—an interpretation supported in later scenes by the picture David's little boy draws of a phantom chasing away wolves, and by David's own radiant look when he and his own doctor father "operate" on the family automobile.

In *Dreams* the old philanderer, Sönderby, has rejected, along with his psychotic wife, his daughter Marianne, that rejection being the ostensible cause of Marianne's alcoholism and loathing for him. In contrast, Henrik—and this is the only thing for which we respect him—refuses to have a child with Susanne because he could not be around while he or she was growing up.

In *Last Couple Out* (1956), a film that Bergman wrote but did not direct, he seems to return primarily to his own youthful problems. Like Jan-Erik Widgren in *Torment,* his teenage protagonist, Bo Dahlin (Björn Bjelvenstam), finds his emotional and sexual urges conflicting with the conventions upheld by inhibited, inconsistent, and suspicious adults. Convinced that almost all the important adults in his life have betrayed him, he confides to a sympathetic teacher that he sees no solution but suicide. The teacher deflates Bo's self-pity by pointing out that betrayal is common, and that in time Bo himself will not be above it, so he had better deal with the problem now as best as he can.

Finally, in *Smiles of a Summer Night* Bergman again draws upon his own adolescence for the portrait of Henrik, but he also reveals his own failings as a father. Though we laugh at Fredrik's charm and ego-trimming, ironic wit, we flinch when he exercises it on his son (for example, "I only bought two tickets [for the theater]. I thought comedy too worldly for a man of the cloth"). Actually, the sybaritic Fredrik considers his son's choice of profession a temporary aberration that, along with his pimples, time will cure. Fredrik even promises Petra financial remuneration if she will speed Henrik's sexual education. When Henrik becomes so miserable over his failure with Petra that he relaxes his defensive formality with his sarcastic father and confesses his terrible unhappiness to him, Fredrik is moved to tone down his archness slightly. He assures his son that sex is just a plaything and that "a young person is always in love . . . with himself and with love itself." When Henrik, without an ounce of irony, says it must be wonderful to be like his father, who knows what love is, Fredrik stares Henrik in the eye and says quietly and seriously, "It's terrible, my son, almost more than one can bear." Henrik's happiness about his father sharing his feelings with him for the first time is profound and moving, but it is cut short. When Henrik admits that after he failed with Petra she remarked, "Better luck next time," Fredrik laughs and praises women for their more realistic view of sex. Bitter that their momentary intimacy has been aborted, Henrik charges his father with "Mak[ing] fun of everything," and later, in front of Mrs. Armfeldt's dinner guests, he declares that he is ashamed to have Fredrik as his father—neither of which statements seems to noticeably discomfit Fredrik.

Like the theme of unhappy adolescence, humiliation and the sacrifice of a character to somehow benefit the protagonist have appeared in Bergman's films from the start. Caligula's humiliation at the hands of the police and his own humiliation of Jan-Erik (*Torment*), among many others, and Johannes's humiliation by his father (*Ship to India*) are just two examples of the former; examples of the latter include Berta's being sacrificed to educate Jan-Erik (*Torment*), and the sacrifice of Birgitta Carolina to enlarge Tomas's self-awareness (*The Devil's Wanton*). In the four films discussed in this chapter, he continues to use both humiliation and a sacrificial victim—the sacrifice often seeming to be God's purposeful work—as part of his picture of people involved in marital and love relationships, but with an important difference. In the earlier films (and several to come) the life of a young woman or young man was sacrificed. In the present films, before Bergman's usually narcissistic protagonist can be joined with the person he or she loves or deserves, or before the protagonist can achieve enlightenment and self-fulfillment, only his or her pride and dignity need be sacrificed. That sacrifice usually takes the form of (often public) humiliation, which Bergman calls "one of the basic experiences" (*BB*, 81). It is the natural and perfect weapon of the Sunday's child, who has a God-given talent for "stripping away facades of lies and deceits that other[s] . . . incase themselves in" (Blackwell, 51). This is especially true of insecure and hostile Sunday's children whose hypersensitive egos are so outsized that it makes them unusually vulnerable to humiliation. People who understand and accept their limitations and life's injustices are not easy targets for humiliation, whose natural prey is those with an inflated view of themselves. Tragedy employs death as punishment for hubris. Comedy, needing only to cauterize, employs the not quite lethal properties of humiliation. Obviously, humiliation is the perfect and natural weapon/tool of an artist whose principle theme is narcissism. It is also understandable that someone who has suffered so much humiliation should so enjoy using it to vent his own hostility.

Sawdust and Tinsel is packed with scenes of public humiliation, but one is justly famous.[9] Had his entire career consisted of nothing but the film's single flashback—the clown being publicly humiliated by his wife—it would have earned Bergman a niche in film history. The situation and the style in which it is presented are important enough to this study to be examined in detail.

From a wagon moving at a leaden pace and swathed in the rain-pregnant, tin-gray, predawn cold, the viewer is suddenly plunged into the action on a sun-glazed hill overlooking the sea. A regiment of cannoneers is practice-firing while other soldiers, in their boredom, drink, gamble, and curse the heat. Our ears are assaulted by the non-diegetic raucous music of an oompahing band. The vigorous and salacious impact of Karl-Birger Blomdahl's music, which counterpoints the image of the phallic cannons spiritedly and deafeningly ejaculating shells, cannot be conveyed in words. Into the midst of this sexually latent situation strides the smiling Alma (Gudrun Brost), swinging her skirt provocatively. Her large facial features heavily outlined by makeup are further exaggerated by the high-contrast photography. An officer (Åke Fridell) with a lickerish grin offers her money to bathe naked with the soldiers. (As the soldiers wait for her decision, we see a cannon aimed diagonally toward the frame's upper left corner, an image that in *Persona*'s opening montage Bergman will make literal with a close-up of an erect penis pointed in the same direction.) Past 40, this former beauty, who still needs to feel desirable, accepts the offer. The mischievous officer sends a boy to fetch her husband, the circus clown Frost (Anders Ek).

He arrives in whiteface and wearing his beloved costume, which sports a giant, grinning sun directly over his genitals (see fig. 5). Frost's own mouth is huge, and his gestures outrageously pompous. Vain, he is about to illustrate that even a man who routinely invites ridicule and physical abuse, who seems beyond embarrassment, is vulnerable to humiliation. Frost descends the hill, striking out ineffectually with his clown's bladder at the crowd of laughing soldiers and town and circus people. Near the water's edge he calls out to the naked Alma, who is off shore frolicking with a handful of soldiers. From a low angle we stare up at his huge, dark mouth calling—mutely—"Alma! Alma!" Eliminating the sound of his voice while the laughter grows thunderous has a nightmarish effect. No stranger to laughter on his own terms, Frost is dumbfounded and turns to search the laughing faces for an explanation as to why anyone would derive pleasure from his pain. In response, the music and the laughter die out. Frost carefully unbuttons his precious costume and slips it off. Dressed now only in his conical clown's hat and his long undershirt, he squats and places his hand over his buttocks to hide his near nakedness. He moves to the water's edge, his bare feet unsuccessfully trying to avoid the small, sharp stones. A boy hides his and Alma's clothes. Finally, it dawns on Alma what her husband is experiencing, and she wades to his side, her stringy blonde hair only partially hiding her breasts. Frost hugs her close to him, his hands shielding her buttocks.

The hilarity, which has become louder than before, again subsides as Frost, his undershirt shredded, looks for their clothes. Giving up the search, he lifts Alma and starts up the steep, stony incline of the beach. The military drill resumes, and a soft, funereal drumming accompanies images of the staggering emotional and physical agony Frost endures as he bears Alma, like a heavy cross, up to the path leading to the campgrounds. We can no more escape the scene's cruelty than Frost can the pitiless sun that saps his diminishing strength. Close-ups of his painted, white, tortured face reveal only black blurs for eye sockets and sequins of sweat that make his flesh look as if it were peeling. His bare feet press heavily on the jagged, hot stones. Wounded in the recesses of his soul and unable to stop the scene of their humiliation from continuously replaying itself somewhere in the dark theater of his mind, he continues to call out "Alma!" At last he collapses. Proud of his sacrifice, Alma, as if at last she shares his agony, holds him in her lap, creating an elemental Pietà, though her seaweedlike hair, blurred-black lipstick, and sweat-dotted face make her resemble a ferocious sea hag. Then, in fact, she turns into a Fury, emitting a silent scream at those around, blaming *them* for what has happened. At last, lifted by his colleagues, Frost is carried back to the circus tent. All the while, the naked Alma supports his head and in his ear whispers promises we cannot hear.

By comparison, the comic embarrassments to the characters in *A Lesson in Love* are mere pinpricks. The same is true, though their pain is somewhat greater, of the major characters who are embarrassed or humiliated in *Smiles of a Summer Night*. Much of the comedy in that film is at Fredrik's expense, and it is his discomfiture that we remember best: the proud, dapper man sitting in a puddle, his ejection from Désirée's apartment in a nightgown, and the act that marks the death of his misguided illusions, his sooty "suicide." *Dreams* is also a film in which the dignity and dreams of all the major characters are punctured in humiliating circumstances—old Sönderby's ordeal and collapse at the amusement park; Marianne insulting Doris, whom Sönderby then coldly turns out of his house; Martha confronting her husband and Susanne in Susanne's hotel room. Only one public humiliation in these films is almost as psychologically excruciating as Frost's.

In *Dreams,* after being spied outside his house, Susanne escapes to a tearoom and phones Henrik. He attempts to cut the conversation short, but she begs him, whispering, not to hang up. Her eyes closed, her fingers approaching the mouthpiece as if in touching it she were touching him, she says slowly and in a slightly louder voice, which is calm only from desperation, "Henrik . . . Henrik . . . I'm not going to cry or make a scene. I just want to see you . . . talk to you . . . no, no, we won't even talk. You won't refuse me that!" He repeats that he is going to hang up. She does not respond, just listens, savoring the voice she may never again hear. Her long silence frightens him, and so he agrees to visit her hotel room later that day. She hangs up the receiver carefully and, still in close-up, composes her face. As she turns, the camera pulls back to reveal the entire room of middle-aged and elderly women staring at her from their tables: everyone has heard her shameless, humiliating supplication. Susanne tries to rush out, but Bergman gives the screw another turn. The clerk demands a coin for the call. Susanne searches her purse for change but turns up only a bill, which the woman refuses to break unless Susanne buys something. Refusing to be held prisoner any longer, Susanne tosses the bill on the counter and flees.

The most noteworthy uses of sacrifice to enlarge the self-awareness of the Bergman protagonist (Fredrik's symbolic suicide in *Smiles of a*

Summer Night aside) are in *Sawdust and Tinsel*. First, there is Frost, Albert's alter ego, who is sacrificed to his wife's narcissism and broken by his ordeal. Afterwards, he is a hostile and self-destructive alcoholic. Bergman represents the double nature of Frost, a repressed Jack figure (and an ineffectual version of *Shame*'s Jan), by yoking his name and the sun image on his costume and, later, by having Albert explicitly characterize him as a man who is "cold as an icicle" and full of fear and who "despise[s] everyone," including himself. Frost's repressed hate is exposed when Albert threatens to shoot someone. Frost recommends that Albert kill himself, or Alma's sick bear, or, with tears in his eyes, Alma: "It would be a kindness." Frost's secret goal is absolute peace, oblivion; his favorite dream is of himself as a shrinking fetus in Alma's womb.

The overall effect of Albert's mauling by Frans is not as mythic as Frost's humiliation in the flashback, but that humiliating beating, Albert's subsequent failed suicide (discussed further in chapter 4), and his killing of Alma's bear approach archetype. Here is a man who has lost his self-respect and sense of human worth, who can no longer believe in himself as a businessman, artiste, husband, father, lover, or as a man capable of defending his honor or brave enough to take his own life. Secretly gratified that his suicide has failed, he vents his self-destructive impulse by killing Alma's ailing bear, with which Bergman earlier identified both Albert and Frost by having them get down on all fours and imitate it. Again, the Bergman protagonist requires a sacrifice in order to be released from his old attitudes. To Bergman, bears (in every other film teddy bears[10]) generally represent security or happiness. By killing Alma's sick trained bear, Albert not only vents his frustration but symbolically reasserts his manhood and rejects the tame, secure life he sought with Agda. He takes revenge—for himself, Frost, the bear, and all men—on women's strength and domination. After killing the bear with the tiger tamer's pistol, however, he finds sanctuary in the stall of Anne's horse, Prince. Crying as he strokes him, he unconsciously relinquishes his image of himself as the virile master of wild animals—the tiger tamer—for one in which he is the trained Prince on whose back Anne can dance. After this elemental contact and purging of emotion, Albert, who had planned to give up the circus and Anne, decides to stay.

Before concluding this analysis of the Gun films, let me say a little more about Bergman's style. The audaciously baroque *Sawdust and Tinsel* is especially interesting. Influenced by his expressionistic models—Dupont's *Variety* and one of his own nightmares—Bergman

enlarges and shapes the story's essentials by using startling camera angles, giant close-ups, dense compositions, and jolting jump cuts and
juxtapositions, and by dramatically expanding his use of what I have
termed psychic or expressionistic neorealism and analectic sound. In
Sawdust and Tinsel he may first heighten the appearance of an actor
(Frost, Alma, and Albert primarily) with heavy theatrical makeup and
then exaggerate it with the original neorealistic look—grainy, halating
whites butting up against blurry blacks. "They thought I was crazy.
We made a negative of the print, and then from that negative we made
a new print and then a new negative. Eventually we effaced every
grain of the image until we got true black and white—and only black
and white" (Kaminsky, 130).[11] The technique is powerfully effective
in making palpable the sensation of scathing sunlight and unrelenting
heat, and it is largely responsible for the feeling of rawness in the
flashback to Frost's humiliation. It contributes immeasurably, as well,
to that scene's mythic quality. This "look" is not the look of the whole
film, however. A scene's content determines its style. For example, to
signal control and airless, domestic serenity, Bergman not only puts
Agda in a homey dress with a high, tight collar but also uses subtle
photographic images and a muted, gray light in her parlor with its
curtained windows, flowers, and fluted bric-a-brac. The very next
scene, Albert's discovery that Anne has visited the actor, returns to
the expressionistic mode. The scene is bleached by the same searing
sunshine of the Frost scene and accompanied by the same drumbeat
and bitingly satirical music—a trumpet blares a dagger note and
mocks, "Waaa, Waaa"—that we heard not only in the flashback but
in the scene in which Albert first brought Anne to town.[12] Startling,
giant close-ups reveal Albert's heart-stopping panic as he finds it difficult to swallow or even breathe. With his handkerchief he fruitlessly
wipes at the beads of feverish sweat on his fat face and neck, the high-
contrast lighting making his wet, pasty face look sickly by contrast to
the extreme blackness of his eyes, mustache, hat, and coat. (Like the
images of Frost and Alma in the flashback, this is among Bergman's
most shocking visual portraits. It foreshadows the smeared, grotesquely painted face of the psychotic Johan Borg in *Hour of the Wolf*.)
Expressionistic neorealism will surface again for the opening nightmare in *Wild Strawberries*. Before and after that (for example, in *The
Seventh Seal* and *The Magician*), Gunnar Fischer, the virtuoso cinematographer who had photographed most of Bergman's films since
1948, would transform these rough, high-contrast images into the

beautifully subtle chiaroscuro images that were partly instrumental in Bergman's coming to the world's attention. (It should be noted, however, that in *Sawdust and Tinsel* the interiors were shot by Sven Nykvist—his first stint for Bergman—and the exteriors by the old pro Hilding Bladh, whose best work reached back to the early forties.)

Sawdust and Tinsel also marks an important step forward in narrative simplicity and fluidity. It contains roughly half as many scenes as *Monika* and only one flashback. With the exception of *A Lesson in Love* (whose flashbacks enrich the story because they deal with only the two protagonists), *Wild Strawberries,* and perhaps *The Devil's Eye* (1960), it would be 15 years before Bergman used another flashback. (The parallel plots in *Dreams*—Susanne's and Doris's dreams are shattered simultaneously—make sense thematically but slightly undercut the film's intensity.)

Bergman was learning to do something else that was enriching his films. In the opening scene of *Smiles of a Summer Night,* after delivering theater tickets to his employer, Fredrik's clerk leaves Fredrik's office and tells his fellow clerk that he made Fredrik blush by mentioning Désirée Armfeldt's name. The viewer, however, recalls no such reaction. The clerk's self-aggrandizing lie characterizes himself rather than Fredrik. This discrepancy is an example of Bergman's interest in filling almost every moment of film with complex information. This impulse to achieve more subtlety and complexity is one reason he increasingly relied on giant close-ups and expressionistic techniques that make subtle feelings large and readable. Bergman has always required that his audiences work at reading his films. Recall his mentors frequently imploring him to simplify. What he does in the scene just described, however, is different from what they were suggesting. An example of his doing too much is found in the scene in *Sawdust and Tinsel* in which Albert cross-examines Anne about sleeping with Frans. Albert's confusing series of manic-depressive reactions and attitudes emotionally and cognitively overloads the scene; even when one reexamines the scene it is difficult to satisfactorily sort things out. Happily, in future films this kind of overloading rarely occurs (an example would be *The Passion of Anna*), whereas the kind of subtle, rich, but clear complexity evidenced in this scene from *Smiles of a Summer Night* increases.

By 1955 the Gun and Harriet periods were essentially over. Bergman had fallen in love and was living with 19-year-old Bibi Andersson, whom he had met when she was 16 while they were filming the Bris commercials.[13] He gave her a small role in *Smiles of a Summer Night*—she appears in Désirée's play—and promised her Ulla Jacobsson's role if the latter's pregnancy became a problem. Bibi Andersson's "ability to stimulate him even in moments of severe depression" (Cowie 1982, 134–35) and her salubrious innocence intangibly influenced that film and those that have established him as a luminary. By now the reader has observed that when Bergman found or fell in love with an actress, he used her in a succession of his films. It is impossible to determine the extent to which his use of them (and of some actors) expressed "new inner developments" in Bergman and the extent to which his subsequent artistic and personal relationships with them provoked these developments (Wood, 15).

To save his career, Bergman had had to concoct a comedy. So he produced the brilliant *Smiles of a Summer Night*. He learned a lesson that in *The Seventh Seal* he shares with his audience. When the squire tells the artist that in painting the grim mural "The Dance of Death" he only causes people to close their eyes to his paintings, the artist replies, "Maybe. But then I'll paint something amusing for them to look at. I have to make a living." *Smiles of a Summer Night,* in fact, made it possible for Bergman really to become Bergman. "I was sitting in the shithouse reading the papers. And . . . I read: SWEDISH FILM GETS PRIZE AT CANNES, SWEDISH FILM CAUSES SENSATION. . . . When I saw it was *Smiles of a Summer Night* I couldn't believe my eyes. So I took the script of *The Seventh Seal* . . . to . . . Carl Anders Dymling . . . [who was] selling *Smiles* . . . to every country you could think of and was in a state of euphoria . . . [and I] said . . . 'Carl Anders, it's now or never!' " (*BB*, 103).

4

God's Mysterious Ways

Seeing *The Seventh Seal* in 1957 was a revelation to many moviegoers. It was the hoped-for proof that an intellectually challenging film could grip one with the same power as Hollywood's wish-fulfilling melodramas. For the audiences exiting the little art theaters, a *film* that dealt with God, agnosticism, and atheism was exhilarating, especially for those who (wrongly) saw this film as shifting the burden of proof from the shoulders of unbelievers to those of the faithful. And in 1957 there was the additional resonance that came from identifying the plague in *The Seventh Seal* with the threat of atomic holocaust (Steene 1972, 51). Pauline Kael sums up much of what it is about Bergman's films that appealed—and still does—to audiences. Along with their eroticism, their "'stark' beauty and exposed nerves," and their capacity to move "audiences deeply by calling up their buried fears and feelings," there is their "semi-intellectual . . . 'metaphysical' content." Although Bergman is not a "deep thinker," she observes, "people come out of his movies with something to think about."[1] *The Seventh Seal* grappled with a subject that audiences hungered to see scrutinized: belief in God.

Virtually every film discussed in this chapter—*The Seventh Seal, Wild Strawberries, Brink of Life, The Magician, The Virgin Spring, The Devil's Eye, Through a Glass Darkly,* and *Winter Light*—reflects Bergman's belief that he has "knowledge" of God's existence and that God intervenes in human affairs (Sjöman, 26). Except for *Sawdust and Tinsel* and *Smiles of a Summer Night,* God is not active in the Gun comedies. In *Sawdust and Tinsel* He intercedes to prevent Albert's suicide after his merciless, humiliating beating.[2] Back in his van, Albert tries to recover his dignity with one courageous, final act. As he sits and looks at his contused face in the mirror, he raises the tiger tamer's gun to his temple, closes his eyes, and pulls the trigger. The gun misfires. He pulls the trigger again, with the same result. In the process of examining the gun, he pulls the trigger again. There is an explosion, and his mirror image has a bullet hole in it. God's intercession has not only saved Bergman's protagonist but suddenly turned the film from its seemingly tragic path onto a (blackly) comic one. In *Smiles of a Summer Night* Malcolm's fundamental cowardice precludes any need for God to intervene in Fredrik's attempt to put a bullet through his head. But along with the cunning gods of comedy—the film opens with a wall decoration showing Cupid touching down on earth—Bergman's god of love is at work. Just as the gods punished Thebes for Oedipus's unnatural crime by preventing all reproduction, God keeps Fredrik's marriage to a woman his son's age unconsummated, and Henrik impotent until he sleeps with Anne. Fredrik has been sent signs (his dreams, and his and Désirée's son) that his relationship with Désirée was made in Heaven, but he willfully ignores them. Part of God's will is effected through Mrs. Armfeldt, her magic wine, and her house of love (which sports that wonderful mechanism installed by a king so that his minister's wife's bed could be transferred secretly into his bedroom). Nevertheless, though Mrs. Armfeldt and her daughter orchestrate the fairy tale–like party—"We have to help [men] find their way"—a greater power is at work, and Its primary, though not sole, concern is Henrik and Anne. Thus, Henrik's suicide attempt results in Anne's bed being ferried into his bedroom and the natural order finally being achieved.

Whereas narcissism in the Gun films is woven into the love and marital relationships, the films in this chapter not only meld the narcissism into man's relationship to God but move it to center stage. From now on, in fact, Bergman structures most of his dramas around the unmasking of prominent, esteemed, especially celebrated people, highlighting the contradiction between their public image and their (often pathologically) narcissistic personalities: the crusader Antonius Block (*The Seventh Seal*), the award-winning Dr. Isak Borg (*Wild Strawberries*), the wealthy landowner Töre (*The Virgin Spring*), the infamous Don Juan (*The Devil's Eye*), the Rev. Tomas Ericsson (*Winter Light*), Judge Abramsson (*The Ritual*), the psychiatrist Dr. Jenny Isaksson (*Face to Face*), and a series of celebrated artists—the magician Albert Emanuel Vogler (*The Magician*), the novelist David (*Through a Glass Darkly*), the cellist Felix (*Now about These Women*), the actress

Elizabet Vogler (*Persona*), the painter Johan Borg (*Hour of the Wolf*), the trapeze artist Abel Rosenberg (*The Serpent's Egg*), the pianist Charlotte (*Autumn Sonata*), the actress Emilie Ekdahl (*Fanny and Alexander*), and the theater director Henrik Vogler (*After the Rehearsal*). This desire to debunk prominent people stems in large measure from Bergman's need to expose his own pathology. Meanwhile, ironically, what he regards as a naive and gullible society was increasingly idealizing and lionizing him.

THE SEVENTH SEAL

The Seventh Seal's genesis was a one-act play called *Wood Painting,* which Bergman wrote in 1954 to provide parts for all ten students in his Malmö City Theater acting class.[3] This group would soon include Max von Sydow, whom Bergman had watched perform at Hälsingborg City Theater and whom Bergman invited in 1955 to become part of his Malmö stable. When, after *Smiles of a Summer Night's* success, Dymling gave Bergman permission to make *The Seventh Seal* (1957), his stipulation of a shooting schedule of 35 days meant that it would have to be filmed at the Råsunda studio. Afterwards Bergman prided himself on having created "a new genre" (Steene 1972, 73) and "a whole epoch [the Middle Ages] with such incredibly simple means" (*BB,* 117, 113–14). For example, a fire hose was used to create the stream in the forest, which was actually a nearby woods. (In shooting, they had to be careful that the surrounding tall buildings did not show.)

The subject of the play was inspired by a church mural Bergman claims he saw as a child. The mural filled the space over two opposing arches. One mural showed "the eagle of Revelation," "Death playing chess with a Crusader," Death sawing down a tree to whose branch a naked man clung, and Death leading "the final dance toward the dark lands." The mural opposite showed "the Holy Virgin . . . walking in a rose garden, supporting the child's faltering steps." In the chancel was "the drama of the crucifixion," which stunned the child Bergman with its "extreme cruelty and . . . suffering" (Steene 1972, 70–71).[4]

Before *The Seventh Seal*'s action begins, a printed statement, a voice-over, a chorus's fevered rendition of "Dies Irae,"[5] and the film's title establish the context: plague-infested fourteenth-century Sweden as the world approaches the terrible hour of God's judgment. As for the title, the book of Revelation (8:1) says that on the day of judgment a new terror is unleashed as each seal of the Book of Life is removed. The seventh seal reveals God to His faithful. Before this seal is removed, however, there is to be half an hour of peace and silence. The voice-over, the aerial camera angle, and, against threatening clouds, the almost motionless, hovering bird—the mural's "eagle of Revelation"[6]—reinforce the separation of Heaven from the earth. Below, beneath hostile gray cliffs that edge the sea, are the two men who, we are told, have returned from the Crusades. The separation also underscores coexisting kinds of time: man, the sun his clock, treking through life toward death, and his soul's journey toward eternity, symbolized by the sky and the sea. As subsequently we will note, there are often disorienting changes of scene like the moves of a knight on a chessboard. Places *are,* and we are not to trouble ourselves with their contiguity—a seashore, a church, a cluster of vacant houses, an inn, Elsinore somewhere to the south, a forest, a castle. This treatment of time and space helps elevate the spiritual drama over material details and is echoed in the church mural, which views time as coterminous, clustering actions not linked by temporal linearity (for example, Death is simultaneously playing chess, cutting down a tree, and leading the dancing dead).

Leaning against a boulder, his sword and chessboard beside him, is a youngish, blond knight, Antonius Block (Max von Sydow). His first name is that of the founder of Christian monasticism; his last name suggests solidity and impenetrability. This is no common warrior but a man with a searching intellect who wants the universe to be as orderly and purposeful as his favorite game. Further along the stony beach is his middle-aged squire, Jöns (Gunnar Björnstrand), asleep on the sharp rocks. The knife in his hand and the scar on his closely cropped scalp testify to the violence in his life. (These two incomparable actors—the former appearing in six, the latter in five, of Bergman's next seven films after this one—would become one of cinema's great acting teams.[7]) Whereas the lean knight's coat of mail emblems his imprisoning self-absorption, the squire's cloth and animal hide outfit indicates not only his slightly inferior social status but his earthy, gregarious nature. Jöns's animal-like growl and rugged appearance belie his superior intelligence, and though he and Block hold different attitudes toward the supernatural, the knight respects his loyal companion's mind.

I am Death.

The Seventh Seal. AB Svensk Filmindustri

It is before sunrise, and the knight seems not to have slept. Troubling thoughts, not danger, are the cause. Rising, he walks to the water's edge and bathes his face, then kneels and brings his hands together to pray. As if it were his shadow, a rock behind him reinforces the idea of his strength and his imperviousness. His ulcerous doubt about God—which in another form infects Europe as the Black Plague—defeats him. The magnified sound of crashing waves overrides all other sounds as he returns to his belongings. As he packs his saddle bags, however, there is absolute silence. Feeling watched, he turns to see a motionless figure in a black cowl and cloak—a faint breeze playing with its hem—facing him a short distance away. So right and intriguing is Death's (Bengt Ekerot) appearance and tone of voice, so matter-of-fact and swift the knight's recognition, that we instantly accept the personification. After the knight admits to Death that he has long felt his nearness, Bergman employs a shot he had experimented with in *Night Is My Future, Port of Call,* and *Sawdust and Tinsel,* now with definitive eloquence and resonance: to a surge of music, with his arm extended shoulder-high to one side, Death advances directly at the camera (us) until his black cape fills the frame and creates total blackness. But then, as if through a doorway, he seemingly walks through the lens so that we are now behind him as he approaches to enfold the knight. A man of unusual self-confidence, his strength deriving from his indifference to matters of this life, Block fires off a challenge: he will play chess with Death, whose skill Block knows of from ballads and paintings, and if Block wins, Death will release him. Death seizes the opportunity. He does it presumably not only to vary what must be the boring task of reaping life but to show off his skill and to learn why this man who is not afraid to die wants to extend his life. For the next shot, the cinematographer Gunnar Fischer etches one of his most dramatic—and film's most memorable—chiaroscuro tableaus: with the brooding sea as backdrop, the two figures, sculpted with backlight, face each other across the black-and-white chess board.[8] Modestly arrogant and smirking, Death mordantly observes that it is "appropriate" that he has drawn the black pieces, leaving Block the white. Then the contest begins. Thus is set up the film's symbolic opposition: light as life, love, and God versus darkness as Death, narcissism, and nothingness.

In the next shot Death has already departed. The knight wakes Jöns and they resume their journey homeward. A little later, as they are riding past a covered wagon and a tethered horse under a huge tree, the camera remains on the new subject and the two men continue on out of the frame. This new, pastoral setting contrasts dramatically with the inhospitable beach where the horses of the knight and squire nuzzled seaweed. Asleep inside the wagon is a troupe of actors: Skat (Eric Strandmark), Jof (Nils Poppe), his wife Mia (Bibi Andersson, who will appear in four of Bergman's next five films), and their infant son Mikael. This, too, contrasts with the first scene, in which the knight was separated from his sleeping companion. These people lie head to head. A mosquito's sting awakens the juggler Jof, whose quick hand smashes it against his forehead, leaving a smudge of blood on his brow. (First used in *Summer Interlude,* this touch of realism may also represent the opening of the sixth seal, which contains an injunction to the attacking angels not to hurt anything "till we have sealed the servants of our God in their foreheads [Rev. 7:3].") Now awake, Jof exits the wagon and chats with the horse. Suddenly, there is a strange quieting, as when Death appeared to the knight, but with a difference: a heavenly chorus and warm sunlight accompany Jof's vision of the Virgin Mary supporting her son's faltering steps in a brightly lit, nearby grove. "The Virgin Mary is real, with the child," states Bergman. "It is not fantasies or dreams or imaginations" (Simon, 33).[9] Beaming with joy, Jof hurries to report his vision to Mia, who is skeptical because on occasion he has lied about having visions. The sequence ends, however, with her in his arms. Their professions of love are accompanied by the heavenly chorus we heard a moment earlier.

We rejoin the knight and squire as they stop before and enter a small, isolated church. As the knight goes to pray, Jöns remains behind to discuss the mural an artist is painting (which supposedly duplicates the mural images Bergman saw as a child). Made refreshingly, blasphemously expansive by the painter's brandy, Jöns, a confessed atheist, mocks God's Crusades and celebrates what he sees as a meaningless world. Meanwhile, at the altar in the rear of the church, Block kneels beneath a large wooden crucifix supporting a carved, shockingly twisted Jesus.[10] Still unable to pray, he turns to confess to a hooded priest behind a barred window, the grid and its shadow perpetuating the chess board motif and creating the impression that Block is a prisoner. As the tormented Block is describing his most intimate feelings of narcissistic emptiness and disgust at his indifference to his fellow humans, we see that the hooded figure is Death.[11] (Ekerot's characterization has already made Death fascinating, but that Death, by his nature seemingly all-knowing and all-powerful, needs to cheat to ensure against failure and to preserve his reputation is an exquisitely humanizing touch.) At first with feigned disinterest and then with daggerlike directness, Death probes his opponent's hidden motives. Because of the deception, their exchanges make riveting cinema. If life is so meaningless, asks Death, why does Block not want to die? "I do!" affirms the knight. But he does not want to die before he has accomplished two things. First, having faced up to his isolating self-absorption, he wants to perform an act out of deep feeling for someone other than himself. Second, he must have proof—"knowledge, not faith"—of God's existence. Block—who is possessed of an unshakeable intuition of a transcendent reality—has given his life to God to use as part of His cosmic design, but He has given no signs that He exists. Acting as devil's advocate, Death suggests that there may be no God, afterlife, or meaning. Then, insists Block, "life is an outrageous horror," a waste. (Von Sydow makes Block's spiritual agony—echoed in the wrenched face and body of the crucified Jesus above him—so palpable that even those for whom these questions are no longer pertinent feel it.) Wanting God to acknowledge *him* is another sign of Block's egoism, and it is pride that now leads him to mention that he is playing chess with Death for his life, that he has not yet lost a single piece, and that he intends to outmaneuver his opponent through a combination of his knight (intellect) and bishop (faith). Death reveals his identity and leaves, promising to rendezvous at the inn to continue their game. Angered at having been duped, Block's epic struggle with Death nevertheless exhilarates him; he feels vitally, heroically alive.

As Block and Jöns leave the church, they discover tied up outside its door a mannish-looking, adolescent woman (Maud Hansson), whom a monk identifies as the witch who caused the plague, and who, the next day at dawn, after the priests have tortured her, is to be executed. Block pauses over her, not from compassion but to ask if she can shed light on his quest. The suffering girl is oblivious to his presence.

Heading for the inn, the two men pause outside a village of deserted houses. As he searches for water, Jöns encounters Raval (Bertil Anderberg), who has been stealing from the dead and is about to rape a girl (Gunnel Lindblom). Jöns recognizes Raval as the seminarian who convinced Antonius Block to perform God's work by regaining the Holy Land from the infidel. Loathing this priest turned thief who has wasted the last ten years of his and his master's lives, Jöns draws his knife. But the girl's scream stops him, and Jöns warns Raval that when next they meet he will brand his face the way "one does with thieves." Afterwards, the girl—who does not utter another sound until the film's penultimate scene—apprehensively accepts Jöns's protection and joins him and the knight.

Outside the inn, the trio are watching Skat, Jof, and Mia perform a play when a droning litany and a swelling tide of human wails and screams slowly drown out the actors' song. A procession of half-naked, limping, moaning, bleeding penitents—some holding aloft skulls, some wearing crowns of thorns, some bent under the weight of huge crosses, some whipping those in front of them—halts in the square. With relish and in a snorting, sneering, guttural voice, a monk (Anders Ek) addresses the terrified bystanders, assuring them that life is sin and death is life's raison d'être. (Bergman says the scene is stagy because he had to shoot it in a single day [Kaminsky, 128].[12]) The knight scoffs at Jöns's "Do they really expect modern people to take that drivel seriously?" But Jöns sassily insists that God, Jesus, and the Holy Ghost are fairy tales.

Inside the inn (called the Embarrassment Inn in the screenplay), fear of Judgment Day is as palpable as the mingled odors of sweat, mead, smoke, and roast pig. The sadistic Raval is there, and under the pretext of punishing Jof for Skat's having run off with Lisa (Inga Gill), the wife of Plog the blacksmith (Åke Fridell), he sinks his knife between Jof's fingers and then forces him to dance like a bear on the table. Exhausted from terror, Jof looks heavenward and raises his hands in prayer: in that instant, the door opens and Jöns enters. Sizing up the situation, he grabs Raval, announces, "I'm a man who keeps his word," and slashes Raval's face with his knife. Meanwhile, Jof snatches the silver bracelet that Raval tried to sell him (and which, earlier, Jöns saw Raval steal from a dead woman) and scurries out the door. The scene is rich. Bergman sets up the atmosphere of the time, makes the point that God uses even atheists to protect His faithful, and, with the image of the blood leaking through Raval's fingers as they clutch his face, satisfies our craving for justice. In addition, in making Jof a petty thief—he will also lie to Mia about how he got the bracelet—Bergman ensures that Jof is not too good to be true. Finally, this violent, claustrophobic scene makes all the more effective the pastoral scene that immediately follows, one in which Block has an epiphany that provides him with the means to fulfill one of his two goals.

On a rise overlooking the sea, Block is distracted from the study of his chess board by Mia fussing over the babbling Mikael. He joins her, his steel mesh dramatically contrasting with her loose clothing and Mikael's near nakedness. In the course of their conversation Mia says that though Jof wants Mikael to grow up to become "the great juggler who can perform the one impossible trick—making one of the balls stand absolutely still in the air" (that is, performing a miracle)—she wants him to become a knight. The practical Mia wants her son to be a doer, but in seizing on the knight as the model for him to emulate she symbolically perpetuates as well the conflict between faith and skepticism. Jof joins them, lying about how he got the bracelet and scared off his persecutors, and then confessing the truth about his cowardice; this and the uninhibited love he shows for his wife and son consolidate our liking for him. Block suggests to him that he and his family not go to Elsinore, which is closer to the plague's center, but come north with him to his castle. Jöns and the silent girl join them, and Jof plays his lute. During these next golden moments the knight tells of leaving his happy life with his new bride—the pattern of Berg-man's Kasper-like characters leaving their wives for a more adventur-ous life is reproduced here—to go on the Crusades. Then he talks of his religious torment: "To believe is to suffer. It's like loving someone in the dark who never answers." With the nurturing milk (in place of wine) and wild strawberries (in place of the wafer) that Mia has pro-vided, he celebrates the unique sense of peace he feels amid this loving family.[13] Raising the bowl of milk and drinking, he concludes this secular mass by saying, "I shall remember our words and bear this memory between my hands as carefully as a bowl of fresh milk, and this will be a sign of great content." To preserve this feeling and to ponder his achievement of the significant act that was one of his two goals, he leaves, ascending the hill toward his chess board. Now, us-ing a shot that he had experimented with in *Monika,* Bergman creates one of the film's most fearsome moments. As Block's face exits the frame, Death's face (which has been present throughout the scene in the form of the actor's death mask hanging on a pole beside the wagon), in extreme close-up and accompanied by threatening musical chords, edges menacingly into the vacated space. The next shot finds Block and Death resuming their game, and we are anxious to know what Death will do with his ill-gotten knowledge of the knight's strat-egy. Intrigued by Block's new equanimity, Death asks why he looks so satisfied. "That's my secret," replies the smiling knight, the holy family for whom he intends to sacrifice himself visible in the distance. Death is surprised further when, after he has taken Block's knight, Block laughs aloud and says, "As you were meant to. . . . Check!" However, Death asking Block if he plans to escort Jof's family through the forest, and his refusal to reveal why he has inquired, erases the smile on Antonius's face.

That evening the little band, joined by the blacksmith Plog (after a delightful conversation with Jöns about the hell of living with or without women), enter the same forest that the Red Cross Knight, Hansel and Gretel, Dorothy, and Young Goodman Brown travel through, the menacing forest of confusion and evil. It is made all the more eerie by analectic sound and Gunnar Fischer's photography. First, they encounter Lisa with Skat, and in an amusing but very theatrical scene the unfaithful wife returns to her husband. Having feigned suicide to escape Plog's wrath, Skat is left behind and takes refuge for the night in a tree. Death arrives and, after some witty repartee based on a passage in Strindberg, ends Skat's life by sawing down the tree.[14] Then Bergman presages the film's ending: life over-comes death; immediately, a squirrel jumps onto the fallen tree's moonlit stump.

The group next meets eight soldiers who have been paid by the priests to burn the witch at the community's execution site. The squire, always anxious, if it is practical, to prevent human suffering, tells his master that it is not worth killing the soldiers because the tortured witch is "nearly dead" (her vigor and alertness annoyingly undermine this observation). As at their first encounter, Block's chief interest in the witch, who claims carnal knowledge of the Devil, has to do with her belief that the Devil can be seen deep in her eyes. Block believes that, if the Devil exists, surely he will know about God. Re-minding us of the imagery of the church's confessional, Block presses his face into the space between the bars of the criblike cart and cross-examines the girl, but all he accomplishes is to make her doubt the Devil's existence and power to protect her from the pain of her exe-cution. When Block turns to ask the monk beside him why the girl has been tortured, he finds himself again facing Death, who quietly inquires (again borrowing from Strindberg), "Don't you ever stop asking questions?" "No! I'll never stop!" shouts the knight.[15] "But you get no answers" is Death's verbal checkmate.

The girl is tied to a ladder that will be dropped into the flames. The squire gives her water, and to his credit, the knight places in her mouth a drug to "still the pain." But he still seems to be looking for answers in her eyes. When the ladder is leaned against a tree, the im-plications of the blazing inferno beneath her slowly penetrate the girl's delusion, and the next few moments are the film's most profoundly moving. The squire moves to save her but is restrained by Block. Standing behind his master's shoulder, the cynical squire, who by now should be inured to suffering, responds with heartrending compas-sion. He asks rhetorically of Block, "Who will look after that child? The angels, God, Satan, emptiness?" and asserts, "It's emptiness, my lord!" From between his clenched teeth, Block insists, "It cannot be!" His eyes filled with tears and barely able to shape the words, Jöns cries, "We are helpless. We see what she sees and her terror is ours. Poor child! I can't stand it!" He rushes off, leaving Antonius Block, tears in his eyes as well, fighting back grief and doubt. Block and his contingent then mount their horses and board their wagon, leaving the girl to her fate. Once again the pattern of sacrificing a young woman of unsavory sexual reputation as part of the process of educating Bergman's protagonist is used. The silent girl, who becomes an increasingly important character from here on, is the one who finds it most difficult to abandon the terrified girl.

The troupe makes camp in another part of the forest. The ominous and unnerving silence is suddenly broken by the cry of the plague-seized Raval. Only the silent girl does not recoil, but her attempt to take him water is stopped by Jöns, who assures her of its uselessness. In midscream Raval dies, and the patch of ground on which his death dance has taken place is beautifully flooded with moonlight.[16] Having collected Raval, Death stays to conclude his chess game with Block. He sits, his back to the group, and smiles wryly as he casually takes the knight's white queen (Mia). Visibly shaken, Block admits he had not noticed her vulnerability. Her loss, of course, would represent his failure to perform the significant, unselfish act. At that moment, Jof, who has been sleeping, miraculously awakens, sees Death and the knight, and alerts Mia, who sees the knight alone at his chess board. Trusting her husband's instincts, however, she gathers up Mikael, and they board their covered wagon and slip out of camp. Watching them over Death's shoulder, Block asks, "Nothing escapes you—or does it?" "Nothing escapes me; no one escapes me," replies Death, confidently. To ensure that Death is distracted, Block sweeps the chess pieces from the board with a clumsy movement of his cape. Then he remarks, "I've forgotten how the pieces stood." Pleased that his presumptuous challenger has had to resort to so obvious a ruse to save his life, Death chuckles. *He* has not forgotten, he assures Block, and he returns the pieces to their former places. As he does, the holy family effects its escape. "You are mated at the next move, Antonius Block." "That's true," says the contented knight, himself becoming someone who sacrifices himself to save Bergman's protagonists. Finally Death informs Block that at their next meeting his time will be up. He will take Block and his companions. His first goal is accomplished, however, and Block is now concentrating on his second, finding evidence of God. He asks Death if at their last meeting he will divulge his secrets. Death's reply, "I have no secrets," dashes his hope. Death, as the early image of him blacking out the screen suggested, is only the cessation of life, a doorway ignorant of what, if anything, lies on the other side of him.

As Jof and Mia drive furiously through the forest, they are hounded by a violent storm, the "Angel of Doom" (the banal, tinny music—the film's worst—trivializes the terror). Frantic, they finally take refuge in the back of their wagon. Meanwhile, Block, Jöns, the silent girl, Plog, and Lisa find relief from the storm and the darkness in Block's castle. He is welcomed by his wife Karin (Inga Landgré), who, having heard he was coming, did not flee the plague with the rest of the household. Her apathetic manner of throwing a final log on the fire may contain within it the remnants of her exhausted anger at her husband's waste of their lives, but otherwise she shows none, not even when he says that he does not regret going on the Crusades. Tired beyond measure, he closes his eyes, and she gently lays her hand on his cheek. Like Mrs. Lobelius (the role Landgré played in *Dreams*), Karin is resigned, content merely to have her husband with her to face their hopeless future. The image of Block's face dissolves into that of the silent girl's, which is immediately superimposed over the image of the group sitting around a wooden table eating their last supper. The shot connects her to Christ. As they eat, Karin reads from the book of Revelation. The room, with its thick, stone walls and deep, dark windows, is lit by torches. Her reading is suddenly interrupted by three echoing knocks at the castle's outer door (calling to mind the dead Commendatore coming for Don Giovanni). The knight dispatches Jöns to investigate. Karin continues reading, and the camera moves in on the silent girl's face as she watches the dark window suddenly being illuminated from without with intensely bright light. Jöns returns, saying he saw no one, but his look betrays that, as he had done earlier when he discovered an ulcerated corpse, he may be trying to protect his friend from a terrible, imminent reality. The silent girl, however, soon senses the presence of the draped figure in the shadows. She rises, and a close-up reveals tears on her smiling face. Block courteously welcomes Death, and everyone is introduced to him. Then, standing in the rear of the group, Block presses his hands over his eyes and face and cries out with pathetic, childlike desperation to the God he hopes and prays "*must* be somewhere . . . [to] have mercy upon us!"—his lack of faith preventing him from realizing that when he achieved his first goal he was in the process of achieving his second. God, Who moves in mysterious ways, *did* "stretch out his hand." Block was part of His plan; just as Jöns appeared miraculously at the inn to save Jof, Block helped save His holy family.

Jöns, his eyes on Death, upbraids his master for his narcissism ("indifference") and for wasting his time praying to an indifferent universe. Echoing Albert (*Sawdust and Tinsel*) and Frid (*Smiles of a Summer Night*), he advises Block to forget his obsession with Death and to "feel to the very end the immense triumph of being alive!" The gentle, bourgeois Karin politely reprimands his indecorous surge of spirit and asks him to be quiet. But true to his character, Jöns vigorously replies, "I shall be silent, but under protest!"

It is given to the silent girl to end this sequence. The endless pain and loss this sensitive, compassionate young woman has endured and observed is at the source of her muteness. Language involves the speaker in relationships, and relationships always mean pain. We almost hear old Mrs. Armfeldt saying, "You can never protect a single human being from suffering. That's what makes one so terribly tired."[17] The camera moves in on the silent girl's face, her tears almost dry, as she kneels before Death. Anticipating relief at last, smiling, she speaks for the first time, uttering Jesus' final words, "It is finished!"

We feel relieved as her face dissolves into the brightly lit face of Mia. The wagon has emerged from the dark forest, and under the morning's cloudless sky it has come to a safe halt near the edge of a cliff overlooking the peaceful sea. The setting is similar to that of the first scene, but the mood, except for a brief moment, is exactly the opposite. Jof and Mia are about to start out when Jof experiences his now classic vision: to the funereal beat of a snare drum, the silhouetted image of Death is leading their former companions in a beautiful, if macabre, dance from right to left—not from left to right as it is usually reproduced in books—along the top of a distant hill. They are moving away from the dawn to the dark lands, and rain, Jof notes, washes away their bitter tears.[18] Mia does not fully appreciate this marveling, tragic vision; she simply smiles with pride at her husband's powers. When the vision is over, Jof, shyly shrugging, turns the wagon about—the death mask conspicuously absent—and, placing his arm over Mia's shoulder, leads her and Mikael (all the other relationships in this story are childless) toward the dawn. Their journey is accompanied by Bergman's musical sign of love, the harp, and the heavenly chorus we heard in Jof and Mia's first scene.

The Seventh Seal's occasional theatricality may annoy after multiple viewings, but the film passes the test of durability. Its passionate frankness and archetypal imagery captivate, and like other filmed morality plays—*The Cabinet of Dr. Caligari* (1919), *King Kong* (1933), *Beauty and the Beast* (1946), *High Noon* (1952), *The Night of the Hunter* (1955), *A Clockwork Orange* (1971)—it benefits from repeated viewings. Like children returning to their favorite books, we enjoy reexperiencing its allegorical journey, its ribald farce, erupting terrors, and bone-deep revelations of belief and feeling, all presented in stunningly composed and photographed black-and-white images. Like the mushroom cloud and Edvard Munch's shrieking figure, some of *The Seventh Seal*'s images, notably its vision of death, have become cultural touchstones. In fact, at times we even may half-imagine that a black-cloaked figure wearing a stocking-tight, black cowl around his chalk-white face is going to attend our own expiring, and that he will be speaking Swedish—with English subtitles across his waist.

This film's greatness also lies in Bergman's ability to make each point on the spectrum of belief compelling. He says he has always felt "sympathy" for the Jönses, Jofs, Mias, and Skats, but "it's with something more like desperation I've experienced the Blocks inside myself. I can really never [cotton to] them, the fanatics. Whether they appear as religious fanatics or vegetarian fanatics makes no [difference]. They're catastrophic people" (*BB,* 117).

WILD STRAWBERRIES

Bergman has great sympathy for the Block-like, 78-year-old, narcissistic protagonist of his next film, *Wild Strawberries* (1957). God's existence, however, is not the central concern of the physician Isak Borg (Victor Sjöström).[19] Borg indicates (in the screenplay) that he believes that death will not answer "the metaphysical question," and in the film, in a mellifluous voice that makes musical almost any words he speaks, he recites a hymn that laments never finding God but rejoices in seeing His traces in one's own "burning heart" and in nature's beauty.[20] (Isak's daughter-in-law Marianne has to provide a significantly forgotten line: "His love is mixed with the very air."[21]) This recitation occurs when Isak is drawn into an argument over God's existence with a trio of young hitchhikers: Viktor (Björn Bjelvenstam) holds that man "believes only in himself and his biological death, everything else is nonsense"; Anders (Folke Sundquist), a ministerial student, argues that all men face death with horror and "can't bear [their] own insignificance"; and Sara (Bibi Andersson), their lovably narcissistic girlfriend, is skeptical, because it is modern to be so, and annoyed that her suitors fight more heatedly over God than over her. Though he may not be like Antonius Block when it comes to the question of God's existence, Isak is like him in his inability to relate to his fellow humans. A nightmare involving his death has terrified Isak. The nightmare and his receipt, on this June day, of his profession's highest honor—the Jubilee Doctorate for 50 years of service—trigger within him a depressing awareness of the disparity between his altruistic public image and his actual character. He senses that he is an unmitigated failure. A lot of what we learn about him, in fact, is ugly. Nevertheless, we admire this elderly man for probing his own character, and we fear that his death may come before he completes his painful task.

His most haunting nightmare opens the film, and it frightens us as much as it does him. Sunlight rakes the abandoned urban landscape so that doorways become wells of ominous blackness. (Bergman had all the walls and floors of this set, built on the lot at Råsunda, painted pure white so they would glare, and as with the flashback in *Sawdust and Tinsel,* he had the negative processed to make the blacks and whites abrasive.) This eerie, sunny setting without warmth and the absence of all ambient sound create the impression that Isak is in the city—Borg means city—of the living dead, disconnected from the world. Even time does not exist, though the amplified beating of his panicked heart stands in briefly for the absent ticking of his handless watch.[22] Bergman snaps us back and forth from long shot to close-up to establish how totally alone this Crusoe is. But then Isak sees he has company, a man wearing a dark hat and overcoat, standing beside a lamppost. Isak approaches this (alter ego) Friday, who has his back to him. When Isak touches the man's shoulder, he turns to face him. Isak is taken aback when he views the man's fetuslike face: every orifice—eyes, nostrils, mouth, ears—is squashed shut so that there can be no communication with others.[23] Isak recoils, and the man dissolves to the pavement, the only sound that of his now empty clothes plopping into a pile at Isak's feet. Some dark liquid leaks from beneath the pile. (In the screenplay for *Fanny and Alexander* Bergman describes the trapped Alex as feeling "his skeleton leaving him and draining out through the soles of his feet and spreading over the . . . carpet.") A horse-drawn, driverless hearse now attracts Isak's attention as it blindly rounds the corner. When it passes Isak, its axle catches on the base of the lamppost, shaking loose its metal and glass lamp in an explosion of amplified, analectic sound. The sound is loud enough to wake the dead, and it does: the hearse, its wheel caught, its rocking springs sounding like an infant's cries, slowly, painfully gives birth to the coffin, which crashes to the pavement. (By yoking birth and death, cradle and grave, a lifetime is subsumed in one image.) The hearse's wheel comes off and nearly crushes Isak. Now free, the hearse clatters off and disappears down the street. (Bergman often assaults us at relatively quiet but hyper-charged moments with gashing visceral-aural-visual images.) Silence again. Isak approaches the coffin, whose lid has been knocked aside. Looking inside, he sees himself, dressed in the formal attire he is to wear at the award ceremony. The corpse grasps his hand, and the two Isaks engage in a dreadful tug of war. This brings Isak awake and out of bed. As in a similar sequence, "The Hearse Driver," directed by Basil Dearden in the six-part British psychological thriller *Dead of Night* (1945), and as does Dickens's Scrooge, he rushes to look out of his bedroom window to reassure himself that he is alive.

The next scene is staged as if we have been summoned by Isak to his study. It is a bit off-putting to find ourselves virtually at floor level looking across a large room at Isak's back as he sits in his thronelike chair at his massive desk, his faithful Great Dane bitch asleep at his feet. (When he leaves the room, the camera is placed even lower and further away, perhaps suggesting Isak's attitude toward and inability to relate to people.) Isak speaks to us in voice-over, observing that "in our relations with other people we mainly criticize them." When he adds, however, "That is why I have withdrawn from nearly all social intercourse [and] this has made my old age rather lonely," our attitude softens. Next, he shows us his family, each member safely framed behind glass: his son Evald (Gunnar Björnstrand), Evald's (pregnant) wife Marianne (Ingrid Thulin), his aged mother (Naima Wifstrand), and his deceased wife Karin (Gertrud Fridh). He does not mention his deceased father, who may be the thirtyish-looking gentleman in the oval frame in the shadows at the rear, and who still plays an important role in Isak's fantasies. (Is he the empty, self-absorbed man in Isak's nightmare?) Isak also informs us that his love for science has been his salvation. It is this for which he is receiving the Jubilee award in Lund. We will come to understand that, in fact, this identification of himself with his work is one result of his early retreat from intimacy and "social intercourse."[24] The truth is that, with few exceptions, and in spite of what the photographs imply, Isak has no memories to fortify his spirit against death. Loving no one, he has cut himself off from relationships, which are the source of sustaining memories. Unlike old Henrik Erneman (*A Lesson in Love*), whose wife, son, daughter-in-law, grandchildren, and chauffeur crowded around his bed on his birthday, and who showed no fear of death, Isak has no sense of place in the succession of generations. Except for his science, which makes him a part of one social group at least, and his belief in God, which joins him with transcendental nature, he is not a part of any shared history (Kernberg, 312). Thus, his terror of death is heightened "precisely because he [finds] himself in a position of narcissistic isolation." He will die and that will be that (Kaminsky, 199)!

The morning of his nightmare is the day he is to receive the Jubilee award. (The confusing time sequence of the narrative generally goes unnoticed, owing to the film's numerous time shifts.) Isak decides that instead of flying, as he had planned, he will drive from his home in Stockholm to Lund. His nightmare has made him want to detour into his past to try to understand what his unconscious is saying to him. This change of plans upsets his housekeeper, Miss Agda (Jullan Kindahl), who had planned to fly with him. A brief, comic scene shows the two septuagenarians, from opposite ends of the house, spatting; she charges him with not thinking of anyone but himself, and under his breath, he calls her an old "cross patch." Marianne, who has left Evald and has been staying at her father-in-law's, has privately decided to return and fight for her marriage. Isak agrees to let her accompany him to Lund.

Naturally, Isak drives. As his big car journeys west, Marianne, who is one of Bergman's most intellectual, self-assured, and forthright women characters, and who is well aware of Isak's dislike of modern women—those who wear slacks, smoke, and speak their minds—eventually vents her opinions about him and his relationship with Evald. But like many Bergman women, she masks her harsh comments with a slight smile in order to abrogate responsibility for the hurt they cause and to disarm retaliation. She tells Isak that behind his "benevolent exterior" and "old world charm" he is "hard as nails" and "utterly ruthless," and that he "listens to no one but [him]self." She reminds him that when she approached him with her marital problems, he told her not to draw him into her squabbles. In addition, he said he had no respect for mental suffering, and that since it was the fashion, she and Evald should see a psychiatrist. Marianne remarks that she also resents that he is needlessly compelling Evald to pay back a debt. This unnerving conversation is punctuated and relieved by three brief, jarring shots from outside the car. They function as visual beats to accelerate or moderate the scene's rhythms. (Though Isak's point of view is dominant, Bergman never relinquishes the omniscient narrator's powers. As with the shots outside the car, he shows us what Isak does not or cannot see or control. Earlier he showed us photographs of Evald and Marianne that were behind Isak, and later, when the hitchhikers present Isak with flowers, Bergman unexpectedly surrounds him with blackness, as if to suggest that the emotions stirred up in him need to settle and steep.) Marianne peers out her side window after calmly dropping the comment that even though Evald will honor his debt, he hates his father. In close-up, we witness the impact of this heart-stopping blow on Isak's heretofore imperturbable old face. (In the nightmare the pounding of his heart underscored his fragility.) We almost expect him to collapse and the car to career off the road, but Isak quickly regains his composure. He tells Marianne that he thinks she is a fine person, that he has enjoyed having her around the house, and that he is sorry she dislikes him. She corrects him; she does not dislike him, she feels sorry for him. He asks if she would like to hear a weird dream he had that morning. We grow angry as she, apparently unwittingly, mirrors his attitude toward her marital problems. She says she is not interested in dreams. Nevertheless, because he believes she is bright, honest, and capable of being judicious, Isak has secretly decided to use her in his journey of self-exploration.

Isak pulls off the highway to visit the vacation house where he spent every summer until he was 20. While Marianne goes for a swim, he returns through memory to his youth, eavesdropping as an old man on his cousin Sara (Bibi Andersson), to whom he was "secretly engaged," being kissed by his older brother Sigfrid (Per Sjöstrand). Then, entering the summer house, he stands outside the dining room and eavesdrops on the brightly lit scene of his lively, extended family (minus himself, his mother, and his father) at lunch. (In Alf Sjöberg's *Miss Julie* [1951], a character likewise reviews a past event, keeping past and present clearly defined.) He listens to Sara tell of her reservations about their engagement; she prefers the "naughty and exciting" Sigfrid to the intellectual Isak, who will only kiss her in the dark. (That he wants their relationship kept secret is evidence that even then he could not completely commit himself to a relationship.[25]) Furthermore, Sara says that Isak's obsession with sin and the afterlife (like Henrik's in *Smiles of a Summer Night*) makes her feel guilty, and his adoration makes her feel unworthy and inferior. Sara, we will discover, remains for Isak an eternally adolescent, spiritual goddess as well as a mother figure (in the Old Testament Sara is Isaac's mother). Her choice of Sigfrid over Isak apparently intensified Isak's fear of deep emotional involvements. Like *Summer Interlude*'s Marie, he afterwards entombed all painful memories and constructed around himself an unbreachable wall of rigid habit. Later in the film, in another dream, Sara mercilessly unmasks his narcissistic illusion that he is still young. Commanding him to look into the mirror she holds up, she says, "You're a worried old man who is soon going to die. . . . [That hurts] because you can't bear the truth." Another truth that emerges is that, unlike him, she regarded love as a pleasurable game that would eventually result in motherhood. (Now 75, Sara has had six children.[26]) In this later nightmare Sara leaves to attend a baby (who, in the screenplay, Isak envies). Dark clouds and a maelstrom of screeching birds suddenly create a feeling of menace. When he follows Sara to her house, first he is shut out of a romantic, domestic scene between her and Sigfrid, and then, unexpectedly, after impaling his hand on a nail while pounding to be let in,[27] he is invited into the summer house, which instead of being the sun-filled, joyous place of his first dream, is gray and dreary. It now houses an amphitheater like the one in which he used to give his polyclinical lectures and examinations. It is his own credentials as a human being that are now examined, and the tests reveal him to be an insensitive narcissist.[28] Isak sees nothing but himself in the microscope, does not know that asking forgiveness is a person's first duty, and is unable to discern that a woman he is given to examine is alive. Then, when his deceased wife's charges of "callousness, selfishness, [and] ruthlessness" are brought against him, his examiner escorts him outside. They pass the charred ruins of a cottage (which may represent his and Karin's hellish domestic life[29]) and go through a swamp (libidinous memory[30]) to a place where Isak is forced to relive Karin's (Bergman's mother's name) unfaithfulness. After the act, she predicts for her partner that Isak's response when she confesses her infidelity will be hollow sympathy—"He'll say, 'My poor girl. I'm sorry for you,' just as if he were God." Most maddening, she continues, will be his unwillingness to face his own sexual itch. He habitually turns from an icily aloof judge into a titillated lover; when she points out his hypocrisy, he silences her with sedatives, and insincerely forgives her and accepts the responsibility for her unhappiness. Karin is another sensual woman sacrificed to an immature male's narcissistic needs. Isak's behavior, as Karin describes it, serves to save him from emotional involvement or the kind of unsavory contentiousness that we witnessed earlier between two habitual practitioners of psychological savaging, Mr. and Mrs. Alman (Gunnar Sjöberg and Gunnel Broström). Soon after Isak, Marianne, and the hitchhikers left the summer house, the Almans' Volkswagen almost collided with Isak's car (Mrs. Alman was slapping her husband at that moment). Because their VW was disabled, they joined Isak's group. Almost immediately they returned to probing, with surgical exactitude, each other's private vulnerabilities. Mr. Alman, for example, informed the group that for two years, because his wife Berit needed sympathy, she claimed she had cancer. Less articulate than her husband, the frustrated Mrs. Alman again retaliates by slapping her husband's face. (To protect the three young hitchhikers, Marianne, who was driving at the time, kicked the Alman's out of the car.) In the nightmare in which Isak is tested, Mr. Alman is Isak's patient and impartial examiner, guide, and ironic alter ego, and Mrs. Alman is the woman—Karin—Isak does not recognize is alive. When the vision of Karin has departed and Isak asks where she has gone, Alman informs him that, like *all* Isak's failures in life, he has repressed the memory: "Removed by an operation, Professor. A surgical masterpiece: no pain, no bleeding." The result? asks Isak. "Loneliness," replies Alman. "Is there no mercy?" inquires Isak, shutting his eyes. Echoing Death's reply to Antonius Block's query as to what lies beyond death, Alman answers, "Don't ask me. I don't know."

Before this last nightmare, we have seen some of Isak's positive characteristics, giving balance to our judgment of his character. His infatuation with Sara—who resembles his cousin Sara (both roles being played by the same actress) and who, with her two boyfriends, he has invited along—tickles us. And when Isak stops for gas in his old neighborhood, the station owners, the Åkermans—the film's benchmark of a happy marriage—greet him enthusiastically. (So identified is Max von Sydow, who plays Åkerman, with Antonius Block that his appearance here invariably gets a laugh.) Åkerman and his pregnant wife Eva (Anne-Marie Wiman) inform Isak that they plan to name their "son" after him because Isak did so much for the people in those parts.[31] Isak is deeply touched, seeming to sense for the first time that what one does out of compulsion and for money can also earn love (Erickson 1976, 11). He looks to see if Marianne has witnessed this affection for him.

Isak allows Marianne to come along when he visits his mother, who lives nearby. This living-dead old woman—"I have felt cold all my life"—is undilutedly narcissistic.[32] When she and Isak, looking at family photographs, linger over a picture of her with three-year-old Isak and his five-year-old brother, all that she seems interested in is how unattractive the fashions of that day made her look; when he asks if he may keep the photo, she replies, "By all means. It's only rubbish."

(Contrast her to Helena Ekdahl lingering over her photo album in *Fanny and Alexander,* and to Bergman's caressing and melancholy little film photo album devoted to his mother, *Karin's Face* [1983].)

Later, this visit and Isak's comment to Marianne that he feels his dreams are trying to tell him "I'm dead, although I'm alive," trigger a rapprochement between the two. Marianne is shocked because Evald had said the exact same thing to her. She asks Isak if he is now interested in hearing about Evald and herself. He would be "grateful," he says sincerely, if she would tell him. She relates a recent conversation she had with Evald during a drive; to create the equation between father and son, Bergman keeps the composition of the frame the same but substitutes Evald for Isak beside Marianne in the car. (This flashback, the only time the narrative is not focused on or controlled by Isak, marks a turning point in his development: he relinquishes "space" to someone else.) The Evald we now meet is like his father, intensely controlled and afraid of emotion, but he lacks his father's "old world charm." Evald, too, has avoided dealing with his and his wife's emotional lives by immersing himself in his medical practice. When Marianne tells him that she is pregnant and intends to have the child, Evald glares at her and gets out of the car, which is parked beside the roiling sea. Oblivious to the steady rain, he is placed with a barren, black tree stump behind him. When Marianne joins him, he insists that she choose between him and the child, because (echoing *To Joy*'s Stig) it is absurd to bring children into this world. He, in fact, "was an unwanted child in a hellish marriage." His grandmother, whom he visits alone, never liked Evald's mother and undoubtedly let him know of Karin's scandalous behavior. Evald is not sure he is his father's son. Marianne recognizes Evald's fear of responsibility as the rationalization it is. "Poor Evald," she says, holding his arm and looking up into his rain-streaked face, "that's just an excuse. . . . You're a coward." "Yes," he says, pulling loose and getting back into the car, "this life sickens me. I will not be forced to live one day longer than I want to." "I know you're wrong," she replies. But he ends the conversation by declaring, "There's neither right nor wrong. One functions according to one's needs. . . . Yours is to live and create life. . . . Mine is to be dead."[33]

Isak asks Marianne why she has told him this story. She answers that when she saw Isak with his mother—that "old woman, cold as ice, more forbidding than death"—and heard Isak call himself "a living corpse," she panicked. "Evald is growing just as lonely, cold, and dead, and I thought of the baby inside me. . . . It must end somewhere." Because this conversation occurs near the end of their journey, after a number of experiences and dreams have shaken Isak and fanned alive the embers of his desire to care about and connect with others, he is able to ask Marianne, "Can I help you?" And from here on, several signs of his altering attitude and state of mind are presented: his uncharacteristic informality in greeting the young hitchhikers as, marching in the procession, he passes them on his way to Lund Cathedral; the radiant glow on his face as he receives, to the blasts of cannons, the honorary doctor's top hat and ring; and his admission (in voice-over) during the ceremony that he discerned "an extraordinary logic" in the day's "jumbled events," a statement made even more poignant by the (diegetic) strains of a doleful cello. Furthermore, that evening, he asks Miss Agda (nurse/mother) for "forgiveness" for having upset her plans and suggests that they be less formal with each other. Rejecting the idea, nevertheless she slyly indicates that she appreciates the offer. (At the film's start her room is a house-length away from his; at its end her room is next to his, and she leaves the door ajar in case he needs anything.) Most important, he calls Evald to his bedside to ask what he intends to do about his marriage. Evald's tone is as formal as his tuxedo, and he sits in the chair he brings to the bedside with his back toward his father. He does, however, confess to his father that he cannot live without Marianne and that he has agreed to having the baby. Isak attempts to cancel Evald's debt, but so locked into a lifelong attitude is his son that he misreads the allusion to the debt as a reminder to pay it. Marianne's entrance aborts Isak's attempt to clarify his meaning, but it is clear that she, with whom Isak has become very close, will bring father and son closer. ("All this business about Evald and his father is so tremendously personal," says an ingenuous Bergman, "I can't sort it out. Nor . . . the relationship between Isak . . . and his old mother" [BB, 148].)

Sara and her suitors show up outside Isak's second-floor window to say good-bye. After Anders and Viktor leave, Sara tells Isak that it is really him she loves, a revelation that helps heal the pain of his own Sara's rejection of him. By this time our feelings of warmth and admiration for this exhausted old man have been reignited. This is not to say that we should believe Isak's character has changed. "He can't," insists Bergman. "I don't believe that people can change, not . . . fundamentally. . . . They may have a moment of illumination, they may see themselves, have awareness of what they are, but that is the most they can hope for" (*Playboy*, 68). But Bergman does believe—to take a line from the Mummy in Strindberg's *The Ghost Sonata*—that those who have erred can be better than themselves because they disapprove of their misdeeds.

All alone at last, but no longer feeling totally alienated from the world, Isak, who began the film by talking to us, does so again. Isak informs us that after sad or worrisome days he recalls "childhood memories" to help calm himself so he can sleep.[34] Not unrelated is Bergman's statement that when he is troubled by "doubt and uncertainty, I take refuge in the vision of a simple and pure love . . . [which] I find in those spontaneous women who . . . are the incarnation of purity." Another stage-managed combination of memory and daydream follows: a series of harp arpeggios, besides creating the mood of love and acting as an audio dissolve, takes us back to the exterior of the sun-bathed summer house. It is swarming with family again (except for his mother and father). Old Isak, in his same overcoat, is again in the strawberry patch where earlier he saw his brother kiss Sara. Sara appears and tells him, "There are no strawberries left"— that is, he cannot recapture his youth or win her. Isak answers plaintively, "I can't find either Papa or Mama." Now Sara is not only the young, blonde Sara with her pageboy hairdo who moments earlier outside his window told him that she would "always" love him, and whose resemblance to his golden, long-haired Sara has facilitated the dissolution of his jammed fixation on her, she is also Bibi Andersson, the "spontaneous woman" who is "the incarnation of purity" and, as Bergman's lover, is partly his mother. Taking his arm, Sara/Sara/Bibi guides Isak/Ingmar over a hill and through fields of golden grass to a ledge above a tiny cove. There, on a rocky peninsula softened by patches of grass, scrub pines, and a background of sailboats in mirror-still water, sit his parents. The lighting of the vision has a crystalline character that makes it almost an audible experience. His father is at water's edge, smoking a pipe, and into a crevice near his feet he has wedged the handle of his fishing pole. A few feet up the bank Isak's mother, also dressed in light-colored clothing, is knitting. The father acknowledges his son's presence by raising his hand casually to his pipe, and his mother, setting down her work, stretches her hand above her wide-brimmed hat and waves happily (see fig. 12). (Earlier, while Isak was visiting his past, he heard someone say that he and his father were out fishing together. He had responded, "I felt a secret and completely inexplicable happiness at this message.") As if he were watching a movie of them, Isak does not return their greeting. The narrow gulf of water and space that separates them is eloquent: they exist as an immutable image of idyllic peace, contentment, and acceptance. Isak (and Bergman) cannot reach them, and he knows an unbridgeable gulf exists between them not only in time but between his image of them and what they actually were (are). As the camera dollies in for a close-up of his radiant, transfixed face and moist eyes, Sara leaves, unnoticed and unmissed.[35] His parents return to their tasks while Isak drinks in this paradise, which has the numinous sublimity of Jof's vision of the Virgin and Child. The emotional hunger that Isak has felt for so long is silenced for the moment.[36] The fantasy dissolves, but it is evident from his face that his self-generated state of grace lingers. He clears his throat, takes his arms from beneath the covers, and awaits a peaceful sleep. The film ends with ascending notes on the harp—this film contains Erik Nordgren's best score for a Bergman film—prolonging the melancholic joy that death, temporarily evicted, only enriches. No other Bergman ending is so tearfully affecting.[37]

In shooting this film, Bergman pried into Sjöström's face. "Sometimes it [was] like a dumb cry of pain, sometimes it [was] distorted by mistrustful cruelty and senile querulousness, sometimes it dissolve[d] into self-pity and astoundingly sentimental effusions."[38] But "not a scrap" of what happens to Isak Borg is meant to be "a study of Victor Sjöström's life," Bergman assures us. It is only about Berg-

Wild Strawberries. AB Svensk Filmindustri

man's life. (It is no accident that the protagonist's initials are the same as the director's.) Isak Borg is a character who had "cut off everything around him—as I'd done. . . . I made it as a rundown of my earlier life, a searching final test" (*BB*, 131–33). Even so, it is the misanthropic, 78-year-old, ailing widower Victor Sjöström who makes Isak Borg unforgettable.[39]

THE MAGICIAN and NOW ABOUT THESE WOMEN

In 1947, for the Gothenberg City Theater's experimental studio, Bergman had staged G. K. Chesterton's *Magic: A Fantastic Comedy* (1913), which involves a conjurer with supernatural powers who performs before doubters, with the result that an atheist who cannot explain one of the tricks almost goes mad and a woman who believes that the conjurer is more than he is falls in love with him. This play, and to a far lesser degree Strindberg's *Advent* (1899) and Pirandello's *Six Characters in Search of an Author* (1921), influenced Bergman's *The Magician: A Comedy*, which celebrates mystery and the power of love by introducing Vogler's Magnetic Health Theater into the Stockholm household of Mr. and Mrs. Egerman and friends. The results are similar not only to those produced by the conjurer in Chesterton's *Magic* but to those produced by Mrs. Armfeldt on another set of Egermans and their acquaintances in *Smiles of a Summer Night*. *The Magician,* however, is far darker than that bright quadrille. Though stunningly photographed, wonderfully acted, intellectually stimulating, thrilling at times, and fun, it is less funny, in part because the "actor who [played] the big comic role was so drunk all the time he couldn't remember his lines or what he had to do. [As a result] about a third of his part had to be cut, which meant that the film lost its balance and became too serious" (*BB*, 123). *The Magician* achieves its comedy and meaning by unmasking pretension, undermining dogmatic conviction, and deflating human magic. This applies even to the early history of Bergman's protagonist, Dr. Albert Emanuel Vogler (Max von Sydow), who, because he possesses a miraculous power to heal—he "*used* to think of himself as a priest," says Bergman (Kaminsky, 125)—has become famous and rich. He has been encouraged in this belief about himself because his grandmother (Naima Wifstrand) possessed inexplicable powers. So successful was he that he retired and "bought a country house." But retirement left him feeling unfulfilled, so he sold everything, bought a coach and horses, and took his show on the road. To commercialize his "secret power," he has even employed a theatrical manager, Tubal (Åke Fridell). It is not long, however, before it becomes disillusioningly clear to him that his miraculous power is nothing more than mesmerism (hypnotism). He carries on, nevertheless, embellishing his performances with tricks, though the added hocuspocus tends to produce suspicion and laughter. Again, the disparity between a person's reputation and his actual self and power is a major theme, the difference between Vogler and Isak Borg being that Vogler knows early on that he is a phony. And critical to Bergman's continuing exploration of narcissism is his protagonist's talent, hypnotism, the consummate means of controlling others.

The deflation of mystery and the unmasking of pretension begin at once. Although the film will end in bright sunshine and on a burlesque note of joyous victory, it opens on a world pregnant with palpable mystery and violence. The year is 1846, but it is as if we were picking up where *The Seventh Seal*'s dance of death leaves off. Milling around a hilltop gallows at twilight is a coach, horses, and a handful of silhouetted figures: Vogler, his male assistant Aman (Ingrid Thulin), little Simson the coachman (Lars Ekborg), and Tubal. Vogler's grandmother is off digging up money she previously buried. A kettle drum and somber orchestral chords promise danger and a thunderstorm.

When the troupe sets out again, they enter an eerily beautiful forest. Reminiscent of Kazuo Miyagawa's photography of the forest in Akira Kurosawa's *Rashomon* (1950), the horse-drawn coach, as shot by Gunnar Fischer, seems to be floating on billowing clouds of ground fog. The coach advances beneath sentinel trees whose branches fan the light of the setting sun into rays. Bergman forces us to heed this hauntingly dreamlike visual world by stripping away all ambient sound and substituting the misleadingly relaxed chords of a guitar. Granny hears a cry that she identifies as coming from "the living dead." It scares young Simson into the coach. In contrast, Vogler, concentrating on the sound, leans forward into a startlingly huge close-up that compels us to study his carefully trimmed black mustache, ebony black hair that hangs down just below his small earrings, and black eyebrows that almost merge with his dark eye sockets. The impression of dignified authority and melancholic aloofness is enhanced by his silence.[40]

After a moment Vogler exits the coach and enters the swamp to search out the source of the ghostly cry. But just as at the gallows, where the portentous silhouettes turn out to be this motley collection of itinerants merely eating lunch, the puncturing of illusions continues. The ghost is Johan Spegel (Bengt Ekerot), a dying, alcoholic actor, lying prone in the muck. That Spegel—the Swedish word for mirror—is to function as Vogler's alter ego and double is made clear immediately. Spegel recognizes that Vogler is wearing a disguise and asks, "Are you a swindler who must hide his real face?" Vogler smiles but listens intently as his double, his head resting on Vogler's shoulder, confesses bitterly, with the obsessiveness that makes him a Bergman creation, that he yearns for a sharp knife that would remove his vital organs from his "meaningless carcass" and scrape away his uncleanness so that his "spirit [can] ascend." Later, sounding like Antonius Block, he tells Vogler that he has prayed "just one prayer in my life. Use me, oh God. But God never understood what a devoted slave I would have been. So I was never used." As with Block, God will answer Spegel's prayer, but, ironically, the actor has mistakenly come to believe that life is nothing more than walking "step by step by step into darkness." Vogler helps Spegel to the coach where—again like Block, who interrogates the dying witch and Death for information about the next world—Vogler peers intently into the actor's face. Spegel apparently expires trying to satisfy Vogler: "I will tell you. Death is. . . ."

When Vogler's coach stops at the Stockholm toll gate for a permit to play in the city, the police take the troupe into custody and deliver them to the home of wealthy Consul Abraham Egerman (Erland Josephson). He is in the midst of entertaining Starbeck (Toivo Pawlo), a foppish parrot whose sole claim to respect is being chief of police, and the debonair, coldly sadistic Dr. Vergérus (Gunnar Björnstrand), senior doctor of the Ministry of Health. They are joined by Egerman's wife Ottilia (Gertrud Fridh), who is still mourning her recently deceased child. Seated before his mocking interrogators, Vogler, indignant and brooding, covers his face with his hand. With a barker's flourish Tubal introduces the troupe and announces that Dr. Vogler is mute (explaining his previous silence, and stirring our sympathy). Dr. Vergérus declares that he believes in neither Vogler's reputed powers nor his muteness, and he subjects him to a humiliating physical examination. Vogler squeezes his eyes closed in mute rage as Vergérus roughly kneads his throat and forces his mouth open to peer into his throat. Ottilia shuts her eyes in sympathetic agony. Vergérus then challenges Vogler's "supernatural" ability to produce visions in others. In close-up, Vogler and Vergérus lock eyes in psychic combat. Vogler's concentrated stare seems on the verge of exploding the mind of his opponent when the latter breaks off the duel and pooh-poohs it as a boring failure. But Ottilia observes that Vergérus experienced something he "doesn't dare" admit. The ironic Vergérus retorts that what she sensed was his regret at being "incapable of experiencing anything," a statement that, with his passionate antipathy to Vogler, betrays in him a deep desire for mystery. When Egerman admits to believing that "inexplicable" powers exist, Vergérus asserts that this idea is catastrophic for science because it means that "logically we would have to accept . . a God." The fool Starbeck says that science can explain everything. The discussion ends with Vergérus and Egerman wagering on the issue. Before they sneeringly dismiss Vogler, after ordering him to put on his show the following morning, Vergérus, another of Bergman's narcissistic scientists who feel they have the right to do what they wish with people, confesses that he would like to perform an autopsy on Vogler—"weigh your brain, open your heart, explore . . . your nerve circuits, lift out your eyes." His statement stirs our memory of Spegel's wish for "a sharp knife that would remove his vital organs" in order to free his spirit to be used by God.

While Vogler and Aman are setting up their apparatus for the morning's performance, Ottilia enters. Grinning, Aman leaves. Dissatisfied with her husband's passivity, Ottilia is sexually excited by the charismatic Vogler, whose seething hatred she takes for spiritual pain. He is the Christ-like figure she has dreamt would come to change her life. In fact, she has just drugged her husband so that Vogler can visit her (separate) bedroom. Egerman, however, is eavesdropping as she reveals this. She also asks Vogler to explain why God has taken her little daughter (the exact question that will be posed in both *Brink of Life* and *The Virgin Spring*). As she speaks, Vogler clenches his fist until his fingernails puncture his palm. Ottilia notices the blood and kisses the wound. After she departs, the frustrated Vogler repeatedly pounds the coffin he is sitting on. Is it anguish over his inability to live up to his image, or—like the actor—his inability to do God's work or perform miracles, or is he once again furious at people trying to use him?

At bedtime it is not Ottilia's Christ-like Don Juan who visits her bedroom but her husband, and he has tears in his eyes. Surprised, she denies her guilt and then, planting the idea, asks if he intends to beat her. He is shocked, causing her to call him a "milksop." Galled by her shameless lies and arrogance, he slaps her face but then, not observing that the blow has stimulated her, begs forgiveness. As he moves to withdraw, she grabs him and pulls his mouth toward hers. Their subsequent night together does not complete their reconciliation, but their union is the first in a series of love relationships revitalized by the presence of the Vogler troupe.

Meanwhile, downstairs in the kitchen, passion is percolating in the form of love, hate, and violence. Picking his teeth, Vogler, his hand on Aman's shoulder, exits the kitchen where little Simson and Rustan the butler (Axel Düberg) are vying for the flirtatious but virginal Sara Lindqvist (Bibi Andersson), and where the imperious widow Sofia Garp (Sif Ruud), impatient to make up for eight husbandless years, is reciprocating Tubal's advances. Granny contributes by selling bottles of her love elixir, a brew that calls to mind old Mrs. Armfeldt's magic wine—that is, until it runs out and Granny substitutes bottles first of colic and bunion medicine and then rat poison. (Granny has a firm grip on reality. She is careful not to "offend the new [scientific] creed because then one might be put in a madhouse.") On the way out of the kitchen Granny meets the Egermans' coachman, Antonsson (Oscar Ljung), and informs him that she just saw "a murderer" hanging from a hook. When he scoffs, the old Cassandra replies, "I see what I see and I know what I know, but nobody believes me." Granny then visits the bedroom of the 16-year-old maid Sanna (Birgitta Pettersson), to calm her fear of the strangers in the house. In a voice that sounds like a whispered groan, the tiny crone sings of love as a strengthening mystery. She so eases the girl's acceptance of adult love that later, frightened, Sanna throws herself into Rustan's arms. Meanwhile, having fallen in love with the virgin Simson, the virginal Sara seduces him amid the fresh sheets in the laundry room.

Bergman now pursues his fascination with unmotivated violence and cruelty. *Fanny and Alexander*'s Aron will observe, "Everything unintelligible makes people angry." Such is the case here. Getting drunk, Antonsson and Rustan vent their inexplicable antipathy to the Vogler troupe. "Seeing a face like Vogler's drives you mad . . . makes me want to bash him." Their brandy-loosened ruminations slow the pace for a wonderfully melodramatic moment of comic terror. Accompanied by thunder and lightning, the resurrected Spegel—earlier in the coach he merely passed out—in his crumpled derby and with his cape swinging theatrically, explodes into the room, plants an axe loudly in the tabletop, and disappears with the brandy. He turns up next in the room where Vogler is preparing the next day's show. Sitting in the prop coffin, Spegel takes a swig of his brandy, and dies. Vogler compassionately hugs his reeking double's head and gently lowers him into the casket, the cloth flaps snapping closed over him.

The Magician. AB Svensk Filmindustri

At this moment, on his way to bed, Vergérus uses his cane to nudge open the door of Vogler's bedroom and eavesdrop on Manda (Aman's real name) as she is removing her male disguise (worn to help her husband avoid the police). He enters as she is washing up and, running his white-handled, phallic cane sensuously down her bare arm, confesses an "unexplainable liking" for her. She emphatically declines his proposition and then assures him that she and her husband have no secret powers. But her wistful "If just once . . ." may shed light on Vogler's earlier act of self-inflicted pain. Just as Consul Egerman does earlier, Vogler is eavesdropping (see fig. 13), and when Vergérus again touches Manda's bare shoulder with his cane, he rushes in, shoves Vergérus down on the bed, breaks his cane over his knee, and throws the halves at him. Vergérus gets up, and they grapple, Vergérus trying to maintain his composure with his wit. Just as Désirée convinces Fredrik to leave before Count Malcolm's anger grows lethal, Manda persuades Vergérus to abandon the field. When Vergérus leaves, Vogler slams the door, paces animal-like, and then stops and repeatedly bashes the back of his head against the wall. When at last his anger subsides, he disappears into the next room. He returns without his makeup. It is one of the film's most disturbing moments. Gone are the false beard, black eyebrows, and hair. In their place are Vogler's natural, cropped, blonde hair and deeply receding hairline, his pale skin and baggy eyes, his weak mouth, chin, and sour expression. His appearance produces in us a visceral reaction bordering on repugnance. Bergman has made us recognize how much we prefer the mask of artifice and mystery to the pallid visage of reality. Do we not feel slightly sad after being shown how moments from our favorite films were created? (This moment and the events that follow also speak to Bergman's fascination with the discrepancy between the artist and the public's perception of the artist, to be discussed at the end of this analysis.)

In bed Manda kisses her mute husband's ear. He turns away. Amused, she reminds him of the beating he recently gave a German prince who was infatuated with her and with whom Vogler thought she had betrayed him. That beating had gotten them jailed for two months. When the prince finally forgave Vogler, he went even further, promising to recommend their show to the Swedish court. Do you think he kept his word, she asks. Vogler shakes his head no. Then our sense of reality is again shattered. Echoing Rustan and Antonsson, Vogler speaks, hissing between his teeth, "I hate them. I hate their faces . . . but I am also afraid, and then I become powerless."[41]

During the performance the next morning the audience, made up of all the household, is delighted when Starbeck reveals the mechanism behind Aman's miraculous levitation and is sent into hysterics when the hypnotized, frumpish Mrs. Starbeck blurts out her contempt for her husband. The audience is horrified, however, when Antonsson—unbeknownst to them, he is also under Vogler's hypnotic power—seemingly strangles Vogler to death and, as Granny foresaw, then runs off to hang himself. In the confusion the troupe substitutes Spegel's corpse for Vogler in the coffin, which is then removed to the attic where Dr. Vergérus prepares to perform his wished-for autopsy on Vogler. The sacrificial pattern is familiar: Spegel, whose overriding wish was to be used by God, dies not only to aid the Bergman protagonist but to help God achieve His goals.

After telling Manda to lock the door to the attic, Vogler sets out to get his revenge on Dr. Vergérus. By means of a series of illusions, and by smashing Dr. Vergérus's eyeglasses so that he cannot identify the corpse, Vogler first rattles the scientist's trust in his senses and then makes him fear that the magician has returned to life.[42] Suddenly feelings nauseous, Dr. Vergérus descends the attic steps to leave, but the door is locked. Returning and seeing Vogler's image in a mirror, the scientist tries to calm himself with reason: "Actually rather interesting," he says to himself. Then a hand emerges from behind the slatted wall and grasps his throat (reminding us of Vergérus squeezing Vogler's throat earlier). To the accompaniment of accelerating beats, like heartbeats, on a kettle drum, the gasping Vergérus breaks loose and falls to the floor. His terror increasing, he crawls backwards as Vogler's towering figure advances toward him. Rapid cutting and a subjective, moving camera make us both the pursuer and the pursued. The increased volume of the drum is joined by a rattlesnake effect on the castanets. Panic-stricken, Vergérus retreats blindly until he cascades down the attic stairs and comes to a stop against the locked door. Vogler leaps and grabs his throat, and Vergérus screams, again and again. The door is suddenly unlocked; it is Manda, come to prevent murder.[43]

But this experience has not made Dr. Vergérus what Bergman calls a "good intellectual," that is, someone who "doubt[s] his intellect, [has] fantasies, and [is] powerfully emotional" (Kaminsky, 125). Having at last identified his terrorizer, Vergérus composes himself and snidely concedes that Vogler gave him a scare, "a slight fear of death." He will not admit that for a few moments the "inexplicable" leaked into his materialistic universe.

In the very next shot Vogler plunges from the summit of his mas-terful revenge to surly servility. Descending the hall stairs, he encoun-ters Ottilia, who, when she thought he was dead, had cried, "I can't bear it any longer," and accused her husband of petty revenge for per-mitting the autopsy. Now, face to face with her savior, without his makeup and wearing Spegel's ragged, undersized clothes, she with-draws into her husband's protective arms. She denies ever knowing Vogler and refuses to pay for the performance. Sardonically, Vogler reminds her, "You thought we were 'twin souls.'"[44] Further down the stairs Vogler meets Vergérus, who also refuses to deal with the real Vogler. He too prefers him made up. Vogler again rushes at him in a manner both threatening and obsequious, calling the doctor "ungrate-ful" but adding "sir" as he reminds him that he at least should be paid for providing the doctor with "a sensation." Vergérus flings a coin onto the floor and, turning to Egerman, demands that he concede that he, Vergérus, has won their bet. Egerman's ironic grin belies his concession.

Most of the plot's conflicts have been resolved. There may be no hard evidence, but based on the pattern of God's intervention in such films as *Smiles of a Summer Night* and *The Seventh Seal,* it seems cred-ible that God has used the Vogler troupe to produce a series of loving alliances in the Egerman household, and that, just as He sacrificed Antonius Block to save His holy family, He has used Vogler—sacri-ficing his double, Spegel—to breach Vergérus's atheism. However, just as He failed to get through to Block, He has failed with Vergérus.

The pseudo-Christ Vogler, denied by Ottilia, is now deserted by two other disciples, Tubal and Granny. Tubal is staying to live with Sofia Garp, and Granny, complaining that Vogler is too "rash," is going to use the money she has squirreled away to open a respectable apothecary shop.

Inside their carriage the depressed Vogler rests his head on his wife's shoulder and holds on to her hand. Wearing her most feminine cos-tume (tucked sleeves, lace cuffs and collar), Manda takes command. Leaning out the window into the drenching downpour, she urges Simson, who along with the stagestruck Sara is staying with the the-ater, to drive them out of there before the police arrest them. Her order comes too late. Starbeck and two coaches filled with police ar-rive and force the troupe back into the house. Vogler, still in Spegel's rags and wrapped in a soggy blanket, just stares at the floor. Starbeck, much to his annoyance, reads to the assembled household an order from the King of Sweden. Vogler is to be escorted at once to the palace where that night, 14 July (Bergman's birthday), he is to per-form.[45] Manda's doting prince kept his word; again love (God) has deviously shaped events. Transfigured, Vogler glares contemptuously at his persecutors, flings his soggy blanket over his shoulder—just as Spegel had slung his cape—and sweeps out and into his coach. To the (nondiegetic) joyous peal of countless church bells, hundreds of peo-ple cheering, and a brass band's zesty march, Vogler's escorted coach—jostling, as it exits the courtyard, an unlit lantern hanging from a hook—races up the cobblestone street to disappear into the bright sunlight at the top of the hill. Suddenly, the music, about to conclude, halts, and the *only* sound is the melancholy squeak of the swinging lantern, which ought to remind us of the gallows at the beginning and, like the actor's death mask in *The Seventh Seal,* may be intended to remind us of the continued presence of death and evil in the world.[46] After this prolonged, playful interruption, the march resumes with an emphatic finale that thumbs its nose at ill fortune and celebrates again the intervention of God and love, or God as love.

Seeing *The Magician*'s world as one governed by a God trying to enrich the lives of His characters and to rid the world of unbelief and hate unifies what may at first appear to be an artistic Rubik's cube— Bergman says that making the film was like playing a game (Kamin-sky, 124)—composed of a period drama, a grimacing comedy-fantasy, a morality play, and a highly theatrical Gothic thriller.

As I have said, Bergman is interested in the discrepancy between the artist and the way the public regards him. As we shall learn in *Persona,* he loathes the public's naïveté. Artists create from a variety of selfish and unselfish impulses and feelings—narcissism, anger, hatred, compulsion, a need to communicate or share, and love. Spegel asks Vogler, "Are you an imposter?" The answer, obviously, is "of course." Shamming is just another motive for and facet of his art, because to prosper the artist disguises his motives, urges, drives, and fantasies. In 1964 Bergman would make his first feature-length color film, *Now about These Women,* one of his "few cinematic fiascoes."[47] (He now says he is "ashamed" of this "superficial and artificial com-edy," which was written by Buntel Eriksson, the pseudonym adopted by Erland Josephson and himself—Bergman is "Erik's son.") This film is an exposé of artists' and critics' need for immortality, the latter achieving it by clinging to the coattails of the former.[48] But just as important, it reveals the discrepancy between the artist's creative achievement and reputation and his actual character. Again, Bergman demonstrates that in spite of what people want to believe, the artist is often amoral, immoral, crude, cold, manipulative, and scandalously narcissistic. Nevertheless, his drama says, the artist is that rare creature capable of imagining and producing works of excruciating beauty, acute sensitivity, and profound compassion. This film's theme relates to the theme of *The Magician,* and significantly, the portrait of Felix, the incomparable artist-cellist who is the protagonist of *Now about These Women,* was based on a German violinist named Jonathan Vogler. He was the husband of the Italian piano teacher of Bergman's fourth wife, Käbi Laretei; her teacher was a woman who, like the film's Adelaide (Eva Dahlbeck), had "to play traffic-cop" to all her husband's women. He was, according to Bergman, "little, fat, boss-eyed . . . demonic . . . utterly lower class, utterly uneducated, utterly amoral . . . but [he was] a fantastic musician" (*BB,* 21; *ML,* 219–20).

When Bergman's contract with the Malmö City Theater expired in 1959, he returned to Stockholm to work for the Royal Dramatic Theater. His reputation had by then made moot the issue of his being up to its standards. In 1963 he would be appointed its head.

BRINK OF LIFE

Bergman made *Brink of Life* (1958) because he owed Nordisk Tonefilm a project and because he wanted to collaborate with his writer friend Ulla Isaksson. A large measure of the film's success is due to its setting in a hospital's maternity ward, whose cloistered feeling makes the outside world seem like another universe. Bergman excises everything random. Nothing outside the hospital is shown, nor, after a few minutes, is anyone, whether visitors or personnel, not involved in the plot. The story is presented with equally expressionistic spareness. Background music, makeup, and theatrical lighting and effects are either eliminated or kept extremely subtle. A few scenes involving hemorrhaging women in labor and women nursing their children even have the feel of a documentary. All of this heightens tension and instantly indicates that the setting—austere halls and wards and a steely delivery room—is designed more for baring character than bearing babies. Childbirth, in fact, serves to a large extent as a metaphor for either failure or self-realization and fulfillment. We are trapped in a place where pain is nakedly exposed, and the women we encounter face hard truths about themselves, their roles as women, and, for one, existence itself.

The drama of this simply plotted story arises from the suffering of three women in one room. Whereas weaving together more than one story was unsuccessful in *Three Strange Loves* and *Secrets of Women,* and slightly weakened *Dreams,* it works here. By confining the story to these three, and by carefully planning his camera placements and movements, Bergman's interweaving of the fates of the three protagonists feels natural. And by photographing each protagonist's intense and raw emotions in extreme close-ups, he obviates questions of contrivance, staginess, or structural woodenness.

Virtually every theme or pattern we have been tracing—and most of them are basic conflicts—comes into play in this film: narcissism, the nature of God, marital conflict, parent-child relationships, sacrificial victims (who also, as in *The Virgin Spring,* help unite an estranged daughter with her family), loneliness, and, to a small degree, the discrepancy between one's public image and one's true self.

The film's credits are superimposed over a hospital door's pressed-glass window, close to which a blurred shadow occasionally approaches. (In *Secrets of Women* Märta, about to leave for the maternity ward, takes just such a shadowy presence as an omen of death.) The doors open, and Cecilia Ellius (Ingrid Thulin), who has started to hemorrhage, is wheeled on a stretcher into the hospital's waiting room. Her husband Anders (Erland Josephson) is beside her. She raises herself into an extreme close-up and asks him what until now she has feared to ask, "Do you really want this child?" He answers that there is nothing that they can do about it now; besides, she shouldn't worry, the doctors will do all they can to save it. She falls back and turns her face from him. (In the background a baby's irritating wail begins and persists throughout the early phase of the Cecilia sequence.) Anders is left behind as Cecilia is wheeled into the examination room. Placed beside the table with the stirrups, she is subjected to what seem a series of time- and life-wasting questions. Then she is left alone. When Cecilia realizes the baby is emerging, she screams for help and then faints. After she revives, she is perfunctorily informed that the baby died because something was wrong from the start, but that the operation they performed will ensure that next time everything will turn out all right.

Cecilia is put in a three-bed room, and the curtains are drawn around her. Her moaning, however, unsettles the other two occupants. Whereas Cecilia's smoking, cropped hair, eyeglasses, books, and job as a secretary to the school board establish the impression that she is a private, even repressed intellectual type, the bovine Christina "Stina" Andersson (Eva Dahlbeck), wearing a checkered maternity dress, hair braided, and, Eve-like, munching an apple—in Bergman's films always a symbol of an imminent fall into painful knowledge—is the film's most lovable and seemingly self-assured mother-to-be. (Isaksson calls this spirited Eve "one of our Lord's creations.") The third woman, her hair in a ponytail and not visibly pregnant, is the gum-chewing, movie magazine–mad, adolescent Hjördis Pettersson (Bibi Andersson). She, we soon learn, has already tried to abort her child and is secretly not taking the pills given her for its prenatal care.

Sister Brita (Barbro Hiort af Ornäs) attends the half-alert, sobbing Cecilia, who, between bouts of vomiting, reveals that she sensed that Anders not only did not want the baby but does not love her. Normally, she would never have shared this information with anyone, but the loss of the child forbids her, she asserts, from ever again being the acquiescent, guilt-ridden wife. Anders arrives bringing a large bouquet of flowers, which he lays on Cecilia's chest as if she were dead. The way he looks down at his wife's upturned face, kisses her forehead, and holds her hand indicates a habit of keeping life at arm's length. He mentions that he feels Cecilia is behaving coolly toward him. This leads her to confess that she now realizes that soon after they married he felt it was a mistake but he was too considerate to admit it. Moreover, it is clear to her that he did not want the baby. He does not contradict her and, as if relieved, inquires when she came to these conclusions. The camera dollies in close to her face. Yesterday, she says, when she was hemorrhaging; she saw his fear and revulsion. Suddenly, her lifelong habit of self-denigration and self-sacrifice, fueled by her guilt over the lost child, dissolves her anger-inspired candor. Almost smiling, she says, "I'm not strong, not fit to live, not fit to be married." She adds that if Anders wants to be free of her she will not object. Until this moment it has been difficult to determine whether Anders, who finds it difficult, if not embarrassing, to express strong emotions, has not been further inhibited by his awareness that Stina and Hjördis cannot help overhearing them. But his reply—echoing Eugen Lobelius's in *Secrets of Women*—to Cecilia's suggestion that they divorce damns him in our eyes: "But everything that we have built up: our home, our books. . . ." Cecilia asks him to leave. Seeming ready to take back the flowers, Anders tells her, in a tone of voice that couples consideration with a stern warning, that he will call to inquire how she is. Aware that what he said has not come out as he intended, he starts to explain but cannot; he then leaves.

Cecilia's guilt is compounded when a visiting doctor callously suggests she induced her miscarriage. Outraged, she flings back at him, "I wanted that baby!"

The story now turns to Hjördis, who phones her boyfriend to ask him to visit her. He responds, "I ain't your husband!" but offers to arrange an abortion. Finally facing what he is like, she rejects his offer and hangs up. On the way back to her room, she passes the nursery and stops to steal a peek at the babies through the window in the door. (Bergman avoids sentimentality by presenting a montage that stays with the babies, making us see them as more than just cute.) When a nurse happens to lower the shade, Hjördis, because she feels guilty about not wanting her own child, takes this shutting-out action to mean that she is undeserving. Just then the hospital's social worker (Anne-Marie Gyllenspetz) happens by and invites Hjördis to her office. As with some of Bergman's other female adolescents who leave their rural homes to enjoy the freedoms (especially sex) of the city, things have turned out badly for Hjördis. Because her mother told her not to come home "dragging a baby," she is afraid to inform her parents she is pregnant. In a message-ridden scene, the social worker reassures the young woman that, in spite of her parents' attitude, society does not condemn unmarried mothers, that the government will force the father to pay his share, that the child will have rights, that Hjördis will receive free maternal care, and that if she goes to work she can make a life for herself and her baby, even call herself Mrs. Unable herself to have children, the social worker tells Hjördis, who sits pouting, to regard the child as a "precious gift."[49] Calling to mind attitudes expressed by Nix (*A Lesson in Love*), Charlotte (*Smiles of a Summer Night*), and Ingeri (*The Virgin Spring*), Hjördis blurts out, "Men are beastly . . . arrogant and vain and have hair all over their bodies. . . . What do you know about it? . . . You've never forgotten yourself, seen a pair of tattooed arms digging into you!" Having let slip more than she intended, she covers her mouth with her hands and rushes out. Alone, she relaxes, kicking her slipper down the corridor (a spontaneous act of Bibi Andersson's that Bergman kept in the film).

Reentering her room, she catches Stina, on whom the story now dwells, off guard. Not wanting to be thought of as anything but a happy hausfrau, but obviously very concerned that her baby is overdue, Stina pretends to be reading. When Sister Brita arrives with beer and castor oil to induce labor, Stina, who has never drunk beer before, begins joking, even zanily addressing her unborn. Suddenly, her smile disappears and she hugs the sister. A line from the Bible—"a sword went through her soul" (Luke 2:35)—has just struck her "like a deep pain." She is also afraid that her joking may bring bad luck. The mood changes again. Announcing with a bow that "Papa is here!" and bearing irises from their garden and sketches for a bathroom shelf for the baby's things, Stina's husband Harry (Max von Sydow) bounces in. The happy couple agree about everything except Stina's desire to have the child baptized.

An hour before midnight Stina goes into labor. As she is wheeled out, she shouts, Frid-like, "Don't be scared, girls, this is life itself!" Hjördis and Cecilia are subsequently unable to sleep, and so they talk. Among other things, Hjördis confides that if someone loved and married her she would like to have the baby. Cecilia suggests that Hjördis give her mother another chance, that she call her to see if she won't accept Hjördis and the baby.

The birth, meanwhile, is going badly for Stina. At first capable of joking, the pain soon has her shrieking and unable to catch her breath. [Earlier in the evening she was lit like a radiant madonna; now her taut face is corpse-pale, and her sweaty hair sticks to her head (see fig. 14).] She cries out in fear when the doctors inform her that they must anesthetize her and use forceps. (Up to this time no fictional film that I know of had conveyed such frightening physical agony.)

The next scene tricks us into believing things turn out well for Stina. It is the following morning, and we watch a nurse push a chest of drawers, each of which contains an infant, into a room and dispense the infants to their mothers for nursing. We assume that one of those drawers contains Stina's child. But this scene is followed by another in which we see an unsmiling Stina being wheeled on a stretcher back into her room. Sister Brita helps her back into bed, gently touches her forehead, and then informs Cecilia that the baby died because Stina's "labor pains were too violent." (After Cecilia's miscarriage, and in spite of the omens—Stina eating the apple, the "sword," learning that Stina's mother's first child miscarried—we turned in wish-fulfilling relief to the robust Stina, and her lavishly anticipated baby achieved a brief existence in our imagination. As a consequence, we feel somehow guilty when we learn that it has died.)

Stina stares at the water glass on her bedside table. Hjördis reaches to hand it to her, but Stina, with cold fury, slaps the hand away. Her exhausted face hardens into a mask of concentrated will, and she grasps the glass. But then she lets loose of it and lays her arm over her eyes. Strong in body and in mind, she is reasserting control over her life. But she also seems to realize how limited that control is, and how limited, too, is her image of God. This metaphysical dimension is raised both in Isaksson's preface to her story—"There is a secret . . . as to why some are called to live, while others are called to die" (Donner 1964, 23)—and now by Stina herself. On his rounds Dr. Nordlander (Gunnar Sjöberg) passes her by, but she suddenly sits up and demands an answer to the question that is asked in *The Magician* and will be again in *The Virgin Spring:* "Why did [my child] die?" From the safety of the foot of her bed, he answers, "I'm just as helpless as you are. . . . There was nothing wrong with you, nor with the baby, but life was denied him. . . . Next time everything will probably be all right." Unsatisfied, Stina falls back and turns toward the wall.

The final scene in this room centers on Bergman's long-standing treatment of loneliness as the greatest hell. Anders's sister Greta (Inga Landgré), dressed in black and, like so many of Bergman's independent, unhappy women, wearing her hair severely (mannishly) pulled back, visits Cecilia. She informs her that Anders broke down after his visit, and that it is her opinion that Cecilia and Anders "suit" each other. When Cecilia says she does not feel strong enough to sustain two people, Greta replies, obviously from personal experience, that loneliness demands even greater strength. Taking Greta's warning to heart, the guilt-prone Cecilia, who still wants to be a mother, gives in.

Hjördis is glad when Dr. Nordlander tells her that she can leave. The ward, she says, makes her feel that "nothing [will] ever be born again. . . . Death [is] all over the place." It is a critical moment: death has led Hjördis to life. She wants her baby. Sister Brita holds the young woman's hand as she phones her parents. Hjördis's response to her mother's "Come home" is the film's most touching positive moment.

Bergman is obviously ambivalent about hospitals and medical professionals; of all the medical staff, Sister Brita is the most humane. Bergman heightens her femininity by having her uniform strap keep slipping down off her shoulder. Though she maintains a professional distance, her compassion is heartfelt; she looks on unhappily as Cecilia and Anders quarrel, and after Stina's loss her face registers a helpless frustration. Then in helping Bergman's chief protagonist—Hjördis— get her life back on track, Sister Brita functions, as do many of the elderly figures in Bergman's earlier films, as God's facilitator.

Barrenness and death have benefited Hjördis. She leaves, the beneficiary of Cecilia's and Stina's miscarriages, the social worker's barrenness, and Sister Brita's apparent childlessness as well as her kindness.

Like *The Virgin Spring*'s Ingeri (whom we will meet in a moment), Hjördis is the focus of God's attention and functions as the saving remnant. Whereas Cecilia's fetus passes out of her like water, and Stina involuntarily kills hers, Hjördis's attempts to abort her baby do not interfere with God's plan, which includes her reunion with her family. Hjördis is not in the Isaksson short story, "The Aunt of Death," on which the film is based. She is Bergman's creation.

THE VIRGIN SPRING

Bergman's affair with Bibi Andersson—though not their friendship—ended at this time, and he became romantically involved with the Estonian-born, internationally known pianist Käbi Laretei, who had fled to Sweden during World War II. Käbi, only four years his junior, had a daughter and was still married to the conductor Gunnar Staern when Bergman took her with him up to Darlarna, where he and Ulla Isaksson went to work (separately) on the screenplay for *The Virgin Spring* (1960). (He also wrote there *The Devil's Eye,* a project that resulted from his contract with SFI to write a comedy as insurance against *The Virgin Spring*'s commercial failure.) Bergman and Käbi Laretei were married in September 1959, and in 1962 their son, Daniel Sebastian, was born.

Bergman had discovered the "blackly brutal," fourteenth-century Swedish religious ballad "Töre's Daughter in Vänge" when he was a university student, and he had tried unsuccessfully to turn it into a play and a ballet. The ballad provided Bergman with a plot he could use to dramatize many of his favorite themes and patterns: narcissism, the discrepancy between self and one's public or self-image, the question of God's existence and nature, the sacrifice of innocents (here not only to enlarge the protagonists' understanding but to unite a family), conflicted marital relationships, and parent-child relationships. Isaksson was a perfect partner, as evidenced in *Brink of Life,* which she also had helped write. The crisp, clinical severity of her narrative style was well suited to the ballad's impersonal point of view. The film's visual style was influenced by Bergman's great admiration for Akira Kurosawa (*BB,* 120) and by Gunnar Fischer's unavailability.[50] As a consequence of the latter, Bergman was reunited with Sven Nykvist, one of the cinematographers he had worked with on *Sawdust and Tinsel.* (This conjunction of events suited Bergman, who had come to feel emotionally incompatible with Fischer. Except for *The Devil's Eye,* immediately following *The Virgin Spring,* and, eleven years later, when Fischer shot the credit sequence for *The Touch,* they never again worked together.)

The first two scenes of *The Virgin Spring* establish that in medieval Sweden, though Christianity dominated, paganism still had its devotees. It is barely dawn when Töre's (Max von Sydow) adopted foundling, Ingeri (Gunnel Lindblom), kindles the fire in the kitchen's open hearth. Dark-complexioned, unkempt, and wearing a rough cloth shift over her ballooning pregnancy, she checks to be sure that no one is eavesdropping and then, opening the chimney hatch in the roof, thrice summons the god Odin. Bergman juxtaposes her actions with those of Töre and his wife Märeta (Birgitta Valberg): he cuts to their bedroom where they are praying to a large carving of the crucified Jesus. Töre, a temperate and pious man, has unquestioning faith in God's justice and mercy. His prosperity as a herdsman and his good fortune as a parent seem evidence of his being one of the chosen, but his yawn, which almost blurs the end of his prayer—"Keep us safe from the Devil's wiles; let there befall us, God, today, no sin, nor shame, nor harm"—indicates a touch of complacency. In contrast, Märeta is obsessed with the Devil, especially his threatening sexuality. This is at the root of her fear that the lusty Ingeri will corrupt their adolescent daughter Karin (Birgitta Pettersson). Partly because that night she has had a (prescient) "evil dream," Märeta ends her prayer by blistering her wrists with hot candle wax, an ascetic act that Töre gently reproves.

Because on Good Friday a "maid" must deliver the candles to the village church, Karin must be the bearer. During breakfast Märeta goes along with Karin's excuse for not going: she has a fever. Noting that she was well enough to attend a dance the previous evening, the amused Töre orders Märeta to get the slugabed on her way and Ingeri to pack a lunch for her. As he was so successful in doing in *The Seventh Seal,* Bergman makes the medieval setting tangibly real with just the thick log buildings and such simple, deft details as the characters dipping their bowls into the community pot.

Hostile to Karin's privileged position and often superior attitude, the loweringly proud Ingeri fashions a sandwich consisting of a live toad between scooped-out halves of a loaf of bread. Meanwhile, Karin says she will deliver the candles only if her mother lets her pretend that she is a princess on a holy mission. To complete this fantasy she must wear her beautiful silk shift and accessories. As is her habit, Märeta appeases her daughter, and soon the blonde girl looks like "a young bride dressed up for her groom." When Töre comes in to check on the cause of the delay, he is so charmed that he acts the groom, lifting his gleeful daughter off her feet and swinging her around. Märeta's exclusion is conveyed in the composition: standing expressionless and motionless on the far side of the room and in the lower right of the frame, she, who we have noted looks much older than her husband, is blocked out of the picture when Karin leans forward into Töre's arms. Töre's exhilaration finally makes him self-conscious. When he sets Karin down and is leaving, he throws a guilty glance at Märeta. Outside, again like a bridegroom, the regal Töre carries the magnificently outfitted "princess" through the barnyard's muck to her horse. She, meanwhile, has convinced him to override her mother's prohibition against letting Ingeri travel with her.

As Karin and Ingeri head toward the hills of unbroken forests that run to the horizon, their less tightly choreographed movements and our escape from the household's claustrophobic interiors into the freedom and vastness of nature[51] affect us viscerally, and suddenly the film also begins to breathe (Donner 1964, 191). When the two young women stop briefly to pick flowers, Karin inquires if Ingeri's child causes her pain. Ingeri answers that someday Karin will find out, to which the proud Karin replies that when that time comes *she* will be "married with honor." Ingeri snidely suggests that passions can override honor, or that a woman may be taken against her will. "I'll break loose," replies Karin. "But if he is stronger?" asks Ingeri, knowingly. She then moves out of earshot as Simon (Oscar Ljung), a farmer, approaches and flirts with Karin, finally setting her on her horse and good-naturedly chiding her for showing off. Afterwards the jealous Ingeri asks what Karin and Simon spoke of. Karin lies, saying, "a way out for you and the child." When Ingeri retorts, "And he said if you lay in the hay with him he'd help?" Karin slaps her face, but then, seeing her foster sister's tears, she quickly utters the familiar "Forgive me." "Don't ask my forgiveness," replies Ingeri, in a tone of loathing that shocks Karin.

Legend has it that when the river god Odin gave up one of his eyes a raven took its place. Bergman cuts abruptly to a giant close-up of a cawing raven and a one-eyed old man who is watching the girls approach. The man, whose hut stands by a stream that blocks the girls' progress, volunteers to lead Karin's horse across while she crosses on a plank. Together again on the other side, Ingeri, probably apprehen-

sive about what will happen when Karin eats the sandwich she prepared, pretends to be afraid to continue. Apprehensive that Ingeri's
hysteria will harm her child, Karin gently touches her cheek and gives
her permission to remain behind, even offering her the sandwiches,
which Ingeri, who made them before she knew she was going with
Karin, refuses. After Karin departs, Ingeri accompanies the old man
into his dark, musty hut. While poking through his clutter of talis-
mans, she hears thumping outside. The man identifies it as "three dead
men riding north." Then he grows lecherous. Ingeri bolts from the
hut and flees into the woods, leaving her horse behind.

About this time Karin, who has paused to bathe in the warm sunlight, becomes intrigued by the sound of a Jew's harp. The player
(Axel Düberg), a balding, scraggly goatherd in his early thirties, is
accompanied by two other males, presumably his brothers. One (Tor
Isedal) is a dark-haired fellow near his age whose tongue has been cut
out and whose slavering speech the balding brother has to translate.
The other brother (Ove Porath) is a twelve-year-old whom the other
two treat both affectionately and brutally. The boy can speak but does
not. Still playing the princess and flattered by their obsequiousness,
Karin offers to share her lunch with them. As the portentous bleat of
one of their goats accompanies the ominously relentless twang of the
Jew's harp, they lead her horse away from the road into a sun-cheered
clearing near a stream. Karin presides over the picnic, reprimanding
her guests with a stare to keep them from eating before she has blessed
the "living bread that from Heaven comes." Only the boy notes the
words. At this moment, Ingeri arrives, but hearing laughter she eavesdrops from behind a hill. So pleased with herself is Karin that she spins
a story that momentarily captures even the trio's imagination: she is a
princess whose father is the king of a great castle, and the goatherds
are "three enchanted princes." Suddenly, their smiles disappear and
they press closer (see fig. 15). The tongueless brother addresses Karin,
and the exchange that follows reminds us of Little Red Riding Hood
talking to the disguised Wolf ("What big teeth you have." . . . "All
the better to eat you with"). Interpreting, his brother says, "My
brother says my lady has such white hands . . . [and] a white neck."
Though wary, Karin's narcissistic fantasy overpowers her instinct, and
she proudly explains that "princesses have no menial tasks . . . [and
their necks are white] so the gold will gleam all the brighter." Their
staring revives her apprehensiveness, so she tries to divert them by
giving the boy the untouched sandwich. As she reaches for the knife,

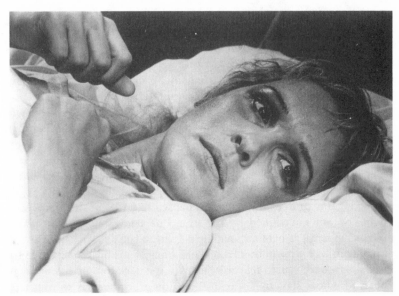

Brink of Life. Nordisk Tonefilm

The Virgin Spring. AB Svensk Filmindustri

the mute snatches it. Frightened, she clutches to her a passing goat (symbol of both lust and sacrifice) and makes the fatal mistake of mentioning that she recognizes its "earmark." The rustlers get to their feet at once, and in the process the boy drops the sandwich, releasing the toad onto the white cloth. Eden and original sin flash through our minds; the sight outrages all three brothers. Karin hurries toward her horse, but the boy tackles her. He is then kicked out of the way as the other two drag her down among the tentaclelike branches of a fallen, dead tree. Watching the rape, her face expressing pain struggling with pleasure, Ingeri picks up a rock, but then drops it. We recall her "But if he is stronger?" and later she will confess to Töre that since she became pregnant she has hated Karin, and that she welcomed the rape.

Afterwards, Karin gets to her feet, holding her dirty silk dress at the stomach and uttering a wheezing whimper. She walks past the men toward her horse, the spidery shadows of the leafless branches appearing as webs across her face and body. Then, before his brother can stop him, the mute hefts a log and brings it down on her head. We do not see the impact; we only hear the thud and, in close-up, watch Ingeri's head jolt backwards as if she had taken the blow. After a moment, Karin raises her head. Blood trickles out of the corner of her mouth and down her white neck. Her eyes fluttering uncontrollably, she looks up at her murderer with a gaze that seems to ask, "Why?" Then her head sinks back lifeless into the sand.

At first, the astonished brother just gapes, but then he joins his mute sibling to strip the corpse of its finery. Karin is left in her white linen shift. The mute then searches her saddlebags. Finding nothing but the Good Friday candles, he stomps on them in a fit of insane frustration. Ordering the boy to wait there for them, the older brothers depart.

With the death of the "May Queen," the beggar monk (Allan Edwall) at Töre's will say later, "winter returns with frozen tears." The boy is surprised when a light snowfall replaces the sunlight. Scooting over to the food, he bites into the abandoned bread but vomits it up. His mouth still dripping, he looks over toward Karin, who seems to be watching him. To silence her stare, he goes to her, scoops up dirt, and throws it on her face. Still terrified, and ignoring the beating he will get for disobeying, he runs into the forest, stopping only to note Karin's following gaze.

That night Töre, looking even more regal in his huge fur coat, waits in his courtyard in the snow and cold for Karin and Ingeri's return. When providence brings the three herdsmen to his gate, he invites them in out of the cold, shares his hearth and food, and promises them employment. (When the action moves inside, the claustrophobic feeling of control returns.) As at breakfast, Töre sits kinglike (and Jesuslike) at the center of the long table. The members of his household sit on either side of him while the herdsmen, for whom this will be their last supper, are across from him. The boy recognizes the grace Töre says as the one Karin said, but he remains silent. Again, when he eats, his internalized guilt prevents him from swallowing; he spits up his milk. After dinner the housekeeper Frida (Gudrun Brost) makes a bed for the troubled child, assuring him that God is merciful. When she inquires if he says his prayers, the boy speaks his first words, "Yes, yes," and presses his hands together. The monk also tries to "comfort" him, melodramatically preaching that when he thinks all is lost he will be delivered to where "evil no longer has power" over him.

In their bedroom Töre reassures the frantic Märeta that Karin must be staying in the village, as she has done before. Sobbing, her hair hanging loose, Märeta confesses to Töre that she loves Karin "more than God Himself," and that she hates Töre because Karin prefers him. Töre sympathetically grips her hands and shoulder, but she is indifferent. He gives up and is soon asleep.

Hearing a scream, Märeta slips on her robe and returns to the dining hall. There is blood on the boy's mouth. Sensing danger, she turns to leave, but the brother who can speak approaches and offers to sell her a silk shift that, he claims, belonged to his dead sister. Birgitta Valberg, whose acting until now has been only competent, makes the most of this dramatic moment. When the brother gently lays the shift across her outstretched arms, Märeta knows that Karin is dead. We hold our breath because a hint of recognition on her part will mean her death. The asceticism that until now we have frowned upon serves her well. Acknowledging the rips and stains, the man points out the intricate and beautiful embroidery. At this instant Märeta, who has not raised her eyes from the shift, draws back almost imperceptibly so that he can not touch it again. Her voice as steady as her face, she says, "I shall ask the master what might be a fitting reward for such a costly garment." Her irony does not alert the profferer. Then, she raises her glance. She does not look into the eyes of her daughter's murderer, however; she turns and leaves. Outside, she sits on the step and, burying her head in the shift in order to suffocate her sobs, rocks back and forth in pain. Then, stifling her grief, she hangs the shift around her neck and with great effort hoists the heavy metal bar into place across the thick door.

Returning to their bedroom, she apprises Töre of what she has discovered. When he steps outside, he finds Ingeri, who lays her head on his chest and begs him to kill her. His first concern is justice. "You *saw* it?" he asks. After she has related what happened, his face turns to stone and he orders her to prepare the bathhouse. He ascends a hill on top of which is a single, young birch silhouetted against the horizon. From a distance and a low angle we watch him—his murderous fury fueling his strength—wrestle it, the leaves whooshing, to the ground. There is something, as well, of the act of rape in this staging. Suddenly, the sky is vacant of the tree's slim form, and he is lying on top of it, breathing heavily. Rising, he shears off branches and returns with them to the bathhouse, where Ingeri has heated the stones. Ingeri attends as the birch whisks flail his naked body in a ritual of purification. (The sound in this and the next scene is almost deafeningly amplified.) Afterwards, he dons his leather apron and orders Ingeri to bring him his slaughtering knife; these are animals to be butchered. He then joins Märeta, who is waiting at the door. Unbarring it, the two of them enter.

Töre first removes the bag from beneath the sleeping mute's arm and empties it, disclosing Karin's possessions. Then the patient executioner sits in his thronelike chair and drives his huge knife into the table so that it is near at hand. (Remarkably, the trio remain asleep.) Now Töre reminds us not of Jesus, but of a vengeful God. When the brothers awaken at dawn, they try to flee. Töre attacks and, after a struggle in which he himself receives slashes to his back and shoulder, drives his knife into the heart of the mute. Almost as if he were again grappling with the birch, Töre wrestles the other brother to the floor and strangles him; seen through the hearth's flames, they seem to be making love. The terror-stricken boy flees into Märeta's arms. Töre rises and wrenches him from her embrace. Lifting him above his head, he heaves the child against the shelved wall, killing him instantly (if not convincingly).[52] He bends over the boy's body and is suddenly repentant. Surveying the scene, he stares at his hands and says, "God have mercy on me for what I have done!" He goes out, leaving the now childless Märeta hugging the dead boy and crying quietly.

Töre herds the household onto the road to retrieve Karin's body. (The sound and/or image of running water is in virtually every remaining shot.) When they reach her, Märeta brushes the dirt from her face, and she and Töre try to embrace her. At last, he rises and walks (away from the camera) down the hill to the stream's edge. There he falls to his knees and grovels in the dirt. (Again, the long shot forces our empathic imaginations to reach out.) Sitting up, his back to us, he looks heavenward. As the camera dollies close enough so that we can see the gash in his shoulder, von Sydow, for the first time, makes Töre fully human, makes his pain—like that felt by Block and Jöns just before the witch is burned—move us to tears. Convulsed with grief, with doubt, with outrage at his own murderous hands, he asks his God how He, just and merciful, could allow the death of innocent Karin and permit his revenge? "I don't understand you!" But Töre's faith and need for a meaningful and just universe sustain him and compel him to add, "Yet, now I beg your forgiveness . . . [because] I know of no other way of being reconciled with my hands. . . . I know of no other way to live." As penance for his sin, he promises to employ his murderous hands building a church on this spot. His body conveys the rest. He stands, raises his arms over his head with palms up and fingers stretched apart, and then slowly drops them to his side. Has God heard? Does He care?

The heretofore excluded sounds of birds return. Märeta and Frida lift Karin, whose head is upside down in the frame—the angle Bergman frequently uses for close-ups of the dead or dying. Suddenly, from the sandy spot on which her head had rested comes a trickle of water that nudges its way down the hill toward the larger stream. The monk kneels, and Ingeri gets down and baptizes her face in the widening stream. She has witnessed the Christian God's power and is instantly converted, giving her soul and that of the new life within her to Him. Faith has sprung from evil and death: God has sacrificed the innocent and the guilty to convert a pagan and her line to Christianity, to enlarge the protagonist's knowledge of himself, and to unify a family—Töre and the smiling Märeta, together again, fully accept their foster daughter and her child as theirs. The tension that has built relentlessly is released with the sound of the spring's frolicking waters and of the nondiegetic choral singing of a religious chant, which foreshadows the devotion that will take place on this spot. The film ends, looking down from above on this holy place and moment.

Even though years later Bergman mocked *The Virgin Spring*'s "totally unanalyzed idea of God" (*BB,* 41), when he finished it he considered it one of his best. Its power and art were recognized by

Hollywood; the Academy of Arts and Sciences named it the Best Foreign Film of 1960.

Chronologically, *The Devil's Eye* (1960) is Bergman's next film, but because thematically it is more closely linked to films that I shall be analyzing in chapter 5, I shall discuss it there.

THROUGH A GLASS DARKLY

Although Bergman published it as the first film of a trilogy, *Through a Glass Darkly* (1961), whose first title was *Wallpaper,*[53] was originally intended to be the second part of a trilogy that commenced with *The Virgin Spring* and concluded with *Winter Light* (Sjöman, 6).[54] "I never planned [*Through a Glass Darkly, Winter Light,* and *The Silence*] as a suite. They just followed one another" (*BB,* 150). In it, as in *The Virgin Spring,* God's nature is clarified as He again sacrifices a young woman named Karin to benefit Bergman's alter ego(s).

Borrowing from Strindberg, Bergman characterizes this and several of his subsequent films as "chamber plays"—that is, in them, as in chamber music, the structure is simplified and the number of instruments vastly reduced, permitting us to concentrate on the timbre and musical line of each. Many of his earlier stories had employed large casts involved in complicated situations set decades, even centuries ago. *Through a Glass Darkly* is a contemporary drama, employing a quartet of actors, in which more than ever character is plot. The rigorously simplified and focused situations in this film and the ones that follow permit Bergman to create hyper-intense, wincingly painful dramas in which desperate or guilt-ridden intimates discover ugly truths about themselves and each other. Ironically, though many of *Through a Glass Darkly*'s dramatic moments occur during witheringly candid conversations, Bergman is also intent on revealing how words can be used to disguise feelings. We recall his comment that, as a child, most crippling to his psyche was the disturbing disjunction between what his mother said her feelings were and what he sensed she actually felt. This cognitive-emotional asynchronism is at work here. Twice in the film a character accuses another of not feeling what he says he feels. Even the Latin term, "constructio ad sensum," that 17-year-old Minus (Lars Passgård) is asked to define relates to this: "a grammatically correct construction is changed to suit the context."

Through a Glass Darkly's first movement opens with a vigorous but dour passage from J.S. Bach's Suite No. 2 in D Minor for Violincello, a montage of the placid sea mirroring—the film's literal title is *As If in a Mirror,* but see 1 Corinthians 13:12 for the source of the English title—bright, fleecy clouds, and then a shot of four swimmers splashing and shouting in the water off an island.[55] Chill air, however, soon sends the bathers heading for shore along the jetty that, like a finger, points to where gray sea and sky imperceptibly merge (see fig. 17). The youngest members of the quartet, Karin (Harriet Andersson) and Minus, are sent to fetch milk from a neighboring farm. This gives Martin (Max von Sydow), Karin's husband and a medical doctor, his first opportunity to talk privately with David (Gunnar Björnstrand), Karin and Minus's father. David, a novelist, has only this day returned from Switzerland. Martin informs him that the schizophrenic Karin has relapsed, and that her condition has been diagnosed as "relatively incurable." Bergman dollies in on David's reaction. He swallows hard and hugs his own shoulders against the chill of the air, and of Martin's news. The fishnet David is holding suggests his unwanted enmeshment; had he received Martin's letter informing him of Karin's condition, he would not have returned home. Martin is aware of David's aversion not only to being involved but to being inordinately important to Karin, and he sees himself, mistakenly, as the only secure point in his wife's life.

On the way to the farm Minus (projecting his own ambitions) shares with Karin the hope that David will write a "great" novel, not just another commercially successful one. But on the return journey Minus, his legs too long for his pants, his turtleneck shirt too short to tuck in, confesses his sexual apprehensions to his noticeably overly fond sister. Girls cannot possibly be interested in him, he says. Suddenly, he plops himself down, spilling some of the milk he is carrying on the black rocks. The suggestion of an involuntary ejaculation—recall Bergman's first, explosive experience—is inescapable. In a state of fury and frustration, and sounding like other adolescents in Bergman's films of this period, he orders Karin to stop kissing and pawing him and informs her that her sunbathing half-naked makes him sick, and that he is disgusted by the way women smell, move, and stick out their stomachs. But, he adds, bursting into tears and not resisting Karin's embrace, what really "tears him up inside" is not being able to talk to his father about his erupting thoughts and feelings. (The fact, which we learn later, that his mother is also schizophrenic must

The Seventh Seal. AB Svensk Filmindustri

Through a Glass Darkly. AB Svensk Filmindustri

exaggerate his apprehensiveness.) His voice breaking with his heart, he stares at the sea and says, "If only I could talk with Papa, but he's so wrapped up in himself," an image that calls up the earlier image of David hugging himself. To Minus's credit, he acknowledges that in this he takes after his father. Later, in fact, he observes that "each of us is in his own cube," an image reinforced by the island (which keeps before us the "horrible fact of our solitude"), by the summer house's thick-walled, cell-like rooms, and by Bergman's propensity for isolating his characters in the frame.

The reunion and the loveliness of the evening inspire David to prepare dinner outside. While they are setting the picnic table in front of the house, the sense grows that the gaiety is forced and that words are out of sync with feelings. Martin cuts his finger and, sucking on it, complains, "I can't bear hurting my fingers."[56] But when Karin shows concern for it, he pooh-poohs the wound. Then David, having just confessed how homesick he grew in Switzerland, informs them that, in spite of his previous promise to stay home, he is leaving for Dubrovnik to lead a cultural tour. The insistent conviviality is replaced by a reproachful silence, which David says makes him feel "like a criminal." Matters grow worse when he distributes gifts, all of which, it turns out, are inappropriate (Minus guesses that they were an afterthought and probably purchased when David landed in Stockholm). As the gifts are being opened, David, on the pretext of needing tobacco for his pipe, visits his room. The static camera outside his open door doubly frames his pacing frantically in and out of view. The feeling of his being trapped in his cube/personality is overpowering. Suddenly, his hands grab his mouth and he tries to stifle the most hair-raising, inconsolable cry ever heard from a male in a film. Again, the long shot, because it does not thrust the character's anguish in our faces but forces our imaginations to pursue it, heightens the impact. At the same time, it respects the mystery of this man who, we will eventually learn, in spite of his determination to be strong and to care for people who need and love him, finds their emotional demands intolerable. (Bergman's sympathy for David is indicated by his placement in front of the window with his back to us and with his arms extended in a cruciform stance.) Wiping away his tears, David returns to his family, who thank him effusively for his gifts and then perform for him the play Minus has written and all have rehearsed.

The Artistic Haunting, or, The Tomb of Illusions tells of a young prince-artist who visits the tomb of a 13-year-old princess forgotten by her husband. The princess emerges and informs him that if he wants her love he must join her in death. He accepts, but when she returns to the tomb to wait for him, he changes his mind because he realizes he needs the world's acclaim. "Well, that's life!" he announces. Besides, he can transform this adventure into an opera in which, of course, his prince *will* choose oblivion. Minus's message registers on David's face, but he hides his discomfort and applauds, shouting, "Author! Author!" When the others go inside, David remains outside, sitting at the picnic table, smoking his pipe, and listening to the chatter coming from the house. As the sun's last rays dissolve behind him, we are sure he is reflecting on his failure as a parent.

While they are preparing for bed, Martin learns that Karin is disturbed that Minus's play upset her father, a concern that, in turn, upset Minus. Putting on his glasses—as we see in *Brink of Life,* where Cecilia's husband Anders wears glasses, they are Bergman's sign for distancing oneself from reality—Martin pressures her into saying she loves him and then reassures her that he will protect her from her fears. (She knows, however, that he does not believe in her fantasies, such as the "sniffing wolves with bared fangs.") In bed—now without his glasses—this sex-starved man, who is considerably older than his wife, whispers, "Dearest little girl. Dear one, I love you," and adds what both know is untrue, "You can never upset me." Turning from his tender advances, Karin utters the familiar "Forgive me," and then says, "Good night."

In this and the next few films Bergman uses illness to signal a character's spiritual and psychological deformity. In his room David is experiencing an anxiety attack (or pain from an ulcer). Unable to sleep, he sets to revising, word by purple word, his latest romantic novel. (In contrast, as we shall see, his diary's prose is simple and brutally direct.) After a moment, however, he looks up from his editing and says, "Oh my God!" Seemingly, this is his acknowledgment that his reason for neglecting his family, his "art," is a sham: he knows that his work is second-rate, and that he uses it as an excuse to escape his family responsibilities.

The cry of gulls—they sound as if they are killing or being killed—awakens Karin, whose hearing, we are told, has grown hypersensitive since her electric shock treatment. Burying her head under her pillow does not shield her from either these cries or her imagined voices. Feeling herself called, she steals out of the room to the front room upstairs. There, she drops her robe and, dressed only in her white nightgown and sandals, presses her ear to a vaginal-looking rip in the wrinkled, discolored wallpaper. The light bouncing off the rippled surface of the sea, which is visible through the window, animates the wallpaper's pattern of wanton-looking leaves, making them look like hellish flames (see fig. 18). A melancholy foghorn periodically moans.[57] Then she (and we) hear whispering behind the wallpaper. Karin returns to the center of the room, falls to her knees, rubs the inside of her thighs, and writhes in pleasure as she reaches a sexual climax. Afterward, she puts on her robe and goes downstairs to visit her father.

We may recall Anne intruding and sitting like a child on Fredrik's lap (*Smiles of a Summer Night*) as Karin sits on David's lap and asks him to read from his manuscript. He begs off reading, carries her to his bed, and tucks her in. "Just like when I was little," she says, and falls asleep immediately. Minus appears at the open window—he does not enter his father's cube—and invites him to help take in the nets.

Outside, joyous at being alone with his father, Minus shows off, talks too loudly and fast, and, after trying to diminish the hurt his play may have caused, reveals—Bergman lends Minus his own experience during the summer of 1940—that he cannot stop writing; 13 plays and an opera have spilled out of him. Is this the way it is for David, he queries. Discomfited by his recent revelation about his own so-called art and the compulsive ease of his son's literary output, David answers no, but he has the good grace to say—echoing Bergman's father's comment about *The Seventh Seal*—that he liked Minus's play "very much."

Karin awakens and, again driven by her voices, furtively removes her father's diary from his desk drawer. (In the foreground, David's black-rimmed eyeglasses evoke him.) She reads the last diary entry aloud: "Her illness is incurable, with bright patches. I have long suspected it, but the certainty is nevertheless more than I can bear. To my horror I find I'm curious. The desire to know its course and the details of her gradual disintegration. To use her." She closes the diary and stares at its cover, then slips it back into the drawer. The cello enters for the second time, adding unfathomable sadness to the revulsion and betrayal she must be feeling. The camera closes in as, childlike, the tip of her thumb slips into her mouth and she gazes out the window. Somewhere out there is her beloved, psychologically rapacious father.

When she returns to her room, the hurt comes out in a restrained whimper; it is not the shallow whining that Harriet Andersson gave to Monika, Anne (*Sawdust and Tinsel*), and Doris (*Dreams*). When Martin asks the reason for it, she confesses to having read the diary but cannot bring herself to repeat what David said about studying her. *Is* her illness "incurable?" she asks. Putting on his glasses, Martin assures her that David misunderstood him. Shifting the subject, Karin asks Martin if he would not be happier with a warm woman who would give him children. He replies emphatically, "It's *you* I love. . . . I don't *want* anyone else," and then he takes refuge in brushing his teeth. "You always say and do exactly the right things, but it's always wrong," she says. He turns to Karin, her image also behind him in the sink's mirror, and replies with impassive directness, "If I do, it's out of love." Unable to meet his gaze, she says coldly, "Those who really love do right by those they love." In a tone of sad vindictiveness, he answers, "Then you don't love *me*." Surprised by his forthrightness, she stares at him with something close to hate.

The film's second movement is largely structured around Karin's three psychotic-sexual episodes. Martin and David have gone off in the motorboat to get groceries. Karin teases Minus about a girly magazine she discovers him reading, then helps him with his Latin,[58] and, finally, informs him about her wonderful experiences with the "others" in the upstairs room to which a stern voice calls her every morning. Taking him up to the room, she explains that when she is here alone she passes through the wallpaper, which gives way like leaves into a bright room. That room is inhabited by people—some of whose faces are radiant, some demonic—who are waiting for God to emerge from the closet. So safe, so close to perfect love and true communication does she feel there that her feelings verge on ecstasy. She can barely endure the waiting. This is why she has sacrificed her relationship with Martin, whom she finds weak. Sane enough to entertain the possibility that she has imagined it all, and sounding like Antonius Block's final prayer, she says longingly that it "*must* be real!" When, however, Minus says that none of it is real to him, she turns on him and orders him out of the room. A moment later, though, she behaves as if none of this had occurred.

A little later, down on the beach, Karin suddenly and supranaturally senses a coming storm and hurries off. After a moment Minus pursues her, searching everywhere. By now we know the house so well that

Bergman places his camera in one spot and lets the sound the character makes locate him: the camera is at the far end of the downstairs hall, opposite the front door. Minus runs in, disappears to check Karin's room and the upstairs wallpapered room, returns downstairs, and runs back outside. This technique also creates the feeling that the character is at the end of a tether that invariably will be reeled in by the director and/or the Director. Minus finds her at last, curled up on a wet plank in the rotten hulk of the beached ship where, undoubtedly, both have often played. Like the upstairs room, this decayed, womb-like hull represents both Karin's disintegration and regression. The disintegration is clear enough to audiences, but what is involved in her regression may not be. Because she has found that loving others is risky and unsatisfying, Karin feels that only God, mixed up in her mind with her father, can satisfy her longing for the kind of total and unambiguous love she experienced as an infant. Short of that, the only unthreatening and reliable love is with herself, that is, masturbation. After herself, her narcissism permits her to accept blood kin, her alter ego Minus, who, because he is younger and sexually frustrated, she can overmaster. So when Minus now approaches and crouches over his silent sister, she, grinning demonically, suddenly grasps him to her. He recoils, but erotic urges win out.

Karin, whose bizarre and dramatic experiences rivet our attention, is, as Robin Wood rightly judges, the film's "emotional center" (Wood, 107), and Minus's fate, like Hjördis's in *Brink of Life,* is the film's ultimate center of concern. But Bergman is most interested, as he establishes in the scene in the anchored boat, in his adult alter ego, the emotionally crippled David. Martin, in an uncharacteristic burst of righteous anger, has waited until after lunch to confront David with what he wrote about Karin in his diary. David confesses his interest in studying Karin's illness, and Martin attacks his father-in-law's "absolutely perverted insensibility." David replies that he loves Karin, but Martin, who, as we have seen, when pushed beyond his sense of rightness can lash out, scoffs, "You . . . *love*! In your emptiness there's no room for feeling." Still smarting from Karin's accusation, Martin modifies her words and applies them to David: "You know how to express things in just the right words, but one thing you haven't a clue about is life itself. . . . You're a genius at pretexts and excuses." "What am I to do?" asks David helplessly. In a tone as close to loathing as he is capable, Martin answers, "Write your book [and achieve] what you want most: a name as an author. Then you won't sacrifice your daughter in vain."[59] His anger dissipating into frustration, he sits beside David (partly hiding him) and calmly charges, "You've got a God to whom you kowtow in your novels, but your faith and your doubt are equally unconvincing. . . . You're empty and clever and now you think you'll fill your emptiness with Karin's extinction. How are you going to mix God up in all this? He'll be more inscrutable." David steps to the back of the boat and, confident that everyone is as weak and selfish, though not as brutally candid, about his feelings as he is, asks Martin if at *some time* he has not wished Karin dead. The logic of his insight, Karin's earlier intuition that Martin would be happier with a "warm" woman, and our own observations of the frustrated Martin make the suggestion plausible, but Martin fires back with convincing—if possibly self-deceiving—rectitude, "Preposterous! . . . You're grotesque!" "That's how *you* see it," replies David. His eyes watering, Martin says slowly, "I love her. I can only stand by helpless and watch her being transformed into a wretched, tormented animal." David returns to sit beside Martin. In a tone completely devoid of self-pity and revealing a frightening will power, he confesses to Martin that in Switzerland he hired a car and set off "calmly" one afternoon to drive full speed over a cliff. However, the "engine stalled [and] the car hung with its front wheels over the edge. I crawled out, shaking all over." We know from Bergman's having dramatized again and again his belief in God's intervention that what David has described is a miracle, though, like Antonius Block, he does not recognize it as such. God intervened to save him. "Why tell me this?" asks Martin. David's stirring answer reminds us of how many of Bergman's characters—Albert, Antonius Block, Isak Borg, Fredrik Egerman, Hjördis—have had to teeter on (or near) the brink of death before mustering the courage to shatter their life-suffocating illusions: "Because, out of the void within me something was born . . . a love . . . for Karin and Minus and you." We are impressed, too, when David affectionately grasps Martin's arm. Our gratification is diminished, however, by what we have seen of David since he returned from Switzerland.

The image of Karin pulling Minus down on top of her is followed with startling abruptness by one of rain pouring furiously into the hull. Besides setting mood, the rain establishes that some time has elapsed since the incest. When at last Karin asks weakly for help, Minus hurries to the house and to his room, where he snatches the blankets off his bed. Before leaving, however, he falls to his knees, looks heavenward, and implores, "God!" The cello's unassuageable lament keens out and persists into the next image of Minus sheltering Karin in his arms.

The rain and music stop. At the sound of the motorboat, Minus runs to fetch David and Martin. When they arrive, Karin tells Martin that she wants to talk privately with her father. Offended and possibly sensing the incest from Minus's behavior, Martin leaves to call the mainland for the helicopter ambulance. Karin tells David, who remains at a distance from her, that she wants to stay in the hospital, but without any more shock treatments; she can't stand "going back and forth" between two worlds. She also tells him about her voices and the room upstairs and hints at the incest. Coming, at last, to stand beside her at the ladder to the hatch,[60] David looks down into her upturned face and asks her "to forgive" him for having fled to Switzerland to write his book at the onset of her illness (which, he adds, resembled her mother's).[61] Is his book a good one? she asks. With a smile of self-contempt, he rounds out Minus's cube metaphor: "We draw a magic circle and shut out everything that doesn't agree with our secret games. Each time life breaks the circle . . . we draw a new circle and build a new defense." Karin replies soothingly, "Poor little Papa." "Yes, poor little Papa, forced to live in reality," responds David, putting a loving arm around his daughter and stroking her hair.

As they are reentering the house, David sees Minus hiding and calls to him, but Minus darts away. Martin's physical awkwardness reveals his increasing insecurity, and at her first chance, Karin escapes his supervision. David and Martin, medical bag in hand, search for her and find her standing in the middle of the upstairs room, speaking to the wallpaper and the closet. Martin pushes past David and goes in. In spite of Martin's imploring look, David remains outside the room—it is as if he were in a closet—watching Karin through the partially open door. Fascinated but frozen, he is unable to enter, and in one shot his shadow is seen retreating slightly. Karin tells the distraught Martin that God's arrival is imminent. When he insists that God is *not* going to emerge from the closet, she orders him to be silent or leave. When he stays, she asks him to kneel with her in prayer. He kneels, rests his head on her shoulder, and repeatedly whispers, "Dearest." The awaited moment seems to arrive. A deafening roar—the motor of the descending helicopter ambulance—is heard. During this acoustic climax, the closet door, seemingly set in motion by the copter's vibrations, swings open. Behind the enrapt Karin's right shoulder we see the helicopter descending past the window like a spider on an invisible thread. Suddenly, Karin's glance drops to the floor and her expression turns to revulsion. She opens her mouth, but her terror at the pursuing vision causes her scream to stick in her throat so that she gags and flees into the window well. Frantically brushing the loathsome vision off her, she recoils from the wall, where it has subsequently crawled, and runs out of the room. Halfway down the stairs she comes face to face with Minus, her recent victim. She stops, permitting the men chasing her to grab her. They all hold her down as Martin hurriedly injects her with a sedative. She struggles but soon becomes groggy and begins describing her horrifying experience. God, she says, emerged from the closet in the form of a spider with "a horrible, stony face"—David's face is behind her—and He tried to force Himself into her genitals. When she prevented Him, He crawled onto her breasts and then onto the wall, which is when she fled.[62] The ambulance man's authoritative knock at the front door—like Death's arrival at the knight's castle in *The Seventh Seal*—ends her narration. Donning a pair of sunglasses to mitigate the painful light of reality (and symbolizing her final withdrawal), Karin follows Martin out the front door. Sobbing, Minus slides down in the narrow space between the wall and stove but, at the sound of the copter lifting off, hastens outside to watch it disappear silently into the heaven of merged sea, sky, and setting sun. The plaintive cello, heard for the last time, hurries us to the film's conclusion.

For the first time, Minus enters his father's room. Employing a birth metaphor, he tells him that when he clung to Karin in the wrecked boat, "reality burst and I tumbled out. It's like a dream, though real. Anything can happen, Papa—*anything*—I can't live like this, Papa." David, whose good intentions repeatedly have been defeated by his emotionally crippling narcissism, realizes that his son's sanity depends on him. Looking at him, he sternly insists that Minus *can* live if he has something to hold onto. "And what could that be?" inquires the agnostic youth. "A God? Give me some proof of God." David hesitates. "You can't," says Minus. David answers that he can. He "hopes," he says, "that love exists as something real." "A special kind of love?" the boy probes, afraid of the answer. "All kinds!" asserts David, relieving Minus of his guilt over the incest, "the highest and the lowest, the absurd and the beautiful. *All* kinds of love."[63] "So, love is the proof [of God's existence]?" asks Minus. "I don't know if love proves God's existence or if love is God Himself," says David, but "that thought helps me in my emptiness and grubby despair."

"Say more," pleads the boy. "Suddenly, emptiness changes to wealth, despair to life," continues David. "It's like a reprieve from the death penalty." Then Karin, concludes Minus, "is surrounded by God since we love her . . . [and] that can help her?" "I think it can," says David, looking Minus in the eye with insistent conviction. As Minus now looks away, his relief is evident. He asks David if he minds if he goes for a run. (Unlike the film's first image, which showed four people almost swallowed up by the sea, in this scene a beautiful sunset has been visible through the window behind David and Minus.) "See you later," says David, and he leaves the room to make dinner. Minus stares after him and, in the voice of someone who has just experienced a miracle, says, "Papa *talked* to me!"

For the moment at least, David has lived up to his responsibilities, but Minus is saved as much, if not more, by the simple act of communing with his father as by his father's philosophy. (Minus is the last troubled adolescent that Bergman would study; Bergman's subsequent films deal with younger or older children.) Nevertheless, at work has been a very active, loving God who has prevented David's suicide, saved Minus's sanity and faith in God, and brought son and father together by sacrificing, once again, a sexually charged young girl. Bergman repudiates this vision of a loving God in his next film, *Winter Light*. In that film he acknowledges what increasingly has been implicit in his stories: a vision of "the Christian God as something destructive and fantastically dangerous, something . . . bringing out in [man] dark destructive forces instead of the opposite."

Before passing on to the next film, tribute must be paid to Harriet Andersson, none of whose previous roles had shown the breadth needed to play Karin, a role that required the actress to convey, among other emotions and attitudes, nubile innocence, childlike defenselessness, the coyness and seductiveness of a femme fatale, demonic cunning, and heart-stopping terror. Her Karin, along with her Agnes in *Cries and Whispers,* are two of the greatest performances ever put on film.

WINTER LIGHT

Having not much liked playing the villainous Vergérus in *The Magician,* one can sympathize with the 53-year-old Gunnar Björnstrand's distaste for the sometimes vicious, sometimes childish Rev. Tomas Ericsson, his role in *Winter Light* (1963). The enervated Tomas, odiously and incurably narcissistic, is incapable of caring deeply for others and barely able to hide his teeming self-hate and suppressed rage behind his priestly garb and behavior. The single appealing quality of this "all-too-horribly-sane" (Wood, 112) but self-deceived narcissist is that he is beginning to face some of the blistering truths about himself and his belief in God.

Not without ambition, the young Tomas had acquiesced to his pious parents' desire that he become a pastor. Tomas packed the pews with his message that "God is love; love is God." He married a woman who, like his mother, "protected [him] from everything [that was] evil . . . ugly . . . [and] dangerous" to his vision of himself, God, or God's world. Tomas claims to have been "crazy in love" with her, but what he loved was actually his image of her and the support she provided. The cynical church organist, Fredrik Blom (Olof Thunberg), asserts that "Tomas has as much knowledge of human nature as my galoshes," and (in the screenplay) that his wife "hadn't a genuine feeling in her whole body, not an honest thought." When she died suddenly (five years before the action commences), Tomas thought about suicide but did not take his life, he rationalized, because people needed him. We suspect that one of his reasons was his belief that God doted on him. After a few years, Tomas took up with another mothering lover, Märta Lundberg (Ingrid Thulin), a grade school teacher who physically resembles his deceased wife. Märta, however, does not believe in God and refuses to play priestess to Tomas's illusions. This is partly why Tomas has been withdrawing from the relationship. Determined to marry him and confident that she can teach him how to love, Märta nevertheless puts up with his rejection and clingingly exploits his childlike dependency. The film opens during the town of Mittsunda's Sunday noon church service on a winter day; Märta is in attendance and even takes communion. She is there not only to make the small congregation—nine people—a little less so, but out of her desperate need to be near Tomas.

Dressed in his black cassock, white bib collar, and black horn-rimmed glasses, the reverend stands almost exactly in the center of the austere, seemingly unheated church's front arch. He is flanked on either side by windows that admit a chill, gray light that robs the setting of mystery.[64] His mechanical mouthing of the communion text, the perfect symmetry of the architecture, and the flat, shadowless light communicate a deathly stasis. When he passes with the wafers and then the chalice, the camera, often behind the communicants, permits us to study the skeptical Tomas's expression as he tries to discover in each face the secret of his owner's belief. As he finishes the service, his head slowly drops forward from disappointment and dizziness. Tomas has influenza, a symbol of his being infected with doubt.[65] Märta and the sexton, Algot Frövik (Allan Edwall), a hunchbacked little man and the single parishioner shot from behind and above, are the only ones to show concern.[66]

The service concluded, Tomas, wracked by fits of coughing, retires to the church vestry, a cell-like room with thick walls, a deeply recessed, barred window, a grandfather clock, and a large carving of the crucified Jesus (the one used in *The Seventh Seal* and *The Virgin Spring*). Tomas cannot go home to bed because he is responsible for holding Vespers at 3:00 P.M. in nearby Frostnäs. Sexton Frövik stops in because he has something important to say to Tomas, but Tomas, who may feel an aversion to the deformed man because of his suffering, puts him off until they meet later in Frostnäs. Mrs. Persson (Gunnel Lindblom), with her husband Jonas (Max von Sydow) reluctantly in tow, enters and sits across from Tomas. The slim, curly-haired fisherman does not look at Tomas while his wife tactfully tries to explain his to her incomprehensible fear of man's destructive nature.[67] Jonas has read that the Chinese, who have been brought up to hate, will soon have the atom bomb, and this news has heightened his anxiety and depression. When Tomas offers trust in God as the antidote, Mrs. Persson's lip drops and Jonas's face registers insult. He turns and impales Tomas's gaze with his own. Conscious of the inadequacy of his platitude and unable to endure this defiant but longing-filled stare, Tomas drops his eyes (see fig. 19). Then, coming around from behind his desk, he sits on its edge, looks down at Jonas, and starts again. He acknowledges that occasionally reality overwhelms our peace of mind and that God seems too remote to help, but, he insists, "we must live!" Jonas fires back, "Why must we live?" Again, Tomas lowers his eyes, and almost inaudibly, he mutters that he does not know. Jonas politely but contemptuously notes that they are wasting each other's time and moves toward the door. Tomas, however, makes him promise that, after he has delivered his wife home, he will return to talk further. The doorway of the vestry frames the trinity of despairing sufferers: Tomas, Jonas, and the Jesus on the wall.

Through a Glass Darkly. AB Svensk Filmindustri

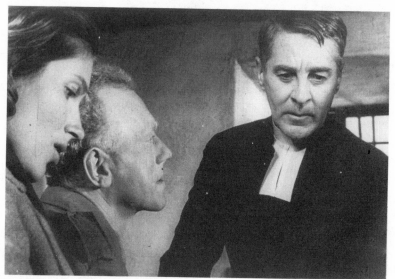

Winter Light. AB Svensk Filmindustri

By himself, Tomas takes out a letter Märta has sent him, considers reading it, but puts it aside and goes out to the altar. Confronting the Jesus suspended on a cross between God's knees, he announces, "Absurd." Concerned about his illness, Märta comes in with a hot drink. He tries to brush her off, but she pursues him into the vestry. She puts her arm around his shoulder, pats his hand, rubs his cheek, and caressingly whispers, "Poor Tomas!" From the first, subtly and not so subtly, Bergman makes Märta, whose excessive, selfless love is oppressive, unappealing. He amplifies the sound when she blows her running nose and calls attention to her continuous dabbing at it, to her swollen eyes, her homely, high-cheekboned face, her unattractive, thick-lensed eyeglasses, her loping walk, her sailor cap, and her big, slightly shabby, fleecy sheepskin coat, which itself magnifies the impression of her suffocating warmth. (That her aggressively oppressive love is distasteful to the germ-fearing Bergman is conveyed when he has Märta take Tomas's head between her mittened hands and, indifferent to catching his flu, kiss him repeatedly on the lips.)

Although Tomas balks at her attentions, he is happy to have someone to confide in. Between spasms of coughing, he covers his face and, nearly in tears, cries, "God's silence. . . . What am I to do?" Reflecting on that morning's service, he asks her why she, who does not believe in God, took communion. "It's supposed to be a love-feast," she replies playfully. She, in turn, inquires if he has read her letter and is annoyed to learn that he has not. Sensing this, his tone turns playful, the first indication, besides his having confided his most personal thoughts to her, that he feels or ever has felt anything for her. (Only in this brief exchange does Björnstrand exhibit the agile wit and charm characteristic of his earlier roles.) When she insists that if he wants her sympathy he must marry her (marriage will also prevent her from being sent to teach elsewhere), he says disingenuously, "Well, we'll see." "Yes, I know. You can't marry me because you don't love me," she says matter-of-factly. Seeing how worried he is about "God's silence," she hugs him again and tells him that God is silent because He does not exist, adding on her way out that what Tomas really needs is to "learn to love." "From *you?*" he asks brutally, turning to stare out the window. She pauses outside the vestry door, on the verge of tears.

Certain that if he can answer Jonas's doubts he will silence his own, Tomas impatiently whispers that Jonas "*must* come!" The grandfather clock unrelentingly hammers out the seconds "so that we feel [Tomas] has a temperature" (Sjöman, 217–18). Tomas sits at his desk and removes from his wallet three rough-proof photographs of his wife, whose resemblance to Märta is striking. He sighs, "My darling," and eases them back into his wallet. Then, putting on his glasses—which he did not need to look at the photographs—he pulls Märta's thick letter (she is excessive even here) from its envelope. As he begins to read, he is replaced by a frontal shot of Märta, sitting in front of a nakedly blank wall, speaking her letter directly at us. This startling, even assaultive device is filmed in literal time and is a quick, personalizing, and dramatic way of conveying the mass of information in the letter. (The germ of this device is in *To Joy,* in which Stig speaks aloud his thoughts and letters to *his* Märta, and, possibly, in Antoine Doinel's interview with the social worker in *The 400 Blows* [1959].) By framing her in this naked space and letting her visually and aurally establish the rhythm of the scene, Bergman lends her shocking charges greater weight; she exhibits an independence and aggressiveness that she seems unable to muster in Tomas's presence. Nevertheless, her nearly unblinking stare—she is not wearing her thick-lensed glasses—the ironical and unattractive smirk that twists her mouth, and her hair, which is worn as the late Mrs. Ericsson wore hers, are all slightly off-putting. She talks about the previous summer, after she and Tomas had lived together for almost two years, when she was stricken from head to foot with an oozing eczema.[68] She reminds Tomas that not only did he not pray for her relief from the eczema but he became so disgusted he began to avoid her. Worse than discovering that he did not love her was the realization that he might be incapable of love. It was then that she realized he was also indifferent to Jesus. (Bergman, recall, was jealous of Jesus because his father was more concerned with Him than with his younger son. Tomas would share that jealousy, as well as find Jesus' suffering distasteful and His unachievable compassion a reproach.) Then the atheist Märta asked God to indicate to her that her suffering and the strong body and spirit He had given her had meaning. Echoing Spegel (*The Magician*), she prayed, "Give my life meaning and I'll be your servant!" All of a sudden she realized that the task she sought was to help Tomas, though, she comments, she does not believe that this discovery had anything to do with her praying. She adds that she would also pray to find out how to show Tomas her love, but that she has too much self-respect ever to pray again. "Tomas," she concludes, "I love you and I live for you. Tame me and use me. . . . I have only one wish: to live for somebody." This final, gentle plea is almost drowned out as the narrative returns to the present and Tomas fumblingly shuffles and tries to force the multitude of pages—the sound is so amplified that it sounds like someone walking through dry leaves—back into their puny envelope. The pages do not cooperate—feelings out in the open cannot be neatly packed away and forgotten. Tomas ends up just pushing the letter aside.

Jonas arrives, still dressed in his Sunday best and still looking like a child made to stay after school.[69] Refusing to look Tomas in the eye, the fisherman waits out Tomas's small talk about boats and again bristles when Tomas suggests that he consult a psychiatrist. Tomas captures his attention at last when he describes the despair he felt after his wife died. But as he continues, Tomas becomes caught up in his own disintegrating faith. He buries his face in his hands, and, unlike David, who asserted a "truth" to save Minus, Tomas tells Jonas—who turns his head aside as if something foul-smelling has been shoved under his nose—that he is not only no good as a clergyman but that he now realizes he has been praying to an "echo-God who gave [him the] benevolent answers" he wanted to hear. When he finally had the courage to look at reality, Tomas's God "turned ugly, hideous—a spider God, a monster." How could a benevolent God have created so much pain and evil? For awhile he shielded his notion of God "from the light" (reality), but he now realizes that if he accepts the position that God does not exist, then evil just *is* and the dilemma dissolves. Tomas concludes, "What a relief! Death is just a snuffing out. . . . There is no creator." So struck is he with this construction that he is unaware of, and essentially unconcerned with, Jonas's departure from the vestry, his despair fueled. The camera dollies in on Tomas's astonished, pensive face as from the window the room is suddenly filled with sunlight. His earlier statement that he shielded himself and his notion of God "from the light" suggests that this burst of light is the sign of His approval of Tomas's arrival at a truer sense of reality. Stunned by his own illumination and loss, Tomas hoarsely echoes Jesus: "God, why hast thou forsaken me?" Walking out of the vestry, he steps up to the altar rail but suddenly collapses in a paroxysm of coughing. When he raises his head, the sunlight illuminates his face. "I am free . . . at last," he says quietly. His coughing, however, brings him to his knees. Märta, whom he has not seen standing nearby, descends upon him instantly, attacking him with her wet kisses. The frightened child-man's hand presses on her face while his fingers sink deep into the fur of her coat. Through waves of uncontrollable sobs he cries out that everything he has believed in is merely "imagination, dreams, lies." Märta's slobbering kisses continue. Finally, he regains his composure and rises, breaking up this Pietà. He has just callously rejected Märta's offer to accompany him to Frostnäs when, from the back of the church, an elderly woman parishioner, in a heartbroken voice, announces that Jonas Persson has shot himself in the head.[70] Ignoring Märta, Tomas gets his coat and rushes out to his car.

The following scene has a complex, if not paradoxical, effect. At the site of the suicide, we are suddenly out-of-doors and viewing Jonas's body from a distance and from a high angle. We are unable to hear the exchanges between the constables, the two boys who found the body, and Tomas and the ambulance men because of the amplified roar of the nearby icy stream.[71] The claustrophobia created by the previous scenes' subdued speech and tightly composed shots in closed-in spaces (Wood, 114) is exorcised, but the relief is undercut by the oppressive roar and the corpse. We both want and don't want to view the body. Bergman's long shot heightens that prurient, mixed desire while at the same time it respects Jonas's privacy and permits us to reflect on the cause of the tragedy: another self-involved Bergman protagonist is indirectly responsible for a death. Will the sacrifice help this protagonist better comprehend himself and his world and God? The situation in the final scene of *The Virgin Spring* is similar to this one but shot differently. In that film the stream near the corpse ripples away lyrically and we hear Töre cry out to the God in whom he unquestioningly believed. In *Winter Light* the stream—the only element in the scene registering rage—like Tomas's new conception of God, churns deafeningly, and human speech is inaudible. The feeling is one of absolute waste and meaninglessness. As the ambulance men remove Jonas, who is wrapped in a tarpaulin, Tomas tries to keep the frozen tarpaulin's flaps folded over the body, but he is as ineffectual in this as he was in returning Märta's letter to its envelope: certain things cannot be hidden. Märta walks up, and Tomas orders her to wait for him in his car. When he finally joins her, we feel sensory deprivation— it is like entering a vacuum. The silence is all the more deafening because Bergman expunges even Märta's voice as she talks to the unresponsive Tomas while he backs onto the highway.

On his way to inform Mrs. Persson, Tomas drops Märta at the schoolhouse where she lives. In no hurry to carry out his unpleasant duty, he asks her for an aspirin. She invites him inside. Waiting in the schoolroom, he sits down at one of the desks, a symbol of Bergman's belief that adults in general are emotionally stunted, and that Tomas in particular is an emotional child incapable of feeling deeply for anyone. Tomas's lack of deep wrinkles and his boyishly short "old Schoolboy haircut" (Sjöman, 61) reinforce this notion. Excessive as usual, Märta returns with a small drugstore. Though he lets her spoon-feed him cough medicine, he refuses her pills. His tone causes her to observe, "Sometimes you sound as if you hated me." When she begs to go with him, he brings her to tears by responding that he wants her to leave him alone. Then, without looking at her, but with his brightly lit face wearing an almost jauntily capricious smile, he loads the accumulated effect of the day's annoyance and pain into a matter-of-fact tone of voice and fires both barrels. It is the cruelest verbal assault in Bergman's films, and we are caught in the vicelike grip of embarrassment and fascination as Märta takes each shot full in the face. Tomas tells her, "I'm tired of your fondling, your good advice . . . your myopia, your fumbling hands, your timidity, your fussy endearments. You force me to busy myself with your ailments, your weak stomach, your eczema, your periods, your chilblains. I'm fed up with everything to do with you." His wife, he throws in, was everything Märta can never be, even though Märta "apes" her. Märta's surprise at his charge, and her simple response, "I didn't even know her," succinctly reveal Tomas's self-delusion. Removing her glasses and wiping her tear-filled eyes, the stunned teacher-mother instructs her cruel and incorrigible child, whom she sees, even though a blur, with inspired clarity: "I've done wrong from the start. Every time I've felt hatred for you I've changed it to pity. You'll never manage. You'll die of hate." (In *The Passion of Anna* Tomas's condition will be called "cancer of the soul.") Tomas lunges, grabs her arm, and spits out, "Can't you leave me in peace!" then heads for the door. But near it he returns and asks her—her hands are placed so that she seems to be praying—"Are you coming to church?" Losing both Father and mother in one day is too much: Tomas needs a crutch. That Märta recognizes his need is evident from her inquiry if he *really* wants her to come or if he is "just afraid again?" But Märta being Märta, she adds, "Of course I'll come. I have no choice." In most stories when the woman continues to love the man who mistreats her it means that he possesses some redeeming qualities. Here, Märta's obsessive need undermines any such conclusion.

Märta drives them to Mrs. Persson's. When Tomas enters the

house, Mrs. Persson leaves the children at the dinner table and closes the door so that they cannot hear her and Tomas. When Tomas informs her of what she seems to have been partly expecting, the pregnant woman eases herself down onto the stairs, and her immediate response is typical Bergman: "I'm alone then." Tomas offers to pray with her. At first she treats his offer as an impertinence, but then she softens her "No" to "No, thank you." Leaving, Tomas pauses on the porch to eavesdrop through the front window as Mrs. Persson, pausing over the dinner table, considers how to tell the children. He does not stay for the painful scene.

On the way to Frostnäs, Tomas and Märta have to wait as a threatening-looking train passes a crossing. Tomas takes that interlude to relate his childhood fears.[72] He does not speak directly to Märta again.

At Frostnäs, a madonna and child decorates the altar of the church and the vestry, not Christ supported by God.[73] And in contrast to the Mittsunda church, which was lit by the winter daylight, Sexton Frövik has warmly illuminated the Frostnäs church with candlelight. In the vestry Tomas asks Frövik what he wished to say to him that morning. Frövik, who obviously has diagnosed Tomas's spiritual problem, reminds Tomas of the time he asked Tomas what he should do when, because of his pain, he could not sleep; Tomas had told him to read the Gospels. Frövik says now that he did and found them good sleeping pills. (The film's one funny line; even Tomas laughs.) However, when he came to Christ's passion, he reflected that the crucified Christ's mere three hours or more of physical suffering were not as bad as the pain he, Frövik, suffers continuously. No, he continues, excusing his presumptuousness, the fact is that Jesus' greatest suffering came when he realized that his disciples had not grasped his teaching and fled or denied him. "To know that nobody understands. To be deserted just when you need someone." Frövik, his evocation of Jesus' doubt affecting even the unbeliever, goes on. "Yet, that wasn't the worst. When Jesus . . . cried out . . . 'God, my God, why hast thou forsaken me?' he thought his Father in heaven had deserted him. He thought his whole teaching was a lie. [That] horrible doubt just before he died . . . must have been when he suffered most. I mean God's silence." Almost in a trance, his pale face aging before our eyes, Tomas whispers, "Yes, yes." For the first time in his life, he is able to identify with Jesus.

Bergman told Vilgot Sjöman that he had "knowledge" that God exists, that he was "convinced that [intercession] is a reality," and that "one can cut oneself off from God" (26). Though Tomas has abandoned God, God has not abandoned Tomas. Like Antonius Block, who demands a sign and is sent a holy family, Tomas has been sent Frövik, who for Bergman "is an angel" (Sjöman, 32), the most Christ-like of all the God-sent intercessors who have assisted his confused, despairing protagonists. But God is not finished.

Sitting in the dark in a pew at the rear of the church, Märta is approached by the organist Blom, who is tipsy. Satan-like, he leans over her shoulder, disparages Tomas, and warns her to escape her unpromising life here. He then visits the vestry to inquire from Tomas if, since no one has arrived, there is to be a service. (If no more than three persons are in attendance, it is the custom not to hold a service.) He then retires to the organ loft to wait for "a sign" of Tomas's intent. Consulting his watch and slyly reminding Tomas that *someone,* Miss Lundberg, is in attendance, Frövik tells Tomas it is time to make his decision. Bergman cuts to Märta setting aside the last of her self-respect. She had said she would never pray again, but now she kneels. In extreme close-up, her face in silhouette so that we concentrate on her words, she half addresses God. "If only we were sure so that we dared show affection. If only we believed in a truth." As she adds, "If only we believed," there is an auditory overlap, and we see Tomas, his bent head in his hand almost exactly as Märta's is in her's, trying to decide. It is a communication remarkably like that in *Night Is My Future,* in which, unseen, Ingrid, at her father's funeral, communicates her confidence to the frightened Bengt in the church's organ loft and he begins to play. Tomas looks up and takes a deep breath—"That's all," says Bergman, "that's needed to indicate the new faith . . . stirring inside the parson" (Sjöman, 32). Delighted, Frövik (whose playful mannerisms keep this film from being a dreary, glacial drama) takes this as the signal. He jauntily snaps on the lights that indicate the service is to commence. Disappointed, but dutiful, Blom sends a joyous hymn swelling through the church. Tomas enters in his priestly garments and faces his congregation: Frövik and, in the rear, Märta. The camera dollies in on her now lovely face (without her glasses) and its barely hidden smile. Staring out at the congregation, but also into that interior screen of projected hopes that so many of Bergman's characters turn to, the film ends with Tomas intoning, "Holy, holy, holy, Lord God Almighty. All the earth is full of His glory." In contrast to *Through a Glass Darkly*'s exhilaratingly hopeful ending, the note of hope struck here is so faint as to be almost inaudible. But Tomas's voice is not that of someone grudgingly tolerant of a life he feels he has no choice but to slog through, or that of a broken man going through meaningless motions in a stale, defunct ritual. It evinces a more vital connection to the sacraments and to life, and it is infused with a willful, if almost imperceptible, freshness and a rekindled faith in a redefined God.

Bergman tells us that his father's taking communion for a sick pastor provided him not only with the ending of *Winter Light* but with a rule he has continued to obey: "*Irrespective of everything, you will hold communion. It is important to the churchgoer, but even more important to you. We shall have to see if it is important to God. If there is no other god than your hope as such, it is important to that god too*" (*BB*, 173–74; *ML*, 273).[74]

The austerely brilliant *Winter Light* is also a record of Bergman's own changing beliefs. Like Tomas, Bergman had previously conceived of God as a shaping, guiding, and protective force. God especially "liked" Bergman, though in making him who he was and in spurring him to become "the best director in the world," He was responsible for the aggression that destroyed Bergman's "connections to other people" (Jones, 57). And His "enormous" (Jones, 56) eye, observing Bergman's every act and thought, was disconcerting and guilt-engendering. Renouncing this conception of God, says Bergman, was like coming "out of prison" (Jones, 60). Almost overnight "I changed completely," accepting both "life as it is with its greatness and its cruelty" (Jones, 58), and himself. Now, he was able to say that Ingmar Bergman "is like that. Now, try to live with him . . . accept him . . . like him" (Jones, 59). Feeling a new self-confidence, Bergman even lost his "literary inferiority complex. I lost, above all, the fear of not being up-to-date and modern."[75] He could make films about other matters, and in the way he wanted. Beginning work on his new film, *The Silence,* he felt that "only now . . . am I starting to be myself" (Sjöman, 206). It was "no longer [a] question of 'God, why?'" (Prouse, 30).

Bergman once claimed that he had nothing in common with Tomas other than their similar experiences of coming to a new conception of God (Sjöman, 33). I do not believe he would maintain that today. What still depresses us at the end of *Winter Light* is our realization that Tomas's pathological narcissism provides little hope for any fundamental improvement in his character. Märta's love, his ego, and a sliver of faith will ensure that he endures, but he and Märta "will have a terrible life" (*Playboy*, 68). The only hope here lies in Bergman's moving closer to the realization that "we're saved not by God, but by love. That's all we can hope for" (*Playboy*, 68).

That is one of the messages in his next films.

5

Fortunate Falls, Mothers, and Dreams

The Devil's Eye, a comedy made between *The Virgin Spring* and *Through a Glass Darkly,* embodies Bergman's pre–*Winter Light* view of God as benevolent and intrusive. This chapter will begin with it because it is the first of several Bergman films structured around the idea of the "fortunate fall": the position that Adam and Eve's taste of the fruit of knowledge was, all in all, a positive achievement, that acquiring a more complex sense of good and evil was worth banishment from Eden and the loss of immortality. It is the Miltonian idea that virtue untested is not virtue. Bergman might call it the sin of innocence since, as we see in *Winter Light,* God appears to be more on the side of knowledge than of ignorance.

Tied into the dramatization of this theme is Bergman's stepped-up exposure of his narcissism. "The people in my films are exactly like myself," he says. "Mostly they're body, with a little hollow for the soul" (*BB,* 190). Almost invariably, the protagonists of the films discussed in this chapter are a pathologically narcissistic Bergman alter ego (male or female) and a naive, vulnerable woman, the latter often played by women—generally Bibi Andersson—with whom Bergman had had a long relationship. The conclusion these films reach is that the hurt these women suffer from their relationships with the pathological narcissists is, for the most part, beneficial, their disillusionment a "fortunate fall."

THE DEVIL'S EYE

In *The Devil's Eye* (1960), a film drama divided into three acts—each of which is introduced by an urbane, sardonic, but unfortunately lamely amusing lecturer (Gunnar Björnstrand)—God is a very active player. Though He seems nostalgic about innocence, His efforts seem to be devoted to making his naive, narcissistic, or idea-obsessed subjects more self-aware and human. In Hell even Satan (Stig Järrel), who wears a business suit and sits behind a desk in a chair whose tips spout little pilot lights, "has gradually become more and more human." Act 1 informs us that Satan has been psychosomatically affected by one of God's successes. Satan has a sty in his eye because 20-year-old Britt-Marie (Bibi Andersson) is about to be married and she is still a virgin.[1] Satan counterattacks with his best, Don Juan (Jarl Kulle). (*The Devil's Eye* is based on a Danish radio play called *Return of Don Juan* by Oluf Bang; it also draws upon some of the staging effects Bergman employed in his 1955 production of Molière's *Don Juan*.) Satan has been punishing the Don by providing him with women whom Satan— announcing, "The performance is over!"—evaporates at the moment preceding consummation. One of history's great narcissists, the Don articulates the condition that prevents Bergman's narcissistic protagonists from enjoying deep and unselfish relationships: "My inside seems burnt out; my skin [is] a thin shell round a void." As Robin Wood sees it, Bergman uses the Don to confess his own struggle with "emotional impotence and spiritual sterility," to confront "the core of his own fears." Don Juan is "in Hell not because he has seduced so many women, but because in doing so he has never really felt anything" (95, 92). The Don is sent to rob Britt-Marie of her virginity and destroy her belief in love. With him goes his servant Pablo (Sture Lagerwall), who wants to "suck at life."

The film's funniest scene occurs when these emissaries (appropriately dressed and speaking the language) arrive in modern Sweden. Satan's most wicked devil, who takes the form of either a monk or a black cat, contrives for them to meet Britt-Marie's father, the vicar (Nils Poppe), who, in the course of events, will also lose his innocence. Although he is obsessed with supernatural evil, this simple, gullible, and indiscriminately good man possesses an unshakeable faith in his God's goodness. Right off, his certainty that his faith in God makes him invulnerable to evil is ridiculed. Certain that the Don and Pablo have appeared providentially to repair his stalled car, he says, "I've always said that the Lord helps his own. . . . It is as if the Devil and his crew put their tails between their legs when I appear." He invites the strangers to the vicarage where he introduces them to his wife Renata (Gertrud Fridh), who, seemingly bed-ridden, is only "dying" of boredom. Then he invites them to his own room, where he offers them a glass of gin from the bottle he keeps hidden from Renata in his cupboard. He also reveals his ambition to match the achievement and fame of one of his predecessors, who trapped a devil in that same cupboard: "I'd make him tell what he knew."

While the vicar takes Don Juan next door to meet his daughter, Pablo slips back into Renata's bedroom and into her bed. She flees into the hallway but only checks to see that no one is observing. She does not recognize the forces warring for her soul, the black cat (little devil) in her path and the cross on the wall. She returns to her room and to Pablo, who she learns understands her character: he senses that her damned-up sensuality finds release only in dreams, the poetry she writes, and the books—for example, *Love*—she reads. Intrigued by this seductive man, but still hoping for the best from her marriage, Renata walks out on him.

Left alone with Britt-Marie—our first sight of her is atop a stepladder with the upper part of her body out of the frame—Don Juan brings her down to earth. Like Anne (*Smiles of a Summer Night*), she wants a father for a husband: the house she is redecorating to live in after she is married is next door to her father's, and what she praises in her 25-year-old fiancé Jonas (Axel Düberg) is his ability to soothe her anger by explaining her feelings, and his being "calm and mannerly . . . almost like a father." And just as her father believes his faith in God protects him from evil, Britt-Marie believes her love for Jonas provides her "a shield" from temptation. That and the fact that Jonas is not expected for another day permit her to accept the Don's dare: to give him an "innocent" kiss to compare with Jonas's. When she takes his head in her hands and kisses him, he trembles, and she feels something that makes her admit that she may be "playing with fire." (In this scene she is often seen against ragged, scorched-looking wallpaper, and the Don, here and later, often has a fireplace behind him.) When she tells him that she prides herself on never having lied to Jonas, the Don scoffs. He has no such scruples; he is motivated by vice, debauchery, and godlessness, and though he may be incapable of love, he knows the real thing. Her love for Jonas, he insists, is "sham love." But it is his inability to believe in the illusion that true lovers "are mirrors which reflect God" that almost brings Britt-Marie to tears. Then "you are dead," she replies. God now intervenes to stop her, for the moment anyhow, from getting further involved: Jonas unexpectedly drives up. He is a day early, he explains, because someone sounding like Britt-Marie phoned him to "come at once," and "then the phone went dead."

In act 2 Jonas, already offended that when he arrived Britt-Marie avoided his kiss, is angered at the dinner table when she labels as boring his talk of the pigs he has bought for their farm. He heads for the door. Stopping him, Britt-Marie asks his forgiveness and kisses him. But when she refuses to explain why she earlier withheld her kiss, Jonas, in a scene that practically replicates Palle's reaction to the selfish Doris's behavior at the beginning of *Dreams,* calls her "selfish and spoiled" and storms out. Less upset than we might expect, she returns to the table in time to hear the Don relating how Don Juan was dragged into Hell by the statue he had invited to dinner. (The scene, shabbily staged, is dramatized.) The story moves Britt-Marie and Renata to tears. The vicar responds with his habitual "Most interesting," which so exasperates Renata that she departs for bed.

At bedtime the vicar, neither unintelligent nor unfeeling, thanks God "for today" and asks Him to rid him of his "childish naïveté" and give him insight into people's pain, in particular, Renata's. Immediately, the opportunity is provided. With adultery on her mind, Renata comes to his room and inquires how he would react if she died or were unfaithful. Lovingly covering her shoulders against the evening's chill, he replies that he would "grieve terribly" if she died. As for infidelity, he "must" love her because love does not cease. Like Ottilia Egerman, who craves passion, even violence, Renata almost screams at this, but the hopelessness of it restrains her. "Good night, my dear," she says, "and wake up to your beautiful world and all the kind people." The vicar assures her that he wants terribly to understand her. Fearing that living with him has cost her the ability to feel deeply, Renata calmly voices the dilemma that will drive the actress Elizabet Vogler (*Persona*) to muteness: "You see me in one part and others see me in another. No one sees my real self." As she is departing, the insight the vicar had prayed for leads him to offer, "If only something would touch your heart, make you feel pity." Ironically, that is what happens. Back in her bed, Pablo reappears. It is not his declaration that she is the loveliest woman he has ever known, but his appeal to her motherly instincts—"my mother wept over my sins . . . showed me tenderness"—that causes her to give herself to him.

The little devil informs the vicar of his wife's infidelity, brings him to her door, and hands him the key so that he can "see abomination, animal lust, [and] get a poisonous bite in your soul to make you human, you who have played your way through life, believing good of everyone." However, this devil underestimates the vicar's interest in the metaphysical. Using gin as bait, the vicar lures the devil back to his room and into his cupboard. Locking him in it, the vicar immediately sets down his great feat in his journal. Having earlier claimed, "My life is a series of fortunate misfortunes," the vicar asserts that "good will come of it, not evil." He is right, but not in the way he imagines.

In the act 3 scene between Andersson and Kulle that follows, there is too little electricity for the scene to be compelling; Kulle's too cool Don robs the film of flair, energy, and fun.[2] (Likewise, in the earlier scenes Lagerwall's Pablo is not as funny as he should be, nor is the lust for life he exhibits as convincing as, say, Åke Fridell's as Frid in *Smiles of a Summer Night*.) Dressed in his bathrobe, Don Juan visits and awakens Britt-Marie. They kiss, this time leaving a sore on her lip, a sign of her infection with evil. Though she is affected by his mysterious power, she insists that she does not love him or long for his body, and that the "mortal wound" he will give her will not affect her love for Jonas. She (like her mother) is giving herself to him because his suffering torments her "more than anything [she has ever] known." Almost miraculously, this living-dead narcissist feels love for the first time, but, too proud to accept Britt-Marie's charity, he leaves.

Later that night the devil in the cupboard informs the vicar that his daughter is being seduced. In dramatic contrast to his reaction to the news about his wife, he flies to and bursts into Britt-Marie's room, awakening her. Is he sleepwalking, she inquires. "Not any more," he replies pensively. But he is wrong; his full awakening takes place in the film's one truly poignant scene, which follows. In the upstairs hall outside Britt-Marie's room, the vicar peers down through the prisonlike bars of the railing and sees Renata and Pablo emerge from her room. Pablo kneels and rests his head against her stomach; Renata kisses him. When Pablo has departed, the vicar quietly whispers down to his wife, "Renata, what's to be done now?" "He touched my heart," she says simply, adding, "but that wasn't the hardest. . . . All the time . . . I pitied you." The vicar does not question this; he only repeats, "And now? You'll stay with me?" "Where would I go?" comes the unsatisfactory reply. "Could we start over again?" he asks. "I don't think so," she says thoughtfully. "Can we change?" he softly, desperately asks. Still thinking of Pablo, but with a slight note of hope in her voice, she answers without looking up at him, "We could try." He concludes the interview by bidding her to go back to bed: "You may catch cold." The chill he should fear is not from the weather but from his emotional distance from his wife: throughout the scene he remains a floor above her. Nevertheless, his innocence has been shattered, and he knows he should love God in the abstract less and humans more. (Instead of letting the ambiguity of this relationship ferment, Bergman unfortunately has Satan later predict that Renata "may . . . become a good wife," and the vicar a "power to reckon with.")

In the morning the Don, desperate, searches out Britt-Marie and begs her to say—even if it is a lie—that she loves him. We imagine the countless women who have asked this of him. Without recognizing the metamorphosis she has produced in him, Britt-Marie sums up what she has learned. Yesterday she was a playful girl excited by his cold desire to hurt her, and she believed her love for Jonas would shield her from danger. Last night she learned that her love shielded her from nothing, that her motherly needs and compassionate character make her vulnerable to evil. Don Juan's (pathological) suffering awoke in her a desire to protect him, but then she realized that the excitement, mystery, or compassion stirred by a suffering but evil person, even one who cannot help himself, does not justify betraying the person one loves. Hurt and humiliated, his inner void having been invaded by unselfish love, Don Juan, proud of both his beloved's hard-won wisdom and having been the one who helped lead her to it, smiles and utters Satan's "The performance is over!" At once he is back in Hell, where Satan punishes him by calling upon the ear devil (Allan Edwall)—a personification of Bergman's favorite device of eavesdropping—so that the Don is forced to hear Britt-Marie speak her wedding vows and attend her cry of pleasurable pain at the marriage's consummation. When they also hear the corrupted but wiser Britt-Marie lie to Jonas about how she got the sore on her lip—"Don't be silly! I've never kissed any other man"—Satan's sty disappears. Satan then inquires if what the Don overheard pained him. Yes, answers the Don, but he can endure it, and besides he is contemptuous of both Satan's and God's "mean little" skirmishes for man's soul. Do what they like to him, Don Juan will never submit to being a puppet for either one.

THE TOUCH

Ten years after *The Devil's Eye* Bergman filmed *The Touch* (1971), his first English-language film. Having heard the story idea, ABC offered to give the famous director a million dollars and the final cut, as well as to pay the salary of the English-speaking actor who would play David.[3] For this film he stripped the earlier story of its comic and metaphysical elements and dramatized only the Britt-Marie conflict. The Britt-Marie character, a 34-year-old married woman with two children, is now called Karin Vergérus; again she is played, now with profound feeling, by Bibi Andersson. The story opens as Karin arrives at the hospital too late—as Bergmann was—to be with her mother when she died. The demise of her mother is the first jolt to the stability of Karin's conventional, safe world.[4] Starting the film with her mother's death implies that it is a contributing factor to Karin's subsequent sally beyond the walls of her Nordic Eden. (Bergman uses an unusual number of fast fades and jump cuts within or between scenes. This nervous, anxious pacing viscerally conveys Karin's sense that she has "lost her footing," that her predictable, conventional world no longer exists. However, in one instance—Karin stands in front of a mirror (the camera) trying on different outfits for her first tryst— the jolting jump cuts also represent her fundamental indecisiveness.) Eden, in fact, is one of the two major metaphors that structure this symbol-laden film about a fortunate fall. During the credit sequence a montage highlights the decayed, ancient wall that encircles the island of Gotland where the Vergéruses live,[5] and the Vergérus home, left to Andreas (Max von Sydow) by his parents, is photographed through banks of colorful spring flowers (see fig. 20). In the fall, after life in this Eden has been corrupted, Karin and Andreas are seen collecting (rotting) apples under their tree. The serpent that Andreas invites into this Eden is a German-born American Jew, David (Elliott Gould).[6] He is, appropriately, an archaeologist. Sometimes charming, sometimes infantile, the self-hating, pathologically narcissistic David (who also laments the loss of his mother) brings id, passionate emotionalism, and violence into the Vergéruses' decorous lives. (The Vergéruses' sex life is good though devoid of the passion—sometimes psychotically rapacious—that David brings to intercourse. The one time Bergman shows Karin and Andreas's lovemaking he tempers and distances it with mirrors and doorways, by dressing the two blonds in cool, all-white bathrobes, and by having Karin unreflectingly take her habitual passive position.) During David's first visit to their home, he cynically asks, referring to her marriage, "Then, everything in the garden is lovely?" Later that evening, while showing slides, Andreas associates Karin with his favorite orchid, which looks like an insect and thus "attracts the interest of flies." Bored, David says he would prefer to see a slide of Karin nude. Amused and intrigued by the American's outrageous humor, Andreas tells him he's sorry but David will have to content himself with *his* (the ownership is important) orchids.

Subsequently, David seduces Karin with the speed of the infamous Don Juan. Her capitulation is sped by her inordinate need, like both Britt-Marie's and Renata's, to mother a mysterious, tortured, and dangerous foreigner. Karin, who instinctively believes that only mothering makes her life meaningful, is masochistically drawn to this swarthy, black-bearded man because, unlike her self-assured psychiatrist husband and her well-adjusted children, he desperately needs her. Karin's attraction to evil is represented when she and David visit the Hamer church (it will be reconsecrated at the height of their closeness). She walks out of the frame, which remains focused on a serpent incised on the church's whitewashed exterior wall; she comes back into the frame, takes off her (protective) glove, and caresses the serpent. David touches her hand at this moment, stimulating her feelings for him. (Two years later, before David abandons her, she again caresses the serpent, but with her glove on. In keeping with the idea of narcissism, the serpent seems to be mating with or devouring itself.) In the church statues of Saint George slaying the dragon and of stern, judgmental-looking saints silently warn her of the danger she is in.

There is another important structural metaphor related to the Edenic metaphor: original sin. Mother/Eve/Karin is also identified with a smiling, well-preserved wooden statue of a pregnant madonna holding a child in her arms. (When the statue has been removed from the dark cavity, Karin and David study it. Karin, pregnant with David's child, and the madonna will be on the left, and David and the child will be on the right.) The statue was discovered when the restorers of the medieval church demolished a wall that had kept it concealed for 500 years. When the madonna is brought out, it is discovered that before she was walled up in darkness insect larva hibernated in her; now the light has awakened them. (Karin first met David in the hospital's dark cloakroom where she had retreated to grieve her mother's death. David's entry is marked by his turning on blinding lights.) The beetles, which are eating away the madonna and child from within, represent both the original sin that Karin's protected life has kept dormant and the muscular atrophy that is an inherited trait in David's (and Bergman's) family. Not surprisingly, the self-hating, self-destructive David finds the destructive insects as beautiful as the statue itself.

David's narcissism causes him to treat the disturbingly compliant, love-wracked Karin as an extension of himself, to use her to satisfy his needs. Impotent during their first assignation, he orders her to a second, which starts out as a rape. As he reaches climax, he involuntarily spews hateful epithets, some having to do with Nazis, others suggesting she is his mother. Amazed, she watches him act out his abusive fantasies on her body, until he screams for her not to look at him. (Here and elsewhere in the film Bergman uses the nondiegetic sound of a screeching buzz saw cutting into wood to further the feeling of nerves being ripped; the buzz saw is also a modern, technological version of the wood-destroying insects.[7]) Aware of his volcanic emotions, David asks for Karin's patience, but he cannot always control his churning emotions. Like Jan-Erik, who rejects Berta because she relapses from the perfect woman he had helped her become (*Torment*), David throws furniture, tears pictures off the wall, and slaps Karin's face because she (his mother-mistress) is not on time for their tryst and has broken her promise not to smoke or drink. When she tries to laugh off his behavior, which she calls "crazy," he acidly orders her to leave. Sobbing uncontrollably, Karin is just leaving the courtyard when the suddenly remorseful David rushes downstairs and, accompanied by the musical love theme, returns her to the apartment for the film's most lyric and tender love scene.

Without such moments, Karin's relationship with David would be unbelievable; at times, we, too, are touched by his vulnerability—for instance, during Karin and David's first tryst when, to resolve their awkwardness, Karin finally asks, "Shall we take our clothes off and go to bed and see what happens?" When David shows Karin his photograph album, the truth of what he says—that his father, who headed a mental clinic near Berlin, sent him, his sister, and their mother to New York when David was four, that all of his relatives were wiped out in German death camps, and that David went to Israel after his mother died—may eventually be called into question, but we do not question the feelings aroused in him by the photograph of his mother (actually Bergman's mother Karin): "Don't you think she's pretty? Sometimes it feels so lonely without mother. Isn't that absurd; after all, I'm grown up."

In spite and because of the pain that this pathologically narcissistic man causes her, Karin is obsessed with him. We find her inability to face the implications of his character infuriating. She understands the way he thinks, she feels for the torment and self-hate he projects onto her and the world, and finally, she even understands—though she will not let herself fully believe—that the love she compulsively offers him ("You're like my newborn child") cannot change him. To stop him from leaving her, she self-deceivingly argues that she can combine her two lives—the one with Andreas and the children and the one with David—into "one wise and good life that benefits other people and makes them happy." She adds that she even thinks that Andreas will accept it.

Dr. Andreas Vergérus, although older, more mature, and infinitely more charming than *The Devil's Eye*'s Jonas, has a relationship with his wife that is similar to Jonas's with the pre–Don Juan Britt-Marie. In Bergman's other films the Vergéruses, in all but two instances medical men, represent rigid rationality or narcissism divorced from human instinct and feelings. Though a busy doctor, Andreas is neither obsessive nor insensitive; he is as warm, paternal, and caring a father, husband, and doctor as the other Vergéruses are hostile and heartless.[8] Like Jonas, Andreas, a psychiatrist, functions as Karin's father and superego as well as her husband. He understands her better than she does herself, is forced to be the disciplinarian with the children, and knows how difficult it is for her to make difficult decisions and adhere to them. For example, because unconsciously she wants more children, he has to remind her to take her birth control pills. He is trusting, but his training has made him uncannily observant: like Jonas, he notes a sore on Karin's lip, the symbolic result of her contamination by evil. When he becomes aware of the affair, he waits for Karin to come to her senses and make up her mind. He tolerates it longer than we do. Two years pass before he finally confronts David (and Karin). It is one of the film's most dramatic scenes.

The doorbell rings while David and Karin are in the bedroom. Expecting someone from the museum, David answers it. Andreas's deep, gentle voice heard asking if he can come in invariably causes audiences to gasp. Inside and sitting facing each other, Andreas responds to David's childish hostility—"It's all so very touching. . . . Go now, Andreas. You've humiliated us both long enough with this ridiculous visit"—with a restrained, soft-spoken affability: "I don't understand why you are so aggressive, David. I like you." But Andreas—von Sydow's incipient smile is magnificent—subtly stilettos his crude opponent. Knowing that Karin is eavesdropping—he passed her coat as he entered—he leaks the secret that he met David when the latter tried to commit suicide. "You were never to speak of it," pouts David. "That's right. Sorry. Forgive me," replies Andreas, playing with his gloves, which he has taken off. Andreas then reveals Karin's greatest weakness: "She hates any form of decision."

As Karin suspected he would, David runs out on her. The scene in which she visits David's empty, dingy apartment—the walls are a grayish bile color—economically and powerfully conveys her anguish. With her discarded love letters to David in her hand, she walks slowly through the vacated rooms. Her own numbed emptiness is so kinesthetically painful that she comes near to vomiting; to equalize the pain, she takes off her glove (reminding us of when she touched the incised serpent) and presses her bare flesh on shattered glass.

Sometime afterward the noticeably pregnant Karin arrives at Andreas's office to tell him that she must visit David in London to find out why he has left her. Andreas responds, "Suffering must have an end. . . . I don't want to be poisoned by hatred and spite; I don't want to hate you." If she goes, he informs her, he will not have her back; if she stays and accepts "for once" the consequences of her acts, he will help her in every way. Karin does not so much decide she must see David again as let the raging force of her need sweep her onward. Typically, she prefers that Andreas tell the children about their separation.

In London Karin discovers that David has a sister, a borderline psychotic, who is partially paralyzed from an inherited disease that David shares. (There may even have been incest; his threatened sister says, "We have everything in common.") Karin's instinct to protect the life within her—and to a lesser degree herself—from David's physical and mental pathology ends her pursuit of him. She returns to Sweden. In the next scene she is inexplicably—Bergman finesses the reconciliation—back in her house. In the middle of the night, very pregnant and uncomfortable, Karin leaves her bedroom, pops her head into the dark, nearby bedroom, and quietly calls, "Andreas, Andreas," in a way that indicates he is there. Receiving no response, she goes to another room and lies on the floor to get comfortable. There is a terrible sense of aloneness about the scene.

Not long afterwards—it is fall—the high-spirited David shows up, blithely expecting to continue their affair. Karin, on the way to an Italian lesson, meets him in a greenhouse by a river. This rounds out the film's metaphorical framing: gone are the conventional flowers that walled the Vergérus Eden (also by a river), but in their place is a humid, artificial jungle consisting of exotic flowers, especially orchids. We recall Andreas's reference to Karin as his (artificially protected) orchid (see fig. 21). David, who looked most natural when he was dressed in his bright orange overalls or when he was digging up skulls, is dressed in a double-breasted suit that makes him seem to be in a straitjacket. Karin tells him that she has had enough scandal, that he has no right to make any demands on her, and that she has nothing more to say to him. She exits the greenhouse. He runs after and stops her. It has begun to drizzle. Looking into her face, he compellingly argues that he has discovered he cannot live without her and that he is not the person who left her. Remembering *The Devil's Eye*'s Don Juan, we entertain the possibility that her love *has* fundamentally changed him: "I think and feel and react differently," he maintains. "Before I met you I could live without living. I didn't care. Nothing mattered." He pleads that he will meet any conditions she sets; he will even take the two children—neither David nor Karin mentions her pregnancy—and provide the security he has always scoffed at. Karin's firm tone and nonvindictive language, embodying the principle of the fortunate fall, indicate not only that she has achieved an understanding of herself and life that she previously lacked but that she can stick to the painful decisions she makes. In one of the most touching speeches in all of Bergman's films, she compassionately describes their relationship and affirms that it is over: "Poor David. I love you so much." "It's not true!" he insists. "That is the truth," she replies. "No one has done me as much good as you; no one has done me so much harm as you. Even so, I'm not coming with you. . . . I feel it is my duty to stay where I am." David has repeatedly accused Karin of being merely a slave of her bourgeois life and out of touch with life's essentials—a charge to which Bergman lends support by showing her doing housework to the beat of parodic music—to coerce her into capitulating to his needs. The "new" David repeats the accusation now, screaming, "I know the real reasons. They're so goddamned rotten and trivial and

The Touch. AB Svensk Filmindustri

The Touch. AB Svensk Filmindustri

cowardly I can't be bothered to go into them! Can't you see the pattern, Karin?" Infuriated by her strength, David knocks the books from her hand and stomps off, still raving. The film ends as we watch the drizzle creating circles that radiate outward in the nearby stream, and the pregnant Karin Vergérus picking up her books out of the dead, brown leaves.[9] We ponder the fact that, symbolically, David and his genetic disease (like the beetles/original sin) will be carried on through Karin's child and its offspring. But her pregnancy and her Italian books—the Mediterranean represents liberation in Bergman's films—symbolize Karin's new and renewed purpose.

Before leaving *The Touch*, I want to testify that after many viewings this disparaged film wears remarkably well, and that, as I have indicated, it contains powerfully dramatic moments and scenes. It is true that it is flawed. Sometimes its symbolically freighted or grammatically correct language undermines its naturalness (for example, "I just wanted you to know with whom you're going to bed"),[10] but Bergman's most serious mistake was forcing Elliott Gould to be more Bergman than Gould.[11] I acknowledge that my criticism is based on my opinion that Gould's success as an actor has been based to a very large extent on exhibiting his personality, not suppressing it. By stripping Gould of his endearingly impish, anarchic manner and his exaggerated but ironic humor, Bergman deprived Gould of the very qualities that make his personality so engaging to audiences.

THE SILENCE

The third film structured around the fortunate fall theme is *Persona,* but for stylistic as well as thematic reasons we must first analyze the film that, except for a comedy, preceded it, *The Silence* (1963). Though usually placed with his religious films, according to Bergman *The Silence* "came quite unexpectedly as the third part of the trilogy" (Sjöman, 32). It is a film of "the *here* and *now.*" (Although one character prays to God, He is, seemingly, absent. Bergman associates Him with the female protagonists' 440-pound dead and buried father [Sjöman, 49, 34–35]. Originally, Bergman planned to show a dying man "of immense age" but cut it because it was "far too symbolic" [Sjöman, 58].)

The abandonment of his old conception of God ("God, why?"), which is chronicled in *Winter Light,* freed him, we recall his saying, to accept life's good and evil and his own personality. He also said that he even lost his "fear of not being up-to-date and modern," by which I take him to mean that not only had his religious theme run its course but he felt strong enough to resist the demands by some critics that he treat more current social issues. He would choose his own issues, which were focused on himself and, as we have seen evidenced in some degree in *The Touch,* his relationship with his mother. This shift from God to mother is signaled at the end of *Winter Light,* where, in place of the Mittsunda church's God and crucified Jesus, there is the Frostnäs church's madonna and child, and where, instead of the unpredictable father (for example, David in *Through a Glass Darkly*), the motherly Märta takes over the "struggle for faith" (Sjöman, 34). With *The Silence,* he maintains, he was "starting to be [him]self" (Sjöman, 206).

Aging and his marriage to Käbi Laretei, a woman closer to his own age, seem to have facilitated Bergman's coming to terms with his complex feelings about his mother. Just as it was no longer a question of "God, why?" he says he no longer felt he had to ask, "Mother, why?" (Prouse, 30), but this did not mean, as it did in his struggle with God, that he would avoid explicit discussion and dramatization of his feelings about his relationship with his mother.

The Silence prefigures *Cries and Whispers,* whose four female characters, Bergman says, represent aspects of his mother. Like that later film, the earlier one centers on the relationship between narcissistic sisters, one of whom is dying. In addition, it involves a caring servant, a child hungering for the love of an unpredictable, narcissistic mother, and a character whose sacrifice enlarges the protagonist's awareness. When Strindberg parceled out his own qualities to his characters, he called it "polymerizing" himself. Besides polymerizing his mother in these films, Bergman, as usual, polymerizes himself. *The Silence,* he says, is "about my private life . . . a personal purgation: a rendering to me of hell on earth—my hell" (Kaminsky, 123).

In *The Silence,* for the first time, Bergman makes a child a major protagonist. His alter ego is the ten- or eleven-year-old Johan (Jörgen Lindström). Bergman treats this frightened, hostile, often unattractive boy, who oppressively dotes on his mother, sympathetically but without sentimentality. (Recall that Bergman's clinging to his mother led her to tell him that he "behaved like a girl.") Anna's (Gunnel Lind-blom) behavior toward her son is based on Bergman's memory of his own mother's toward him. Anna is alternately seductive and rejecting. (When they return to Sweden, in fact, she plans to deposit him for a year with his grandmother.[12]) Anna also shares the adult Bergman's voracious sexual appetite. In contrast to the unintellectual, easy-going, lusty Anna, the third protagonist, Anna's dying sister Ester (Ingrid Thulin), is an intellectual who fears her instincts and is patho-logically driven by a need to control. So "close to himself" is Ester that Bergman confessed that he "thought of masking [the similarity] in some way" (Sjöman, 190).

Because the way this story is told is bound up with its theme, and because stylistically *The Silence* differs dramatically in degree (not in kind) from Bergman's earlier films, instead of treating its style after my discussion of the themes, I must deal with style first. *The Silence*'s style evidences Bergman's strong desire to achieve greater interioral-ity. Probably based on his growing belief that his mother's dual mes-sages were what caused the most psychological damage, he explicitly called attention in *Through a Glass Darkly* to how words distort or mask what a person actually feels, how spoken language can be subtly out of sync with tone of voice, gesture, or facial expression. "Words are used to conceal reality, aren't they?" Using more and larger close-ups, he tries not only to dramatize this contrapuntal dissonance—"in the tension between image and word a new dimension is created"—but to urge his viewers to look for truth behind or at the edges of his characters' masks. The "expression around a person's mouth and . . . the angle of his eyes and the skin around the eyes" (Steene 1972, 43–44), he writes, can directly convey that person's naked "mental move-ments." To become a Bergman aficionado one must learn to read his actors' most subtle facial, gestural, and tonal cues. This kind of sub-tlety partially accounts for Bergman's opinion of the silent film as the "most sophisticated form of communication" (Cowie 1970, 182).[13] It also helps explain why his style grows continually sparer. He is excis-ing everything that might distract his audience from garnering the meaning conveyed through these complex aural-visual chords. It helps explain, too, how "he can let almost nothing happen and still keep his audience captivated" (Donner 1966, 227).

Studying music with Käbi Laretei seems also to have had an effect on his films, by contributing to the liberties he was taking with nar-rative (*BB*, 181). He structured his films more fluidly and musically and more like dreams, which, like music, bypass intellectualization and reveal authentic feeling to us. When he began the screenplay of *The Silence*, he said that not only would the film "be a dream" but he would "call it *The Dream*" (Sjöman, 192), and he told Sven Nykvist to give it "the character of a dream," though without resorting to cinematic clichés.[14] It may also be that returning to the netherworld of his childhood for his picture of Johan and his mother liberated him from naturalism, from any "fear of not being up-to-date and modern." He could freely experiment with dream techniques. In fact, departing from what he had done in his previous films, in *The Silence* he occasionally blurs the distinction between the real world and the characters' mental-emotional worlds.

The Silence opens with a loud noise—the whistle of the train he is on—awakening Johan from his sleep literally and, eventually, figuratively.[15] Frightened to his feet, he thrusts his pale, moist face (in extreme close-up) at us. Sharing the stiflingly hot compartment with him is his mother, a big-boned, attractive woman around 30 and her sister, a frailer, slightly older woman. They are Anna and Ester, respectively, though—and this contributes to the divorce from reality—we do not learn their names until the film is half over. Her flesh beaded with sweat, her lips and teeth slightly parted, Anna is leaning against the seat and staring blankly; slowly, very slowly, she fans herself with a book. Ester is dressed in a long-sleeved suit, and her hair, in contrast to her sister's loose style, is pulled back. She sits upright, and her skin is unaffected by the clammy heat. Her dignified expression hides her physical discomfort. The three travelers are on their way back to Sweden after a vacation—the familiar Bergman pattern of returning home—and are presently passing through Timoka, a country whose language is incomprehensible even to Ester, who is a translator.[16] One of Johan's first acts is to ask her what the printed message on the card on the window means. After telling him she does not know, she suffers a paroxysm of coughing, from which her handkerchief comes away stained with blood. Anna tries to help her, but Ester—like the angry Stina slapping away Hjördis's hand *(Brink of Life)*—pushes her sister to the floor and stumbles out of the compartment. After a moment, however, she is back in her seat, accepting Anna's aid. Anna closes the compartment door, shutting out Johan, the first of more than a half-dozen times he will be "shut out" in the film.[17]

Another action that all three protagonists, but especially the outsider Johan, partake in is eavesdropping. After being shut out of his compartment, Johan peeks into other compartments and stares out the window. A wartime setting is established by the soldiers on the train and by the army tanks that speed by on the adjoining track. Bergman uses analectic sound to show the latter as they pass by on flatcars, each with a cannon extending from its turret. In place of the ambient sound is a steady, low-pitched hum, which creates a dreamlike sensation. In several critical instances what each of the protagonists sees in the outside world—to varying degrees—is a projection of his or her own feelings or fears. The soldiers and the tanks with their erect (phallic) cannons, for example, represent, in part—as does his reaction to the soldiers on the train—Johan's fear of masculine authority and sexuality. We have seen a number of Bergman's characters stare at inner screens onto which they project their hopes and dreams; in this film real windows often become the frame for the characters' mind-screens.[18] The next shot, however, is a reverse shot, from outside the train. Anna has exited their compartment and is standing behind Johan, who is looking out the window. What we see are railroad signals, boxcars, and staves of tracks reflected in the window over the images of Anna and Johan.[19] He has the palm of his hand flat against the glass, a shot that foreshadows the same actor, at the opening and closing of *Persona,* reaching out toward a translucent screen on which he sees giant faces of mother figures.

The subdued screech of the train's brakes as it enters the station is abruptly replaced with the close-up din of street noises—barrels rattling on a cart, car horns, men hawking headlines—and the scalding sunlight associated with Bergman's nightmares. Because of Ester's illness the trio is going to lay over in Timoka, and they have been transported, in dream fashion, seamlessly from the train and into the seclusion of hotel rooms. (Ester's and Anna's large rooms are joined by a door.) From the window in the room he shares with his mother, Johan safely looks at the threatening babel below. It soon becomes apparent that Bergman is using the incomprehensible Timokan language and the evident preparations for a civil war not only to establish place and mood but to heighten and symbolize the feelings of isolation, hostility, and fear that exist between Anna and Ester, who are also involved in a civil war.

As Anna readies herself to take a bath, Johan puffs up his cheeks and loudly blows out the air, an act that either exorcises his discomfort with the tension between the two women or releases the erotic feelings that have built up from watching his mother undress.[20] His joy at being invited to wash his mother's back, made amply clear when he stops rubbing it and lays his forehead against it, causes Anna to smile, pat his cheek, and send him into the other room to take a nap. A jump cut helps convey the rejection he feels, and the ensuing game his anger: Johan's hand, acting as an airplane, comes up out of a valley created by the puffy linen hills of the bed's lusciously thick feather bolster, and suddenly, accompanied by the sound effects he makes, his other hand rockets up to explode the plane. Moments later, after ordering him to strip to his underwear, Anna, fingers wiggling as she advances, kisses and coats him with delicious perfume and then, naked, slips in beside him under the quilt and goes to sleep.

Parallelism—or to use the musical term, counterpoint—is this film's most common structural device. Another scene involving sensuality follows. The alcoholic, chain-smoking Ester, in mannish pajamas, is in bed reading, drinking, and listening to romantic music on the radio.[21] She stops, gets out of bed, and goes into the adjoining room where, standing over the sleeping Anna and Johan, she lightly touches their hair. Then she returns to her room and looks out her closed window. (Strangely, the music from the radio in the room ceases, and though she does not open the window, the street noises are not muted.) Below, she sees-projects an emaciated horse pulling a wagon piled high with furniture and driven by a man in a bowler hat; the image evokes a feeling of uprootedness and death (see fig. 22).[22] (One of this image's antecedents is in Victor Sjöström's *The Phantom Chariot,* another in *Monika*—the used-furniture dealer who appears near the start and finish of the film. A similar image appears in *The Serpent's Egg* and *Fanny and Alexander.*) When Ester turns from the window, the romantic music returns. She shuts off the radio and, noting that she is out of brandy, rings for the hall porter.

The man who arrives, wearing a worn but immaculate suit of tails and thick, black, horn-rimmed glasses, is tall, slender, and elderly (Håkan Jahnberg). Throughout this scene Ester is viewed reflected in the wardrobe mirror, whereas the old man—there is something of the faithful old horse about him—is viewed directly. He cannot speak any of the languages Ester plies him with, but a glance at the empty bottle's label animates his wrinkled smile, and he leaves. Singing, Ester dances over to a chair, sits, and lights another cigarette, wiggling it up and down between her clenched teeth so that it resembles a bouncing penis. The camera suddenly dollies in on her as a loud drone replaces her singing. At first we mistake it for merely an air-raid siren, but it is also an expressionistic device to convey the lonely Ester's despair and panic. Only after the porter returns and she has taken a drink does it cease. Calm again, she asks the old man to write down the word in his language for *hand*. He writes "KASI." A bell rings in the hall; endearingly, he raises high his long, old legs, slaps his face as if to say, "No rest for the wicked," and leaves. Under the influence of the romantic music, her perusal of her sister, the brandy, and her fear, Ester now gives herself over to her emotions. Just as Anna rubbed perfume over Johan's body, Ester rubs the paper with KASI on it across her face and, falling backwards onto the bed, closes her eyes. As she screens her incestuous fantasy in her mind, from behind her head we watch her unbutton her pajama top, rub her breasts, and masturbate. (As in *Through a Glass Darkly,* the need for complete sexual control expresses itself in onanism and love of a younger sibling.) Her upside-down face is grotesque at the moment of orgasm. The camera then ascends so that not only are we looking down on the lonely woman staring into space but we are nearer the (announced) planes suddenly roaring past.

Johan, again jolted awake by a fearsome sound, sits bolt upright in bed. It is as if his previous air war fantasy has materialized. Frightened by the continuing roar, he calls to his mother, but she groggily reprimands him for bothering her and goes back to sleep. The roar ceases only after Johan has dressed himself in his short pants, white shirt (buttoned protectively to the neck), and wire-rimmed glasses. He holsters his cap pistol under his belt and steps into the hotel corridor. Johan's adventures in the gloomy hotel's labyrinthine, empty (typically Bergmanesque) halls begin when he brazenly shoots a hotel handyman who is atop a stepladder changing a bulb in one of the huge, glass chandeliers that hang from the arched, high ceilings. The flabbergasted man looks down at Johan from his vulnerable position at the ladder's crotch. Lowering his gun, Johan, as earlier, fills his cheeks with air, noisily expels it, and cautiously backs away. Next, he takes cover behind a large armchair and aims his gun at the old porter sitting in his closetlike station. When the old man tries to make friends, Johan flees to the far end of the corridor. A moment later, however, he bows an unthreatened greeting to a male dwarf who courteously doffs his hat. Next, Johan comes upon and studies a huge reproduction of Rubens's *Dejanira Abducted by Nessus:* the naked Dejanira, Hercules' wife, is dismounting the centaur Nessus, to whom

The Silence. AB Svensk Filmindustri

The Silence. AB Svensk Filmindustri

Hercules had given her to transport across the river. An arrow of Hercules' is in Nessus's heart because he attempted to rape her (see fig. 23). The naked, fleshy woman and the fearsome horse-man heighten the hypersensitive Johan's anxieties and oedipal fears, even as the arrow represents his hostility. (Like the child Bergman, who was afraid of all animals, Johan, we will learn, is afraid of horses.) Suddenly terror! The porter has snuck up behind him and grabbed him. Johan wrenches free and flees the disappointed old man.

Though as we watch the film we have no trouble understanding the parallel cutting—that is, that sequential scenes are often taking place simultaneously—the story's breaking into three strands, Ester's, Anna's, and Johan's, creates a problem for my verbal narrative, in which transitions have to be more explicit. The problem of transition is especially important in this film whose scenes are often meant to be seen, in one way or another, as parallel in subject matter. The scene following Johan's study of the painting containing the centaur and naked woman is a good example. At the very time Johan is looking at the painting, Ester, in her bedroom, is *on all fours* spying on the naked Anna—framed by two doorways—cooling her underarms and breasts in the tap water of her bathroom's sink. When Anna notices her sister in the mirror, she smiles. It is meanness as well as a desire to maintain her privacy that a moment later causes her to stand where Ester (and we) cannot see her as she dresses. The shot's canted angle suggests something is amiss.

After creating shadow monsters on the wall, Johan stops at the open door of a room inhabited by a Spanish theatrical troupe of male dwarfs. He shoots three men, one of whom charges at him dressed in a lion's head. His victims play dead. Holstering his pistol, he enters their room, his glowing face testifying to the security and pleasure he feels with these childlike men. The film's concern with sexuality, including Johan's sexual ambivalence, continues as the little men slip a dress on the delighted boy and a man in a monkey mask leaps up and down in a courting ritual. To Johan's dismay, however, the little man he bowed to earlier enters, scolds his colleagues, gently removes Johan's dress, and politely ushers him out. Again the world has betrayed and rejected him. After looking about to see that no one is watching, he purges his irritation. He urinates on the floor.

The unseen emergence of Johan's penis is paralleled in the subsequent image—an extreme close-up of Anna's lipstick emerging from its metal tube—which, in addition, indicates what is on Anna's mind.

As she slams out of the room, the jealous Ester stifles a scream, triggering another spasm of suffocation. It is as if her body were revenging itself for her life-denying control. Sounding like the terrified Dr. Vergérus in the attic (*The Magician*), Ester, when she is able to breathe again, cries out, "This is bloody humiliating . . . ! I must keep my head. I'm known for my clear logic." But unlike Vergérus, she prays, "Dear God, do let me die at home." Grasping for the open brandy, she knocks it over on the bed and falls off the edge trying to retrieve it. Helpless, she rings for the porter. A giant close-up of his wrinkled, compassionate face fills the frame, and Bergman leaves it there for such an inordinate length of time that we get the impression we are seeing into his very emotions and thoughts. Jabbering incomprehensibly, this asexual combination of Sister Brita (*Brink of Life*) and Frövik (*Winter Light*) returns her to bed and helps her freshen up. When he gathers up the soiled linen and leaves to get her something to eat, he has created a feeling of cleanliness, forgiveness, and acceptance.

Possibly at that same moment, in a bright, smoke-filled, oppressive café that seems to be frequented only by men, Anna is encountering another waiter (Birger Malmsten), but he is young, dark, and virile. She orders an ice cream sundae and buys a newspaper, which she quickly throws away because nothing in it is intelligible, apparently not even the concert featuring music by "J.S. Bach," whose name blares out in bold letters. When the waiter contrives to get a close look at her legs, his face conveys a quality of pent-up yet tender energy.

Lonely, bored, and hungry, Johan at last enters Ester's room. She shares with him the food—for all three characters food corresponds with emotional needs—brought her by the porter. Out of loyalty to his mother, however, he does not let her touch him. Instead, he promises to "draw something nice" for her. The face he draws, which has a "cruel, twisted mouth" with two fangs and earrings—daggerlike slashes—through its big ears' lobes, is his mother's.

A less hostile but more sexual artistic performance is taking place at the variety theater that Anna has gone to. Onstage, each member of the troupe of dwarfs bends over and grabs the waist of the man in front of him. The result is a long, centipedelike body that snakes around in front of, incongruously, a Greek temple. Anna is sitting in the balcony alone except for a man and woman who are uninhibitedly coupling. She watches them, and their sordid ecstasy fascinates and repels her and stirs her own carnal feelings. Taking a deep breath and unable to take her eyes off the couple, she backs toward the exit door. When she reaches it, however, it sticks, trapping her. It is as if she were imprisoned by her lust; the searchlight, which had earlier panned the balcony, adds to the prison metaphor. Throwing her weight against the door, she finally bursts out of the darkness and into the thundering sunlight of a hot, dusty street being repaired with pungent, steaming tar and by earsplitting jackhammers. The narrow sidewalk bordered by dirty walls is crowded with men, many of whom wear sunglasses and all of whom wear dull, gray clothing. Dressed in white, Anna contrasts glamorously with the file of sullen males passing like drones headed for their workstations or for tawdry stage shows or for surreptitious sex. It is a drab image of a proletarian Balkan country in which totalitarian control (like Ester's) is eroding its population's sense of individuality. But the men also seem a projection of Anna's need for an anonymous male. She returns to the café. Now the presence of a few women at the outdoor tables relieves the grubby menace of this male world. A silent exchange of glances with the waiter communicates her need.

Twirling his pistol, the lonely Johan journeys once more through the empty hallways of the dingy hotel, a relic of a pleasure-seeking past whose baroque voluptuousness, combined with its apparent emptiness, creates an aura of sensuality and death.[23] When Johan stops to watch the porter in his station eating his lunch, the old man wins the boy's smile with his performance: he makes a puppet out of one of his sausages. But when he reprimands the little phallus and unexpectedly bites off its head, Johan glares at him. Half a chocolate bar and an invitation to sit on his lap regain the boy's favor. To further amuse him, the porter takes a set of worn photographs out of his wallet and gives them to Johan to peruse. The pictures show a man and a woman, possibly his mother and father, side by side, and a boy, probably the porter, standing with family members around the coffin of his mother. The sad memories they provoke in the man trigger a trancelike reverie and unintelligible muttering. He is oblivious when Johan slips off his lap and runs to hug his mother, whom he hears returning. As we watch from a distance we see Anna, certain of a confrontation with Ester, prevent Johan from entering the room with her. When she is gone, he hops away along the border of the rug until he becomes aware that he still has the porter's photographs. Carefully, maliciously, he slips them under the rug and flattens the slight bulge. His jealousy of the husband in the photo, his guilt at having run off with the old man's beloved photographs, and his hostility toward Anna for having rejected him again—right now he may want her as dead as the mother in the photograph—could account for his literally and figuratively burying his feelings along with the photographs under the rug.

Anna enters her room and undresses. Ester comes in, notes Anna's soiled dress, sneers, and returns to work in her own room. The tightening of Anna's jaw muscles betrays her seeming calm, as does the amplified sound of her combing her long hair: the friction from the strokes sounds like a brush fire. She paces like a great, lithe, caged cat. Fed up with being on the defensive, she invades her self-righteous, controlling sister's room to tell her to stop spying and mind her own business, adding, "To think I have been afraid of you."

The film's second movement takes place that evening. Ester looks out the window as bells ring out from the uninviting church across the noisy square. What she sees—a handful of responding worshipers, the man with the emaciated horse and another load of furniture disappearing into the darkness, and youths playing war with wooden guns—speaks of uprootedness, violence, and a breakdown in religious belief. Turning from the window, she listens intently to one of Bach's Goldberg Variations on the radio.[24] It provides a refreshing relief. The harpsichord's clean, clear notes create order and momentarily transform the dreary surroundings. The porter, who now enters with Ester's tea, recognizes the music. In fact, the music seems to unite the quartet of listeners. Anna, who earlier did not even seem to recognize Bach's name, asks about the music. Our eye is directed past Ester and the porter through the doorway to the other room to a Pietà: Johan in Anna's lap, being caressed and kissed. The porter names the composer of the "mooseek"; his stress on the first name, "*Johann* Sebastian Bach," requires that we connect the artist to Bergman's homunculus alter ego. As a matter of fact, Johan subsequently comes and sits in the connecting doorway. Like the music, he functions both as a connector and a "ground" to help discharge the electric hostility that has built up between the two poles. His act also represents his venture away from his mother's body-centered behavior and closer to Ester's intellectual-artistic sensibility.

Under this influence, Ester thoughtfully informs Anna that she is not up to traveling, so she and Johan should leave Timoka that evening. Anna replies that she cannot leave her sister behind. For a moment we believe that Anna has had a change of heart—until we realize that her real reason for staying is another rendezvous she has planned with her waiter. Instructing Johan to read to Ester, she starts for the door. Suddenly, shutting off the uniting music, Ester shouts, "Go while your conscience lets you!" Anna stops in her tracks. Again sending Johan out into the hall—his exit through Ester's door signals a further step in his altering allegiance—Anna readies herself to face Ester. Turning out the lamp, she stands by the window, knowing that Ester will come to her. She does. The subsequent shot is the precursor of the yin-yang, Picasso-esque shots that Bergman would use to equally brilliant effect in *Persona* and would thereafter become a signature composition: Ester faces us, but half of her face is hidden by Anna's profile lit by the moon and the streetlights. The impression is that there is one face: one eye (Ester's) faces us while the other eye and nose facing left are Anna's. The composition visualizes each sister's desire for and rejection of the other's qualities (see figs. 24, 25). Ester, who ten years earlier had blackmailed Anna into recounting the details of a sexual experience, envies and is repulsed by Anna's promiscuity. Their deceased father and Ester, we learn, have made Anna feel worthless and guilty not only for not being intellectual but for being the slave of her sexuality. Anna now uses that sexuality to torture her ambivalent sister. Flauntingly, she tells of having had sex that afternoon with a man behind a pillar in a cool, dark corner of the church. Ester listens, her unblinking eyes glistening and her tongue unconsciously wetting her lips. When Anna has finished, Ester returns to her room, sits on the edge of her bed, and asks Anna to come sit beside her. Anna complies. Ester rests her head on Anna's shoulder and pleads that she not meet the man because—like her incestuous desire, also a symptom of Ester's narcissism—it humiliates her (Ester). Then she carefully, repeatedly, kisses Anna's cheek. Aware that she is revealing more than she wants, Ester assures Anna that what she feels is not jealousy. Skeptical, Anna unoffendingly pushes her sister away and leaves for her tryst. Ester, says Bergman, "loves her sister, finds her beautiful, and feels a tremendous responsibility for her." However, she would "be horrified if it were pointed out that her feelings were incestuous." Ester's need to control Anna, he adds, "as her father had controlled [Ester] by his love . . . is a despotic love . . . [and] the beginning of Death" (Prouse, 30).

The waiter appears in the hallway. Johan is eavesdropping as Anna goes to him, kisses him passionately, and then disappears with him into a nearby room. From a distance—the camera is near the ceiling

The Silence. AB Svensk Filmindustri

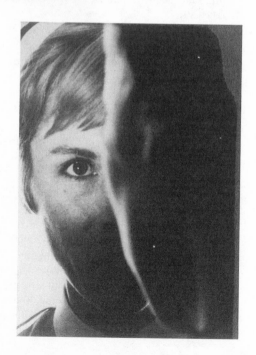

Persona. AB Svensk Filmindustri

of a vaulted archway over the juncture of halls—we watch Johan sneak up to the door, put his ear to it for a moment, and then wander down the hall in our direction, the rug runner determining his direction. We are looking almost straight down on him as he steps into the center of a circular design in the rug. Underfoot in the center of the circle are back-to-back *E*s, which may suggest coupling or emotional gridlock. The dominant feeling of the shot is isolation and loneliness. As he walks slowly down the dark hall toward his room, the quiet drone of the siren returns, this time expressing Johan's desolate feelings.

We next see Johan in bed reading Lermontov's *A Hero of Our Times*. We do not see the passage, but as pointed out in chapter 1, the protagonist's description of his character could well apply to that of the future Johan (or Bergman, or Ester): "Whether it is my upbringing that made me thus or whether God created me so, I don't know: I only know that if I am a cause of unhappiness for others, I am no less unhappy myself. . . . My soul has been impaired. . . . My main pleasure . . . is to subjugate to my will all that surrounds me. . . . My love brought happiness to none, because I never gave up anything for the sake of those whom I loved. I loved for myself" (Lermontov, 39–41, 159).

Putting the book aside, Johan quietly and slowly enters Ester's room, where the panning camera establishes his subjective point of view. He studies his sleeping aunt from the foot of her bed, then moves to the table near its head. After a moment he becomes aware of room-shaking vibrations, which draw his attention to the window. Looking out, he sees a camouflaged tank clumsily (like the hearse in *Wild Strawberries*) negotiate a narrow turn, advance toward the hotel, and stop across from him in the dimly lit square. Its cannon is erect. (At this moment his mother is having sex with the waiter.) As earlier, the view from this window is both real and a complex projection: in addition to being a threatening, male symbol, the tank is Johan's cap pistol made Brobdingnagian. Ester, awakened, interrupts his vision by asking him to read to her. His face, which usually camouflages his intense hostility and fear, noticeably brightens. He tells her that he would rather put on his Punch and Judy show (which she has seen before), and she accedes. He subsequently turns a tall chair toward the foot of her bed and, hiding behind its high back, raises the two puppets over its top. From behind him we watch as, talking gibberish in a high, whiny voice, Punch smashes Judy over the head with his club and she sinks down out of Ester's sight. Ester asks what Punch is saying and why he doesn't sing something today. Johan replies that when Punch is afraid he cannot sing and he speaks a funny language Johan does not understand. Suddenly, his suppressed emotions erupt, and his generally impassive expression cracks. Sobbing, he rushes to Ester and throws himself into her arms. At that very moment the prowling tank noisily departs the scene, but only we see it.

Until this scene the viewer may have found Bergman's direction of Jörgen Lindström puzzling—his acting has been called wooden. Up to now this sneaky, selfish, and fearful mama's boy has seemed unappealing and nearly affectless, but this scene permits us to understand the strategies that Johan employs to cope with his enormous fear of and hostility toward a world he finds so unresponsive and threatening. Now the matter of language and understanding (introduced by Punch's unintelligibility) is pursued. Self-possessed again, Johan asks Ester why she is a translator. So one can read books written in a foreign language, she answers. At his request, she promises to write down the few words that she has learned of this country's strange and unintelligible language. Aunt and nephew seem to have broken down the barriers between them, but unexpectedly, again out of loyalty to his mother, Johan shies away from Ester's touch—observing, however, that his mother apparently does not like being with either of them. Why do you say that? asks Ester. He answers, why else would she leave them to pop into a room with a man?

The language motif is carried on in the next scene. "How nice it is we don't understand each other," says Anna, kissing the scratches she has left on her lover. Shoving her hands deep into his pockets as he stands at the mirror combing his hair, she adds, "I wish Ester were dead," and then she confesses how she has always hated being regarded as dumb by her father and her sister. At that moment she hears Ester at the door, crying and asking to be admitted. Exasperated, Anna decides to give her sister a full dose of what earlier she served up only in part. Turning off the lamp, she unlocks the door and crawls onto the waiter's lap. When Ester reaches the bed, Anna turns on the lamp and kisses and caresses him. As in the scene in *Monika* after Harry finds Monika in bed with her lover, Ester and Anna are now made to look imprisoned by repeatedly being shot through the bars of the foot of the bed (see fig. 3). As the bemused waiter looks on from behind her, Anna, like a caged animal, keeps lunging at the bars; she rightly identifies Ester's harping on moral principles as her way of achieving control. Rising above the bars and whispering through clenched teeth, she accuses Ester of being afraid of her and of hating everything, including herself. Ester defends herself with smugness, preceded by Bergman's formulaic "Poor Anna." The defeated Anna begins laughing and falls prostrate on the bed. Ester leaves, but her pensive expression acknowledges that she has been shaken by Anna's insights. Anna's hysterical laughter immediately turns into pathetic, uncontrollable sobs, which excite the waiter. He raises her slip, gently embraces her, and thrusts his member into her anus.[25] Physical pleasure and pain join the morass of emotions Anna is experiencing at this moment.

Ester is leaning against Anna's door when the dwarfs, returning after their last performance, parade past her. They are emblems of stunted emotional as well as physical growth and appear in scenes involving perverted or unseemly sex.[26] Their costumes—two are dressed as groom and bride (the latter taking swigs of liquor from a bottle) and one as death—mock Ester and foreshadow her fate. In the morning, when Anna is about to leave the sleeping waiter, the door resists opening. As in the variety theater, she is again trapped in her tawdry, sexual prison, a point also made by the attention paid to her act of slipping on her handcufflike bracelets. Blocking her escape is Ester, lying unconscious.

The narrative's third movement begins with Anna telling the bed-ridden Ester that she and Johan are leaving on the 2:00 P.M. train. She then takes Johan to breakfast, leaving the porter with Ester. After an hour Ester is furious that they have not returned and, as had Anna, launches into a monologue that is incomprehensible to her companion. Wiping her moist brow, chest, and armpits with the bed sheet, she intellectualizes her disgust for human physical processes, and in the course of her remarks she alludes to her own obviously inappropriate marriage and an unwanted pregnancy. "Erectile tissue. It's all a matter of erection and secretion. . . . A confession before extreme unction: Semen smells nasty to me. . . . I found I stank like rotten fish when I was fertilized.[27] I wouldn't accept my wretched role. But now it's too damn lonely. We try out attitudes and find them all worthless. The forces are too strong. I mean . . . the horrible ones." (*Persona*'s Elizabet Vogler will also loathe her uncontrollable sexual urges.) She yawns, unexpectedly provoking another suffocating spasm. She flails grotesquely backwards and forwards on the bed until, at last, she is able to breathe. She screams, "I don't want to die alone!" The droning, deafening siren peals forth once more, effacing her voice. (As is often his habit, Bergman photographs her deathly expression from above and behind so that her face is upside-down.) Grabbing the sheet and pulling it over her head, Ester silences the siren; the impression is that she is dead. Suddenly, however, Johan, who has returned with his mother, whisks the sheet off her face, thus resurrecting her. Sensing his fright, she reassures him that she is not going to die. Then she bids the porter to hand Johan the *"important"* letter she has written him. Impatient to leave, Anna calls Johan to her, but surprisingly, instead of obeying, he crawls under the bed. When the annoyed porter drags out the little rebel, Johan throws his arms around Ester and kisses her until Anna gently pulls him away. Ester assures Anna that it is just as well that she and Johan are leaving, but Anna, having decided that she is no longer her sister's keeper, replies coldly, "I didn't ask your advice," and departs, Johan in tow. After the angelic porter also leaves, the camera dollies in on Ester staring at the ceiling.

The film's last movement continues the physical movement toward home. As the train pulls out of the station, Johan studies his mother, who is watching the rain beat against the window of their compartment. When she sees him looking at her, she guiltily lowers her eyes. He then turns to the letter from Ester. Threatened, Anna intercepts it. Reading, "TO JOHAN: WORDS IN A FOREIGN LANGUAGE," words she considers of no consequence, she hands the letter back to him and returns to the window, which she opens. A roar of noise pours into the compartment. As Susanne does in *Dreams,* Anna thrusts out her head and luxuriates in the driving rain as it bathes her arms and face. Deliciously baptismal, the rain seems to cleanse her guilt along with the sweat. We feel some of the same relief—at escaping the heat, the hotel's claustrophobia, deathly Timoka, and the dying Ester's hopelessly sick view of life. The film has posed the question, "Am I my sister's keeper?" A compassionate stranger and a little boy answer yes, but Anna's answer is no. For her, it is not that simple. We know from the intensity of her reactions that Ester is an important part of her—she admits that she is proud when Ester recognizes her as a good driver—and that she even harbors a trace of love for her dying sister. Yet we sympathize with the vital Anna's Cain-like hate and instinctive sense that to preserve her sense of self she must abandon her life-denying, vampiric sister. Her mistake, of course, is in believing that Ester's death will end her guilt. The way Johan stares at his mother suggests that his experience of the last few days has borne in him more than just a discriminating wariness. After repeatedly being rejected and betrayed by his mother, and having seen her abandon her own sister, he knows he will have to be more guarded—more consciously critical—as he enjoys the exquisite pleasure of her rare company. And Anna senses that Johan, whose build, countenance, and interests more closely resemble Ester's than her's, may also be developing her father's and Ester's censorial, if not moralistic streak. The scene's acoustic climax—the pounding of the train's wheels and its screaming whistle, the latter suggesting the deafening siren and, perhaps, Ester's last screams—makes it clear that Anna will never escape her guilt.

The film ends as it began, with an extreme close-up of Johan, this time puzzling over the foreign words that he mouths. In the beginning, even for Ester, "the word" was unintelligible. Why did she consider her letter "important"? What "secret message" does its words convey? We have seen that the inability to communicate—Johan's inability to understand what Punch is saying and what causes him to thrash Judy—or the desire not to communicate—Anna's desire that her waiter not understand her reasons for hating her sister, and Ester's confession of her deepest feelings only to herself—are the result of fear, hostility, and narcissism. Robbed by hate and selfishness of the ability or desire to communicate is like being sick in a hostile country that does not speak your language. Ester's horror of loneliness and death—again, it takes death for the Bergman character to achieve self-knowledge—has forced her to recognize how her narcissism has isolated her. Though she cannot change, her act of communication (by letter) conveys her realization that to be fully human one must get beyond narcissism and learn to empathize, as did the angelic old porter, with the feelings and suffering of others. Ester, says Bergman, "represents a distillation of something indestructibly human, which the boy inherits from her. . . . [It is] the impulse to understand a few words in another language" (*BB*, 183, 185). *The Silence*'s world, he says, is "utterly without god": "only the hand—fellowship—is left" (Sjöman, 222). The letter's two translated words are *hand* and *face*. "What matters most of all in life is being able to make . . . contact with another human. Otherwise you are dead. But if you can take that first step toward . . . understanding, toward love, then . . . you are saved" (*Playboy*, 68). If *Through a Glass Darkly, Winter Light,* and *The Silence* are a trilogy, it is because each ends with this contact: Minus's father talks to him, Tomas conducts the service for Märta, and Johan reads Ester's letter.

The difficulty Johan is shown to be experiencing in making out "the strange language" may be meant to show that spoken, written, and gestural languages are inadequate for grasping and conveying our complex mental and emotional experience. In *Persona* Mr. Vogler will complain how difficult he finds it to explain to his boy why Mrs. Vogler has rejected them both: "One loves someone, or one says one does. It's intangible . . . as words, I mean." In *The Touch,* after making love for the first time, David tells Karin (over the phone), "There's something important I'd like to tell you that I've never told anyone. . . . I'd like to tell you. I have no words. I'm illiterate." Images, like faces and hands, speak directly to us; they are more easily understood than the words *joy, spirit,* or *anxiety,* which, in the screenplay but not in the film, are the Timokan words Ester translates. To convey these complex feelings it takes not only words but images, tones of voice, compositions, music, sound effects, and rhythms—that is, all the elements of film. The double messages conveyed in Bergman's parents' words forever remain a caution: "Words ['Forgive me' and 'Poor So-and-so'] are used to conceal reality." He has been training us to see that we must penetrate words, smiles, and touching to get to the true feelings, that we must be crafty, even eavesdrop, if we are to get behind the multitude of masks. The film medium, especially its revealing close-ups and dream-making techniques, more and more becomes the message. "I dig for secret expressions. . . . Behind each face there is another and another and another. The actress's face gives you, in enormous concentration, that whole series of faces—not a single moment, but at different moments in the same performance or, sometimes, during a close-up. In each thousandth part of a second an actor gives you a different impression, but the succession is so rapid that you take them all as a single truth" (Kaminsky, 121). In *The Silence* and *Persona* Bergman says he experimented with "how far I could go without words" (Steene 1972, 44); cinema, he said, is "so sensitive an instrument that it should be possible to use it to illuminate the human soul" (Geduld, 188).

PERSONA

Persona (1966) is one of this century's great works of art, as well as one of its most complex. The following analysis is certainly not going to capture the film's richness of meaning and style, but by using the themes we have been tracing to interpret it I believe sense can be made of much that has confused or eluded viewers and critics. One of the latter has written, "Everything one says about *Persona* may be contradicted; the opposite will also be true" (Cowie 1982, 231). The films in this chapter—and several later chapters—are about the effect of Bergman's narcissistic personality on people, especially women, with whom he has had close relationships. We know that he writes a role with the actor or actress who will play it in mind. Bibi Andersson, the protagonist in the majority of the films in this chapter, remarks that whenever she read a new script for a film Bergman asked her to be in, she tried to figure out "what side of me he is trying to use now. . . . When I read *Persona* I wasn't flattered. I didn't understand why I had to play this sort of insecure, weak personality when I was struggling so hard to be sure of myself and to cover up my insecurities. I realized that he was totally aware of my personality (Andersson, 41–42). The drama (essentially a two-character one) of *Persona* is ignited when Bergman brings the character Bibi plays (Alma) into contact with the character, played by Liv Ullmann, who represents the worst side of his own personality (Elizabet).

Persona opens with an autobiographical "poem," a sort of visual haiku. Creating a strongly physical beat, this montage flashes by so rapidly that what Bergman said about an actor's performance applies: "In each thousandth part of a second an actor gives you a different impression, but the succession is so rapid that you take them all as a single truth" (Kaminsky, 121). The ideas wrapped in these images are highly solipsistic, but their meaning can be intuited and the whole film enjoyed without fully comprehending either the meaning or the film—as with dream. The narrative that follows the poem, though nowhere as persistently elliptical or esoteric, maintains this oneiric mode.[28] *Persona* is incomparable, in fact, because of its success in merging realism and the dream mode. It replicates one's ability in dreams to be the mysterious figures one has conjured up, and it approximates dream's erosion of the clear demarcations between time, space, and ego. Furthermore, as with dreams, it completely makes "one's awareness of time vanish" (Sjöman, 212), while making "time as duration . . . a dimension of space."[29] In *2001: A Space Odyssey* (1968) Stanley Kubrick probed the mysteries of outer space and at the end simulated breaking through the space-time barrier. Two years earlier, in *Persona,* Bergman had used dream techniques and extreme close-ups for a face odyssey that climaxed in his breaking the space-time-psyche barrier, and in his photographing a dissolving ego. (*Persona* probably could not have been created much earlier. The enlargement of film's vocabulary by such techniques as the jump cut and the freeze frame, made popular in the 1960s by French New Wave directors, seems to have liberated Bergman.) The film also employs a more musical structure than *any* previous commercial, nonanimated film with a linear narrative. Just as a piece of music exists both all at once as the printed score and in time as it is played, the short (only 84 minutes), intense *Persona* feels like it simultaneously exists all at once and as a narrative. It also approaches music as it moves us from place to place and from moment to moment in waves—of emotion, of images, of scenes. Unlike most films, *Persona* does not allow the viewer to feel anchored to clear actions developing in identifiable space and chronological time.

The poem that opens *Persona* begins with the screen dark. Slowly, parallel with the bottom of the frame, the image of a movie projector's left carbon arc begins to glow. Then, the right arc glows, resembling an erect penis as it emerges diagonally from the lower right. The two arcs touch and ignite. Kawin calls the explosion of light produced by this mating, "intercourse" (106); the light will realize, give identity to, the images imprinted on the film strip. This opening image establishes the film's rhythmic, structural, and thematic patterns: moving from sleep, or lack of self-awareness, to consciousness and self-knowledge. The image also prefigures the psychological fireworks that will result when the film's two protagonists are forced into close contact, and it symbolizes what Bergman sees as a key source of his creativity—aggression and sexual energy.

As the film starts up and passes the projector's lens, the numbers count down to the first image, which makes this connection between sexual energy and creativity explicit: it is a photograph of an erect penis also aimed diagonally toward the upper left, like the projector's right arc (see figs. 26, 27).[30] Next, playful, braying music accompanies an upside-down, momentarily frozen image of a scratched, animated cartoon (circa early 1900s). In addition to foreshadowing the momentary breakdown of the film during the later narrative, this image may allude to one of Bergman's first films as a child, about which he said, "If you looked into the lens upside-down, [the woman] vanished to the left" (*BB*, 8). The sound of film being pulled past the lens by the projector's sprockets now accompanies a shot of a real child's pudgy

Persona. AB Svensk Filmindustri

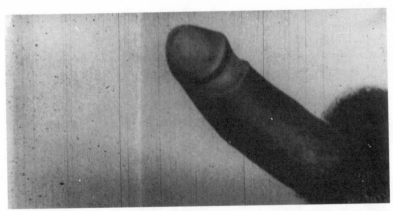

Persona. Stig Björkman. *Ingmar Bergman*

230

hands imitating a magician's gestures: . . . "shadows' unceasing movements controlled by me. . . . Hypnosis and magic."[31] There follows a snippet of the staged farce—based on another of his childhood films—that Bergman re-created for *The Devil's Wanton*; significantly, it is about a man prevented from going to sleep by, among other things, a spider, Death, and the Devil. The next set of images refer to Bergman themes. First, an ominous, hairy spider—Bergman's spider-God—is photographed against a halating, white background. Second, there is a reference to God's sacrificial victims: to discordant music, a lamb with its throat cut is bled and gutted, and the executioner forces us to look closely at its staring eye. Bergman says that Alma "provided some blood and meat" for Elizabet, the film's other character (Simon, 32). The third image evokes those characters who, like Birgitta Carolina or Antonius Block, consciously sacrifice themselves: a hand, seemingly the victim's own, holds the wrist of a melodramatically lit hand as a black spike is hammered—the sound crushingly magnified—through its palm; syrupy blood emerges from the wound. These thematic shots are followed by shots related to Bergman's location and state of mind when the idea for *Persona* came to him. We see soiled snowbanks, hospital grounds and buildings, and then, in the hospital's morgue, images of rigid hands, feet, and the waxy, sunken faces of corpses. We hear the echoing sound of voices, doors slamming, dripping water, and the nagging ring of a telephone. The last sound awakens a female corpse—her eyes suddenly pop open—whose face is seen (typically) upside-down in the frame. It also awakens a seemingly dead boy—Bergman's young alter ego in *The Silence*. Johan (the 13-year-old Jörgen Lindström) sits up, puts on his wire-rimmed glasses, and continues reading *A Hero of Our Times*, the book he was reading in *The Silence* (suggesting that we, too, are embarking on a narrative journey). After a moment, however, he is distracted by the huge, at first out-of-focus faces (of Bibi Andersson and Liv Ullmann) emerging on what seems to be the outward projection of his mindscreen. As these alternating faces continue to dissolve in and out of each other, the boy tries to caress them.

Bergman helps us with some of these images. He tells us that in March 1965 he was in the hospital suffering from (among other things) an infection of the inner ear that forced him to cancel his plans to make a four-hour film to be called "The Cannibals" as well as his trip to Amsterdam to receive the Erasmus Prize, which he was to share with Charles Chaplin.[32] (Bergman's colleague Kenne Fant went in his place and delivered Bergman's "Snakeskin" speech. In it, he confessed that for 20 years he had worked in a kind of rage, born of the "dammed-up hunger of my childhood," to communicate "dreams, sensual experiences, fantasies, outbursts of madness, neuroses, the convulsions of faith, and downright lies."[33]) Bergman administered the affairs of the Royal Dramatic Theater, of which he was still the head, by phone from his hospital bed. He says about *Persona's* opening poem: "I . . . began with the projector and my desire to set it in motion. But when the projector was running, nothing came out of it but old ideas, the spider, God's lamb, all that dull old stuff. My life just then consisted of dead people, brick walls, and a few dismal trees out in the park. In hospital one has a strong sense of corpses. . . . So I made believe I was a little boy who'd died, yet wasn't allowed to be really dead, because he kept on being woken up by telephone calls from the Royal Dramatic Theatre. Finally he . . . lay down and read a book . . . and suddenly two faces are floating into one another" (*BB,* 198–99).[34] The shots showing Bergman's alter ego reaching out to caress the lips and noses—as a child left alone in a hospital morgue, Bergman caressed the corpse of a dead woman—of the seductive, teasingly elusive faces suggest an infant reaching out to his mother's face or breast. Arguably, Bergman as the boy, and we the audience, "are both linked at the mother's breast, the screen, caught in a dream in which we want to return to a sense of oneness with the eternal world."[35] In the reverse angle, the boy reaches toward the camera, making *us* the mother substitute who can provide the attention and love for which he hungers. This segment climaxes and ends with the dizzying, high-pitched whir, which has accompanied the boy's groping, growing louder as the alternating faces become sharper. Bibi Andersson has her eyes closed, an important detail because near the film's end this image returns and her eyes are open.

The credits that follow are virtually indistinguishable from the previous poem; they pass rapid-fire and are alternated with two sorts of images. First are images that will appear in the subsequent narrative: the famous footage of the Vietnamese monk immolating himself, Alma's and Elizabet's faces (sometimes half in shadow), *The Devil's Wanton's* farce, and the boy's (Bergman's) face (which appears ten times, more than any other image). (In the credits Bergman just uses Jörgen Lindström's face, not his name.) The second kind of image does not reappear: there is, for example, a shot of seaweed, and a shot of a pair of lips arranged vertically so that they suggest a vagina (a companion to the penis). The latter image may allude to the huge photograph of a pair of lips that opens Bergman's *Dreams*. (*Dreams'* very title makes it an appropriate reference here, but since the coming together of like images is the most important motif in *Persona*, the image of two lips is especially fitting.) These images and credits alternate so rapidly that they become almost subliminal; thus we are alerted to expect that what follows will be more visual than verbal, and that we should be prepared to use our noncognitive as well as our cognitive abilities. The cognitive frustration we feel during the poem and credits makes the subsequent narrative come as a relief.

Persona is the story, par excellence, of narcissism and a fortunate fall. As the pure white screen out of which she materializes suggests, Sister Alma is a tabula rasa. She became a nurse partly because her mother was a nurse and partly because it satisfies her need to "mean . . . something to others." Like Britt-Marie (*The Devil's Eye*), this pretty 25-year-old is marrying a man she only "likes a lot." Being committed to a profession and to marriage, however, makes her secure and happy: "That's all settled. It's inside me . . . it's a nice, safe feeling." Like Britt-Marie's Jonas, Alma's Karl-Henrik knows her mind better than she does, but Karl-Henrik upbraids her for going "around like a sleepwalker," meaning that she—like Karin (*The Touch*)—is unable to think through important decisions or assert her will. (Alma will later marvel at her patient doing what *she* wants, regardless of what everyone else expects.) Alma's position as the youngest child and only girl in a family of seven brothers goes a long way toward explaining her habitual self-denial, as well as the seductive appeal for her of being in charge of a patient who is mute: "People tell me I'm a good listener. . . . No one has ever bothered to listen to me the way you [do]. . . . I've been surrounded by boys all my life."

Elizabet Vogler contrasts dramatically with the acquiescent Alma. Like Renata (*The Devil's Eye*), who complains that "no one sees me as my real self," Elizabet, a famous actress, suddenly decided to cease playing the roles life had imposed upon her or to which she had acquiesced. She took to bed, refused to speak, and finally entered a hospital. She has been mute for three months when her psychiatrist assigns Sister Alma to her. We are in attendance when Alma, as nervous as if she were being called on the carpet, is summoned. The psychiatrist, a handsome, self-assured woman, is wearing a white medical coat and sits behind a desk in an antiseptic white office. (Satan's office in *The Devil's Eye*, though darker, was emotionally warmer.) Alma stands facing the desk from a distance. As the psychiatrist relates Elizabet's case history to Alma, shots illustrating it are inserted, creating the impression that the minds of the psychiatrist and the omniscient author/image maker are somehow connected. The omniscient author also shows us Alma's fidgeting hands behind her back, and in the next scene, by means of a shot from under Elizabet's bed that catches Alma shifting her weight from one foot to the other, he reveals her secret discomfort. We are further made aware of his presence when, as he did in *Secrets of Women,* Bergman expressionistically dims the light on Elizabet's face.[36] "One consciousness," says Bergman, quoting Strindberg's preface to his *A Dream Play,* "is superior to [all the images]: that of the dreamer. For him there are no secrets."[37]

Alma tells the psychiatrist that, only having been a nurse for two years, she feels she may not be up to dealing with a woman who "won't speak or move because she *decides* not to." As if intrigued by the experiment, this female Vergerus (God, Satan, or Bergman) nevertheless throws the lamb to the mute, pathological lion, who, says Bergman, is "a monster because she has an emptiness in her" (Simon, 32). Before falling asleep that night, Alma, who idolizes the actress, whispers Elizabet's name into the darkness, in what is almost a lover's incantation.

Through a Glass Darkly's David says he repeatedly has to redraw a protective circle around himself to keep out reality; Elizabet's psychiatrist will warn her that "reality is diabolical. Your hiding place [muteness] isn't watertight. Life trickles in from the sides and you're forced to react." As Alma slips off to an apparently dreamless sleep, Elizabet is having a nightmare. In it, she is lit by the glow from a television monitor placed near the foot of her bed as she paces her hospital room. A male, English-speaking news commentator describes U.S. planes from Guam dropping bombs on Vietcong positions, but his narrative is inappropriate to what we see and hear on the monitor, which now completely fills the movie screen: the image of the Vietnamese Buddhist monk immolating himself, and a man trying to snap his photograph. The monk is another of those "moralistic moralists" like Antonius Block and those strong-willed individuals like Elizabet of whom Bergman is "scared stiff" but with whom he identifies (*BB,* 257). The image sends Elizabet cowering into the far corner of her room. Her hand flies to her face to shield it from the flaming image and to stifle her silent scream, but she does not stop staring. (Artists, says Bergman, "see friends and relatives torn apart by conflicts, but the cannibal in them is always ready waiting to note down, to observe" [Sjöman, 159].) Elizabet's dream replays—we see it—the burning monk falling onto his left elbow, and with each close-up the assaultive sound grows louder. Then sound and picture cease as mysteriously as they materialized, and only the relieved Elizabet's panting is heard. Her Electra-like strength of will has managed even in her dream to shut out the unpleasant image. Her ability to shut out unpleasant reality is characteristic. Earlier, after first laughing at it, she angrily had turned off her bedside radio as a woman in a soap opera was pleading, "Forgive me, my darling. . . . Your forgiveness is all I crave. . . . What do you know about mercy?" Subsequently, when Alma reads a letter to Elizabet from her husband that contains a photograph of their son, she snatches the letter out of Alma's hands, crumples it, and tears the photograph in half when the husband describes Elizabet being overcome by sexual passion (something Ester also hated). Later Elizabet will also walk away from the psychiatrist as she describes Elizabet's (Bergman's) "constant hunger to be exposed . . . to be seen through," and later yet, she will walk out on Alma when she voices an unflattering truth about her patient.

Again calling attention to his omniscient control, Bergman (in voice-over) informs us that the psychiatrist sends Alma with her patient to the psychiatrist's summer home, and he describes their settling in. In a series of scenes that blur chronology, Alma, who has to do all the talking, becomes increasingly infatuated with her idol, who is attentive and seemingly affectionate. Alma has doffed her uniform for an open-necked, short-sleeved dress, whereas Elizabet wears a protective, long-sleeved turtleneck. In one stunning set of shots, sunlight, like the reality the psychiatrist talked about, leaks through the brims of their straw hats to produce lovely, sliding freckles of light on their shadowed faces. Alma's growing identification with Elizabet is stressed by shots that make her head appear to be on Elizabet's neck and Elizabet's hands appear to be Alma's. But their differences are also being clarified. Reading from a book, for example, Alma asks Elizabet if she believes the author's statement that our desolate existence, "inexplicable cruelty," and "terror at the thought of extinction" are the sources of our creation of God and salvation. (Bergman illustrates her words with shots of a barren, rocky terrain.) Thoughtfully and with absolute conviction, Elizabet shakes her head yes. From behind her protective dark glasses, Alma replies emphatically, "I don't."

As Alma progressively reveals her secrets, she even finds herself examining repressed sexual feelings. Her most memorable secret is of once having sunbathed naked with a stranger, a woman her age, and their having had sex with two very young boys, an experience so liberating that the sex Alma had that night with her fiancé was unique.[38] Bergman rightly says that "[you] experience [Alma's story] all deep down inside you, in your own cinematograph—much more . . . brutally, honestly, and voluptuously than I could ever show" (*BB,* 208). (Alma's narration, in fact, vies with one in Jean-Luc Godard's *Weekend* [1967] for the honor of being the most erotic in film.)[39] The implications of this story for Alma's feelings for Elizabet are inescapable. Later, in bed beside Elizabet, Alma begins sobbing. Throwing her arms around Elizabet, she confesses that she subsequently became pregnant but acceded to Karl-Henrik's desire that she abort the fetus. Like a mother who considers her crying child's pain exaggerated, the smiling Elizabet tries to soothe Alma's inconsolable grief by stroking her hair and patting her face.

In the morning, after a sleepless night and a lot of wine, a tipsy, deliciously relaxed Alma caresses Elizabet's cheek and tells her that though Elizabet is prettier Alma believes they look alike and that she could change herself into Elizabet if it were not that the actress has too large a soul. Then, imagining that Elizabet *tells* her to go to bed, she retires and dreams that Elizabet comes through the fog-filled house to her bedroom, stands beside her, and, just as Alma is in the habit of doing, brushes Alma's hair (now boyishly cut) off her forehead. The exquisite merging of the two continues as Alma rests her head on Elizabet's shoulder and Elizabet, closing her eyes, lays her face on the back of Alma's neck so that her lips just touch it. It is an erotic, swanlike ballet of arching arms, caressing hands, and elegant, sensually intertwined necks.[40] This tactile, melancholy dream is enriched by the periodic moan of a foghorn and by the gauzy, white curtains that, like ghosts, billow into the room, gently pushed by puffs of gray fog.

The next scene, the following morning, opens with a jolt, created by Bergman's use of off-screen space: Elizabet, a still camera at the ready, pops up from below—right in front of the movie camera—and snaps our picture. It is another device to make us aware of the storyteller/image maker, but it also pulls us into the story by forcing us to recognize ourselves as eavesdroppers. Alma is deeply disappointed and confused to learn that Elizabet not only did not tell her to go to bed the previous evening but did not visit her.

Eavesdropping is the mechanism Bergman uses in the next scene, a pivotal scene almost as powerful as the one in *Through a Glass Darkly* in which Karin reads in her father's diary that he is studying her psychological disintegration. Driving to the post office, Alma is unable to resist the unsealed letter—has it been left open, as it appears, from Elizabet's haste to get it off, or from an unconscious desire to have Alma read it?—that Elizabet has written to her psychiatrist.[41] Alma stops the car and reads it. Elizabet, after acknowledging that she feels some healing has occurred, says she finds it "fun studying" Alma, who is a "tiny bit in love" with her and who (referring to the beach orgy and the abortion) suffers because her "ideas don't tally with her acts." For some time mist or drizzling rain have encased the island and created a blurry ambience; now the rain is gone, and though the day is still gray and overcast, everything is clear and sharp. As Alma reflects on Elizabet's statements, she appears in a brief shot that places us halfway across a small pond at whose edge she stands. At her feet, Narcissus-like, is her perfectly mirrored reflection, suggesting the emergence of that other self we glimpsed in her story about the orgy and in her dream. Feeling betrayed and rejected, she silently puzzles over the sort of person with whom she is dealing. Hands in the pockets of her shiny slicker, one leg—she is wearing high boots—advanced, her body is turned away slightly but her head faces us over her shoulder. Her stance projects determination and bitterness.

In the next scene bright morning sunlight replaces the recent scenes' grayness. As we have noted, Bergman believes long shots heighten emotion; the brutal is "more terrifying from a distance" because it enables "you to experience it all deep inside you." Bergman now makes us eavesdroppers from the shadows of the trees about 30 feet away from the house. ("It was from [Mizoguchi] I pinched [this] long shot which I regard as among the most successful I've ever made" [Kaminsky, 110; *BB*, 109, 209]). Barefoot and wearing a black bathing suit and black straw hat, Alma emerges from the cottage carrying a glass of orange juice. Sitting on a bench against the building, and beginning to soak up the sun, she accidentally knocks over the empty glass, which shatters on the flagstone walk. She sweeps up and disposes of the shards. When she has finished, she sits on the step and lights a cigarette. After a moment she notices that she has missed a large shard and picks it up. She immediately replaces it, however, as she hears Elizabet preparing to join her. The camera closes in—the film's basic structure—on Alma as Elizabet joins her outside. Beneath her hat brim, Alma's eyes are fixed on the shard that the passing Elizabet's bare feet miss twice. As Elizabet approaches it for the third time, Alma gets up and goes into the cottage. We are forced to imagine—we hear Elizabet's cry—this first drawing of blood. Looking out the window, Alma sees Elizabet holding her cut foot. Alma unflinchingly meets Elizabet's puzzled, outraged stare. Suddenly, the right side of the acetate film strip bearing Alma's image splinters off (a visual correspondence to the shattered glass), leaving that side of the white screen glaring from the light from the (imaginary) projector's lamp. Alma's complete image returns momentarily, but the film sticks in the gate and her face slowly melts from the buildup of heat. (In *Fanny and Alexander* Alex's anger will immolate his hated enemy.) Finally, the film slips off the sprockets, and all we see is the tabula rasa, the totally white screen.

Bergman has several explanations for this interruption,[42] but one thing is certain: it momentarily deprives the viewer of his sugar-tit fiction—the pleasure of looking and the druglike pleasure that narrative provides by drawing one out of oneself. On first viewing, people invariably moan because they think that the film has actually broken and burnt. Besides reminding us that this is a film, the deprivation ties into the poem, which ends with the boy reaching out to the screen/ breast. The regeneration of the image-making/storytelling process, which draws from Bergman's as well as Alma's mind, is accompanied by garbled voices insanely repeating a phrase. First, footage appears from the slapstick comedy that appeared in the poem: Satan and Death pop out of trunks and, with a robber and a policeman, violently chase the man in the nightgown. The Devil's presence is emphasized; violent and primitive, he seems to have burned his way through Alma's brittle, adult mask (film) to produce a momentary film death. Whiteness again possesses the screen. Then comes a distorted cry of excruciating pain, followed by the sound and image (from the poem) of the spike being hammered through the hand whose wrist the victim, himself, seems to be holding. The camera next moves so close to an eyeball that its veins are in sharp focus and we feel that we are about to break through sight into the mind. (When the projector has been turned off, Bergman writes in the screenplay, "I think the shadows will continue their game [of] . . . reach[ing] out toward the senses, deep inside the retina, or into the finest recesses of the ear" so that they are as alive in the audience as they are in their creator, "their rage surviv[ing] . . . without the help of the picture frames.") Music gradually replaces the electronic, otherworldly sounds, and as if this dreamer, who has had a momentary breakdown, has gotten his or her dream back on track, an out-of-focus, ectoplasmic figure (Elizabet) floats in slow motion toward us through curtains. The action has just returned to normal speed when the image maker freezes the frame to adjust all the elements so the dream can proceed properly. A loud, sharp note on the violin accompanies the picture's snap into focus as it picks up the narrative at the exact same location—though at a later time that same day—it broke down. But there is this difference: it is Elizabet, worried about Alma's whereabouts, who is looking out the window.

Apropos of the filmic regeneration that has just taken place is Bruce Kawin's proposal that this film takes "shape not only in the director's imagination but also in the mind of the work," that is, even though the film is incapable of itself being self-conscious or conscious, it "can imitate consciousness . . . give the impression of presentational autonomy, and of self-awareness. . . . In this context, every frame in *Persona* makes manifest a dialectic—perhaps the most characteristic one in modern art—in which the self-conscious artist and the self-conscious audience engage across the self-conscious mind of the work" (111, 115–16).

Elizabet at last locates Alma sitting on the stone wall of the terrace. She is wearing insolently black sunglasses and pretending to be reading. Elizabet touches her nurse's cheek with the back of her hand and then sits down and begins slitting the uncut pages of her book (suggesting both an opening up of what has been sealed away and a sense of violation of the virginal). After a few moments have passed, Alma interrupts her to beg her to talk. She says she can no longer bear the silence. (In *The Touch* Karin tells David, "I can't bear your silence; that's the only thing I can't bear," a reference not only to the hated treatment Bergman received as a child but, one suspects, to a punishment that he himself employs.[43]) The freckles of light created by the sunlight filtering through Elizabet's straw hat remind us of the pair's earlier closeness, but Elizabet's silence, black shoulder, and the stone wall behind her are her only answer. Framed on the left by a wiry, thorny tree and on the right by a ship's figurehead of a woman, which Bergman says he likes "because she is made of hardwood" (Kaminsky, 112), Alma screams, "I always thought great artists had compassion, that they created out of this compassion and a need to help. But that is silly!" In the hospital, when Alma told Elizabet that she admired artists and felt that art was important "especially for people with problems," Elizabet smiled, reflecting Bergman's contempt (*BB,* 211) for the belief that artists—actors, writers, or directors—necessarily possess their fictional characters' compassion, morality, or unselfishness. When Elizabet still does not speak, Alma rips off her black glasses, acknowledging that they were meant to signal her hostility as well as to help her distance her emotions. Then she bursts into tears and noisily busies herself gathering up the dishes and pots from the picnic table. When Elizabet joins her, Alma's anger leads her to confess that she read Elizabet's letter and to charge her with laughing at her behind her back. Furious, Elizabet walks away, but Alma grabs and shakes her, screaming that she will *make* her talk. Elizabet slaps Alma's face and shoves her against the wall. Alma rebounds, spitting. Elizabet slaps her again, bloodying her nose. Blood has been drawn by both sides. A jump cut to Alma wielding a pan of boiling water. Elizabet cries out, "No, don't!" Alma sets down the pan, goes up to Elizabet, taunts her about her fear, and asks, "What sort of person are you? Or did you think, 'I'll remember that face, that inflection, that expression.'" As if to tear off Elizabet's mask, Alma grabs her cheek. When she lets go, Elizabet feels to see if there is any blood; finding none, and suddenly regarding Alma's unhappiness and the situation as absurd—seemingly, only death (the burning monk) can get to her—she unexpectedly smiles, though she tries to suppress it. Frightened by her own emotions and defeated by Elizabet's, Alma, sobbing and already looking apologetic, goes inside to wash her bloodstained face. The slow disappearance of Elizabet's smile as Alma departs, and her offer to Alma of a cup of coffee when she emerges from the bathroom, lead us to hope that maybe, at last, she feels some compassion. Alma, who has stopped crying, accepts the cup and poses a question: Doesn't lying and just settling for surfaces—as, until now, she has always done—make living with people easier? For the moment, we may feel that Alma's position is reprehensible compared with Elizabet's heroic purging of the dross of insincerity and role playing. But Elizabet's act, as Steene perceives (1968, 115), is an act of integrity only "as long as no one else is involved." Bergman now reveals how much Alma has matured by demonstrating that she fathoms Elizabet's narcissism more clearly than does even Elizabet's psychiatrist (whom, in the screenplay, he mocks[44]): "People like you can't be reached," says Alma. "I wonder if your kind of madness isn't the worst kind. You act healthy, act so well that everyone believes you. Everyone except me, because I know how rotten you are." Elizabet's reaction, hidden from Alma because the actress's back is to her, makes it clear that Alma has hit a nerve. Checking her impulse to reply, Elizabet hurries from the house. Alma, her hand flying to her mouth to net the truths she has let escape, whispers, "What am I doing?" and races after her patient.

A short distance away, with scrub bushes between the two women and us, the camera tracks with Alma running along the rocky shore in pursuit of Elizabet. Over the sound of the waves we hear her pathetic, heartbroken plea for Elizabet to forgive her. At last Elizabet turns and lets her catch up. The camera comes in on Alma's tearful face. Elizabet looks her in the eye, then turns and continues up the beach. The cruelty of this rejection renders Alma incoherent. Her cry "I won't! I won't!" may mean she refuses to beg any longer; or it may convey a thought expressed later in a dream, "No, I'm not like you"; or, given that her identity may be dissolving in her desperation and hysteria, she may be imagining herself as Elizabet and vocalizing the rejection: "I won't forgive you." Backing away and still sobbing, she runs toward the sea and throws herself on the rocky beach, pressing her face against the jagged stones. A dissolve indicates a passage of time. Alma has not left the shore, but now she is a tiny figure in black, sitting huddled amid mammoth, gray boulders. Her fresh, innocent expression has been replaced by a lightless stare and the repose of an angerless, possibly suicidal despair. Throughout, Lars Johan Werle's heavily electronic musical score is flawlessly wedded to the film's images and moods; now, an electronically modified, high piano note is slowly repeated and eerily combined with low, foghornlike notes and a droning, oriental-sounding instrument. The motionless Alma remains on the giant boulders even as darkness settles. Meanwhile, Elizabet, who has been worriedly peering out the window, stops pacing and lights a kerosene lamp. After a moment she casually flips open a book. A photograph drops out it—one of the most famous photographs from the Holocaust. It pictures Warsaw Jews being herded by German soldiers through the streets. Intrigued, Elizabet props it up against the lamp, turns up the light, and bends close to study it. A subjective camera and montage indicate that she is focusing on the seven- or eight-year-old boy separated from the prisoners on his left and the soldiers with rifles on his right. He is carefully dressed in a cap and overcoat, short pants, and knee-length socks. His arms are raised as if he were a dangerous criminal; under his cap his frightened, uncomprehending face remains brave. In front of him on the left (his right) is a woman also with her arms raised—she must be a mother—whose head is turned as she addresses over her shoulder a frenetically inquisitive, slightly older boy. Amid the crush of bodies behind this boy peeps the face of yet another tiny boy (see fig. 28). From the start, the increase in the speed of the panning and cutting from one figure or bunching of figures to another conveys Elizabet's deepening absorption. Her scrutiny is accompanied by a screaming whine, like that of a diving plane, which increases in volume and pitch until the feeling of terror and panic reach a crescendo with her finally zeroing in on the first boy, especially his little, upraised hands. Then the shot fades to black. The context forces us to conclude that Elizabet is attempting to penetrate—as we have been forced to do with her—the emotions in the faces and gestures in the photograph, not merely to "use" them, but because she has connected her treatment of the suffering, essentially innocent Alma with the German soldiers' treatment of these people, whose innocence is symbolized by the child. The transition from the shot of the boy to Alma in the next scene underscores this identification. As in Elizabet's nightmare about the suicidal monk, this

Persona. AB Svensk Filmindustri

photograph seems to have touched some deeply buried but still sensitive spot in Elizabet, though as usual with a Bergman narcissist, it takes a brush with death to reach it. Since on the following morning she returns to society, we may assume that she is ashamed of her cruel behavior even though she cannot escape her pathology.

More important than what is going on in her head is what is going on in her victim's. Alma is about to fight back. In her dream that night Alma works not only to get the upper hand over Elizabet but to break through Elizabet's calcified humanity. (The means Alma uses to respond to her view of the world being shattered—a dream—is almost as important as the fall from innocence itself.) The scene opens with her dreaming that she is convulsively fighting off a nightmare. A voice on the radio in Alma's dream announces part of her goal: "What means can I use to make you listen?" Then, like the corpse—the living dead—in the film's opening poem, Alma suddenly comes alive, her eyes open. After a moment she hears Elizabet's husband calling his wife, and Alma goes to him in her stead. (Earlier, Alma said that her only passionate love affair had been with a married man who became bored with her: "I was never quite real to him." Because he, too, smoked, she identified him with Elizabet.) In Alma's dream, Elizabet, dressed in her black turtleneck and black headband, is present at the meeting and is usually seen over Alma's shoulder in an Edvard Munch–like composition. Alma insists to Mr. Vogler (Gunnar Björnstrand) that she is not his wife, but he is made blind in her dream to facilitate his mistake (it is night and he is wearing dark glasses). To disguise her aim of making Elizabet jealous while she is trying to teach her how to love, Alma has Elizabet place Alma's hand on her husband's cheek. Mr. Vogler professes his love for Alma-Elizabet and informs her that what counts in a relationship is the effort one makes to understand not only the other's good resolutions but the often uncontrollable "forces" (like sexuality) that can rule them. Alma's reply, "We know each other's thoughts," foreshadows her clairvoyance in the next episode. During Alma's conversation with Mr. Vogler, Elizabet's back—she is facing us—is to the couple, but because this is a dream, Alma can see her face just as we do; in fact, we are made conduits of the dream. As in the close-ups of Marie in *Summer Interlude,* the right side of the frame momentarily cuts Elizabet's face in half. This technique not only adds to the impression that the film is getting closer to her psyche, it is yet another halving that foreshadows the upcoming merge of Alma's and Elizabet's faces. [This composition

Edward Munch. *Jealousy* (1895?), 25-1/2″ × 39″, University of Michigan Photographic Services. Bergen kommunes kunstsamlinger (Bergen Billedgalleri, Rasmus Meyrers Samlinger and Stenersens Samling).

Persona. AB Svensk Filmindustri

seems to have been inspired by Edvard Munch's *Jealousy* (see figs. 28, 29).]

Still trying to provoke passion in the apparently bored, even disgusted Elizabet, Alma, like Renata capitulating to the love-deprived Pablo (*The Devil's Eye*), has sex with Mr. Vogler. Afterwards, however, she can no longer maintain the sham. Her adultery, her lie to Mr. Vogler—"You're a wonderful lover"—and her having so successfully become Elizabet that she feels "cold and rotten and bored," are all so guilt-provoking that again Alma convulsively tries to wake up. The last shot, however, is of Elizabet's enigmatically vacant face, half of which is in ominous shadow. The struggle has been fought on Alma's dream turf, but Elizabet has won the first round.

Having failed to awaken wifely feelings, the dream combat continues with Alma trying to awaken maternal feelings. Alma catches Elizabet sitting at a table secretly studying the pieced-together halves of her son's photograph. (The halves also foreshadow the facial merge, and the photograph calls to mind the Jewish boy.) Dressed like Elizabet in a black turtleneck shirt and a black headband, Alma sits across from her and clairvoyantly describes Elizabet's past. Elizabet became pregnant when someone said that the only thing she lacked was motherliness. The pregnancy, however, made her hate her swelling body and fear not only the pain of childbirth and the possibility of dying but the resultant responsibility. She attempted to have the fetus aborted but failed, and the boy was born deformed. (In Bergman's films deformed or sickly children represent their being unwanted and unloved.) Elizabet responded to his "ugly body and . . . moist, pleading eyes" and his "strange and violent love" for her with hate, cold indifference, and revulsion. (Earlier, when we saw Elizabet's nightmare, we had to be struck that the image of the burning monk had been part of the film's opening credits, which almost seemed an extension of Bergman's opening poem. "If she can dream about it, it's because . . . it's I who am giving her her dreams" [*BB*, 253]. If this is the case, Alma should be able to tap into Bergman's omniscience, an ability that would explain her present clairvoyance.) Alma now repeats the same story word for word, but whereas the first time the camera was on Elizabet's reactions—which confirmed the truth of the assertions—the second time it is on Alma. When she has finished the second telling, she slowly becomes aware that her empathic invasion of Elizabet's pathology is eroding her sense of self. She tries to fight off her loss of identity but cannot. Alma once told Elizabet, "You could change yourself into me like this [snaps her fingers]"; all of the devices I have noted, including repeated elisions, blurrings, halvings, and doubled time and space, facilitate what we and Alma (and Elizabet) now see and experience: the right side of Elizabet's face momentarily invades and replaces the right side of Alma's. Realizing what is happening, Alma moans, "No! I'm not like you. I don't feel as you do. I'm Sister Alma. . . . I'm not Elizabet Vogler! . . . *I'd* like to have . . . I love. . . ." But again Elizabet defeats her. The grotesque Siamesing of foreheads, noses, lips, chins, and agonized, moist eyes fascinates and forces us to experience what it feels like to lose control of one's sense of self, what I was referring to when I said that in this film Bergman photographs a dissolving ego.

Alma tries a third time to assert herself over Elizabet. For this assault she has strengthened her identity by abandoning Elizabet's penchant for black; she is dressed in her nurse's uniform. Her face determined, even hostile, Alma again faces Elizabet across the table and tells her that she has "learned quite a lot," but, she insists, "I'll never be like you. . . . You will never reach me." The silhouette lighting of this head-to-head encounter almost completely eliminates their individuality, thus undermining Alma's assertion. Sensing this and again resisting, Alma pounds on the table and covers her face with her apron. Turning her back on Alma, Elizabet faces us and, like a ventriloquist's dummy, mouths the words that Alma, her face no longer in sharp focus, is uttering aloud. It is more than just a moment of psychic overload. According to Bergman, "She [Alma] has been driven nearly insane by her resentments so that words. . .can no longer be put together by her. But it is not a matter of psychology. Rather, this comes at the point inside the movement of the film itself where words can no longer have any meaning" (Kaminsky, 111).

Like waves washing on shore, Alma dreams yet another scenario that may give her dominion: she has Elizabet's mouth caress and then bite into her (Alma's) wrist. (Besides calling to mind Munch's *The Vampire,* this image also recalls the previous images of the impaled hand.) As the blood oozes from between Elizabet's lips, Alma grips Elizabet's hair and, breathing deeply from the pleasure that comes with this perverse union, holds Elizabet's head in place. Then she pulls it away and, with teeth bared and crying, screams to fight off her own vampiric qualities that she feels exist, monstrously magnified, in Elizabet. Uncontrollably and repeatedly, she slaps Elizabet's face, but she has been defeated again.

Alma finally stage-manages a victory. Her recognition that Elizabet is feeding off of Alma's psychic health, and that she is capable of resisting Elizabet, has fortified her. She now replays her first encounter with Elizabet in the hospital. Alma had been ill at ease then, but now Elizabet's eyes are closed and she appears to be in a trance, defenseless. As church bells (signs of victory) ring in the background, Alma places Elizabet's frowning, oily face on her shoulder and has her say, "Nothing." In total command, Alma answers, "That's right. That's the way it shall be."[45] The image then dissolves to the lovely image Alma created in her first dream: Elizabet, standing behind Alma, reaching around and pulling back and caressing Alma's hair. This time, however, Alma does not rest her head on Elizabet's shoulder.

Gasping, Alma awakens from her dream. Leaving her bed, she discovers Elizabet packing her suitcase (until we see Elizabet back at work, this image is all that indicates Elizabet has left the island). In uniform, Alma tidies and closes up the house. As she is leaving, she stops momentarily before the hall's full-length mirror and reenacts the dream image of Elizabet pulling her hair off her forehead. Suddenly, as happens to Isak Borg before going to sleep at night, her cherished vision appears: Elizabet, one hand on Alma's shoulder and the other stroking—their hands overlapping—Alma's hair (see fig. 31). The fact that the image is not perfectly superimposed, as it was when she

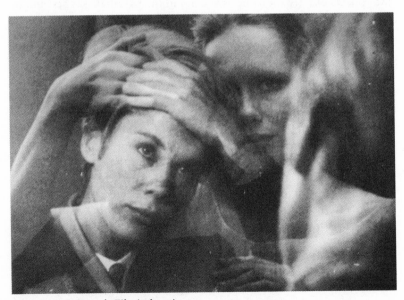

Persona. AB Svensk Filmindustri

dreamed it, indicates that Alma retains her own identity. When the vision dissolves, her hand is still resting on her hair, and a semblance of a smile forms: she will remember Elizabet fondly. Though she has had an experience that has hurt her deeply and destroyed her naïveté, her goodness and wholeness remain. Like Karin (*The Touch*), Alma is saying, "No one has done me so much harm as you. No one has done me so much good." (Bibi Andersson, in fact, believes Alma's experience "will change [her] life" [Andersson, 44].) Outside, we look past the wooden figurehead as in the near distance Alma locks the cottage door. The figurehead's huge, upward-tilted, painted face stares out of the frame at us. As was often the case with Elizabet, her back is to Alma. The figurehead's hardness and dark, curled, carved hair evoke Elizabet, but Alma, too, partakes of its strength. It may also represent hope: in another context Liv Ullmann, possibly using a metaphor suggested by Bergman, writes, "I was like a figurehead on an old ship. She who is standing seemingly so proud at the bow and plows through the waves and gazes ahead" (Ullmann, 158). The very next shot is a close-up of Elizabet playing Electra. Her face is a painted mask: her lips are parted, her glistening eyes are staring dead ahead. Like the figurehead, her black hair is curled into carved-looking ringlets and pasted against her forehead. When she turns and looks at us she appears exactly the same as she did in the psychiatrist's account of the day she suddenly realized she was unhappy with her condition. Bergman's later assessment is that she is intelligent, gifted, and sensible, that she possesses emotions but is immoral—by which I think he means that she is pathologically narcissistic. His prognosis is that she will go on, "but she's a monster because she has an emptiness in her" (Simon, 32). The film gives us hope that at least she better understands herself.

Bergman cuts back to Alma, walking along the beach road to catch the bus. Then he cuts to Elizabet again, but now she is in the midst of a film shoot: the buzzer calls for silence, and the crane bearing the 35mm camera, Sven Nykvist, and the camera operator descends for a close-up of her (living-dead) face, which is reflected upside-down in the glass fronting the lens. Next, he cuts to the bus that Alma boards and pans with it until it is out of sight; the pan continues downward, to the barren, gravelly earth. This last image may suggest the effects of Bergman's lifelong feeling of unrequited affection for his mother, an interpretation supported by the following image: Bergman's alter ego, Jörgen Lindström, is still, as in the beginning, reaching out to the two faces—Alma's and Elizabet's, Bibi Andersson's and Liv Ullmann's (the former, significantly, now with her eyes open)—on his mindscreen. These mother substitutes tantalizingly float in and out of each other and grow vaguer. As the boy seems about to give up, he is suddenly replaced by the image of the tail end of the film's last reel slipping off the projector's rollers. The absence of film in front of the sound exciter lamp produces static, the carbon arcs separate and darken—photographing them from the opposite side acts as a further framing device—and the screen returns to black.

Before leaving this extraordinary film, it should be noted that none of Bibi Andersson's earlier film work prepares one for the astonishingly complex performance she gives here. She makes Alma's self-centered, childlike candor endearing, her pain profoundly affecting, her instinctive viciousness sympathetic, and her final soundness totally persuasive. *Persona* is significant, too, because it introduced Liv Ullmann to moviegoers, and under Bergman's tutelage she became one of cinema's greatest actresses. After making *Persona*, Ullmann became Bergman's lover, had a child by him, and, for the next dozen years, was the female protagonist of virtually all his films.

CRIES AND WHISPERS

In 1971, a few months after he received the Motion Picture Academy's Irving Thalberg Memorial Award—Liv Ullmann accepted it for him—and after *The Touch* had been released, Bergman began filming *Cries and Whispers* (1972), the final film to be treated in this chapter.[46] If *The Touch* is a version of *The Devil's Eye, Cries and Whispers* is a version of *The Silence,* but it also draws on themes, strategies, characters, and devices from Bergman's other films. Joined to his exploration of destructive and dehumanizing narcissism and the fortunate fall is the theme of the innocent whose death almost brings together alienated family members, as in *The Virgin Spring* and *Through a Glass Darkly.* Like *The Silence, Cries and Whispers* also involves antipathetic sisters—characters hungering to mother or to be mothered—a caring outsider, and a "secret message." Like *Persona,* it employs the revenge dream, and once more Bergman makes his audience aware that he is the image maker/storyteller.

Bergman says that all the women in *Cries and Whispers* represent aspects of his mother. (As in *The Touch,* the father is never mentioned, though the various males in the film can be read as representing aspects of his character.) But given that in the process of polymerizing himself Bergman transposes genders to distance or disguise his own feelings, to some degree he is in all the characters. He is even in the saintly Agnes. Just as some of his characters keep him honest about his worst qualities, she partly reflects, as have several of his earlier characters, his desire to be better than he is.

Because stylistically *Cries and Whispers* is the antithesis of *The Silence* and *Persona,* I feel it necessary—as I did in dealing with both of those films—to comment first on its style. *Persona* opens and closes with a black screen and at important times uses a glaring white screen at its base. *The Silence*'s base, or set of primary colors, is also black and white—the fades are to black—but its claustrophobic grayness is what sticks in the memory. The base color in *Cries and Whispers* is an orange-red. It is the primary color of the omniscient image maker's dream screen. When a scene ends, the fade is not to black but to red. Besides calling attention to the filmmaking process, these "red-outs" deprive us of that restful closure that black provides; instead, they create a feeling of low-key excitation, of free-floating anxiety, even of discreet or latent violence, all of which contribute to the film's underlying violence. (The film's dominant set, the interior of a house, is decorated in a darkish red that eventually becomes oppressive.)

Cries and Whispers is stylistically different from *Persona* in other ways. *Persona* (and to a lesser degree, *The Silence*) progresses in waves and blurs distinctions and lines of demarcation between images (with fog, mist, or silhouette lighting), between scenes (with elliptical jumps in time), between characters (Alma and Elizabet), and between interior and exterior worlds (physical or psychological). *Cries and Whispers* is more novelistic and theatrical. Bergman, like a novelist, speaks to his audience and even stops the action to insert character-defining episodes from his characters' pasts. He narrates the transitions into these episodes, but his voice is absent when a character recollects or reads about the past even though we also see it illustrated. As for theatricality, the action takes place largely in one setting, a summer house in Sweden, and the film's fabric is woven of mise-en-scène more than giant close-ups. (The sophisticated filmgoer cannot help but be aware of the presence of Bergman and Nykvist as he or she watches the extended tracking shots that follow the characters down the long halls past the great windows. It is worth noting here that Sven Nykvist's cinematography for this film won him an Academy Award.) Furthermore, the action, instead of flowing seamlessly, is more formal, progressing in segments or scenes that are often presented as a montage. The style is also more painterly, stylized, and self-consciously artificial. Bergman, for example, further calls attention to the filmmaking process by bracketing each of the aforementioned flashbacks with a chiaroscuro, extreme close-up of the face of the person involved. In the first of these bracketing close-ups, he lights the left half of the face and leaves the right side's features so deep in shadow that they are indistinguishable (reminding us of shots in *Persona*). As soon as the flashback concludes, the closing bracket appears; the same close-up that opened the flashback appears, except that now the right side of the person's face is lit and the left side is in deep shadow. These bracketing images are accompanied with whispering—the sound of guilt and hostility, a kind of aural equivalent of the red-outs.[47]

Cries and Whispers opens with a montage that evokes serenity, eternal beauty, and false promises of security. We see mist, weathered, classical statues, and the dawning sun's rays sliced up by the trunks and motionless branches of huge trees on the spacious grounds surrounding a white, fin de siècle manor house.[48] A duck or two and a bell are heard in the distance. We are transported inside the house where the sense of timelessness is contradicted by the camera's slow pan of a variety of elegant, ticking, and chiming clocks—one of the film's motifs—in seemingly empty rooms. It is 4:00 A.M. The camera continues its journey past Maria (Liv Ullmann), asleep in a chair. Just as we begin to crave more visual and audio stimuli, the camera takes us into the adjoining room and approaches the sleeping Agnes (Harriet Andersson), whose gaunt face contrasts dramatically with Maria's fulsome beauty. An imminent spasm of pain causes her to open her eyes and, when it arrives, wrenches her features and makes it difficult for her to breathe. A tear runs down her sallow skin, and she bites her fever-cracked lips and the side of her mouth to help muffle her cry; she will not bother the others with pain below a certain threshold. When the pain has retreated, she leaves her bed. Her pure white nightgown (and the white fireplace and bed curtains) stand out against the red walls, rug, blankets, chairs, and screen. She resets the stopped clock on the fireplace—her time is not yet up—raises the window shade, quickly takes in the view, and then steps to the door. She shakes her head and smiles tolerantly at Maria, who is supposed to be "sitting up" with her. Before getting back into bed, she writes in her diary, "It's Monday. I'm in pain." Agnes has cancer.

Bergman's next montage defines the characters' distinguishing characteristics. Maria, who has not outgrown her childhood narcissism, is shown in her bedroom, her doll lying on the bed near her head and she, sucking her thumb, scanning the elaborate doll's house nearby. Rolling over, she looks lovingly at the painting of her deceased mother, who, except for her black hair, is Maria (Ullmann plays both). Next is the hate-filled Karin (Ingrid Thulin). She is dressed in dark blue and sits in a black chair working over the ledgers. The chime of a clock causes her to drop her pen and glasses and to look at her "too large" hands. Finally, we see Anna (Kari Sylwan), the family's bovine domestic. She is kneeling at her bedroom shrine to her dead daughter and praying. In rote fashion, probably as she was taught as a child, she thanks God for letting her experience a new day (like the vicar in *The Devil's Eye*) and asks Him to look after her little girl who, in His wisdom, he has taken. Her simple faith prevents her from asking the anguished question, "Why my daughter?" that Ottilia (*The Magician*), Töre (*The Virgin Spring*), and Stina (*Brink of Life*) ask. In fact, with her eyes still on the shrine, she takes a big red apple out of a bowl and sinks her teeth into it, an act that not only establishes her earthiness but promises a (fortunate) fall (see fig. 32). The nondiegetic Chopin Mazurka that is heard during her prayer heightens the sense of her contentment, and it segues us back to the ailing Agnes, not a mother remembering a dead, beloved child, but a child remembering, as she does "nearly every day," her dead, beautiful mother. Agnes, though often rejected, loved her mother "utterly and jealously." She recalls (in flashback) her mother in a long white dress strolling through the manor's manicured grounds and then sitting in a white, wicker peacock chair. (The whiteness connects her to the cold statues in the opening montage.) Agnes tells us that she resented her mother's preference for her younger sister Maria—the narcissistic mother favored the child who resembled her physically and temperamentally—while scolding Agnes for her perpetual solemnity.[49] (Karin, interestingly, never alludes to her mother, and as a child Agnes seemingly was not jealous of her older sister.) What Agnes remembers most fondly, however, is the occasion when she was discovered eavesdropping, as was her wont, on her mother, who then summoned her. Her mother wore such a sorrowful look that Agnes, moved almost to tears, reached up and touched her mother's cheek. That moment of contact—"We were close"—is the first moment of grace in this film in which touching, though not always sincere, is the first step in showing caring.

A watercolorist, Agnes is painting a white rose that reminds her of her mother when the doctor (Erland Josephson) arrives.[50] The pressure of his hand on her lower abdomen is too much, and she gently removes it to her chest in a way that bespeaks a profound loneliness. He responds with a professional smile and a Bergman pat on the cheek. Out of her hearing, he perfunctorily informs Karin that Agnes's end is near. On his way out he is detained by Maria, with whom he has had an affair. Hidden behind a door, he touches her neck, and she pushes his hand to her breast (an echo of Agnes's act). They caress and kiss passionately, but apparently remembering his resolve not to get involved with her again, he pulls away and leaves. Her half-smile seems to be in response to her momentary success and to her embarrassing rejection.

Bergman interrupts the action to insert a flashback about this lushly erotic woman. Maria's bracketing close-up begins with her slowly opening her eyes and with the hint of a self-satisfied smile playing around her mouth. In voice-over, Bergman tells of the doctor visiting the manor one night to tend to Anna's sick little girl (both of his patients die). Afterwards, because of the hour and the absence of Maria's husband, the doctor accepted her invitation to stay overnight. At din-

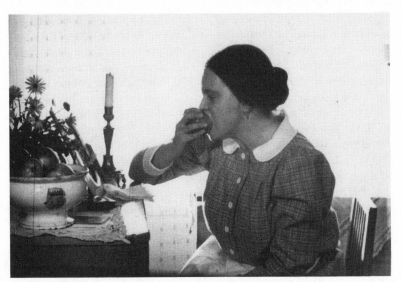

Cries and Whispers. AB Svensk Filmindustri

ner, Maria, oozing sensuality, sat at his side as he lustily consumed his meal. Later, in a red lace peignoir that highlighted her ample cleavage, and wearing that puffy, saccharine smile Ullmann uses to project self-satisfaction, Maria visited him. The red room and the two candle flames reflected in the doctor's spectacles suggested something satanic about him. Before they made love, he placed Maria before a mirror and, giving her beauty and incipient wrinkles their due, described her general indifference and her calculating and self-satisfied character.[51] Feeding on his scrutiny, she smiled and informed him of what he also knew, that he was just as selfish, cold, and indifferent.

The doctor was gone by the time Maria's husband, Joakim (Henning Moritzen), returned in the morning. Joakim read Maria's infidelity in her face and small talk. After patting her face, and their little daughter's, the humiliated and ineffectual man retired to his study where he tried, unsuccessfully, to commit suicide. Maria entered in time to see the letter opener he had used drop to the floor from the slight puncture in his chest, and to hear him call, pathetically, for help.[52] Maria, who has an aversion to all unpleasantness, backed out in disgust. (We learn that Joakim and the marriage survived.) The flashback ends with Maria's bracketing close-up wearing a serious look, and with the sound of whispering.

Anna responds late at night to Agnes's whimpering. Surpassing both Sister Brita (*Brink of Life*) and the porter (*The Silence*) in her need to mother, Anna undresses, gets into Agnes's bed, and cradles her against her bare breast until she falls asleep. But it is not long before Agnes (her head upside-down in the frame) is writhing in pain. Dry-vomiting, her mouth gaping, she tries, in deep, wheezing gasps, to suck air into her suffocating lungs while, with the little energy she has left, crying for help. We, her sisters—Maria finally covers her face and turns away—and Anna watch, terrified and helpless. When the seizure ends, the three women dotingly undress and wash Agnes and change her nightgown. Afterwards, Maria reads from Dickens's *Pickwick Papers* (1837). Agnes is manifestly pleased but, exhausted, soon falls off to sleep. The others retire to the adjoining room. [Bergman's costuming and arrangement of the women in these scenes is inspired by Munch's *The Death Chamber* and *By the Death Bed* (see figs. 33, 34).] The tide of pain and suffocation soon returns. Lunging at the foot of the bed, Agnes screams, "Can't someone help me?" (Harriet Andersson's performance stands as a touchstone; Agnes's death throes are the most excruciating and convincing *ever* filmed.[53]) The seizure finally

Edward Munch. *By the Death Bed* (1895), 35-3/4″ × 48-1/2″, University of Michigan Photographic Services. Bergen kommunes kunstsamlinger (Bergen Billedgalleri, Rasmus Meyrers Samlinger and Stenersens Samling).

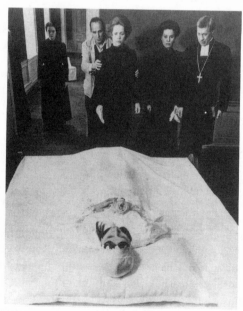

Cries and Whispers. Svenska Filminstitutet

relents and Agnes dies, but before she does, she turns, smiles at Anna, who is alone with her in the room, and then glances briefly outside. As she does, the light grows slightly brighter. The sisters and Anna immediately lay out the body; revealing Agnes's gnarled feet and showing the little finger on one hand catch on the other makes the reality of her death unimpeachable.

As he recites the traditional prayer, the pastor (Anders Ek) is backed by the red walls.[54] Then he moves so that he is backed by the bright window. Now, from his heart, he expresses ideas familiar from Bergman's earlier films. Agnes's faith, he admits, was greater than his; she was Christ-like. Consequently, he bids her to ask God to show those "here on this dirty earth under this empty, cruel sky" that their lives have meaning, and to thus relieve them of their anxiety and profound doubt. A panning shot unites all the principals around Agnes's body and then moves in on Anna.

Again Bergman interrupts the action to insert and introduce a flash-back about Karin. The bracketing close-up shows Karin, almost gagging, with her eyes open. There is more whispering. Then she closes her eyes and her face grows calmer. Bergman tells of the night that Karin and her diplomat husband, Fredrik (Georg Årlin), a man 20 years her senior according to the screenplay, stopped off at the manor. We are present at another dinner scene, but in contrast to the reds and the eroticism of the dinner in Maria's flashback, black and white dominate and the mood is chill. Instead of sitting beside her male companion as Maria had, Karin, the blue-black of her high-collared dress matching her thick hair, sits stiffly across from her elderly husband at the elegantly set table. She almost seems a hired companion. In a coldly sociable manner, he invites her to have seconds of fish with him. She declines. (Recall Ester's comment, "I smelled like rotten fish when I was fertilized.") Anna serves him. Puzzled by Karin's anxious silence and smirk, Fredrik, a sneer always at the ready, eats without inviting small talk. At his announcement that he is going to ready himself for bed, Karin, her emotions as tight as a watch spring, loses control and involuntarily knocks over her wine glass, which shatters. The red stain on the white tablecloth cries out violation and repressed pain. When Fredrik is gone, she enigmatically observes aloud—she will repeat it four times in the next few minutes—that everything is "a tissue of lies," an attitude that calls to mind Ester's and Elizabet Vogler's renunciation of the roles they felt trapped in, especially motherhood.[55] The broken glass gives Karin an idea. Selecting a shard, she retires to her dressing room and places it on a silver plate. Anna helps her undress, a process that involves removing layer after layer of concealing clothing. Finally, she stands naked in front of two large oval mirrors, but, unlike Maria, who enjoyed the doctor making her look at herself in a mirror, Karin doesn't even so much as glance in the mirror at her body. After donning her nightgown, she, for whom any intimacy is difficult, suddenly slaps Anna. It is a reprimand for Anna's expression, which mirrors Karin's own self-hatred and disgust. Repentant, Karin asks Anna to forgive her, but Anna refuses.

When Anna departs, Karin fingers the glass on the elegant silver plate. Then she takes it and, sitting in a chair, pulls up her nightgown and mutilates her genitals. After her initial pain, her facial reactions—which is all that we see—are erotic; smiling, she runs her tongue around her lips.[56] Rising, she enters the bedroom, where Fredrik, a man who would seem to take his sex the way he takes his sugar, is sitting reading. He smiles a welcome. When Karin is in bed and Fredrik comes to stand at its foot—there is a blood-red pillow there—she spreads her legs, exhibiting her bloody crotch. Her face expresses spite coupled with a curious exaltation. She tops off her repudiation of her humiliating sexual connection to her husband and to her own urges by smearing the blood over her mouth—she almost resembles a clown—and licking her lips. Fredrik grimaces, but unlike Maria, who recoiled at the sight of blood from her husband's self-inflicted wound, Fredrik is more startled than deeply affected. The flashback ends. The bracketing close-up starts out with Karin with her eyes closed, but then she opens them. On the sound track are agonized cries.[57]

Once again, Bergman structures a film around the sacrifice of an innocent. In *The Virgin Spring* the sacrifice converts a pagan to Christianity, teaches the protagonists about themselves and their God, and brings them together as a family. In *Cries and Whispers* Agnes's death almost brings together her alienated, narcissistic sisters, Maria and Karin—the former swimming in boundless self-love, the latter drowning in self-hate. In addition, the death of the saintly Agnes teaches Anna, like the vicar in *The Devil's Eye,* that she must make her Christianity more human.

Agnes's death so affects Maria that she seeks out and admits to her standoffish older sister that though she is childish and superficial, she "can't stand distance and silence." Furthermore, she is asking Karin to be her friend at this time because she senses "that something decisive is going to happen, something that's going to change our whole lives."

Karin seems to snub her sister's request; instead of answering, she reads aloud from Agnes's diary a passage that probably refers to Anna, who is eavesdropping on the reading: "I have received a gift of human contact and kindness. I think it is called Grace." Agnes's death, Maria's overture, and Karin's own need momentarily soften her iron control, corrosive self-hate, and "hate of any [physical or emotional] contact." Sensing this, Maria gently runs her fingers over Karin's face. Tears fill Karin's eyes, and she lets herself be embraced, but suddenly she pulls away and screams that she does not want to be touched, and that her guilt "won't let [her] breathe."

A little later they again sit down together. Karin uses as a pretext their need to decide what to do about Anna, whose services, with the death of Agnes and the sale of the house, will no longer be needed. Though the two women sit at the sides of the dining room table, not at its ends, Maria's placement across from Karin is intended to evoke the scene between Fredrik and Karin. Again Karin is dressed in blackish blue, and she knocks over an (empty) glass. After a moment she explains her earlier behavior. Keeper of the ledger, and the victim of a brutal superego, Karin is as judgmental as was Ester. She confesses that she cannot stop hating and condemning; she hates her body (which her husband considers ugly), Anna's "imploring eyes," and Maria's "cold, little smile," caresses, and false promises. She even has considered suicide. Her confession and accusations make Maria very uncomfortable. Though Karin tries to maintain control of her emotions, it is obvious that the more she says the more she wants to pour out. Her hate seems to swell and literally be about to explode and splatter her psychic viscera against the red walls. She flees the room and, leaning against the closed door, emits a scream so primal that it sounds like the one produced by Agnes's cancer. It contains her regret for rejecting Maria; she may have lost her only chance for human contact. Maria hurries out of the dining room at just this moment. Karin stops her and begs her forgiveness, adding hopefully, "Perhaps you do want to know me." The blurred image of Agnes's corpse with Anna kneeling beside it is visible deep in the frame. Maria turns, and both sisters, crying happily, embrace and passionately stroke each other's faces; it is as if touching transfers feelings directly into the other's psyche. The camera, swinging back and forth, frames and caresses their faces and movements while from their mouths spill forth (soundlessly) words of praise, forgiveness, promises, and love. Bergman knows that words cannot convey what humans feel or what feelings do, so while their lips move we hear Bach's sadly joyous Saraband No. 5 in D Minor for violincello. It soothes, elevates, and bridges.

This loving scene is followed by one that reveals Anna's dark side. Like Alma (*Persona*), Anna dreams her revenge. She resurrects the Jesus-like Agnes to vent her own anger and punish Karin and Maria who, she knows, do not love—or deserve to be loved by—their sister. Because this is a dream, not history, Bergman does not narrate entry into it. He does, however, bracket it with a close-up of Anna, but it is the left, not the right, side of her face (eyes open) that is dark. The dream begins with Anna kneeling beside her dead child's empty crib. That she is viewed through its bars may be meant to underscore her obsessive, imprisoning involvement with her dead child and her obsessive need to mother (her "imploring eyes"). Suddenly, Anna hears a baby's cry. She hurries out and dutifully asks Karin if she doesn't also hear the crying, which Anna cannot get out of her head. Karin appears catatonic. Standing as limp as a stringless puppet, she mutters, but no words are emitted. Maria is in the exact same condition. (Like Elizabet at the end of Alma's dream, they are helpless and thus ready to be used.) Anna then hurries to Agnes, who is laid out in bed wearing a baby's bonnet. Agnes tells Anna that she is dead but unable to sleep or leave her sisters and Anna. Anna tries to explain away Agnes's state as being merely a dream, but Agnes replies that it may be a dream for Anna, but it is not for her. Then she has Anna summon Karin. After she arrives, Karin tells Agnes that she does not love her and then flees. Maria is summoned. Anna sadistically has the corpse hug and try to kiss Maria, and when Maria runs away, screaming—jump cuts add to the panic—Anna has the doors resist her escape.[58] Alone at last with Agnes, Anna announces self-righteously, "I'll stay with her!" A cut suddenly displays Anna, her eyes closed, in bed holding Agnes in her lap, Agnes's head resting peacefully beneath Anna's large, bare breast. Anna's dream ends with this Pietà, which establishes her sense of her life's meaning. Besides being represented as the apple-eating Eve (like *Brink of Life*'s Stina), Anna is the Eve who keeps losing her children to death. Here she sees herself as the mother of the crucified Christ (Agnus Dei means the lamb of God).[59] Anna is also presented as the saving remnant, the keeper of the flame. Almost the first image of her in the film—it is the image that also introduces Ingeri in *The Virgin Spring*—shows her, at dawn, blowing dormant embers to life. In the bracketing image that now ends the sequence, Anna opens her eyes.

After the funeral the sisters and their husbands, dressed in heavy black coats, gloves, and hats (the women's with black veils) and sitting in a semicircle on chairs with white protective covers, discuss giving Anna notice. The abrupt shots of the four underscore their lack of feeling for each other. Except for Joakim, who suggests she be given a small sum and that they help her find new employment, they behave as if Anna were a common menial. Anna, who has been eavesdropping, is called in. Acknowledging Anna's close relationship with Agnes, Karin offers her some article of Agnes's. With barely disguised anger, she refuses "anything at all." Fredrik sneers in German at her false pride. Feeling that their duties are completed, the four rise to bid Anna farewell and to leave. The mode becomes (heavy-handedly) subjective from Anna's point of view: each of the four approaches and looks slightly to the right of the lens as he or she bids her good-bye. Significantly, Karin drops her veil before doing so, and Maria makes the kind of shallow gestures that make her feel good: she caresses Anna's cheek and asks Joakim to give her a little money. Anna takes it.

The last two scenes resemble *The Silence*'s last two. Near the door Karin reminds Maria—as in the scene of their reconciliation, Maria is on screen left, Karin on the right—of their resolve to get closer: "You touched me. Don't you remember?" The need for contact that Maria felt after Agnes's death has passed. "I can't possibly remember every silly thing," she answers with saccharine exasperation. Despairing, Karin's eyes fill with tears, and she draws back from her sister's meaningless kiss. "Pity," says Maria, and like *The Silence*'s narcissistic Anna, she turns and leaves her lonely sister to what, for Bergman, is psychic death. We are left to contemplate the fact that, unlike the sacrifices of the Karins of *The Virgin Spring* and *Through a Glass Darkly*, Agnes's sacrifice fails to reunite the members of her alienated family. Agnes does, however, have an effect on Anna and us.

The cries and whispers persist. Alone and bitter, Anna turns to Agnes's diary, which she has taken in spite of what she told the family. She treats it as sacred scripture, having wrapped it in cloth. She lights a candle and reads aloud from it. Its "secret message" is more explicit than Ester's. After a moment her voice is replaced by Agnes's and the image of the candle's flame dissolves into Agnes's face. We are where we were when the film opened, but now the cold statues and serenity are replaced by the four lively women walking the mansion's manicured grounds. The relief we feel at emerging from the baroque house's obsessive reds, whites, dark blues, and deathly blacks into the out-of-doors enhances what follows. It is a late but still bright after-noon in early September; autumn's dying leaves and grass wear a golden patina. As we listen to Agnes's words, we see her, Karin, and Maria, carrying white umbrellas and dressed in wide-brimmed hats and lacy, white, wide-skirted dresses, run to and sit down in a white, wooden four-seater swing. Anna, dressed in gray, stands beside it and rocks it. The camera is stationed behind and between Maria and Karin, who are facing Agnes. As Agnes's voice-over statement cli-maxes, the camera dollies in past her sisters' framing shoulders to set-tle on her thoughtful face, the brim of her hat a halo around her head. "My sisters have come to see me," she says. "Like the old days, we are together. All my pain was gone. The people I'm most fond of in the world were with me. I *felt* their presence. This is happiness. I experience perfection and I feel gratitude to my life which gives me so much." She smiles and closes her eyes, locking in the experience. Unlike Isak Borg, whose final vision of his parents is consciously idealized—we know his mother is not as he remembers her—Agnes knows her two sisters. Not only does she not judge them, she luxu-riates in their best behavior and their mere presence. It is a forgiveness and acceptance so sublimely spiritual that it transforms the film, tem-porarily erasing the memory of her agonizing death and our sour knowledge of Maria and Karin. Its effect on Anna as she reads and experiences it vicariously is similar to that of the miraculous spring on Ingeri. She takes on Agnes's extraordinary humanity and is freed from her obsession with her daughter's death, her hate for Karin and Maria, and her pat faith. After the image of Agnes's serene face comes the film's final image, which is presented with the omniscient narrator's authority. Printed on a reddish-orange background is, "And so the whispers and cries faded away."

In 1967 Bergman underwent a minor operation for which he had to be anesthetized. Accidentally, he was given too much. "Six hours of my life vanished. I don't remember any dreams; time ceased to exist, six hours, six micro-seconds—or eternity. . . . The lost hours . . . provided me with a calming message. You were born without pur-pose, you live without meaning, living is its own meaning" (*ML,* 204).[60] "The only life that exists for me," he says elsewhere, "is this life, here and now, and the only holiness that exists is in my relations with people. And outside, nothing exists. When I . . . began to un-derstand that . . . it gave me a marvelous feeling of relief and secu-rity. . . . I don't believe in any afterlife because *this* life gives me everything I need; the cruel, beautiful, fantastic life. For me, the meaning of everything is life itself" (Marowitz, 12–18). Out of these convictions grows Agnes's definition of grace as the "gift of human contact and kindness."

A final judgment of *Cries and Whispers:* earlier I described it as a version of *The Silence.* As drama, however, I feel that even though *Cries and Whispers* contains scenes—primarily those centering on Agnes—that rank with the most moving ever filmed, three of the film's four main characters are less authentically complex than their counterparts in *The Silence. Cries and Whispers'* Maria, Karin, and Anna are essentially types, and the melodramatic flashbacks meant to deepen our understanding of their characters (and the film's stylized, color-coded world) actually reinforce this impression. These three women are, to be sure, rounder than the film's stock Bergman characters—the ambivalent mother, the cynical doctor, the doubting pastor, the weak or cold, imperious husband—but compared with Agnes they seem more two-dimensional, more programmed. All in all, I think the gray world and vital characters of the less self-conscious (pretentious) earlier film make it a more complete and substantial work than the film modeled on it.

Bergman's intrusion at the very end of *Cries and Whispers* to tie it up reminds us that in a very important sense these people and their story exist as a kind of dream in his mind. As we have noted in this chapter, Bergman was increasingly presenting his films so as to keep his audiences aware that his stories are extensions of himself, that he has dreamed them. Even his theatrical work began to draw on this sense that the story is an extension of the writer. Recently a critic reviewing Bergman's production of *A Long Day's Journey into Night* (1955) concluded that "Bergman appears to have conceived this work as the dream of Edmund Tyrone, which is to say of the character's surrogate and creator, Eugene O'Neill himself. . . . The entire action seems to be enshrouded in fog, suggesting that the whole play is a memory. . . . [Edmund] hovers on the edge of the set, an eavesdropper on the scenes in which he doesn't participate. At such moments, O'Neill and his character are identical, and his whole dead family is being dreamed onto the stage."[61]

In the next chapter we find that Bergman would continue to make the world of his films an extension of his own mind, but in these films he no longer focuses on the naïveté of the women in his life. He now focuses on his own pathological narcissism.

6

"This Time He Was Called ..."

In *Hour of the Wolf, Shame, The Ritual,* and *The Passion of Anna*—the four films that immediately followed *Persona*—and in two that were made over a decade after it, *The Serpent's Egg* and *From the Life of the Marionettes,* Bergman continued his study of pathological narcissism and his debunking of those people—most of them artists—whom society admires, romanticizes, or even lionizes. He uses these films, in fact, as case histories in which he dramatizes the struggle of his various narcissistic alter egos, now generally male, to survive identity-threatening, sometimes horrifying situations. As we shall hear Bergman himself say to the audience at the end of *The Passion of Anna,* "This time he [my alter ego] was called Andreas."

There is much of Bergman's Jack Kasparsson in the male (and in one case, *The Passion of Anna,* female) protagonists of these films. Each of them tries to escape responsibility; in *Hour of the Wolf, Shame, The Passion of Anna,* and *From the Life of the Marionettes,* the protagonist takes refuge on an island and/or in fantasy, or he lapses into madness. In *The Serpent's Egg* he disappears into the anonymous German masses. Each gets involved with people or situations that permit him freer expression of his sexual and violent urges. And whereas in his earlier films Bergman's alter egos were generally permitted to express their homicidal urges only in nightmares (Bo in *Eva,* or Bertil in *Three Strange Loves*), except in *Hour of the Wolf,* where the attempt fails, each of these protagonists murders or causes a death. In several cases the protagonist's fear of his own repressed violence is so great that he undergoes a reaction-formation that leaves him ineffectual, socially inept, and sexually sterile. Unlike earlier Jack Kasparsson–like characters, none of these protagonists are permitted to return home, and with the exception of *The Ritual,* at the end of these films the male protagonist's state of mind, fate, or whereabouts are uncertain.

Except for *The Ritual,* the male protagonist's female companion, usually played by Liv Ullmann, tries to sustain him, although from his perspective at some point she betrays him and thus hastens the disintegration of his ego and the emergence of the destructive impulses he has been struggling to suppress. In *The Passion of Anna,* in which the female protagonist is more pathologically unbalanced than the male, she actively and unambiguously tries to destroy him. (In contrast to *Sawdust and Tinsel,* the betrayal does not lead to heroics on the male's part or to a reconciliation.) Furthermore, an attitude toward relationships found in Bergman's films as early as *The Devil's Wanton*—in which Birgitta Carolina and later Sofi recognize the severity of Tomas's narcissism but accept him nevertheless—reemerges with new power: women recognize that the men they love are too narcissistic to be capable of real love, and that essentially what their men want in their sexual partner is a mother. These women accept these relationships, nevertheless.

Significantly, unlike the films that precede them, Bergman widens the focus in these films to show the social and even political forces at work on his characters. In *Hour of the Wolf* the society seems to be composed of a decadent aristocratic family and their friends; in *Shame* the characters become caught up in a Swedish civil war; in *The Ritual* three artists are investigated by a government censor; in *The Passion of Anna* the Vietnam War provides the context for the action, which includes the police pursuing an animal killer and vigilantes terrorizing an innocent man; in *The Serpent's Egg,* which takes place after World War I in a disintegrating Germany, the protagonists become involved in an insidious political-scientific plot; and in the contemporary society shown in *From the Life of the Marionettes* we encounter characters from government, business, and the underworld.

In *The Devil's Eye, Persona, The Touch,* and to some extent *Cries and Whispers,* Bergman explores how a sane or normal person sustains her humanity after having been drawn into the orbit of a psychologically cannibalistic predator; in so doing, these films adopt primarily the normal, vulnerable person's point of view. In the films discussed in this chapter, by contrast, Bergman largely subordinates the sane protagonist's view of the world to that of the pathological protagonist. Doing this in *Hour of the Wolf,* Bergman realized too late, was a mistake.

HOUR OF THE WOLF

Hour of the Wolf (1968) is based on a script written the year before Bergman made *Persona* (*ML*, 205; *BB*, 195–96, 215) and was to have been a four-hour film called "The Cannibals." Making the dominant point of view that of "a man who is already mad [and becoming] crazier" reduces what could have been the story of a woman's fascinating struggle to remain sane to a case history of a madman: "Had I made it from [Alma Borg's (Liv Ullmann)] point of view it would have been very interesting . . . see[ing] an absolutely sane woman go crazy because she loves the madman she married. She enters his world of unreality, and that infects her. Suddenly, she finds out that she is lost." Bergman found the results "boring," but only after the film was finished. So he went back and tried to shift the focus by creating a frame, something like the one in *The Devil's Wanton*. It consisted, says Bergman, of my "sitting on the film set and telling the actors how the idea had come to me: a woman [Alma] had come to me with [her famous husband's] diary . . . and then I asked her to tell me, in front of a microphone, what their life together was like. Initially, moreover, I was supposed to have known this boy, somewhat as in E. T. A. Hoffmann's well-known plot. . . . We even re-shot some scenes, but it was too late" (Kaminsky, 131–32).[1] Bergman decided to eliminate most of the frame, keeping only "the sound track that you hear during the credits" (Björkman, et al., 45) and the scenes of Alma being interviewed. Thus, the story is filtered through her perspective, but Johan Borg's (Max von Sydow) diary, which is essential for much of what we know about his interior life, is actually the heart of the story.

One reason Bergman was defeated in his attempt to shift the balance to Alma was that in making her so uncomplicated and stable, her husband's demons, with whom she has to interact, come across less as personified projections of his various neuroses than as real demons from a netherworld. (Like *The Devil's Eye's* Don Juan and Pablo, they seem like hellish figures who have taken on human form to invade our everyday world.) It is very possible that Bergman wanted to keep the situation ambiguous. As suggested in chapter 1, this Sunday's child may have experienced at some time what he believed *was* another reality, a demonic world like that encountered in the fiction of his model, E. T. A. Hoffmann. Nevertheless, these problems may weaken the film's narrative integrity but they do not ruin its dramatic effectiveness. The raw, nakedly confessional feel of this film seems, to use one of its characters' phrases, to be the result of literally turning inside out the psyche of its protagonist. Bergman called *Hour of the Wolf* a "very personal picture" about demons who "were born in the events [the artist] lived through as a child and have taken their place beyond the boundaries of consciousness" (Meryman, 66–67). At another time he said it was about demons who dissociate Johan Borg "from his gift for life and . . . destroy him and themselves" (Björkman, et al., 79, 81).

This black-and-white film opens with a printed statement informing us that a few years earlier the "painter Johan Borg vanished without a trace from his home on the Frisian island of Baltrum,"[2] and that a few months afterwards his wife gave Bergman her husband's diary, which, with what she told him, is the basis for what follows. Then, as the white credits appear on the black background, the sound track is filled with the racket made by the crew setting up the scene and Bergman talking, laughing, and, finally, shouting, "Camera! Action!"

The camera moves in on a weathered, wooden picnic table sitting beside a barren tree at the moment the reluctant Alma, eight months pregnant, her hair pulled back and tied in a bun to keep it off her scrubbed face, is cued to exit her thatched-roof plaster-and-stave cottage. As she approaches, she slips a jacket over her peasantlike clothes, then sits at the table. The apples beside her on the table (probably symbols of fruitfulness) actually seem to heighten the feeling of loneliness and unrelieved grayness. She turns her head aside and, nervously twisting her wedding ring, says that she has no more to tell the filmmaker (and us). Besides, she adds, the director has the diary. With the chill wind whipping strands of her hair against her forehead, and at times having to fight back tears, she nevertheless continues talking. In that somewhat high-pitched, almost whiny little girls' voice Ullmann uses to evoke dependency or helplessness, she confides that she and Johan came to this island just after they married seven years before because he was afraid of meeting people. She injects that she is proud that he liked the fact that she did not talk a lot. It was their custom, she continues, to return to the mainland before winter. In fact, she will soon return there to have their baby. She finally details what happened after they returned to the island the previous May. They arrived home at three in the morning, and she was happy to see that (like her) the apple tree in front of their cottage was in bloom. Johan, however, was annoyed at finding footprints under their kitchen window. Almost immediately, the pattern that had grown worse in recent years reasserted itself: Johan's painting began to go badly; he could not sleep and was afraid of the dark. Alma hesitates and lowers her head at these painful memories. The image then fades out.

Having established the authenticity of his source, Bergman proceeds to dramatize the memory. Its visual images, in conjunction with its analectic sound, make it as eerie as any scene he ever filmed: the camera tracks with and extremely close to the side of the prow of a large motorboat as it glides into shore with a feeling of inevitability. Gloomily beautiful, this compelling shot is held so long that it becomes portentous. Then, from the front, we see Johan in the bow using an oar to guide the boat clear of rocks and through the calm, weedy cove to the shore. Another extremely long (in duration) shot of them unloading the boat, during which not a word is exchanged and the only sound is the chugging motor, compounds the ominousness. Finally, the boat slowly backs off out of sight and hearing behind a jutting rock, another shot whose duration makes us hyperconscious of time. We are left with a sense of sad finality and feel abandoned and isolated. Then Alma heads up the steep path past the high, jagged pillars of rock.[3] Johan follows, pushing the wheelbarrow loaded with their belongings and supplies. The *only* sound is the high-pitched, irritating whine of the wheelbarrow's rusty wheel.

A handful of brief scenes establish the progression of Johan's psychosis. At first he and Alma are happy; he coaxes her to sit under the blooming apple tree so that he can sketch her neck. But in the next scene he arrives home from sketching looking worried and distracted. As he moves among the wind-driven, drying sheets that Alma has hung on the clothesline, their flapping resembles and sounds like the wings of giant birds. The next scene takes place at night. Afraid of the dark, Johan, fortifying himself with drink, also is keeping Alma awake until dawn. At the moment, he is forcing her to look at his sketches of the creatures he is certain are pursuing him. As he excitedly turns the pages and describes each one, the camera stays on the incredulous Alma's concerned face. One sketch is of a man he calls a harmless homosexual, probably Bergman's first explicit reference in his films to his own homosexual impulses, and possibly one reason he would say, "I was terribly aware that I was running a risk by making *Hour of the Wolf*" (Björkman, et al., 79). Among the other demons are an old woman whose face will come off when she removes her hat (his fear of death), a "schoolmaster with a pointer in his trousers,"[4] spider men, and a bird man related to *The Magic Flute*'s Papageno. (*Vogel* being the German word for bird, the bird man is related to Bergman's family of Voglers—the homicidal magician Albert and the vampiric Elizabet.[5]) Alma dozes off in spite of herself, but Johan shakes her awake (see fig. 35). The scene becomes even more tense as Bergman makes time palpable by having Johan track the second hand of his ticking wristwatch for a full minute. At the end—"a minute can seem an eternity"—he and we feel as if we have been holding our breath underwater. When Johan, fatigued from sleeplessness and drink, finally permits Alma to talk, she observes that people who live together for a long time come to think and even look alike. He scoffs at this, and while she is responding, he falls asleep, the usual response of a Bergman male when a woman reveals her private thoughts to him. The tension dissolves as the pregnant Alma half drags Johan to bed.

The tension returns with the next scene. While at the pump, Alma senses something behind her and looks around to find an old woman (Naima Wifstrand) dressed in a turn-of-the-century outfit and leaning on a cane. She offers Alma her cold hand—Isak Borg's mother says she always feels cold—and after letting it slip that she is 216 years old, she changes that figure to 76. She disappears as mysteriously as she materialized, but not before insisting that Alma—the wind, the waves below, and the eerie screech of gulls drown out some of her words— read Johan's diary, which she informs Alma he hides in his black satchel under his bed. This encounter between the unquestionably stable Alma and the old woman, and the latter's special knowledge— though Alma certainly knew of Johan's diary—lends weight to the idea that the demonic forces on this island are real, not merely the result of Johan's hallucinations. As for the old woman, since we have already encountered in this study a number of grandmotherly or grandfatherly characters who intervene on behalf of Bergman's pro- tagonists, we can speculate about whether she wants Alma to be better informed so that she can help her husband, or whether she is trying to draw Alma into his psychosis. In the screenplay, this ancient tells Alma that Johan's "big failing" is that he "distrusts me." She could be a figure like Mean from Bergman's play *To My Terror:* "Mean and Grandmother ['an unfeeling hag'] are mythic figures who 'never die,' projections of good and evil forces in [the protagonist]" (Steene 1968, 31).

Like Karin (*Through a Glass Darkly*), whose demonic voices tell her to read her father's diary, Alma does as she is told, though guiltily. Bergman films Alma from an angle near the satchel on the floor so that the satchel seems to draw her to it. The clock's loud ticking—it stops during each flashback—heightens our sense that Johan could come in at any minute and discover Alma lying on the bed reading his diary. The first entry (in flashback) is from late July: it recounts the island's owner, the sardonic Baron von Merkens (Erland Josephson), inviting the famous painter to a dinner in his honor at the castle. Though wary, Johan accepts. The second entry recounts how Veronica Vogler (Ingrid Thulin) materialized at the edge of the sea where Johan was sitting and trying, fruitlessly, to draw. The rocky shore— its barrenness manifesting his creative impotence—is bathed in Bergman's nightmarish sunshine. Fittingly, the bare feet and legs of this lusty hallucination enter at a distance and at the top of the frame near Johan's bent head.[6] When she is before him, she alone talks, reminding him of moments from their violent sexual past and telling him of a threatening letter she has received; it promises that the end is near and that "the springs will dry up and other fluids will moisten [her] white thighs." He becomes oblivious to everything except her. As he unzips her dress and caresses her sides and arms to the voluptuous sound of the gentle waves licking at the stones, the film's one erotic, heterosexual moment occurs. The last entry—Johan's return to the cottage interrupts her reading—describes Johan's encounter with Curator Heerbrand (Ulf Johanson), who claims that, like Johan, he too can "finger souls and turn them inside out." As he dogs Johan's steps, his reference to the painter's unsteady nerves causes Johan to scream, "Shut up!" and to knock down his pursuer, bloodying his nose (the usual symptom of violence in Bergman's films).

Alma fixes Johan's lunch and tells him how she has spent her allowance. Her primary purpose is to force him to acknowledge her as more than his quiet maid, bed partner, model, and motherly companion during sleepless nights. Also, by engaging him with solid numbers, she hopes to anchor him to reality. Johan just eats, responding to her account and her tears with an indifference indicating that everything but his inner life is irrelevant. He hands her a wad of bills and passively accedes to her proposal that she buy his son (presumably by Veronica) a birthday present (probably Bergman's comment on his relationship to his own children). Johan is puzzled, however, when, having apprised Alma of the baron's dinner invitation, she answers, "I know." He turns—she has left the table—and looks into the lens.

Suddenly, the camera is subjective. Presaging the shot he will use when the cold-hearted family bids goodbye to Anna near the end of *Cries and Whispers*, Bergman places the camera between Alma and Johan and uses a wide-angle lens to slightly distort the approaching faces that introduce themselves: the baron, his wife Corinne (Gertrud Fridh), his mother (Gudrun Brost), his brother Ernst (Bertil Anderberg), and their guests—Archivist Lindhorst (Georg Rydeberg) and Curator Heerbrand (*ML*, 220). At the elegantly laid dinner, the camera dizzily circles the table, moving back and forth or swish panning from speaker to speaker (often, as in *Smiles of a Summer Night*, through candle flames) and creating the impression of swirling conversation and of eyes darting from one bizarre person to another.[7] The amplified sound of the clattering dishes and glasses and the callous, explosive laughter and ugly, often shrapnel-like verbal exchanges disorient and intimidate Alma and Johan, who are separated by Lindhorst. Having already drunk too much, and drowning in the raucous, unintelligible clamor, Johan, sweating, runs his finger inside his tight collar. Some of the tasteless or hostile statements shock Alma (and us), but she is attentive when Veronica Vogler is mentioned. The camera is on Alma when the baron says, "What hatred in those eyes." Johan is grateful when at last dinner is over and Alma is beside him, her hand lovingly covering his, which is resting on her shoulder.

All retire to the library where Lindhorst performs Mozart's *The Magic Flute* on the stage of his puppet theater.[8] The cacophony of the previous scene is replaced by the exquisite harmony of music and song, but we are taken aback when we realize that tiny Tamino is unsupported by strings and is, in fact, flesh and blood.[9] Behind and above his stage Lindhorst, resembling a grinning Bela Lugosi because of a shadow cast across the lower half of his face, watches Alma and the tipsy Johan, the latter's eyes closed against this further confusion of reality and fantasy. On the little stage Tamino, searching for Pamina and deceived by the Queen of the Night's dark forces, stands before the Temple of Wisdom lamenting his inability to perceive underlying truth. His "When will my eyes see the light?" is answered by an invisible chorus: "Soon, soon . . . or never."[10] This craving for light is bound up with his quest for Pamina, which is for "love as something perfect."[11] According to Bergman, he is actually asking, "Does Love live? Is Love real?"[12] When the aria is over, the roving camera settles on the face of Alma-Liv Ullmann for a giant (eyebrows to lips) close-up; it is Bergman's "double declaration of love, tender hearted but hopeless" (*ML,* 217). Afterwards, Lindhorst explains that Mozart, mortally ill when he wrote this opera, must have felt the "soon . . . or never" with "secret intensity," and then he asks Johan to comment on the fact that this great opera was commissioned. Stepping forward, his smile wine-induced, Johan articulates the theme of so many of Bergman's recent films—that there is a difference between the artist's public image and private motives, that the title "artist" does not make a person special. With pompous modesty, he emphasizes that he has not sought his fame; like other artists, he creates from freakish compulsion, not from choice.[13] Furthermore, his appreciation of the "unimportance of art in the world of men" keeps him "immune from exaggerating the significance of his work." (Bergman has often claimed, perhaps rather ingenuously, that he did not "work to win immortality, *sub specie aeternitatis"* [Björkman et al., 78], and that he believed that "art no longer ha[d] the power . . . to influence the development of our life" [Kaminsky, 89].) Applauding his candor and profundity, the group presses in on him. So oppressively close are they that the baron's mother, attempting to place a rose in his hair, cuts his face with her fingernail. Recoiling, he pushes her backwards into the arms of the chortling crowd. Embarrassed, Alma chides him for having drunk too much and takes him outside. Separating themselves a bit from the others, who have joined their stroll, Alma quietly observes that the two of them never kiss anymore. Johan is about to kiss Alma when he hears Heerbrand tell about being knocked down and having his nose bloodied. "Must it be like that?" Heerbrand asks, posing the very question that in *Persona* Alma puts to Elizabet after the latter has slapped her and bloodied her nose.

Back in the decaying castle, Corinne wants Johan to see his portrait of Veronica Vogler that she has bought and hung in her bedroom.[14] Johan wants to leave, but Alma insists on seeing it. Once in front of the painting, however, Johan is oblivious to everything else, and Alma is almost as engrossed. As the scene progresses a more complex picture of Alma emerges; her image, in fact, is often repeated in a mirror. She reveals a defensive, almost angry expression that we have not seen before, and she snaps up the opportunity to confirm for Corinne that she and Johan have no secrets from one another, not even his scandalous five-year affair with Veronica Vogler, of whom, she insists, she is not jealous. Finally left alone with the portrait, the worried Alma studies it.

After the party, Alma and Johan, silhouetted by the sun that lingers at the horizon,[15] head home along the cliff overlooking the sea. The sea's roar and the howling wind force Alma, now distraught, to shout her confession that she read Johan's diary. Then she turns to Johan, who is behind her, and, crying, tells him that she knows that these evil forces want him to themselves, but that she is going to fight them. When Johan does not respond—he doesn't even take his hands out of his pockets—her expression hardens and she begins to sob. Backing away from him, she doubles up, making us conscious of her pregnancy. (Neither ever mentions their unborn child, which Johan may regard as a threat to Alma's total devotion to him.) Johan comes and places his hand on her shoulder, but she breaks away. He approaches again, but she pushes him off and paces among the sparse trees. Putting his hands back in his pockets, he saunters off, leaving her behind.

In the screenplay, during their stroll at the castle, Johan has an interior monologue that ties in with Tamino. He wonders if Alma, whose "own feeling is so great that it fills her need to the brim," is capable of feeling his longing for a love so total that he would exist with his loved one in a "wordless affinity" that obviated either lover's playing roles, judging one other, or making the other suffer. It would be a love that renders useless such words as *captive, distance, void, punishment, forgiveness, guilt, confessions, nightmares,* or *revenge;* it would be a relationship in which his lover would understand "all his thousands and thousands of changing moods." This perfect love is, of course, pure narcissism; one can only have this kind of relationship with oneself. When Alma draws away from Johan's touch, according to the screenplay, he "realizes in a flash that her grief applies only to herself . . . [that for] the first time she is leaving him outside." This is the turning point in Johan's attitude toward Alma; during most of what follows nothing is of consequence to him but his own inner life. The screen fades to black, and the film's title reappears. ("It's good for people to be woken up a moment, then drawn back into the drama," says Bergman [*BB,* 222].) As when the film appears to melt and break during *Persona,* the jolt out of our illusion produces in us a sense of desertion, which reinforces the effect of Alma literally being left behind and Johan feeling deserted by his mother-wife.

The film resumes with eerie, electronic sounds and the image of Alma and Johan's little cottage, its window the single point of light, silhouetted in a black universe. It *is* the hour of the wolf.[16] Inside, as if he were defying the hellish powers that lick at his psyche, Johan watches the flames of the matches he strikes edge toward his fingertips. Suddenly, he is hit by a migraine memory, and pressing his fingers against the bridge of his nose, he recounts how as a child he was punished by being locked in a dark wardrobe where, he was told, there lived a little man who gnawed off the toes of naughty children. When he was finally released from the wardrobe, Johan was whipped by his father and made to ask for forgiveness from his tearful but complicitous mother.[17] Von Sydow's almost uninflected baritone voice makes his account as gripping as Sister Alma's narrated beach escapade in *Persona*. Following this story, Johan caresses Alma's face and confesses how he got what he told her was a snake bite, a story (either because of its homicidal or homosexual implications) he says he never thought he could tell anyone. Though not sure if it actually took place or was merely a hallucination, he nevertheless swears Alma to secrecy.

This incident is not narrated but presented as a flashback. Dressed only in bathing trunks and posing seductively, a demon (Mikael Rundqvist) barely into his teens hovers about and antagonizes Johan, who, shirtless and barefooted, is fishing off the edge of a cliff (see fig. 36). (The fishing rod seems to extend from Johan's crotch, furthering the sexual overtones.) Ultimately, the lithe youth leaps onto Johan's back and coils his arms and legs in a strangling embrace. (Johan can only achieve this forbidden union by disguising it as violent resistance.) Close shots with a hand-held camera heighten the vertiginous struggle, and a compound of sounds—a rapidly marching beat, a wavering drone magnified to sound like a swarm of bees, and, at the scene's climax, shrieking flutes—conveys Johan's panic. To free himself, Johan flings himself backwards, crushing the boy's naked flesh against a wall of rock. Before slipping to the ground, the boy emits a painful cry from his dark-lipped mouth, the first natural sound in the scene. We assume that the boy has been totally defeated, but suddenly, snakelike (a wood-block creates a pseudorattlesnake effect), he sinks his teeth into Johan's bare foot (we may recall Elizabet's vampiric bite into Alma's arm in *Persona*).[18] Johan instinctively seizes a nearby rock and hammers the boy's head, each of the eight blows a dull thud in

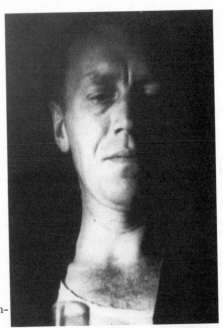

Hour of the Wolf. AB Svensk Filmindustri

Hour of the Wolf. AB Svensk Filmindustri

the midst of a jumble of electronic sounds. Afterwards, Johan picks up the limp body and slides it over the edge of the cliff into the sea.[19] We watch the boy sink from sight, but before disappearing for good, his head returns to the surface and his blood-streaked face revolves so that we and Johan can see it. As he floats up into and then down out of sight, his hair undulates like a beautiful sea anemone. (Bergman will increasingly call attention to the beauty in violence and destruction. Remember David's attitude toward the beetles in *The Touch*.)

When Johan's flashback is finished, the ticking of the clock is the only sound until Heerbrand (able to go "through locked doors," like Hummel in Strindberg's *Ghost Sonata*) hammers loudly three times on the locked front door and then enters. The sinisterly cheery man invites Johan to a party at the castle, adding that Veronica Vogler will be there. Before he departs, he gives Johan a pistol, whose purpose clearly is to eliminate the troublesome Alma. The mention of Veronica fuels Alma's jealousy, but when she cross-examines Johan about this old relationship he is not forthcoming. Intent on having it out, Alma gets his diary, which she obviously has been studying, and reads him an entry: "My obsession became at last a torment to us both. I . . . spied on her jealously. I think my passion stimulated her, but she never knew her own mind. We had frightening scenes utterly devoid of reason. We moved from town to town to escape her relations and lawyers." Johan tries to wrench the diary from her, but when he fails he toys instead with the pistol. Alma finishes reading: "We carried out the Bible's words that man and woman 'shall be one flesh.' Then her husband took her away. I was taken to a hospital and we didn't see each other for several years."[20] Feeling defeated, Alma says she should not have believed him when he once said that he liked her because God had made her "all of a piece," and that she "had whole feelings and whole thoughts."[21] Besides, she adds, she hates talking to his demons and seeing him run after Veronica. Sobbing and sensing his intent, she admits that she fears that if she stays he may murder her. In a tone of lethal loathing, Johan orders her to go outside, and as she heads for the door he fires the pistol three times (each explosion heightened by a crashing cymbal). Like Kasper, who abandons his wife to revel with members of the underworld (resulting in his death), the shooting of Alma marks Johan's capitulation to his violent and erotic urges, and his demise.

Near the end of the film Alma tells us that, when Johan shot at her, only one bullet grazed her arm and that she pretended to be dead.

Then, when he ran out, she hid the pistol and herself. He returned after "some minutes," looked demented, talked to himself, wrote in his diary for several hours, then packed his satchel and headed into the woods. What happens in Johan's mind, his adventures in the castle during those "some minutes," takes 15 minutes of film.

The third gunshot acts as the sound of Johan breaking through the castle doors. The spatial disorientation in the labyrinthine castle and delaying encounters swell the sexually obsessed Johan's bewilderment and frustration as he searches for Veronica. He meets the baron's mother, whose foot Johan-Bergman must kiss in a variation of the wardrobe punishment, and he meets the baron (another former lover of Veronica's), who is sobbing. The baron's jealousy is so great that it literally drives him up the wall; spiderlike, he walks up the wall and across the ceiling. Johan next comes upon Corinne listening to an elegantly dressed harpsichordist, Mr. Kreisler (Lenn Hjortzberg), and he watches as the old woman's face comes off with her hat and as she drops her eyeballs into a wine glass.[22] Lindhorst is the last to delay him. He lends Johan his dressing gown and silk pajamas and prepares him for the tryst with cosmetics that leave Johan looking and smelling humiliatingly effeminate. At the door to Veronica's room, at the end of a long corridor filled with screeching birds, Lindhorst changes into a giant bird and disappears.[23]

Inside the bare room, and on a primitive catafalque, is Veronica's corpse. (Is embalming fluid the fluid she was warned would moisten her white thighs?) Removing the sheet that covers her, Johan, his anguish visible behind his grotesque mask, whispers her name and (in close-up) caresses her naked body from head to toe.[24] Suddenly, just as Mrs. Alman's corpse comes alive in *Wild Strawberries*,[25] Veronica, laughing loudly, obscenely, carefreely, sits up, clasps Johan to her, and smothers his face with kisses. And just as in *The Magician* Albert Vogler (von Sydow) takes his wife Manda (Thulin) by the throat, Johan, hungrily, violently, takes Veronica Vogler by the throat, returns her kisses and caresses, and then gets on top of her. Almost immediately, however, he is aware of eavesdroppers, and when he looks up, he sees the covey of demons clinging like bats or perched like birds around and above the doorway and in the window well. Laughing raucously and attempting to get Johan to attend to her, not them, Veronica slides her hand down his face, smearing his makeup. Dismounting from her, Johan, his lower arms still in the sleeves of his open dressing gown, falls to his knees in unbearable psychological pain. He buries his smeared, skull-like face in his hands and then, drawing them away, looks directly at us. In a variation of the silent girl's final words in *The Seventh Seal,* he whispers, "The limit at last has been reached and I thank you. The glass is shattered, but what do the splinters reflect?" Johan's id and superego—in the screenplay he realizes that "deep down . . . pardon doesn't exist"—have shattered his ego. (One thing this very derivative film is eminently successful in achieving is exteriorizing what it must feel like to be a psychotic trying to keep one's head above the black waters of psychic oblivion.) The camera moves so close to his mouth that it becomes a blurred, black hole shaping inaudible words. An extended blast from a hunting horn announces a climax, the opening of the void. The image dissolves into a negative and then a positive image of the murdered snake-boy—his face streaked with blood, his hair undulating like sensuous seaweed—rising to and hovering just beneath the surface of the black waters of consciousness. Finally, his head sinks from sight and back into a negative image.[26] Not Alma's "murder" but his suppressed homicidal and homosexual impulses are the crimes that Johan feels are cardinal.

For a moment the film returns to the present as Alma tells of following Johan when he left the cottage for the last time. We watch as she finds him in a swamp. He is nearly catatonic. He looks at her and affectionately runs his muddy fingers down the side of her face. She responds by cradling his head on her breast. A dissolve indicates a passage of time, and when the camera pulls back, Johan is gone and the baron is standing beside Alma. He leads her, frightened and guilty for not having remained vigilant, until she can see Johan in the distance. Johan takes a few steps toward her, but like an exhausted, defeated stag, he turns to face his attackers, who are lined up behind him. (Throughout the film people frequently come from deep in the frame toward the camera.) Heerbrand steps forward and thrice slaps him; the baron's mother slashes his jugular with her claw-sharp fingernails; and Lindhorst, his face alternating with that of a black bird—the bird is frightening even in the momentary freeze frame—strikes Johan in the temple with his beak. More blood gushes forth. Johan sinks to the ground but, clutching the top of a log, heroically pulls himself up. The covey retreats. Alma, who at first covers her eyes, then screams a silent scream and watches in horrified fascination, rushes to the spot, but Johan and his demons have vanished. She gathers his satchel and heads home.

Alma finishes the interview and brings the film to an end by looking directly into the camera and asking us if the demons she saw were real or whether she just shared Johan's psychosis. Did she love him so much that she lost her perspective, or did she not love him enough? Did her jealousy lead to the increased hold the demons had over him? Our faith in Alma's sanity and our sense, early on, of the hopelessness of Johan's mental condition render the question irrelevant. After a long pause Alma admits she knew Johan did not really love her, though once, she happily asserts, he "definitely" told her he felt good being close to her. The films ends with her staring at us, imploring us to help her in the face of her uncertain future.

THE RITUAL

Written in 1967, rehearsed for four weeks, and shot in nine days in the spring of 1968 at SFI's Råsunda studios, *The Ritual* (1969), though it was released as a theatrical movie outside of Sweden, was made for Swedish television because at the time Bergman did not want to meet the exhausting demands of a movie project. This accounts for the film's nine designated scenes and its heavy reliance on close-ups, dialogue, flat lighting, simple sets, and mise-en-scène. The decor, which consists of "just blank walls, a curtain or so, and a few bits of furniture" (*BB,* 67), reinforces the feeling—the same effect created by *Brink of Life*'s hospital—that little life exists outside the film's five sterile sets and cramped, claustrophobic frames.

The story involves the harassment by a government censor of three cabaret actors who call themselves the "Riens" (the "Nothings"). ("Nothing," the only word Elizabet Vogler speaks in *Persona,* seems to acknowledge a void at one's center that leads to psychopathic behavior.) Bergman polymerizes himself into all five of the film's characters. Three of them are the actors who comprise the cabaret trio: the hypersensitive, nymphomaniacal actress Thea Winkelmann (Ingrid Thulin), her husband (and when necessary, pimp) who is also the trio's shrewd, suave, and fatherly manager,[27] Hans Winkelmann (Gunnar Björnstrand), and finally, the homicidal Albert Emanuel Sebastian Fisher (Anders Ek), who murdered his best friend and is Thea's lover. (Sebastian's first two names link him to *The Magician*'s violent protagonist, who exacts revenge on *his* troupe's persecutors. Bergman conveys Sebastian's lethal, volcanic interior expressionistically by showing him setting aflame the very bed he is sitting in the center of, and by having him wear dark glasses like those Karin [*Through a Glass Darkly*] and Alma [*Persona*] wear to contain their fury.) Bergman's fourth alter ego is Judge Abramsson (Erik Hell) of the Court of Appeals. The judge, who senses he soon is "going to die" from his bad heart, is driven by self-hate and violent erotic needs that, repressed, emerge as ill-smelling sweat; like Kasper *(Kasper's Death)*, Judge Abramsson is drawn to those who act out what he represses. Finally, largely for reasons of cost, Bergman himself plays the role of the cowled, Catholic priest to whom the anguished, atheistic judge confesses. (The scene conjures up Antonius Block's confession to Death.[28])

In his handling of these artists, the judge goes beyond his responsibility as an official to investigate a possibly "pornographic" cabaret act. He probes the performers' personal morality and behavior. Though he claims he was assigned their case by lot, we suspect that he contrived to get it; in the film's last scene he admits, "I wanted to see your number at close quarters. Perhaps, I wanted to take part in it, or it was the secret need to. . . . I don't know. . . . I don't understand your relations or mine to you." The respectable, unmarried judge is tired of sublimating his aggressive and sexual urges. Though he can say, "I am incapable of aggressiveness, I just feel utterly powerless," he not only slaps Thea eight times as he tries to rape her, but during his participation in a private performance of the banned "rite" he is composed in the frame so that he seems almost to be touching the erect penis fastened to Sebastian's crotch.

The artists soon have this lonely, duplicitous man's number. Seeing how difficult it is for him to resist Thea's devouring sexuality, Hans offers her to him and then lures him into participating in the questionable play he is investigating. Immediately, the roles of victim and victimizer switch. In what is a kind of reenactment of Johan Borg's demise at the hands of the bird man and his cohorts in *Hour of the Wolf*, the actors—the men-priests wearing stylized, artificial genitals, and Thea with her breasts exposed—wear fearsome bird masks (recall Bergman's fear of birds) and threaten the elderly man with a knife, beat him, and humiliate him. The judge half welcomes this treatment and rightly points out that his persecutors humiliate themselves in the process. In *The Magician* Vogler's sadistic act of almost scaring Dr. Vergérus to death is ultimately intended to force the doctor to entertain the possibility of God; here the judge has a heart attack, but he is not scared to death as much as he dies from a surge of instinctual energy brought about by the ritual's animalistic power. But unlike

Vergérus, who refuses to learn from his experience, the judge's last words are, "I understand!"

Just as *Persona* opens with our being made privy to Elizabet Vogler's medical history, and *Hour of the Wolf* with our being made privy to Johan Borg's diary, once again Bergman treats his story as a kind of case history. *The Ritual* opens with the image of the judge's eye seen through a magnifying glass as he inspects his file on the Riens. The comic conclusion of the film-file consists of our being told that after the judge's death, and after the Riens had been fined for their "pornographic" piece called "The Ritual," they gave interviews and went on holiday.

In the dialogue of this wordy, sometimes repetitive television film, Bergman touches on a wide range of his concerns, some of which have only appeared in interviews, but for audiences familiar with Bergman's biography and films, none of what he admits or asserts comes as a surprise. With regard to his art, he points out that each member of the creative group makes an indistinguishable contribution to the finished work, that art no longer seems necessary to people's lives, and that the artist's freedom is a terrible responsibility. More personally, he confesses that he neglects his children, longs for his deceased parents, and fears loneliness. The exposure of the judge's private feelings through personal confrontation, confession, and, finally, the ritual conveys Bergman's belief that we welcome the humiliation of having our hidden motives revealed. Hans claimed that the ritual (art) satisfies our childlike "sensual longing" for humiliation, and, the film implies, the ritual satisfies our need to experience the primitive emotions of eros and violence. The artist helps us cope with and exorcise these powerful, Dionysian emotions by ritualizing them. Hans holds up "the bowl of blood above his head to mirror the face of the god" (Thea, who is behind his back) and thereby drive the god away (*BB*, 240–41).

SHAME

Part of the context of *Shame* (1968), Bergman's next film project, has to do with his having "loved" Hitler and been "a little pro-German fanatic" when he was an adolescent. "After [World War II]," he says, with heavy irony, so many Swedish, Scandinavian, English, and American heroes told us what the German people should have done under the pressure of the dictatorship. . . . All these very, very clever people telling us what the German civilians should have been thinking and saying; how they really should have reacted to the concentration camps. All this was terribly painful for me, because I'm not very courageous and I hate physical violence. I don't know how much courage I would have if somebody came to me and said, "Ingmar, you are a very talented man, we like you very much; be the head of the *Schauspielhaus* [National Theater]; if not, you know what will happen to you, your wife, and your children. And, you know, we are having some difficulty with the Jews, and we don't want them in the Theatre; you will fix that for us." . . . And I don't know . . . at all how I would have reacted. (Simon, 38–39)

"How much of the fascist are you and I harboring inside ourselves? What kind of situation is needed to turn us from good social democrats into active Nazis?" (*BB*, 232). These are some of the questions *Shame* asks. One of his masterpieces, *Shame* is as sure-handed and unerring as *Hour of the Wolf* is tentative, narrow, and flawed. Bergman places his pathological alter ego in a wartime situation in order to dramatize the worst-case scenario of how he imagines he might have behaved. This time the protagonist is called Jan Rosenberg (Max von Sydow), his name the only explicit indication that he is Jewish. Bergman probably makes Jan and his wife Eva (Liv Ullmann) Jews not only because Jews are associated with the arts (and violins)—until the war both Jan and Eva were violinists with the Philharmonic—but because of the Jews' suffering, especially in this century. Bergman, recall, had just used the Jewish boy in the Warsaw ghetto (*Persona*) as a symbol of the innocent suffering. Casting against type, then, Bergman shows that Jews can be as vicious or as loving as anyone else. Making his protagonists artists also continues his assault on the sentimental belief in, as he puts it in this film's screenplay, the "colossal sensitivity of [the artist's] soul": "The artist lives exactly like every other living creature that only exists for its own sake" (Kaminsky, 91).

But the middle-aged Jan is a Bergman protagonist before he is a Jew or an artist. Like Bergman, who claims he "hate[s] physical violence," Jan is filled with rage and destructive urges. Jan, however, has repressed these urges and in so doing has undergone a reaction-formation. Overtly he is meek and passive, sometimes to the point of groveling. One reason he does not press his will on others is that he is desperately afraid of alienating those on whom he depends as buffers against decision making, against the responsibilities of adulthood, and against discomfiting reality.[29] He lies to others and to himself to hide his ineffectuality, but ironically, his ineffectuality ensures that his desires are not taken seriously, thus further fueling his rage. He is represented as physically awkward, just as the ineffectual Tomas is early on in *The Devil's Wanton*. Jan is hypersensitive, hypochondriacal (his supposed bad heart has saved him from being drafted), and totally self-involved. Events, however, are about to lance his impacted emotions. Jan's narcissism and inordinate dependence on his 28-year-old wife Eva obviate any meaningful love on his part.

His passivity and ineffectuality force Eva, who tries not to nag and would rather not usurp his authority, literally to wear the pants in the family: the very first scene shows her moving decisively about the house dressed in men's pajamas, the top unbuttoned male-style so that she is bare-chested. This bit of nudity, the last we see, is, except for one suggestive scene, devoid of sensuality, like all the sexuality in this film. Eva, who always wears men's clothing, has almost lost the image of herself as a sexual object. On the verge of anger, she has to urge Jan to get out of bed, to shave, and not to make them late for their appointment. Ironically, her strength, forced to the fore by his weakness, hardens Jan's retreat from reality and masculinity. As for Eva, her name gives us a clue to her real character: more than anything else, Eva wants to be a mother. She is denied fulfillment by Jan's (probably) psychologically induced sterility. That Eva dislikes constantly having to prod her husband and that she would happily fulfill the traditional female role is evident whenever Jan is affectionate. At those moments she glows (Ullmann looks more naturally beautiful in this black-and-white film than in any other Bergman film).[30] Seven years of marriage, however, have taught Eva that Jan is incapable of real love. Nevertheless, though she repeatedly threatens to leave him, it is not surprising to find that, being a Bergman female, she feels that being alone is the more intolerable condition. (She is further threatened by knowing that when she and Johan did once separate, he had an affair.)

As the film's white-on-black credits appear, we are bombarded by a drumbeat, blasts from a machine gun, and brief, confusing, and generally incomprehensible radio exhortations or questions from different political leaders, among whom are Hitler and Mussolini, Chamberlain and Roosevelt, and Robert Kennedy (as a member of the McCarthy committee). We are relieved when the mosaic of noises ends. The narrative commences with darkness and seeming silence, which, after a moment, is exploded by the amplified alarm of a clock. (Dramatic juxtapositions of silence or relative quiet with eardrum-shattering sound, and darkness with sometimes blinding light, occur throughout the film. Most of the film's lighting, however, is flat and gray, and the occasionally grainy texture of the image suggests documentary.) The alarm runs down as we wait for someone in the dark room to respond. At last a figure in men's pajamas rises from one of the separate beds and noisily raises the blind, letting the glaring daylight do what the alarm failed to do. Silhouetted, the person's gender remains a mystery until she approaches the camera.

Bergman typically frames his stories with his protagonists in similar postures, places, or situations. *Shame* opens with Jan and Eva, side by side in separate beds, awakening to what soon will be an alarming reality. The film will end with them lying side by side on the verge of death. (At the start the camera angle is low, emphasizing Eva's activity and control; at film's end it is looking down on the motionless, helpless pair.) The film also opens and closes with the recounting of a dream. Jan, for whom sleep is partially an escape, sits up, puts on his glasses, takes a pill, feels his tooth, checks his foot, and without hesitation or embarrassment tells Eva, who is dutifully performing her morning ablutions, that he just dreamed that the now four-year-old war was over and the two of them were again sitting beside each other at the Philharmonic and rehearsing Bach's Fourth Brandenburg. He adds that he awoke crying.

At breakfast Jan has still not washed and is in his pajamas. He notes Eva's bad mood, which disappears when he kisses the palm of her hand and suggests they buy a bottle of wine with some of the money they will receive from the mayor for their loganberries. (They support themselves with what they raise.) Smiling, she leans over and kisses him on the mouth. His response is to press her hand on the imagined swelling from his wisdom tooth. This, and learning that he has failed to pay the phone bill—without a phone they cannot get orders—revives Eva's exasperation. Jan's escapism manifests itself not only in his not wanting the phone to operate but also in his having moved to this island when the war started, and in his having "fixed" the car and the radio so they do not always work. Bergman now begins to integrate the two civil wars that this film documents, the private and the national. As they leave the house, Jan is disturbed by passing troop transports and the church bells ringing on a weekday. His dream and the supposedly disconnected phone that keeps ringing, even though when Eva answers it there is no response, are other omens of the trouble to come.

Sitting in their small station wagon and finally about to leave, Eva, noting the weather, sends Jan back for his leather jacket. As she waits for him to return, we study her from the vacant driver's side. She is wearing dark (protective and hostile) glasses. She waits and waits, sighing deeply. In the distance the church bells rhythmically beat out the time, speeding up after about the twenty-third chime. Finally, she mutters aloud, "Oh, Christ!" and slams out of the car. In two shots Bergman has conveyed the history of her having to do things herself if they are to get done, and of Jan's unpredictability and unreliability. Inside, she finds him sitting on the stairs, crying like a frightened child. "Shut up!" he replies when she asks him to try to control his hypersensitivity. Removing her dark glasses (never to wear them again), she asks his forgiveness. They return to the car and, at last, leave.

On the road to the ferry to the mainland they stop at a stream where their friend Filip (Sigge Fürst) is fishing. Typically, it is Eva who gets out of the car to purchase one of his catch. The roar of the stream prevents Jan from hearing what seems to be a serious conversation, so when she returns Eva recapitulates it for him (and us): Filip told her the radio has reported that the invasion is imminent. Jan's response that it is better to "know nothing" exasperates Eva, who replies, "Your escapism drives me mad!" But when he tells her how lovely she looks (her loose hair hangs down past her shoulders), a smile blossoms on her lovely face, and they kiss.

The ferry is crowded with soldiers and military vehicles, one of them a sedan containing Mayor Jacobi (Gunnar Björnstrand) and his wife (Birgitta Valberg) who, returning from their cottage, are on their way to see their son. They engage the Rosenbergs in conversation, arranging for the delivery of the berries and enthusiastically planning to get together some evening soon to make music.

When Jan and Eva arrive at the center of town, they encounter a storm of sound comprising church bells and a deafening procession of pig-nosed tanks and troop trucks pulling cannons. Bergman next employs a jump dissolve (which is distractingly inappropriate to what is essentially a straightforward presentational style) to convey in two shots Eva starting off to deliver the berries and her return. Delighted at having been paid extra, she kisses Jan, whose reaction makes it clear that he is embarrassed by public displays of emotion. As they enter a square that houses the antiques shop where they intend to buy a bottle of wine, it is as if they have sailed into the quiet eye of that hurricane of noise created by the church bells and the grinding and clanking war machinery. Outside the antiques shop Eva excitedly lingers over a wooden cradle. Leaving behind the bright out-of-doors, they enter the dimly lit shop, which at first seems abandoned. At last the shop's middle-aged owner Lobelius (Hans Alfredson), dressed in an ill-fitting army uniform, emerges, looking as if he has been crying. He informs the couple that he has been called into service even though he has a bad foot and has not handled a weapon for 20 years. This man represents one of Bergman's greatest fears. No one cares about him, not even the woman he pays to come in once a week to clean the place and have sex with him. It is no surprise then that the proprietor's thoughts turn to his mother. He sets before Jan and Eva his most prized object, his mother's eighteenth-century, Meissen porcelain musical statuette. As the trio sample the delicious Moselle—a close-up of the white liquid in an elegant, cut-glass goblet makes the experience almost tactile—they also drink in the statuette's delicate beauty and music. Meanwhile, Bergman cuts—supposedly a subjective shot—to other objects around them that evoke our civilized heritage: a painting of a royal family, a carved cherub, and a ship's wooden figurehead (which is also seen in *Persona* and *The Passion of Anna*). Afterwards, Jan and Eva buy a bottle of the wine; uncomfortable about the owner's plight, they enthusiastically platitudinize about his fate, then depart.

Bergman cuts from the antiques shop's dark interior to Jan and Eva, both a bit tipsy, outside their house, picnicking on their fish and wine. The natural sounds, the sunny, pastoral setting, the daisies on the old wooden table, and their intermittent clinking of their wine glasses convey how relaxed they feel. After the first brief shot in which the camera views Jan from behind Eva, it is placed behind Jan and remains there, fixed on—celebrating—Eva's face. Their occasionally humorous (the film's only intentional humor) conversation provides crucial information and insight. Both are trying to be upbeat, though whenever Eva mentions anything that makes Jan uncomfortable, his defense is to lean over and caress her face. He tells her he has the radio working. She tells him she is going to study Italian again. Jan suggests that they make music every morning. "In the morning? You!" replies Eva, good-naturedly. Growing reflective, she informs Jan that she feels unfulfilled not having children. She wants three by the time she is 40. She adds that maybe childlessness is what is wrong between them. Smiling and joking, Jan fills her glass, pats her face, and, assuring her that he is referring only to the immediate future, vetoes the idea. She persists, carefully suggesting that he should let himself be examined by a doctor because it may be that his affairs have affected his fertility. Becoming sexually excited, Jan sidetracks the conversation by professing his love for her, but she points out matter-of-factly that he loves only himself. Without actually disagreeing with her, and using an idea that Bergman categorically rejects, Jan maintains that he can change his character: "I'm no determinist." The camera now moves in on Eva's puzzled expression as she downs more wine and queries, "What's a determinist?" When Jan starts to define it, she interrupts, laughing, "I don't give a damn who you are as long as you mend the sink!" The scene draws to a quick close with Jan deciding that they will put off cleaning up; he leans over and kisses her. Eva closes her eyes, smiles, and sinks under the table, and after snatching a daisy off the table, Jan follows her.

Before totally destroying this idyllic mood, Bergman symbolically reestablishes his characters' fundamental natures. The very next shots catch the sterile Jan emerging from the outhouse, and the frustrated Eve, Eva, feeding her rabbits. Suddenly, jet fighters scream overhead. To shield themselves from both the deafening roar and the explosion of a plane that crashes nearby, they drop to the ground and cover their faces and ears. Instinctively drawn, as ever, to someone else's suffering Eva goes to the crashed jet's pilot, who is hanging by his parachute from the branches of a tall tree in the nearby woods. Just as instinctively, Jan tries to stop her. She slaps his face; screaming "Coward!" she escapes his grasp and continues on her mission. By the time Jan has located his rifle and reached the dying man, Eva is headed home to call an ambulance. Soldiers suddenly appear, however, and warn them to get out because enemy paratroopers are nearby. Jan and Eva hurriedly load their small station wagon with bedding and necessities, but when they are ready to leave, its motor won't start. Speechless with exasperation, Eva storms into the house, leaving Jan behind kicking the station wagon. Another jump dissolve: it is a half-hour later and almost dark. Jan finally has gotten the station wagon started and they are just driving away when armed soldiers, camouflaged and their faces blackened but otherwise indistinguishable from the soldiers Jan and Eva saw earlier, block their path and drag them out of the car. In what follows Bergman brilliantly reproduces the mind-boggling

confusion experienced by people caught up in a war in which one does
not know from what or from whom—both sides speak the same language—one is being liberated, and that terrifying feeling, experienced
by soldiers and civilians alike, of knowing only what is immediate
and proximate. The officer in command calls in his camera crew to
interview the "liberated" Jan and Eva. Wide-eyed with terror, Eva
identifies herself and proclaims that (like Bergman) she has never
bothered with politics. Jan's response is to feign a heart attack. The
interview ceases as the soldiers are scared off by the sound of gunfire.
Eva has practically to carry Jan back into the house. There, as they
huddle over a candle flame, she cries out that she suddenly realizes
that she will never have children.

At dawn, house-shaking explosions and blinding, strobelike flashes
make it imperative that they escape. So panicked is Jan that Eva has
to order him to put on his boots. He does, however, note that they
have no food. He suggests they take some chickens, which leads to a
bit of black slapstick comedy. Unwilling to chop off their heads, he
decides to shoot them with his rifle (a phallic symbol that combines
sex and violence). He sets up a chicken in front of him, aims from
point-blank range, and fires. He misses. "Oh God, I'm so tired of
you!" screams Eva. On their way at last, they are unable to escape
danger. As shells burst on both sides of the station wagon, the camera
stays focused primarily on their faces. By remaining largely inside the
car—it abandons their point of view only once to show dead bodies
on the roadside—the camera creates a fearful sense of being trapped
and vulnerable. The effect of the shelling is liquidation: every house
or barn is afire, and everyone they come across is dead. They pull up
to a house, and a child's corpse momentarily renders Eva oblivious to
the falling shells. A few moments later, finding their only escape
route, a bridge, blocked by an overturned tank, Jan experiences mental gridlock. Eva has to shake him out of his catatonia. They return
home and, on entering, huddle together on the steps leading upstairs
(where earlier Jan had sat crying). The pumping of antiaircraft and
tank guns sounds like someone pounding on their front door (like
Death knocking on the castle door at the end of *The Seventh Seal*),
and only a short time passes before an explosion blows one of the
huge, double front doors off its hinges and into the house. When at
last the barrage ceases, they cautiously step outside and silently view
the devastation. A bird is heard. (Life goes on in spite of man's impulse
for destruction. Bergman has said, "I really believe that somehow hu-

manity will survive. It's a part of human nature: knock it down and build it up" [Lejefors, 39].) They bring back to the house the goods they had stuffed into their car. Jan carefully checks his precious violin's case for signs of damage.

That night, dressed in pajamas, they huddle around that sacred object as Jan tells Eva the story of its Viennese maker, a man Jan seems to admire for having been able to return to creating after losing a leg while fighting Napoleon. As up-tight as the strings he plucks, Jan—who earlier, we recall, had suggested they begin practicing again—does not play the instrument because, he lies, he has hurt his hand. Eva also demurs. The faith in the future that makes creating beauty possible and necessary is ebbing away. Taking off his glasses, Jan, in another of his bursts of affection, asks Eva if she likes—loves—him just a little bit. She smiles and answers yes. They are about to embrace when he suffers a leg cramp. As a consequence, he limps to his bed (the image of the taut strings and the crippled violin maker come together). After Eva has gotten into bed and turned out the light, there is a pregnant silence. Jan, who lacks the courage to ask, responds like a child frightened of the dark when she lifts her blankets and says, "Come here to me."

A few days later Jan and Eva Rosenberg are arrested. The economy of the scene is splendid, reminding us of the shot of Alma breaking her orange juice glass in *Persona*. Bergman places his camera at the edge of the woods quite a distance from a house just off the road that employs its first floor as a store. Except to pan slightly at the end of the scene, the camera remains still. From that spot we watch Jan and Eva drive up, meet a man (Filip), and enter the store. Almost immediately an army troop truck roars up and pulls into the drive next to the house. Soldiers burst out, enter the store, and lead out several prisoners, including Jan and Eva, who are helped into the rear of the truck. Filip and two women remain in front of the store after the truck has noisily departed. A slight pan follows Filip as he walks from the front of the store, across the road, and up toward the camera. Besides creating a sense of expectancy and mystery, and reestablishing Filip's importance to the plot, this virtually static long shot lets us enjoy the titillation of eavesdropping while being safely distant from the trouble. It also heightens the opposite effects that will be created in the very next scene: a jostling, subjective, hand-held camera tries to suggest how it feels to be a prisoner being herded like cattle into the schoolhouse headquarters. (Bergman and Nykvist use the hand-held camera, which had become very popular, more in this film than in any previous one.)

The cattle metaphor is appropriate, but more so is the context. In *Winter Light* Bergman had Tomas take out his childhood frustrations in a schoolroom, thus emphasizing that children still inhabit our adult bodies. Here, Bergman uses the school setting and our own childhoods to make us experience the fear and humiliation these prisoners feel in the face of mysterious and frightening powers. The prisoners wait childlike in the school corridor, sit at children's desks in rooms plastered with children's drawings, and are quizzed by omnipotent authorities.[31] Eva and Jan are even shown a visual aid in which words are literally put in Eva's mouth. (The invading army's interview with Eva is doctored so that she enthusiastically welcomes the liberators.) Later, they are also offered candy by a callous doctor, given lunch, and then, because the Rosenbergs are teacher's pets ("I forbade them to touch you"), made to wait apprehensively outside what could be the principal's office. Finally, they are sent home.

Just before they are called in to be interrogated, Eva whispers to Jan that she feels as if they are in someone's dream. She wonders what that person will do when he awakes and is ashamed of what he has permitted to take place in his dream. After her interrogation Eva is charged with traitorous action, then grabbed around the neck by a soldier and dragged into a room containing other prisoners, some whom have been tortured or are dead. When the soldier grabbed Eva around the neck, she called to Jan for help. After pausing to remove his glasses, he makes only a feeble effort to aid her. Moments later, when he is thrown into the same room, he screams that he has been beaten and, moaning, crouches in the corner. Examining him, Eva finds no sign of any such beating, and so she turns and offers to help feed a man whose arm has been dislocated. But unlike Jan, he gratefully declines and, ignoring his pain, feeds himself. Their eating is interrupted; they are all herded outside into the darkness and the cold to observe a man's execution and await their own fates. Mayor Jacobi arrives and presides. He commutes the man's sentence to a life of penal servitude and moves among the prisoners, using his cane like a cattle prod to separate the innocent from the guilty. Jan and Eva, among the former, are sent to wait in Jacobi's office. The subsequent brief scene in that cold office between the three of them contains the germ of the tragedy to follow. The burned-out Jacobi, bundled up in his overcoat, orders a vehicle to transport Jan and Eva home. When they are gone, the camera focus on his thoughtful but almost expressionless face as he pulls a little electric heater closer to himself with his cane. This cane, besides suggesting weakness, continues to symbolize his authority and, like Dr. Vergérus's, will soon become a phallic symbol. Jacobi then opens a magazine, but he immediately looks up: he realizes that he wants—and knowing Jan, thinks that he can have—Eva.

The action jumps forward. We learn and infer from Eva and Jan's dialogue that in the subsequent weeks Jacobi has coerced and seduced the couple into accepting his protection. Jan and Eva, to different degrees, have sold their integrity for little luxuries and the "feeling of safety." As a result, they have begun to hate—their hate is now as close to the surface as the potatoes they dig from the mire—themselves and each other and to blame each other. Jan's growing laziness is manifested in his desire to quit digging and go inside to listen to the radio Jacobi gave them. Disgusted, Eva tells him to go ahead, and she charges him with having grown servile before Jacobi. Jan countercharges that she too has been groveling. Eva screams that that is a lie, and that she cannot wait for the war to end so that she can leave Jan. Her fury at a peak, she swings at him, misses, and falls to her hands and knees in the mud. As she sits there sobbing, Jan asks her forgiveness. "Do you mean it, or is it just hot air?" she asks. But she falls into his arms even though she knows the answer.

The next scene shows us Jan, still in his pajama top, and Eva, both sitting half-drunk at the table and unsure even of what day it is. In contrast to this dissoluteness, from the transistor radio comes the clean sound of a harpsichord playing sacral music (Bach), which for Bergman represents that "small holy part" of every man's mind that, when it has "dried up, it's the end of your life." *Shame* is about a time, says Bergman, "when music is dead" (Freedman).

A knock at the door turns out, not unexpectedly, to be Jacobi. On entering, he steps into Jan's slippers because his own shoes are wet. Oedipal, Edenic, and Last Supper imagery inform the following scene, in which Jacobi joins Eva and Jan at the table. Jacobi gives Eva a ring and Jan a first edition of a Dvořák piano trio. Although from the moment she admitted him to the house Eva has been cool to him, she accepts the ring. As Jan leaves to answer another knock at the door (Filip, now a guerrilla leader, is stopping by to warn Jan not to befriend Jacobi) we remain behind to hear Jacobi call Eva "my dear." Aware that Filip's men are in the woods nearby, Jacobi describes them as possessing a "terrible idealism." A smile softening her mocking observation, Eva suggests that Jacobi is no different. Jacobi does not reply but asks Jan if he can kiss Eva. It is up to Eva, replies Jan; he laughs uncomfortably as a reluctant Eva joins Jacobi in an embrace and a kiss and then caresses his head, which he rests on her bosom. She reminds him of the danger he is putting them in. Afraid she may alienate their benefactor, Jan frowns and tries to explain away her admonition. Jacobi reminds them that he can have them sent to a labor camp. He turns on Jan and inquires if he is an artist or a good-for-nothing. Jan chooses the latter. Jacobi, à la Caligula (*Torment*), smashes his cane on the tabletop and threateningly intones Bergman's continuing attack on the artist: "The Sacred Freedom of Art! the Holy Slackness of Art!"[32] (Jacobi's part is sketchily written, and in a moment the role will be lumbered with Bergman's personal history. The emotional credibility and final success of Jacobi depend largely on Björnstrand's acting.)

When Jacobi goes out to urinate, Jan and Eva, trying to sober up, agree they must get him out of the house. When Jacobi returns, he notes that the woods are swarming with Filip's men. He assures Jan and Eva that they need not worry because there is an armistice covering this part of the island. Nevertheless, he has a premonition that even though he possesses no secrets, he will be captured and tortured. These thoughts of death lead him to sit beside Eva and have her "touch"—she looks embarrassedly toward the smiling Jan—his head, his eyes, and then his crotch. "Can you feel me?" he inquires. "Yes," she replies. Taking Jan's hand, he asks, "What about you?" Jan, drunk and uncomfortable, says he does not understand, and as Jacobi explains, Jan begins to doze off. "Strange," Jacobi muses, half to himself and half to Eva, "I have only experienced human intimacy a few times. Always in connection with pain." "Go now, please," says Eva, and leaving Jan asleep at the table, his head resting on his arms, she gets up and walks into the bedroom. Jacobi follows her. Standing, he informs her that she is to be his heir—the ring he gave her now takes on symbolic meaning—and now he hands her a wad of money, his total savings. Then, sitting on the edge of Jan's bed and facing her, he tells her that two days before he saw his son, who is on leave, feeding his 19-month-old boy; the child sat securely in his father's lap and, when he had eaten enough, fell asleep. This episode reminds him of another son, himself, and his (Bergman's) old mother. The camera moves closer to his face as he relates that a few years before he was notified one morning that she was dying from her heart condition;

when he arrived at her house, she was already dead. He spent an hour just sitting and looking at her. Now, leaning forward and putting his hand on Eva's shoulder, he confesses that he took his present job because he was afraid of being sent to the front, and he asks her if she is sorry that he is there? "No," she replies. She fully understands his meaning, because she tells him that she has never been unfaithful to Jan. Jacobi moves toward her, but she stops him with the comment, "Not here." Eva's decision to offer herself—more as a mother than a lover—is influenced by Jacobi's talk of his son, grandson, and mother, by his need for intimacy, an intimacy of which Jan is incapable, by Eva's awareness that he may be killed, by her tipsiness, and finally, by Jan's cowardly complicity. Like many of Bergman's women Eva feels compelled to mother someone in pain. She leads Jacobi out of the house and into the greenhouse—into the garden—as church bells, omens of both good and ill, sound. There, when Jacobi tries to kiss her, she turns away, but when his head rests in her lap she takes it and brings it toward hers. Born of fear and pity, their lovemaking is also a warding off of emptiness and despair.

Jan awakens with a hangover and stumbles into the bedroom where, sitting on Eva's bed, he accidentally touches the money she was indifferent to. His head still not clear, he looks at the wad of bills and then says, sternly, "Eva!" He rushes outside, his hand on his heart, shouting "EVA!" Jan, who has seldom stood fully erect, whose hands dangle when he walks, and whose movements have always been tentative and awkward, is now almost comic as, still in his pajama top, he prances gingerly in his stocking feet on the stony ground. He almost reminds us of the betrayed, humiliated Frost walking on sharp stones and calling for Alma. That he is without his slippers remind us of who is wearing them. Jan returns to the house, sits at the table, puts the money in his back pocket, and begins his search again. As he passes the window, he obviously sights Eva and Jacobi leaving the greenhouse because now he speaks her name with a wrenching sob, climbs the stairs, and sits where we saw him sitting and crying earlier in the movie. Then, with his hand covering his face, he movingly cries, "Eva." He is behind the door when Jacobi opens it but waits outside. Eva comes in, hands Jacobi his cane, closes the door, and faces Jan. This time she does not criticize him for being hypersensitive. His grief is legitimate, so she tells him, "Cry, if you think it helps," then walks into the kitchen. Jan joins her immediately and begins to question her about the money. They are interrupted by Filip, who has

Jacobi in tow. The two men go directly to the bedroom. After a moment Eva and Jan are summoned there. Sitting on the edge of the bed with his cane between his legs, Jacobi informs Eva that Filip will free him in exchange for the money he gave her. Ready to go along with the bargain, Eva says that Jan has it. Jan (shown in one of the film's few giant close-ups) denies knowing anything about the money. Jacobi swallows hard but maintains his dignity, seeming to regard Jan's response as predictable and probably even justifiable. Though resigned to the inevitable consequence, Jacobi now has to concentrate to keep his hand steady when he lights a cigarette. Eva (in another giant close-up) pleads with Jan to turn over the money. Filip, his face heretofore an impassive mask, looks annoyed as he "divorces" Eva and Jacobi by removing the ring Jacobi gave her. Then Filip gives his men orders for the house to be searched. Taking Jan outside and again asking for the money, Filip is even more impatient when Jan again denies ever having seen it. (The firmness with which he lies foreshadows the strength he shows later.) Jan will have revenge for Jacobi's paternalistic tyranny and for cuckolding him.

Jan's knowledge of the sin committed in the garden brings on the destruction of his world. In the next few minutes the soldiers, with childish exuberance, destroy the house.[33] We hear and see a concert of destruction augmented by a hand-held camera and amplified sound: windows are smashed, mirrors machine-gunned, pots scattered, the piano brutalized; one after another the chickens are beheaded (reminding us of Jan's impotence with his rifle earlier), and grenades are set off inside the house. Jan picks up his broken violin from the rubble and tenderly inspects it. Unexpectedly, he is thrown to the ground by Filip, who for the first time shows anger.

Meanwhile, knowing he has only a few minutes to live, Jacobi, who is sitting on a wooden bench by the house, enjoys his cigarette and studies the sky. Filip comes to him and, honoring his stoicism, softly pats him on the head as a sign to move to the place of execution. In a long shot using deep focus, we see Filip stand Jacobi beside a cart, return to the near foreground, and hand Jan the executioner's pistol. Jan walks away from us deep into the frame toward Jacobi. When he nears him, Jan grasps the gun with both hands—like the rifle, it combines violence and potency—and then drops it, shaking his head no. Standing nearby, Filip's rigid form compels Jan to pick up the pistol. He does and, in a replay of the chicken scene, shoots at Jacobi and misses. (The sound of the gun is realistic, not amplified; a puff of smoke blown by the strong wind confirms each shot.) He shoots again, and this time fells Jacobi, who cries out. Moaning and trying to get out of sight, Jacobi tries to crawl behind the cart. Seemingly energized by the experience, the stocking-footed, awkward Jan staggers around to the other side to cut him off and fires again. Until now Eva has been watching, but now she presses her face to the wall and flinches with each shot. At last Filip gives the signal for a soldier with a machine gun to finish the job. With obvious contempt, he takes the pistol from Jan and orders the house torched. As the conflagration spreads, Filip's men sit Jacobi's corpse in a wheelbarrow, pile their booty on top of him, and depart.

Jan and Eva try to escape the heat of the burning house by retreating inside the greenhouse.[34] After a moment Jan turns the money out of his pocket. Seeing it, all Eva can do is stare unbelievingly at his back, but later she asks why he did not give Jacobi his money. Jan replies that they would have killed Jacobi anyhow. She screams at his lie, and when she emits a heartbreaking sob, he slaps her twice across the face. The satisfying feeling of killing Jacobi, and the fire that has destroyed Jan's last ties—especially his violin (*BB*, 229)—to civilized restraint, have kindled the embers so long banked inside him. His former habit of repressing his feelings has been replaced by an uninhibited confidence and a heretofore unrealized sense of manly expression and control. His former self-centeredness is now accompanied by an assurance that he needs and can trust no one, and that from now on he alone will determine his fate. All of this is signaled by his abandonment of his horn-rimmed glasses and by the tempo of his physical movement. He now moves vigorously, lithely, and with purpose.

Eva and Jan have exchanged roles, except that unlike her he is indifferent to all humanity, including her. When she trips as they are moving through a barren, charred landscape, he impatiently watches until she starts to get up, then moves on. One day on returning to their greenhouse they are held at bay by a young, uniformed deserter (Björn Thambert) with a machine gun. When he lets them approach, Eva's mothering instinct immediately awakens when she sees that he is exhausted, scared, and suffering from a dog bite. She offers to feed him and bandage the wound. Thrown off guard by her kindness and his own exhaustion, the boy, Johan, collapses in sleep into her lap (like Jacobi), but not before mentioning that he has to get to Hammars. Jan takes the boy's machine gun, wakes him, and at gunpoint orders him outside. The lad begs Jan not to kill him, and when Eva tries to intervene, Jan shoves her across the greenhouse and marches the boy off.

For a moment Eva just sits there thinking, and then she runs after them. From a very high camera position we look down at the area, but she is the only living thing we see. At the distant sound of machine-gun fire she drops to the ground, surrounded by stones and rock walls. After a moment she sits up, puts on her gloves—no more touching—and screams her way back to the greenhouse, where she finds Jan putting on the boy's boots—the second exchange of shoes in this film. (Like *Hour of the Wolf*'s Johan, Jan has killed a boy, ironically named Johan.) Jan extorted from the boy the information that a fishing boat is leaving from Hammars. When Eva shakes Jan and demands to know what he has done to the boy, he answers by shoving her to the floor. "I'm not coming," she responds, seeming to have lost all hope. Looking at her with cold indifference, he utters the last words he will speak in the film: "It'll be simpler if you stay." Eva gets up, sits in a chair, and stares at him; finally, her look softens into resignation. She cannot survive alone, and besides, nothing is worse than loneliness. "We'd better have something to eat before we go," she says. The thought may already have crossed our minds that the abuse inflicted earlier on these two by the establishment's officials or by the revolutionaries or by the war itself is nothing compared to the emotional cruelties these two have inflicted on each other.

Making their way to Hammars with their few possessions, Jan and Eva are seen moving from right to left on top of a hill, an image that evokes *The Seventh Seal*'s dance of death. They pass a file of people carrying a coffin toward a burned-out church: some people have held on to their beliefs. Bergman may be implying by this juxtaposition that though we may not believe in a deity we must at least keep firmly rooted inside us the moral values associated with God. Otherwise, we are dangerous and lost (*BB*, 232).

Eva's plan to learn Italian and the importance she has put on telephones, cars, radios, and relationships make her the symbol of the need to make contact, to communicate; now, at Hammars, as they (and others) wait for the boat, she asks Jan, "What's it going to be like if we can never talk to each other any more?" The arrival of the motorized fishing boat may be what prevents Jan from answering, but it is clear he is not interested in her question. When they get to the boat, the drama is composed of ironies: Filip is the captain of the little boat, and Jan pays him for their passage with Jacobi's money.

It is not long before the small boat is out of fuel and the men have to row; some days Filip steers, some days he rows. Before dawn one morning Jan awakens and, before rolling over and going back to sleep, watches this big man, his face as impassive as usual, silently lowering himself over the side into the sea.

Soon the food and the water have run out. A bearded man, whom we have seen hugging his wife—Jan and Eva are shown in separate shots or are seen one behind the other—dispenses the last sugar cubes, scraps of bread, and drops of water, leaving himself little more than a swallow. A day or so afterwards, the passengers wake to a terrible stench: the boat is trapped in a slick of swollen, human offal floating in life jackets.[35] Jan and another man exhaust themselves fruitlessly shoving the bodies clear with an oar.

From a great distance the boat appears to be a speck in the universe, a dot on a gray sea that melds with a gray sky. Accompanied by Eva's voice in close-up sound, the shot dissolves into a shot of the boat's interior, its passengers lying inert as they await death. A medium close-up looks past the horizontal Jan's face to Eva's, which is turned slightly toward us; both their heads are wrapped in scarves, and their eyes are closed (see fig. 37). Eva is describing a dream she has just had. She was walking along a beautiful street bordered on one side by elegant white houses and on the other by a park under whose trees "ran cold, dark green water." Then she came upon a high, rose-covered wall. Suddenly, a plane roared down and set the roses afire. (At this, both Eva and Jan open their eyes.) The reflection of the burning roses in the clear, dark green water was, she remembers, beautiful. Their daughter—the word causes Jan, whose sullen, embittered face has remained motionless, to blink three times—clung to her. Eva now looks puzzled as she says that throughout the dream she knew she should remember "something important that someone had said," but she cannot.[36] She closes her eyes, and the film ends.

In this dream Jan is present only as the progenitor of Eva's child. Eva is the creative, mothering principle, and she experiences the world in both its domesticated and violent forms as beautiful. Even though reflected through the greenish water darkly, the blazing roses are, along with the feel of the baby's wet mouth on her cheek, the most beautiful part of the experience. Eva's dream presents not only humans' love of conventional beauty but their fascination with violence and destruction. We recall the soldiers' joyous razing of Jan and Eva's house, and we remember that in *The Touch* David finds the beetles destroying the madonna and child as beautiful as the statue itself. In *The Ritual* Sebastian says, "Lilies shoot up from the arsehole of corpses." These Siamese urges to create and to destroy are part of

Shame. AB Svensk Filmindustri

human nature, the film argues, and therefore war can never be deleted from human history.

Because it ends with no mutual feeling between its two doomed protagonists, *Shame* is Bergman's most despairing film to date. Significant, if unstressed, signs of hope do, however, appear in the film: the dignity in death exhibited by both Jacobi and the self-sacrificing Filip; the married couple in the boat who impartially minister to each other's and their fellow passengers' needs before attending to their own; the hope and love in Eva's dream; the emphasis on the importance to civilization of moral and humane traditions and behavior. As for Jan, whom at first we pity and laugh at and then come to fear and hate, we do not dismiss him because, like Bergman, we can never be absolutely certain what, given extreme circumstances, we ourselves might do to survive.

Shame differs from the films that preceded and would follow it in that it conveys his themes without overtly calling attention to Bergman. But for the two jump dissolves and a few shots from an omniscient point of view, our immersion in this devastating film's gritty and grim reality remains undisturbed and total.

THE PASSION OF ANNA

Distancing and authorial intrusion are very much a part of *The Passion of Anna* (1969), Bergman's first color film since *Now about These Women*.[37] (This time, Bergman says, he and Nykvist did not approach color "by the book," which he feels hurt the earlier film.) In *The Passion of Anna* it is immediately clear that the omniscient storyteller/image maker is presenting his story as a case history, almost as if he were the psychiatrist in *Persona;* Bergman subtitles the film *L 182,* a reference both to the production numbers given films—*Winter Light,* for example, is L 186—and to the numbered boxes containing photographs of people in various psychic states kept by one of the film's protagonists, Elis Vergérus (Erland Josephson). This passion to study psychic states is one goal of *The Passion of Anna,* and it is a characteristic of all of Bergman's Vergéruses (the most horrifying of whom will be *The Serpent's Egg*'s Hans Vergérus). The script for *The Passion of Anna,* according to Bergman, was "more a catalogue of moods than a film script." (Bergman had problems filming *The Passion of Anna.*

Because he had not worked out all the technical problems beforehand, he says he had to reshoot several scenes [*BB, 261*].[38]) Asked whom he modeled his Vergeruses on, Bergman replied, "Myself" (*BB, 126*). In addition to the subtitle *L 182* and the credit "A Film by Ingmar Bergman," Bergman makes us recognize this film as his construct by opening it with his own voice-over, thumbnail history of the male protagonist, Andreas Winkelmann (Max von Sydow), by subsequently narrating several of the transitions, and by speaking the film's last words. Periodically, too, he distances the audience by interrupting the narrative to interview his actors about their roles. He intends their responses, which are mostly scripted, to round off the film's "four clean acts" (*BB, 222*).[39] Finally, Bergman also calls attention to the filmmaker at work by fragmenting the narrative and by occasionally employing unusually amplified sound (usually in conjunction with extreme close-ups).

Except possibly for *Cries and Whispers, The Passion of Anna* more than any other Bergman film of this period makes one conscious of Bergman experimenting just to experiment, and most of it works. (I feel interviewing his actors is the single experiment that does not work. Besides presenting information that is redundant, the self-conscious playfulness of this device undermines one of the film's strengths, the impression of ruthless candidness; to no great effect, the distancing also impedes the momentum of fate's implacable advance, another of the film's noteworthy achievements.) This film feels looser and more spontaneous than his previous films. He often jettisons conventional transitions. The very jarring ellipses that result remind the audience of the storyteller and contribute to the impression that this is a case history, not a conventional, seamless, and fluid narrative. Because these ellipses often occur as Bergman introduces new information about situations we thought we already understood, we are brought up short and, thus, made aware of a reality outside the film's. In this connection, the feeling that reality cannot be shaped or fully comprehended even by the storyteller strengthens both the story's fatalism and the impression that the mystery involved is impenetrable.

Bergman frames the film with his own comments and presence, but as is his custom, he also provides a visual frame. (As often noted, in many of his films the last image's similarity to the opening image calls our attention to the changes that have accrued in between them, for example, *Dreams* and *Shame*). *The Passion of Anna* ends with Andreas mentally broken and crawling on the ground under what seems to be a bright sun; Bergman magnifies this image until instead of fading out it grains out. The opposite effect opens the film. Andreas is on his hands and knees, climbing up his very steep roof to repair its tiles. Sven Nykvist's subtle imaging of what Andreas sees and hears—delicate chimes, bells, a dog's bark, the random rattle of sheep bells, and a beautiful and peaceful landscape—contrasts dramatically with the ending's grainy, blurred, raw imagery. Even though Andreas has taken refuge from society and conflict here on the island, this image of him on the roof suggests that reality still leaks through his defenses. For a moment, however, he is able to pause in his work and smile at the beauty and peace of his pastoral, island world, giving the impression that he is a man at harmony with himself and his environment. The steep roof, however, and omens—the sudden appearance of a parhelion (the illusion of three suns[40]), the sheep suddenly being spooked—cue us to his essential instability and the dire events to follow. The parhelion causes his weathered face and expression to darken, and he suddenly quits work. As he descends, the precipitousness of his position is underscored when his pail of cement slips and clatters along the tiles and falls off the roof. Even on the ground he swears under his breath at the pail because he still cannot get it to stay upright. The terra-cotta shards of roof tiles that litter the ground, and the use of a hand-held camera, further the impression of fragmentation, insecurity, and instability.

Educated, modest, capable of tenderness and caring, Andreas nevertheless feels an emptiness within that weakens his sense of self and his morality. He feels, and is, a failure.[41] His wife has left him, and his fear of descending into sinkholes prevents him from following his profession as a geologist. He has been in prison for tax evasion, drunk driving, hitting an officer, and forgery. The last offense is emblematic of his weak ego, and his drunkenness and violence hint at the rage suppressed behind his passive, humble manner. This suppressed violence is conveyed to us early on in a panning close-up that connects Andreas's inexpressive, bearded face with the head of a hammer driving in a nail, the sound amplified to fit the giant close-up. Lacking self-respect and strong convictions, and thus experiencing a state of free-floating humiliation, Andreas is a variation of *Shame*'s Jan—but with the crucial difference that Andreas knows and faces up to his character. Called a "whipped cur" to his face, he accepts the epithet, but he knows he is capable of striking out violently if whipped too long or too hard. When later we learn that the man whose life

Andreas seems to be reliving was also capable of being warmhearted or cold-bloodedly ruthless, we should not be surprised. Duality, in fact, is a characteristic of almost everyone and everything in the film. Each of the five protagonists is different from what he or she seems, and the seemingly peaceful island is infected with violence. Even fire variously symbolizes vulnerability, passion, love, anger, and evil.

Though he has retreated to this island, at heart Andreas is no hermit. Unlike the sick, elderly Johan Andersson (Erik Hell), who has reconciled himself to his reclusiveness, Andreas needs people. In part, they help obscure the loneliness and emptiness he feels. After coming down to earth from the roof in the scene just described, Andreas approaches and invites Johan to visit him. Though he is unsuccessful, Andreas is pleased when a limping stranger, Anna Fromm (Liv Ullmann), drives up and asks to use his telephone. His fatal need for involvement causes him to pretend to leave her alone in his study and then stand in the hall and eavesdrop on her conversation. The camera zooms in on his face, beside which is an ornamental bell whose spikes suggest a crown of thorns; the light reflected through the stained-glass window in the door casts a cross on the wall. Hearing Anna burst into tears, he slips outside. When the upset woman joins him outside, she responds coolly to his friendly gestures. After she has driven off, he thinks about what he has done and laughs.

"What do you think of Andreas?" Bergman's voice asks Max von Sydow, unexpectedly interrupting the narrative. The gist of the actor's reply is that playing Andreas is hard because Andreas hides his emotions. Bergman's cognizance of the difficulties that this can create for the action is reflected in his alternating extremely high shots with low shots, long shots with close-ups, and in his frequent use of a hand-held camera to photograph Andreas. These devices not only help energize this impassive, uncertain, almost aimless character, they enhance the general feeling of disorientation, unpredictability, and mystery. The interview ends with a white-out that not only foreshadows Andreas's final situation but acts as a transition to the next scene, in which Andreas is lighting his kerosene lamp to examine the contents of Anna Fromm's forgotten purse. Once again Bergman is able to jump the action ahead by means of eavesdropping. The only object of interest in the purse is (à la *Persona*) a letter. It is from Anna's deceased husband. Andreas reads it aloud: even though he loves her, writes Andreas Fromm, he is leaving her because continuing their marriage can only lead to "physical and psychical acts of violence." As Andreas reads the last sentence again, to himself, the camera pans the typed words, which are thrust at the viewer in an extreme close-up. The restrained, portentous diction and the slow, amplified, fateful tick of a clock alarm us. We will learn that after receiving this letter, Anna's husband and child were killed and she was crippled when the car she was driving crashed nearby.

The next scene takes place on a cold, windy night soon after Anna's visit. Andreas drops by the Vergéruses, at whose home Anna is re-cuperating, to return her purse. When Eva (Bibi Andersson) and Elis Vergérus come to the door, Nykvist's warm, golden lighting of the space behind them is so inviting that we want to enter. Andreas is asked to, but, poised on the knife edge of his fear of involvement, he begs off until another time.

The next scene occurs some days afterwards. While in the snowy woods collecting pine cones for burning, Andreas glimpses someone running in the distance. He then discovers and saves a puppy that has been hanged. Taking it home, he feeds and talks to it. As mentioned earlier, the film is purposely elliptical about time. Sometime after this event, he comes upon Eva Vergérus lying motionless across the front seat of her car. Because of the preceding scene we fear the worst, but a touch awakens her. She informs Andreas that she often naps in the daytime because she is unable to sleep at night. Then, just as Anna had done, Eva drives off leaving him puzzled. Their encounter, how-ever, leads to a dinner invitation at the Vergéruses. "Not knowing quite why," says the narrator, Andreas accepts.

Once there, Andreas feels a sudden affection for his hosts. After a brief establishing shot of Andreas, Anna, Eva, and Elis sitting around the dining room table, Bergman isolates each one for a single, unin-terrupted shot. (Like the larger interviews with the actors, these shots also make the actors seem like puppets.[42]) Andreas and Anna are framed alike, their fates thus subliminally interwoven: deep in the frame there are tall candles on either side of them. In contrast, Eva has two short, warmly bright candles next to her right shoulder, and Elis—just as Bergman does with Josephson's devilish doctor in *Cries and Whispers*—is shown with the fireplace's leaping flames behind him.

Their wide-ranging conversation provides thumbnail portraits of each. The most vulnerable and insecure is Eva, whose name (like that of the childless Eva in *Shame*) underscores her desire to be a mother. (She was once pregnant, we will learn, but the fetus was killed when she received an overdose of a sleeping drug.) Her overdependence on males is demonstrated when she is asked if she believes in God. She looks at Elis and asks, "Do I?" and then confesses that she does, that she came to believe when, sitting on her atheistic father's lap, she saw God represented as a fatherly, bearded, flying figure in a book entitled *Light*. However, if she had children, she says, she would not teach them to believe as she does. "Why?" she is asked. Stymied, she is grateful to Andreas (ironically) for suggesting it would be from principle, that she would want the children to make up their own minds. Elis, we also will discover, does nothing to help Eva achieve self-confidence, nor will he satisfy her need for personal fulfillment. Thus, she pretends she does not want a child.

We quickly perceive a number of things about Elis. He has made cynicism his chief defense against disappointment and suffering. (The only time Eva has seen him cry was when their baby died. Never again will he open himself to such pain.) An eminent architect, he delights in cynically labeling the cultural center he is designing for Milan as nothing more than a mausoleum in which to house meaninglessness. He is an insecure man who masks his anger and fear of failure with jokes, smiles, and whistling, and who artfully and sadistically uses his money, sardonic humor, and his hobby of photography to study, control, and humiliate others. He is a Vergérus after all.

Anna, in contrast to Eva, is a willful woman crippled by guilt and one who supports herself with a crutch of illusion. On the phone at Andreas's we witnessed a vulnerable, desperate Anna; now we see a hint of the anger she can muster. She is outraged with Elis's contempt for his work and excitedly insists that one must devote one's life to truth. Take her marriage, for example. It was a success, she says, not only because she and her husband strove for spiritual perfection but because they were absolutely honest with each other. Suddenly, Bergman submerges himself in Andreas's mind, and again, to the amplified ticking, the giant close-up of the line from Andreas Fromm's letter fills the screen: "I know that we shall only . . . bring on terrible mental disturbances, physical and psychical acts of violence."

Andreas stays over at the Vergéruses' and sometime during the night is awakened by Anna, who is having a nightmare. She repeatedly screams, "Andreas!" Sitting up in bed, he listens. Besides pondering her relationship with his namesake, Andreas has to be wondering if—even hoping that—she is calling to him.

In the morning Elis shows Andreas his attractive studio in a converted windmill. From floor to ceiling are numbered boxes containing photographs of people in all states of emotion. At one time, says Elis, he "collected only pictures of acts of violence." Ominously exhaling cigarette smoke, Elis shows Andreas photographs of both Anna and Andreas Fromm (Birger Malmsten), whom, he comments, Anna loved with insane intensity. Laughing, and making it seem that he is almost proffering his wife, Elis adds that Eva was Andreas Fromm's mistress for a year, but that one day she just left him; Elis has never asked why. Anna and Eva are inseparable friends, Elis adds. The more Andreas hears the angrier he becomes, but it shows itself almost exclusively in the amplified sound made when he sets down his empty whisky glass. (Four shots of Andreas include Bergman's "hardwood" figurehead.[43])

At home Andreas's need for a woman and his sense that he is somehow getting embroiled again cause him to get drunk and visit his wife's pottery studio, which remains just as she left it. Sitting at the pottery wheel—we may remember Nix and David throwing pots in *A Lesson in Love*—this unproductive man spins it, sending his gin glass flying. He steps over the shattered glass and goes outside. His exit is shot from high overhead and from a distance; he appears trapped. Mounting his bike, he rides drunkenly across the yard and runs into a wall. He leaves the bike behind and stumbles across the street into the snowy woods. Shot now from treetop height, he seems all the more insignificant and trapped. Convinced that his voice has no weight, and he himself no substance, he repeatedly screams (recalling Anna) "Andreas Winkelmann! . . . Winkelmann!" (the Swedish word for "corner") at the gray sky, as if it might answer and confirm his identity. But the only reply is from a melancholy foghorn guiding ships through the fog. Andreas slides down against a tree and slips into unconsciousness. (The color of the setting is practically black and white, further depriving the scene of warmth.) As if heaven-sent, Johan Andersson, this film's interceding angel, appears and saves Andreas from freezing to death. Calling "Andreas!"—Andreas's name *has* been heard—the ailing old man loads the raving, hostile figure onto his cart and takes him back across the road. Inside Andreas's house Johan props him up in a chair, but Andreas immediately slouches off it and onto the floor. Realizing he has done all he can for Andreas, Johan puts a pillow under his head and leaves. Andreas's puppy rushes in and licks his savior's face. Johan's intervention and this amusing expression of instinctual affection momentarily counter the film's growing bleakness.

Bergman now questions Liv Ullmann about her conception of Anna. Wearing a wide-brimmed, bright red, floppy felt hat, Ullmann stresses Anna's lying and cheating to make the world fit her idea of how life should be. Bergman opens the interview by having Ullmann come into focus and ends it with her going out of focus.

The fateful pattern is taking shape. Having been left alone for three days by her husband, Eva visits Andreas—they stand on either side of his roaring bonfire—with the clear intent of sleeping with him. Andreas shows her around, even taking her to his wife's pottery studio, which leads to his confiding that he is divorced "in a way," and that "perhaps" his wife will come back. He is even noncommittal when Eva asks if he misses his wife. They return to the house. Like the bonfire, the light from the amber sunset that suffuses the house's interior foreshadows and facilitates what is going to happen. Eva begins drinking and puts "Always Romantic" on the phonograph. She informs Andreas that when she dances Elis gets embarrassed. She adds that even though she truly loves Elis she always wants to pay him back for his sarcasms, and that she simply does not know how to make him appreciate her love. Maybe, she ruminates, he is tired of her. Standing behind the sitting Andreas, she lays her forehead against his head, and while he kisses the back of her hand, she reflects, "What is this deadly poison that corrodes the best in us, leaving only a shell?" (In *The Devil's Eye,* Don Juan confesses, "My inside seems burnt out, my skin a thin shell round a void.") Drowsy, she asks if she can take a nap. Andreas settles her on his couch, puts a pillow under her head, and gives her his puppy to hold, all of which calls up the previous scene. Then he turns off "Always Romantic." Now the only sound is the faint tick of the clock. Andreas takes this opportunity to wash the dishes; the sound of the dishes hitting against one another is highly amplified. We recall von Sydow's complaint that Andreas does not project what he feels. It is the case that in the editing of the film Bergman almost always shows Andreas's face before revealing what he sees, be it a parhelion, Anna's phone call, the hanging dog, or Eva asleep in her car. Likewise, it is often the case that Bergman will cue us to a character's feelings by means of such exterior details as colors or sounds. In *The Silence,* for example, it is the magnified sound of Anna's comb passing through her hair. In a moment, the color of a phone will clue us to Elis's jealousy. Now it is the magnified clatter of the dishes that hints at Andreas's sexual feelings.

When Eva awakens, having overslept, she immediately phones Elis, whose habit it is to call her at home when he is away. Unlike when he eavesdropped on Anna, Andreas inquires if she would prefer to be alone while she talks to Elis; she says no, so he hears her lie to Elis that earlier she met Andreas, but that now she is home alone. It seem clear that just as Eva knows which of Elis's smiles means he is angry, she also knows that he knows she is lying. Beautifully silhouetted against the blue sky outside the window, Eva unexpectedly starts sobbing, lamenting that she feels unneeded and unloved. Then she and Andreas begin to make love. Suddenly, there is a close-up of the phone ringing. As Andreas answers it, Bergman cuts to Elis's hotel room as he tells Andreas that he just called Eva at home, and he is worried because she did not answer. Would Andreas look in on her? He hangs up, his jealousy symbolized almost entirely by both the abrupt way he puts down the phone and the phone's redness. Afterwards, Eva and Andreas continue making love, the film's only lyric and erotic scene.

In the morning Andreas gives Eva his puppy, a gesture we assume is motivated partly by his awareness of her childlessness, and partly by a desire to reassure her that she was not a "dreary" love partner. When she leaves, she will join Elis for two weeks, but Andreas makes her promise to visit him again. Before she tears herself away, she passionately and repeatedly kisses him. After she is gone, Andreas returns inside. He feels an overpowering sense of loneliness, which the clock's ticking through the empty rooms underscores. Whistling, he walks into a giant close-up and then turns and walks deep into the frame. He ends up lying on his bed. Now, not a foghorn but church bells are heard in the background. Loathing his irresoluteness and moral bankruptcy, he suddenly emits a cry that might, were it less self-concerned, rival David's in *Through a Glass Darkly*.

In the next scene we learn that eight sheep belonging to one of Andreas's neighbors have been found with their throats cut. The police take snapshots (calling Elis to mind). Evoking images from the German death camps, Andreas helps drag the bloody sheep into a huge pit.[44] In voice-over, Bergman announces that there is a "madman on the island." On first viewing, this statement makes audiences think that they are watching a traditional murder mystery, and so they begin speculating about who is perpetrating these unmotivated cruelties. (The culprit, of course, is Bergman, who says, "Unmotivated cruelty . . . never ceases to fascinate me" [*BB,* 40].)

In exchange for Elis's signature on a loan authorization, Andreas has agreed to transcribe Elis's notes for his Milan project and to sit for photographs. When, in the next scene, he arrives for the sitting, the cordial Elis impales him, the second Andreas to be Eva's lover, on a

stool under grueling lights. Then, using the finest of cameras,[45] Elis
circles his passive, dizzied prey, snapping his picture and grilling him
with humiliating questions. Elis has discovered that Andreas was in
prison; he inquires, finally, if Andreas is a "whipped cur" or if he bites.
Anger rising in his gorge, Andreas replies, "Wait and see," but then
quietly adds, "No, I don't think I will." Eva enters, and Elis leaves
almost at once; with him gone, the recording of Bach's music that has
been counterpointing Elis's cynicism and cruelty ceases. Alone, Eva
tells Andreas that she thinks of him constantly, and she calls him "my
dear." We are stunned when next she informs him that Anna has told
her about her affair with him, and that she, Eva, forgives him. But,
she warns, be careful, because it is "hard to be sure about Anna's feelings." The return of Elis, wearing a sly smile that broadcasts his suspicions and anger, ends the conversation.

We are profoundly unsettled, not to say disoriented, to find that
Bergman has kept from us something as important as Andreas dropping Eva and launching an affair with Anna—who has long been absent from the film—and to learn that their affair has been going on for
months. Part of our discomfort is caused by the ease with which Andreas drops Eva for Anna. It can be argued that Bergman's view of
his story as a case history justifies not only jettisoning this chunk of
time and events but ignoring the expected transition and dropping
prominent characters—except for Bergman's interviews with Bibi
Andersson and Erland Josephson, Elis and Eva now totally disappear
from the film.

Another word about this last scene: Bergman uses Elis to comment
on his own art. Elis points out that even a facial close-up 40 feet high
leaves a character's feelings and motives ambiguous. He shows Andreas photographs of Johan Andersson, who became a hermit when
he lost a lawsuit, and then of Eva. She is smiling. Actually, says Elis,
he took the photo, without Eva's knowledge, just when she was starting a migraine: "I don't reach into the soul with these," he asserts, "I
just register the interplay of forces. Then you look at [them] and give
rein to your imagination." He concludes, "You can't read another person with the slightest claim to certainty, not even physical pain."[46]

Now the narrator Bergman tells us that Anna, who employs herself
translating, and Andreas, who employs himself transcribing Elis's
notes, are living together in relative harmony, without quarrels or passion. When we think about it, we understand why this "whipped cur"
might be attracted to the passionately self-assured Anna. Odd as it is

that we are never shown a love scene between these two that is comparable to the lyrical, erotic one between Andreas and Eva, an explanation is provided by the narrator's description (the implications of which for Bergman and Ullmann's relationship are disconcerting). These lovers seem to enjoy an emotion that "is not quite love, but instead an intricate exchange of self-interests, a sensual companionship enabling each to become closer, not to the beloved, but to himself" (Zweig, 105). The scenes that follow (with the exception of Bergman's interviews) document the progress of the personal relationship between these pathological protagonists and document some of the varieties of violence in our world.

In another of the great scenes-arias in film history—an uninterrupted monologue shot as a giant close-up—Anna, wearing her girlish, self-satisfied smile, describes to Andreas her ideal marriage, emphasizing how between her and her husband there was no dissension, pretense, suspicion, or hatred. When, however, she begins to describe the accident that killed her husband and child, it is as if it happened to someone else and she were watching the event as a movie in her head. In a tone and manner that seem prurient, she makes the accident scene visible to us—Andreas halfway through the windshield with his throat cut, their son sprawled on the ground with his neck broken, and her own shinbone sticking through her stocking. As her submerged pain and guilt near the surface, almost imperceptively her eyes redden and water, her supercilious smile fades, and she confesses that she never thought life would be daily suffering.[47] The expression that accompanies this statement reveals the enormity of her need to deny reality (see figs. 38, 39). And again, in extreme close-up and accompanied by loud ticking, the line from her husband's letter is called up (by Andreas or Bergman?) on the screen.

One day, after Anna and Andreas have helped Johan Andersson dislodge his cart from a bog, they learn from him that because he was once in a mental hospital people are accusing him of being the animal killer. "Me, cruel to animals?" he laughs. Because the police have not been able to do anything and he has nowhere to escape to, he is certain, he tells Andreas and Anna, that he will be killed.

Johan's suffering is not the only pain that intrudes on Andreas and Anna's happiness. As they unflinchingly watch on television the Vietnamese police chief unexpectedly shoot his prisoner in the head—like most, though not all, of the physical violence in this film, the climactic act is left to our imaginations—a small bird smashes into their house.[48]

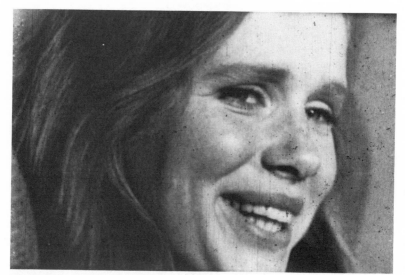

The Passion of Anna. AB Svensk Filmindustri

The Passion of Anna. AB Svensk Filmindustri

Anna's spontaneous response is for Andreas to put it out of its misery, but she utters a little moan when he crushes its head with a stone. It is only after she has buried it, and while they are washing the dirt and blood off their hands, that she inquires, in a flat tone, if it could have survived. A little later, during a chess game (domestic combat[49]), she asks Andreas why the bird was flying around at night. That she is, in part, thinking of the insomniac Eva is made clear when, after Andreas has answered that it might have been "afraid of something," she asks him to confess that he and Eva had an affair. When he lies, Anna, believing that she believes in truth or nothing, sweeps all the chess pieces onto the floor.

Bergman interrupts to interview Bibi Andersson, who says she hopes that the plot will save Eva, and that Eva will "work with the deaf who are in even greater isolation." Bergman ends the interview by bleeding the color out and overexposing the shot.

A scene that may be a continuation—after some interval—of the scene that was interrupted shows Andreas and Anna sitting side by side as the lamp goes out. Andreas tries to kiss Anna, but breathing heavily and laughing rather demonically—light glints off one of her eyes and off her teeth—she grabs his throat. Before he can kiss her, finally, he has to pry loose her strangling fingers.

At Easter time Anna Fromm's guilt—her last name is Swedish for "pious"—over the death of her husband and son emerges in a nightmare that she recounts to Andreas. It starts in color, but the color bleeds away until the scene, in both its setting and photographic look—grainy black and white—replicate that at the end of *Shame*. The lifeboat filled with dead bodies drifts into shore, and Eva-Liv Ullmann-Anna is the *only* survivor. After disembarking, she hurries along a road that runs through *Shame*'s barren and burned-out landscape, which is inhabited only by women. When she approaches them, they run from her as if she were cursed. Then she and the other women fall in stride with a woman (Barbro Hort af Ornäs) who is on her way to her son's execution. Eva-Anna throws herself at this Mary figure and begs forgiveness—but she is rejected, undoubtedly because she has shown no contrition. Now dressed as Anna, not Eva, Anna runs, accompanied by the fast ticking of a watch or a time bomb. She comes upon the dead bodies of her husband and son. Like Munch's shrieking figure, she soundlessly screams "Andreas!"—thus replicating her response to her nightmare the night that Andreas slept over at the Vergéruses.

The next scene commences with Bergman's camera panning up from the shards of roof tiles on the ground in front of Andreas's house to a police car that parks in front of his door. The police have brought a sealed suicide note from Johan Andersson that is addressed to Andreas, the only man who has treated him with respect. (The police are portrayed as mere note takers; they will never track down the madness on the island.) Andreas reads the note aloud; the emotion that wells up in him almost prevents him from finishing. Johan recounts how after a mob came to his house, struck him in the head with a stone (like the bird), urinated on him, knocked out his false teeth, and got him to confess to what he had not done, he fainted. When he awoke and realized he could never again look anyone in the face, he hanged himself. (The hanged puppy flashes through our minds.) Anna listens impassively, and after the police have gone, Andreas finds her sitting in the pottery studio, "praying." She says she is praying for Johan, but Andreas accuses her of praying for herself, for her own vision of the world. (Bergman has said, "The idea of the Christian God as something destructive and fantastically dangerous, something . . . [which brings] out in [people] dark destructive forces instead of the opposite . . . is one of the main motifs in *A Passion* " (*BB,* 164). When Anna raises her head to look at Andreas, her expression is one of hate.

In the scene that follows Andreas pays his last respects to Johan. Just as Jacobi *(Shame),* Karin *(The Touch),* and Bergman studied their mothers' corpses, Andreas sits by the bed and studies Johan's, at one point placing his hand over Johan's folded, calloused hands. A picture of Jesus is on the wall above Johan's head. Ticking is the dominant sound. From the window a stream of light illuminates the body, as it will the saintly Agnes in *Cries and Whispers.* Johan is another character whose death helps the Bergman protagonist gain insight into himself and the world. To a degree, Andreas identifies with this lonely, humiliated man, but more than that he seems to be in awe of Johan's strength of character and self-respect. Also foreshadowing *Cries and Whispers,* the scene ends with a fade to red.

In voice-over, Bergman tells us that though Andreas and Anna argue, it is never venomously, and that they have lived together quietly for a year. But then he presents Andreas daydreaming about women he has slept with; the brief flashback is shot subjectively from his position on a bed. Looking up at the woman—she seems to be a nurse—he has just slept with as she is getting dressed, he hears her diagnose his character. It is Bergman's most vivid metaphor for the pathological condition he has spent his career tracking. Andreas, she says, has "cancer of the soul." This brings Andreas out of his daydream. Typing translations in another room, Anna senses that he is remembering an old flame and asks him what he is thinking about. As he did about his affair with Eva, he lies. Anna gets up, limps to the refrigerator where she removes a huge bowl of milk, walks to where he can see her, and drops it, pitifully crying out his name. He rushes to her, and they embrace over the spilled milk.

For the next scene Bergman replaces the naturalistic lighting with cameo lighting and places Andreas and Anna against a black background, just as in *Winter Light*'s letter scene he placed Märta against a plain, white background.[50] Using shot/reverse shot, he shows Anna looking up at the distressed Andreas and catches her facile response that she fully understands what he feels, when it is clear from her unmodulated tone that she does not. Through Andreas, Bergman launches into a monologue about the walls he has built around himself that prevent him from being "warm and tender and alive." It is what in his autobiography Bergman calls the Bergman family's motto: "Don't disturb, don't intrude!" (He imagined asking his mother why he and his siblings were "given shame and guilt instead of love and forgiveness? . . . Why was I incapable of normal human relationships for so long?" [*ML*, 283–85]) Next, he speaks of the crippling effects of failure and the humiliation of letting people trample on one. Like most people, he asserts, he lives without self-respect and with the sickness of humiliation. As a consequence of being so infected, the freedom he and others want in order to take control of their lives turns to poisonous self-hate. He cannot stand himself any longer, but neither can he escape his condition. (The island is the symbol of his entrapment.) And he has noticed that the "worse off people are the less they complain," and that they finally become silent. Bergman here inserts a shot seen previously of old Johan shaking his head. Unfortunately, this extended, abstract, and complicated speech is, for those with or without a knowledge of Bergman's personality and earlier work, extremely difficult to grasp. This may be what Bergman is referring to when he says that, though he "very much" likes *The Passion of Anna,* he has "the feeling that it doesn't reach the audience."[51]

Bergman disrupts the narrative for the last time to interview Erland Josephson. Sitting amid stage props, Josephson ignores the camera. He calls Elis's analysis and categorization of others' suffering simply his way of coping.

In the next scene Bergman amplifies the sound to make us *experience* the tension between Andreas and Anna. At breakfast they are overly formal. The salt and pepper shakers, moved like chess pieces, thump loudly as they are set down on the checkerboard tablecloth. When Andreas wipes his mouth with his napkin, it sounds like he is crumpling cellophane, and when Anna spreads butter on her toast, it sounds like she is using a rake instead of a knife. Her chewing sounds like someone walking on thick, dry snow. After breakfast Andreas sublimates his pent-up anger in splitting logs. We never see him set up a log, only the exertion on his face and the axe descending to halve log after log. A hand-held camera enhances the energy in each blow. A long shot of the wood pile that quickly forms represents just how profound his frustration and anger are. Slightly hysterical, Anna comes outside to inform him that they are finished. She says that the lies he has told about his marriage and divorce have destroyed their relationship. She reminds him of how, in contrast, she and her husband lived by the truth. Having to shout over the wind boosts the level of the building pressure. When she screams that he is not her master, that he cannot order her about, he lunges at her, sinking the axe blade into the wall beside her head. Though we are thrust back in our seats, we share Andreas's hostility and thus join the list of potential murderers on the island. He chases her, screaming and crying, about the yard. Catching her, he slaps her. When she hits back, he knocks her to the snowy ground. Just as Anne let loose her veil in *Smiles of a Summer Night,* Anna unfastens and drops her red bandanna, gets up, and limps inside. The camera lingers on the blood-red cloth on the battlefield's pure white snow (an image that calls to mind the earlier image of the blood-stained snow around the murdered sheep). Symbolically, blood has been shed, and the breach seems irreparable.

Inside, Anna retreats to her bedroom and covers her body with her blanket and her head with her arms. When Andreas enters the house, he paces from room to room, finally sitting down at Anna's typewriter. The ticking, which once again is noticeable, is suddenly blotted out by the siren of a fire engine that passes, its lights flashing. Andreas calls to Anna, but when she does not respond, he runs off to the fire.

The scene that follows materializes the passions of the previous scene. When Andreas arrives, the inferno, the flashing police beacon, and the sound of screaming cattle add to the dizzying terror as he is told that the madman poured gasoline on a horse in the stable and set it on fire, and that for a long time the blazing animal has run about, refusing to die.[52] "The war in *Shame*" says Bergman, "now manifested itself for me in . . . a more surreptitious way. In the cry of animals . . ." (*BB,* 253). Anna arrives with the car, and Andreas immediately gets in. Just then—to the sound of a kettle drum being struck—the immolated horse is dragged onto the back of a truck.

As they drive, Andreas, who, except in the long speech on his emptiness and humiliation, has not uttered more than a sentence at a time, now speaks easily and naturally. Openly afraid of what has happened to them, he tells Anna that (like his namesake) he wants his freedom back, adding that had they really loved one another they might have made it. (This is one of the few instances in which a Bergman character finds hell together worse than hell alone.) Silent, scarily impassive, Anna stares straight ahead. Close-ups of her steering and shifting gears and exterior shots of the tires splashing muddy water out of chuckholes—accompanied by the beat on the kettle drum now associated with the dead horse[53]—are ominous. So, too, is the little toy bear—Bergman's symbol of security that here reminds us of the puppy—swinging by its neck from the rearview mirror. Anna's silence provokes Andreas to smile and mock her so-called ideal of truth. He reveals at last, with relish, that he read her husband's letter. Anna does not blink; she speeds up. Continuing, Andreas tells her that her talk of loving the truth "was all lies." The mud-obscured windshield and the fogged side windows increase our feeling of being trapped. Preferring oblivion to losing her construction of the world, Anna suddenly heads the speeding car off the road. "Are you going to kill me too," he shouts; he avoids his namesake's fate by grabbing the wheel and turning off the ignition. As they sit there, silent but for their heavy breathing, the ticking is heard again, low but very fast. Calling her insane, Andreas asks why she even came to get him. "To ask your forgiveness," she replies. Like the Mary figure in Anna's Easter nightmare, Andreas, dumbfounded, rejects her suspect plea and gets out of the car.[54] Anna starts the motor and drives off.

Preventing Anna from killing him is a victory of truth over illusion, but Andreas has no illusion to sustain him, and the truths he knows about himself are unbearable. A long shot now shows this lone figure trapped in a wasteland in which he, a rotted tree stump, and a telephone pole (communication) are reflected in pools of water. Stymied, Andreas's thinking and feeling processes seem to experience meltdown. He has no sense of purpose; nor does he have the strength, like

Johan, to commit suicide. He paces rapidly back and forth in increasingly smaller circles. The ticking, which sounds more like that of a time bomb, increases in volume. The sky grows brighter than Elis's punishing spotlights, and like an object under a microscope, the pacing Andreas is tracked down by an optical zoom. As his image, along with the photographic grain, is being magnified, he lies down on the ground, rolls over, then gets to his hands and knees. Like the immolated horse that refused to die, he crawls in excruciating psychic pain. (The moment bears some similarities to Frost's physical and mental collapse in *Sawdust and Tinsel*.) The magnification of the image continues until finally, to the beat of the drum—which is like a modest explosion—Andreas is atomized, an image difficult to relate to. Bergman ends the film by saying calmly, "This time he was called Andreas Winkelmann."

Bergman's deterministic view of character, his fate-driven plot, and his case history approach, which elides and telescopes events, tend to make *The Passion of Anna* feel a bit too programmed at times, maybe a little thin. They also tend to make the film's patently violent, painful world feel too hermetically sealed. A shot that comes after Andreas almost splits Anna's head with the axe asserts this symbolically: inside the house we watch a moth beat its head and wings against a window. But as in *Shame*, Bergman lets some hope leak into the world of *The Passion of Anna*: Eva, Johan Andersson, the woman who cries over her sheep, Andreas when he is tender and caring, the Milanese for whom Elis builds monuments, and Anna's attacks of guilt suggest the existence of enduring positive values. Color, used to capture the beautiful as well as the bleak, also helps vitalize and alleviate the monochromatic, *Shame*-like despair. And we are aware that the creator of this fictional-autobiographical world, even if he cannot put into practice what he knows it takes to be psychologically healthy, still is capable of speaking out for wholeness. Soon after finishing this film, in fact, Bergman said that he believed "that every human being has a sort of dignity or wholeness in him, and out of that develops relationships to other human beings, [and this includes the] tensions, misunderstanding, tenderness, coming in contact, touching and being touched, the cutting off of contact and what happens then. That's what is fascinating. I feel I have come . . . into an enormous field, and I can now get started. . . . Because of that I made *A Passion* and my documentary [*The Fårö Document* (1970)] and . . . I am writing my new picture [*The Touch*]" (Simon, 29–30). As we have already seen,

The Touch focuses on a character not unlike *The Passion of Anna*'s dependent Eva, the difference being that Karin's journey toward becoming her own person, though painful, is successful.

The Passion of Anna stresses the danger of reality-denying idealism and exhibits a variety of destructive urges that exist in human nature and human institutions. Possibly most important is Bergman's analysis of how self-centeredness, weakness, and humiliation metamorphose into emotional paralysis and then into violence. *The Serpent's Egg* continues this examination on both a personal and a social level.

THE SERPENT'S EGG

The script for *The Serpent's Egg* (1977) was completed for producer Dino De Laurentiis in late 1975, before Bergman's contretemps over taxes and his self-imposed exile from Sweden. Made in Munich, it was his costliest film to date—$4 million—and his second English-language film (*This Doesn't Happen Here* was simultaneously shot in both Swedish and English in 1950). Some of the film's protagonists have their origin in an unfinished filmscript he wrote in 1965 about two acrobats who lose their partner and are stranded in Varsovie [Warsaw] during the German occupation. "One of them . . . fell sick . . . [and] from then on it was to have been about the [younger] man's experiences, how the city gradually draws him down into itself, how their friendship goes to pieces as the older man gets sicker and sicker" (*BB*, 181). (*The Silence*, of course, has to do with illness forcing a trio to stay in a country on the brink of war, and with disintegrating relationships.) His reading that the CIA had conducted experiments in which men voluntarily took drugs so that the psychic results could be studied had influenced a screenplay Bergman wrote in 1967. It concerned a scientist who shut people up in his laboratory to observe their responses after he had "expose[d] them to various psychic pressures" (*BB*, 231). As for the *The Serpents Egg*'s setting, Berlin in 1923, Bergman drew on an adolescent experience of his own in that city (*ML*, 130–32), on Siegfried Siwertz's short stories, on Hans Fallada's *A Wolf among Wolves* (1937) and *Little Man, What Now?* (1932), and on Bertolt Brecht and Kurt Weill's *Threepenny Opera* (1928). Twice before, in his radio play *The City* and in *The Silence*, Berlin had been Bergman's model. The city fascinated him because it possessed a "demonic suggestiveness" that had to do with a "sense of sinking into [the city's enormity and] . . . becoming anonymous within it" (*BB,* 181).[55] To be sure, the audience's response to this film depends on this specific historical setting; nevertheless, in spite of the documentary touches, audiences must also view *The Serpent's Egg*'s Berlin as a quasi-historical, metaphorical setting for Bergman's usual protagonists and themes.

For this semipolitical film Bergman reunited the three actors (two males by proxy) from his other "political" film, *Shame*. Liv Ullmann returned to play the Eva-like Manuela, a former member of a famous acrobatic trio and the ex-wife of its "catcher," Max Rosenberg (Hans Eichler). Max's brother Abel (David Carradine) is the third member of the troupe, which two months before disbanded because Max injured his wrist. Like Eva—though slightly less self-assured and independent than her—Manuela is overly compassionate and in desperate need of companionship. To survive in depression-era Germany after her separation from Max, she performs as a singer and dancer in a Berlin cabaret and as a prostitute. Heinz Bennent, who plays Dr. Hans Vergérus, markedly resembles Gunnar Björnstrand's Dr. Vergérus (*The Magician*), and like his predecessor, Hans is obsessed with demonstrating a theory. (The character also is related to *The Passion of Anna*'s Elis Vergérus, who takes still photographs of people in pain or being violent.) Finally, though decidedly not the pathological narcissist that *Shame*'s Jan Rosenberg is, Abel Rosenberg is another sulky Jew filled with self-hate and repressing "an excess of rage." Abel is played by the American David Carradine, whose face vaguely resembles Max von Sydow's.[56] *The Serpent's Egg* is similar to *The Magician, Shame,* and *The Ritual* in that the artist-protagonist is arrested and/or sadistically humiliated, and similar to *Hour of the Wolf* in that the protagonist finally has a mental breakdown and disappears. It has the most in common with *The Passion of Anna* because once again a "madman" is responsible for mysterious deaths, and because photographs—here they are movies, thus more clearly evoking Bergman—are taken of people undergoing unendurable stress. Most salient, however, *The Serpent's Egg* enlarges on Andreas Winkelmann's point about the effects of humiliation: "Most people have to live without a sense of self-esteem. Humiliated at heart, stifled and spat upon. They're alive and that's all they know; they know no alternative. Even if they did they would never reach out for it. Can one be sick with humiliation? Is it a disease we have all caught?" *The Serpent's Egg* opens with silent, monochromatic shots of a sidewalk crammed with gloomy-faced middle-aged and elderly Germans advancing in slow motion toward us (see fig. 40). (The camera is in front and above them.) These shots

The Serpent's Egg. Rialto Film

alternate with the credits, which are accompanied by a sassy jazz score whose irresponsible joy mocks the claustrophobic shots that sandwich them. Similar shots, composed primarily of young Germans, appear at the film's climax to illustrate Hans Vergérus's prediction that in a decade the impatient children of these sheeplike Germans, who are "far too humiliated, too afraid, [and] too downtrodden" to revolt against their condition, will, at the behest of some leader who can articulate their anger and mobilize their idealism, create a bloody revolution.

In documentarylike voice-over, the narrator—probably because this is an English-language film, it is not Bergman—informs us that it is Saturday, 3 November 1923; that because of inflation money is weighed, not counted; and that people in Germany have lost faith in the future. Abel Rosenberg, who we learn has been drinking steadily since his job ended with the circus, comes through the arch at the end of his street and stumbles toward us along the wet cobblestone street. Like all the other streets in Berlin, this one seems to emanate the damp, evil air that poisons people and relationships and feeds social decay. Abel is wearing what he almost always wears—a hat, a shirt and tie, a brown sweater under a suit jacket that does not match his pants, brown and white shoes, a scarf, and an earring in his left lobe. He stops in front of the boardinghouse where he and his brother room. Smiling, he hums along with the family sing-along that emerges. The singing and a warm, inviting light swathe him when he enters. His accidentally walking in on a woman in a bathroom fore-shadows this somewhat shy and inept man's habit of inadvertently getting into trouble (opening a door to trouble will be an important image). Unmarried, unemployed, and an American Jew who speaks no German, the 35-year-old Abel is the quintessential outsider. His loneliness is underscored when, after the landlady gives him his key and a dinner tray for him and his brother, he pauses outside the parlor door to watch the family singing and rocking in unison from side to side. (We may recall Isak Borg longingly eavesdropping, in his mem-ory, on his family at lunch.) A close-up shows him trying to sing in German, and then we see him bounce up the stairs, go down the hall, and, with his foot, push open the door to Max's room. We look past him and see Max sitting up against the head of the bed with his mouth open and his blood and brains splashed against the wall behind him. The singing downstairs is the only sound as the dazed Abel sets down the tray, disappears behind the half-open door, then comes out of the room. Bergman zooms in on Abel's shadowed face as he paces back and forth, like Andreas at the end of *The Passion of Anna*.[57]

Two metaphors structure this story. The first has to do with de-scending into increasingly shocking realities. Max's wrist injury ended their aerial act and forced Abel—whose response to social problems is, "I couldn't care less. I swing on my trapeze, I eat, sleep, and fuck"—down to earth to face some hellish realities. He will descend further: into basements, morgues, and underground labyrinths. The second metaphor is biblical. The use of Abel as a name recalls what is also the theme of *The Silence,* Cain's question, "Am I my brother's keeper?" It is also relevant that Abel was born in Philadelphia, the City of Brotherly Love, that his and Max's father died recently, and that Solomon, the Jewish cabaret owner, refers to the persistent rain as "the Flood." Two other facts are important: Abel refused to seek a new partner after Max injured his wrist, emphasizing his dependence on his brother for his living and for self-expression, and the brothers recently had a fistfight over a whore. Since, as I shall note, this film alludes to several other films, it is not merely fanciful to recall that in the television show "Kung Fu," the chief source of David Carradine's fame, he played the self-reliant loner Kwai Chang Caine. The hypersensitive, fear-ridden, self-hating Abel, in fact, is simultaneously Abel and Cain(e), but unlike Johan Borg, Jan Rosenberg, or Andreas Winkelmann, he, like Kwai Chang Caine, cares about his brother's (brothers) killers and is capable of something that approaches the heroic.

The next morning Abel reports to police headquarters. Church bells are heard in the distance as he looks out of the inspector's window, past the several cacti on the sill. He is looking at a stone angel when the red-haired and red-bearded Inspector Bauer (Gert Froebe) arrives.[58] Without removing his black overcoat, he questions Abel and becomes impatient with him—the inspector is already annoyed at having to come in on Sunday—for having no idea why his brother killed himself. Intimidated by authority, Abel is obsequious and speaks rapidly like a guilty child (Carradine's oddly cadenced speech rhythms somehow fit his lumpy body). He spills out what he imagines Bauer wants to know until Bauer, no anti-Semite, inquires if Abel is Jewish. Abel bristles. Bauer ends the interview warning Abel not to stay in Berlin: German unemployment is bad enough without the economy having to support him.

On his way to inform Manuela about the suicide, Abel unexpectedly meets and is invited to lunch by the ebullient Papa Hollinger (Georg Hartmann), the Jewish owner of the circus. (Abel demonstrates his contempt for the bourgeois by parking his hat on one of the restaurant's marble busts.) Hollinger reads aloud to Abel a newspaper editorial about Jews traveling the countryside with portable gallows to butcher the citizenry. The alcoholic, generally impassive Abel seems concerned only with his schnapps. Finally, however, he blurts out that he does not believe in all this "political crap." Jews only get into trouble when they are stupid, and not being stupid, he won't get into trouble. Warmly thanking Hollinger for the money he has given him, Abel departs.

At the Blue Mule, a claustrophobic cabaret that smells of greasepaint, sweat, liquor, cheap sex, and cheaper perfume, he orders a beer and joins the sparse audience to watch Manuela's performance. Heavily made up and wearing a green wig and a scanty outfit, she sings an obscene song in a raspy voice. Hers is a mediocre talent.[59] Afterwards, passing a shirtless female impersonator and a fat midget, specimens of the sordid backstage life that Bergman has presented ever since *Ship to India* (and also the setting for the climax of *From the Life of the*

Marionettes), Abel visits Manuela's cramped, moldy dressing room. Manuela is a simple person who is virtually immune to hostility or neurosis and generally straightforward and honest. She is sincerely happy to see her neurotic, former brother-in-law and is shocked but not surprised at the news, bluntly delivered, of Max's suicide. Abel mentions that a few weeks earlier Max had taken a job that, though it paid well, he refused to discuss. Then Abel gives Manuela an envelope from Max. It contains dollars he apparently earned from that job and a note that is practically illegible; the only phrase that Abel can make out is, "There's poison going on." Manuela's next number is coming up, so she hurriedly dresses. A few moments later, while following her toward the stage, Abel is stopped in the wings by a short, well-dressed, blond gentleman with glasses. The man maintains that he knows Abel, recalling that as kids at their parents' cottages they had their first cigarettes together, and that Abel had an older sister named Rebecca.[60] Abel pretends not to know Hans Vergérus and curtly walks away. Instead of leaving, however, near the cabaret's entrance Abel gives money to a woman and takes her upstairs.

When Abel leaves, it is nighttime. He stops to watch an elderly Jew being beaten by some young men and forced, with his wife, to scrub the sidewalk. The old man's pleas for help are ignored by passing policemen. When the three bullies advance toward Abel, he runs, taking shelter in a family-operated bar where, to settle his nerves, he smokes and gets drunk. When Manuela arrives at the Pension Holle, her home, she finds Abel lying in the arched doorway. (In their late films Bergman and Nykvist developed a predilection for shooting through rectangular arches. In this film curved arches vie with hard rectangular arches.) She helps him inside and upstairs to her cluttered, Victorian-style room, the walls of which are punctuated by arched windows and covered with blue-flowered wallpaper and posters from the Hollinger circus. As she is helping him out of his coat and sweater, the seemingly cynical and impassive man suddenly breaks into sobs and holds her.

In the middle of the night hall noises familiar to Manuela awaken Abel, and he awakens her. He is photographed through the bars of the railing. (This becomes a visual motif that underscores Abel's being trapped. The camera generally anticipates his movements, thus creating the impression of his limited choices. Contrast this treatment of Abel with the way the camera lets characters move out of the frame in, say, *Through a Glass Darkly*.) He mentions to Manuela that he ran into Hans Vergérus, whom he remembers seeing last when the circus was in Heidelberg, and who he does, in fact, remember as a youngster. Hans, the son of a supreme court justice, was even then an outsider; no one liked him, but everyone thought him a genius. He was in love with Abel's sister Rebecca. Abel also recalls that Hans once dissected a live cat to show Abel how its heart worked. When Abel asks Manuela if she saw Hans in the wings, she arouses our suspicions by covering her head with her sheet as she says no. Thoughts of Max return and set Abel to crying again. He gets up and goes to the window. Bells sound in the distance as his attention is drawn (a slow zoom) to someone waking and walking through a large, well-lit apartment across the street, and then below to workers filing onto a trolley that will take them to their daily toil. Then he watches three elderly people drag and push a wagon piled high with salvaged furniture and household goods, and a horse-drawn wagon moving along the snowy, shiny cobblestone street and disappearing into the darkness. We remember that similar images of loneliness and uprootedness are seen by Ester (*The Silence*) outside her window in Timoka.

Just as in *Shame* Jan Rosenberg wakes up crying and keeps being visited by fits of tears, at breakfast Abel again breaks into tears. He tells Manuela about the old Jew begging the police for help and being ignored (but not about being approached by the bullies himself, and running). Manuela, whose voice sounds even more nasal and wispy than before, only replies that she has an extra job she must rush off to. She evades revealing the nature of her employment by flashing that familiar, vague Ullmann smile and by patting Abel's cheek, the Bergman cue for insincerity. After she has left, unaware that Manuela's landlady, Frau Holle (Edith Heerdegen), is watching him through the door, which she has pushed open slightly, the suspicious Abel rifles through Manuela's drawers.[61] He finds a wad of dollars and pockets most of it. Afterwards, as he is leaving the building, Frau Holle calls him into her room and to her bedside—she pretends to be more of an invalid than she is—and, in a treacly, casual tone, assures him that Manuela has told her about him and that he is welcome to stay with Manuela for awhile. Frau Holle's spying and intense scrutiny of others make us distrust her, but we respect this old woman's uncanny incisiveness. She senses that Abel has been crying, and she describes Manuela, whom she regards like a daughter, as a kind but dangerously naive person who is too unconcerned with what is happening about her. Frau Holle is also suspicious of Manuela's extra job.

In one of Abel's rare escapes from the imprisoning frame, Bergman ends the scene with Abel walking out of the frame, leaving it filled with a close-up of Frau Holle's enigmatic face.

When he returns to his boardinghouse, Abel finds Inspector Bauer waiting to take him to identify a dead woman. (When they leave the boardinghouse, Bauer gives money to an organ grinder and his monkey. This may be a metaphor for the kind of control Bauer is going to exert over Abel in the next sequence, or a reference to the organ grinder in Fritz Lang's *M* [1931]—Bauer alludes to another madman operating in Berlin—or a reference to *The Cabinet of Dr. Caligari* [1919], in which an organ grinder and his monkey stand at the entrance to the fair where the mysterious, murderous Dr. Caligari operates. Other allusions to Lang's *M*, as well as to his Dr. Mabuse series, follow momentarily.[62])

At headquarters, Bauer takes Abel down to the morgue. Abel becomes increasingly nauseous as he recognizes the woman laid out there as Max's fiancée. Then he recognizes another woman, one who once helped him to his room when he was drunk. Abel also identifies a boy from the cabaret. (A male corpse reminds Abel of his recently deceased father. Is this an expression of guilt on Bergman's part?) Bauer expresses heartfelt outrage at the insane and painful ways these people died. Back in his office the intimidating inspector informs Abel that seven mysterious deaths have taken place in Abel's vicinity. The seemingly indifferent Abel asks why Bauer is concerned by "a few paltry deaths" when in Germany a catastrophe could bring everything to an end the next day. The gruff, authoritative man delivers a humane and modestly heroic speech. He does his job for his own sake. He knows that people are starving, that money is worthless, that communists are agitating, that the government is confused, and that in Munich there is "a Herr Hitler . . . preparing a *Putsch* with thousands of starving soldiers and uniformed madmen." It may be, he continues, that "nothing works properly except fear," but he—and millions of petty officials like him all over Germany—do their jobs "to create a little patch of order and reason in the midst of a chaos of hopeless dissolution." Then, after stationing men outside his door, Bauer sits down to write a letter, letting the insinuation that Abel knows something of the seven deaths drive the alcoholic, hypersensitive Jew to the end of his tether. After pacing about, Abel lets out a hysterical scream and leaps past the guards at the door. Like a giant monkey, the athletic Abel easily negotiates the maze of stairs and halls that catacomb the bowels of the building, but every outlet is barred. He is inevitably trapped and carried to a cell, where, to quiet his hysterical screaming, he is knocked unconscious. (The impression evoked by this scene—and the film—is that in running from one's fate one runs into it.)

Hours later Abel is ushered into a room that, except for his guard and Manuela, is virtually bare. He is seated at a wooden table across from Manuela and soon notes that she is unable to concentrate on what he is saying. A moment later, she faints. Revived, she explains that she is just upset because her money was stolen from her apartment. Then she confesses that her extra job is in a "classy" brothel. Bauer arrives, frees Abel, and, looking at the couple strangely, decides not to tell Abel what he is "wondering about" (possibly that Manuela is Hans's mistress).

At the cabaret that evening, while onstage a bride (the female impersonator) and her groom mime the consummation of their vows, the drunk Abel visits Manuela's dressing room and finds Hans there. A bachelor, Hans asks Abel and Manuela if they would like to have dinner with him. When he softly caresses Manuela's cheek, Abel—just as Albert Vogler attacks Dr. Vergérus when Vogler discovers him making overtures to his wife (*The Magician*)—is upon him, slamming him against the wall, yelling that he should go to hell, and threatening to punch him. Mending his dignity with a smile and offering his regrets, Hans leaves. When Abel and Manuela return to Frau Holle's, she informs them that she has changed her mind about Abel staying there. (The script says that Frau Holle is Jewish; it seems likely that Hans, for reasons we shall discover, has coerced this change.) Frau Holle is distraught when Manuela screams that, if Abel has to go, so will she.

Upstairs Abel asks Manuela, who is visibly sicker, if, how often, and why she has slept with Hans. Responding as Eva *(Shame)* might were she asked why she had slept with Jacobi, Manuela says that though she is not sure she loves Hans, "I'm fond of him. Maybe he needs a little kindness and pampering." Then, uttering a small, dry cry, she begs Abel to be kind to her and hugs him, but he pushes her off. When she persists and sits beside him, he turns his back.

In the morning Abel secretly follows her. First, she goes into a church. (Outside, framed through three huge arches, is a dispirited file of demonstrators marching to the beat of a snare drum and carrying placards seemingly written in Hebrew.) Abel eavesdrops as Manuela detains a harried American priest (James Whitmore)—yet another outsider—hurrying to his next service. Fighting back tears,

Manuela finds it difficult to speak until the impatient man orders her to "come to the point!" She then confesses that she is sick and can no longer bear the inexplicable guilt she feels for failing to save Max. She also feels guilty for not being able to help Abel, who, though he is frightened, refuses her help. "Is there no forgiveness?" she asks. Having donned his black overcoat and galoshes, the priest asks her if she would like him to say a "special" prayer for her? "Would it help?" she inquires. "I don't know," he says; setting down his black briefcase, he kneels on the stone floor. The camera is behind him and shoots past his curly gray hair, wire-rimmed glasses, and deeply wrinkled face to focus on Manuela's desperate expression as he offers a prayer that calls to our minds the prayer of the pastor in *Cries and Whispers*. It is one that, its metaphysics aside, sums up the position Bergman has held ever since his hospital stay around the time of *Persona*: "We live far away from God, so far away that no doubt He doesn't hear us when we pray to Him for help. So we must help each other . . . give each other the forgiveness that a remote God denies us. I say you are forgiven for your husband's death."[63] Then he says to Manuela, "I beg *your* forgiveness for my apathy and indifference. Do you forgive me?" Reaching up, she touches his head and answers, "Yes, I do." Though his subsequent, hurried act of ushering her out verges on the comic, this scene provides Manuela, whose part is not richly written, with an angst that at last makes her interesting.

After departing the church, Manuela crosses a walled, swampy, rat-infested lot near St. Anna's Clinic—one of the children playing there thrusts a dead rat toward us—and enters a shabby building. Abel follows her inside only to find that they are in a ground-floor apartment. The ailing Manuela is exhilarated. Just before he attacked Hans in her dressing room, she informs him, Hans had offered them rent-free this recently vacated apartment. Moreover, Hans has a job for Abel in the clinic's archives. "Please say it would be nice," she begs. Abel rejects Hans's "charity" and walks out. Overcome by hopelessness, Manuela, seen here for the first time with her long hair hanging down around her shoulders, watches through the barlike windows as Abel walks away through the rain and mud. Then he stops, seeming to realize that he has no place and no one to go to. When he returns, she rushes to him. They embrace and kiss and, arm in arm, enter the bedroom to make love for the first time.

In the next scene it is evening. At the cabaret a chubby, inept belly dancer is performing onstage, and Abel is sitting, talking to Solomon

(Walter Schmidinger), the cabaret's Jewish owner. Solomon's thin black mustache, his conspicuously large, white teeth, and his eye-glasses make us fix on his face. Suddenly, men in policelike uniforms invade, smash the mirrors and chandeliers, corral the actors and au-dience in front of the stage, and read them a diatribe on the Jewish responsibility for the perpetuation of obscenity. As the leader reads, the camera picks out Abel and Manuela, who hold each other, and the grotesquely painted faces of the absurdly costumed actors. The leader of the jackboots then takes Solomon's head and, after carefully re-moving his glasses, slams it a dozen times against the tabletop (be-neath the picture frame). Holding the bloody blur that was once his sharp nose and large, white teeth, Solomon collapses under the table. (Bergman represents physical violence more graphically in this film—though still discretely—than he did in *The Passion of Anna*.) Finally, the intruders torch the cabaret. The image of the flames dissolves into Abel's face—suggesting Abel's inner rage—and acts as the transition into the next scene, which takes place later back in Manuela and Abel's dreary new apartment. Disturbed by the periodic sound and vibra-tions of a nearby engine, Abel is unable to sleep. Just as Johan Borg keeps his pregnant wife awake because he cannot sleep, Abel awakens the sick Manuela. The gin she gives him finally brings uncon-sciousness.

For a few moments the pace of the next scene is livelier as Abel jumps off the bus near the archives of St. Anna's Clinic and is greeted by Drs. Soltermann (Fritz Strassner) and Silbermann (Hans Quest). They lead him down winding steel stairs and through a maze of shelves containing hospital records. His journey into this catacomb is shot with the dollying camera disturbingly close to his face. When he arrives at his station, it is a barred cell containing a table, an unshaded light bulb, and confidential files containing "reports of inconceivable human suffering" that he is to transfer, without reading or removing them from the premises, to different folders. The clinic, headed by Dr. Vergérus, has always had a great "reverence for humanity," they assure him. Before leaving him alone, the doctors lock him in. At lunchtime he is led out. During his lunch break he visits Manuela, who is now working in the hospital laundry. She tries to be cheery, but Abel is very concerned about how ill she looks.

As Abel heads back to the clinic, Hans Vergérus suddenly pulls him back from the curb and claims he just saved him from being hit by a car. He also inquires how Abel likes his new job and again suggests that the three of them should get together some evening. Abel, however, abruptly excuses himself and returns to work. As he is again being led to his cell by Dr. Silbermann, the frightened man cautiously whispers to Abel that "horrible . . . experiments with human beings" are being carried out at the clinic.

That evening at their small dinner table Abel is sitting on the left and Manuela on the right. Visible between them on the wall facing the camera is a mirror. Abel is almost crazy from a headache that he insists must have something to do with gas or with the periodic rumbling of the unidentifiable motor. (The rumbling noise-vibration begins to affect us.) His argumentativeness and shoving the heretofore passive Manuela in the face finally provoke a reaction. She pounds the table and shouts that if he cannot stop acting like a lunatic he should leave: "I've done what I could to keep us going; now I can't go on. . . . I don't give a damn about your fear . . . about you!" Knowing Abel to be incapable of a deep relationship, yet more afraid of being alone than of his behavior, she soon tells him that she doesn't want him to leave. Abel hugs her briefly but pulls away and lies down on the bed. Blindly, almost unconsciously, she gropes her way to his side and again they embrace. Suddenly he grabs his head and moans, "I can't . . . I can't stay like this!" and once more walks out of the frame. We next see him putting on his coat (his actions reflected in the large mirror behind him), taking money from Manuela's purse, and leaving. The last shots are close-ups of Manuela, alone, her sunken face exhibiting that absolute hopelessness and indifference that is often evident in the very ill. Her head sinks forward, and her long, stringy hair almost covers her eyes.

During his midnight peregrinations Abel passes a cart whose horse has collapsed and is being carved up. Asking him if he wants to buy some meat, its owner thrusts a handful of its bloody flesh into Abel's (and our) face.[64] Abel next stops in at a club that features a jazz band composed of black and blackfaced musicians. Muscling his way through the wall-to-wall dancers to the bar, he buys a bottle of liquor, stuffs the bills in the bartender's mouth, and leaves. Later, drunk and having just encountered two trucks full of armed soldiers, he catches sight of a shop window bearing the name "A. Rosenberg." His self-hate and ambivalence about being a Jew spur him to pick up a huge cobblestone from a nearby construction site and heave it through the window.[65] The middle-aged Mr. Rosenberg (Toni Berger) rushes out into the street and slaps Abel, who at first passively shields himself with his arms. Finally, to stop the barrage, Abel grabs the man's wrists and walks him backwards until Mr. Rosenberg happens to trip over a sand mound. When Abel offers to help him up, Mr. Rosenberg finally looks scared. By now, the short and stocky Mrs. Rosenberg (Erna Brunell) is upon Abel, screeching and slapping him. Unexpectedly, Abel hugs her to him, tries to hold her breast under her coat, and kisses her. (His attraction to this much older woman must relate to Bergman's feelings about his mother.) Mrs. Rosenberg's surprise at this behavior is conveyed in her three short, whimpering cries.

Having run from the old couple, Abel soon finds himself on Steinstrasse, defined as hell by Mikaela (Lisi Mangold), a patrolling prostitute who entices Abel to her basement apartment.[66] In that reddishly lit den her coworker, Stella (Grischa Huber), is with a young American black man named Monroe (Glynn Turman). Naked except for his band jacket—he may be one of the jazz musicians seen earlier—he is screaming in fear of Stella's genitals and rationalizing his impotence. Reminding us of the cabaret act in which the female impersonator pretended to copulate, Monroe insists, "I'm not a queer." Abel bets cash that Monroe cannot make it with Stella. Monroe accepts, and with the women laughing like harpies, he makes an excruciating effort. He has to masturbate to get an erection, and as he does the camera zooms in on Abel's face as he watches. Monroe then mounts Stella but is unable to penetrate her. When Mikaela grabs the prize money, Abel, possibly from guilt, slaps her face and then forces her to the floor for sex. A jump cut follows. Abel awakens in the middle of the night and leaves the sleeping Mikaela's bed. On the way home he passes the steaming but clean bones of the horse. The narrator, whose report on day-to-day social and economic conditions contributes to a feeling of inevitable hopelessness, says that this is 7 November and that there is no milk in Berlin.

The next scene parallels the one in *Torment* in which Jan-Erik, after abandoning Berta, has a change of heart and returns to her apartment only to find her dead. Back in his and Manuela's apartment Abel is sitting down to take a drink when he notices a trickle of blood oozing from the corner of her mouth. He screams and shakes her, but it is useless. Again, the death of a promiscuous woman is the occasion for the narcissistic protagonist to gain insight into himself and his situation. Here it also results in "heroic" action. As he is screaming, Abel is surprised by a flash coming from behind the mirror. Someone is photographing them. He breaks the mirror, and then others in the apartment, to discover cameras behind each one. Crawling through one of the openings, he descends into yet another catacomb. At one point a hand (as in *The Magician*) emerges from the edge of the frame to push him down the elevator shaft, but when he senses its presence and spins around, no one is visible. A few moments later, however, that person attacks and wrestles him to the floor. In the struggle Abel forces the man's head over the edge of the elevator shaft so that the descending elevator decapitates him, squirting blood in Abel's face.

Abel arrives late for work that day, but he is as calm and self-possessed as if he had just come from reading philosophy. Led this morning through the labyrinth to his workplace by Dr. Soltermann, Abel wrestles the keys from him when they arrive at the cell. Aware that he is physically no match for Abel, Soltermann just smiles and proclaims that "a savior is born" in Munich, one who is going to deliver the German people. The fact that millions of lives will be sacrificed is irrelevant, he maintains, because "there are plenty of human beings." Abel knocks him unconscious, unlocks a small iron door that opens into a room, and enters. Inside is a movie projector, a turntable for playing the disks that contain the sound that accompanies the film images, and a phonograph horn for amplifying the sound. Suddenly, Hans, wearing wire-rimmed glasses and dressed in a doctor's white lab coat, enters, locks the door, and, after amiably confessing that he foolishly disregarded Dr. Soltermann's warning that Abel would be a problem, begins projecting for Abel some "interesting" movies that document his experiments. For the rest of the scene Abel, his haggard expression a permanent mask, is silent; like us, he watches the experiments in muted fascination and horror. This is the most riveting instance of "eavesdropping" in Bergman's canon of films: First, we see a woman locked in a room with a baby whose ceaseless crying finally drives her to kill it. "Unfortunately," says Hans, "our camera didn't manage to document the actual deed . . . our apparatus is still defective." Next, we see Hans revive a hungry man who, for money, has volunteered for a sensory deprivation experiment. Then we see the boy whose corpse Abel saw earlier in the morgue. He is given a drug that causes such mental pain that he tries to kill himself with the unloaded pistol Hans has provided him. A few days after being released, Hans informs Abel, he shot himself. Hans shows embarrassment when he tells Abel that this was the experiment for which both Max and his fiancée volunteered. "He himself wanted to try out the Thanatoxin," Hans tells Abel. "I advised him not to, but he insisted. . . .

They were very attached to each other and lived for a time in one of the apartments that you yourself. . . ." Finally, there is the filmed record of the experiment with a colorless gas that puts the emotional system out of order: Bergman's camera zooms in for a giant close-up of Abel from his watering eyes down to his upper lip. He puts his hand over the left half of his face but (like Elizabet Vogler watching the monk immolate himself) watches, through his spread fingers, a couple like Manuela and himself sitting at a table arguing and finally coming to blows. Hans finds the scene almost farcical. Afterwards he comments, "Repeated exposure to the gas can cause permanent damage." He insists, however—and in the present situation he has no reason to lie—that he never experimented with Abel and Manuela. In fact, he takes Abel in a friendly fashion by the back of the neck and, glancing down with absolute sincerity and without his glasses, says, "I always liked you and Manuela. She showed me an affection which I think was sincerely meant. Against my better judgment I tried to help you." (We recall, however, Abel and Manuela's awareness of gas and the cameras recording their lives and her death. Did Hans's overly conscientious colleagues disobey his orders?) Abel's expression is one of disbelief to the point of near catatonia, but he does remove Hans's hand from his neck. "I'm not a monster, Abel," says Hans. "What you have seen are the first faltering steps of a necessary and logical development." He adds that he knows that Abel has informed Inspector Bauer, a fact that, besides explaining Abel's puzzling earlier calm, makes him one of the few Bergman characters who acts heroically for others, not just for themselves. When Bauer and his men arrive momentarily, continues Hans, he will bite on the cyanide capsule he holds in his hand.

In the meantime Hans enlarges on his goals. He will not burn the records of his experiments because he knows that the law will file them away and in a few years science will unearth them and build on them "on a gigantic scale." He predicts, too, that the imminent revolt of that "scatterbrain" Adolf Hitler will be "a colossal fiasco" because he "lacks intellectual capacity and every form of method and he doesn't realize what tremendous forces he is about to conjure up. He will be swept away." Hans shows Abel another silent movie—it is *The Serpent's Egg*'s opening, slow-motion, monochrome shots of adults, now followed by shots mainly of children and teenagers. These latter, says Hans, will in ten years (1933) marry their idealism to the festering hatred inherited from their parents, and under the inspiration of some great leader demanding sacrifice, they will create, through blood and fire, "a new society unequaled in world history." It will not be a society based on the unrealistic notion that man is basically good, but on the recognition that mankind is an ill-constructed lot. "We [will] exterminate what is inferior"—he almost spits out this word—"and increase what is useful." The memory of the bodies in the morgue connects with our knowledge of the Nazi death camps when the smiling Hans adds, "Do you know what gave us the most trouble with these experiments. . . . It was getting rid of the bodies. . . . Dr. Eichenberg designed an incinerator . . . but we couldn't afford to build it."

Hans takes up a hand mirror, throws down his cigarette, and, as he slowly raises the capsule to his lips, tells Abel that he is free to repeat what he has just heard; no one will believe him, however, "despite the fact that anyone who makes the slightest effort can see . . . the future. It's like the serpent's egg. Through the thin membranes you can clearly discern the already perfect reptile." For someone familiar with Bergman's attitudes, the image can also be taken as a metaphor for how childhood humiliations and fears become the adult's neuroses and psychoses. The silence is broken by the sound of the police storming the sealed metal door, shouting and pounding. But it holds. Nevertheless, the fanatical empiricist puts the capsule in his mouth and bites it. Then, bringing the light from the overhead lamp to bear on his face, he scrutinizes his agonizing death throes in the mirror he has been holding. Like Albert Vogler studying the face of the dying actor, or Antonius Block staring at the face of the dying "witch," we, Abel, and Hans watch his spasms with horrible fascination until he collapses.

What makes Hans so frightening is his humanity, his thin but genuine affection for Manuela, and his faith in the hostile Abel. Just as Conrad's Kurtz is not mad, neither is Hans, but like Kurtz, Hans's "soul" is mad. His obsession about perfecting mankind has made him indifferent to human suffering. He is neither amoral—he knows that his acts are considered monstrous—nor anti-Semitic. He is just anti-imperfection, thus, antihuman. He is Bergman's most passionately idealistic monster, an Anna (*The Passion of Anna*) incapable of guilt.

The drumming on the metal door is deafening. Muttering to himself and shaking his head from side to side—like Andreas Winkelmann pacing—Abel begins to go to pieces. He unconsciously backs up until he is against the rough cement wall and his face is lit by a bare light bulb hanging there. But then Bergman breaks the pattern of photographing him through bars, or tracking, panning, or zooming in on him in order to keep him caged in the frame: Abel walks toward the door—and out of the frame. Just as he leaves the frame (foreshadow-ing the film's conclusion), the image blurs; without losing a beat, the camera pans down to his head, which is in sharp focus just as he is awakening from a two-day sleep. He is in the prison's white-tiled in-firmary. Raising his head and squinting at the sunshine coming through the window, Abel half listens to the ebullient Bauer, who, having just entered, is helping him drink some water. It is 11 Novem-ber, and Bauer, another of Bergman's guardian angels—recall the mar-ble statue outside his office window—has made arrangements with Papa Hollinger for Abel to return to the circus in Basel. A constable has been assigned to accompany him to the train, and the state will pay his fare. Beaming with pride, Bauer also announces that Hitler's Putsch in Munich was—he uses Hans Vergerus's exact words—a "co-lossal fiasco": "Herr Hitler and his gang underrated the strength of the German democracy." Bauer departs, leaving Abel staring out the win-dow as if he had never seen sunlight before. ("It is the bright day that brings forth the adder. . . . [T]hink him [Caesar] as a serpent's egg / Which, hatch'd, would, as his kind, grow mischievous, / And kill him in the shell" [*Julius Caesar,* act II, scene 1]). Then, turning, Abel clutches at his own image faintly mirrored by the white tiles. Is he afraid that he is yet another case history being filmed by the likes of Hans or, for that matter, Bergman?

The film's final shot is of Abel, dressed as usual and with his hands in his pants pockets. He is walking toward us but against the crowd on a Berlin street teeming with traffic. As in *The Passion of Anna,* the authoritative narrator reenters: he informs us that Abel escaped his police escort, disappeared into the crowd, and was never seen again. It seems that having discovered that the unrelenting evil in man knows no bounds, that we are all victims and tormentors, the famous acrobat could not return to his fantasy world high above the hoi polloi. He rejects notoriety and, unlike Stig in *To Joy,* rejects being a worker bee in the artistic community. Having survived, he chooses total anonym-ity among the gray masses. The narrator might well have added about Bergman's protagonist, "This time he was called Abel Rosenberg."

FROM THE LIFE OF THE MARIONETTES

Susan Sontag describes Bergman as "one of those oppressively mem-orable geniuses of the artistic dead-end, who go very far with a limited material—refining it when they are inspired, repeating it and parodying themselves when they aren't."[67] *From the Life of the Marionettes* (1980), which Bergman believes "belongs among my best films" (*ML*, 264), is no parody. It deals with the same characters and themes found in *Hour of the Wolf, The Ritual, The Passion of Anna, Face to Face,* and *The Serpent's Egg,* but the determinism at work is richer and more complex.[68] For the film's two main protagonists, Bergman drew on Peter and Katarina Egerman, a warring, married couple who appear briefly in *Scenes from a Marriage* (1973) (to be dealt with in the next chapter).[69] *From the Life of the Marionettes,* which contains an unparalleled number of autobiographical allusions, also represents Bergman's most definitive use of his marionette alter ego, Jack Kasparsson. In this film he is Peter Egerman, a man whose repressed sexual and aggressive drives refuse to be denied any longer. So tormented is he by his realization that his life has been a lie that, like Kasper, he wants to flee the stifling, self-destructive roles imposed on him by his bourgeois existence and his marriage. Whereas Kasper's escape results in his demise (as indicated in the title, *Kasper's Death*), in *From the Life of the Marionettes* Peter's attempt to escape results in the murder and rape of a prostitute (who represents his mother, his wife, and himself) and, like Johan Borg and Andreas Winkelmann, in his going mad.

Another familiar Bergman pattern structures *From the Life of the Marionettes:* the sacrifice of a young sexual wanton—though psychologically she strikes us as probably the most innocent and normal person in the film—as a means of helping Bergman's protagonist better understand himself. Finally, by the end of the film we understand that Peter's pathological narcissism, which manifests itself in part as a need for absolute control, is homicidal and suicidal.

Bergman once again brackets the narrative with basically the same scene, and he begins and ends this black-and-white film with color sequences. Finally, the narrative is again conceived of as a kind of case history. The story is structured as a police investigator's report on the factors behind Peter's murder of the prostitute called Ka. Each episode, in fact, is introduced with titles typewritten in white on a black background.

The film's central question is not, "Who murdered Ka?" but, "Why did the distinguished Peter Egerman murder a prostitute?" The narrative is another of Bergman's investigations into what at first appears to have been an unmotivated act of violence. (Although presented in a rather mechanical, enervated style, virtually every scene seeps rage.) The film opens in color: Peter Egerman (Robert Atzorn), dressed in a suit, tie, and French cuffs and cuff links is standing, resting his head on the bare shoulder—she is naked from the waist up—of the prostitute Katarina Krafft (Rita Russek), called Ka. Ka is affectionately caressing his head when suddenly he knocks her to the floor. She flees into the red room in which, during business hours, the girls perform before peephole audiences. He pursues, catches, and strangles her; we only hear her gasping and see her legs convulsing. Afterwards, he props her up face down on the stage that serves as a bed and begins caressing her in preparation for anal intercourse. At this point the color, like Ka's life and Peter's "sanity," fades away. The subsequent black-and-white scenes set out to try to understand Peter's motives and actions.

Twenty hours later, in a small, gray, bare room at police headquarters, the psychiatrist Mogens Jensen (Martin Benrath) sits across a desk from an unseen inspector (Karl-Heinz Pelser) who is taping the doctor's testimony. (In the course of the interviews we will recognize that some of Peter's history is Bergman autobiography: for, example, Peter bit his nails to the quick as a child, his brother is an ambassador, and his sister is married to a well-to-do businessman.) Peter phoned Dr. Jensen to come to the scene of the murder soon after he had finished with Ka. Jensen does not reveal that recently Peter had suddenly visited him to tell him that he was afraid of his dreams (like Bertil's in *Three Strange Loves*), and his thoughts of killing his wife. Peter said he had been having them for over two years, and they were getting progressively more real. Nor does Jensen confess his failure to follow up his intuition that Peter was dangerous. Understandably, Jensen also does not mention that he used this visit to get Peter's wife to his office so he could seduce her. (Unbeknownst to Jensen, Peter eavesdropped on this unsuccessful seduction attempt. Jensen is unaware that the police have a letter of Peter's that reveals this information.) This episode, which took place on a Saturday *two weeks before the murder,* comprises the next scene.

In Dr. Jensen's office the boyish Peter admits, as will his wife Katarina (Christine Buchegger), that he is not very good at articulating his feelings and impulses. Not surprisingly, he also confesses that his lovemaking with Katarina is without feeling, and that for two years now he has dreamed of murdering her. ("When I was younger," writes Bergman, "I was tormented by loathsome dreams: murder, torture, suffocation, incest, destruction, [and] insane anger" [*ML,* 174].) Bergman's dramatization-imaging of the dream Peter subsequently relates involves bright, nightmare lighting. Just as in her dreams Alma tries to get control over Elizabet (*Persona*), Peter tries to get control over Katarina in his. She, however, mocks his cowardice: when he places his straight razor against her throat—Bergman mimics the shot from *Persona* in which Alma dreams that Elizabet's head is close behind hers—she smiles (see fig. 41).[70]

Having heard Peter's dream, Jensen's prescription is either institutionalization and thought-erasing drugs or a therapy session with him later that week. Jensen does not answer Peter's question about whether he should tell Katarina about his obsession. He just informs Peter that he must go because another patient is about to arrive. Peter senses that the doctor is going to contact Katarina, so he only pretends to leave. Undetected, he overhears Jensen phone Katarina and, when she arrives, hears him not only attempt to get her to go away with him but sleep with him then and there. (As increasingly will be his habit, Bergman frames the couple we and Peter are watching through a square arch. It is a theatrical impulse that makes his characters appear to be actors on a brightly lit stage.) When Katarina goes into the bathroom to undress, Peter watches her silhouette on the glass bathroom door as she combs her hair; it is an image reminiscent of his dream. Subsequently, Katarina informs Jensen that because of her love for Peter she has had a change of heart. Though he swears he is not being sarcastic, Jensen makes the same snide reply David makes to Andreas in *The Touch*: "How touching." Katarina then tells Jensen that she not only is afraid of him but fears he is trying to disrupt her marriage. A slow zoom in on Peter reveals his pleasure at what she says next. She regards Peter as a child who is part of her ("here inside me"), and she believes they quarrel because they are both children who refuse to mature. The scene ends with her expression of the goal that many of Bergman's characters would like to reach—to consume their loved ones and to invade and/or be invaded by them so as to totally share their physical and psychical states. Katarina is sad that she cannot experience Peter's feelings (or he hers).[71] This film will demonstrate that trying to reach someone else's inner privacy is so threatening it will provoke rejection.

A week after the murder the inspector interviews Peter's mother, Cordelia Egerman (Lola Müthel), a former actress; her husband coerced her into retiring to care for their family. (Katarina, who dislikes and is jealous of her mother-in-law, will later speak of her to Peter as "a decaying symbol of your father's goddamn tyranny.") Mrs. Egerman is like *Autumn Sonata*'s Charlotte, whom we will meet in the next chapter, in that she redirected the energy she had previously devoted to her art to controlling her children, especially the Bergman-like Peter. Though no longer on the stage, Mrs. Egerman is still the actress. Her lack of spontaneity is symbolized by her extraordinarily thick eyeglasses. Though she rejects any suggestion that Peter's upbringing could have a bearing on his horrible act, her revulsion at the memory of Peter's ugly bitten nails when he was a child is stronger than her reaction to the murder. The flashback that accompanies her description of Peter's recent visit to her is far more revealing than her words: in this candle-lit scene, the warmest and most invitingly photographed in the film, Peter drinks in his seductive mother's show of affection. Significantly, the scene ends with a freeze frame of son and mother embracing. It is the *only* freeze frame in the film. She also remembers that during that visit she talked to Peter about seeing to the repair of her decaying mansion—thus symbolically tying him to the past—and she recalls his remarking how tired he was.

Five days before the murder, Peter, unable to sleep, gets up and takes Nembutal and brandy. Concerned, Katarina joins him and tries to discover what is troubling him. She does not understand his half-hearted response—"There's no way out"—which increasingly becomes a barometer of how close he feels his half-imagined fate is, but it stirs her to recount a bothersome, recurring insight of her own: she feels that everything that belongs to her is going to be taken away and she will be left with "nothing." Like the Johans in *Hour of the Wolf* and *Scenes from a Marriage*—husbands who fall asleep while their wives are confiding to them their most serious thoughts—Peter too has drifted off to sleep. And as Alma (*Hour of the Wolf*) does after her drunk, exhausted husband falls asleep during her confession, Katarina helps Peter to bed.

Obviously pleased with *The Serpent's Egg*'s silent, slow-motion cinematographic-poem, which pictures the silent, sheeplike movement of people, Bergman creates a similarly cold, gray, droning impression in *From the Life of the Marionettes,* but in this poem the images are accompanied by discordant piano chords and a faint drumbeat. He shows the autobahn at dusk, cars bumper to bumper, head and tail lights reflected on wet pavement, and, silhouetted against the darkening sky, a tall, gray concrete and glass building, topped by a crane that looks like a huge praying mantis. Bergman pans up the side of a mazelike office building and dissolves to Peter in his dark office, *an unspecified time before the murder.* In a mechanical, uninflected monotone he is dictating to his female secretary a complicated business letter involving tough negotiations. Though successful, and the son of the firm's founder, whose Rembrandtesque portrait imposes itself on the room, Peter has come to find business an utterly empty activity. He uses it to exercise his suppressed aggression. Impeccably dressed and wearing narrow glasses that drastically age his boyish looks, he stands over a lamp—that is, when he is not moving in a trance around the room. His fingers follow the lamp's stem upward and hover near its helmet-shaped shade as if he were contemplating strangling or crushing it. Later, sitting behind it, he seems to be wearing the metal helmet of an electric chair.

The next scene occurs *four days before the murder.* Another slow-motion montage introduces Katarina at work. It is composed of living female mannikins modeling dresses and coats (to satisfy more sophisticated fantasies than those aroused by the prostitutes performing in the film's climactic sequence). When Peter arrives to take her to the lunch being held at his mother's, Katarina is frenetically preparing her staff for a fashion show. (Peter habitually takes his business associates to his mother's because he feels "it is important for her" and because they consider it an honor to be in the presence of this symbol of a glamorous past.) Ignoring his comment that he is tired, Katarina, who intensely dislikes her mother-in-law, purposely provokes him into going without her. When he has left, she accepts an invitation to the apartment of Tomas Isidor Mandelbaum (Walter Schmidinger), a homosexual coworker.[72] For a considerable length of time the camera remains at a distance, permitting us to take in almost the entire apartment, which Mandelbaum, known as Tim, simultaneously describes. More important, the distance sets us up for the longest monologue in close-up that Bergman ever filmed. The monologue is transfixing not only because Schmidinger is electric, but because unlike Peter (except in his dreams) and Katarina (who says she has "never given a thought to the mind"), Tim is able to candidly describe and analyze his inner life. (Our interest in Peter and Katarina depends heavily on their inner lives, but their semi-inarticulateness about such matters, besides making them atypical Bergman characters, keeps them from achieving that intimate psyche-to-psyche proximity with the audience that occurs in the best of Bergman's films.) Tim attributes his being "in closer touch with [his] feelings" to being homosexual. Removing his eyeglasses—Bergman's sign that a character is going to face the truth (recall Mrs. Egerman's thick glasses)—Tim stares at himself close up in a mirror. (Ironically, a white mask is seen above his head.) After alluding to his fear of aging unattractively and becoming undesirable, he kneads his face with his hands and says that even though he sees himself as a youth the mirror reveals "a little old man" whose body and mind prevent him from achieving his dream of closeness and tenderness. He catches himself up on this half-truth, admitting that his love is also wildly jumbled up with lust, savagery, mad excitement, and terror, and he tells of seeking out dangerous, possibly homicidal lovers. He then sums up the Bergman marionette theme that is at the heart of this film: "I'm governed by forces I cannot master . . . can't [even] control," by forces that even fight each other. His dreams "of closeness, tenderness, fellowship, self-forgetfulness, [and] everything that means life and beauty" are opposed by his desire for "violence, filthiness, horror, [and] the threat of death." He sounds like Eva, who in her final dream in *Shame* sees beauty and violence as co-manifestations of human nature: "At times," says Tim, "I think it is one and the same urge. . . . My dreams were perhaps too beautiful, and as punishment . . . you have your orgasm with your nose so far down in the shit that you nearly choke." Breaking off, he goes up to Katarina and reenacts another gesture from *Shame:* just as Jacobi asks both Eva and Jan to touch him to help establish his being alive, Tim asks Katarina to place his hand against her cheek and tell him if she can feel *"that it's me."* She does and starts to nod her head yes, but ends up by firmly shaking it no.

The next scene takes place *three days after the murder* and consists of a subtly humiliating interrogation of Tim by the inspector. It is reminiscent of scenes in *Shame, The Ritual,* and *The Serpent's Egg* and was undoubtedly influenced by Bergman's arrest and interrogation on tax matters. At the start the defensive Tim spars (wittily, he thinks) with his examiner, who maintains a cool, even ironic distance. (Like Bergman, he observes the varieties of deception and fumbling rationalization.) But in time Tim regards him more as a father confessor, finally admitting to him that he loves Peter, whom he sees as dying psychically, and who he is certain was interested in him. His ambivalent aim was to rescue Peter from his loveless marriage, but also to get back at Katarina, whom, like Peter, he both likes and dislikes. He felt he could accomplish his aims by bringing Ka and Peter together, an act for which now he feels guilty. Pleading helplessness before the forces he told Katarina about earlier, he concludes, "Certain wise people consider that man . . . follow[s] prescribed patterns, which from birth are a fixed condition, or [are] the drive of our senses."

The following scene commences with Peter, like Märta in *Winter Light* and Karin and David in *The Touch,* speaking to us through a letter. Though never sent, he wrote it to Dr. Jensen *after he visited the psychiatrist's office* and witnessed Jensen's attempt to seduce Katarina. Peter does not dwell on this, however; he is too intent on describing his dream about Katarina: From high overhead the image zooms down to Peter and Katarina, both wearing pajamas and sleeping side by side, he on his back, she on her stomach. The brightness and lack of defining space conveyed Peter's feeling that he was floating in free sensuality. He noticed that the lower part of his body felt connected to the "nice, strong scent of a woman's moistness, sweat, saliva, [and] the fresh smell of thick hair." Just as Johan Borg (*Hour of the Wolf*) runs his fingers over the naked corpse of Veronica Vogler from her head to her toes, Peter, his eyes closed, twice raised his head and caressingly moved it down past Katarina's face and neck to rest it on her naked breast. His consciousness, he writes, was "intensely concentrated in my hands, or rather fingertips; on every finger I had a little eye, which . . . registered all this gleaming whiteness and the floating itself." A few shots later he remarks that he was not sure whether he was experiencing death or the life force in this dream.

As with *Persona*'s Alma, who tries several scenarios in order to gain control over Elizabet, Peter's dream starts over. Again from overhead, we look down at the couple, who are now completely naked. Feeling trapped in this totally closed space, Peter muttered to himself not to panic or try to escape. When he spoke to Katarina, who was awake, she was indifferent to him. This response excited him into wanting to make love. When he was on top of her, however, he found that he was impotent. Like Veronica Vogler, she smiled, which made him furious. To prevent himself from killing her, he drew away and covered his face with his hands. What follows is accompanied by a drum and a maddeningly irritating electronic sound that has the effect of the beelike noise that accompanies Johan Borg's murder of the boy demon. In a medium close-up and in slow motion, Peter lashed out at Katarina, who flinched but then began to enjoy the violence. Her hair whipping from side to side and her lips curling in pleasure, she pummeled him until he withdrew, shielding his head with his arms and hands. Strangely, after he spoke to her—the screen is filled by a zoom-in on his giant, hate-filled eye staring through strands of her hair—the next image, accompanied by a lyric flute, is of him lovingly coiled around her, his head resting on her breast ("sudden intimacy without reserve"). Though her arms were around his neck and she was stroking his hair with one hand, she looked slightly apprehensive. A jump cut, and suddenly Peter was sitting over her; a rapid pan down to her head reveals blood streaming from beneath it. Her throat had been cut. (The parallel between this scene and Johan's encounter with Veronica in *Hour of the Wolf* is even closer in the screenplay. In it Peter says that demons are present in this scene, "faces that observed us with excitement and ruthless interest, pallid, scornful faces with no pity." In addition, in the screenplay the last line of this scene is the last line of the parallel scene in *Hour of the Wolf:* "The mirror is smashed, but what do the splinters reflect?") Peter jolted awake and checked that Katarina was in bed beside him, unhurt. Peter concludes his unsent letter by asking if there is any help for him, and querying whether this dream isn't, in fact, his single contact with true reality.

In the following scene, which takes place *two days before the murder* of Ka, Peter threatens to commit suicide by jumping off the roof of his apartment building (an act alluded to in *Scenes from a Marriage*). He is rather easily persuaded to return inside by a friend, Arthur Brenner (Heinz Bennent). Soon, and in front of Arthur, Peter and Katarina are again viciously and humiliatingly talking about divorce. Katarina laughs at Peter's impotence when he tried to sodomize her; Peter claims that he has a trick for bringing Katarina to orgasm and speaks of having almost strangled her with her necklace (foreshadowing his strangling of Ka). When Peter leaves to take a nap, he sarcastically suggests that Katarina and Arthur have had an affair, an insinuation that the screenplay confirms, and then he utters Christ's "Woman, behold thy son! Son, behold thy mother!"

Later Katarina, beside him in bed, apologizes for the way she behaved in front of Arthur. Peter rejects her tears and labels the formulaic Bergman refrain—her "It was my fault, forgive me, darling"—as her "gramophone record." Wallowing in hostility and indifference toward everything, he expounds on his great fear of disorder and details what he compulsively does to maintain order and then what he perversely does to destroy it. Puzzled and frightened, Katarina just stares at him.

Three weeks after the murder Katarina visits her mother-in-law. Outside the decaying mansion the camera settles on a headless statue of Cupid. Peter's mother mouths motherly platitudes, but her obvious preoccupation with her own loneliness and well-being—she has not even visited her son in the psychiatric hospital—provokes Katarina into pointing out her selfishness and insensitivity. Katarina then confides that her own life has altered totally. Although she has "never been able to enter into someone else's feelings or thoughts," she thinks she understands Peter's loneliness. Moreover, she is confident that he will never return to reality. Worst of all, she finds speaking about it difficult. In fact, she is haunted by Ka's death. At this moment, Bergman inserts Ka's image.

This allusion to Ka leads into the next sequence, which takes us back to *fifty minutes before the murder*. In that sleazy temple of modern sexual freedom, the porno peepshow, the image zooms in on the little window in a small booth. Reflected in it is the seemingly indifferent but fascinated face of Peter watching a naked woman writhing suggestively a few feet away on a bedlike platform. Pulsating red lights and a throbbing disco beat behind a heavily breathing songstress assault us.[73] When the doorman closes up for the day and shoos the men out of the booths, he gives Peter (prearranged by Tim) permission to stay behind with Ka. In her basement dressing room, which reeks of sweat, makeup, and fecal matter, the half-naked brunette sits and follows Peter's directions as to what makeup to wear. They go to her room, but its lack of windows so oppresses Peter that Ka takes her bedding and spreads it out on the performance platform in the main room. As Peter grows drunk on her cheap wine, he begins to strike her as odd. (She mentions that one of the girls had offered to stay as protection, but that she had concluded it wouldn't be necessary.) When at last she is in his arms kissing him, he learns, fatefully, that her name is Katarina. Within moments he is repeating, "There is no way out," but he fights back the compulsion swelling inside him by trying to flee. Paying her off, he puts on his overcoat and tries to leave, but all the doors are locked. "You'll have to stay," says Ka. (Peter is unable to achieve what it took Bergman 40 years to achieve. As Bergman puts it, he finally found the key that would free what his senses told him "from that closed room" they inhabited, thus permitting them to reach his emotions [*ML*, 94, 118].[74])

Trapped, Peter returns and sits down. His hands and arms hang in front of him as they had when he stood over the lamp in his office. When he complains of the smell, Ka poetically describes how the seasons smelled to her when she was six years old and her mother took her to Denmark: "Winter smelled of snow and coal stoves and damp gloves. . . . The spring smelled of melted snow in the deep ditches and fresh birch leaves at Easter and rain." After she helps him remove his overcoat, he lays his head on her shoulder. We have reached the moment that opened the film. The major effect of this framing is to make us conscious of how much we have learned about the internal and external forces that have driven Peter to what at the film's start seemed an unmotivated act. Though on the one hand the back-and-forth time scheme that encircles the murder has virtually destroyed our sense of logical and sequential order, on the other hand it has infused the narrative with the feeling of a weaving and woofing fate that is deviously and inevitably driving Peter into a no-exit situation.

For the last time Peter repeats what he said to both his mother and Katarina, "I'm tired," an indication that he can no longer fight back his aberrant fantasies. The dissolution of the line between fantasy and reality in Peter's mind has been facilitated by the smells, the lurid red lights, the wine he has drunk, the locked doors, and Ka's affection and idyllic childhood memories. At last, because, in his mind, being aroused by this wife-mother figure—whose behavior corroborates her foulness as well as his own—justifies their mutual destruction, Peter gives himself over to his dream scenario, which is now so familiar to him as to be prescriptive: he murders this woman whose tenderness, tragically, has emerged in the form of motherly comforting (see figs. 41, 42).

At this point Bergman borrows from Hitchcock. At the end of *Psycho* Norman Bates has totally withdrawn into his paranoid, schizophrenic world and is undividedly his mother. To make sure that viewers feel they understand Norman's behavior, Hitchcock imports a psychiatrist to explain Norman's thoughts and actions, momentarily turning the dramatization into a case history. But in reducing what we have seen of Norman for almost two hours to this brief summary, Hitchcock is mocking both psychiatry's assumption that it can explain a human being and our willingness to accept that assumption.

The next episode takes place in Dr. Jensen's office *a month after the murder*. Dr. Jensen sits preparing a summary analysis of Peter Egerman. In his preface to the screenplay of *From the Life of the Marionettes* Bergman says that Jensen's summary is far from the truth. In spite of this warning, which also can be regarded as Bergman's attempt to distract us from truths about himself, we must listen to Dr. Jensen because many of his insights are valid. It is true that Jensen was overly impressed with Peter's mother, causing him to underestimate her nar-

From the Life of the Marionettes. AB Svensk Filmindustri

From the Life of the Marionettes. AB Svensk Filmindustri

cissism and seductiveness. But he did recognize that her domination of Peter, who felt an extraordinary affection for her, in conjunction with Peter's weak relationship with his father had led to a latent homosexuality that damaged Peter's relationships with women and put him at odds with himself. Jensen further points out that because early in his life Peter could not find a way to express or even acknowledge his aggression toward his mother, he cut himself off from his true emotions and adopted the attitudes and roles that society assigned him. His development of a strong sense of self-discipline and duty not only led to his achieving social success but reinforced his separation from self. Acceptable levels of drug and alcohol ingestion made it possible for him to avoid facing the causes of his "inexplicable anguish." Then Peter's dependency on his strong-willed wife Katarina replicated his relationship with his mother. Though he is intimidated and even made impotent by women, Peter is drawn to them. To achieve potency, freedom, and pleasure, he learns that he has to achieve control and dominance over them. The disaster occurs when Peter flees his everyday world and enters the sexual underworld, where the supporting inhibitions and restrictions that have held him together are absent—even the police drop in for quickies. It is tragic and fateful that having repeatedly dreamed of killing his wife he meets a prostitute in this setting whose name is the same as his wife's. His hatred of the dominance of his mother-wife and his indecent love for her emerges, encouraged by the soothing behavior of the sexually arousing Ka-Katarina-mother toward her child-man. In fact, just before Peter murders Ka the camera lingers on a wall poster of a mother with her two small children. In addition, Peter's being aroused by the innocent Ka demonstrates that he is not in control himself—an avalanche of incomprehensible and uncontrollable emotions are released that can only be quashed or ordered in the acts of murder and rape. Peter achieves mastery—the need for narcissistic control—through the killing and the sodomy. "Only someone you kill can you possess—or rather be completely master of," comments Dr. Jensen. In fact, this pathological narcissism, this need for absolute control, is what makes Peter a potential suicide: "Only someone who kills himself possesses himself entirely."

During these last sentences and afterwards, we eavesdrop with Katarina and a nurse on Peter. It is, of course, *some time after the murder.* Again we are looking through a little window, this time not in the booth of a pornographic peepshow but in the door of Peter's cell on the psychiatric ward. He is playing chess against a computer, and like Antonius Block, he has just lost his knight to his superior opponent. As if an oracle, the computer ambiguously and ironically flashes a message in English, "You missed the mate." Afterwards, Peter, still obsessively devoted to order, straightens his sheets, stands (like David in *Through a Glass Darkly*) in a cruciform position at the window, and then lies down on his bed, forgetting his sexuality and grasping, in close-up, his orange teddy bear, Bergman's symbol of childhood and security.

As the two women watch Peter, the black and white associated with the case history is now replaced by the exaggerated color that accompanied Peter's actualization of his fantasy. The black and white had viscerally conveyed to the audience the gray life that Peter felt had bled away his true self, his "real" feelings. The color has returned with his regression into the reality of his nurturing fantasies. Dostoyevky's "underground man" asserts that the only response to a world in which all of man's choices and actions can be predicted and thus controlled is to go mad. Peter, aware of being the marionette of an interior puppeteer, unconsciously senses this, that the only way to regain his freedom, his control, is to obliterate reality. This is madness as suicide: "Only someone who kills himself possesses himself entirely."

In *From the Life of the Marionettes* it is Bergman, not his protagonist, who confesses and accepts the forces that have crippled and made him unhappy. It is Bergman who has reconciled himself with his past and himself. Reconciliation, as we shall see, is largely what the remainder of his films are about.

7

Revolt, Recrimination, and Reconciliation: Bergman's Colic Mellowing

The films in this chapter cover the years between 1973 and 1993 and bring us to the end of Bergman's career as a film director (though not as a writer of screenplays and books). Except for *After the Rehearsal* (1984), whose protagonist is essentially the elderly Bergman, *Sunday's Children* (1992), whose protagonist is essentially the young Bergman, and his documentary *Fårö 1979*, these films either have women protagonists or, as in *Fanny and Alexander*, treat the fates of the women protagonists equally with the fate of the character who functions as Bergman's alter ego. (Males *are* the primary protagonists of two other films made in this period—*The Serpent's Egg* and *From the Life of the Marionettes*. In *The Best Intentions* [1992] and in the novelized version of the film [1993], characters who represent Bergman's mother and father are co-protagonists.) And most of these films involve a woman becoming aware that she is being suffocated or crippled psychologically by her relationships with her parents, grandparents, and/or husband, and by the roles society expects her to play.

It is useful for understanding what follows to repeat just a bit of the biographical information mentioned earlier. In 1971, after a brief affair with Malin Ek, Bergman married his present wife, Countess Ingrid von Rosen,[1] who had four children. Their relationship, along with the effects of the aging process on his perspective, seems to have ameliorated Bergman's lifelong bitterness over his upbringing. Though he does not discount the faults of either parent, he is now able to admit his intense and overwhelming love for his mother and to take a larger view of his father. He is also able to show his enjoyment of life, which many of his earlier films and statements have obscured. One of Ingrid von Rosen's qualities that Bergman appreciates—besides her facial resemblance to his mother—is her talent for managing his social and family affairs. She has, for example, arranged periodic family reunions that have reunited Bergman with his alienated children. On the other hand, Liv Ullmann reports (see chapter 1) that in some ways Bergman's treatment of his present wife is not very different from his behavior in his earlier relationships, so we have to assume that von Rosen has done most of the adjusting.

SCENES FROM A MARRIAGE

After *Cries and Whispers* Bergman wanted to do something "small," a television project that he, Nykvist, and a tiny crew could shoot "quickly." The resulting film, *Scenes from a Marriage* (1973), was released in two forms: the version I shall analyze, six 50-minute television episodes (shot in 16mm), and a 155-minute theatrical version that was blown up to 35mm and retains the same six divisions.[2] It has also been turned into a play, consisting of eight scenes plus interludes.[3] For the two protagonists of this film, which is largely a duet, he chose Liv Ullmann and Erland Josephson, using, as he often does, their personal mannerisms to enrich the roles.[4] Ullmann's previous performances in Bergman's films have demonstrated her astounding range, and she continues to appear as Bergman's chief female protagonist. His longtime colleague Josephson has come to replace Max von Sydow and Gunnar Björnstrand (who died in 1986) as Bergman's primary male protagonist and alter ego.[5] Josephson's major roles in Bergman's films have progressed from weak, passive characters to weak, hostile, even sinister characters to strong, vulnerable, likable egoists. He was the self-conscious, patronizing Anders Ellius, who welcomes his wife's miscarriage, in *Brink of Life;* then he was *The Magician's* too polite and reserved Consul Egerman, who comes to recognize violence as the path to his wife's affection. Next, in *Hour of the Wolf,* he was the sinister, jealous Baron von Merkens, and in *The Passion of Anna* he played the garrulous but insecure, jealous, and cruel Elis Vergérus. We last saw him as the self-assured and illusionless doctor in *Cries and Whispers.* In *Scenes from a Marriage,* especially early on, that egoism comes across as smugness. But overall, the bearded Josephson relaxes—even slouches—and warms his persona, making Johan, the character he is playing, avuncular and bearishly professorial. "I've often played slightly ironical, skeptical, cold academics, leaning more towards the intellectual than the intuitive side," Josephson observes, adding that "the intellectual in Sweden is so intent on being an intellectual" that it takes alcohol to help him get in touch with his intuition (Josephson, 3–5).

Given its episodic structure and its subject matter, *Scenes from a Marriage* might at first be taken as a soap opera. But on viewing it one recognizes that it has eschewed the titillating excess and unreality of soap opera's alternating plots involving a myriad of interconnected characters. Its concentration (sometimes claustrophobically) on the in-depth documentation of one marriage and on the internal growth of its two protagonists signals the audience that analysis and constructing a case history, not the false climaxes of melodrama, are its ultimate aims. The protagonists of this film will mirror the worst and most hateful in us, but we never hate them. Their generosity, tenderness, striving for understanding, and, above all, their personal growth earn our admiration and affection.

The film's nonpoetic, realistic dialogue and grainy images further the impression of pseudo-cinema vérité.[6] In addition, although the metaphorical titles of the sequences elevate and universalize the drama, this film's world differs from most of Bergman's earlier films in its unblinking, sometimes mundane realism and in being time-specific, largely symbol-less, and nonexpressionistic. *Scenes from a Marriage* is direct, simple, and familiar; its trivial details, tasks, and concerns—the furniture of common domestic life that David violently rails at in *The Touch*—accrue until the audience feels capable of stepping into its protagonists' shoes. The detailing of their inconsistencies, contradictions, and vacillations helps make them more three-dimensional than their environment. The boundaries of Johan and Marianne's story are the boundaries of their emotional and philosophical life. "This picture is not about a milieu; it is about a marriage, and we are interested in the faces" (Nykvist, 897). Bergman's statement, "It wasn't until *A Passion* [*of Anna*] that I really got to grips with the man-woman relationship" (*BB,* 178), applies even more comprehensively to *Scenes from a Marriage*.

Scene 1, "Innocence and Panic," opens with Marianne and Johan, purportedly "an ideal married couple," being photographed and interviewed at home for a women's magazine. (Off-screen we hear

Bergman posing the family.) Though it is obvious that Bergman's script is mocking the interviewer (Anita Wall), she functions to give us a quick biography of this couple. Married 10 years, the 42-year-old Johan, an associate professor at the Psychotechnical Institute, and the 35-year-old Marianne, a specialist in family law—divorce in particular—have two daughters and a full set of in-laws. Though we never meet them, except for Marianne's mother, we learn that Johan's father is a doctor and his mother is very motherly; Marianne's father is a lawyer, and she and her mother are on good terms but have never been intimate. Just as in *Persona,* where Alma felt compelled to follow in her mother's footsteps, it was decided early on that Marianne would follow in her father's and go into the law.

Marianne and Johan married on the rebound from failed relationships. When she was 19, Marianne fell madly in love, married, had a child who soon died, and divorced; Johan had had a "much-discussed affair with a pop singer," who eventually dropped him. Marianne and Johan met frequently at political and amateur dramatic events. They lived together, helping each other to recover from their unhappy relationships and get back to their studies. Everyone, including their parents, thought they made a perfect couple, and being "terribly" in love, they married.

When the slightly shy—she holds onto Johan's hand—Marianne is asked to define herself, she responds that she is "married to Johan and has two daughters." When the question is put to Johan, he describes himself in a facetious and world-weary manner. His polished apathy and wry dismissal of life's absurdities, even though for him life is no joke, are his ways to avoid exposing his real feelings and to cope with his fear and "unnecessary guilt." He tries to shock his questioner by answering that he does not give "a damn about anything" and by revealing his need to see their parents because "it reminds me of my childhood when I felt I was protected." Marianne's replies are more earnest because she feels honesty is expected of her and because she half-consciously wants to take stock, to pursue some incipient doubts. Her sense that something is amiss accounts for her mention of a friend's comment that Marianne and Johan's "very lack of problems [in their marriage] is in itself a serious problem." The camera moves closer here, as it often does when a comment comes close to a truth or to submerged anger. Asked to describe their marriage, she says she finds Johan's balanced, cautious behavior calming, but she rejects his apathy. She believes instead in "fellow-feeling," by which she means caring about everyone. Asked to define "happiness," she offers her life as it is now; asked to define "love," she initially offers romantic love but immediately qualifies her response, pointing out that romantic love is (as Frid points out in *Smiles of a Summer Night*) so rare that striving for it becomes oppressive. In her law practice, she says, she has seen people collapse under its impossible demands. In its place she proffers just showing kindness, affection, tolerance, and humor toward the person with whom you live. With this modest goal, "love is not so important." We sense her uncertainty about and dissatisfaction with her answer. Marianne is beginning to sense that the price she has paid for the security she has achieved is internalized anger and the suffocation of self.[7] Admitting that she is confused, she ends the interview with the boilerplate lament that people are forced to play roles. The hearty laughter that introduces the next scene implies that the cover-up will continue.

The day the article appears, Marianne and Johan have their married friends, Katarina (Bibi Andersson) and Peter (Jan Malmsjö)—who will become the protagonists of *From the Life of the Marionettes*—to dinner. All "send up" the sugary idyll, but it sparks the guests, who have drunk too much, to savage each other, reminding us not only of the degrading violence of the Almans in *Wild Strawberries* but of Edward Albee's *Who's Afraid of Virginia Woolf?* (1962).[8] (In the process someone quotes Strindberg: "What is more horrible than a husband and wife who hate each other?") As their reason for not being able to agree on a divorce, Peter and Katarina cite the interdependency of their personal and business lives. Privately, however, Katarina admits to Marianne that she likes having sex with Peter, who she knows is impotent with other women, and she derives satisfaction from understanding his "misery and disgust and panic and [the] aching void he feels." Moreover, even though Peter tries to make her feel guilty by threatening suicide and accusing her of being a "man inside," he alone understands her "need" for a double life. Peter, borrowing words from *The Touch*'s David, mocks Marianne and Johan's perfect marriage as "all too goddamn touching" and then agrees (seemingly) to divorce Katarina. But they continue exchanging white-hot insults so that Katarina soon is in tears. We wait for her to retaliate just as we have been waiting for the long ash to drop off her cigarette. Finally, she does: just as the verbally overmatched Mrs. Alman retaliates by slapping her husband's face, Katarina throws her brandy in Peter's face. His laughter hiding his pain, Peter begs his embarrassed hosts' forgiveness, and he and Katarina leave.

Tidying up afterwards, Johan and Marianne agree that they could never feel about or treat each other in this manner. In the subsequent scenes we will note that these two have found that by accepting each other's masks and by substituting candor for truth they can avoid hard decisions and possibly insoluble conflicts. We now watch Johan deflect analysis of their marriage with false reassurances, decoy ideas, kisses and hugs—just as Jan does with Eva in the picnic scene in *Shame*. Marianne, who has gotten pregnant in the hopes that a child might shake them out of their complacency, takes this opportunity to reveal her pregnancy. Johan receives the news amicably, though without enthusiasm; he finally utters what she half-heartedly feels: they do not want their routine disturbed. Nevertheless, they back into deciding to have the child, a decision negated immediately by an abrupt cut to Johan visiting Marianne in her white, austere hospital room after the abortion. They avoid mentioning the fetus, and though Johan does his best to ease Marianne's "awful remorse," when he has departed she pulls the covers over her head and sobs.

Scene 2 is entitled "The Art of Sweeping under the Rug." Marianne is increasingly concerned about the effect of habit on their marriage, so with Johan's support she attempts to break off their weekly dinners with their parents—typically, she wants Johan to make the phone calls—but she caves in to her mother's expectations. When Marianne leaves the room, Johan hurriedly dials another number, but her return forces him to hang up. As events soon will reveal, Johan is having an affair. Ironically, Marianne, who believes that Johan's love of tidiness precludes this possibility, says she almost wishes that one or both of them might be unfaithful just to get them out of their "little squares," a metaphor partially realized in the static camera's tight framing of the actors. Driving to work, Marianne admits to Johan that she is not as sure of her identity as he is of his. Her inability to take responsibility for her actions is pointed up when Johan insists that she pay the many parking tickets she has acquired.

A chilling scene follows. Marianne consuls a Mrs. Jacobi (Barbro Hiort af Ornäs), whose marriage, as Marianne notes, also seems "ideal." Now that her (unloved) children are on their own, Mrs. Jacobi wants to end her loveless marriage, which has done more than just stifle her potential for love. In forcing her to suppress her true feelings, it has numbed her capacity to feel. An unforgettably expressive close-up of her hand moving across the wooden table's grainy top illustrates her point that "I can touch [this], but the sensation is thin and dry. . . . It's the same with . . . music, scents, people's faces and voices. Everything's getting meaner and grayer, with no dignity."

Meanwhile, in his office at the Psychotechnical Institute, Johan is subjecting his longtime friend and colleague (and later mistress) Eva (Gunnel Lindblom) to an experiment. He does not reveal its purpose, but he seems to be measuring how little frustration it takes to erode one's poise and patience: "Take this pen . . . [and] when I put the light out you'll see a brightly shining fixed dot on the wall in front of you. Try to touch it with the point of the pen. If you miss it you must draw a line until you reach it." When Eva tries and fails, Johan shows a Vergerus-like pleasure at her irritation. (A clue to the experiment may be Bergman's declaration that "I work only with that little dot, the human being; that is what I try to dissect and to penetrate more deeply, in order to trace his secrets."[9] Then, to support his own (as yet unrevealed) moral weakness, he encourages the nervous Eva to break her six-day abstinence from cigarettes: "Now you'll have a bad conscience and that's nice too. One must seize every chance of enjoyment these days." Eva, who has come to deliver her judgment of some poems Johan has written, gets revenge. Standing before a fresh target, she calls his poems confusing and juvenile. She also confesses her and his colleagues' disappointment with him; they had considered him the most talented member of their group. When she learns that he has not shown the poems to his wife, because Marianne is "not interested in poetry," Eva reprimands him. Annoyed, Johan writes off Eva's judgment as the result of her having given up cigarettes and says that he knows *one* person who will like them.

Frightened by her interview with Mrs. Jacobi, Marianne calls Johan and invites him to lunch. She brings with her to the café brochures for trips they could take, but Johan responds unenthusiastically and talks instead about the dilemma between making a choice that may turn out wrong and staying in an unending rut. Sensing that he is slipping away from her, Marianne professes her fondness for him and suggests that they talk about their unsatisfactory sex life, but Johan, who is absolutely charming, scotches that too.

Arriving home that evening after seeing *A Doll's House,* Johan waggishly expounds to the defensive Marianne some of his (Bergman's) conclusions about women: they like sacrificing themselves for men;

they uncritically accept the notion that they "have a very special talent for affection"; and though they lament their lack of equality with men, they avoid the responsibility that equality requires. He also repeats Bergman's saw that married couples inevitably tire of each other. When they broach the subject of Marianne's increasing disinterest in sex, she becomes upset, and they retreat from the subject under the cover of laughter. A moment later, however, Johan makes an advance. She gently rebuffs it, but later in bed—whenever Marianne removes her glasses she becomes more emotional—she thinks better of her decision. By then, of course, Johan's urge has waned.

Scene 3, "Paula," dramatizes Johan's informing Marianne that he is passionately in love with a 23-year-old woman named Paula, with whom he is going to Paris for six months.[10] The fast zoom in on Marianne's face conveys her feeling of suddenly being crushed. Johan describes his bad conscience, voices how absurd he appears to himself, wonders whether he shouldn't scrap the affair, and admits that in spite of everything he loves Marianne more now than before—all comments that make the situation more, not less painful. Marianne's first response is to try to ingratiate herself by mothering him. Then she suggests that he delay his departure, scheduled for the following day, so they can work things out. Desperate, she finally threatens not to be there when he returns to Stockholm. His response, that for four "bitter" years he has wanted to ditch his "good" but suffocating family life, dazes her.

She *is* successful in getting him to stay the night. Trying to size up her competition as she waits for him to get undressed and joins her in bed—his nakedness as he changes into his pajamas reinforces the scene's candor—she asks to see Paula's photo. This inspires Johan to describe his sex life with Paula, whom he characterizes as young and insecure, and their scandalous behavior during a tryst in Copenhagen. At last, overcome with the shame of his life-saving "catastrophe," Johan stops pacing and falls sobbing into Marianne's arms.

In the morning, still wearing her black-and-white-striped night-shirt, which suggests that it is she who feels indicted, Marianne packs Johan's suitcase, tends to his bleeding cuticle, and, her eyes full of tears, makes him breakfast—all of which "indecent" attentions increasingly irritate him (and the viewer). As they eat, they tidy up practical details and social obligations.[11] Typically, Bergman saves the long shot for the most painful moment. Through a doorway framed by gray walls and backed by red curtains, we watch Marianne, her arms around Johan's neck, make a last plea for a fresh start. But Johan breaks loose, bids her good-bye, and, in ironic contrast to *A Doll's House,* walks out. The sound of the door shutting sends Marianne to the window to watch him drive off. Utter aloneness and shame affect her stomach like a suddenly descending elevator. She takes refuge in her bed and buries her face in her pillow. Suddenly, she grasps at a straw. Phoning a mutual friend, she asks him to intercede. Her hope is dashed, her humiliation compounded, and her anger inflamed when she learns not only that the friend has already tried but that many others know of the affair. She slams down the phone. Eyes closed and almost gagging, she bites her hand to keep from screaming. Then she takes refuge deep, deep under the bedding.

Scene 4, "The Vale of Tears," takes place six months later. Because Paula is in London, Johan has called and asked to visit Marianne. (She arranges for the children to sleep at an aunt's.) Ibsen's Nora says, "I don't know what will become of me. I don't know where I'm going; I only know that I can no longer bother about what others say. I must find my own way." Marianne has taken only baby steps in that direction because reconciliation with Johan is what she most wants. The initial moments of their first date find the usually self-confident Johan, though gracious and flattering, as nervous as Marianne. His inquiry after the children brings on an upbraiding from Marianne: not only has he forgotten their birthdays, but he has not even called them. We will learn later that the jealous Paula has prohibited him from contacting his family, but obviously he finds her prohibition congenial. When the conversation turns to Marianne, she is defensive about having taken a lover and even about having altered things in the house to suit her own needs. Their kissing stimulates Johan sexually. Marianne entertains his suggestion that they have sex, postponing it until after dinner. Over dinner he mentions that he feels a new self-confidence, which is partly based on the possibility of a lucrative and exciting professorship at an American university. If the position is offered him, he will leave Paula, whose emotional storms and subsequent pleas for forgiveness have come to sicken him. He adds, however, that he is grateful to Paula for having taught him how to brawl and be physically violent.

Reflecting on his and Marianne's marriage, Johan says, has confirmed his belief that making houses, rituals, friends, and parents the source of one's stability is a mistake: "Your security [must be] inside yourself." Furthermore, the sooner one accepts that "loneliness is absolute," that everything is pointless, and that unhappiness is life's norm, the better; then one can get on with things. This philosophy, he (Bergman) concludes, helps him "placate the great emptiness" that pains him physically, "like when you were little and had been crying and the whole inside of your body ached." Sensing, without fully understanding, some deeper disillusionment behind his flurry of words, Marianne simply replies that he is too theoretical for her. What she does know is that even though she is happy she has not been able to stop worrying about his loneliness and fear, and she has not stopped loving him or blaming herself for their breach. Though she hates what he did to her, she does not want anyone else. He suggests sarcastically that she see a psychiatrist. She is, she says. Part of her therapy, she adds, is to write down her dreams, memories, and thoughts. She is delighted when Johan asks to hear what she has written, but when she returns with her notebook, he forces himself on her, drawing her down onto the floor. (A shot that reminds us of the Picasso-like union of faces in *The Silence*—this time horizontally arranged—shows Johan's eye just behind and above Marianne's two eyes, which are facing us.) Crying, she tells him that she has resolved not to have sex with him after all because of the hopeless loneliness she would feel when he is gone. Johan returns to the couch and encourages her to read from her journal. The camera zooms in for a tight close-up of her face as she commences. The entries—written in *Changing*'s flowery, free-association style, and illustrated with snapshots of Ullmann at various ages and often showing her false, defensive smile—focus on the reasons Marianne does not know exactly who she is: her mother forced her to conform and be "agreeable," and her father coerced her into becoming a lawyer even though she wanted to be an actress. Reflecting on her past, she recognizes, has helped her to realize that placing other people's desires over her own is not unselfishness but cowardice, and that "outward security demands a high price: the acceptance of a continuous destruction of the personality." What kind of woman might she have become, she wonders, if she had been true to her talents? Is it possible to reawaken them? Glancing up from the diary, she sees that Johan is asleep, and she smiles sadly.[12]

She leaves the sleeping Johan to talk to her boyfriend David on the phone, and then she returns and gently awakens Johan. What follows is a salient example of the film's rich characterizations: a character's convictions are overridden by complex and achingly conflicting feelings. On his way out Johan opens the door, then closes it, then opens it again, and finally turns and rushes into Marianne's awaiting arms. In bed, they kiss and giggle and caress, and Johan compliments Marianne's body. So content are they that they agree not to make love, but just lie there and hold hands. A phone call from David interrupts their quiet loving. When Marianne answers the phone, David's jealousy over Johan being there—typically, Marianne has involved herself with another of Bergman's childish and violent men—causes Marianne to tell him to behave "like a grown-up man *for once*." Finally, she breaks off their relationship. Because it has always been difficult for her to express her anger openly, she is pleased with her act. But she is soon sobbing to Johan about the "responsibility" she feels to look after him and to repair their marriage.

Sleep will not come to Johan, so he decides to leave. As he is dressing, Marianne discloses a letter she has received from Paula. In it, Paula predicts that Johan will contact Marianne and says she will no longer prevent Johan from seeing Marianne and the children. The letter ends with a declaration of Paula's love for Johan, whom she describes as the "gentlest, kindest, and most affectionate person" she has ever known, but who, in spite of what he pretends, is deeply unsure of himself. Irked, Johan scoffs at Paula's comments, then kisses Marianne goodbye. She kisses his hand. The sound of the outer door slamming and the starting of the car are accompanied by a jarring zoom into a tight close-up (eyebrows to mouth) of Marianne, who is staring at us.

Scene 5, "The Illiterates," opens with Marianne, smartly dressed, moving with a heretofore unobserved vitality, arriving at Johan's office with their divorce papers. After they open a bottle of brandy, we learn that Johan is experiencing a midlife crisis, that he is still living with Paula—whom he believes is having an affair—and that he has been passed over for the position in the United States. As with Tomas (*Winter Light*), his mental state is symbolized by a cold. Marianne has fallen in love and is about to go abroad. Her old compulsion to mother is noticeably absent; in fact, at her instigation they have sex, and she gets on top, moving up and down in a relaxed rhythm. Afterwards, she admits that she is pleased that she no longer feels any commitment to Johan (see fig. 48).

As soon as they turn to the divorce agreement, Johan begins to haggle over details, provoking Marianne to suggest that he take the papers and go over them at home with Paula to make sure Marianne hasn't "diddled" him. They argue about the children, their expenses,

their behavior, and their alienation from their father; Marianne remembers how he doted on them when they were little. Johan waxes
philosophical, observing that people are intellectual and emotional illiterates who know a lot about math, geography, and their bodies but
nothing about their minds and feelings. Marianne yawns. Johan, who
has drunk more brandy than has Marianne, complains that he no
longer knows who he is. Not noting his dagger glances—Bergman's
men do not cope as well with humiliation as do his women—Marianne happily notes that his suffering only produces in her a "faint
sympathy," which she takes as evidence that she is free of him, free to
live her own life.

Johan's sarcasm and old attitude that he knows what she is thinking
better than she does produce the kind of venomous exchange that earlier passed between the brandied Katarina and Peter. Johan condemns
Marianne's habit of using sex to punish or reward his behavior, and
says that he has felt hate and disgust during and after sex with her.
She screams back that she was justified; it was the only weapon she
had against him and their parents, who were always nagging her to
neglect her professional interests for her homemaking. Suddenly, it
dawns on Marianne that Johan does not want a divorce, and she demands that he admit it. In a broken voice, his hands cradling his head,
he cries and confesses that he feels like a "failure . . . scared and home-
less." He adds that he finds living with Paula unendurable; he is bound
to Marianne more deeply than he thought. Reaching over and patting
his face, Marianne points out that it would be a mistake to restart their
marriage. Then her anger suddenly flares, and she reminds him that
she once begged for what he wants now. As Marianne vents her hate,
we are reminded of the nightmares of Tomas (*The Devil's Wanton*),
Bertil (*Three Strange Loves*), and Peter (*From the Life of the Marionettes*)
in which they murdered their wives: "I'm proof against that gaze of
yours. I've hardened myself. If you knew how many times I've
dreamt I battered you to death, that I murdered you, that I stabbed
you, that I kicked you . . . what a goddamn relief it is to say all this
to you at last."

At last, the venom exhausted, she admits that she is tempted "to
start all over again together. I'm much stronger now and more independent. I could really be of help to you when you're having a rough
time of it. I feel such tenderness for you, Johan." She catches herself
in time, however, and informs him, "Wisdom and common sense tell
me that we must [divorce]." Suddenly it strikes her that because she

is her own woman she doesn't care whose name she bears; she calls a cab to go home to the man who is waiting for her. She does not see Johan lock the door.

Johan now expresses the idea that shapes the film: "If only we could meet as the people we were meant to be, and not as people who try to play the parts that all sorts of powers have assigned us." Noting that Johan is too drunk to drive, Marianne insists he share her cab. Johan, however, turns hostile, refusing to give her the key to the door. When she tries to laugh off his absurd behavior, he hits her, bloodying her nose. She fights back, and they are soon wrestling on the floor, breathing heavily. (Bergman, like Strindberg, makes us feel the embarrassing but joyous relief of venting hatred at the person one blames for making one act so badly. The hatred Johan feels is for himself for not having lived up to his ideal conception of himself.) When they pause, Johan still refuses her the key. Marianne swears at him, and he screams over and over, "I could kill you!" and knocks her down and kicks her. They wrestle and screech until they are both exhausted.

Finally, Johan asks her if she is all right and offers to help her up. She refuses his help, telling him she does not want him near her. He gives her the key, and she goes to wash her bloodied face. Sobbing, Johan goes to the desk and finalizes the separation with two sweeps of the pen. On her return Marianne also signs the papers, gathers them up, and, without another word, leaves.

The sixth (and final) scene, "In the Middle of the Night in a Dark House Somewhere in the World," takes place three years later. It opens with a brief scene in which Marianne visits her temporarily invalided mother (Wenche Foss), who immediately tries to pressure Marianne into attending a small ceremony—a "formality"—to inter Marianne's father's ashes. It is scheduled for the morning Marianne is committed to a court case. Marianne resists the pressure from her mother, indicating how strong she has grown.

Subsequently, mother and daughter chat, and Marianne inquires about her marriage. Her mother's description of her placid marriage, of her guiltless regrets about what she and her husband might have done differently, and of the influence on her of her own parents nearly recapitulates entirely Marianne and Johan's experiences. As she is leaving, Marianne notes that she and her mother never before exchanged such confidences. Both look forward to more discussions.

At his office Johan—mellow to the point of aloofness—breaks off his affair with Eva. Swearing, she tries to irk him by reminding him that at his last physical examination the doctor told him he had shrunk a couple of inches, and by trying to get him to admit that her replacement is his young, "motherly" secretary. Eva is wrong about the woman. Having accidentally met at a play a year earlier, Johan and Marianne, both remarried, have been carrying on an affair.

The start of the next scene refreshingly, though briefly, replaces the film's insidious claustrophobia with an exhilarating liveliness and openness. The camera cranes down on a traffic circle—there is more activity than usual on a Bergman street—as church bells seemingly celebrate the lovers' rendezvous. Marianne drives up, gets out of her car, and runs to kiss Johan, who is behind a tree. Then, getting into his car—she almost gets run over in her headiness—they drive to what was once their own country house but now belongs to Marianne and her husband, Henrik. (Both Henrik, a senior physician, and Johan's wife, Anna, are out of town.) Because the place raises too many memories, they move to a nearby cabin belonging to Fredrik (the friend Marianne called the night Johan left her). While Marianne "tidies up" the clutter—a verb Bergman has Marianne use repeatedly to emphasize her and Johan's compulsion for domestic and emotional order— her gaze settles on Johan starting the fire. Echoing both Paula's and the doctor's description of him, she tearfully tells him that he is handsome, gentle, and kind and has "grown so small in some way." Johan, apparently incapable of hostility, explains that in fact he has found his "right proportions." He has accomplished this by accepting his limitations. He no longer feels driven to live up to his father's expectations. The mellow mournfulness struck in his speech permeates this scene.

A large, paper lantern that looks like a sun with a catlike face[13] grins down at them as they eat dinner and talk. They soon discover that they no longer feel the need to lie to each other or to make do "with convenient half-truths." They can speak truths they cannot share with their present spouses. It strikes them that the full communication required for a healthy relationship is impossible under the constraints, habits, commitments, and pressures of marriage. The bond between them is stronger than any marriage contract and permits each to hear what the other is actually saying. The respect each shows for the other's differences is poignant, and we recognize that it is the mark of their growth.

When the conversation turns to their marriages, Johan quickly grows impatient.[14] He complains instead that his life has only the meaning he gives it. Like Antonius Block and other Bergman characters, he wants "something to long for . . . something to believe in." Her eyes closed and running her finger over his forehead, Marianne, exhibiting what he refers to as her "boundless and eternal female strength," tells him that for her part she enjoys life and interacting with people, even the compromises. Once again Bergman has framed his narrative: we recognize these attitudes as ones she glibly expressed in the opening sequence. Now, however, they ring with a conviction forged from painful experience. Talked out, Marianne and Johan kiss and prepare for bed.

"Any drama is worthless that does not deal with metaphysical questions," Bergman has said. He now poetically elevates this drama by pursuing the metaphysical concern that Johan injected. The final scene opens with a shot of a beach lit with a purplish cast and the sinisterly forlorn lowing of a foghorn. Marianne awakens from a nightmare, cries out, and leaps out of bed to frantically pace the room (the lantern's grotesque grin presides). When Johan is finally able to coax her back and into the safety of his arms, she describes her dream: she, Johan, and their daughters were walking along a dangerous road, and she began to slip and sink in the soft sand. When she reached up to the others for help, she discovered that she had no hands, just elbow stumps. What causes such a dream of one's ultimate aloneness in a hopeless existence, she asks? Maybe, says Johan, "in your extremely well-ordered world there is something you can't get at." Does this hopelessness apply to everyone, she inquires? I believe so, says Johan. Marianne then describes her ability to sometimes identify with Johan (or with others) to such a degree that she not only knows what he is feeling and thinking, she momentarily feels a "great tenderness" for him and is able to forget herself. What grieves her, however, is that she is not totally able to efface her sense of self, and that she believes she has never loved anyone or been loved by anyone in a totally self-less fashion. Johan comforts her by saying he believes that they do love one another, but in "an earthly and imperfect way": "Here I sit with my arms around you . . . in the middle of the night in a dark house, somewhere in the world. And your arms [no stumps now] are around me. I can't honestly say I have any great insight or fellow-feeling. . . . I don't know what the hell my love looks like. I can't describe it and I hardly feel it in everyday life." "And," she inquires, "you think I love you too?" Yes, he says, but he adds that he believes that if they talk about it too much it may "give out." Satisfied, Marianne sinks deeper into his arms, with the intent of falling asleep there. But again reality interferes. They are not going to sit there, says Johan, because his leg is asleep, his arm hurts, and he's cold and sleepy. Bidding each other good dreams, they snuggle under the blankets. Unlike the timeless fantasy that eases Isak Borg into sleep, the peace that now presides is based on a real communion—triumphant in that each is embraced by the one person in the empty universe who understands him/her—as much as that is possible. It is a serene moment in time that seems to last forever. What comes to mind may be Bergman's statement, "If you take that first step toward communication . . . understanding . . . love, then . . . no matter how difficult the future may be . . . you are saved" (*Playboy*, 68). This is not to say that questions do not remain to be answered in Marianne's and Johan's lives. Bergman comments, "People think there is an optimistic end to [*Scenes from a Marriage*]. I don't think so, because I know these two people, Johan and Marianne. They are coming now into real difficulties, new lives, new compromises, and they have to go ahead with that" (Jones, 67). Nor should we forget their metaphysical and psychological apprehensions, which dominate the last moments of the drama.

Like other Bergman marital twins (*A Lesson in Love*'s Marianne and David Erneman, *Smiles of a Summer Night*'s Fredrik and Désirée), Johan and Marianne's "marriage"—as the film's title emphasizes—transcends legalisms and conventions. The natural impulse is to lament that they cannot live with this honesty on a full-time basis. Certainly one of the reasons they do not remarry each other is that it would entail hurting others. Besides, their affair is exciting. Having heard him say it in so many of his earlier films, no one is surprised to hear Bergman saying once again that monogamy is a generally inadequate arrangement and that one person cannot play all the roles that a partner requires. I wouldn't be surprised either if Liv Ullmann isn't echoing Bergman, who has maintained close relationships with his former lovers and wives, when she comments that there is a lot "to be gained by breaking up [a relationship] . . if you can keep the friendship. I'm not saying that it's better than having the relationship. That's of course the best thing. But if you can't have that, it's a lovely thing to have a friendship with someone you've been close to. It's like a brother or sister—closer than a friend."[15]

This film's strength derives from its verisimilitude in laying bare Marianne and Johan's physical and emotional bonds, and from its demonstration that the mysteries of attraction are inexplicable. By the end these two people perfectly complement each other. Marianne's need to mother remains, but now at least she takes her own needs seriously; Johan provides her a bearish sense of security, part of which is based on his ability to rationalize for both of them the metaphysical and interior voids they sometimes feel. I also think audiences find valuable the film's message about reducing our demands on love. Marsha Kinder, necessarily employing numerous qualifiers, deftly sums it up: "The film implies that if we have the strength to take a relationship as far as it will go, to discard as many false masks as possible, to live through the outbursts of hatred and violence, to confront honestly our full range of feelings, we may discover an emotional capacity that is much deeper and richer than we expect. The doubts are never quieted, the struggle is never over, the confusion is never eliminated, but the imperfect love comforts and survives."[16]

The dramatic and substantive success of *Scenes from a Marriage*, in Sweden at least, was evidenced by the fact that on the nights the series ran phones all over the country were left off their hooks, and that after the series concluded, we are told, the divorce rate dramatically increased (Cowie 1982, 291).

THE MAGIC FLUTE

Bergman now felt he was ready to undertake a project he had put off for 20 years: the filming of "the most . . . difficult opera ever written," Mozart's *The Magic Flute*.[17] The success Bergman had just had with making *Scenes from a Marriage* for television and with shooting in 16mm[18] encouraged him to go that route again, much to the annoyance of the other producers at Swedish TV, whose projects had to give way to Bergman's almost $4 million production. He shot the film in 1974 and released it in 1975 (Cowie 1982, 295–99). Although he tried to match the probable color scheme of the original 1791 performance, as he frequently does with works he interprets Bergman made significant changes in *The Magic Flute,* partly, it seems, to stress his own major themes. Tamino (Josef Köstlinger) becomes obsessed with finding "the goal and purpose to his life" and is promised that if he passes three tests, not only will he win his beloved Pamina (Irma Urrila) but he will be accepted into Sarastro's (Ulrik Cold) brotherhood and have revealed to him the mystery of life. He will also be assured of Heaven at his death. Love is the force that will help him reach God and defeat the meaninglessness represented by Pamina's mother, the demonic Queen of the Night (Birgit Nordin), who wants to control the world. As in *A Lesson in Love, Smiles of a Summer Night,* and, ironically, *Scenes from a Marriage,* Pamina and Tamino are marital twins, their joint destinies signaled by their paired names. In Pamina's ambivalence toward her deceitful, selfish mother is found the theme of ambivalence toward—and often reconciliation with—one's parents that will become central in *Face to Face, Autumn Sonata, From the Life of the Marionettes, Fanny and Alexander,* and *After the Rehearsal.* That ambivalence—even Tamino proclaims, "All is hypocrisy"—is in the original opera. However, Bergman alters the story to make Sarastro the father with whom the estranged Pamina is finally reunited, and who orders her to follow his counsel if she is not to waste her life. (Whenever Sarastro refers to his wife-enemy, he exhibits a scary near loss of his sage composure.)

The opening of the film resembles that of *Cries and Whispers.* Instead of a sunrise, however, a golden sunset shimmers across a duck pond and birds chirp wildly. As the camera lingers on the silhouetted image of a neoclassical statue on the grounds outside the baroque Drottningholm Court Theater, the overture commences. Bergman then plucks us out of this world of manicured nature and ushers us inside into a world of total artifice. A slow zoom moves in close on a fresh-faced young girl (Helene Friberg) staring at the floating neoclassical figures painted on the curtain, whose rise all await. This girl represents the childlike attitude Bergman wants us to adopt before this fairy tale. Bergman also uses her face (and during the overture a couple of other faces) as a visual note to which he repeatedly returns. Her expressions cue the changes in the opera's moods. (After awhile, her unblinking intentness, incipient smile, and glistening lower lip become annoying.) Her face is also made part of a montage of expectant, posed faces belonging to men and women of a variety of ages and races, among whom are Erland Josephson, Sven Nykvist, Bergman himself, and portraits of Mozart. These faces, which distract us from the overture, seem to be meant to demonstrate the opera's universal appeal.

That we are intended to have a jolly good time is signaled as the curtain rises and from behind the colorfully painted flats appear a strutting, Muppet-like dragon and Tamino, shrieking. To establish the coexistence of theatrical and filmic spaces and audiences, Bergman has Papageno (Håkan Hagegård), who now arrives on the scene, sing directly to us. Bergman's approach to filming this opera is to respect and not overpower the stage with film devices. He does not, however, deny himself what film can enhance, open up, or intensify. He is very successful in creating a protean sense of place, and soon both the worlds onstage and backstage feel almost as familiar as our own homes. Backstage during *The Magic Flute* we see the machine producing the thunder and the huge wooden wheels that raise and lower the flats. (As far back as *Ship to India* and *Summer Interlude* Bergman has had a penchant for revealing the mundaneness and even sordidness of backstage life; in *The Devil's Wanton* he delighted in puncturing filmmaking's special effects.) And when, as with a child's pop-up book, a twist of the wrist enlarges this world by fluidly and imperceptibly moving us into the film studio for big effects, we smile at the seamlessness and take delight in the filmic devices, some of which we may recognize from Bergman's earlier films. Portraits in lockets come to life as in *Summer Interlude*. When Tamino enters the Temple, Bergman shows him from virtually the same oblique, overhead angle and with the same lighting effects he used for the crazed Johan Borg's entrance into von Merkens's castle in *Hour of the Wolf*. And the seemingly disembodied hands that enter from the edge of the frame to place a lock on Papageno's mouth call to mind the hand that floats in from the edge of the screen in the attic scene in *The Magician,* or the murderous hand that will threaten Abel Rosenberg in *The Serpent's Eye*.

The opera's characters move, with a minimum of jarring, from relatively natural sounding dialogue into arias and back again. (The queen's vocal straining in critical passages may cause some to long for the artificially cultivated voices that Bergman eschewed.) Though not all of his singers are accomplished actors—Hagegård is a delight—Bergman catches some subtle expressions in close-ups. The queen's sideways glance as she deceives Tamino, and later, her final, quick, defiant smile as she is swept into the void, are striking moments, as is Pamina's Elizabet Vogler–like act of peeking through her fingers with fascination and horror at her terrifying mother. As for Sarastro, we remember Ulrik Cold's searing dark eyes. Bergman also stresses reality-establishing details that would be unavailable to theater audiences, possibly the most memorable being the hole in the glove of the speaker (Erik Saedén) as he rests his hand on Tamino's shoulder. Most of the invention, however, comes from Bergman and Nykvist's expressionistic lighting—for example, Monostatos's (Ragnar Ulfung) rust-red, leering face behind Pamina's chalky blue face (Nykvist, 954–55).

There is lots of evidence that Bergman had as much fun filming the opera as he hoped his audience would have watching it. His characters smilingly flip placards with the printed text of the more sententious passages they are singing. During intermission he shows, among other things, the queen backstage continuing to break the law by smoking a cigarette under a "No Smoking" sign, and the dragon strolling about. We also watch Pamina beating Tamino at chess. But it is three little boys who play the spirits, descending in a hand-propelled balloon—a flying machine—while barely able to suppress their laughter, who provide the surest sign of Bergman's attitude. The first act of the opera is spritely and continuously engrossing. In the second part, which is notoriously problematic, even with Bergman's excisions and rearrangements to help focus and intensify our attention, some scenes fall short. The most salient example—in a scene that foreshadows the dream sequences in *Face to Face*—is Tamino and Pamina's journey through hellish flames as maggot-white, naked, and featureless bodies impotently writhe and try to ensnare them.

FACE TO FACE

Like *Scenes from a Marriage,* Bergman's next film, *Face to Face* (1976), was both serialized for television (in four 50-minute episodes) and released as a film. Its New York run played a role in Woody Allen's *Annie Hall* (1977). *Face to Face* is the film that Alvy, accompanied by Annie, refuses to see because they are two minutes late. Cognoscenti will recognize not only Allen's tribute to his favorite filmmaker but the connection between the subject of his idol's film and his own—a woman finding her identity.

Face to Face also raises questions that stem from Bergman's personality. Near the end of the film the psychiatrist Jenny Isaksson (Liv Ullmann), who is recovering in the hospital from a suicide attempt, comes to understand that the origin of her problem and of her damaged personality is the guilt and fear she incurred during her youth. She asks her friend and doctor, Tomas Jacobi (Erland Josephson), if she is part of "a vast army of emotionally crippled wretches wandering about calling to each other with words which we don't understand?" It is a question that calls to mind Marianne's (*Scenes from a Marriage*) lament about being incapable of loving unselfishly.[19] Tomas, who understands perfectly and seems to share her condition, expands on the state of psyche she describes: "I wish that someone or something would affect me so that I can become real. . . . To hear a human voice and be sure that it comes from someone who is made just like I am. To touch a pair of lips and in the same thousandth of a second know that this is a pair of lips. Not to have to live through the hideous moment needed for my experience to check that I've really felt a pair of lips . . . to know that a joy is a joy and above all that a pain has to be a pain." Tomas's words also presage Bergman's description in his autobiography of his longtime psychological condition: "My senses did indeed register the external reality, but the impulses never reached as far as my emotions. [My] emotions [were not] linked with [the] impressions of my senses. . . . [For] forty years . . . I existed on the memory of feelings. I knew perfectly well how emotions should be reproduced, but the spontaneous expression of them was never spontaneous. There was always a micro-second between my intuitive experience and its emotional expression" (*ML,* 118). *Face to Face* climaxes with these questions.

At the film's start, Jenny, in Bergman's words, is "a well-adjusted, capable, and disciplined person, a highly qualified professional woman with a career, comfortably married to a gifted colleague and surrounded by . . . 'the good things of life.' It is this admirable character's shockingly quick breakdown and agonizing rebirth that I have tried to describe. . . . [I have also tried to show] the causes of the disaster as well as the possibilities to this woman in the future."[20] Jenny Isaksson, another of Bergman's struggling marionettes, is an extreme version of Marianne (*Scenes from a Marriage*) in that she sees herself as "a puppet . . . reacting more or less to external demands and stimuli . . . [while] inside there is nothing but a great horror." But even more than Marianne, Jenny resembles Dr. Isak Borg (*Wild Strawberries*), whose first name she shares. She too is a doctor oblivious to the sickness of her existence who is alerted to her problem by a vision of death. And largely by means of a series of dreams she too returns to the scenes of her crimes and the crimes perpetrated against her. Like Isak, she encounters her living corpse in a coffin, stands trial as a doctor (in the screenplay), and explores her youth. Furthermore, like Isak she comes to realize that even though she cannot fundamentally change, she now can—and must—behave differently, especially with her offspring, whom she has caused to hate her. Finally, like Isak's story, Jenny's ends with an epiphany—the sight of her loving grandparents—and with the promise of a better tomorrow.

As the credits roll we hear faintly lapping waves and look down into greenish, unfathomable waters representing the unconscious. (In *The Passion of Anna* an almost identical shot is accompanied by a statement that "the warnings beneath begin to reveal themselves.") A dissolve sets us face to face with Jenny as she puts on her dark glasses, which she (like *Through a Glass Darkly*'s Karin) wrongly hopes will soften reality's appearance. (1 Corinthians 13:12: "For now we see through a glass, darkly; but then face to face: now I know in part; but then shall I know even as also I am known." St. Paul's vision is of passing through death to meet God face to face. What follows is a secularized resurrection in which Jenny will pass through death to a new view of life.) This close-up is followed by a medium-long shot that shows Jenny as a small, isolated figure standing alone in the middle of a white void, her virtually empty living room. The only objects the furniture movers have left are a plant and a telephone, symbols of life and communication. As Jenny takes a farewell look her echoing footsteps call attention to the absence of the possessions that have served as her buffer against emptiness. (In *The Touch* it is the death of Karin's mother that jars her loose from her firm moorings.)

Until their new house is built—by which time her husband Erik (Sven Lindberg) will have returned from a meeting in Chicago—Jenny is going to live with her grandparents. But instead of going directly there, Jenny stops off at the psychiatric hospital to visit her patient Maria (Kari Sylwan). Strangely, under Jenny's treatment the psychotic Maria has regressed to the oral stage (presaging Jenny's later regression). Ironically, the infantile Maria intuitively understands her doctor's repressed anguish. "Poor Jenny," she says, and reminding us of Ester's (*The Silence*) final message to Johan, "hand," "face"—an allusion to the need for human contact and love—Maria, muttering "brow, cheek, eye, mouth," tries to touch Jenny's face. Startled as well as repulsed by Maria's sensuality, Jenny stiffens and, nearly in tears, flees the room. Later, when we come to understand that the face Jenny presents to the world and to herself is largely a mask, we will understand why she subsequently diagnoses Maria's psychotic behavior as an act. Another irony is that at this time, unlike Maria, Jenny is never in touch with her deepest feelings.

Later that day, as she enters her grandparents' building, Jenny is again unsettled, this time by an elderly woman's (Tore Segelcke) smile at her from beneath a black veil. (This woman's antecedents are the veiled figure in Birgitta Carolina's dream in *The Devil's Wanton*, the apparition of death Märta sees through the pressed-glass door of her parents' apartment in *Secrets of Women,* and in *Summer Interlude* Henrik's death-associated aunt, who stops to stare at Marie when she returns to the tragic scene of her youth.) Subsequently, Bergman's camera draws our attention to the yellow (later blue) tulips in the stained-glass window in the door to Jenny's grandparents' apartment. They are replicas of those that decorated the door of Bergman's grandmother's apartment, the only place he could be himself, and they also symbolize the joy that as a child Bergman experienced there.

Jenny is welcomed by her grandmother (Aino Taube), with whom the nine-year-old Jenny came to live after her parents were killed in a car crash. Her grandmother assigns her to her old room, which she has refurbished with familiar objects from the attic. Jenny enthusiastically greets her grandfather (Gunnar Björnstrand), who is being terrorized by senility, but does not hug him. Instead, she responds, as she often will, with that forced smile that Ullmann characters often use to hide pain or to ease the tensions they feel at having to deal with people. Her grandfather's thoughts of death—he keeps trying to connect with life by poring over the family photo album—contribute to Jenny's own preoccupation with it. That night Jenny's dream is visited by the veiled woman she met in the hall. As the woman advances Jenny is horrified to discover that one of her eyes is as dead as a black agate. Jenny awakens trying to scream.

At work the next day, when Jenny does not follow through after asking her colleague, Dr. Wankel (Ulf Johanson), not to smoke in her presence, we are reminded of Jenny's comparison of herself to her grandmother, who, she said, accepted the situations in which she found herself. The cynical doctor's questioning of the efficacy of psychiatry further weakens Jenny's self-assurance. That afternoon Jenny attends a party given by Wankel's wife, Elisabeth (Sif Ruud), who has separated from him in order to develop her own personality, a state she seems well on the way to having achieved. Dressed in red, the flighty and frenetic woman appears intoxicated with life. Her flamboyantly colorful, plant-filled apartment contrasts dramatically with both Jenny's empty living room and her grandparents' Victorian apartment, which is crowded with overstuffed furniture and family photographs. Fighting the aging process and trying to escape her deadening habits, Elisabeth is having an affair with Mikael Strömberg (Gösta Ekman), a homosexual 26 years her junior, whom, along with his paramour, she mothers and supports financially. The desperation with which she pursues her doomed pleasures tempers our mockery with pity. However, her candid statement—which echoes Bergman's about himself—that she is "happy more or less," and that now at least she "know[s] that it's *my* feelings and sensations, since there's no gap between myself and what I experience," forces us to qualify our initial impression of her as merely a flighty fool. Whatever her sad delusions, in this regard she is healthier than Jenny.

Elisabeth introduces Jenny to Dr. Tomas Jacobi, whom she describes as "mixed up," and who turns out to be Maria's half-brother. When Tomas invites Jenny to dinner, she turns him down, but when he does not press the matter, she is reassured and changes her mind. She calls and breaks her date with her exasperatingly immature lover who, she later tells Tomas, is not even as nice as her husband. They are to meet in front of the restaurant, but not until the moment before Tomas sees her there is she sure that she wants to broach a new relationship. (The restaurant is on a typical Bergman street—empty except for the two protagonists.) After dinner they drive out to Tomas's suburban home. Jenny learns that he is divorced from his wife, who (like Käbi Laretei) is a pianist. Jenny feels surprisingly relaxed until Tomas asks about her breasts. Before she insists that Tomas call a cab to take her home, Jenny, in a speech almost as chillingly humiliating as Katarina's to Peter (*Scenes from a Marriage*), imagines their lovemaking, dissecting its progress in cruel, deadening clichés. But something about this bearded doctor's ease, openness, and frankness intrigues her. As she is leaving, she does not discourage the idea of his telephoning her.

It is almost 3:00 A.M. when Jenny enters her grandparents' apartment. Instead of going to bed she sits, illuminated by a thin shaft of light, in a dark corner. After a moment, her insomniac and shuffling grandfather—his slippers seem too big for him—comes in and heads for the grandfather clock, which, he says to his wife, who trails him, is running down and needs repair before it stops altogether. Her grandmother reassures the prickly man that the clock is all right and that he will not, as he also fears, be sent to a nursing home. Her grandfather confesses his humiliation—"Old age is hell"—and then proffers, "Forgive me." Assuring him that he can sleep near her, her grandmother leads her grandfather back to bed. Jenny has tears in her eyes.

Suddenly, she is startled by the ringing of the phone. She answers it and then leaves. We recognize her destination—her empty house. Upstairs, in what had been her own bedroom, Jenny finds Maria unconscious and virtually naked on the floor. To remind us of the connection between Jenny and Maria, Bergman shoots from the far end of the hall so that the two sick women are in the same frame, separated only by the wall that connects the two bedrooms. The bright morning light from the window illuminates Jenny as she sits on a chair in the corner and picks up the phone to call for an ambulance. Suddenly, a man (Birger Malmsten) and an adolescent boy (Göran Stangertz), who but for his jeans is naked, step into the picture. The young man is very gentle with Maria, with whom, it seems, he has had sex. In what is perhaps the worst bit of plotting Bergman has ever devised, it turns out, according to the older man, that Maria requested that they remove her from the hospital and bring her to Jenny. Then he grabs Jenny and holds her as the youth tries to rape her—as in Peter Egerman's murder of Ka in *From the Life of the Marionettes,* we see only her thrashing lower right leg. After considerable effort the boy gives up, complaining, "She's too tight." Before giving Jenny permission to call the ambulance, and leaving with his companion, the older man takes money from her purse, a fitting conclusion since, as we shall learn, she wanted the intercourse. Jenny is frighteningly calm as she makes the call.

There is an abrupt visual and audio cut to Jenny and Tomas that very night. They are attending a piano concert in a small, crowded hall. The pianist (Käbi Laretei) is playing Mozart's Fantasia in C Minor. Jenny is so tense—she flinches at each loud note—that she cannot concentrate on the music. Feeling as if she were in another world, she observes with puzzlement those around her who seem transfixed by the performance.[21] The music's power, delicacy, and drive provide a poignant counterpoint to an expression of her seismic—or paralyzed—thoughts and emotions. And the music continues, accompanying her and Tomas on their drive to his place. When they arrive, Jenny is still as tight as a piano string. She asks Tomas for something to make her sleep, and then, calling to mind Jenny's grandmother's soothing words to her grandfather, she also asks him to let her sleep there and to only keep her company by sleeping beside her. In bed, both dressed in pajamas of a disquieting brown color, she informs Tomas of the attempted rape and the fact that though at first she was frightened, she began to find the rape absurd, and then she wanted the boy to penetrate her. She startles Tomas by suddenly erupting into harrowing convulsions of hysterical sobbing and demonic laughter (Nykvist, 954–55). When at long last she is able to control herself, she asks him to drive her to her grandparents'.

There, she sleeps for days, awakened for only a brief moment by her grandmother, who informs her that she and Jenny's grandfather are committed to staying the weekend in the country with friends. It is Sunday when Jenny again awakens. Her anxiety seems to have passed because, as she makes breakfast and calls Tomas, she is wearing her familiar smile. She has just apologized to Tomas for her behavior the night of the concert and suggested that they go to a movie when, in the mirror, she sees the death apparition. Without explanation, she hangs up and, as if in a trance, paces, ignoring the ringing phone. She runs her fingers over the edge of a wooden chair, but like Mrs. Jacobi (*Scenes from a Marriage*), she seems unable to feel anything.

Considering herself a failure as a doctor, wife, mistress, and, as we shall learn, mother, and being a person whose primary defense against life's disjunctures is total control—"If you force everything to be as usual then it *will* be as usual. . . . That's how it is with me"—suicide is the only answer because, as we are told in *From the Life of the Marionettes,* suicide is the ultimate control. Jenny places the suicide note she has written to her husband on the table near her bed, sits on the bed, and, her hand shaking, swallows—Bergman forces us to experience the whole, awful, gagging process—handfuls of sleeping pills. When she has emptied the bottle and lain down to await the pills' effect, a subjective camera represents her surveying her childhood room. We hear the ticking of her watch and her humming and then we see her hand come up into the frame to trace the vine design on the wallpaper. After a few moments her hand falls from sight and we hear her deep, relaxed breathing. The camera continues to pan the room. After settling on the picture of a twin-towered castle, the image dissolves.[22]

Up to this point, without dispensing with the rich suggestiveness and complexity of art, the film's episodic and elliptical structure, its concision and sometimes unbearably realistic directness, have approached the style of case history. A discordant and—I agree with Bergman here—not wholly successful change of mode now occurs as Bergman turns to the sort of stage expressionism that we find in Strindberg's *Ghost Sonata*. The cause, says Bergman, is that he experienced an embarrassing failure of inspiration. As a consequence, the "dreams [that] were to become tangible reality . . . became synthetic" (*ML*, 232, 73).

Probably because Little Red Riding Hood was a favorite tale of Bergman's as a child, Jenny in her dream appears in a red robe and an embroidered, tight-fitting red cap.[23] She is at home with her stern grandmother, who is reading her a scary fairy tale. It is about a girl who is wandering through the passageways of a castle that belongs to a wicked, old woman and her husband, and who is unable to find anyone in whom to confide. Jenny complains of the disgusting smell of old people, especially her grandmother. When she begins to wander through the altered rooms of her grandmother's apartment, a voice like Tomas's warns her not to go through a door (death) because behind it are unknown horrors. Then, the dead-eyed apparition of death appears and Jenny flees—she actually feels the urge to awaken—but she finally gives herself up to the woman, who enfolds her in her shawl. With renewed effort Jenny rejects this comfort and wakens to find herself in the hospital with smelly, sickeningly green tubes extending from her nose; Dr. Jacobi is beside her. (When she inexplicably hung up the phone on him, Tomas investigated.) The overhead camera may suggest that a higher power once again has intervened to save a Bergman protagonist, and it foreshadows another Jacobi (again played by Josephson) demanding a miracle to help Fanny and Alexander escape. The drugs that remain in her system soon send Jenny back to sleep. Her dream continues with her now wearing a doctor's white coat over her red outfit. Hurrying past her grandmother, Tomas, and the twin-towered castle, she enters a room filled with her "patients," one of whom is Maria, who looks like a ticker-tape machine; words printed on a long tape emerge from her mouth.[24] In addition to Jenny's grandfather and her daughter Anna (Helene Friberg), there is a woman who, like the old woman in Hour of the Wolf, peels off her face to reveal her psychic ulcers. Except for Anna, who flees from her mother, Jenny treats all of them—their hands reaching out to grasp her remind us of the lost souls in Hell trying to grasp Tamino and Pamina—with a placebo concern that thinly disguises her disgust for their psychic dread and pain. Tomas reappears and tells her that she can only help her patients when she learns to respond in their words and feelings, not just in her own. Jenny awakens for the second time.

No sooner has the tube been removed from her nose than she is confronted with her fashionably dressed husband Erik, who has returned from the United States to visit her. When he comes in, the slow zoom-out indicates the distance between them. Erik is uncomfortable with the situation and seems deeply concerned. He says he blames himself for her suicide attempt, though he cannot fathom what he has done; he is not concerned enough to offer to cancel his next day's flight back to the States to chair a committee. With that familiar insincere smile of Ullmann's, Jenny reassures Erik by assuming all the responsibility. "Forgive me," she says. Finally, he kisses her on the temple and promises to call their daughter at camp before he departs. He is almost out of the room when he returns to tell her, "Take care of yourself," and to perform that other self-conscious Bergman ritual: laying his hand on the side of her face. Love is never mentioned.

After he has left, Jenny erupts into another of her wrenching sobs and buries her head in her pillow. The image of the stained-glass tulip on the door of her grandparents' apartment is the segue back into her dream world and to herself as a child. In this dream Jenny (still in her red outfit and tight-fitting cap) confronts her dead parents and her ambivalent feelings for them. (Are these the people the little girl in the fairy tale was searching for to confide in? And is the mother's Bergman-like black beret meant to incorporate Bergman in the idea of the neglectful parent?) Jenny is angry because their deaths cheated her out of the opportunity to confront them with her unresolved feelings about them. Screaming, she pounds first on a table and then on her beloved, crying father, whom her mother tries to shield. Jenny recalls the love they shared, their unintentionally hurting each other, and her own ambivalence: "It's always the same! First I say I love you, then I say I hate you, and then you turn into two scared, guilty children. Then I feel sorry for you and love you again! I can't go on any longer!" The dream ends as the now capless Jenny rushes from them into a corner and pounds her head. With this Jenny awakens for the third time.

Tomas is at her bedside, he informs her that he is now her doctor. Setting aside concern with herself for a moment, she asks the cuddly, mellow man to talk about himself. He reveals being unhappy that his five-year love affair with the young male actor Jenny met at Elisabeth Wankel's party has ended. Unlike the suicidal Jonas Persson (*Winter Light*), on whom another Tomas laid his problems, Jenny listens with sympathy and is neither shocked nor disappointed by what Tomas has said.

In Jenny's final dream she acts out her self-hatred. Her sinister grin turns to outright laughter as she immolates her deceased double (recall *Wild Strawberries*), who is laid out in a coffin. After the coffin has been sealed and set aflame, pounding and cries for help are heard from within.[25] When Tomas, standing nearby, begins to weep, she tells him not to. He replies, however, that his tears are not for her. The fourth nightmare ends.

Awake and dressed in a hospital gown and a pair of white socks, Jenny gets out of her bed. She utters a careless laugh and tells Tomas that she realizes that the source of her fear of death is the death of her parents,[26] her dog, and, when she was 14, a cousin. The cousin died of polio just a few days after the two of them had been kissing under the dining table—a Bergman experience. (In one of the dreams she admits to her grandfather than she is as afraid of death as he is and facilely prescribes for his ailment while she is thinking of something more important.) It is also her fear of death that makes her afraid to risk loving, and it is a source of her frigidity. Then, like other recent Bergman female protagonists, she complains of having had to play roles as she was growing up that kept her from being herself. She recalls that her father, whom she favored, liked her to cuddle him, and that her mother was jealous of the affection they showed each other. She also recalls that both her grandmother and mother "despised" her father, feelings that contributed to Jenny's guilt about physical contact with men.[27] Her distrust of adults also came from witnessing her beloved grandmother's "savagery" in making Jenny's mother cry: "It's horrible with faces that change so that you don't recognize them." Then, in a passage in which Bergman again uses a child to represent the parent's pathology—recall Elizabet's reaction to her unwanted and deformed child (*Persona*)—the ambivalent Jenny describes her infant Anna's strange cry: "It wasn't like other babies', she didn't cry with rage or because she was hungry and wet. It was more like real sobbing. It was heartrending, and sometimes I wanted to hit her for crying like that and sometimes I was beside myself with tenderness."

Rushing about the room in her white gown and ankle socks, Jenny grows increasingly hysterical. As she comes face to face with her repressed, unrelenting guilt and anger, she screams that she cannot live any longer with these memories and feelings. She fights off Tomas, who attempts to calm her. Suddenly, unconsciously, she speaks with different voices. Starting off with her own adult voice, she regresses until she is speaking in her voice as a young girl being either obsequious or defiant with her grandmother. Then her voice becomes that of the domineering, punitive grandmother. In this manner she relives shouting matches, slaps, and the terrifying punishment of being locked in a dark closet. For a few moments she is lying on the floor in a fetal position, reminding us of the infantile Maria. Throughout this primal experience, Tomas, the gynecologist and friend, tries merely to be a midwife to the emergence of these childhood experiences and fears. Bergman says, "I had read Arthur Janov's *Primal Scream* [1970], a powerful and controversial book I admired. It propounded a psychiatric therapy with participating patients and relatively passive therapists. . . . I was extremely stimulated and started developing a television film in four parts along Janov lines" (*ML*, 231). This influence should not come as a surprise given that since the 1960s, as we have noted along the way, Bergman's films have often been clinical in approach and, at times, similar to modified case histories.

Jenny finally regains her calm. As they talk, Tomas, in an act of commiseration, describes his own feelings of never being "real" (in the passage that I referred to earlier). He also informs Jenny that on the following day he is moving to Jamaica and that he does not foresee coming back. He gently rejects her offer to accompany him. Even though our knowledge of his bisexuality has caused us to limit our expectations for the relationship, as has Jenny, Tomas's departure strikes one as just too obviously an authorial device to get him out of the picture. This story is meant to be one of self-confrontation, rebirth, and reconciliation with self, others, and life, not the chronicling of a love affair. So, after watching Jenny face herself, it is time to see how strong, independent, and wise her experience has made her. A nurse enters and announces that Jenny's daughter Anna is waiting to see her. Tomas bids Jenny good-bye, advising, "Take care of yourself and those who are fond of you," a comment that acts as foil to the next scene.

Jenny's interview with the 14-year-old Anna, who wears her hair loose, exactly like her mother, is brief and devastating. As she did with Erik, Jenny tries to assuage any guilt on Anna's part, but she does not recognize that asking this uncomprehending child for forgiveness is beside the point. The rejected Anna just wants Jenny to assure her that she won't try to commit suicide again. For a moment Jenny fails to connect her own loss of her parents with Anna's reaction. In fact, Jenny is impatient with what she regards as Anna's obtuseness. As a consequence, Jenny is stunned when the impassive girl says, "You never liked me anyway" (the partial truth of which Jenny had faced earlier in her dream). Reassuring her mother that she is able to manage her own affairs, Anna departs, returning to camp and a 17-year-old boy with whom she is in love.

The image of the stained-glass tulip cues us to Jenny's return "home." She now recognizes the love that exists between her and her grandmother, in spite of the pain and hatred that once passed between them. After a little small talk she senses *something* has changed. Her grandmother tells her that her grandfather has had a slight stroke and will probably "never get up again." Looking down at her hands and then at Jenny, she sighs resignedly and says, "Well, that's how it is." With convincing affection, and seeming to measure her own problems against those of her grandparents, Jenny smiles, runs her finger across her grandmother's face, and is on her way to visit her grandfather when her grandmother signals her to wait for a moment. Now the film's emotional direction pivots toward the rebirth promised by the church bells on the Sunday Jenny attempted suicide. Like *Wild Strawberries, Cries and Whispers,* and *Scenes from a Marriage,* this film ends with a profoundly poignant and charitable epiphany. Her hair hanging naturally over her shoulders, leaving visible her wedding ring on the chain around her neck, Jenny, her reposeful face slightly eclipsed by the doorway, watches her grandmother attend to her grandfather. In voice-over, Jenny, who said she once had laughed sarcastically at the idea that "love and death merge and include each other," says to us, "I stood for a long time looking at the two old people and the way they belong together. I saw them approaching that mysterious and awful point where they must part. I saw their humility and dignity, and for a short moment I knew that love embraces all, even death" (see fig. 43). Then she steps into the library and, face to face with the camera, phones the hospital, informing them that she will return to work in the morning. As she leaves the apartment, Bergman focuses on the blue tulip: spring and rebirth.

By film's end Jenny is in touch with her feelings and understands her psychological limitations and possibilities. Aware that "anyone who's constantly afraid of dying can't get much pleasure out of living," and now able to see life and death holistically, she no longer despairs over or is terrorized by old age and death. And because she comprehends that hers is not the only suffering in the world and understands that love—the holy grail that Bergman has sought all his life and has found in satisfactory measure only in others—is sustaining, she may be able to forgive and reconcile herself to others and to herself. The prognosis is good; we sense that she can now listen to Maria without having Maria's needs spelled out on a tape, and more impor-

Face to Face

tant, we sense that Jenny and her daughter Anna will be reconciled. As for the elderly man/artist who has lamented and exploited the fears and pains of his youth, Bergman seems to be saying to him, "Grow up! Get on with it!"

Before passing on to the next film, tribute must be paid to Liv Ullmann's performance in *Face to Face*. Not only is it a benchmark of this incomparable actress's staggering range, it is one of cinema's most daring, demanding, and fully realized performances. Nowhere has Ullmann's desire that audiences not think "this is an actress," but rather "this is a person," been so completely achieved.

Just as *Face to Face* was appearing on Swedish television in April 1976, Bergman, in response to being accused of tax fraud, left Sweden in voluntary exile. He settled in Munich finally, and there made the almost epic-sized *The Serpent's Egg*. Its failure in the United States— one critic dubbed it a "major disaster"—probably was a factor in his return to the chamber play form for his next film, which he made in Norway.

AUTUMN SONATA

Because of his bad experiences with his two previous English-language films, *The Touch* and *The Serpent's Egg,* Bergman insisted on shooting *Autumn Sonata* (1978) in Swedish. He refused to shoot in English even though the film would feature one of Hollywood's most famous stars, Ingrid Bergman (who vigorously supported the idea of working in Swedish), and all the actors could speak English with the same accent. There was another potentially serious problem with the project, however. Ingrid told Ingmar, "You know I'm living on borrowed time" (*ML,* 183–85). She was undergoing radiation treatments for a cancer that had metastasized, and she was scheduled for surgery after the film was completed. Nevertheless, she "went on working as if nothing" were the matter.

Both Bergmans had wanted to work together, but their different work habits caused conflict. Ingmar, who did not like to rehearse a lot before shooting, had to adjust to Ingrid's desire to rehearse a great deal. And she did not like his ten-minute takes, the long monologues, the numerous close-ups, and the story's lack of humor—"I asked Ingmar if we could put some jokes in," Ingrid said, "but not . . . Ingmar. He's too serious."[28] Perhaps the director did not sufficiently honor his actress's anxieties over her illness; he wrote: "It was one big fight with Ingrid. . . . [Because she was a star], if someone tried to tell her anything, she wouldn't accept it" (Marker and Marker 1983, 7). In the beginning, she "was very angry because when we were shooting I didn't look at her. . . . I said, 'If I hear that your voice is correct, I know that you look correct" (Wolf, 37). Afterwards, in spite of her complaints, Ingrid remembered the experience positively and was proud of the finished film.[29]

With *Autumn Sonata* Bergman returns to his favorite mode, poetic and symbolic realism. The film also impresses one as having been made by an artist for whom the film medium has become practically as unconscious a process as breathing. Bergman's direction is simple and direct. For example, he illustrates conversations about the past with the relevant action, inserting scenes so seamlessly that the past—its impact anyhow—seems to be part of the present. We also re-encounter familiar devices and themes. Bergman again frames his narrative with the same setting and with similar actions. In fact, with the exception of the shot early on of Charlotte (Ingrid Bergman) arriving at her daughter Eva's (Liv Ullmann) home, the flashbacks, and the few shots of Eva visiting the cemetery and, near the end, of Charlotte on a train, we never leave Eva's home. This framing, and other patterns of repetition, contribute to the sonatalike form of *Autumn Sonata* (which has similarities to *The Ghost Sonata*). The sonata generally begins with theme A (Eva) in the home key, then adds the contrasting but closely related theme B (Charlotte) in a different key. After developing these themes, it ends by returning to A in the original key, but now with B in the same key.

Besides being musical in form, the film is often quite theatrical. In the beginning, for example, Eva's husband Viktor (Halvar Björk) stands *Our Town*–fashion near the camera (the proscenium) and tells us about his wife, who is visible behind him sitting at her desk in the adjoining room (she is slightly out of focus and framed by two prosceniumlike doorways). The physical distance between them also hints at an emotional gap between them. Viktor's quiet, confidential tone simultaneously distances us and creates a sense of intimacy. It distances us by alerting us to the filmmaking process, and draws us to him because he is secretly taking us into his confidence. Viktor's eavesdropping on Eva is the first of several instances of eavesdropping in the film; in fact, Bergman employs the device more in this film than in any other, with the exception of *Fanny and Alexander*.

Several Bergman character types also reappear. In the screenplay we learn that Viktor—the name of the adolescent atheist in *Wild Strawberries*—was a minister but has lost his faith. Charlotte's daughter Helena (Lena Nyman) is the child whose physical disability and mental suffering are the result of being inadequately loved, and whose saintly nature is the chief touchstone by which we measure her sister and mother, who are emotionally crippled people incapable of loving fully or of accepting love. Charlotte, a celebrated pianist,[30] is another of Bergman's destructive, narcissistic parents and artists. (Ingmar and Ingrid sharing a last name strengthens their identification.) Eva is another Bergman child locked in a love-hate relationship with a parent, and another Bergman woman obsessed with mothering. This film is primarily Eva's story: a child avenges herself on an insufficiently loving parent but subsequently achieves an understanding of herself and that parent that permits reconciliation. Another Bergman theme that reappears is (or seems to be) an interceding God, and a character (Eva) who desires to be used by God. As with her predecessors Antonius Block (*The Seventh Seal*), Spegel (*The Magician*), and Märta (*Winter Light*), Eva's wish is fulfilled, and as a consequence she is set free from imprisoning self-absorption to be reconciled with her mother, her husband, and herself.

The narrative begins after the credits, which are backed by a splash of autumn watercolors and accompanied by a recorder and harpsichord playing Handel's Sonata in F, Opus 1. Viktor, who not surprisingly is a good deal older than his 38-year-old wife, quietly relates to us the history of their relationship. He emphasizes his inability to ease her psychological problems. He describes himself as having only vague expectations from life. He says he met Eva, then a journalist, at a church conference, and that two or three days later he proposed marriage. When Eva visited the parsonage, which is beautifully located near a fjord, she said it felt like home. She accepted his proposal, but she confided to him "that she was incapable of loving." (Later she refers to him as her "best friend," someone she "can't imagine [living] without.") Viktor now reads to us from one of Eva's books a passage that calls to mind statements made by Marianne and Johan (*Scenes from a Marriage*) and Jenny and Tomas (*Face to Face*): "I don't know who I am. . . . If anyone loves me as I am, I may dare at last to look at myself. For me that possibility is fairly remote." Viktor—he is the film's other touchstone—professes that he loves her in exactly this way, but that he is unable to make her feel it, reminding us of what Martin feels for Karin (*Through a Glass Darkly*) and Märta feels for Tomas (*Winter Light*). One of the sources of Eva's problem is her mother, whom she has not seen for seven years and with whom she now desires a closer relationship. Viktor tells us at this very moment Eva is writing to her mother to invite her to visit the parsonage for a "few days or weeks." The death of Leonardo, a fellow musician and for 13 years Charlotte's lover, has provided Eva with the needed pretext. Though none of Eva's reasons for inviting her mother to visit are clear in her own mind, they include curiosity over whether her mother has changed, a desire to mother her mother (a way, in part, of controlling her), and wanting to settle old scores. Eva is placed so that as she reads her letter aloud to Viktor, a crucifix is continuously in view over her shoulder.

Charlotte's arrival is (fittingly) heralded by the sound of the powerful motor of her Mercedes. (After the camera has followed her approach up the winding road, it settles on a cluster of roses, possibly with the aim of setting up false expectations on our part, or of foreshadowing this rose's thorns.) Unseen, Eva watches her mother's arrival from a second-floor window and then descends to face her. Their facades effusively greet each other, and then Eva shows Charlotte to her upstairs room. Charlotte hides her discomfort behind a constant flow of talk, describing how she tended Leonardo on the last day of his life, dwelling on the superficial details of his dying and on her own discomfort during his last hours. Charlotte, we learn, stopped living with Leonardo when his illness became terminal. Her rationalization for their "hardly ever" speaking of his illness when she did visit his villa at Naples is that "it would have displeased him." Obviously aware of her distaste for other's pain, Leonardo apparently sent her from his hospital room moments before his death. Finishing her story, Charlotte turns to the mirror and asks, almost coercively, how she looks and if she has changed.[31] Never a pursuer of self-knowledge, Charlotte does not catch the sad irony of Eva's response: "You're just the same." The truth of this judgment is emphasized when, after Eva has bragged in a modest fashion that she recently held a musical evening in which she played the organ and talked about each piece, Charlotte counters with the news that in Los Angeles she played and talked five times to audiences of 3,000 children. When she notices, however, that Eva is crying, she chides herself for talking only about herself. Typically self-effacing, Eva replies that her tears are from the joy of seeing her mother.

Eva wears little or no makeup, unattractive, greenish clothes, and large, unbecoming granny glasses, and for the first half of the film she has her hair braided and pinned across the top of her head. In addition, she repeatedly exhibits the artificial, puffy, thick-lipped smile and whiny, childishly obsequious, and soft-throated voice that Ullmann employs when her character is feeling weak or regressing. Furthermore, her awkward movements reflect her discomfort with her body. Pauline Kael says Ullmann gets "so far inside the dullard [Eva] that there isn't a shred of beauty in her face or body . . . and there's a wormy sanctity in her smiles."[32] There is, however, a viper behind the self-pitying Eva's frumpy appearance and mousy manner. She now informs her mother that Helena, Charlotte's other grown daughter, is no longer in the nursing home where Charlotte placed (abandoned) her but living with Eva and Viktor at the parsonage; Lena, as she is called, is, in fact, in the next room.[33] Charlotte does not hide her anger at being tricked—she would not have come had she known—and insists they get the encounter over at once. Lena suffers from a degenerative nerve disease that has robbed her almost totally of speech and controlled movement—again, as in *The Touch,* Bergman invokes the genetic disease that crippled his grandfather and brother. Charlotte and we (though not Eva) find the visit excruciating. Except for yes and no, Lena's words are unintelligible, so her attempt to express her overpowering joy is harrowing. Bergman frames the faces of the three women in the same close shot, but unlike Eva's and Lena's, Charlotte's face, as if she were the outsider, is in profile. Even though at moments the practiced joy that Charlotte exhibits is belied by looks of distress that border on an impulse to flight—the revulsion Elizabet Vogler (*Persona*) feels toward her deformed but mother-worshiping child comes to mind—Charlotte's performance is convincing. She even kisses the rapturously happy Lena, who has a cold—we learn later that Charlotte, like Bergman, is "afraid of sick people"—and she enthusiastically suggests to Lena that they spend time together. Before leaving the room, she presents Lena with her wristwatch, an act that represents how Charlotte deals with her guilt.

The next scene finds Charlotte alone in her room. She is wearing a bathrobe whose whiteness suggests she is getting down to essentials. Charlotte, who heretofore we have judged to be little interested in self-examination and incapable of self-incrimination, faces her bathroom mirror and says, "This hurts, Charlotte. It hurts. Hurts. Hurts." Pacing, she fights back tears and, as she will do whenever she feels threatened, lights a cigarette. In a passage that is crucial in establishing the limits of her narcissism, she soliloquizes that in spite of herself she actually felt motherly compassion in Lena's presence: "Damn it, to think I can't lift her up and carry her to my bed and comfort her like when she was three years old. That soft, torn body, that's my Lena!" As significant, she asks herself—and at that moment downstairs Eva is asking the same question about Charlotte *and* herself—"What was I longing for so desperately" from this reunion? Just as in *Through a Glass Darkly,* after finally returning to his two parent-hungry children (one irremediably ill) and his helpless son-in-law, David decides to cut short his visit and flee to Yugoslavia, Charlotte decides to cut short her visit to four days and then go to Africa. Talking nonstop to herself, Charlotte enters the shower. It is one of the film's rare moments of humor.

Meanwhile, Eva is carping about her mother to Viktor, whose considered movements as he dutifully folds the dinner napkins define him as slowly and deliberately as do his words. Their conversation leads him to reassure Eva of his longing for her. Her reply again calls to our minds *Through a Glass Darkly*—Karin's words to her husband

Martin: "You always say the right words and do exactly the right things, but they're wrong, even so." It is also a reiteration of Ingmar Bergman's complaint about the dissonance between words and their meaning. Eva replies, "Those are very pretty words. . . . I mean, words that don't mean anything real. I was brought up with beautiful words. Mother is never furious or disappointed or unhappy; she is 'pained.' . . . If you say you long for me when I'm standing here in front of you, I begin to be suspicious." Viktor is as direct as Martin is with Karin—"You know quite well what I mean," he says—but unlike the staring, unsmiling Martin, he laughs and backs off.

Confuting her daughter's prediction that she would show up for dinner exploiting her mourning status, the vivacious Charlotte appears in a "divine" red dress, pearls, and bouffant hairdo, all in dramatic contrast to Eva's green dress, with its white Peter Pan collar, and her American Gothic hairdo. Charlotte's appearance also gives us a measure of her grief for Leonardo. (Just as Victor Sjöström's star quality and old-world charm make the narcissistic Isak Borg sympathetic, Ingrid Bergman's star quality lends something intangibly positive to Charlotte's narcissistic character.) Following dinner, Charlotte receives a telephone call from Paul, her American agent, with whom, she says, she has worked for 30 years. (Paul is played by Gunnar Björnstrand, whom Bergman began directing 31 years earlier, in 1946, in *It Rains on Our Love*.) Her spirited conversation, which is in English, is partly the result of her relief at talking to someone with whom she feels comfortable. Paul offers her an exorbitant fee to play a concert. Even though it is scheduled during a period of time that she had set aside for herself, the more than financially secure Charlotte accepts.

When they retire to the living room, Viktor radiates pleasure because things are going so smoothly between Eva and her mother. Eva, who has been diligently studying the piano to please her mother, is asked to play. As Charlotte listens to Eva's (Käbi Laretei's) rendition of Chopin's Prelude No. 2 in A Minor, her facial expressions shift from aesthetic pain to an almost tearful (maybe embarrassed) smile of motherly pride (see fig. 44). When she has finished, Eva's fingers dart to her mouth as if she had been caught stealing. Then, recognizing her mother's obvious disapproval of her interpretation of the work, she tries to hide her hurt by requesting that the professional demonstrate how it should be done. Sensing Eva's pain, Viktor retreats helplessly to a chair by the window. Charlotte, who has pondered

Chopin's character in a way she never has her daughter's, describes her approach to the piece. In the process she sums up her own approach to life. This prelude must not be played sentimentally or mawkishly like an old woman, she says, as if she were lecturing a master class; the evident pain must never show and the music may even sound ugly—that is, until the end, when Chopin's "proud, sarcastic, passionate, tormented, furious, and very manly" spirit emerges triumphant. She demonstrates, playing with an elegant stoicism. For a while Eva, sitting beside her on the piano bench, watches Charlotte's fingering, but then she raises her eyes to study her mother's impassive face. Eva's pouty, brooding expression cannot hide her kaleidoscope of reactions, among which are admiration, longing for love, and hatred. One might say that much of Bergman's art is defined by the juxtaposition of these two women's faces with the counterpointing music. When Charlotte finishes and takes up her coffee cup, the scene ends. We view the trio from a distance and through an arch. The sense of isolation is overpowering, and all is silent, except for the rattle of Charlotte's cup in her saucer.

The next day Charlotte comes upon Eva sitting in the warmly decorated and lit upstairs nursery. Charlotte is surprised to learn that the room has remained unaltered ever since Erik, Eva and Viktor's four-

Autumn Sonata. AB Svensk Filmindustri

year-old son, drowned. As we shall learn, Erik was the second child Eva has lost, and just as Eva and Elis (*The Passion of Anna*) were devastated by the death of their child, so have been Eva and Viktor by Erik's death. Eva entreats her mother to sit and listen to how she has reacted. First of all, she says, her mother must recognize that "the reality we perceive with our blunt senses" is merely one of "countless realities." "Sometimes," she continues, "just as I'm falling asleep, I can feel [Erik] breathing against my face and touching me with his hand." Her statement calls up not only what we learn were Leonardo's dying words to Charlotte—"This time next year I'll be gone, but I'll always be with you just the same. I'll always think of you"—but Bergman's story of once feeling his deceased mother sitting beside him. (In *Autumn Sonata* this idea of coexisting worlds will play into Bergman's invocation of the past through flashbacks in such a way that the past seems almost to coexist with the present.) Eva concludes by echoing Bergman's position on God before he said he ceased believing in Him: God contains everything from great good to terrible destructiveness, and "man is God's image."

Charlotte, who had dismissed Leonardo's idea about life after death as "theatrical," is disturbed by what Eva has said to her, and that evening she is further distressed when Viktor and Eva show her slides—giant close-ups—of Erik. When she thinks Eva is upstairs tending to Lena—Eva is actually eavesdropping—Charlotte tells Viktor that she finds Eva's neurotic ideas appalling. Viktor responds by telling Charlotte about Eva confiding to him early on that she was "incapable of loving," and by describing how Erik's birth changed her. The child not only gave meaning to her life, his presence made her uncharacteristically indifferent to whether others approved or disapproved of what she did. And for almost four years the three of them were gloriously happy. As for himself, when Erik died he found that the previous grayness of his life returned intensified, and he stopped believing in God (according to the screenplay) because He let children suffer and die. It is evident to us that Eva has also compensated for the loss of her child by doing church work and mothering surrogate children—Lena, Viktor, and now her mother, who, she believes, has been weakened by Leonardo's death.

As Eva tucks the insomniac (as was Bergman's mother) Charlotte into bed that night, there is a moment of friction, but their professions of love for one another defuse it. However, viewers familiar with Bergman's films recognize their constant touching of each other's faces as his code for their ambivalent and superficial feelings. When at last she is alone, Charlotte again soliloquizes, changing her mind about buying Viktor and Eva a new car. She will give them her Mercedes and buy a new one for herself.

Possibly influenced by Eva's account of feeling Erik's touch, Charlotte "dreams" that a female hand gently grasps her own. She responds, but when the hand desperately caresses her face Charlotte screams and wakes up—somewhat as Maria flees the dead Karin's embrace in *Cries and Whispers*. She heads downstairs and on the way encounters Eva, whom she has awakened. Charlotte does not confide her dream, but she does tell Eva that she loves her. Ironically, this statement provokes from her daughter first a trickle and then a flood of pitiless, cathartic accusations, some based on Bergman's autobiography, and some fictional. And as Eva's petulant tone hardens and becomes unforgiving, we withdraw the loyalty to her that has been built up by our recognition of how sinned against she has been. We do not transfer our loyalty to Charlotte, however, but adopt a more impartial stance. In fact, without ignoring Charlotte's severe limitations as a mother, we allow her other qualities and feelings, those we have observed or now discover, to temper our previous condemnation. These include her artistry, her permed confidence, her endurance, her "love" for her husband and Leonardo, her pain, and her infantile needs.

Eva indicts her mother for having crippled her. The first charge is that when Charlotte left her loving husband Josef (Erland Josephson) for an eight-month affair, it fell to Eva to comfort him. As we study Charlotte's astonished, aged face and hear her husky but lilting voice exclaim, "Eva, you hate me!" we may recall Isak Borg hearing his daughter-in-law tell him that his son hates him. Meanwhile, Lena, the upstairs barometer of the emotional storm taking place below, cries out from a nightmare. This momentarily postpones the confrontation. Eva leaves to comfort her sister. At her bedside Bergman lingers on Eva's and Lena's grasped hands, calling up the image of the clutching, hungry hand in Charlotte's dream.

Downstairs again, and framed by flames from pudgy red candles, Eva reinforces her courage with wine. Soon tipsy, she hurls more charges, some of which are those that Jenny lodges against her parents and grandmother in *Face to Face,* and some of which echo Bergman's complaint against his mother that her words and tone were not always in synchronization. Eva complains that her mother's words belied her actual feelings. Although Charlotte said she loved her daughter, for example, she repeatedly abandoned Eva to concertize. In a flashback we see Charlotte, from a distance and through a prosceniumlike door, sitting at a piano that separates her from her adoring child Eva (Linn Ullmann), who is sitting like a puppy on the floor. (The long shots employed for these "memory" scenes contrast with the film's dominant mode, which is medium and extreme close-ups.) Then, says Eva, continuing her accusations, when Charlotte did decide to put her career aside to stay home, things became worse. Guilty at having neglected her daughter, Charlotte devoted her ferocious and now frustrated energies to reshaping her 14-year-old, who already felt ugly: "There wasn't a shred of the real me that could be loved or even accepted. . . . I became more and more . . . annihilated. I said what you wanted me to say, I made your gestures." A shot of Viktor shows him standing near the camera—the present—eavesdropping on the two women, who are busy in the near distance excavating the past. Eva, in a cry for understanding uttered in a voice that increasingly approximates Lena's, desperately tells Charlotte, "I didn't realize I hated you because I was quite convinced we loved each other and that you knew best. So I couldn't hate you, and the hatred turned into an insane fear." Eva then indicts her mother for coercing her to abort her baby when she was 18 years old and had fallen in love. Charlotte's reason had been that she regarded the boy as a "nitwit." Charlotte responds to the charges by pointing out that Eva is damning her for both taking an interest and not taking an interest in her daughter. At that moment, apparently struck by the hopelessness of the situation, we see Viktor withdraw.

Eva, the weak-willed child grown strong from misfortune and festered memories, sums up for the accused and we the jury. She admits she hates her mother, whom she sees as an "emotionally crippled" escapist who hates both her and Lena. Her hair literally down, and standing close behind and looking over Charlotte's shoulder, Eva poignantly and brutally charges, "I was little and malleable and loving. You bound me, you wanted my love, just as you want everyone else to love you. . . . People like you . . . are a menace. You should be locked away and rendered harmless." Charlotte absorbs the blow, covering her face with both hands. When she removes them, her magnificent face is stripped of pride and hope. Eva asks a final, violent question: Must a daughter pay for the mother's disappointments and unhappiness? "Mama, is my grief your secret pleasure?"[34] Eva's charges have somehow awakened Lena, who, babbling but unheard, rolls herself out of bed.

It is 5:20 A.M. Charlotte is downstairs lying on the floor to ease her back pain,[35] and probably for the first time in her life she relinquishes her defensiveness to present a "horrible picture" of herself. She articulates Bergman's belief in the hereditary cycle of neuroses. Because her parents never touched her "with caresses *or* punishments," she was "completely ignorant of . . . tenderness, contact, intimacy, warmth." Only through music was she ever able to show her feelings. Thus, she became a frightened child. "I've never grown up. My face and body age, I acquire memories [she cannot, however, remember the faces of her mother, her daughters, or Leonardo] and experiences, but inside the shell I'm, as it were, unborn." She admits to not only having been afraid of Eva's emotional demands but to wanting Eva to recognize that she, Charlotte, felt like a helpless child. (Earlier, Eva also repeated the now familiar idea of Bergman's that "grown-ups are still children who have to live disguised as grown-ups.")

Lena has crawled out of her room and over to the hall bannister. She is listening as Eva relates how one Easter when the family was together, Lena, who was not so ill then, fell in love with Leonardo, who had secretly kissed her. On Good Friday Leonardo played all of Bach's suites for unaccompanied cello. Again there is a flashback in long shot. Leonardo is playing the fourth suite, and its mesmerizing effect on everyone in the room is apparent. Lena, all traces of her illness gone, sits enraptured, her face made radiant by a warm, haloing sunset and candlelight. Bach, Bergman has said, "called this state his joy, a joy in God. . . . Bach's piety heals the torment of our faithlessness" (*ML,* 43, 281). The next day, motivated by jealousy, Charlotte left four days earlier than she had planned. Before departing, however, she suggested to Leonardo, who she knew could not resist following her, that he stay on a few days because he was doing Lena so much good. Leonardo, of course, departed with Charlotte. That night—it was Easter night—the Christ-like Lena experienced a kind of death as her illness returned worse than ever. The flashback over, Eva informs her mother that she holds her mother responsible for Lena's illness and for deserting them both. Eyes furrowed with a hatred that Ullmann's characters have not shown since *Persona* and *The Passion of Anna,* Eva concludes with words similar to those of Isak Borg's judge: "There can be no forgiveness." Charlotte challenges Eva's assertion that she is "entirely" to blame for Lena's condition, but Eva demands that her mother recognize her guilt. In a merciless close-up Charlotte, her reddened eyes pleading for mercy, asks, "Eva, darling, won't you forgive me for all the wrong I've done? I'll try to mend my ways. You must teach me . . . help me. I can't go on any longer, *your hatred is so terrible*. I haven't realized I've been selfish and childish. Can't you put your arms around me? At least touch me! Help me!" As mother and daughter look into each other's eyes—Eva's hate-filled stare is unwavering—the story turns to the eavesdropping Lena, who is thrashing about on the balcony. Overcome with compassion, she cries out in her babyish voice to a mother who, symbolically, has never heard her. Now Lena's words are intelligible: "Mama. Come! Mama. Come."

A score of short scenes that juxtapose Charlotte and Eva follow. The next shot takes place on the following day. After the searing night encounter we just witnessed, Charlotte has fled the parsonage and is now aboard a train. With her in the compartment is her agent Paul, to whom she speaks in English. She tells him that she wishes Lena, who has gotten worse, were dead. "Do you think it's cruel of me to talk like that, Paul?" Paul, who knows that their friendship is based in part on his ability to let her vent her neurotic energy and to make no emotional demands on her, never responds verbally to her rhetorical questions or monologues.[36]

An abrupt cut finds Eva sitting on the wall around the lush green graveyard where Erik is buried. To view her, we have to look past the gravestone on which are carved his name and a crucifix. Eva muses rather self-satisfiedly that she so scared Charlotte that she may never see her mother again. As for her own meaningless life, though she wants to stop feeling, she is afraid to commit suicide. She will therefore carry on with her duties, hoping that God will someday use her and thus free her from her self-absorption.

The narrative cuts back to the train. It is sunset, and Charlotte is looking out of the window at the lit-up houses that line the tracks. In Swedish she laments, "I feel shut out. I'm always so homesick, though when I get home I realize it must be something else I long for."

The story returns to Eva walking among the gravestones. Suddenly, she feels Erik stroke her face. This convinces her that they will never leave one another. Is he also trying to tell her something else?

Charlotte, in the meantime, has come to sit beside Paul. Holding his hand and speaking English again, she tells him that she could not manage without him. They laugh. Then her melancholia returns. She turns back to the darkness outside, but the window offers only the reflection of her face.

At that very moment Eva arrives in front of the invitingly lit parsonage. Looking up at Lena's window, she surmises that Viktor must be informing Lena of Charlotte's departure.

The story cuts to Lena's bedroom, where, until near the end of the scene, the camera remains on Lena. Troubled and feeling powerless, Viktor had confusedly aired his doubts about Eva inviting Charlotte to visit them, causing Lena to cry out hysterically. Unable to understand her garbled utterances or control her thrashing, Viktor runs from the room, screaming for Eva. (Like Martin [*Through a Glass Darkly*], this husband is also ineffective in a psychological conflict between children and their parents.)

Bergman ends the story by once again using the suffering of an innocent young woman to bring about both a positive change in his protagonists and a more realistic understanding of God's nature. Charlotte, Eva, and Viktor, whose faith, we are told, depends on Eva's, are the beneficiaries of the suffering Lena's loving and forgiving spirit. As at the beginning of the film, Eva is once more seen in the distance writing at her desk. Though at first we do not see him, Viktor again speaks to us. As in a sonata, his first sentence about eavesdropping is exactly the same as that of his speech at the film's opening. He adds that Eva's guilt at "driving her mother away" has made it impossible for her to sleep. He appears in the shot just as Eva comes the length of the house and hands him the letter she has written to Charlotte. Pausing on her way upstairs to tend to Lena, she suggests he read it before he posts it. This time, however, so sure is she of what she is doing that she does not wait for his reaction. Viktor reads it aloud. It reveals a peace and confidence in Eva that has been born of facing the truth about herself, and of the necessity of forgiveness. (It also affects us because we know this is Bergman speaking to his parents.) "One must learn to live; I practice every day. . . . *I have realized that I wronged you.* I met you with demands instead of affection. I tormented you with an old soured hatred which is no longer real. I want to ask your forgiveness." Eva thus joins the saintly ranks of Lena, Frövik (*Winter Light*), and Agnes (*Cries and Whispers*). She will forgive and accept her emotionally crippled mother and, like Eve, the mother of mankind, embrace her (the film's initial title was "Mother and Daughter and Mother"). As usual in Bergman, blood bonds are unseverable. On the word *forgiveness*, Bergman cuts to a chin-to-eyebrow close-up of Eva, and just as in *Winter Light* Märta—who prays to be used to help another virtually hopeless narcissist—speaks her letter, so Eva speaks the rest of hers: "I don't know if you will read [this]. . . . But I hope *all the same* that my discovery will not be in vain. There is a kind of mercy . . . the enormous chance of looking after each other, of helping each other, of showing affection. . . . I will never let you go again or let you vanish out of my life. I'm going to persist! I won't give up, even if it should be too late." Bergman now throws us a tether of hope by ending his film with an epiphany that pushes us beyond our "blunt senses." An identical chin-to-eyebrow close-up of Charlotte's distraught, washed-out face, her eyes lowered as she reads the unseen letter, fills the screen. Eva's voice continues: "I don't think it is too late. It must not be too late." At these last words, Charlotte looks up directly at us, and for a long time stares, giving the words time to sink in. Then, the subtlest hint of a smile appears. Thus is the sonata completed. The hope this shot promises is buttressed by the next—the film's final—shot. It starts on Viktor's smiling face and then pans down to his hands folding the noisy pages—this is an important document—and slipping them into the envelope. (Contrast this with Tomas trying unsuccessfully to slip the noisy pages of Märta's letter into its envelope in *Winter Light*.) Again we should recall Bergman's own words: "What matters most of all in life is . . . [making] contact with another human. Otherwise you are dead. But if you take that first step toward communication . . . understanding . . . love, then . . . no matter how difficult the future may be . . . you are saved" (*Playboy*, 68).

FÅRÖ 1979 and KARIN'S FACE

Before proceeding to the last full-scale film that Bergman has written and directed, a word about two nonfictional films he made. Ten years after his first documentary about the island of Fårö where he lives, Bergman released an updated, more optimistic documentary tribute: *Fårö 1979*. Then in 1983 he filmed, in 8mm and with a special lens, a 14-minute tribute to his mother, *Karin's Face*. It is composed of still photographs he "had stolen" from the family album (which Bergman's hands are seen opening). Typically, the same image—his mother's aged face as it appeared on the passport issued her just a few months before she died—brackets the film. The montage of photographs that follows is accompanied by a piano or by complete silence. Bergman poetically traces Karin's growing up, her marrying, and, in the last years, her presence at large family gatherings. Bergman's camera longingly lingers, almost caresses, his mother's face. There are also a few quick shots that asymmetrically frame one of her or his father's eyes, undoubtedly meant to suggest disturbing aspects of their characters. The first photograph we glimpse after the opening passport photograph—which Bergman returns to repeatedly as a kind of homing note—is a group shot that contains little Ingmar, his brother, and his sister. The penultimate photograph, however, is of just Ingmar on his mother's lap (*ML*, 286–88).

FANNY AND ALEXANDER

Making films, if an exhilarating activity, is nevertheless an exhausting one. "When you get to be sixty-three, you have a leg that hurts, you have a bad stomach, you have an eye that doesn't function very well, you have a shoulder that hurts—you . . . become a little bit of a ruin. . . . These are signals, warnings to take it easy" (Marker and Marker, *SR*, 38). Also taking its toll was the sense that he had overmined his creative lode—his character and problems. When he "scrutinized [his] recent films," they struck him as lifeless. As a consequence he announced that though he would continue his work in the theater, his next film would be his last, a declaration that was strengthened when the film turned out to be one of his most joyful experiences, and one of his greatest successes. He quipped, "Better to stop now when everything is perfect." *Fanny and Alexander* (1982), the longest and most expensive film in Swedish history, was released in a movie version (written first) and then in a five-hour TV version, for which he wrote additional material. The film won Academy Awards for cinematography, art direction and set decoration, and costume design, as well as the award for Best Foreign Film of 1983.

The film contains virtually all the themes, character types, and narrative and visual devices we have been tracing: eavesdropping, death, humiliation, narcissism, reconciliation, imagination, a sacrificial victim, and miracles—one in which God intercedes to save Bergman's alter ego through one of His elderly agents. There is the character who

questions God's existence, a child who is involved in a love-hate relationship with his parents, a character who forswears the materialistic
life to get in closer touch with God's will, and a woman who discovers
herself as she rebels against her dominating husband.

   In this film Bergman polymerizes himself into a larger variety of
characters than usual: an elderly professional actress "who has lived a
lot and is very surprised, though without bitterness, to find that suddenly she is old"; an elderly Jew who, along with his nephews, has
influence with God; an ebullient uncle with an Olympian appetite for
women; a narcissistic bishop who must achieve total control of his
immediate world; a theater director who loves his actors and loves to
create order through art; a beautiful young mother of a "thousand
masks"; and a hostile, imaginative child. Bergman regards all of his
characters as children: "Grown-up children and very old children,
wise children and cruel children—but they're all of them children"
(Marker and Marker 1983, 8). Having reached a point in life where he
"can see wider and understand more" (Kakutani, 26), the Bergman of

Fanny and Alexander. Svenska Filminstitutet

Fanny and Alexander evidences a warmer compassion and more openly gives life's pleasures their due. As will be his tendency in his last films, he offers a more sweet than bitter picture of childhood, family, and life, but without backing away from felt truths: his young alter ego is still closer to his grandmother than to his beautiful, self-centered, and sometimes formal mother. Finally, just as Shakespeare gives free rein to his imagination in his farewell drama, *The Tempest,* so does Bergman in his.

Fanny and Alexander opens with the camera panning down past the inscription, "Ei Blot Til Lyst" (Not Only For Pleasure), above the proscenium of the cardboard theater of Bergman's young alter ego. When the camera reaches the candle-footlights, the curtain and the rear flat rise magically—Alex does not operate them—to reveal ten-year-old Alexander Ekdahl (Bertil Guve) dreamily contemplating his cutout characters and scenery (see fig. 45). (Later, the Ekdahls' real theater will be introduced with precisely the same camera, curtain, and flat movements.)[37] Compelling us to recall the increased number of shots through prosceniumlike doorways in Bergman's recent films, this theatrical framing prepares us as well for the countless number of such shots in this film. It also announces that what follows will be transformed by imagination and art, viewed through the proscenium of the memory of the puppeteer Bergman. As for young Guve, Bergman elicits a subtly expressive performance from this 12-year-old. Alex is as hypersensitive as young Ingmar—"I was a worm"—and as Johan, Bergman's fragile alter-ego in *The Silence,* but Alex is spunkier and far more appealing than either. Like those two, he keeps his thoughts and feelings hidden behind a guarded expression, but his deep brown, penetrating eyes—contrast the effect of Fanny's light blue eyes—stand out against his pale complexion like glistening, dark jewels to capture our attention and symbolize his role as observer.[38] Alex is also as reserved as his predecessors—that is, until he is pressured into responding. Then, in fact, the drama is created by his keen intelligence and his surprisingly direct and shrewdly slippery use of language to cope with those who tyrannize, humiliate, or disappoint him.

This sparely plotted, episodic film—there are five major sequences—conveys a considerable amount of meaning through the textures and lighting of its settings. Nykvist's expressive images are never heavily chiaroscuro. Soft light and shadows sculpt faces, but the stress is on the textures of flesh. In the opening sequence, to energize and loosen up the stagelike, symmetrical compositions, the camera moves or the lens zooms to follow and interweave the characters' paths. The decor of each sequence is different and contrasting. The first major sequence, for example, takes place in the apartment of Alex's grandmother Helena (Gunn Wållgren), which is decorated in red velvet and with old paintings. The second takes place in his parents' apartment, which is decorated with contemporary paintings and paler colors; even the color of the costumes is less intense. In contrast to the first sequence, this sequence's camera movement is more subdued, thus slowing the rhythm of the action.[39]

Bergman also relies heavily on symbols—Jesus and Ishmael are two obvious examples—and foreshadowing. An example of the latter is the Christmas pageant staged by Alexander's father, the theater director Oscar Ekdahl (Allan Edwall). In it Jesus is saved from Herod through the intervention of an angel (played by Oscar's wife Emilie [Ewa Fröling]), thus foreshadowing the miraculous deliverance of Alex (also in the pageant) and his eight-year-old sister Fanny (Pernilla Allwin) from the malignant Bishop Edvard Vergerus (Jan Malmsjö). (The bishop and his family are in attendance at the pageant.)

The visuals and sound effects are critical in realizing and dramatizing the film's contrasting philosophies of life: the repressed world of Bishop Vergerus is as austere, gray, and cold as that of the colorfully extroverted Ekdahls is ripe, tolerant, and warm. Bergman begins with the Ekdahls. They and their apartments are sanctuaries for love, pleasure, and imagination in a cold and threatening world, which is symbolized by the icy river churning deafeningly through the city and by the cold wind that quietly wails through the children's bedroom. This contrast is first delineated by Oscar, who tells his troupe—his family—of actors that he loves working with them in creating little, orderly worlds that provide audiences with either an escape from harsh reality or an elucidating reflection of it. At first we are tempted to smile and turn away from the stumbling, distracted speech of this exhausted, melancholy man. But we do not because we realize that he also speaks for Bergman, who, like Shakespeare's Prospero, is summing up what is important in life, and because Oscar-Bergman senses that soon his revels will be ended. At the film's conclusion Oscar's brother, Gustav Adolf Ekdahl (Jarl Kulle), will make a parallel speech, citing the inescapable evil that prowls "the world like a mad dog."

The Ekdahls are a sensual lot, their world as full-bodied as its corseted women. With the notable exception of Oscar, the brothers are oversexed (like their deceased father), a condition that partly accounts for the failure in life of the undisciplined ne'er-do-well Prof. Carl Ekdahl (Börje Ahlstedt),[40] but that adds to the irresistible charm of the generous, philandering restaurateur Gustav. The huge, tastefully overstuffed apartment of Alex's grandmother, Helena, seems like a nest for pleasure, especially during the film's opening and closing scenes.

Let me return for a moment to the film's opening scene, to the lonely Alex as he abandons his little theater to wander through first his parents' apartment and then his grandmother's, calling out for their absent occupants. In his grandmother's bedroom he leaps joyously onto her bed and covers himself with her blankets, an image that definitively conveys his love for her. Then, in another room, he sits under a large table and, as if in a trance—the tinkling of a music box reinforcing the gossamer mood—acts out the child Bergman's experience of seeing his grandmother's marble statue of Venus move. This is followed by a shot of his long, shapely fingers pressing against the glaze of ice on the window and melting an iris-shaped peephole. What he sees outside is familiar to us from *The Silence* and *The Serpent's Egg*: passing an almost mocking cluster of bright flowers in the snowy square is a horse-drawn wagon piled high with the possessions of an uprooted family. This image contrasts with the Christmas scene that will follow and foreshadows Fanny and Alexander's experience.

The narrative proper begins in Helena's apartment on Christmas Eve 1907, some days after this last scene. The Christmas trees laden with Swedish flags and decorations, the golden light from hundreds of candles, and the long table and sideboards spread to cornucopian redundancy with holiday food and drink make us long to enter the image. This scene of cross-generational affection and high spirits reaches its climax when family, friends, and servants link hands in a singing chain—led by septuagenarian Helena—to wind through the maze of halls and rooms. These images of the extended family joyously celebrating, feasting on, life establish the heart of the film. Pauline Kael captures the distinctive quality of Bergman's direction here: "The pacing . . . is relaxed, assured—[the events in this scene] almost seem to be happening in real time, yet Bergman sustains a tone of wonder and expectancy. His off-hand technique is masterly—from time to time the images seem ceremonial, like prized photographs of family occasions."

After the guests have left and the families have returned to their apartments—it is now three o'clock Christmas morning—materfamilias Helena sits on her sofa and airs her worries about aging and about her family to her sometime lover, the elderly Jewish merchant and money-lender Isak Jacobi (Erland Josephson).[41] Like the other Ekdahls, Helena will not deny her sexuality; she began an affair with the pious Isak when her husband was alive, and he remains her closest friend. A generous man, he lies to her about having loaned money to her ne'er-do-well son Carl. She tries to savor her melancholy, but tears refuse to come on cue. Typically Bergmanesque, Isak fights sleep as she launches into what he calls one of her "soliloquies." Giving the film's most natural and unforgettable performance, the 70-year-old Gunn Wållgren (who—we are reminded of Ingrid Bergman—knew that she was dying of cancer) makes the life-loving, weary matriarch of the Ekdahls the most endearing and poignant elderly character to appear in a Bergman film since Victor Sjöström's Isak Borg. A proud woman, she insists on her authority while, in most cases, tactfully attending to her family's best interests. She is most poignant later when, confronted with countless photographs that await mounting in her black picture album, she senses the futility of the task. At that moment our awareness of time is underscored by the sound of a clock's pendulum.

Except for Emilie and the exhausted Oscar, whom we see kiss only once—a quick but affectionate peck after the curtain has descended on the Christmas pageant—the night air is charged with sex. At bedtime, while Helena and Isak are remembering aloud how their affair began, Alex is engaging in an explosive and sexually stimulating pillow fight with his younger kin and a bout of tickling with the family's lame, voluptuous, adolescent nursemaid, Maj (Pernilla Wållgren). Breaking this up, Gustav's wife Alma (Mona Malm) giddily notes to a bubbly Emilie that her little son "kisses like a real man." When the children are left alone, Alex frightens them with ghost stories illustrated with slides projected on the wall from his new projector.[42] He is then visited by Maj, who kisses him repeatedly on the ear and reassures him that he is still her sweetheart. But she angers him by telling him he cannot visit and sleep beside her this night. Back in her room she is visited by Gustav, who feeds her oysters, promises her a coffee shop, and then has her bounce on his "wooden leg"—until the bed collapses. When he returns to his own bedroom, saddened by having been gently mocked by Maj, Gustav's indefatigable sexual appetite is whetted by the sight of his stately, robust wife. Perky and forbearing, Alma tolerates her husband's mistresses to preserve her marriage and herself. Dutifully, she props herself against the bed to satisfy his badgering—but enjoyable—attentions. (Later she expresses her jealousy of Maj by unexpectedly "boxing" her ear.) Outside their door their daughter Petra (Maria Granlund), like some other young females in Bergman's films, registers displeasure at her father's behavior and her parents' sexuality. Meanwhile, the middle-aged Carl, who in an earlier scene had won the children's affection as well as the audience's by producing a flame-extinguishing fart, is at home a few floors below acting out a Bergman love-hate scene with his long-suffering, mothering German wife, Lydia (Christina Schollin). His angst is heightened by thoughts of death and his awareness of his failed life. (The film's first sour note was struck earlier when Carl raged at his wife for interfering with his and his chums' drunken singing.)

This Christmas sequence concludes with the Ekdahls joining a picturesque torchlight procession of jingling sleighs and laughing pedestrians heading through the early morning darkness to the cathedral. Not only is it rare in a Bergman film to see more than just a few people on the streets—and then, as in *The Silence, Shame,* or *The Serpent's Egg,* it is to underscore a bleak, herdlike ambience—it is rare to see so much joyous activity. The final image of this sequence is of the bundled-up Alex's contented face as the horse-drawn sleigh he sits in joins the procession.

When the story resumes, Alex's secure world is disrupted. Alex is engrossed in a rehearsal of Shakespeare's *Hamlet* and watching his inept father play the ghost of old Hamlet; as he bids young Hamlet to exact revenge on his mother's (Emilie plays Gertrude) new husband, Oscar suffers a stroke. Alex, who is sitting beside Filip Landahl, an old actor (Gunnar Björnstrand), instinctively rises at his father's collapse—the camera zooms in—but sits back down and makes no effort to get involved in the frightening experience. A handful of actors ignominiously cart Oscar home like a sack of flour through the ankle-deep snow and biting cold. Maj has to fetch the reluctant Alex. Later, he and Fanny are playing checkers in a room in which the window is made to seem a crucifix; when they are summoned to their dying father's bedroom, the terrified and revolted boy holds back, buries his head in his grandmother's lap, and even tries to escape under his father's bed. Like the dying Leonardo (*Autumn Sonata*), who told Charlotte that he would always be with her, Oscar tells Emilie, as usual dressed in red, that "nothing" will ever separate them. He next asks to see Fanny and then Alexander. When Alex finally takes his father's hand, the grotesque sounds arising from the expiring man's gaping mouth cause the boy to recoil against the far wall.

That night Alex and Fanny are awakened by terrifying screams. Unseen, they approach the parlor where Oscar is laid out. ("As a child, I had often stood in the dark dining room at home, peeping into the salon through the half-open sliding doors" [*ML,* 37].) The partially closed sliding doors frame the coffin like the curtains of a proscenium. Through it, Fanny and Alexander, standing in the dark, watch their actress mother pace back and forth, periodically emitting wrenching screams. We are aware of two things: the trauma being suffered by the two children, and the peculiarly forced quality of Emilie's terrifying bursts of grief. Framed as it is, it suggests a performance, a guilt-driven attempt to produce feelings for her husband that she has never had.[43]

At the funeral Alex expresses his anger at life by muttering all the obscenities that he knows, while his sister smiles approvingly at him. Afterwards, during the formal funeral dinner, Fanny and Alex suspiciously eye the officiating bishop, who comforts their attractive, pale, silent mother; Alex seems to sense that, like Herod, this bishop may threaten not only his access to his mother but every man-child. Later, the two transfixed and moist-eyed children discover Oscar's ghost (appropriately dressed in a white suit) sitting, picking at the keys of the harpsichord. He stares back at them sadly.

Returning home from school one beautiful spring day, Alex is summoned before his mother. With her is the handsome, suave Bishop Vergérus. Emilie permits the bishop, another Bergman narcissist for whom relating means making others an extension of himself, to reprimand the taciturn Alex for one of his flights of imagination: telling his schoolmates that his mother intends to sell him to a circus.[44] (Bergman has said that many of his own childhood punishments were the result of his inability to distinguish between "lies and truth" [Cavett].) One is not to use God's gift, this "force" of imagination, for lies, the bishop instructs Alex. In spite of the pipe-smoking bishop's smile and soothing rhetoric, he pats Alex roughly, squeezes his neck, and audibly hammers his finger against Alex's head, betraying the anger he feels at not being able to control the child. Then, Alex's worst fears are confirmed. Emilie joyfully, then tearfully, announces that she and the bishop are going to marry. Widowed, the bishop is a man in every way different from Oscar: younger, handsome, authoritative, ascetic. Alex's subtly hostile glances at his mother reveal how betrayed he feels. As they all kneel in prayer, Alex notes that his sad father, lit with a sympathetically ghostly sunlight, is watching from the adjoining room.

When Emilie takes the children to visit the bishop's palace, the Vergéruses' asceticism shocks by comparison to the Ekdahls' hedonism. (Even the bishop's cowed, pallid, rat-faced female servants contrast with their spirited, plump Ekdahl counterparts.) As do Henrik (*Smiles of a Summer Night*), Raval (*The Seventh Seal*), and Ester (*The Silence*), the Vergéruses hide their appetites and potential for violence behind a mask of asceticism. The bishop loves music, theater, simple but elegant clothes, and beautiful women; when we later learn that he is in debt, we are not surprised. During this initial visit by Emilie and the children, the lighting both disguises and reveals the Vergéruses' real character. The bishop and Emilie discuss their forthcoming marriage in a severe but elegantly simple room whose walls are bathed in a lovely, Vermeerian, salmon-pink light coming from a recessed window and two shoulder-high candles. In the close-ups, however, white walls presage the harsh reality.

Our perplexity about the nature of Emilie's grief over Oscar and her fascination with the urbane, pietistic bishop dissolves when we hear her response to the bishop's request that, when they marry and she moves into his household, she leave behind not only all of her possessions but all her friends, habits, and former ways of thought. They will live, he promises, in an "atmosphere of purity and simplicity." Emilie embraces the divestiture, explaining that she has long considered her life empty and has never felt anything—hurt or happiness—deeply. Bright, passionate, and latently strong-willed, she welcomes this opportunity to hone her soul and live a purer, more intense existence, and, one concludes, to be loved in a passionately unadorned manner. Though reluctant to ask her children to make sacrifices for her happiness, at the bishop's request she promises to try to convince them to leave their toys behind.

After the marriage ceremony at the Ekdahls' (Oscar is there), the rebellious Alex performs a (real or imaginary) crashing belly flop onto a table, and Helena expresses her misgivings as she watches the bishop parade his beautiful wife down the street to his palace. At the bishop's Emilie immediately finds herself in a struggle over the children's upbringing—she fights for control as if she loved them deeply—not only with the bishop but with his hard, shrewd mother, Blenda (Marianne Aminoff), and his hysterical sister, Henrietta (Kerstin Tidelius).[45] Throughout this sequence the children seem imprisoned in the palace, specifically in their room, which is lit by a cold, sunless winter light coming through barred windows. Alex's refusal to converse with his stepfather almost leads, in one instance, to the bishop—Uncle Edvard—depriving the lad of his teddy bear. Afterwards, Emilie scolds Alex for his hostility to them both, insisting that Alex is no Hamlet, she no Gertrude, and Uncle Edvard no Claudius.

We are given a respite from the dungeonlike mood of the bishop's residence. It is a year later, and a melancholic Helena, dressed in white, receives several visitors at her country house during a sun-saturated rainfall. Walls of windows illuminate the airy rooms, which are colorfully decorated with wicker furniture and gauzy curtains. Oscar, in his white linen suit, is the first visitor. His caress (as Bergman's camera does in *Karin's Face*) of his sleeping mother's face awakens her. After a bit, they speak about the theater. Helena tells him that she enjoyed being an actress, but that she preferred her pregnancies and motherhood. When he died, she admits, it "shattered reality" for her, but she accepted it. She adds, probably summing up Bergman's present outlook on life, "Oddly enough, it feels better that way. . . . I just don't care if nothing makes sense."

Next, a pregnant Emilie pays a secret visit. She confesses that her life with the tyrannical bishop is intolerable. Her comment that "I hate him so violently that I could . . ." indicates that she has at last experienced one "deep" emotion. She also informs Helena that the bishop has refused to divorce her and that she has confirmed that if she leaves him it will be regarded as desertion and the law will take away her children.

Meanwhile, hoping to ingratiate herself with the bishop, his maid Justina (Harriet Andersson) betrays Alex. Justina's stringy hair is pasted to her scalp, and her face and body are gaunt; wearing narrow, wire-rimmed glasses that sit askew on her nose, and picking at a self-induced stigmata, she informs the bishop of Alex's claim that the ghost of the bishop's last wife told Alex that when she and her two girls tried to escape from the room in which the bishop had locked them, they drowned. (The bishop's strong reaction can be read as either confirmation of the story or outrage at the tale and the teller.) An inquisition follows. (The lightning and thunder that accompany the bishop's insistence that he has truth and justice on his side take us back to the graduation ceremony in *Torment*.) Alex, supported by Fanny, denies the charge, but with pious brutality the bishop lashes the intractable lad into a sassy submission. We only hear the eleven resounding strokes of the rug-beater on Alex's naked buttocks and see their complex effect on the four attending females—Fanny, Justina, and the bishop's mother and sister. The bishop then has Alex locked in the dimly lit attic. (The whipping, the hand-kissing apology, and the incarceration combine punishments from Bergman's childhood.) When the bishop, exhibiting his warmest demeanor, turns with soft words to Alex's ally Fanny, she icily rejects his touch, thus squelching his feeling of victory over Alex. (Film audiences invariably applaud her spirited loyalty, which helps establish her as more than just Alex's more secure, less imaginative, and impressionable foil.) On her return home Emilie, divining the situation, wrestles the key from Henrietta and rushes to her bloodstained son; to the mournful strains of a cello, they embrace. Behind this Pietà is a huge, discarded cross bearing the carved image of the crucified Jesus.

Some days afterward Isak, in an upholstered throne affixed to the top of the flatbed of a horse-drawn wagon, loudly arrives—presumably at Helena's instigation—at the bishop's door. The dignified but cunningly obsequious moneylender allegedly has come to purchase a large wooden chest from the bishop, to whom Isak has been lending money. The hostile Henrietta reluctantly summons her brother, and when he retires to his study to examine the bill of sale, old Isak, revealing a set of skeleton keys, rushes upstairs and unlocks Alex and Fanny's room. They are there alone. He hurries them downstairs— Alex has his teddy bear—and hides them in the chest, first covering them with a small black cloth. When the bishop reenters, Isak raises the chest's lid for the suspicious man's inspection, and then closes it. A few moments later the bishop, still suspicious that Isak is trying to trick him, suddenly turns violent. Shrieking that Isak is a "Jewish swine," he knocks him to the floor and viciously shakes him by the lapels of his coat. Henrietta intervenes, and she and her brother dash upstairs to check on the children. Rising to his knees, the outraged and distraught Isak raises his clenched fists heavenward and screams (see fig. 46). To the sound of a cello, a blinding flash of white light fills the room. And Isak's demand for a miracle is answered. Upstairs, the bishop enters the children's room and sees them prone on the floor and Emilie standing nearby. He obeys her order not to touch them.

Fanny and Alexander. Svenska Filminstitutet

When he returns, the heavy chest is being loaded onto Isak's wagon. Before departing, Isak and Emilie exchange knowing smiles as Henrietta leads her away.

The dreary austerity of the palace is now replaced by the dusty, mysterious clutter of Isak's shop.[46] Living with him are his two orphaned nephews. The older is 20-year-old Aron Retzinsky (Mats Bergman, Ingmar's son).[47] Aron is a puppet maker, but he has the additional responsibility of acting as warder for his androgynous and dangerous 16-year-old brother, Ismael (Stina Ekblad). After midnight, dressed in Aron's ample nightshirt, Alex leaves his bed (and his teddy bear) to find a privy. He loses his way in the maze of antiques, uncanny curios, masks, and almost human-sized puppets. In a smoke-enhanced scene Oscar again visits his son. He bemoans his inability to help his family. This young Hamlet, Alex, dismisses his ineffectual father's ghost. (In the screenplay Bergman injects more autobiography. Alex also speaks of his shame at seeing his father pushed around by his wife and mother-in-law.) If his father is with God, asks Alex, why has he not persuaded God to kill the bishop? In fact, queries the young Antonius Block, has his father actually *seen* Him, and does He really care about anyone? Worried about his son's hatred, Oscar counsels Alex to "be gentle with people" and then disappears for good.

For the remainder of this sequence—it reminds us of *Autumn Sonata*'s ending—Bergman employs parallel cutting to present the events at the castle with those at Isak's. While Alex is talking to his father, the bishop and his pregnant wife, both unable to sleep, are sitting at the dining room table (reminiscent of *From the Life of the Marionettes*). She is drinking a cup of broth in which she has dissolved a few sleeping pills. Unaware of the pills, he asks for her cup, but she claims she hears the cry of his dying Aunt Elsa, a grotesquely obese woman whose feverish, sweaty, bleeding flesh and dementia seem to represent the perverse effect of the Vergéruses' sick and deformed, age-old philosophy. While he goes to check, she dissolves more pills in the broth. On his return, he drinks it. (This Gertrude turns the tables on Claudius.)

Meanwhile, at Isak's, Alex is suddenly frightened into tears by an animated puppet that claims to be God. After exposing the deception, Aron sets forth his uncle's belief that "ghosts, spirits . . . demons, angels, and devils" exist, and that "everything alive is God or God's thought, not only what is good but also the cruelest things." (Ismael will soon say to Alex: "The truth about the world is the truth about God.") Dissatisfied, Alex maintains his skepticism, insisting that if God does exist, He is "a shit and piss God and I'd like to kick him in the arse."[48] Aron accedes, explaining that his knowledge of magic has made it possible for him to do without the supernatural. He deals in the understandable; he leaves it to his audiences to provide the mystery. He then shows Alex a 4,000-year-old luminous mummy that breathes and turns its head.

Simultaneously, back at the castle Aunt Elsa turns her head toward the bedside kerosene lamp that the bishop lighted for her. In their bedroom the bishop, his pajamas buttoned to the neck, is contrasting himself with Emilie. He alludes to her once having told him that because she was "always changing masks" she did not know who she was. Poignantly, tragically—he is another Bergman character who *needs* to expose his real nature—he confesses his inability to ever change: "I have only one mask. But it is branded into my flesh. . . . I always thought people liked me. I saw myself as wise, broad-minded, and fair. I had no idea that anyone was capable of hating me." It is Alex's hatred he fears most. (Bergman: "There's a lot of me in the bishop, rather than in Alexander. . . . He's haunted by his own devils" [Cowie 1982, 339].) The drug takes effect: the bishop grows dizzy and blind. He sobs in desperation as he realizes the cause. Undermining the humanizing effect of his earlier, startlingly candid confession, and demonstrating the truth of his statement that he is incapable of change—identifying him as a typical Bergman character—he viciously threatens to punish Emilie if she does not help him. When he collapses on the bed, Emilie flees to the Ekdahls'.

Alex and Aron hear Ismael singing. Aron unlocks Ismael's door and introduces him to Alex. The brothers kiss (incest?) and then the seemingly gentle, androgynous Ismael—who is described in Genesis as "a wild man . . . [whose] hand will be against every man, and every man's hand against him"—sends Aron away. Perceiving Alex's desire to destroy the bishop, the clairvoyant Ismael also sees Aunt Elsa knock over the kerosene lamp, which sets her afire. Ismael, who represents himself as Alex's "guardian angel," slips Aron's nightshirt from the terrified but passive boy's shoulders, embraces him from behind, and persuades him that they are one person and that he will help Alex with his "evil thoughts," his hatred of the bishop. Bergman has said he keeps open the channel to his childhood: "I am very much aware of my own double self. The well-known one is very under control; everything is planned and very secure. The unknown one can be very unpleasant. I think this side is responsible for all the creative work; he is in touch with the child. He is not rational, he is impulsive and extremely emotional. Perhaps it is not even a 'he,' but a 'she'" (Kakutani). Alex is in the embrace of an awesome imaginative force. According to the bishop's earlier statement to Alex, the source of that imagination is God. Now, like a child burning holes with sunlight concentrated through a magnifying glass, this force is focused through the lens of Alex's hate. (Alex is the dreamy youth who soon will become the master of the magic lantern, which will project the large and intense products of his imagination and feelings.) Ismael pictures in words the bishop dreaming of praying at an altar before a crucifix (like Claudius) and crying out like Jesus, "My God, My God, why hast thou forsaken me?" Functioning as the amplifying conduit of Alex's searing malevolence, Alex-Ismael telekinetically sees and causes—we share their clairvoyance, which is shown twice—the bishop's aunt, her monstrous body now a blazing torch, to burst screaming from her room into the hall.

Suddenly we are jerked out of this terrible nightmare vision. It is later that morning, and we are home safe and sound at the Ekdahls' with Emilie and the children. The rather officious police (like tax in-

spectors) arrive to inform Emilie that Aunt Elsa entered the unconscious bishop's room and flung herself on him, setting him ablaze. A
shot of his charred body suffering indescribable agony is followed by
a shot of Alex eavesdropping on the conversation. The bishop's death,
they have concluded, was the dreadful result of a complex set of circumstances. Given the pattern of supernatural activity in this tale,
Bergman, besides providing Emilie with an experience that has made
her feel deeply for the first time in her life, seems once again to have
called upon an inscrutable and dangerous God to intervene on behalf
of one of his alter egos in order to save him from one of his/His devils.
However, Alex's guilt (to some degree oedipal) concerning his role in
the bishop's death lingers. One night shortly afterward, while casually
walking down the hall in his nightshirt, Alex is suddenly approached
from behind by an unmistakable presence. The sudden close-up of the
bishop's black-and-white priestly garb and a momentary freeze frame
(the only one in the film) of his gold crucifix unfailingly produce an
audible shudder from all audiences. The handsome bishop's "ghost"
knocks Alex to the floor and announces, "You can't escape me!" (Not
surprisingly, Bergman's deterministic philosophy of character carries
over into the next world: Oscar remains ineffectual, the bishop evil.)

Large feasts have marked every important Ekdahl family event—
Christmas, death, birth; they also frame the film. Another banquet
opens the film's final sequence (see fig. 47). Emilie's and Maj's newborn girls are being christened (the pageant involving Jesus' birth was
the first half of this frame). A tearfully happy and proud Gustav—he
has a new, albeit illegitimate daughter, for whom the family shows its
subversive tolerance[49]—circles the round table and shares his "simple
wisdom." He celebrates life's unending renewal (his and Emilie's new
daughters), and he justifies enjoying the world's pleasures with one's
loved ones while there is still time. He also praises the actors—kissing
Gunnar Björnstrand on the head—for giving people "supernatural
shudders and mundane amusements." His acknowledgment of the evil
always and everywhere afoot in the world hardly tarnishes the mood
of epic wish fulfillment.

Afterwards, Maj pleads with the Ekdahl women to coerce the be-
nevolently narcissistic "second-rate Napoleon," as Helena calls Gustav, to free her to live her own life in Stockholm. (Getting Gustav to
give her her freedom will be easy. He has taken an interest in the new
young nanny [Lena Olin].) Clearly, the women are in charge from
now on. Again dressed in red (her "passionate" color), Emilie, who
has decided to take charge of her theater company, persuades Helena

to return to the stage, a sign that even this elderly woman, who earlier lamented that dirt and horror were engulfing the world's happiness, is capable of growth. The film ends in the same vein it began in: Alex's interest in theater is the framing device. The final image is of Alex, he who has learned something of the complexity of life, and who may become a great stage director or filmmaker. His eyes closed, Alex rests his head in the lap of the one adult who nurtures his imagination, his beloved grandmother—at the film's start she offered to play with him—as she reads the introduction to August Strindberg's *A Dream Play*. What she reads applies to this film, which also has woven dark melodrama, fairy tale, religion, magic, and supernatural experience into an enchanting, sun-filled, and joyous "tapestry," as Bergman refers to this film: "Anything can happen; everything is possible and probable . . . on a slight groundwork of reality, imagination spins and weaves new patterns made up of memories, experiences, unfettered fancies, absurdities and improvisations." Though this is not included in the film, Strindberg continues, "One consciousness rules over . . . all, that of the dreamer; for him there are no secrets, no illogicalities, no scruples, no laws."[50]

Fanny and Alexander. Svenska Filminstitutet

AFTER THE REHEARSAL

When Bergman finished *Fanny and Alexander,* he reiterated that, because making pictures was getting harder and his health poorer, it would be his last feature film; he also said, "Naturally I'll go on making films for television . . . [because] a TV film isn't so difficult; it lasts about an hour, 50 minutes. That means a shooting time of two or three weeks, not . . . six months" (Marker and Marker, *SR,* 38). "And the crew isn't so big, and costs aren't so high" (Marker and Marker 1983, 5). The next film he directed after *Fanny and Alexander,* and his last, was the made-for-television *After the Rehearsal* (1984), "a kind of essay on what I think about the theater and the work I have done" (*Positif* 289). In it Erland Josephson once more plays the Bergman surrogate; he is the theater director Henrik Vogler (the surname, as by now the reader is well aware, of several of Bergman's artist-protagonists). This film again deals with an older man's attraction to a young woman, and with the ambivalence of a child—that same woman—toward a parent (her mother), and her complaint about being forced to play unwanted roles in life. But the main themes of this very personal film are, first, the supreme importance to Bergman of his art. His "one really great joy" is inspiring and directing actors and experiencing the magic that they and he can create. The second theme has to do with Bergman becoming reconciled to the mixed blessings of aging. Like old Mrs. Armfeldt (*Smiles of a Summer Night*), Henrik cannot avoid getting involved in inevitably messy and guilt-laden human relationships. Demands on his limited energy invade his life through the stage door or enter from the wings of his memory. Also like Mrs. Armfeldt, he has reconciled himself to his distance from people, and to his inability to spontaneously involve himself in life as others experience it. In this film he makes us lamentably aware of the exertion needed to be not only diplomatic but sociable. On the other hand, mellowing age has its advantages. He is more reconciled to life's psychological crimes and misdemeanors, more able to resist sexual urges—with their inevitable complications—and more patient. Although both of the characters with whom we see him interact drive him to momentary anger, his anger is short-lived, a brief trumpeting by the old elephant to scare off life's uncooperative disruption of his plans and the demands that people keep making on his limited energy. Although the compassion he shows is often a product of consummate acting, he is now more tolerant of and sympathetic toward others' suffering, even when he knows it, too, is partially acted. If generally calmer and more tactful than he used to be, when pressed he is still candid: "If I took off the mask and said what I feel, you would all turn on me in fury." More important, his values have matured: whereas once he would have approved of his actress aborting a child in order to save his production, he can now disapprove of sacrificing a life for mere art.

Overall, even though it does not take much to make him expatiate, we sense that Henrik is bored with repeating what he has said over the years, and with talking about things of little interest to anyone but himself. In fact, his inability to avoid getting fired up when he thinks about his art is inspiring, and at the end of the drama we smile when we learn that his paramount concern is that his instrument—his mind, feelings, and body—remain in working order.

Henrik has just finished a rehearsal of Strindberg's *A Dream Play,* the play Helena is reading aloud to the young Bergman surrogate at the end of *Fanny and Alexander.* On the theater's deserted, almost bare stage—the large, white puppet's head that represents God in *Fanny and Alexander* is viewed momentarily—Henrik awakens from a catnap, raises his head, and, in voice-over, soliloquizes about the pleasure of solitude after rehearsal. (This chamber piece with its solos and duets is musical as well as dreamlike.) His reverie is interrupted by 23-year-old Anna Egerman (Lena Olin), who plays the lead part in the play and is the daughter of his former mistress, the actress Rakel Egerman (Ingrid Thulin), and his friend Mikael Egerman. "Distance and boredom. Distance and anxiety . . . I want you [Anna] to go," Henrik thinks. It is clear, however, that he is not altogether unhappy that she has come, though he sees her pretext—a lost bracelet—for what it is. Indeed, Anna has returned to confront her elderly director with her infatuation for him and with her perception that he is attracted to her. The conversation, however, turns to Anna's hatred for her dead mother, whom Anna remembers as "false" and always sad. It was her mother's insincerity, she says, more than her alcoholism (from which she died) and violence that finally made her daughter hate her. We are reminded of Alexander's final encounter with his father's ghost as Henrik accuses Anna of lacking sympathy—the primary quality of the woman she plays in *A Dream Play.* She replies that only through hate has she been able to forget her mother completely. Henrik muses that with age he has come to believe that the living are like ghosts and that the dead are not dead: Anna's mother, therefore, is still stricken by her daughter's hate. If that is true, says Anna, with moist eyes, I am glad.

She then asks Henrik why he chose her, someone so young and inexperienced, to play the lead in this, his fifth production of *A Dream Play*. Aglow, Henrik describes his lifetime love affair with the actor's ability to create illusion, his own method of working with actors, and the acclaim he has received for making plays work by reshaping, even rewriting them. Twelve-year-old Henrik (Bertil Guve, who played Alexander) is seen sitting in the wings. In the process Henrik reassures Anna about her talent and provides her with an alternative approach to a scene with which she has been having difficulty. As Anna tries it out, suddenly moving into and then out of the role of Indra's daughter, we experience the magic of acting.

Anna says she is also troubled by the roles she finds herself expected to play outside the theater (like Elizabet Vogler), and she is reminded again of her mother, who seemed never to stop acting. Henrik warns Anna that offstage she also acts too much and thus "steals power" from her stage work. He then tries to get her to leave so he can finish his nap, but when she lingers, Henrik (the "Wolf") calls to "Red Riding Hood" (Anna is dressed completely in red) to sit beside him on the couch. A pain in his leg immediately leads to his noting that he is her father's age, but then he grows sentimentally retrospective and identifies the various plays in which the scattered pieces of furniture on the stage—old friends—have been used. Anna's claim that it was studying her argumentative parents' self-conscious gestures and inflections that in fact led her to the stage triggers another memory: Henrik recalls Rakel visiting him there on the stage one rainy day eleven years earlier. The memory materializes (Anna remains silent and motionless on the couch): tipsy, the 46-year-old Rakel, wearing a red dress under her raincoat, enters and asks Henrik (whose appearance does not change) to take her to his room to make love. Henrik's unspoken thoughts again express his aversion to involving himself in demanding relationships: "Distance. Indifference. Boredom. Fear. Powerlessness. Helpless rage. Distance." He is simply tired of having to deal with human beings, except as artists for his plays. Desire and professionalism are compounded, however, with a genuine concern for Rakel's pathetic condition, and even though at moments she infuriates him, he treats her with tender regard. The justice of Anna's description of her mother as always "performing" is immediately evident.

The ostensible reason for this once great actress's visit is to express her humiliation at having been given so small a role in his production of *A Dream Play*. Making only the slightest effort to hide his exasperation, Henrik reminds her that when he offered her the role a year earlier, she wept with gratitude at his not having forgotten her. He inquires if she is still living at home with Mikael and little Anna. (A 12-year-old [Nadja Palmstjerna-Weiss], also dressed in red, replaces the older Anna on the couch.) He learns that Rakel has been hospitalized for her alcoholism: "I have a white cubicle for my screams, my prayers, my vomit, and my fears." Rakel next complains that little Anna plays up to and sides with her father; then she asks for Henrik's reassurance that as an actress she was "the best." When he confirms it, she can only tearfully voice her plaguing awareness of her physical decay. (Thulin invokes *The Silence* with the line, "I stink like a rotten fish," and when she blows her nose in a dirty handkerchief, we recall her Märta's cold in *Winter Light*.) Then she proudly displays her firm breasts and her thighs—still "smooth as girl's"—and invites Henrik to her small apartment behind the theater. He demurs, lying that he has an appointment. Her self-disgust and terror at living become increasingly evident. She demands reassuring lies but responds angrily when Henrik patronizes her; being a Bergman character, she needs the truth. Mikael's lying, she claims, provoked the violence that led to her being forced into the hospital. While trying to calm her, Henrik, sounding like Anna, thinks, "Go to Hell where you belong! I never want to see you again. I've wiped you out; you don't exist!" Henrik continues his conversation with Rakel while the viewer hears his thoughts. This device, along with the insertion of actors who represent Henrik and Anna as children, and the background repeatedly and magically changing, call attention to the director's imagination controlling the film.

Rakel pleads to know why Henrik will not trust her with a large part. When he says that he dares not, she launches into lines by Dionysius from Euripides' *The Bacchae* (calling to mind Thulin's role in the earlier television film *The Ritual*). Like her daughter earlier, in an instant, through word, tone, and gesture, this "instrument" magically and completely transforms herself into the revengeful, commanding god, and then, in another instant, the righteous anger disappears and she is once more the pathetic but momentarily self-satisfied Rakel, casually lighting a cigarette.

Henrik is provoked into admitting his distaste for the messiness of life: he hates these emotional outbursts, and he has "no time for [people's] problems except as keys to the text or as impulses for the actors." His work must be disciplined, clean, controlled—an "operation." As she prepares to leave, however, he salves her hurt: "You are always in my thoughts." "Kindly said," she replies tearfully. He tells her to return to her apartment and he will come to her in an hour. She dances off, and he thinks, "Always the way: lies and reconciliations, guilty conscience, fear, and suppressed curses, and pity . . . always the way."

He returns to the couch and affectionately rubs little Anna's face, but when he reaches for her hand it is the older Anna's. At last she reveals the reason for her visit: the way "Uncle Henrik" looks at her has led her to think that he is flirting. Henrik's evasive directness is artful. Yes, he loves being beside her, loves her being bound to him professionally and emotionally, loves her beauty, her unique talent, and working with her. Then he lets his jealousy flare, belittling the young director, named Peter, with whom she is living. She brings his performance to a sudden halt by informing him that she is pregnant. He restrains his obvious anger—her pregnancy will show by opening night—and he stops short of encouraging her to abort after she has suggested it. After all, he says, it is only a play and this is a child.[51] She volunteers to quit the play, but he is emphatic about her staying; it was only having her in it that made him want to stage it once more. She, we now learn, is more ruthless than he: she has already aborted the child and has even ended her affair with Peter. Then why, asks Henrik, did she put him through all this? To make him show his feeling, she answers, kissing him on the lips. Saddened a little by her callousness, he takes her hands and pushes her gently away, adding, to her displeasure, that she is very like her mother. She informs him that she wanted the child but let herself be persuaded by Peter—the child was not his—to have the abortion because she wants to be in the play.

On her knees, Anna puts herself in Henrik's hands, but he explains that he has grown accustomed to living alone and that all he can give her, along with fatherly "concern and affection," is his professional experience. He is too old and too near the end to play a ridiculous role in her "play." He confesses that he has worried about how she regarded him physically and that he is also wary of her: "You are so like your mother. . . . I think you could be cruel. You lie to manipulate others. . . . You work me . . . to brighten your relationship with Peter." (Earlier, Rakel had said that Anna was like Henrik in precisely this way.) She tries to get him to touch her breast, but he sadly backs off from this "absurd situation." If only he were ten years younger, he muses, putting his arm around her shoulder. He walks her around the stage and conjures up the scenario of how their relationship would have developed and dissolved. It is a delightful passage that enlivens this heavy, static, often recondite drama, and the overhead shot that reveals the actors' blocking marks subtly makes the moment resonate with the countless scenes that have taken place on this spot. When he finishes, she says that she feels miserable. (We speculate that their conversation may also have softened her attitude toward her mother.) Suddenly, however, she recalls her radio rehearsal and starts to leave, stopping only to note the sound of church bells and to ask Henrik if he hears them. "I'm getting hard of hearing," he replies, "haven't you noticed?" Then, recognizing that he is sad, she adds, "I don't want you to be sad." "It's not your fault," he reassures her, and she departs.

At the very moment one is ready to indulge in the not unpleasant pain of responding to love refused and the disappointments of old age, Bergman has his sad, cunning old director—whose work is his raison d'être—end the film by remarking, "What worried me most just then was that I couldn't hear the bells."

This less than totally engaging film may strike even those interested in Bergman's personal and professional careers as too preoccupied with discussions of actors, directors, and their relationships, as self-indulgent to the point of presumptuousness. Why should one care about Henrik Vogler's thoughts and feelings simply because he represents Bergman? These viewers will also be impatient with the numerous passages in which Henrik's companions seem to be there primarily to feed him topics on which Bergman wants to descant. In addition, one would like to fathom these characters' true selves, but they don emotions so facilely that it is impossible to be certain of what they actually feel. As a result, one loses concern and grows to distrust them, enjoying the acting "turns" rather than caring deeply about the characters. One must hope that Bergman intended this reaction. The roles, however, are expertly acted, as one would expect. As the alcoholic, neurotic actress wallowing tearfully in her fear of aging and death, Bergman's old colleague Ingrid Thulin achieves a terrible, pathetic power. Lena Olin, who since has achieved international fame, uses her disarmingly and deceptively childlike face to soften the strong, ambitious, embittered Anna, who is less unsure about how to manipulate people than she is about her acting abilities. As Bergman's self-portrait, Erland Josephson is somewhat elephantine. The stress placed on his fatigue contributes greatly—if dangerously—to the dramas heaviness. His portrayal of the sage Henrik is low-key, patient, grandfatherly. His performance is more tender than taut, thus undercutting our association of his character with the more dangerous—and possibly more interesting—Bergman.

Since this film Bergman has continued directing for the stage and opera. "Movies are an obsession, [a necessity of nature . . . like hunger or thirst]; the theater, on the other hand, is an agreeable métier which one pursues with tranquil joy. You spend four or five hours a day rehearsing with actors, and if a scene doesn't come off, well, then it'll work tomorrow or next week. . . . Film is incredibly demanding; it requires a permanent mobilizing of all your strength" (Sorel, 1, 19). The absence of this pressure has surely contributed to the mellowness we increasingly feel in the screenplays—*The Best Intentions* and *Sunday's Children*—he subsequently has written for others to direct. And according to his colleagues, the mellowing is also noticeable in his behavior. He has begun, they say, to exhibit "a tolerance, open-mindedness and sheer pleasure they rarely if ever saw during the years he was creating films."[52]

THE BEST INTENTIONS

The Best Intentions (1992) "is about ten years of my parents' life—ten important, decisive years, from 1909, when they meet, to early summer of 1918, when this author was still inside his mother, preparing to emerge into life."[53] Produced by Swedish Television (to date the most costly film ever made in Sweden), Bergman's script was directed by the Academy Award–winning director Bille August (*Pelle the Conqueror* [1987]). Like *Fanny and Alexander,* the story has been released as both a series for television (consisting of four 90-minute programs) and a three-hour feature film. (The TV and film versions were shot simultaneously; some scenes were shot in two versions, and some were added to the film version for clarity and continuity.)

Set against his earlier statements about and filmic portraits of his parents, Erik and Karin, Bergman's portrait of them in *The Best Intentions* (where they are renamed Henrik and Anna[54]), is markedly rounder and more compassionate. Nevertheless, broadly applied are the brush strokes highlighting his parents' dark sides and, in spite of their periods of happiness, the inevitable tragedy of their match. The film opens, for example, with the handsome, blond Henrik Bergman (Samuel Fröler), a young man planning to enter the ministry, proudly informing his hated grandfather that he refuses to visit his dying grandmother, who wishes to beg his forgiveness for having abandoned him and his mother. (Later Henrik will learn that his grandfather was the actual culprit.) We immediately sense that we are in the presence of someone whose character has been fundamentally warped by the intensity and depth of his hate. Furthermore, both Henrik and his wife Anna (Pernilla August, who, like Fröler, closely resembles the character she plays) will be seen treating not only each other with revolting cruelty but, in one of the film's most affecting scenes, a talented, desperate, and helpless child, who surely is a fictional stand-in for Bergman. (Bergman's script alters a great many facts for dramatic purposes. For example, the families of second cousins Erik and Karin knew one another, Karin's father did not die until years after Ingmar's birth, and it wasn't until after Ingmar's birth that the queen heard Erik preach and offered him a post in Stockholm.)

The drama peaks early in a classic no-holds-barred Bergman confrontation between Henrik and Anna's strong-willed mother Karin Åkerblom (Ghita Nørby), who disapproves of Henrik marrying Anna. Henrik's being lower-class and formerly engaged to a waitress, Frida Strandberg (Lena Endre), forms part of Karin's resistance, but of far greater importance is her profound sense that he suffers from "deep and early wounds beyond healing or consolation" and her absolute certainty that the marriage will be a "disaster." This latter attitude, we discover later, is shared by Henrik's own doting, pudding-faced, and self-denigrating mother, Alma (Mona Malm). This conviction of Bergman's that it would have been better if these two—he calls them "fire and water"—had not been bound together threads the story and is stressed in the film's last shot. The final scene shows the married couple—they have a four-year-old son, Dag, and Anna is pregnant with Ingmar—reconciling after a violent break and long separation. The scene begins with Henrik following Anna, her mother, and little Dag into a park. When Karin and Dag wander off, leaving Anna sitting on a bench, Henrik approaches unseen and sits on a bench a short distance from her. When at last she senses his presence and turns, she is very happy he is there, but before reconciling, she insists on certain terms. Henrik gives in without a fight, and both are happy. But the last shot of the film shows Henrik on his bench, separated from Anna by a narrow gulf of grass.

At the start of the film and their relationship, the story follows the familiar romantic route. Candid conversations and lyric love scenes put us in the young couple's corner aligned against Anna's parents, who for several reasons, class prejudice included (which the spoiled Anna shares), oppose their relationship. We take heart when Henrik's fiancée Frida tells Anna that she gives up any claim to him, though her description of him increases our ambivalence. He is a person, she says, for whom things have never gone right "in his miserable life," but who is the best and kindest person she knows. He is someone who needs love "so that he does not have to hate himself so much," and only Anna can help him avoid "fall[ing] to pieces." The romantic pattern continues as Anna discovers that she has tuberculosis and goes to Switzerland for the cure; her mother subsequently takes her to Italy for the summer in the hopes that travel will help her forget Henrik; Anna's father, Johan (Max von Sydow), takes her side against his wife; and Karin overrules Johan's intervention (in an act of eavesdropping that calls to mind the unsealed envelope in *Persona*). Getting caught up in this pattern, in fact, causes us to misjudge the depth and complexity of Anna's mother's resistance, and to misread her hardness and determination as only narrow-minded willfulness. Not until Karin replies to Anna's charge that she will never forgive her mother for her interference—Henrik's misjudgment of his grandmother should ring in our ears—do audiences begin to reconsider their alliance: Karin very slowly asks, "Whom will you never forgive? . . . Is it me you'll never forgive? Or our friend? Or life perhaps? Or God? . . . My poor little girl."

Johan's sudden death causes Karin, who is with Anna in Venice, to confess her deception and to accede to the marriage. Anna hurries back to Sweden. The staging of her visit to Henrik's apartment alerts us to the fact that August is going to reference some of Bergman's films. The green walls of Henrik's apartment and his rolled-up mattress call to mind a similar scene in *The Touch*. In *The Best Intentions*, however, Henrik, unlike David—whom Karin finds has walked out on her—unexpectedly appears. Anna's gift to Henrik of a statuette of Mary also seems a reference to the symbolic statue of the Virgin that plays such an important role in *The Touch*.

The first signs of conflict between the couple come when Henrik, now a priest, takes Anna to inspect his new post in Forsboda, a northern wilderness town beginning to roil with conflict between the factory workers, who are struggling for higher wages and better working conditions, and the owners. When Anna and Henrik are shown around the old rectory, Anna hides her dismay at its dilapidated condition but shocks the officials by indicating that the renovations should also take her needs into consideration. Henrik silently simmers and refuses to look at her, let alone take her side. Almost immediately afterwards they quarrel about Henrik's wish to get married in his new parish instead of having the "impressive" wedding in Uppsala Cathedral that they have carefully planned. When Henrik charges Anna with being spoiled, she retaliates by upbraiding him for his lower-class habits, such as not cleaning his nails and smelling of sweat. Then, when she begs his forgiveness for what she has said, he swings at her. She screams that he is "insane." Calming at last, they agree to take what has just transpired as a caution.

After a beautiful wedding in Uppsala—there is, however, something portentous about one set of the vows being heard in voice-over—Anna gives in to Henrik's wish that they forgo their honeymoon to Italy to immediately begin work. And once situated in the harsh conditions of Forsboda, Anna, a trained nurse, is almost heroic in carrying out the duties of the minister's wife—visiting the poor and sick, and making her home an inviting center for their religious community. Soon she gives birth to Dag and accedes to Henrik's idea of sheltering in their home an exceptionally bright, neglected, and abused young boy, Petrus Farg (Elias Ringquist), whose talents she has encouraged. Partly because of pressure from Anna, however, Henrik stops the disgruntled workers from using the chapel any longer for their meetings.

When around Christmas Anna's brother Ernst (Björn Kjellman, who closely resembles the young Bergman) visits them, at first Anna claims that she is deliriously happy. But it soon becomes clear that she is hurt by Henrik's continued hostility to her mother, his jealousy, and his inability to let go and enjoy pleasure. The catalyst that brings her unhappiness to a boil is the offer from the Swedish queen to Henrik to become the court chaplain at the Royal Hospital in Stockholm, where a new parsonage will be built just for them. Because he feels his life's task is to tend to the poor, Henrik rejects the offer. Anna is furious that he does not ask for her opinion and depressed at having to continue at Forsboda.

Back home, Pastor Bergman has run-ins with the town's leading manufacturer, Nordenson (Lennart Hjulström), a strong-minded, lonely man who slanders Henrik's religious practices and inflated sense of power. This criticism combined with the rumor that the Bergmans are going to move to Stockholm causes people to ostracize them. Even those who believe that Henrik has rejected the queen's offer react negatively because they find it a foolish and condescending sacrifice to stay "in this wretched place." Learning this reaction of his parishioners only strengthens Henrik's resolve to stay. But the re- jected, fatigued, and newly pregnant Anna—who has also checked to see that the queen's offer still holds—is no longer willing to endure this life. It is little Petrus, who makes her feel guilty because she can- not love him, whom she strikes out at. She angrily tells Henrik, who tries to get her to be more charitable, that she is tired of being the boy's substitute mother; she wants him sent back to his folks. Petrus eavesdrops on their conversation, and the next day his desperation causes him to try to drown Dag. Henrik stops Petrus in time and mercilessly beats him; Anna watches with cold indifference and then turns her back on the bleeding, nearly unconscious boy lying in the snow.

One day Anna breaks into tears. They are not just for her guilt over Petrus's eviction but stem from her profound unhappiness with her life and the "traitorous" act she has planned. When Henrik finally forces her to voice what is bothering her, she tells him that she has written and gotten her mother's permission to return home with Dag, and she is leaving. This time, Henrik's shouting and blows do not shake her resolve. "I forbid you to go!" he screams. "You forbid noth- ing!" she spits back.

Henrik writes to Anna. She misses him but refuses to return. Two important scenes follow. After Managing Director Nordenson com- mits suicide, Henrik comes at last to understand the man's horrifying despair. Then he self-pityingly explains his own alienation to a woman who is interested in him: "I'm best living on the extreme edge of the world. . . . I have to live in privation. Only then can I possibly become a good priest. I am not created for larger contexts." Articu-

Scenes from a Marriage. AB Svensk Filmindustri

The Best Intentions

lating this vision seems to provide catharsis, because in the next scene Henrik is in Uppsala, with the intention of accepting the queen's offer and reconciling himself with his family and the "larger context," but the composition of the film's very last shot—Henrik and Anna on separate park benches—warns us against giving in to feelings of un-alloyed joy (see fig. 49).

SUNDAY'S CHILDREN

The Best Intentions ends with Ingmar, the Sunday's child, about to be born, a fact that brings this study full circle. So too does *Sunday's Children* (1992), the film directed by Bergman's 30-year-old son Daniel from his father's script. Practically a sequel to *The Best Intentions, Sunday's Children* dramatizes scenes that occur ten years after the former's final scene. The setting of *Sunday's Children* is Bergman's parents' summer home, which Pastor Bergman visited on weekends, and from where he biked to give sermons in local churches. We recall that on occasion he took little Ingmar—in the film he is called Pu (Henrik Linnros)—with him, and that it was during these trips that Ingmar felt closest to his father—played by Thommy Berggren in the film— that is, until one of his father's unexpected black moods exploded into violence.

EPILOGUE

As I end this book and look back on my 15-year journey through Bergman's life and films, I am reminded of the advice given by one of my teachers. After first suggesting that the graduation ceremony for Ph.D.s should consist of incinerating the graduate's dissertation and placing the ashes in a small vial that could be worn around his or her neck, he advised that anyone embarking on the long and exhaust-ing task of writing a dissertation should choose a worthy subject: by-pass writers whose work is of limited consequence and interest for a writer—he cited Shakespeare—who will richly reward the time and energy to be spent.

Bergman is just such a subject. Rarely has he committed the cardinal sin of being boring, and before he appeared on the scene, who would have thought it possible—or permissible—to so bluntly interrogate and mercilessly wrench confessions from characters in a movie? And what director of sound films has so expressively used actors' faces to dramatize stories? To say he is one of this century's most outstanding artists is only to give this Sunday's child his due: if you recall, a Sunday's child is said to be "capable of perceiving supernatural phenomena, of divining truth, and of stripping away the facades of lies and deceits that others encase themselves in."

NOTES AND REFERENCES

Preface

1. Edith Sorel, "Ingmar Bergman: 'I Confect Dreams and Anguish,'" *New York Times,* 22 January 1978, hereafter cited in the text.

2. During one period he was wary of the press because it portrayed him variously as a prima donna, a temperamental wild man, or a Svengali who used hypnosis to induce great performances from his actors—attributes gleaned, for the most part, from the way he behaved in his late twenties and early thirties when he manifested immaturity and insecurity about his abilities as a stage and film director in hysterical outbursts. He would meet these charges by pointing out that his achievements in both media could not have been produced by someone who was undisciplined, erratic, or threatening to his crew and fellow artists. By 1959 he was not only Sweden's best-known and most powerful filmmaker and the most influential force in Swedish theater—as he continues to be today even though he is retired from filmmaking—but an international celebrity. As a consequence, even his personal life came under the scrutiny of the international media. The English press swarmed after him, for example, when he and Käbi Laretei married and visited London.

He says he dreads interviews, even to the point of feeling nauseous beforehand. Having granted an interview, however, he is fastidious about showing up on time and is known to have sent a telegram to warn that he was going to be a few minutes late. He may start out nervous, but as the interview progresses he invariably relaxes and may, in fact, take control of it. Those interviewers who employ a scorched-earth approach soon find their own earth scorched, and those who try to wring out of him interpretations of his films or want him to confirm the rightness of their own can expect to be scorned. In 1972, for example, he told Charles Samuels, "I'm not interested in what *you* think! If you like, ask me questions! But I'm not interested in hearing what you think!" Later in this interview Bergman admitted, "I can say the most astonishing things because I am perfect at giving interviews." Stuart Kaminsky, ed., *Ingmar Bergman: Essays in Criticism* (New York: Oxford University Press, 1975), 104, hereafter cited in the text.

More subtly, Bergman may exert control by becoming acquiescent. One interviewer found that when Bergman is wary of a question, "his eyes glaze over and he will halt in the middle of a sentence for an extraordinary length of time. One's instinct is to help him out with the words, and that, I began

to suspect, was precisely what he was waiting for, for then he would agree
benignly to whatever one said. One needed to summon up every reserve of
sadism within oneself to sit out the pauses in relative silence." Derek Prouse,
"Ingmar Bergman: The Censor's Problem-Genius," *Sunday Times* (London),
15 March 1964, 30, hereafter cited in the text.

    3. Bernard Weinraub, "Bergman in Exile," *New York Times,* 17 October
1976, 15; this series of articles is hereafter cited in the text as Weinraub (and
date).

    4. Vilgot Sjöman, *L 136; Diary with Ingmar Bergman,* trans. Alan Blair
(Ann Arbor, Mich.: Karoma, 1978), 18, hereafter cited in the text.

    5. Harry Geduld, *Film Makers on Film Making* (Bloomington: Indiana
University Press, 1967), 184–86, hereafter cited in the text.

    6. Author's conversation with Vilgot Sjöman, February 1979.

    7. "The Dick Cavett Show," ABC, 14 May 1971, hereafter cited in the
text as Cavett.

    8. Cited in Birgitta Steene, *Ingmar Bergman: A Guide to References and
Resources* (Boston: G. K. Hall, 1987), 213, no. 173.

    9. Jan Aghed, "Conversations avec Ingmar Bergman," *Positif* (Paris)
121 (November 1970): 41–46.

    10. Quoted in Birgitta Steene, *Focus on "The Seventh Seal"* (Englewood
Cliffs, N.J.: Prentice-Hall, 1972), 122, hereafter cited in the text.

    11. Robin Wood, *Ingmar Bergman* (New York: Praeger, 1969), 61, here-
after cited in the text.

    12. If there are factual errors in what I record, they are probably due to
the fact that when I began this project many years ago I had no access to a
moviola and films were not yet available on videotape. I repeatedly ran the
scenes I was analyzing through a movie projector, simultaneously describing
into an audiotape recorder all the elements I saw and heard. Afterwards, I
transcribed this information.

Chapter 1

    1. Ingmar Bergman, *The Magic Lantern,* trans. Joan Tate (London:
Hamish Hamilton, 1988), 1, 22, 289–90; hereafter cited in the text as *ML.*

    2. Marilyn Johns Blackwell, ed., *Structures of Influence: A Comparative
Approach to August Strindberg* (Chapel Hill: University of North Carolina
Press, 1981), 51, hereafter cited in the text.

    3. Peter Cowie, *Ingmar Bergman: A Critical Biography* (New York:
Charles Scribner's Sons, 1982), 239, hereafter cited in the text.

    4. Frank Gado, *The Passion of Ingmar Bergman* (Durham, N.C.: Duke
University Press, 1986), 13, hereafter cited in the text.

    5. Richard Meryman, "I Live at the Edge of a Very Strange Country,"
Life, 15 October 1971, 66, hereafter cited in the text.

    6. Bergman says about his own childhood, "I was born hysterical. . . .

[I] was haunted by gloomy visions of the future and . . . afflicted by violent attacks of weeping. . . . [I] was afraid of my father, my mother, my elder brother—everything. . . . [I] was afraid of all animals. I was a very scared little child." At a production of *Red Riding Hood,* he "allegedly sobbed so loud at the girl's fate that he had to be removed from the premises," and when, at six, he saw the silent, tinted film of *Black Beauty,* he became so upset when the horses were trapped in the burning barn—a situation he would reuse in *The Passion of Anna* (1969)—that he was in bed for a week. John Simon, *Ingmar Bergman Directs* (New York: Harcourt Brace Jovanovich, 1972), 37, hereafter cited in the text; Oscar Hedlund, "Ingmar Bergman, The Listener," *Saturday Review,* 29 February 1964, 48; Kaminsky, 100; Cavett; Vernon Young, *Cinema Borealis: Ingmar Bergman and the Swedish Ethos* (New York: Avon, 1972), 10, hereafter cited in the text; Edwin Newman, "My Need to Express Myself in a Film," *Film Comment* 4 (Fall-Winter 1967): 60, hereafter cited in the text.

7. Ann-Sofi Lejefors, "Bergman in Close-up," *Sweden Now* 1 (1983), 39, hereafter cited in the text.

8. Ingmar Bergman, *Bergman on Bergman,* ed. Stig Björkman, Torsten Manns, and Jonas Sima, trans. Paul Britten Austin (New York: Simon and Schuster, 1973), 173–74, hereafter cited in the text as *BB.*

9. Ingmar Bergman, "My Three Most Powerfully Effective Commandments," *Film Comment* 6 (Summer 1970): 9–12, hereafter cited in the text as "Commandments." Bergman's parents bear a remarkable resemblance to the picture many clinicians paint of the parents of narcissistic patients: "chronically cold" and covertly but intensely aggressive. Usually the mother is someone who appears to perform "well on the surface in a superficially well-organized home, but with a degree of callousness, indifference, and non-verbalized, spiteful aggression." The father is likely to be "self-absorbed" and to rebuff his "son's attempt to be close to him," thereby depriving the child of the needed merger of his own self-concept with his idealized image of his father. The absence of this merger also deprives the child of "the opportunity for gradually recognizing" the father's shortcomings and thus his own. Another consequence of the cold parents' "inability to be the joyful mirror to [the] child's healthy assertiveness" is to cause the child to feel "emotionally unresponded to." The child's self-esteem sinks; he grows depressed and "a deep sense of uncared-for worthlessness and rejection, an incessant hunger for response" and reassurance develops in him. Otto F. Kernberg, *Borderline Conditions and Pathological Narcissism* (New York: Jason Aronson, 1975), 234–35, hereafter cited in the text; Heinz Kohut, M.D., *The Restoration of the Self* (New York: International University Press, 1977), 5, 56, 130, hereafter cited in the text.

10. Alan Cole, "Ingmar Bergman, Magician," *New York Herald Tribune,* 8 November 1959; this series of articles is hereafter cited in the text as Cole (and date).

11. Jörn Donner, *Three Scenes [Conversations] with Ingmar Bergman* (documentary film, 1975), hereafter cited in the text as Donner 1975.

12. This punishment also appears in August Strindberg's autobiography *The Son of a Servant* (1886) and Hjalmar Bergman's *Granny and Our Lord* (1926).

13. A. Alvarez, "A Visit with Ingmar Bergman," *New York Times, Magazine,* 7 December 1975.

14. Erik Erikson, *Identity: Youth and Crisis* (New York: W.W. Norton and Co., 1968), 181, hereafter cited in the text.

15. Frau Holle was, he learned much later, a popular Mediterranean representation of the goddess of love.

16. Mikhail Lermontov, *A Hero of Our Times,* trans. Vladimir Nabokov (New York: Doubleday, 1958), 126–27; hereafter cited in the text.

17. [Interview with Ingmar Bergman], *Positif* 289 (March 1985): 19, hereafter cited in the text as *Positif* 289.

18. August Strindberg, *The Son of a Servant,* trans. Evert Sprinchorn (Garden City, NY.: Doubleday, 1966), 239, 20, 14, 21, 74–75, hereafter cited in the text as Strindberg, *Servant.*

19. "I am a Conjurer" *Time,* 14 March 1960, 61, hereafter cited in the text as *Time.*

20. Bengt Forslund, *Victor Sjöström: His Life and His Work,* trans. Peter Cowie (New York: Zoetrope, 1988), 26, hereafter cited in the text.

21. Ingmar Bergman, *Four Screenplays,* trans. Lars Malmström and David Kushner (New York: Simon and Schuster, 1960), 19, hereafter cited in the text as *Four Screenplays.*

22. This experience will be alluded to in the script of *Hour of the Wolf* and dramatized in adult terms in that film.

23. The emotionally unresponded–to child responds abnormally. "During an excited, overly enthusiastic, hyperidealistic adolescence devoid of meaningful interpersonal attachments, the childhood fantasies often become transformed by an intense devotion to romanticized cultural—esthetic, religious, political, etc.—aims" (Kohut 1977, 5–6).

24. Hannes fell in love with Ingmar's sister Margareta and would have married her had he not been shot down, as a pilot, during the German invasion of Poland.

25. In *Fanny and Alexander* Emilie Ekdahl expresses similar sentiments: "All I bother about is myself. I don't bother about reality either. It is colorless and uninteresting; it doesn't concern me. Wars and revolutions and epidemics and poverty and injustices and volcanic eruptions mean nothing to me unless in one way or another they affect the part I am just playing."

26. Jörn Donner, *The Personal Vision of Ingmar Bergman,* trans. Holger Lundbergh (Bloomington: Indiana University Press, 1964), 80, hereafter cited in the text as Donner 1964.

27. In *Face to Face* Jenny tells Tomas about "a cousin [who] died of polio. I was fourteen then. We had sat under the dining table kissing on Saturday, the next Friday he was dead."

28. Bertil Pehrsson, [summary of interview with Bergman on Swedish TV, 4 March 1973], *Films in Review* 24 (August-September 1973): 448.

29. Birgitta Steene, *Ingmar Bergman* (New York: Twayne, 1968), 22, hereafter cited in the text.

30. In Strindberg's short story "The Reward of Virtue" (1884) the protagonist's mother dies and he "felt as if he had lost a friend, for during the year that she had lain ill he had got to know her personally . . . [and] as she ceased to be the mother of her household and was simply an invalid, the old-fashioned disciplinary relationship, which always comes between parents and child, disappeared." *Getting Married,* vol. 1, trans. Mary Sandbach (London: Victor Gallancz, 1972), 51.

31. Peter Egerman's mother recounts her son's refusal to visit his dying father in the screenplay of *From the Life of the Marionettes* (1980), and much earlier, in *Secrets of Women,* another Bergman surrogate, Martin Lobelius, refuses to attend his father's funeral but eventually relents. Failure to reach a dying mother's bedside in time is dramatized in *The Touch* (1971).

32. Liv Ullmann, *Changing* (New York: Knopf, 1977), 221–22, hereafter cited in the text.

33. Michiko Kakutani, "Ingmar Bergman: Summing up a Life in Film," *New York Times Magazine,* 26 June 1983, hereafter cited in the text. Bergman told Vilgot Sjöman of a dream in which his mother metamorphosed into his wife Käbi Laretei (Sjöman, 135).

34. In Kakutani (28), he implies that her visit was in 1983, in *ML* (283) that it was in 1980. Was it a recurring experience? In *Fanny and Alexander* he re-creates it in reverse: a dead son visits his mother.

35. Not surprisingly, the sequence Bergman likes best in Federico Fellini's *La Dolce Vita* (1960) involves Marcello achieving a short-lived intimacy with his always distant father. "Ingmar Bergman: A Candid Conversation with Sweden's One-Man New Wave of Cinematic Energy," *Playboy*) (June 1964): 66, hereafter cited in the text as *Playboy.*

36. James Baldwin, "The Precarious Vogue of Ingmar Bergman," *Esquire (April 1960): 132.*

37. Ingmar Bergman at 70—A Tribute," *Chaplin* (1988), 53, hereafter cited in the text as *Chaplin.*

38. These flash transformations may also take the form of tenderness: "Sometimes I seem to have seen him so overcome by emotion that it makes him helpless with compassion" (Sjöman, 153).

39. B. J. Bertina and Frenk Van Der Linden, "Ingmar Bergman: 'I Am the Master of Humiliation," *Los Angeles Times,* 10 June 1984.

40. According to Kernberg, the narcissist has an unrealistic conception

of himself and of others. In his fantasies, he confuses his conception of his actual self with the ideal image he has of himself and his parents. This confusion inflates his image of his actual self, but that is the image with which he identifies. He does this to escape being dependent on those he has learned to distrust—parents and other authority figures. Aspects of himself that contradict this inflated view of himself he either represses or projects onto other people or things. What follows is a "vicious circle of self-admiration, depreciation of others, and elimination of all actual dependency" (Kernberg, 228, 233).

41. Lars-Olof Löthwall, "Ingmar Bergman," *Take One* 2 no. 1 (September-October 1968): 16.

42. Egil Törnqvist, "Ingmar Bergman Directs Strindberg's 'Ghost Sonata,'" *Theater Quarterly* 3, no. 11 (July-September 1973), 8.

43. William Wolf, "Face to Face with Ingmar Bergman," *New York,* 27 October 1980, 34, hereafter cited in the text.

44. Lewis Freedman [interview with Ingmar Bergman], broadcast by National Broadcasting Laboratory for U.S. public television, 14 April 1968, hereafter cited in the text as Freedman. Again, Bergman seems to be drawing on Strindberg, who in *Inferno* (1897) writes: "When I got back and opened the door of my room it seemed to me that the whole place was filled with animate and hostile beings. There was not a bit of room anywhere, and I felt as if I were pushing my way through a crowd of people as I tried to reach my bed. Resigned, and resolved to die, I sank upon it. But at the last moment, just as I was suffocating in the grip of the invisible vulture someone pulled me from my bed and the hunt of the furies was on again. Defeated, all my courage gone, driven frantic, I yielded to the Unseen and abandoned the battlefield of this unequal struggle." August Strindberg, *Inferno,* trans. Mary Sandbach (London: Hutchinson, 1962), 139.

45. Steve Lohr, "Bergman's Next Film Project: A New Twist on an Old Romance," *New York Times,* 3 September 1989.

46. G. William Jones, ed., *Talking with Ingmar Bergman* (Dallas, SMU Press, 1983), 60–61, hereafter cited in the text.

Chapter 2

1. August Strindberg, *Lucky Pehr,* trans. V. S. Howard (Cincinnati: Stewart and Kidd Co., 1912), 174.

2. Walter Johnson, ed., *Four Plays by Hjalmar Bergman* (Seattle: University of Washington Press, 1968), 269.

3. Michael Bro is the name of the husband-pimp in *To Joy* (1950). The character type reappears as the dying, alcoholic actor who hungers for divine purpose in *The Magician* (1958).

4. Depressed personalities often suffer an "unconscious sense of guilt. The harsh internal punishment inflicted by the superego consists in the im-

plicit dictum that they do not deserve to be loved and appreciated, and that they are condemned to be alone. . . . Because of their badness they have destroyed their [parental figures] and are therefore left alone in a world now devoid of love" (Kernberg, 214–15).

5. A similar portrait of a sadistic teacher appears in Strindberg's *The Red Room*. In *Hour of the Wolf* one of the demons is a schoolteacher with a long wooden pointer like Caligula's.

6. A graffito in the exam room at school pictures him with horns, tail, and pitchfork. Sjöberg underscores his volcanic inner life by dressing him in a suit and overcoat in sweltering heat and having him close the classroom's windows and compel his students to wear their jackets. Later Sjöberg projects the shadows of rivulets of rain running down the window panes onto the classroom walls so that they appear molten. Bergman stokes our antipathy to Caligula by indicating that even nature responds with suicidal loathing to this man's attempts to connect: Caligula tells of a cat he stroked sinking its teeth and all 20 claws into his hand; it did not let loose even after Caligula immersed hand and cat in a water barrel. A doctor had to cut away the drowned cat.

7. Any material changes Bergman made had to be approved by Lorens Marmstedt and Herbert Grevenius, his superiors at SFI.

Clearly in this film Bergman was again thinking in terms of puppet and puppetmaster. Early on, a small crowd (which includes the captain and Bergman in his familiar beret) watches the Kastner Puppet Theater perform a story about a boy fighting for his life with an alligator.

8. Bergman's script for *Eva* (1948) is built around another Jack Kasparsson-like protagonist, Bo Fredriksson (Birger Malmsten). He has left to escape from his brutal father and his own guilt for being responsible for the death of a little blind girl. While away, he becomes involved with an immoral couple (Eva Dahlbeck and Stig Olin) who tempt him with adultery and drive him to dream of homicide. He is saved when he returns home and reencounters and marries his wholesome childhood friend Eva (Eva Stiberg).

9. Milan Kundera says in *Life Is Elsewhere,* trans. Peter Kussi (New York: Penguin, 1986), "Tenderness is fear of maturity. . . . Tenderness is also fear of the physical consequences of love. It is an attempt to take love out of the realm of maturity (in which it is binding, treacherous, full of responsibility and physicality), and to consider woman as child" (112).

10. Linnéa, whom Bergman gives a mannish appearance, is, with the exception of Hans Vergérus *(The Serpent's Egg),* Bergman's most cold-blooded character.

11. The stories of the two other female protagonists—Viola (Birgit Tengroth), Bertil's former mistress, and Valborg (Mimi Nelson), a lesbian who years before was a colleague of Rut's and now tries to seduce Viola—are, through parallel editing and flashbacks, woodenly interlaced with the successful central plot involving Rut and Bertil. Two grotesquely narcissistic Jack Kasparsson–type males also affect events. There is Dr. Rosengren (Hasse Ek-

man), an unprofessional psychiatrist who warns his patient, Viola, that unless she accepts him as her "God," lets him "sculpture [her] personality," and sleeps with him, she will end in a padded cell, and Raoul (Bengt Eklund), a married, laughably pompous and callous cavalry captain—a forerunner of *Smiles of a Summer Night*'s Count Malcolm—who impregnates Rut and then leaves her when she refuses to have an abortion.

12. The marriage scene in the film was staged at the very town hall in which Bergman and Lundström had been married.

13. In Bergman's play *To My Terror* (1948), Paul, having failed in his literary career and been reduced to rewriting textbooks, likewise leaves his wife and takes a depraved mistress.

14. The cardinal has been interpreted as Bergman's father, the dead as Bergman's five children from his two marriages, the water and "soft channel bottom" as the womb, and the tower being "shaken" by the vision of the "dark, boundless sea" as Bergman's fear of death (Gado, 124–25).

15. Seeing her as Death makes her victory over the pastor in a chess game a foreshadowing of *The Seventh Seal*. The pastor is also the first in a long line of Bergman characters—Antonius Block, Dr. Vergérus in *The Magician*, David in *Through a Glass Darkly*, Elizabet in *Persona*, the demons in *Hour of the Wolf*, Ellis in *The Passion of Anna* and Hans Vergérus in *The Serpent's Egg*—who, for creative or intellectual reasons, try to benefit from someone's suffering or death. The pastor tells Marie he is spending time with the "corpse," as the aunt refers to herself, not out of Christian duty but to gain insight into death.

16. Ironically, Björk was pregnant while the film was being made. It is worth noting that in *The Devil's Wanton* a fish represents Birgitta Carolina's baby. In *Secrets of Women,* especially for Rakel, fish are associated with sexuality. Rakel is afraid of a fish that is clearly identified as a phallic object, and she will talk about the time she went fishing and hooked her husband.

17. In the play Kaj is the central figure, and his attempt at adultery with Rakel fails, though it leads to Eugen's accidental shooting of Kaj's pregnant wife, Mia. In the film the adultery takes place in the bathhouse—a possible reference to Bergman and his sister once having been reprimanded for playing naked in the bathhouse.

18. He made Bris (Breeze) soap commercials, which were made to be shown in film theaters prior to the feature. In accepting the project of making these nine short commercials, Bergman demanded the same movie equipment, cameraman (Gunnar Fischer), and control (including final cut) that he had in making his films. The firm of Sunlight and Gibbs acceded, stipulating only that he had to include in each commercial the statement that bacteria, not sweat, is what makes a person smell, and that Bris kills the bacteria. Bergman subsequently presented this message in a comic manner that mocked it even as it drummed it home. Maaret Kaskinen, "Soap Opera à la Bergman," in *Chaplin.*

19. "I was to be reconciled to one of my wives in Copenhagen. We were staying in the home of some close friends, who'd gone away. They had given us their key, and when we got home in the evening, drunk and happy, with everything fully prepared, we put the key in the door—and it snapped off. No chance of finding a locksmith. So we spent the night on the stairs" (*BB*, 67).

20. Bergman says Olof Molander could "put two actors opposite each other at a table and devote the rest of the time to analyzing the characters" (Sjöman, 104).

21. After Harry's first date with Monika, the Jack-like Lelle (John Harryson), an old boyfriend whom Monika calls crazy, insults her and beats up Harry. One lovely night in the archipelago, Harry and Monika leave an outdoor dance when they hear Lelle's voice. Later, in a scene missing from American prints, they fight with Lelle when he tries to torch their boat. Swedish censors also cut a drunken, orgiastic love scene between Harry and Monika.

22. Harry's train crosses a trestle shrouded in a soft, mysterious mist and enters a dark tunnel. The sexual symbolism seems intentional.

23. This play is in the tradition of *The Difficult Hour* (1918), a set of short, expressionistic plays by Pär Lagerkvist in which the characters are encountered "still clinging to life, contemplating the absurdity of living and waiting . . . for God to answer [their] prayers" (Steene, 25).

24. Quoted in Young, 35. Jack's guilt is heightened both by his having had his oedipal fantasy satisfied with the death of Bro and by his identification with the director/God. "The essence of the Oedipal complex is the project of becoming God!" We are

impelled by a powerful desire to identify with the cosmic process" in order to escape our "horror of isolation." And we all want to be unique; this is especially true of the artist, who "wants to know how to earn immortality as a result of his own unique gifts. His creative work is at the same time the expression of his heroism and the justification of it. . . . How can one justify his own heroism? He would have to be God. Now we see even further how guilt is inevitable for man: even as a creator he is a creature overwhelmed by the creative process itself. If you stick out of nature so much that you yourself have to create your own heroic justification, it is too much. . . . The more you develop as a distinctive free and critical human being, the *more* guilt you have. Your very work accuses you; it makes you feel inferior. What right do you have to play God? . . . In other words, he knows that the work is he, therefore "bad," ephemeral, potentially meaningless—unless justified from outside *himself* and outside *itself*. . . . To renounce the world and oneself, to lay the meaning of it to the powers of creation, is the hardest thing for man to achieve—and so it is fitting that this task should fall to the strongest personality type, the one with the largest ego. (Ernest Becker, *The De-*

nial of Death [New York: Free Press, 1973], 98, 15–152, 172, hereafter cited in the text).

In *Torment* Caligula's last cry in the dark hallway is for light and against the incomprehensible and uncontrollable forces that control him. Fourteen years after Jack, Antonius Block will utter almost the identical prayer, but with "we" superficially replacing "me." "From our darkness we call out to thee, Lord. Have mercy on us because we are small and frightened and ignorant. . . . God, You who are somewhere, who *must* be somewhere, have mercy upon us."

25. Providence acts in the same manner in Charlotte Brontë's *Jane Eyre* (1847). Jane hears the suffering Rochester, who is miles away, and she rushes to his aid: "I saw nothing: but I heard a voice somewhere cry . . . and it spoke in pain and woe wildly, eerily, urgently. 'I am coming!' I cried'" (Boston: Houghton Mifflin, 1959), 398. In F. W. Murnau's *Nosferatu* (1921) sensing Jonathan's peril in a far-off land, Nina awakens, and her loving concern forces the Nosferatu to temporarily abandon his pernicious designs on Jonathan.

Earlier Bengt and the former lumberjack Ebbe, who was being tutored by Bengt in French, had arm wrestled, and of course Ebbe, in part fired by jealousy, won. Unbeknownst to Ingrid, Ebbe pursues her as she searches for Bengt, and when he confronts them he tries to reassert his hegemony over her. Caneless for the first time since his blindness—like Johannes's hump, Bengt's blindness is the symbol of his emotional immaturity and insecurity as a man—Bengt challenges Ebbe. When Ebbe knocks him to the ground, Bengt expresses his gratitude to Ebbe for being the first person to treat him as an equal. (This blow liberates Bengt just as Johannes's slapping his father liberated him.) Realizing he has lost Ingrid, Ebbe leaves.

26. In *Three Strange Loves* the cross-cutting of Viola's death with Bertil's simultaneous "murder" of and revelation of his need for Rut might suggest that her death is, similarly, a sacrifice that mysteriously redounds to Bertil's development.

27. We are deprived throughout this dubbed film of Sjöström's vocal power. Bergman says that he did not come to understand the joy Sönderby speaks of for another 30 years (*ML,* 159).

28. Part of Schiller's verse is, "He who has a wife to treasure / Let him swell our mighty song . . . / Good and God, all things are natures, / And with blameless joy are blessed."

29. Lise-Lone Marker and Fredrick J. Marker, "The Making of *Fanny and Alexander:* A Conversation with Ingmar Bergman," *Films and Filming* (February 1983): 9, hereafter cited in the text.

30. Although Bergman believes it was owing to Sjöström that the "entire production wasn't cancelled," actually it was Dymling, who, even after viewing many of the botched rushes, gave the go-ahead. Sjöström's diary reveals that he was relieved to be free of this decision.

31. Bergman adds that when he wanted to direct a film based on his own script (*The Devil's Wanton*), it was Marmstedt who supported and encouraged him. "It was magnificent. So I'm really deeply in his debt" (*BB*, 26).

32. Bergman heeded these admonitions. The film opens with Bengt being shot and blinded during his military training because he is trying to save a puppy that has wandered onto the firing line. In addition, Zetterling's physical and spiritual beauty is winningly emphasized in such scenes as when, after happily awakening one morning, she walks naked and carefree across her room, and later when, as Bengt had done, she runs her fingers over her face to "find out how freckles feel."

33. These scenes benefited from Bergman's need to shoot them from "a single camera position in order to get as much as possible done in a working day" (Sjöman, 112).

34. In *Secrets of Women* Nilsson, as Märta, shows herself, in the shots immediately following the birth of her child, as a creature of flesh, sweat, and instinct rather than as just a performer.

35. In *The Passion of Anna* Bergman used only Malmsten's photograph, and the role he was assigned in *Face to Face* is tiny.

36. Peter Cowie, *Sweden 2* (New York: A. S. Barnes, 1970), 103, here-after cited in the text.

37. Ghosts of various sorts play roles in this story: Erland lives with the ghost of Marie's mother; the ghostly faces of Henrik and Marie float up out of Marie's diary; Henrik's aunt seems to be a ghost when Marie meets her after disembarking; a ghost appears in the animated sequence; Erland's seemingly deserted house has its furniture covered in white sheets and Marie hears a ghostly pianist playing Chopin; and the ballet master remarks that the theater is filled with ghosts.

38. The notable exceptions are the melodramatic music in the dinner scene in *Smiles of a Summer Night* and the tinny music during Jof and Mia's escape through the storm in *The Seventh Seal*.

Chapter 3

1. Pierre Marivaux, the eighteenth-century playwright and novelist, is the only influence Bergman cites. Other possible influences are Shakespeare, Molière, Mozart (*The Marriage of Figaro, Don Giovanni, The Magic Flute*), Max Ophüls (*La Ronde*), Jean Renoir (*Rules of the Game*, though Bergman claims not to have seen it at that time), and Franz Lehár. In 1954 at Malmö Bergman had directed *The Merry Widow*, which contains the standard—tragic, comic, romantic, and commenting—couples of operetta.

2. Bergman suggests that the costume manager Mago (Max Goldstein) provided the cap. This film marks Bergman's first collaboration with Mago, who had left Nazi Germany when he was 12—just before the war—and became a cartoonist for Stockholm's evening paper, *Expressen*. In the late 1940s,

Mago began to design sets and costumes. Bergman saw Mago's work in an amateur production of *Julius Caesar* and eventually hired him to work on *Sawdust and Tinsel*.

3. This is just one of the many paradoxes in the film. Take Anne and Frans: she is a beautiful strong woman who smells of sweat and manure. A seemingly shrewd woman, she poses as a helpless female supplicant in order to dominate him. However, Frans, a thin, perfumed, effeminate man, easily deceives and dominates her. The many mirrors in this film are used in part to suggest that things are not what they seem and to underscore the paradoxes.

4. Jacobsson was pregnant when the film was made, and Mago designed costumes that kept her condition disguised (Cowie 1982, 130–31).

5. The German silent film *Schatten* (*Warning Shadows* [1923]), directed by Arthur Robison, vaguely resembles this film; it includes a shot in which antlers appear above and as part of the shadow of a potential cuckold's head.

6. The allusion to Nora's interruption of Torvald in *A Doll's House* has to be as intentional as Bergman's wanting us to see the sexual image—a man riding a unicorn—on the back of Fredrik's chair.

7. The province of Skane—the location of Ryarps Castle, where these scenes supposedly take place—has a reputation as a place where strange things happen. People from Skane are often considered magical in Swedish tales.

8. David Sylvester, "The Films of Ingmar Bergman," *New Statesman*, 18 October 1958, 518.

9. This whole film, in fact, is built on humiliation: Albert is publicly or privately humiliated by city officials, the theater director Sjuberg, Agda, Anne, and Frans. Anne is privately humiliated by Albert, and privately and publicly by Frans. Frans is privately humiliated by Anne and, before he gets his sadistic revenge, publicly by Albert. (The scene in which the police, who are concerned with public order during the opening-day parade, tear up the circus posters, seize the circus horses, and leave the performers to pull the wagons—as the townsfolk jeer—was excised from the American prints.) When the circus caravan enters the town's outskirts at dawn, the sleeping, bourgeois community's hostility is represented by a large dog that lunges and yelps at the passing caged bear.

Albert's confrontation with Sjuberg seems patterned on Jack's with the director/God in *Jack among the Actors*. Albert is pushed to the front of the stage and interviewed by Sjuberg, who at first is only a voice emanating from the dark auditorium. The conceit is perpetuated when the magisterial, bearded Sjuberg, in top hat, cape, and tails and carrying a cane, becomes visible. The camera angle is so low that the chandelier high above seems like a halo around his head. He treats Albert and Anne, and Albert's request, with that snide, mock-serious manner and tone that Björnstrand effected so deliciously: "Suppose we get vermin in our costumes, scabies, lice." When Albert asks innocently and without hostility, "Why insult me?" Sjuberg relents somewhat and turns his contempt on himself and his fellow actors.

10. In Bergman's radio drama *The City,* Joachim Naken is berated by his teddy bear for not living up to his childhood dream of joining the circus.

11. In fact, this absolute black-and-white contrast is just one of the story's many extreme contrasts: silence versus sound; physical weakness versus strength; love versus hate; manic versus depressive behavior; claustrophobia versus openness; perfume in contrast to sweat; order versus chaos; sun versus cold; tranquil bourgeois existence versus an active and exotic circus life; domesticated versus wild animals. In addition, Bergman's analectic use of sound is joined to an effect common to silent films and to those made at the beginning of the sound period, an effect Bergman had also experienced in his own dreams: silent films used music and sound effects, and the early sound films often presented much of the spoken dialogue in titles; Bergman just eliminated the titles (*BB,* 87).

12. As Albert confidently and proudly leads Anne into town to borrow costumes from Sjuberg, a brash march and the sound of a mocking cock's crow are heard on the sound track. The camera cues us to Bergman's satiric view by panning up from the water flushing the gutters to Alma and Albert straddling the dirty torrent while effecting an easy stylishness that is undercut by their swagger.

13. Bergman wanted Bibi's sister, who was "very beautiful and . . . a dancer," for a one-minute fairy tale, but someone recommended he give Bibi a chance. Bibi recalls, "He pulled the classic joke on me. I was sixteen . . . still in school, and had hardly been kissed. . . . The story was about the princess and a man who looks after the pigs. She wants something he has . . . and [in return] he wants a hundred kisses. . . . After about fifteen [kisses] Ingmar said silently, 'Stop,' to the cameraman, while we went on and on . . . [kissing] for ninety-eight kisses. And everybody laughed" (Cavett).

Chapter 4

1. Pauline Kael, *I Lost It at the Movies* (Boston: Atlantic-Little, Brown, 1954), 245–46.

2. Bergman may also be alluding to God when, in the flashback and after Frost's destructive ordeal, his colleague Jens looks questioningly up at a bright but silent sky.

3. Gunnar Björnstrand and Bibi Andersson were in the cast. In the fall of 1955 Bengt Ekerot, *The Seventh Seal*'s Death, successfully produced and directed the play for the Studio Workshop of the Royal Dramatic Theater.

4. The play and the film draw on a number of sources: Bergman's *Kasper's Death* (Steene 1972, 121). Pär Lagerkvist's *The Hangman* (1933), and Strindberg's *The Saga of the Folksungs* (1899)—the flagellants and the aural effect at their entrance clearly come from this play—*The Great Highway* (1909), and *To Damascus* (1898–1904) (the silent girl is probably based on the

plague girl). Alf Sjöberg's 1942 film *The Road to Heaven,* in which personified religious concepts intervene in human affairs, is also an influence. It was based on a modern morality play by Rune Lindstrom; its imagery was inspired by the naive painters of the nineteenth-century Dalarna province and by Victor Sjöström's 1918 film *Ingmarssönerna (The Sons of Ingmar). The Road to Heaven* still charms audiences. In it, Mats Ersson's fiancée is burned as a witch and the naive Mats sets out for heaven to seek justice. On the way he encounters, among others, the Devil and God, both dressed in period costumes. Mats gets distracted from his goal, but when he is lying on his deathbed, God, wearing a frock and top hat, helps reawaken his purpose and Mats ends up in a pastoral heaven.

5. Hearing Carl Orff's *Carmina burana* (1937) influenced Bergman's decision to make the film.

6. The screenplay refers to a sea gull.

7. Originally, Bergman offered von Sydow the role of Jof, but then he changed his mind and assigned him to play the knight. Von Sydow was unhappy with the change because he knew from reading the play that the knight had few spoken lines. But Bergman assured him that the part would be much enlarged.

8. In *Lucky Pehr's Journey* it is at sea's edge that Per persuades Death not to take his life.

9. This scene was inspired in part by Georges Bernano's *The Diary of a Country Priest* (1936) (Cowie 1982, 144).

10. The mural was painted and the statue carved by Bergman's set director, P. A. Lundgren.

11. In his chapter "The Subjective Experience of Emptiness," Dr. Kernberg distinguishes between the emptiness the narcissist feels and normal loneliness: ". . . a sense of loss of contact with other people. . . . Life no longer seems to make sense, there is no hope for any future gratification or happiness, there is nothing to search for, long for, or aspire to. . . . [This] feeling of emptiness comes close to the feeling of loneliness, except that loneliness implies elements of longing and the sense that there are others who are needed, and whose love is needed, who seem unavailable now." Narcissists, in contrast, "feel that they can no longer love anybody nor is there any reason why anybody should love them; the human world has become emptied of meaningful relationships among people" (213–14).

12. When the procession leaves, the camera precedes it, looking down obliquely from a steep, high angle that has it enter the windowlike frame from the lower left and climb diagonally upwards—making the effort of the penitents all the greater. A dissolve follows—camouflaged by a cloud of smoke from the censors—to the middle of the procession. Immediately, another dissolve takes us to the stragglers just vacating the frame on the right. Bergman used a similar transition on the procession that carries Frost in *Sawdust and Tinsel.* Besides wonderfully eliding time, this maneuver sustains the illusion of a large number of people with only a few and, in *The Seventh Seal,* creates the illusion that we are scrutinizing an exotic, centipedelike creature through

a giant microscope. In fact, by the end the feeling is that the penitents have departed in the final sense.

13. The strawberries have several associations. Besides being a favorite food of Bergman's, they are associated with the Virgin as well as with the pleasures of the flesh. In *Wood Painting* Plog says, "She's as tempting as a patch of wild strawberries," and Jöns uses berry picking as a euphemism for sexual intercourse. In *Summer Interlude* Marie shares her private patch of wild strawberries with her young lover Henrik.

14. In Strindberg's *Dance of Death* (1901) appears the following dialogue, which closely resembles Death and Skat's exchange: CAPTAIN: 'Do you think I'm going to die?' CURT: 'You will as everybody. There will be no exception made in your case.'" *Plays*, trans. Edwin Björkman (New York: Charles Scribner, 1912), 181, hereafter cited in the text.

15. In *To Damascus* the mother asks, "Do you never tire of asking questions?" The stranger replies, "Never! You see, I long for the light." *August Strindberg: The Plays*, vol. 2, trans. Michael Meyer (London: Secker and Warburg, 1975), 95, hereafter cited in the text.

16. "When we shot that moment, suddenly the sun came out" (Kaminsky, 128).

17. Her words echo those of the old gentleman in Strindberg's *Storm* (1907): "Human beings are more likeable at a distance. . . . If one doesn't allow oneself to get involved, one cannot be hurt." *August Strindberg: The Plays*, vol. 1, trans. Michael Meyer (London: Secker and Warburg, 1964), 396, 412, hereafter cited in the text.

18. "We'd packed up for the evening and were just about to go off home. It was raining. Suddenly I saw a cloud: and Fischer swung his camera up. Several of the actors had already gone home, so at a moment's notice some of the grips had to stand in, get some costumes on and dance along up there. The whole take was improvised in about ten minutes flat" (*BB*, 115).

19. In *A Lesson in Love* the views on God and death of another 73-year-old, David's father (Olof Winnerstrand), are the most sanguine in Bergman's films. When his granddaughter asks if he believes in God, he replies, "If by God you mean life, then I do. I believe in this life and the next and all kinds of life." "But death?" she queries. "Just a part of life," he assures her. "How dull if everything were always the same. You die and begin a new life."

20. He is sitting on the terrace of the Golden Otter Inn overlooking Lake Vättern.

21. The hymn they recite was written by Johan Olof Wallin (1779–1839).

22. Rochelle Wright connects the old watch without hands (and other details) to Hjalmar Söderberg's *Doctor Glas* (1905) (*1978 Annual Film Studies*, Purdue University). Donner mentions a smashed watch that appears in Sjöström's *Karin Ingmarsdotter* (1920). An optometrist's shop with just such a pair of glasses (without the deterioration) over its door existed in Stockholm and can be seen in Arne Sucksdorff's 1947 film *People of the City*. Even more intriguing is the set design for a scene in Karl Grune's expressionistic film *Die*

Strasse (1923): it can be seen in Lotte Eisner's *The Haunted Screen* (Berkeley: University of California Press, 1969), 253. The set contains a similar street with a sign made up of a pair of eyeglasses that flash on and off, and it also contains Emil Hasler's sketch for a street scene for Fritz Lang's *M* (1931) that shows a lamppost identical to the one in Borg's dream.

23. The dummy . . . was constructed from a balloon and a silk stocking" (Cowie 1982, 158).

24. Erik Erikson, "Dr. Borg's Life Cycle," *Daedalus* (Spring 1976): 25.

25. At the start of the film, when Isak is about to leave his study, he stops before a chess board (which automatically calls to mind Antonius Block). He cannot, however, make up his mind to make a move.

26. Except for her character in *Scenes from a Marriage,* all of Bibi Andersson's characters want children.

27. Bergman says that "the most painful of accidents is hurting my hands, and so it seemed to me that when the old man hurt his hand it was a great pain for him, and a prelude to the painful trial he will then undergo." Hollis Alpert, "Style Is the Director," *Saturday Review of Literature* (23 December 1961): 40. Isak's act prefigures Karin Vergérus's in *The Touch:* she presses her bare hand on broken glass so as to equalize the pain she feels at discovering her lover has left her.

28. In Strindberg's *A Dream Play* a similar dream-examination occurs. An officer is examined by a schoolmaster in a classroom of boys. The logic of the officer's answers is correct, but he fails because he is "not mature yet." In that play there is also an award ceremony in Lund Cathedral.

29. We see these ruins when Isak and Marianne first visit the old summer house. Is the charred ladder related to the one in *The Seventh Seal* to which the witch, who believed she had had carnal intercourse with the Devil, was tied?

30. Hundreds of snakes were supposed to be all around them, but those collected for the scene escaped through a hole in the studio's terrarium (*BB,* 141). "I must have been splashing about in psychoanalytical ideas," adds Bergman. Erikson says Sara "is, as first loves are apt to be, both the female other and the feminine Self—that is, the Self which such a man considers too feminine to acknowledge" (25). He adds that Isak turns again to Sara, who personifies the young mother, because there "is an infantile trauma behind these scenes of seduction with which, it is clear, he has unconsciously colluded in his adult life [the Karin scene]. It is what Freud has called the primal scene, the child's observation or imagination of parental lovemaking that makes an Oedipus out of the boy and alienates him from his own Id—the snaky swamp—as well as the betraying parents" (14).

31. In the screenplay she is described as so pregnant she looks "like a strawberry in her red dress."

32. "Narcissistically disturbed individuals tend to be unable to feel warm or to keep warm." Heinz Kohut, M.D., *The Analysis of Self: A Systematic*

Approach to the Psychoanalytical Treatment of Narcissistic Personality Disorders (New York: International Universities Press, 1976), 64, hereafter cited in the text. Mrs. Borg is not as vindictive as Henrik's aunt (*Summer Interlude*), who confidently asserts that she will outlive her nephew and he will never get his inheritance. Mrs. Borg simply takes an amused but perverse pleasure in her grandchildren's impatience with her longevity: "It's thrown all these young people's calculations out."

33. Bergman's reading of Eiono Kaila's *Psychiatry of the Personality* (1946, [4th ed.]) greatly influenced *Wild Strawberries:* "His thesis that man lives strictly according to his needs—negative and positive—was shattering to me, but terribly true. And I built on this ground" (*Four Screenplays,* 21).

34. "When I am dropping off to sleep at night, or if I take it easy for a moment in the afternoon, when I'm in that state between dreaming and waking—and that's an enchanted state—suddenly with no difficulty I can recall memories from my earliest childhood: lights, scents, voices, movement, remarks people made that still seem so secretive, impossible to understand like when I was a child."

35. Bergman describes the situation that preceded this close-up. Sjöström was upset because Bergman had not stopped filming, as promised, in time for Sjöström to go home for his daily whiskey. Both men were angry, but then Sjöström suddenly said to go ahead with the shot. Bergman set it up and told Victor what he was to act—the seeing of his parents. "I already had the feeling that this was going to be a catastrophe. But we had to take it because I had been urging him all day. . . . And suddenly we got it. . . . It's strange. If we had been in a good mood, if we had been just sentimental . . . I think it would have been very bad. . . . We didn't rehearse, didn't press it out. . . . And that face has so very much about experience, about tenderness, about an old man's sadness for life's going away" (Cavett).

36. A passage from Strindberg's *The Pelican* comes to mind: addressing his sister as they are about to be consumed by flames, a young man speaks of their narcissistic mother, who literally deprived them of material and emotional necessities, and who already had been consumed by the conflagration: "Mama is not coming with us, poor Mama she is not with us. . . . Can she have been left ashore? . . . We can't enjoy ourselves without Mama. There she comes now!—Now our long summer vacation is starting!" *Strindberg's One-act Plays,* trans. Arvid Paulson (New York: Washington Square Press, 1969), 368, hereafter cited in the text as Strindberg, *One-act Plays.*

37. In 1958 Sjöström won the prize for best actor at the annual film festival in Argentina. That same year, at the Swedish Film Academy's Silver Jubilee, he won the seldom awarded Gold Plaque. He died on 3 January 1960.

38. J. C. Stubbs, "*The Seventh Seal,*" *Journal of Esthetic Education* 9, no. 2 (1975): 62–76.

39. Carl Anders Dymling helped Bergman convince Sjöström to play the part.

40. Vogler's appearance also derives from von Sydow's role as Alceste in Bergman's 1957 stage production of Molière's *The Misanthrope*, which also featured Gertrud Fridh.

41. This last remark foreshadows future von Sydow characters who suffer from reaction formations—for example, Johan in *Shame* and Andreas in *The Passion of Anna*.

42. In Strindberg's *Advent* the judge closes a cabinet door and a ghost flings it open again. The judge remarks, "I won't be scared. Everything has a cause: ratio sufficiens. This door must have a spring with which I am not familiar. It surprises me that I don't know it, but it cannot scare me." Earlier, "a clock begins to strike and keeps it up as if it never meant to stop." *Plays*, 3d series trans. Edwin Björkman, (New York: Charles Scribner's, 1913), 161, hereafter cited in the text.

43. Bergman says that *The Magician* "corrects" *Sawdust and Tinsel* (Kaminsky, 132). He may mean that Albert Vogler is more successfully able to achieve the revenge that eludes the Albert in the earlier film.

44. In *Magic* the conjurer says to the disillusioned Patricia, who has fallen in love with this stranger she believes is a fairy spirit, "[I] destroyed a fairy tale that [I] was bound to destroy" (New York: G. P. Putnam's Sons, 1913). In *Six Characters in Search of an Author*—which Bergman says influenced *The Magician* (Sjöman, 102)—Pirandello uses the phrase "kindred souls" to describe a clerk's relationship with his employer's wife, whose baby, like the Egermans', has died. *Classics of Modern Drama: Realism and After*, ed. Alvin Kernan (New York: Harcourt Brace, & World, 1965), 235.

45. Bergman says this plot twist is based on his having felt unappreciated and then unexpectedly being awarded "a grant out of the King's Fund" (*BB*, 127).

46. In *Port of Call*, after Berit has been locked out of her mother's apartment, there is a similar shot of a shielded electric light swinging in the wind.

47. He and Sven Nykvist experimented with 18,000 feet of Eastmancolor before they began the film. The colors often establish emotional temperature (for example, red equals passion) or symbolize character (for example, the critic Cornelius [Jarl Kulle] is almost invariably dressed in simple black and white).

48. Erland Josephson, "Ingmar Bergman: Director and Close Friend," in brochure from the Swedish Film Institute, *Swedish Film 84*, (1984): 4, hereafter cited in the text; see also *BB*, 151.

49. Bergman made this pout an important gesture in the repertoires of both Harriet and Bibi Andersson.

50. Fischer had contracted to shoot a film at that time in northern Sweden for the Disney company.

51. Bergman told Dick Cavett that in *The Virgin Spring* he "especially" worked in the Swedish tradition—so eloquently manifested in Sjöström's films—of showing man's destiny being played out in the Swedish landscape.

52. Stanley Kauffmann finds the vengeance scene "so long [that] it verges on the ridiculous," and he points out that Töre and Märeta's noisy entrance and Töre's removal of the bag from under the mute brother—without the "edgy" sleepers stirring—is incredible. *A World on Film* (New York: Dell, 1967), 278.

53. Given this title, one has to consider Charlotte Perkins Gilman's short story "The Yellow Wallpaper," published in Sweden in 1959 as "Den gula tapeten," as an important influence on the film. It is a story of a schizophrenic woman married to a "practical" physician (*"perhaps* that is one reason I do not get well faster") who "has no patience with faith . . . and . . . scoffs openly at any talk of things not to be felt and seen and put down in figures" (9–10). In her diary the woman chronicles her aversion-fascination with the flamboyant designs on the patchy, discolored wallpaper in their room at the "top of the house," a room that used to be the nursery (12). Though at first she resists, when "the sun is just so" she sees a figure moving "behind" the designs (18). The story concludes with the husband fainting as he realizes how far her disease has progressed (New York: Feminist Press, 1973).

Another influence, one that Bergman acknowledges (*BB,* 164), is Anton Chekhov's *The Seagull* (1895). This play involves a young man like Minus, Treplev, who worships his actress mother but resents her career, which keeps her from spending time with him: "It seems to her that she is working for humanity, for *the holy cause of art*" (my italics; in *Shame* Bergman uses this precise phrase). Like Minus, Treplev writes and stages (at twilight) a play for his mother. In it, Treplev's girlfriend, Nina, plays the role of a spirit working for the dead after all life on earth has become extinct. The companion of Treplev's mother, the famous writer Trigorin, speaks of the oppressive compulsion of writing and, like David, uses the life around him as fodder for his creating. In fact, he turns Nina's ensuing insanity, partly as the result of Trigorin's rejection of her, into a short story. *Best Plays of Chekhov,* trans. Stark Young (New York: Modern Library, 1956), 7.

Other influences are Strindberg's *Easter* (1901) and *Storm Weather* (1907) which Bergman had recently staged, and Bergman's earlier film *The Devil's Wanton,* in which Birgitta Carolina visits the room of a lunatic painter at sunrise and hears voices and sees "moving, strange, excited, raging, laughing faces" in the patterns of the wallpaper. In addition, Bergman told Sjöman that as a young man he had "lived with a woman who from time to time was subjected to commands. Voices gave her orders" (26). Bergman says that he drew on her for Karin. Nor should we forget Bergman's own experiences in which he could not distinguish between the real and imaginary.

54. Bergman was distracted because he became interested in another idea whose appeal to him is understandable: a story about the rise and fall of the Swedish sculptor Johann Tobias Sergel (1740–1814) and his relationship with a woman younger than himself, a relationship that starts out "as carnal lust [and] matures into deep affinity." This story may have been one inspiration

for *The Devil's Eye* (or even *Now about These Women* or *Hour of the Wolf*) because the idea came to him while reading about "an egocentric young nobleman at the time of Gustav III. His wife is deeply attached to him, but he casts her aside for all kinds of affairs. 'He's the man who cannot accept love, who rejects right, who can't put up with it'" (Sjöman, 5).

55. Very close to Gotland, this island, which soon would become the center of Bergman's filmmaking, is called Fårö, or Sheep Island. It is also a military base.

56. In the screenplay Karin sucks on Martin's cut, thus evoking the vampire theme.

57. In mixing the sound for this film Bergman sent the prop man Karl-Arne Bergman to record the real sound of a foghorn because the artificially created sound was unsatisfying. The foghorn used here and in his later films is one "that regulates itself by means of real Chinese hair. Damp makes the hair contract" and creates the unmatchable, woeful moan (Hedlund, 48).

58. In Strindberg's chamber play *Easter,* Eleanora talks to Benjamin, a boy Minus's age whom she dubs her "little brother," about failing his Latin exam. She also tells him that she "can see what another can't," and that her hypersensitivity forces her to hear "groaning in the telephone wires. When people talk badly about each other on the telephone, the copper complains." Strindberg, *Plays, 2,* 289, 287.

59. In the screenplay David later tells Karin, "When [your] Mummy died I had my big success [a novel], and it meant so much more to me than her death. I was even secretly glad."

60. The ladder may evoke the young witch in *The Seventh Seal* who imagines she had intercourse with the Devil.

61. Significantly, in the screenplay, David left Karin with her grandmother. In *The City* Joachim Naken laments, "I have buried myself . . . in my faith in a so-called artistic activity." Again, it is in vain; his art does not fill his emptiness.

62. In Strindberg's *Easter* Eleanora tells Benjamin about her illness: it was "not a sickness unto death, but to the glory of God. . . . I wanted good, and evil came. I avoided the light, and the darkness came." Strindberg, *Plays, 2,* 290.

63. Based on Saint Paul's doctrine of grace, the Gnostics believed that adultery, incest, lying, even murder were not sinful if they "were done freely, in a state of illumination." Then they were signs that God was acting through the ego. Paul Zweig, *The Heresy of Self* (New York: Basic Books, 1968), 259–60, hereafter cited in the text.

64. Not satisfied with the "artificial idea of what real light looks like" in the films they had seen, Bergman and Nykvist began working on a completely new lighting technique, trying to capture how light "actually behaves." Theirs was "a new lie instead of the old one" (*BB,* 174).

65. Björnstrand was seriously ill while he was shooting this film. His heavy work schedule—he was also performing in a Buntel Eriksson film com-

edy—was one reason. He took medicine that was prescribed by Bergman's doctor, but it made his condition worse. When he stopped taking it, he immediately improved.

66. The high angle supports his role as "angel," but the fact is that Bergman had to use it because at that time they had to use the crippled prop man Karl-Arne Bergman—on whom the role is partly based—to stand in for Edwall. He was used as well in the wafer part of the communion. Someone also kneeled in for the eight-months pregnant Gunnel Lindblom. By the time the scene in which Tomas visits Mrs. Persson at home was shot, Lindblom had delivered and they had to pad her and use facial makeup.

67. Simon's description of Mrs. Persson's speech is superb (153).

68. The eczema was based on that of Ellen Lundström, Bergman's former wife.

69. Partly to keep the time scheme realistic, Bergman considered making this whole interview a hallucination.

70. Not since *Three Strange Loves* had a Bergman character successfully committed suicide.

71. Two cameras were used, but shooting from a distance made it impossible to get the microphone close enough to pick up any speech.

72. In the screenplay, Tomas's insecurity as a child is made explicit in an incident that has an autobiographical ring. Tomas tells of awakening out of fright one night and finding the vicarage empty. He ran screaming in search of his father: "I'd been left without Father and Mother in a completely dead world. I was sick with terror. Father sat up and watched over me all night."

73. Chance contributed to this: the "Skattingby Church happened to have a Madonna" (Sjöman, 191).

74. Influences on this film included Igor Stravinsky's *Symphony of Psalms* (1930); an idea Bergman had of a man locking himself in a church and saying, "God, I'm staying here until . . . you've proved to me you exist"; a clergyman telling Bergman that a fisherman committed suicide the day after he had counseled him; and Bergman's discovery that the churches he visited in preparing the film were practically unattended and overseen by an indifferent clergy.

75. Charles Marowitz, "The Man of *Cries and Whispers:* As Normal as Smorgasbord," *New York Times,* 1 July 1973, hereafter cited in the text.

Chapter 5

1. The theme is based on the Bergman-invented notion that "a young woman's chastity is a stye in the Devil's eye" (Young, 200).

2. Kulle knew he was wrong for the part. He told Bergman, "Look, I can't do this role. This isn't a young, vital Don Juan! It's an old, burnt-up fellow, completely worn out, a tragic figure. He's not my type." "He was right and I was wrong!" says Bergman (*BB,* 149).

3. Bergman chose Elliott Gould for the role after seeing *Getting Straight* (1970).

4. Though the mother's wedding ring is emphasized, her husband is never mentioned.

5. Except for this sequence, which Bergman's former cinematographer, Gunnar Fischer, photographed, the cinematography is Sven Nykvist's.

6. "The film was done in Swedish, and we did an English version . . . for places where [people] don't [like] to read subtitles. . . . In the Swedish film we speak English with Elliott Gould, which would be natural." ABC, however, "just took the English version. . . . I just hated it because I think it's very silly that Max von Sydow and I talk to one another in broken English." Bibi Andersson, "Dialogue on Film," *American Film Institute* 2, no. 5 (March 1977): 38, hereafter cited in text.

7. Bergman's use of amplified, close-up sound for phone conversations is also jarring at first. Late in the film he uses cameo images of David and Karin speaking their letters to each other, an effect that somewhat resembles that of Märta speaking her letter to us in *Winter Light*.

8. It was evident to Gould and others that David's role was modeled after Bergman, who had fallen in love with the Countess Ingrid von Rosen at first sight and married her a few months after *The Touch* opened.

9. When at the film's start David had asked her about her marriage, Karin replied, "It's very difficult to speak about that sort of thing, especially when you speak a foreign language." Her experiences have provided her with the self-assurance to learn another foreign language.

10. Bergman puts some of the blame on the English dialogue coach (Jones, 65–66). The most badly written *and* acted moment is when David, about to run out on Karin, declares that his and Karin's spirits are one, and he thrice utters, "Forgive me."

11. Bergman told Gould that he thought it tragic that Gould was not playing Shakespeare and Ibsen. Later, after an incident in which Gould felt Bergman had rejected him, he described Bergman as "a boy, a mean, smart, sensitive boy" (Meryman, 71–72).

12. In a rather chilling reference seemingly to Jonas in *Winter Light*, Johan is told he will go sailing with Uncle Persson.

13. It is also the case that, owing to problems with camera rattle, Bergman first shot the scenes with sound and then without (Sjöman, 203).

14. Sven Nykvist, "Photographing the Films of Ingmar Bergman," *American Cinematographer* (October 1962): 627.

15. Recall that, in *Winter Light*'s screenplay, Tomas tells of being frightened awake one night by a train whistle and running to find his father.

16. Bergman came upon the name Timoka in one of Käbi Laretei's Estonian books of poetry; it means "appertaining to the executioner [or hangman]." He made up the other words.

17. As well as being sent to his grandmother's when they return to Sweden, in the course of the film Johan is shut out of the pullman compartment, sent out of the bathroom where his mother is bathing, banished from the dwarfs' room, ejected from his hotel room when Ester wants to talk to Anna,

shut out of the room where his mother has her assignation, and taken out of the dying Ester's room.

18. For an explanation of the term *mindscreen,* see Bruce F. Kawin, *Mindscreen: Bergman, Godard, and the First-Person Film* (Princeton: Princeton University Press, 1978), hereafter cited in the text.

19. This is an effect similar to the one Bergman used in *Three Strange Loves,* though there it is the threatening silhouette of bombed-out German buildings that is reflected in a train compartment's window.

20. In *Persona*'s screenplay Alma, after having enticed Elizabet into sucking blood from her arm, "blows up her cheeks like a child blowing a balloon and then lets the air leak out between her lips with a faint bubbling noise."

21. Her alcoholism and Anna's insatiable sexual hunger are rooted in their "feeling of emptiness" (Kernberg, 213–14).

22. Bergman's use of sound to establish two different realities, and this horse-drawn vehicle, may have been suggested by the 1945 British psychological thriller, *Dead of Night* (mentioned earlier in connection with *Wild Strawberries*) in which a hearse appears outside of a hospital window in a dreamlike vision presaging death.

23. The hotel is the Siljansborg at Rättvik. Alain Resnais's hotel in *Last Year at Marienbad* (1961) may have been an influence.

24. It is no. 25, the "Saraband." Bach wrote these variations for J. T. Goldberg, who played them to soothe his sick, insomniac patron, Count Keyserling. Ingmar and Käbi had worked together on Bach, and Ingmar even had planned to take off the year to study Bach.

25. Bergman wanted Lindblom to play the scene naked, but she refused (*Chaplin,* 53–54). In Sweden some viewers so objected to the film's sexual content that they made life-threatening phone calls to Bergman, and someone even sent him a letter "containing filthy toilet paper." In Sweden and elsewhere censorship or its threat helped make the film a box-office success. See Cowie (1982, 215–16) for a more detailed account of the film's reception.

26. Wood sees the dwarfs as the heroes of this film because of "their robust and uncomplaining acceptance of their lot. . . . They have their lives to get through as Ester has hers, and they seem to be making a better job of it" (136).

27. The association of sexuality with fish appears several times in Bergman. In *The Devil's Wanton,* in Birgitta Carolina's nightmare, her baby turns into a fish; in *Secrets of Women* a phallic fish frightens Rakel; in *Cries and Whispers* Karin (Thulin), before slashing her genitals, watches her hated husband eat fish; in the unfilmed "The Petrified Prince" (1975) a woman, indicating her pudenda, tells her son that he came "out of that big hole with its smell of tainted fish"; and in *After the Rehearsal* Rakel (again Thulin) will say about aging, "I stink like a rotten fish. My skin exudes a putrid moisture. . . . I breathe decay."

28. As he set to work on *The Silence* Bergman said he wanted to make a film called "The Dream" that would "be a dream." He also talked of making a film called "The Big Picturebook," which would not "be a film with dramatic composition throughout . . . only pictures, *pictures, pictures.* . . . As in a dream. Not an ordinary passage of time, but dream time" (Sjöman, 58–59).

29. Agnes C. Schuldt, "The Voices of Time in Music," *American Scholar* (Autumn 1976): 549–59.

30. This shot is cut from available prints in the United States but can be seen in Stig Björkman's film *Ingmar Bergman* (1971). Recall, too, the phallic cannons in *Sawdust and Tinsel.*

31. David Shipman, *The Story of the Cinema* (New York: St. Martin's Press, 1982), 8.

32. Bergman wrote in a small part in "The Cannibals" for Liv Ullmann, to whom Bibi Andersson had recently introduced him.

33. *Bergman: "Persona" and "Shame,"* trans. Keith Bradfield (New York: Grossman, 1972), 12, hereafter cited in the text as *Persona.*

34. Bergman is not consistent about what provoked the idea of the merging identities (*BB,* 195–96; Simon, 39).

35. Robert T. Eberwein, *Film and the Dream Screen* (Princeton: Princeton University Press, 1984), 137.

36. The scene continues with Elizabet staring at the ceiling, her face in silhouette. Then she closes her eyes and, lips slightly apart, rests her left hand on her forehead. From the radio beside her bed comes the "Adagio" from J. S. Bach's Violin Concerto in E Major. The violin's almost human voice conveys a profoundly melancholic and painful longing that underscores the chasm between Elizabet's confused anguish and the music's ability to express deep, compassionate feelings in a pure, direct manner. This shot, with its rapid, kinesthetic progression from light to dark, compacts a whole day's anguish and loneliness into approximately 82 seconds. Yet the darkness and music seem to promise a tranquil sleep. This is not to be the case.

37. *Six Plays of Strindberg,* trans. Elizabeth Sprigge (New York: Doubleday, 1955) 193, hereafter cited in the text.

38. This situation calls to mind *Through a Glass Darkly's* Karin and Minus.

39. Ironically, Bergman was going to cut this scene, but Bibi Andersson asked if she could just change some words that she felt no woman would say. He agreed. "He was embarrassed and so was I . . . to do the scene. We shot it in one long close-up in one take. . . . We started rehearsing at nine, and we were through at eleven. . . . Then we saw it, and he said, 'I'll keep it. It's so good. But I want you all by yourself to go into the dubbing room because there's something wrong with the sound. . . . I had been talking very high, very girlish. So the whole monologue was dubbed afterward, and I [lowered] my voice . . . [which] I dared to do when I was totally alone and no one could watch me. . . . That might be what gives the scene a certain intimate quality" (Andersson, 43).

40. "I remember the studio was full of smoke because it was going to be this kind of blurry thing. Ingmar had a mirror [for us to look into], and we also knew that one of the big problems with the shooting was how to compose the frames, when there were only two people all the time, without just having a reverse over one shoulder. How do you make us move in the same shots so that it will still have movement and be interesting? . . . He wanted a mirror. He said, 'It will be very beautiful.' He also said, 'Move and we'll see.' So we moved. Liv pulled my hair back, and I took her hair. We didn't know what to do, and we just tried to make the frame look interesting. Finally, he said, 'That's it,' and they shot it" (Andersson, 43).

41. Bergman confesses, "Anything written or left behind tempts me so much that I'd read it if I could" (Kaminsky, 111).

42. Bergman says the interruption serves "to wake up the audience for a bit, only to re-immerse them in the drama. . . . If you distract the audience temporarily from the course of events and then push them into it again, you don't reduce their sensibility and awareness, you heighten it" (Cowie 1970, 193); he also says that this simulated breakdown represents the time when he got ill and his "inspiration . . . suddenly dried up" (*BB*, 222, 202).

43. Strindberg's *The Stronger* (1890) is a play for two women, one of whom does all the talking. She says to the other, "Why don't you say something? You have not uttered a single word all this time. You've just let me go on talking. You've been sitting there staring at me only, and your eyes have drawn out of me all these thoughts which were lying in me like silk in a cocoon" (Strindberg, *Plays, 2,* 174). This play has to be one of the sources for *Persona.*

44. At the end of the screenplay the psychiatrist, like Satan in *The Devil's Eye,* is again found behind her desk in a "mildly triumphant" mood. She says, "I was convinced all along that [Elizabet] would go back. . . . It is difficult, of course, to analyze her innermost motives, with such a complicated mental life as Mrs. Vogler's. But I would put money on strongly developed infantility. And then of course all the rest: imagination, sensitivity, perhaps even real intelligence. (*Laughs.*) Personally I would say you have to be fairly infantile to cope with being an artist in an age like ours. (*The doctor is very pleased with what she has said, particularly the last bit.*)" (*Persona,* 99).

45. In the screenplay Alma's last words undercut her development: "I really do like people a lot. Mostly when they are sick and I can help them."

46. Bergman published the script of *Cries and Whispers* in the *New Yorker* (21 October 1972): 38–74.

47. In Strindberg's *Dance of Death* Alice says, "Behind the silence I hear voices—mutterings, cries!" (Strindberg, *Plays,* 238–39).

48. This was shot on location in an old mansion near the town of Mariefred near Mälar Bay, where Bergman reportedly once lived.

49. One of the scenes Agnes recalls is of their red-headed Aunt Olga using a magic lantern to tell the story of Hansel and Gretel. Bergman often pictures the world as one where lonely, frightened children are abandoned by

parents. P. Adams Sitney ("Color and Myth in *Cries and Whispers," Film Criticism* [Spring 1989]: 40) quotes from Bruno Bettelheim's *The Uses of Enchantment: The Meaning and Importance of Fairy Tales* (New York: Random House, 1977) with regard to Hansel and Gretel: "The mother represents the source of all food to the children, so it is she who is now experienced as abandoning them, as if in a wilderness. It is the child's anxiety and deep disappointment when Mother is no longer willing to meet all his oral demands which leads him to believe that suddenly Mother has become unloving, selfish, rejecting. . . . [The gingerbread house] is the original all-giving mother, whom every child hopes to find later again somewhere out in the world" (159, 161).

50. In the screenplay Agnes speaks for Bergman: "In the old days, I used to imagine that my creative efforts brought me into contact with the outside world, that I left my loneliness. Nowadays I know that this isn't so at all. In the end all my so-called artistic expression is only a desperate protest against Death. Despite this, I keep on." The screenplay also suggests that from childhood on Agnes let her art keep her from living "among people."

51. In Strindberg's *The Creditors* (1890), two men examine a woman's photograph: "I see nothing but an affected flirt, bent on making a conquest. Do you see the cynical expression about her mouth—which she never lets *you* see? Do you see these glances in search of a man who is not you? Do you see the extreme low cut of the dress, the way she has done her hair, and how her sleeves have been loosened and pushed up?" (Strindberg, *One-act Plays,* 113).

52. Joakim calls to mind Eugen Lobelius (*Secrets of Women*).

53. Max von Sydow believes her performance in *Through a Glass Darkly* is the greater. Liv Ullmann says Harriet Andersson's performance was "one of the greatest" she has ever seen, and she was surprised that Harriet "spent all her time joking, dancing, and playing the clown" (Michel Ciment, "Jouer avec Bergman: Entretien avec Liv Ullmann," *Positif* 204, (March 1978): 36, hereafter cited in the text.

54. This was Ek's last film with Bergman. Around 1977 he developed blood cancer.

55. In Strindberg's "For Payment" (1886) a frigid wife considers "everything natural . . . unclean" (258). When her husband's ideas about platonic love are punctured, he says it is "like having a finely woven tissue of lies dragged from his intelligent mind. . . . What infernal putrefaction there was under all this deceitful morality" (277). When he finds a booklet entitled *Voluntary Sterility* in his wife's drawer, he comments, "It was really fear, fear of discomfort of being a mother. . . . It had become a disgrace to be a mother, to have sex, to be reminded that you were female" (281–82). *Getting Married,* vol. 2, trans. Mary Sandbach (London: Victor Gallancz, 1972), hereafter cited in text as Strindberg, *Married*.

56. The husband in Strindberg's "For Payment" drives his wife's needle into his finger, "as if he wished to experience the delight of suffering" (Strindberg, *Married,* 281).

57. Bergman might also say, as he did about the film melting after Elizabet cut her foot in *Persona*, that this scene, which recalls the razor across the eyeball in *Un Chien Andalou* (1928), wakes up the audience.

58. Here is Bergman's description of his encounter with a female corpse when he was ten years old: "Then I saw that she was watching me from under her half-lowered eyelids. Everything became confused. . . . Algot [the caretaker] had told me about a colleague of his who had wanted to play a joke on a young nurse. He had placed an amputated hand under the covers on her bed. When the nurse did not appear for morning prayers, they had gone to her room, where she was found sitting naked, chewing on the hand. . . . I was now going mad in the same way. I hurled myself at the door, which opened by itself. The young woman let me escape. . . . I tried to portray this episode in *Hour of the Wolf* but failed and cut it out. It recurs in the prologue of *Persona* and receives its final form in *Cries and Whispers*, in which the dead cannot die but are made to disturb the living" (*ML*, 203–4).

59. There is never any mention of her child's father.

60. The paragraph concludes: "This insight has brought with it a certain security that has resolutely eliminated anguish and tumult, though on the other hand I have never denied my second (or first) life, that of the spirit" (*ML*, 204).

61. Robert Brustein, "The Dreams of Ingmar Bergman," *New Republic*, 29 July 1991, 30.

Chapter 6

1. The allusion to E. T. A. Hoffmann is quite conscious (*BB*, 218). Other influential works not mentioned in the text are Federico Fellini's *Juliet of the Spirits* (1965), Alfred Hitchcock's *The Birds* (1963), and *Psycho* (1960), and Hieronymus Bosch's fifteenth-century painting "Garden of Earthly Delights." Most of the borrowings are, however, from Hoffmann's tales "The Sand-Man," "The Golden Pot," and "Kreisleriana" (*The Best Tales of E. T. A. Hoffmann*, ed. E. F. Bleiler [New York: Dover, 1967], hereafter cited in the text). Besides the names Lindhorst, Heerbrand, Veronica, and Johannes Kreisler, which Bergman took from "The Golden Pot," Bergman uses elements of Hoffmann's characterizations, imagery, plots, ideas about personality fragmentation and the supernatural, and Hoffmann's habit of "breaking into the dramatic action to analyze a piece of music." Stig Björkman, Torsten Manns, and Jonas Sima, "Death at Dawn Each Day: An Interview with Ingmar Bergman," *Evergreen Review* (13 February 1969): 45, hereafter cited in the text as Björkman, et al.

In "The Sand-Man" (1816–17) Hoffmann concluded that the only narrative strategy he could use to tell the story of his hopelessly unstable, depressed protagonist, Nathaniel, was to "present [life] as 'in a glass darkly'" (196). Large segments of the story are therefore conveyed through letters. We learn that Nathaniel was traumatized during his childhood by Coppelius, whom Nathaniel identified with his father. Hiding in a dark cupboard to spy on his father and Coppelius, Nathaniel observed that the fire they labored over made his father's face "an ugly, repulsive Satanic mask. He looked like Coppelius" (188). In a scene that parallels Johan being locked in a closet where a little man threatens to bite off his toes, Coppelius discovers the young spy and threatens to burn out his eyes. Though Nathaniel's father intervenes, Nathaniel faints. He awakens in his tearful mother's arms. Thereafter, Nathaniel is haunted by the demonic Coppelius, who later reappears as a lens maker named Coppola.

Until he becomes obsessed with possessing the beautiful Olimpia—a wondrous puppet created by an associate of Coppola's, Professor Spalanzani—Nathaniel loves Clara, who, like Bergman's Alma, is an unaffected, not very talkative person with a prosaic temperament and a "deep and sympathetic heart" (197). Clara delights in Nathaniel's work, that is, until he tries to initiate her into his mysterious ideas and experiences. Though she does not say so and tactfully avoids the subject, Nathaniel knows that she finds "his dark, gloomy, wearying mysticism" (199) distasteful. When, however, she insists his demons exist only "in his own mind" (198), he is furious. His gaiety returns briefly in a scene in their garden that parallels the early scene in *Hour of the Wolf* when Johan sketches Alma under the apple tree; when Johan has Alma pull her hair back to display her neck and shoulders, the allusion may be to Hoffmann: "Painters averred that [Clara's] neck, shoulders, and bosom were almost too chastely modelled, and . . . one and all were in love with her glorious Magdaline hair" (196). Nathaniel's passion for the "statuesque and soulless'" Olimpia serves as a perfect symbol for his narcissism. She, as well as the "glass" (spyglass) through which he observes her, are mirrors that reflect himself. "He fancied that she had expressed in respect to his work and his poetic genius the identical sentiments which he himself cherished deep down in his own heart, and even as if it were his own heart's voice speaking to him. . . . 'Oh! What a . . . profound mind! Only you—you alone understand me'" (209). One day in Spalanzani's apartment Nathaniel comes upon him and Coppola physically struggling for the possession of Olimpia. When Coppola wrenches her from Spalanzani, her eyes pop out onto the floor. The destruction of Olimpia (Nathaniel's self-image) leads to his "raging with the harrowing violence of madness," and he attempts to murder Clara. When he is prevented, he commits suicide. The story's final image is of Clara, a few years later, married and with two children.

"The Golden Pot" (1814) is the story of Anselmus. It divides his history into 12 "vigils" (a staying awake in order to protect or watch). In the last vigil Hoffmann informs us that until now he has been unable to confide the "singular manner" in which he learned the story of this young man who was unable to stop what appeared to be his fantastical hallucinations. ("Is the Devil in this man?" asks an acquaintance [3].) But, says the author, the necromancer Archivarius Lindhorst, the guiding force behind Anselmus's "malignant fate," has written him that he no longer minds this story being "divulged through the press" (67). The story is as follows: During a psychedelic experience Anselmus fell rapturously in love with a snake named Serpentina. At the same time Anselmus attracted the love of the beautiful Veronica, the daughter of a distinguished citizen. Because he is a talented draftsman, Anselmus is recommended to the mysterious Archivarius Lindhorst. (Lindhorst's father died nearly 400 years earlier; in *Hour of the Wolf* the old woman with the hat says she is 216 years old.) Like Bergman's Baron von Merkens, who once invited to dinner an artist whose painting he purposely hung upside down, Lindhorst humiliates Anselmus when he samples the youth's drawings. He hires him, nevertheless, informing him that Serpentina is one of his own daughters, that she returns Anselmus's love, and that Anselmus will have her if he is able to resist the "hostile Principles" that assail him. In addition, sounding like Pamina's father, Sorastro, who instructs Tamino about important mysteries and how to win his hidden daughter (*The Magic Flute*), Lindhorst tells Anselmus that if he is to achieve "happiness in the higher life," he must undergo "a season of instruction: belief and full knowledge will lead [him] to the near goal" (35), but only if he always bears Serpentina in his thoughts. Veronica, meanwhile, enlists a clairvoyant witch to rescue Anselmus "from the phantoms, which were mocking and befooling him . . . and . . . would at last prove his ruin" (49). The crone gives Veronica a mirror in which she and Anselmus can view each other. (The old woman in Bergman's film informs Alma about Johan's diary so that Alma can better understand him.) When Veronica looks in the mirror, however, she too looks like a snake, thus identifying her with Serpentina. (In Bergman's film Alma's jealousy links her with Veronica). In this contest for Anselmus between the witch and Lindhorst, Lindhorst wins. The description of their struggle bears on *Hour of the Wolf*'s bird imagery: The wind blows Lindhorst's greatcoat so that it flutters "in the air like a pair of large wings. . . . It seemed as if a large bird were spreading out its pinions for flight" (22). Lindhorst appears to become a kite that cries out and soars into the sky. Later, wearing a flowered, glittering dressing gown, Lindhorst leads Anselmus through a long corridor into a greenhouse where he is surrounded by deafening, jeering sparrows. Later yet, in a scene that resembles the demon's final, lethal attack on Johan, the witch commands her spirits to "bite [Anselmus] to death!" Lindhorst takes the form of a parrot to fight the witch's associate, who is in the form of a cat. When the former has the latter by the neck, "red fiery blood burst down over his neck"; then, "with his strong wing, [the parrot] dashed the cat to the ground and . . . with his sharp bill picked out his glowing eyes" (60). At the moment of the witch's defeat, Veronica's mirror shatters, and she realizes that she has forever lost Anselmus. Veronica's father believes that she too has "cracked," but like Clara in "The Sand-Man," Veronica immediately and contentedly accepts a proposal of marriage from her father's friend Heerbrand. Anselmus and Serpentina disappear from this world to mythic Atlantis.

In the last vigil Hoffmann visits Lindhorst, who not only tells him about what happened but alludes to Hoffmann's close friend Johannes Kreisler, from whom Bergman may have borrowed the name Johan. Kreisler was the early nineteenth century's "foremost Romantic music critic" (v) and the pseudonym of E. T. A. Hoffmann. His success as a critic and artist was due in part to his near pathological sensitivity, which contributed to his mental instability. Kreisler's temperament and consequent indiscretions repeatedly brought him trouble. He was first exiled to a small Baltic town; then, as the result of drawing caricatures of the local military commander, he and his wife, a woman, like Alma, whose talents were domestic rather than intellectual, were sent to a wilderness village in central Poland. This was not his last exile.

Music was Hoffmann's "first love and his true love." He so honored Mozart that he "changed his middle name from Wilhelm to Amadeus," and in his writing he frequently refers to Mozart's work (xiii). Johan Borg meets Kapellmeister Kreisler at the castle.

Also related to *Hour of the Wolf*'s demons is the fact that Hoffmann's "work is permeated with the concept of personality fragments coming to separate identity and acting as characters" (xix), and that Hoffmann characteristically blurs the line between dream and reality, the real and supernatural. Hoffmann breaks into the fourth vigil, for example, to inform the reader that the rapturous and horrifying otherworld glimpsed in dreams "lies much closer at hand than you ever supposed" (18), and speaking as a man on intimate terms with this other reality, he advises the reader to open himself to its marvelous presences. Johan Borg's nightly vigils mirror Hoffmann's, which were "plagued by [a] dread of night and would frequently, as the biographies tell us, awaken his wife and make her stay up with him when his overwrought imagination filled him with an unspeakable fear (543). See also Robert Rosen, "The Relationship of Ingmar Bergman to E. T. A. Hoffmann," *Film Comment* (Spring 1970): 28.

Finally, "A Golden Pot" poses the question, "Are you not aware that madness is infectious?" (61).

2. In Michelangelo Antonioni's *L'Avventura* (1960) Anna disappears without a trace from a volcanic island.

3. Like the opening scene of *The Seventh Seal,* this scene was shot at Hovs Haller.

4. In Jan-Erik's nightmare in *Torment,* Caligula threatens to put out Jan-Erik's eyes with his pointer; in Hoffmann, Coppelius threatens to blind Nathaniel. Symbolically, both threats are threats of rape.

5. "Vogler . . . evokes the word *bird*. To me birds have always been something demoniacal, mysterious, and dangerous. I'm afraid of birds . . . since I was a child" (Björkman, et al., 45).

6. "At first one only sees her feet; and she comes closer and closer. This is the only sequence in the entire film that was shot continuously. I.e., there are two takes of the same shot and a dissolve in the middle, which one doesn't

see, because the beginning of the second take was better than the beginning of the first, and the end of the first was better than the end of the second. I'd envisaged that sequence clearly. But then the shore and the location looked different from what I'd imagined when I'd written it, so I began experimenting" (*BB*, 112).

7. Max von Sydow recalls: "Bergman wanted to have the whole dinner table conversation . . . all in one take. His idea was to give the actors something near to the kind of continuity in performance that you get in live theater. Sven . . . was seated in front of us, and the table at which we sat was partly surrounding him. . . . I remember Nykvist's total precision in his panning technique—because when you pan from one face to another as fast as he had to do, it's very difficult to stop each pan at a moment when you have an ideal composition on each person" (Cowie 1982, 243).

8. When Bergman wrote "The Cannibals," he was scheduled to stage *The Magic Flute* in Hamburg. Illness forced him to cancel both projects.

9. In *Summer Interlude* Bergman suddenly animates Henrik's and Marie's drawings, but our recognition that Tamino is human comes closer to the shock we experience at the merging of Elizabet's and Alma's faces in *Persona*.

10. Tamino's question is not far removed from Jack's cry in *Jack among the Actors*: "God . . . help me . . . it is so damned dark. Help me to find a way out. Let it be lighter!"

11. In the screenplay Lindhorst notes that, like Pamina's Alma's name (as well as Veronica's, we note) ends with a consonant and an *a*. "There's nothing in the text that requires [the chorus's partial syllabilization of Pamina's name— 'Pami-na'] . . . which is completely illogical," says Bergman. "You can't find any rhythmic, musical, or logical justification for it. And it becomes a sort of incantation," the formula for the embodiment of perfect love (Björkman, et al., 78).

12. "The greatest of all questions [is] . . . 'Does Love live? Is Love real?' . . . The answer comes . . . [in the] code word for love: 'Pa-*mi*-na still lives.' Love . . . is real in the world of human beings."

13. Pär Lagerkvist writes, "The inner compulsion must be there no matter how it may have originated. That inner compulsion . . . alone gives imaginative writing meaning and vitality. . . . [It is a situation in which there is] no longer a choice or an external chance. But the compulsion from within." *Modern Theater: Seven Plays and an Essay,* trans. Thomas Buckman (Lincoln: University of Nebraska Press, 1966), 30.

14. Near the end of this scene Corinne hikes up her dress to show a bruise on her inner thigh, the result of another man's advances, which she has used to spur her husband's jealousy. She asks Johan to give her another because this one is losing its power. This duplicates the situation in *The Magician* in which Mrs. Egerman (also played by Gertrud Fridh) wants Albert Vogler (also von Sydow) to come to her bedroom. When Mr. Egerman (also Josephson) turns up in his stead she is sexually stimulated by his violence.

15. Some shots in this scene resemble Munch's *Summer Night*.

16. It is, Johan explains to Alma, the hour most people die and most children are born, when nightmares come, and when, if we are awake, we are afraid.

17. For a psychoanalytical reading of this film, see Lynda Buntzen with Carla Craig, "*Hour of the Wolf:* The Case of Ingmar B," *Film Quarterly* (Winter 1976–77): 24; and Gado.

18. In Strindberg's *Son of a Servant,* his young, autobiographical character, Johan, has an argument with his father that he characterizes as a "wrestling match." "Johan was flat on his back, but he could still bite. A schoolboy had once stung him with a clever reply and now he heard the same bee buzzing in his ear." (Strindberg, *Servant,* 128).

19. Bergman says Johan's story was based on one of his dreams (Simon, 30), but it has other possible antecedents. In *Ship to India* Captain Blom tries to drown his son; in *Three Strange Loves* Bertil dreams he crushes Rut's head with a bottle. Fish have always been sexual symbols in Bergman's films (*The Devil's Wanton, Secrets of Women, The Silence, Cries and Whispers*); in addition, if the boy is interpreted as a combination father-mother image, this scene is connected to the final memory in *Wild Strawberries:* "The sun shone brightly. . . . Down at the beach on the other side of the dark water a gentleman sat. . . . He had taken off his shoes and stockings and between his hands he held a long, slender bamboo pole. . . . Farther up the bank sat my mother. . . . I tried to shout to them but not a word came from my mouth." In *A Hero of Our Times,* the book the Johan of *The Silence* is reading, Pechorin, the protagonist, struggles with an almost demonic woman who tries to kill him. That struggle resembles Johan Borg's: "She suddenly jumped up, twined her arms around my neck, and a moist, burning kiss sounded upon my lips. . . . [M]y head swam, I crushed her in my embrace with all the force of youthful passion, but she, like a snake, glided between my arms, whispering in my ear: 'Tonight.'" That night, aboard a small boat, she tries to murder him: "I tried to push her away, but she clung to my clothes like a cat. . . . [Recall the cat that sunk its teeth into Caligula's hand and his having to drown it before its hold could be released.] The boat rocked, but I regained my balance . . . my rage gave me strength, but I soon realized that in agility I was inferior to my adversary. 'What do you want?' I cried, squeezing her small hands hard. Her fingers crunched, but she did not cry out; her serpent nature withstood this torture. . . . I braced my knee against the bottom of the boat; with one hand I seized her by the hair, with the other got hold of her throat; she released my clothes, and I instantly shoved her into the waves. By that time it was rather dark: once or twice I glimpsed her head amid the foam, and then I saw nothing more" (Lermontov, 77–78).

20. The passage seems to refer to Bergman's affair with Gun Grut. "Our love tore our hearts apart and from the very beginning carried its own seeds of destruction" (*ML,* 161). In 1971 Gun was killed in a car crash in Yugoslavia.

21. In Pär Lagerkvist's *The Man Who Lived His Life Over* (1928) the husband, David, says to his wife Anna, "We must be like you." Anna replies, "I'm too simple a person!" David reiterates, "Yes, like you. . . . Pure in heart . . . good and quiet like you . . . and faithful as you are, beloved. . . . So that there will be peace." Anna answers, "Oh my dear . . . so you say . . . and so you used to say when we first met . . .—And you've said it since, though not so often of course." *Five Modern Scandinavian Plays* (New York: Twayne, 1971), 401.

22. "Perhaps I did not give the audience a sufficient indication of where the funny bits would be, for *Hour of the Wolf is* a black comedy—every action in it has two faces, one dark, one light. The audience *should* laugh when von Merkens walks up the ceiling. . . . It is grotesque, like a horror picture, and don't forget that I was brought up on those horror films of the Thirties like *Frankenstein* and *Dracula*" (Cowie, 1970, 196).

23. Through Lindhorst, Bergman makes us experience the humiliation his actors feel having to play out in public his neuroses and fantasies. Only an actor as psychologically sound as a Björnstrand or von Sydow could endure these roles. Bergman says, "As an actor, Max is sound through. Robust. Technically durable. If I'd had a psychopath to present these deeply psychopathic roles, it would have been unbearable. It's a question of acting the part of a broken man, not of being him. [There is] a subtle detachment which often exists between Max and my madmen" (*BB*, 120).

24. In the screenplay Johan also describes his first experience of a naked, voluptuous woman, a corpse in the hospital morgue. This experience provides details for Johan's upcoming encounter with Veronica Vogler: "I drew the sheet off her. . . . I gazed at [her] for a long time. . . . Then I . . . touched her face, her ears, her shoulders, her breasts. I let my fingertips glide over the curve of her hips, the auburn tuft of hair covering her genitals, her long thick thighs."

25. In addition, the corpse of the dead actor seemingly comes alive in *The Magician*; Ester (again Thulin) comes alive when Johan pulls the sheet off her face in *The Silence;* and corpses, among them the boy-Johan, come alive in the morgue at the start of *Persona.*

26. In Bergman's 1973 production of *The Ghost Sonata,* the milkmaid that Hummel murdered and then drowned reappears at the moment the mummy verbally assaults him. According to Bergman, Hummel thinks, "All right, I can stand all this, just as long as you don't start talking about the Milkmaid I've murdered. At this point the Milkmaid appears. Produced by Hummel's anguish." Lise-Lone Marker and Frederick J. Marker, *Ingmar Bergman: Four Decades in the Theater* (Cambridge: Cambridge University Press, 1982), 74–75, hereafter cited in the text as Marker and Marker, *IB.*

27. In one scene Hans stands in front of a circus poster of a bear, Bergman's symbol of security.

28. This confessional scene, during which Bergman inserts shots of a statue of the Virgin, may also strike us as Bergman confessing to himself. Part

of the confession has to do with his childhood fear of being left alone in the dark: "It's evening and it's dark and I'm afraid. My mother has shut the door. I know that no one can hear me if I call." A similar passage appears in the screenplay for *Winter Light,* but with the emphasis on Tomas's father.

29. The origins of this neurotic conflict, according to Horney and Freud, go "back to early childhood. But for [Horney] the critical feature of the early years is the child's helplessness and dependency on others, as well as his inability to comprehend what makes his parents so loving and available sometimes and irritable or withdrawn at others—so that the world often seems . . . frightening and capricious." Paul L. Wachtel, "Karen Horney's Ironic Vision," *New Republic,* 6 January 1979, 26.

30. Ullmann says that Eva was easier for her to play than either Elizabet (*Persona*) or Alma (*Hour of the Wolf*) because by then Bergman knew her well enough to be able to write what she calls her "divided personality" into the film (Ciment, 35).

31. Bergman's mother's name (Karin), an arrow-pierced heart, and a boy's name are carved on the back of the chair Eva is sitting in.

32. In Strindberg's *There Are Crimes and Crimes* (1899), a character says that the career of the artist appealed to her "craving for freedom and fun—as they call it" (Strindberg, *Plays 2, 77*).

33. Shooting this scene was like a wonderful game. When an actor complained about a minor cut, Bergman laughed his famous laugh and retorted, "Never mind, it was fun wasn't it?" Because something hit him in the face while he was panning to the machine guns, Sven Nykvist worried that he had closed his eyes, but the shot turned out all right (Freedman).

34. Liv Ullmann got so upset when the heads of the chickens were falling that she left the scene. She also tried to get away from the burning house, but Bergman shouted, "Oh, don't be so scared, silly woman. Get closer, get closer!" "I hated him for days," says Ullmann, "but now when I see [the film] I understand. . . . He doesn't care about me or the house or anything. He wants the picture" (Freedman).

35. Bergman says he got this image from a photo series in *Life* magazine (*BB*, 233), but the following passage from Selma Lagerlöf's *Jerusalem* comes remarkably close: "The people on board noticed that there was a dark object floating on the surface of the water. By and by it came closer, and soon one could see that it was a corpse. . . . One could tell from his clothes that he was a sailor. He floated on his back with calm face and open eyes. He had not been so long in the water that he had had time to swell up. . . . But when the sailors turned their eyes from him they almost cried out, for without their noticing it, another corpse had turned up right at the bow. They barely missed sailing over it, but at the last minute it was driven away by the swell. Everybody rushed to the railing and stared down. This time it was a child, a prettily dressed little girl. . . . Soon thereafter, one of the men called out that he saw yet another corpse, and so did another man who was gazing in a different

direction. They saw at the same time five corpses, they saw ten, and then there was a whole flock. They could not count them. The ship rocked very slowly forward among the dead bodies, which surrounded it as if they wanted something. They surrounded it on all sides . . . as if they wanted to make the voyage with them across the sea. The skipper had the helm turned to catch some wind in the sails, but it helped little; the sails hung limp, and the dead continued to follow them. The sailors grew more pale, and quieter . . . they could not escape the dead." Selma Lagerlöf, *Jerusalem* (New York: Doubleday, Page, and Co., 1915), 224–26.

36. In Strindberg's *To Damascus* a character has a vision in which he is no longer in the present but dead, and his soul is "where a great river runs like molten gold in the sunshine, and roses [Love] flower with vines upon the wall; and a white pram stands beneath an acacia tree. But the child sleeps, for its mother sits by it knitting, knitting a long, long strip which comes out of her mouth, on which is written: 'Blessed are they that mourn, for they shall be comforted'" (Strindberg, *Plays, 2,* 159). Bergman calls Eva's dream a "dream of lost love" (*BB,* 235). He will use the strip coming out of the mother's mouth in *Face to Face.*

37. The film's Swedish title is *A Passion, (En Passion),* but because of Allan Dwan's film *Passion* (1954), to avoid confusion its U.S. distributors decided to release it with a different title: thus, *The Passion of Anna.* The film's actual title is *Passion* because the suffering, intense emotion, and obsessiveness covered by the word *passion* apply to other characters besides Anna.

38. "We had to do these re-shootings within a framework of forty-five days. Because we couldn't get it the way we wanted, we re-shot a great deal. The more sensitive sort of color film wasn't available. . . . The editing, too, was a terrific job. I had . . . much more material than usual. The first cut took out about 3,400 metres . . . and that had never happened to me before. Now its about 2, 750. Even that's an unusually long film to me" (*BB,* 262).

39. Except for the interview with Liv Ullmann—whom he wanted to defend Anna on her own—Bergman wrote out the characters' lines (Ciment, 34). In her AFI interview (*American Film Institute 2,* no. 3 [March 1973], 5, hereafter cited in the text as Ullmann 1973), Ullman's remarks are confused about what exactly was done. Von Sydow has indicated that though this is one of his favorite films, he does not like these inserted interviews.

40. "Such celestial phenomena have been omens of violent events or catastrophes of various sorts. For me it's an old familiar sign" (*BB,* 255).

41. Andreas bears some resemblance to Mr. Y (and Elis to Mr. X) in Strindberg's play *Pariah* (1890).

42. This scene was one of the last shot, so the actors knew their characters. The night before shooting Bergman went over with them generally what they should talk about. He shot the characters one at a time, and then let the conversation take its course. Bergman was especially happy with the "wild and shrill and strange" note that crept into Liv Ullmann's voice as she de-

fended her marriage (*BB,* 258). Ullmann recalls, "One day a lady came and she made a beautiful dinner. First it may have been Max von Sydow's turn. He drank red wine and all of us could ask him questions. He had to answer as the character and the camera was on him all the time. [Bergman] did the same thing with all four of us. Then he cut it together" (Ullmann, 1973, 5).

43. Bergman has since made this figurehead the emblem of his production company, which, in tribute to the man who developed the first successful movie camera projector, Louis Lumière, is called Cinematograph.

44. In his documentary on Fårö, *Fårö Document* (1970) Bergman interviewed a sheep breeder about the slaughterhouse on the island (*BB,* 264).

45. Elis uses motor-driven Nikon and Hasselblod cameras, then the Ferrari and Rolls-Royce of still photography.

Asked what he garnered about Bergman from this scene, Max von Sydow replied, "It tells me about a man who is very sensitive and very afraid of being handled by other people. A man who is very anxious to stay in command and who is very good at being in command" (Meryman, 70).

46. "One morning during the shooting of *The Magician* Gunnar [Björnstrand] had a frightfully bad migraine. Instead of postponing the take, Ingmar and Gunnar agreed to take the scene just then, while the migraine was at its worst. The extra tension in the face, the pain in the eyes—it would all be very effective in a close-up." Björnstrand said later, "People don't understand that sort of thing. They haven't a clue as to how the artists work. They'd only think it seemed cruel" (Sjöman, 63–64).

47. Though the shot, "made almost six months after the rest of the film," was rehearsed, it was captured on film on the first take. Bergman had begun having his actors dub in the sound in the studio, though he always had a supporting sound track made on location (*BB,* 257).

48. "Last summer [1968] some birds happened to hit against the window-panes of the house where I was staying in Fårö. . . . But I would never have gone over and touched them. I wouldn't have dared. I've been wary of them too long" (Björkman, et al., 45).

49. In *The Touch,* over a game of chess, Karin lies to Andreas about her love affair with David.

50. Bergman will use a variation on this for the letter sequence in *The Touch.*

51. Frederick J. Marker and Lise-Lone Marker, "Why Ingmar Bergman Will Stop Making Films," *Saturday Review of Literature* (April 1982): 38, hereafter cited in the text as Marker and Marker, *SR.*

52. *Black Beauty* was the first film Bergman ever saw. "About a stallion. I still recall a sequence with a fire ['everything was red']. It was burning, I remember that vividly" (*BB,* 6).

53. The camera angles and the editing in this scene are reminiscent of some in *Wild Strawberries.* As Marianne and Isak are driving to Lund, she

brutally exposes his selfishness. Later, Isak swerves off the road to avoid hitting the Almans' car, which has pulled in front of them. The Almans almost smashed into them because Mrs. Alman slapped the face of her husband who was driving.

54. In Strindberg's *To Damascus* the character called the Stranger walks out on the woman who has tried to destroy his pride and honor. She asks, "Can't you forgive?" "Yes, I forgive you—and go. . . . Why should I stay here to let myself be torn to pieces?" "Have you no sense of duty?" she counters. "Yes; the most important one. To save my soul from total destruction. Goodbye!" (Strindberg, *Plays 2,* 140.)

55. Bergman, often too ready to dismiss some films others have judged to be failures, says that *The Serpent's Egg*'s "failure was mainly due to the fact that I called the city Berlin and decided to set it in 1920. . . . I created a Berlin which no one recognized, not even I" (*ML,* 130–32).

56. Elliott Gould says Abel was written for him, but that De Laurentiis prevented the casting. Guy Flatley, "Elliot Gould Speaks Well of *Silent Partner*," *New York Times,* 2 September 1977.

57. "On the first day of shooting," reports David Carradine, "Ingmar walked me through the scene where I discover my brother's dead body. To dramatize my dazed condition, I was ordered to walk into a closet and sit down. That's when I realized I was in a Bergman picture." "A Day on Bergmanstrasse," *Time,* 14 February 1977, 78.

58. Bauer is the name of the Riens' agent in *The Ritual.*

59. Originally, Manuela had two big numbers, but Bergman cut them— probably, says Ullmann, because he thought they would be too autonomous. She liked playing these scenes because they were different from anything she had previously done (Ciment, 31).

60. Hans is undoubtedly named after Hannes, the boy with whom, as a youth, Bergman stayed in Germany, and who, when he returned with Bergman to Sweden, fell in love with his sister.

61. *Frau Holle* was the name of the first film Bergman bought as a child.

62. Among the references are the hurdy-gurdy player, the mention of Inspector Lohmann, who is working "on another case that seems insane," the sinister Mabuse's insidious and subterranean crimes, and camera angles that call to mind the entrapment of "M." There are also organ grinders with monkeys in Bergman's *Secrets of Women* and *Sawdust and Tinsel.*

63. In Hans Fallada's *Wolf among Wolves* (New York: G. P. Putnam's Sons, 1938), a character says, "We ought to tell that to God, but he's got a bit fed up with his job in the last five years [1918–23] and he's deaf in one ear" (297).

64. The horse was obtained live from a slaughterhouse. Bergman wanted to show the horse dying, but the German SPCA would not allow it, though the organization did permit him to kill it. Then Carradine objected. Bergman, he says, "reasoned that the horse was dying anyway, and he

thought the art was worth it. . . . I pointed out to him that I thought a live horse was a much more artistic thing than a dead horse. Or a movie, for that matter. And he didn't see that. He actually felt that the art he was creating was more important than life. Ingmar draws the line someplace, he doesn't kill people." Paul Bartel, "Another Evening with David Carradine," *Take One* (July 1978): 19.

65. Bergman cut out scene 14 in which Abel, talking to Manuela, goes on at length about Jews being poisonous, diseased, abnormal people who should be exterminated.

66. The high-angled shot looking down on the narrow cobblestone street almost exactly duplicates a key shot from *M*.

67. Robert Boyers and Maxine Bernstein, "Women, the Arts, and the Politics of Culture: An Interview with Susan Sontag," *Salmagundi* nos. 31–32 (Fall 1975–Winter 1976): 35.

68. Ingmar Bergman, *From the Life of the Marionettes,* trans. Alan Blair (New York: Pantheon Books, 1980), v–vi. Bergman explains that in this film, as in *Face to Face,* he is interested in the question of how it is that a well-adjusted and established person suddenly suffers a mental breakdown.

69. Katarina is the name not only of the woman who seduced Alma into having sex with the boys on the beach in *Persona,* but of the woman in Andreas Winkelmann's daydream who says he has "cancer of the soul" (*The Passion of Anna*).

70. In a dream in *Persona* Alma bends over the supposedly sleeping Elisabet and says, "I can see the pulse in your neck." Peter, preparing to bring his razor into place, says, "I touched her very lightly, a tiny pulse is throbbing at her neck."

71. Near the end of *Scenes from a Marriage* Marianne will elaborate on this important feeling.

72. Like Bergman's costumier Mago (Max Goldstein), Tomas Isidor Mandelbaum's name is condensed to TIM. He is named Tim, says Bergman, after a now deceased, gay personal secretary of his, a man who suddenly turned to "sexuality of the most brutal kind." Some of Tim's lines, says Bergman, are borrowed from the real Tim (*ML,* 195). In the screenplay Bergman describes Tim as, like himself, "hyper-sensitive" and possessing especially "keen hearing."

73. This performance room was designed by the same production designer who created the prostitutes' basement apartment in *The Serpent's Egg*.

74. To help him recover from the breakdown that came as a result of his income tax affair, Bergman took notes on the "torments tearing [him] to pieces." He tried to determine if it was forgiveness he was after, and if so, whose—"The Tax Authority? Detective Karlsson? . . . Your enemies? Your critics? Will God forgive you? And give you absolution?" (*ML,* 94–95). He later wrote up this investigation into his hysterical behavior and gave it the working title, "The Closed Room."

Chapter 7

1. She was a countess by virtue of her previous marriage to Count Jan Carl von Rosen.

2. Sven Nykvist recalls: "We had to shoot 5 1/2 hours of cut film in . . . 42 days. . . . The reason we decided to shoot it in 16 mm was because we were assured that the finished film would be shown only on television. Basically, we had to shoot a 50-minute episode each week. . . . On Monday and Tuesday . . . we had rehearsal, with only Ingmar, myself and the actors present. . . . There was a lot of dialogue to learn. On the third day, Wednesday, we were ready to shoot and we would start at 9:00 A.M. with camera rehearsal. We tried to time each scene so that it would run 10 minutes long in a single continuous take—just enough to fill a magazine load of film. During that 10 minutes we made many camera moves and zooms, and that was very difficult for me, because I not only had to light the set, but I was also the camera operator, as is the custom in Sweden." Sven Nykvist, "Sven Nykvist, ASC, Talks about Filming Ingmar Bergman's *The Magic Flute*," *American Cinematographer* (August 1975): 932–33, hereafter cited in the text. Worth noting, too, is that Bergman always budgets money to reshoot after he sees what the first shots add up to artistically.

3. The play version appears in Frederick J. Marker and Lise-Lone Markers, eds., *Ingmar Bergman: A Project for the Theatre* (New York: Frederick Unga, 1983), 149–215.

4. Erland Josephson comments: "We got to know the characters so well that . . . we did not in fact have lengthy discussions about each sequence, nor did we improvise stretches of conversation" (Cowie 1982, 285).

5. In some cases Max von Sydow was not available. He told me that he turned down the "grim" role of Abel Rosenberg in *The Serpent's Egg* (14 October 1991).

6. The film's huge success in Sweden led to its being shown in the United States, where it was cut down to two and a half hours and blown up to 35mm. Sven Nykvist thought that this version might hurt his reputation as a cinematographer because of the graininess and tight close-ups. "I photographed [*Scenes from a Marriage*] in the 1.33 format because we had been assured that it would be shown only on television. We never thought that it would be blown up for theatrical release. If I had known in advance . . . I would have moved back a bit and given the compositions more space." He used the very grainy Eastman negative 7254 both because it was the only 16mm color negative available at the time and because "it was very, very important to have the extra speed because of all the moves that had to be made and the necessity for staying in focus. . . . I hoped it would be written in the titles that it was originally shot in 16mm, so that people would understand the reason why it was so grainy." But when he saw the 35mm version in a theater in Stockholm, he found that the shots looked quite sharp: "I dis-

covered . . . what I call 'grain sharpness.' The grain, as it is blown up, stays sharp and creates an impression that the picture itself is sharp. . . . On every picture I . . . [learn] something" (Nykvist, 897, 899).

7. Shooting this film was "like shooting a documentary," says Ullmann. "I felt very connected to the role. It is a moment of my life when I began to be directly concerned with the feminine movement and by my need for freedom in so far as I am a woman. I have been completely supported by my roles and my work and I have never been permitted to really be myself. This film was a stage in my attaining consciousness. There wasn't symbolism, strangeness, neurosis; everyone could relate to it; it was you and me, and in this event it was me" (Ciment, 36).

8. Bergman had staged Albee's play in 1963.

9. *Theater* (New Haven), 11, no. 1 (Fall 1979).

10. This scene was the first one he wrote (Cowie 1982, 285) and is a near facsimile of Bergman's telling Ellen Lundström of his affair with Gun Grut (*ML,* 161).

11. Liv Ullmann says, "There is a scene which I regret is not in the short version. At breakfast I tell [Johan] that I am going to speak to the maid, and he tells me that she already knows, that she came one morning" and caught him with Paula. "I like the reaction of my character. . . . Inside, she is in agony, but on her face there is a smile. This scene seemed much more dreadful than if she had learned on the telephone from her friends that they knew about it. A woman maintains, in effect, personal relations with people who help with the house" (Ciment, 36).

12. In *Now about These Women* Tristan reveals his humiliation to Madame Tussaud, only to be further humiliated by her falling asleep.

13. Birgitta Steene identifies it as the kind of lantern used in "the most Dionysian of Swedish events, the annual carnival-like crayfish party in late August." "Freedom and Entrapment," *Movietone News* (11 May 1975): 16.

14. In the screenplay only, discussion of Anna's unquestioning devotion to Johan leads Marianne to observe (and Liv Ullmann could be speaking for herself and Bergman), "First it was your mother who adored you and thought you were a genius. And then a whole succession of women who have behaved in exactly the same way. . . . I wonder what it is in you that sabotages all natural maturity." Admitting that he does not have Marianne's "gift for feeling love," Johan confidently provides his discouraging answer to her question: "I'm a middle-aged boy who never wants to grow up . . . a child with genitals, a fabulous combination when it comes to women with maternal feelings . . . [and] I don't *want* to mature."

15. Virginia Wright Wexman, "An Interview with Liv Ullmann," *Cinema Journal* 20, no. 1 (Fall 1980): 72–73, hereafter cited in the text.

16. Marsha Kinder,[review of *Scenes from a Marriage*], *Film Quarterly* (Winter 1974–75): 53.

17. "Bergman on Opera," *Opera News,* no. 24 (5 May 1962): 13.

18. Nykvist, 953. By this time Kodak's versatile new negative stock, 7247, was available.

19. In a speech excised from the film, Jenny almost duplicates Marianne's statement. Jenny says, "Once only in my life have I *understood* another human being. For one short moment."

20. Ingmar Bergman, *Face to Face,* trans. Alan Blair (New York: Pantheon Books, 1976), vi.

21. Also in the audience are Bergman's wife Ingrid and son Daniel.

22. Bergman could see a twin-towered cathedral from the two-story house at no. 12 Trädgårdsgatan, where he spent a lot of his childhood (Cowie 1982, 7).

23. As a child when he wet himself Ingmar was made to wear a "red . . . skirt for the rest of the day" (*ML,* 8).

24. "But the child sleeps, for its mother sits by it knitting, knitting a long strip which comes out of her mouth, on which is written: 'Blessed are they that mourn, for they shall be comforted'" (Strindberg, *Plays,* 2, 159).

25. In several places Bergman talks of corpses who still seem alive, and in several of his films—*Wild Strawberries, The Magician, Persona, Hour of the Wolf,* and *Cries and Whispers*—they do come to life. In fact, an excised passage in the screenplay of *Face to Face* is Jenny's account of being at a dead cousin's funeral and believing he was still alive in his coffin.

26. Liv Ullmann's father died when she was six.

27. Ullmann was aware that many of these experiences were "Ingmar's anxieties and childhood experiences that he was using me to share" (Wexman, 76).

28. Judy Klemesrud, "Ingrid Bergman: No Regrets at 65," *New York Times,* 7 October 1980, 19.

29. Ingrid Bergman, with Alan Burgess, *My Story* (New York: Delacorte Press, 1980), 573.

30. Ingrid Bergman played a pianist in her first international film hit, David O. Selznick's *Intermezzo* (1939). (Earlier, in 1936, she had played the same role in Gustav Molander's Swedish film of the same title.)

31. When Hitchcock screened this film, on her first entrance he said, "She looks old; they've shot her badly." *Esquire Film Quarterly* (April 1982): 100.

32. Pauline Kael, *When the Lights Go Down* (New York: Holt, Rinehart, and Winston, 1980), 479.

33. Both Ingrid and Ingmar felt guilty for neglecting their children. One of Ingmar's many children is named Lena, another Eva.

34. Liv Ullmann convinced Bergman to let her substitute her "more human" version of this speech for his more "abstract" one (Ciment, 32).

35. Bergman notes, "All pianists have had backache . . . [and] like to lie down flat on the floor" (*ML,* 183).

36. Interestingly, Max von Sydow told me he does not remember ever hearing Gunnar Björnstrand speak English and is not sure that he could (14 October 1991).

37. This shot of the proscenium stage resembles not only *The Magic Flute* scene in *Hour of the Wolf* but one of Bergman's Bris soap commercials (*Chaplin*).

38. Nykvist used an "eyeballer," a light on the camera that reflects in the actor's eyes to give them a "live" quality.

39. For further discussion, see Bruce A. Block, "Sven Nykvist, ASC, and *Fanny and Alexander,*" *American Cinematographer* (April 1984): 50–58.

40. Bergman devotes chapter 3 of *The Magic Lantern* to his Uncle Carl.

41. Josephson's family was among the first Jewish families permitted into Sweden in 1792.

42. Bergman says his first box of slides had "a pretty picture on the lid of a young man in a sailor suit showing moving pictures of fighting lions to an impressed family." David Shipman, *The Story of the Cinema* (New York: St. Martin's Press, 1982), 8. Photographs of little Ingmar show him in a sailor suit, and Alex and Fanny are frequently seen wearing a variety of sailor suits.

43. In the screenplay Bergman indicates that both her children were by another man.

44. See *ML,* 79–80.

45. Bergman's father grew up in a household of women.

46. In Uppsala a Jewish friend of Bergman's grandmother ran a store just down the street from her apartment. Bergman used to buy short films from him and, with other children, listen to him tell fairy tales and gawk at his mummy.

47. This film served as a family reunion. Besides Mats, Bergman's daughter Anna played Miss Hanna Schwartz, his son Daniel was a grip, and his former wife Käbi Laretei was Aunt Anna, the woman who plays the piano at the Christmas party. Bergman's daughter Linn Ullmann was to play Alex and Fanny's older sister, Amanda, a role that was cut when she was unable to appear. In addition, old lovers and colleagues—Harriet Andersson, Gunnar Björnstrand, Allan Edwall, Jarl Kulle, Erland Josephson—are brought together here.

48. See *ML,* 275.

49. See *ML,* 53.

50. Strindberg, *Six Plays,* 193. "There is a dark romantic chord running through Scandinavian literature, art, theater, and music, right up to the present day; Swedenborg, Sibelius, Hamsun, Kierkegaard, and of course Strindberg," says Bergman. "That theme is also a bit crazy, magic if you like, and a lot of us have that influence in our blood." Peter Cowie, "Ingmar Bergman—The Struggle with 'The Beyond,'" *New York Times,* 26 October 1980.

51. See *ML,* 42.

52. William A. Henry III, "Still Shy, but Not Retiring," *Time*, 24 June 1991, 66.

53. "Filming of Ingmar Bergman Script on Life of His Parents," *Nordst, Jernan-Svea*, 16 August 1990, 15. Bergman says he finds this period from 1900 to the start of World War I fascinating because "it's terrible . . . so obscene . . . the start of a new age. It's a time so double and so cruel and so filled with deceit. The peace is so full of holes." At the same time, it is an "extremely rich period artistically—in drama, in literature, in painting. . . . Can it be that the pressure from the society was so enormous, so perverse, that the artists could only express themselves indirectly? In hidden ways?" (Marker and Marker 1983, 9).

54. Henrik was Bergman's great-grandfather's name, and Anna was Karin's mother's name.

SELECTED BIBLIOGRAPHY

Primary Sources (Not fluent in Swedish, the author has not consulted all of the following.)
Essays, Articles, Letters, and Other Miscellaneous Writings

"Några huvuddrag i Selma Lagerlöfs författarskap" (Some Main Features in Selma Lagerlöf's Works). Unpublished student essay, Palmgrenska School, Stockholm, Spring 1937.

"*Himmelrikets nycklar:* Sagospel, drömspel, vandringsdrama" (*The Key of Heaven:* Fairy Play, Dreamplay, Station Drama). Unpublished undergraduate thesis on Strindberg's play, University of Stockholm, Fall 1940.

"Blick in i framtiden" (Look into the Future). Unpublished manuscript, Swedish Radio Archives, Stockholm; 1944.

"Skoltiden ett 12-årigt helvete" (School a 12-Year Hell). *Aftonbladet* (30 October 1944): 1, 16. Bergman's account of his school years.

"Svensk film och teater: Ett samgående eller motsatsförhållande" (Swedish Film and Theater: Collaboration or Competition?). Unpublished lecture, given 3 February 1946 in Höganäs City Hall.

"Om att filmatisera en pjäs" (About Filming a Play [*Crisis*]). *Filmnyheter* 1, no. 4 (1946): 1–4. Bergman says he did not like the script until he created the character Jack.

"Den bästa novellen" (The Best Short Story). *Vecko-Journalen* 38, no. 7 (1947): 6. Comments on Erland Josephson short story.

"Ruth." *Filmnyheter* 2, no. 11 (1947): 1–4. IB's interview with himself about the main character of *The Woman without a Face* being based in personal experience.

"Det förtrollade marknadsnöjet" (The Magic Country Fair). *Biografbladet* 28, no. 3 (Fall 1947): 1. Tribute to Méliès and the magic of film.

"Tre tusenfotinfötter" (Three Centipede Feet). *Filmjournalen* 29, no. 51–52 (December 1947): 8–9, 53.

"Kinematograf" (Cinematograph). *Biografbladet* 29, no. 4 (Winter 1948): 240–41. Bergman talks about childhood experiences that affected his decision to go into film.

"Själva händelsen" (The Event Itself). *Filmnyheter* 3, no. 20 (1948): 4–7. IB tells of his auto accident, which became idea for *Eva*.

"Brev från Ingmar Bergman" (Letter from IB). *Terrafilm 10 år.* 1948. Stockholm: Terrafilm, 20.

"Filmen om Birgitta-Carolina" (The Film about Birgitta Carolina). *Stock-*

holms-Tidningen, 18 March 1949. Essay on the genesis of *The Devil's Wanton* and a description of Birgitta Carolina.

"Blad ur en obefintlig dagbok" (Pages from a Nonexistent Diary). Unpublished manuscript in Archives of Swedish Film Institute (SFI). Bergman talks about his obsession with filmmaking, 1950, 4 pp.

"Fisken: Fars förs film" (The Fish: A Farce for Film). *Biografbladet* 31, no. 4 (Winter 1951): 200–25.

"Ni vill till filmen?" (So You Want to Get into Movies?). *Filmjournalen*, no. 36 (9 September 1951): 14, 16.

"Vi är cirkus!" (We Are the Circus). *Filmjournalen*, no. 4 1953: 7, 31. Essay comparing filmmaking and the circus.

"Det att göra film" (Making Film). *Filmyheter 9*, no. 19–20 (December 1954): 1–9. Essay.

"Sex frågor till Ingmar Bergman" (Six Questions to IB). *Bildjournalen*, no. 38 (1956): 8–9. IB talks about himself as bourgeois.

"Why Do I Make Films?" (1954). Reprinted in Harry Geduld, *Film Makers on Film Making* (Bloomington: Indiana University Press, 1967).

"Ingmars självporträtt" (Ingmar's Self-Portrait). *Se*, no. 9 (3 March 1957): 33–34.

"Dialog" (Dialogue). *Filmnyheter* 13, no. 11 (1 September 1958): 1–3. Conversation between IB and an imaginary writer.

[Untitled editorial on high taxation on films in Sweden]. *Filmrutan* 2, no. 1 (1959): 1.

"Varje film är min sista" (Each Film Is My Last). *Filmnyheter* 14, no. 9–10 (19 May 1959): 1–8.

"Extract in Memory of Victor Sjöström." *Sight and Sound* 29, no. 2 (Spring 1960): 98–100. Hommage to Sjöström, who died in 1960.

"Förbön" (Prayer). *Chaplin* 2, no. 8 (14 November 1960): 187, 189. Under pseudonym of Ernest Riffe, Bergman attacks himself.

"Away with Improvisation—This Is Creation." *Films and Filming* 7, no. 7 (September 1961): 13. Based on an interview with Bergman by Bengt Forslund.

"Ormskinnet" (The Snakeskin). Essay originally written as acceptance speech for the Erasmus Award, 1965. Published as preface to Swedish edition of *Persona* (Stockholm: Norstedt, 1966), and, under the title "Snakeskin," in *Film Comment* 6, no. 2 (Summer) 1970: 14–15.

"Fantastic Is the Word." *Film World*, no. 3 (1968): 4–5. Account of genesis of *Shame*.

"Schizofren intervju med nervös regissör" (Schizophrenic Interview with Nervous Director). *Chaplin* 10, no. 84 (October 1968): 274. Again using the pseudonym Ernest Riffe, Bergman interviews himself and comments on critics trying to define his values.

"My Three most powerfully effective Commandments." *Film Comment* 6 (Summer 1970): 9–12.

MANDRUP-NIELSEN, MADS. "Jag skulle vilja slå ihjäl er" (I'd Like to Kill You). *Röster i Radio/TV,* no. 15 (7–13 April 1973): 6. Another [Riffe-like interview] in which Bergman attacks progressive, politically conscious young critics and provides a lengthy analysis of *Scenes from a Marriage.* Mads Mandrup-Nielsen is supposedly a 28-year-old film scholar who interviews Bergman.

"Trollflöjten" (The Magic Flute). Unpublished music score, libretto, and IB commentaries on his version of the opera. 1974. SFI Archives.

"Der Wahre Künstler Spricht mit Seinem Herzen" (The True Artist Speaks with His Heart). *Filmkunst* 74 (1976): 1–3. Reprint of speech delivered at Goethe Award ceremonies, 28 August 1976. IB briefly addresses the humanistic, psychological, and professional bases of artistic creativity.

"Nu lämnar jag Sverige" (Now I Leave Sweden). *Expressen,* 22 April 1976, 4–5. Open letter explaining why his arrest by tax authorities compels him to leave Sweden.

"The Closed Room." 1976. Unpublished account of what Bergman considered his exaggerated and inappropriate reactions to being arrested for tax evasion.

Books

Laterna Magica (The Magic Lantern). Translated from the Swedish by Joan Tate (London: Hamish Hamilton, 1988; New York: Penguin, 1989) Autobiography.

The Best Intentions. Translated from the Swedish by Joan Tate (New York: Arcade Publishing, 1993). Novel.

Bilder (Pictures). 1990. To be published in English in the fall of 1993 under the title *My Life in Film.* A book-length evaluation of his films.

Program Notes

During his two years directing at Mäster-Olofsgården, Bergman published several notes and essays in Stockholms Förenade Prästerskap (Stockholm Associated Clergy). Among them were:

"Till främmande hamn" (To a Foreign Port), no. 3 (1938), 3 (Bergman writes, in this stencil publication, about his first Mäster-Olofsgården production, Sutton Vane's *Outward Bound);*

"Experiment-teater" (Experimental Theater), no. 3 (1939), 24; "Lycko-Pers resa" (Lucky Per's Journey), no. 3 (1939), 5; "Experimentteatern igen" (Experimental Theater Once More), no. 9 (1939), 3; "Vår lilla stad" *(Our Town),* no. 1 (1940); "Teatraliskt i stan" (Theatrics in Town), no. 2 (1940), 1; "En saga" (A Fairy Tale), no. 3 (1940), 4; *"Ringaren i Notre Dame" (The Hunchback of Notre Dame),* no. 4 (1940), 6; 'Ett spelår år tillandalupet" (A Year's Repertory Has Come to an End), no. 5 (1940), 8, 14.

"*Hets:* Kniv på en varböld" (*Torment:* Knife on a Boil), 1944.

Untitled program notes for plays IB directed in 1944: *Rabies*, (1 November) Strindberg's *The Pelican* (25 November), Sune Bergström's *Reduce the Morale* (12 April), and Franz Werfel's *Jacobowski and the Colonel* (9 September). Bergman's untitled program note for his unpublished adaptation of a segment of Olle Hedburg's novel *Rabies* at the Hälsingborg City Theater is considered by some his defense of the postwar disillusionment in the literature of the Swedish *fyrtiotalist* (a member of the disillusioned, metaphysically oriented generation of Swedish writers).

"Möte" (Encounter), program note to IB's play *Rakel and the Cinema Doorman*, 1946.

"I mormors hus" (In Grandmother's House), program note to IB's play *To My Terror*, 1947.

"Leka med pärlor" (Playing with Pearls, 1951.) Bergman describes the source of the script for *Summer Interlude*.

"Ingmar Bergman intervjuar sig själv inför premiären på *Sommaren med Monika*" (IB Interviews Himself before the Opening of *Summer with Monika)*, 1953. Reprinted in *Filmnyheter* 8, no. 2 (1953): 4–5.

"Aforkstiskt av Ingmar Bergman" (Aphoristic by IB), 1956. Program note in Swedish and German for the opening of *The Seventh Seal*.

Untitled program note to *The Seventh Seal* for American opening, 1957 (reprinted in Steene, *Focus on "The Seventh Seal"*).

"Kära skrämmande publik" (Dear Frightened Public), 9 October 1960. Program note in which IB, in a dialogue with an imaginary viewer, stresses that *The Devil's Eye* is a comedy.

"A Page from My Diary," 1960. Program note for opening of *The Virgin Spring*.

Untitled program note for the opening of *Through a Glass Darkly*, 1961.

"Kommentar till serie ö" (Commentary to Ö Series), 3 September 1973. IB's comments on nine of his films that were being shown in retrospective at SFI in Stockholm.

Short Stories

"Hets (Pressure/Frenzy) and "Marie," Summer 1937. Unpublished.

"En kortare berättelse om en av Jack Uppskärarens tidigaste barndomsminnen" (A Short Tale about One of Jack the Ripper's Earliest Childhood Memories), *40-tal*, no. 3 (1944): 5–9. Translated into French by A. Amlie under the title "Un souvenir d'enfance de Jack l'eventreur," *Cinéma* 59, no. 34 (March 1959): 39–44.

"Sagan om Eiffeltornet" (The Tale of the Eiffel Tower), 1953. Unpublished.

Plays, Radio Plays, and Plays Adaptions

Stage adaptation of Hans Christian Andersen's tale "The Tinder Box," 1941. Manuscript lost.

"Kaspers död" (Kasper's Death/Death of Punch), 1942. Unpublished stage play.

"Tivolit" (The Fun Fair), 1943. Unpublished stage play.

"Rabies," 1944. Unpublished stage adaptation of Olle Hedburg's novel *Rabies* (1944).

Jack hos skådespelarna (Jack among the Actors). (Stockholm: Bonniers, 1946). Drama in two acts.

"Ett dockhem" (A Doll's House), 1948. Unpublished adaptation of the Ibsen play.

"Kamma noll" (Come up Empty), 1948. Unpublished script for a comedy (play).

Moraliteeter (Morality Plays), (Stockholm: Bonniers, 1948). Publication of three plays under one title: *Dagen slutar tidigt* (The Day Ends Early), *Mig till skräck* (To My Terror), and *Rakel och biografvaktmästaren* (Rakel and the Cinema Doorman).

"Staden" (The City), 1951. Unpublished radio play.

"Mordet i Barjärna" (Murder at Barjärna), 1952. Unpublished play.

Trämålning (Wood Painting) (1954). Reprinted in Steene, *Focus on "The Seventh Seal."* One-act play.

Film and Television Scripts or Synopses

"Hets" (Pressure/Frenzy/Torment), 1943. Unpublished.

"Kris" (Crisis), 1944. Unpublished.

"Det regnar på vår kärlek" (It Rains on Our Love), 1946. Unpublished.

"Kvinna utan ansikte eller puzzlet föreställer Eros" (The Woman without a Face, or, The Puzzle Represents Eros), 1947. Lost synopsis.

"Skepp till Indialand" (A Ship to India), 1947. Unpublished.

"Fängelse" (Prison), 1948. Unpublished.

"Hamnstad" (Port of Call), 1948. Unpublished.

"Trumpetspelaren och vår herre" (The Trumpet Player and Our Lord), 1948. Unpublished synopsis that became *Eva*.

Till glädje (To Joy), 1949. *Filmjournalen* 32, nos. 12–20 (1950).

"Medan staden sover" (While the City Sleeps), 1950. Unpublished.

"Sommarlek" (Summer Interlude), 1950. Unpublished.

"Frånskild" (Divorced), 1951. Unpublished.

"Kvinnors väntan" (Waiting Women), 1952. Unpublished.

"Sommaren med Monika" (Summer with Monika), 1952. Unpublished.

"Gycklarnas afton" (Eve of the Jesters), 1953. *Filmjournalen* 35, nos. 25/26–38 (1953). Serialized as a film novella.

"En lektion i kärlek" (A Lesson in Love), 1953. Unpublished.

"Kvinnodröm" (Women's Dreams), 1954. Unpublished.

Sommarnattens leende (Smiles of a Summer Night), 1955. See *Four Screenplays*.

"Sista paret ut" (Last Couple Out), 1956. Unpublished.

"Det Sjunde inseglet" (The Seventh Seal), 1956. See *Four Screenplays*.
"Smultronstället" (The Wild Strawberry Place), 1957. See *Four Screenplays*.
"Ansiktet" (The Face), 1958. See *Four Screenplays*.
"Djävulens öga" (The Devil's Eye), 1959. Unpublished.
Four Screenplays of Ingmar Bergman. Translated from the Swedish by Lars Malmström and David Kushner. New York: Simon and Schuster, 1960. First publication of IB's scripts in any language: *Smiles of a Summer Night, The Seventh Seal, Wild Strawberries*, and *The Magician*.
"Lustgården" (The Pleasure Garden), 1961. Unpublished.
"Såsom i en spegel" (Through a Glass Darkly), 1961. See *Film Trilogy*.
"Nattvardsgästerna" (The Communicants), 1962. See *Film Trilogy*.
"Tystnaden" (The Silence), 1962. See *Film Trilogy*.
"För att inte tala om alla dessa kvinnor" (Now to Speak about All These Women), with Erland Josephson, 1964. Unpublished.
Persona. Stockholm: Norstedt, 1966.
"Vargtimmen" (Hour of the Wolf), 1966. See *Four Stories*.
"Falskspelet" (False Play), 1966. Written after *Smiles of a Summer Night*, the filming of which discouraged IB from filming "Falskspelet."
A Film Trilogy. Translated from the Swedish by Paul B. Austin. London: Calder and Boyars, 1966. Screenplays of *Through a Glass Darkly, Winter Light*, and *The Silence*.
"Skammen" (The Shame), 1966.
"En passion" (A Passion), 1968. See *Four Stories*.
"Riten" (The Rite), 1968. Published in Swedish in *Filmberättelser* (Film Stories), vol. 3 (Stockholm: Norstedt/Pan), 7–55.
"Reservatet" (The Sanctuary), 1969. Unpublished play for television.
"Fårö-dokument," 1969. No script located.
"Beröringen" (The Touch), 1970. See *Four Stories*.
Persona and Shame. Translated from the Swedish by Keith Bradfield. London: Calder and Boyars; New York: Grossman, 1971.
"Viskningar och rop" (Whispers and Cries), 1971. See *Four Stories*.
"Scener ur ett äktenskap" (Scenes from a Marriage), 1972.
Scenes from a Marriage. Translated from the Swedish by Alan Blair. New York: Pantheon Books, 1974. Script for the television play, plus four-page preface.
"Anskite mot ansikte" (Face to Face), 1974.
Face to Face. Translated from the Swedish by Alan Blair. New York: Pantheon Books, 1976. Script, plus letter IB wrote to his artists and crew before filming.
Four Stories of Ingmar Bergman. Translated by Alan Blair. London: M. Boyars; Garden City, N.Y.: Doubleday, 1976. Scripts to *The Touch, Cries and Whispers, Hour of the Wolf*, and *The Passion of Anna*.
The Serpent's Egg (Ormens ägg). Translated from the Swedish by Alan Blair. New York: Pantheon Books, 1977.

"The Petrified Prince," 1977. Unpublished.

Autumn Sonata (Höstsonat). Translated from the Swedish by Alan Blair. New York: Pantheon Books, 1978.

"Fårö-dokument 2," 1979. No manuscript available.

From the Life of the Marionettes (Aus dem Leben des Marionnettes). Translated from the Swedish by Alan Blair. New York: Pantheon Books, 1980.

Fanny and Alexander (Fanny och Alexander). Translated from the Swedish by Alan Blair. New York: Pantheon, 1982.

"Efter repetitionen" (After the Rehearsal), 1983. Unpublished.

"Den goda viljan" (The Best Intentions), 1990. Unpublished.

"Söndagsbarn" (Sunday's Children), 1991. Unpublished.

Secondary Sources

Interviews

Aghed, Jan. "Conversations avec Ingmar Bergman." *Positif* (Paris) 121 (November 1970).

Alpert, Hollis. "Style Is the Director." *Saturday Review of Literature* (23 December 1961).

Alvarez, A. "A Visit with Ingmar Bergman." *New York Times Magazine,* 7 December 1975.

"Avskedsintervju" (Farewell Interview). In program for Björn-Erik Höijer's play *Requiem,* 1946.

Béranger, Jean. "Recontre avec Ingmar Bergman." *Cahiers du cinéma* (Paris) (October 1958).

Bertina, B.J., and Frenk Van Der Linden. "Ingmar Bergman: 'I Am the Master of Humiliation.'" *Los Angeles Times,* 10 June 1984.

Björkman, Stig, Torsten Manns, and Jonas Sima. "Death at Dawn Each Day: An Interview with Ingmar Bergman." *Evergreen Review,* no. 13 (February 1969).

———. *Bergman on Bergman.* Translated from the Swedish by Paul Britten Austin. New York: Simon and Schuster, 1973. Interviews with IB in January 1968, February 1969, and April 1970.

Björkman, Stig. *Ingmar Bergman* (film), 1971. Björkman documents the making of *The Touch* and interviews IB, cast, and Nykvist.

Bonisteel, Roy. "Man Alive" (CBC), 1970. Television interview.

Cavett, Dick. "The Dick Cavett Show" (ABC), 14 May 1971. Interview in Stockholm with IB and Bibi Andersson.

Champlin, Charles. "Bergman on Hollywood Pilgrimage." *Los Angeles Times,* 9 November 1976.

Cole, Alan. "Ingmar Bergman, Magician." *New York Herald Tribune,* 25 October, 1 November, and 8 November, 1959.

[*Continental Film Review*]. Transcription of IB's press conference on *Shame. Continental Film Review* (London) (December 1967).

[———]. "Bergman Talks about His Life and His Films." *Continental Film Review,* 1, no. 6 (1973).

Cowie, Peter. "Ingmar Bergman—The Struggle with 'The Beyond.'" *New York Times,* 26 October 1980.

Donner, Jörn. *Three Scenes [Conversations] with Ingmar Bergman* (documentary film), 1975. Donner interviews IB about his life, values, and films.

Freedman, Lewis. Television interview with IB. National Broadcasting Laboratory for U.S. public television, 14 April 1968.

Grenier, Cynthia. Interview with IB. *Oui,* no. 3 (March 1974).

Hedlund, Oscar. "Ingmar Bergman, The Listener." *Saturday Review of Literature* (29 February 1964).

Jacobs, James. "Ingmar Bergman at Work." *Positif* no. 204 (March 1978). Transcription of a documentary shot on the set of *The Serpent's Egg.*

Jones, G. William, ed. *Talking with Ingmar Bergman.* (Dallas: SMU Press, 1983). Seminars at Southern Methodist University, Dallas, 7–8 May 1981, including question-and-answer periods.

Kakutani, Michiko. "Ingmar Bergman: Summing up a Life in Film." *New York Times Magazine,* 26 June 1983.

Lejefors, Ann-Sofi. "Bergman in Close-up." *Sweden* Now 17, no. 1 (1983). Originally published in the monthly *Månads Journalen* (November 1982).

Löthwall, Lars-Olof. "Ingmar Bergman." *Take One* 2 no. 1 (September-October 1968).

———. "Moment of Agony: Interview with Ingmar Bergman." *Films and Filming* (London) (February 1969).

Marker, Frederick J. and Lise-Lone Marker. "Why Ingmar Bergman Will Stop Making Films." *Saturday Review of Literature* (April 1982).

———. "The Making of *Fanny and Alexander:* A Conversation with Ingmar Bergman." *Films and Filming* (February 1983).

Meryman, Richard. "I Live at the Edge of a Very Strange Country." *Life* (15 October 1971).

Newman, Edwin. "My Need to Express Myself in a Film." *Film Comment* 4 (Fall-Winter 1967).

Pehrsson, Bertil. Summary of BTV Interview in Sweden, 4 March 1973. *Films in Review* 24, no. 7 (August-September 1973).

Peter-Sundgren, Nils. "Meeting with Bergman." *Positif* 204 (March 1978).

[*Playboy*]. "Ingmar Bergman: A Candid Conversation with Sweden's One-Man New Wave of Cinematic Energy." *Playboy* (June 1964).

[*Positif*]. Interview with IB. *Positif* 289 (March 1985).

Prouse, Derek. "Ingmar Bergman: The Censor's Problem-Genius." *Sunday Times* (London), 15 March 1964.

Samuels, Charles Thomas. Interview with IB. In *Encountering Directors,* New York: Putnam's, 1972. Reprinted in Stuart Kaminsky and J. Hill, eds., *Ingmar Bergman: Essays in Criticism.* New York: Oxford University Press, 1976.

Sorel, Edith. "Ingmar Bergman: 'I Confect Dreams and Anguish.'" *New York Times*, 22 January 1978.
"I Am A Conjurer," *Time*, 14 March 1960.
Weinraub, Bernard. "Bergman in Exile." *New York Times*, 17 October 1976.
Wolf, William. "Face to Face with Ingmar Bergman." *New York*, 27 October 1980.

Bibliographies

Steene, Birgitta. *Ingmar Bergman: A Guide to References and Resources*. Boston: G.K. Hall, 1987. Contains a short biography and critical evaluation of IB and his films, synopses of the plots of all the films, their credits, notes, reviews, and critical commentaries. Lists the writings about and by IB, his other professional activities—radio and TV talks and interviews, direction of stage, radio and TV plays, stage and screen performances, production of films by other filmmakers—and the awards, prizes, and honors he has won. Also includes archival sources and film distributors. Not without errors.

Books

Bergman, Ingrid, with Alan Burgess. *My Story*. New York: Delacorte Press, 1980.
Bergom-Larsson, Maria. *Ingmar Bergman and Society*. Cranbury, N.J.: A.S. Barnes, 1978. Focuses on IB's understanding of self and of the bourgeois world's dreams and myths.
Björkman, Stig, et al. *Bergman on Bergman*. See *Secondary Works—Interviews*.
Blackwell, Marilyn Johns. *"Persona": The Transcendent Image*. Urbana: University of Illinois Press, 1986. Profusely illustrated, close reading of *Persona*.
"Ingmar Bergman at 70—A Tribute." (Stockholm: *Chaplin*, 1988). Slight and substantive articles about IB by his colleagues and admirers. A special issue of *Chaplin*.
Chiaretti, Tommaso. *Ingmar Bergman*. Rome: Canesi, 1964. Treats IB's work through *Winter Light;* includes script for *The Silence*.
Cowie, Peter. *Sweden 2*. New York: A.S. Barnes, 1970. Cowie's early study of IB.
———. *Ingmar Bergman: A Critical Biography*. New York: Charles Scribner's Sons, 1982. This well-researched book, the first biography of IB in English, presents the most complete overview of his life and films through *Fanny and Alexander* and contains a bibliography and a lengthy, if not always accurate, filmography. Cowie's comments on Bergman are cautious, and his critical evaluations of the films are safe rather than exciting. (An updated version was published by New York: Limelight Editions in 1992.)
———. "Max von Sydow: From *The Seventh Seal* to *Pelle the Conqueror*." (Stockholm: *Chaplin*, 1989). A special issue of *Chaplin*.

Donner, Jörn. *The Personal Vision of Ingmar Bergman*. Translated from the Swedish by Holger Lundbergh. Bloomington: Indiana University Press, 1964. Critical study of IB's films through *Now about These Women*. Many of Donner's insights and judgments hold up.

Eberwein, Robert T. *Film and the Dream Screen*. Princeton: Princeton University Press, 1984.

Erikson, Erik. *Identity: Youth and Crisis*. New York: W.W. Norton and Co., 1968.

Forslund, Bengt. *Victor Sjöström: His Life and His Work*. Translated from the Swedish by Peter Cowie. New York: Zoetrope, 1988. Deals with Sjöström as IB's mentor and as an actor in IB's films.

Gado, Frank. *The Passion of Ingmar Bergman*. Durham, N.C.: Duke University Press, 1986. Compelling psychoanalytical study of IB, drawing on his plays, stories, and films through *After the Rehearsal*. Valuable biographical material included. Because the bases for his analyses are IB's screenplays, not the completed films, many of Gado's interpretations of the films are suspect.

Gibson, Arthur. *The Silence of God: Creative Response to the Films of Ingmar Bergman*. New York: Harper and Row, 1969.

Guyon, François D., and Béranger, Jean. *Ingmar Bergman*. Lyon: Premier Plan, SERDOC, 1964. Expanded version of Béranger's *Ingmar Bergman et ses films* (1960), which singles out such IB themes as childhood nostalgia, couples in torment, and the flow of time.

Harcourt, Peter. *Six European Directors*. Baltimore, Md: Penguin Books, 1974.

Höök, Marianne. *Ingmar Bergman*. Stockholm: Wahlström och Widstrand, 1962. Critical study of IB's works through *Winter Light*. Insightful about his relationships with his actresses and crew.

Jones, G. William, ed. *Talking with Ingmar Bergman*. See *Secondary Works— Interviews*.

Kaminsky, Stuart, ed. *Ingmar Bergman: Essays in Criticism*. New York: Oxford University Press, 1975. The first section consists of essays on IB's life and themes and interviews. The second section consists of reviews and studies of several IB films from *The Seventh Seal* to *Scenes from a Marriage*.

Kawin, Bruce F. *Mindscreen: Bergman, Godard, and the First-Person Film*. Princeton: Princeton University Press, 1978. Kawin focuses on IB's *Persona* and *Shame*. Valuable for understanding point of view in film.

Kernberg, Otto F., M.D. *Borderline Conditions and Pathological Narcissism*. New York: Jason Aronson, 1975.

Kohut, Heinz, M.D. *The Analysis of Self: A Systematic Approach to the Psychoanalytical Treatment of Narcissistic Personality Disorders*. New York: International Universities Press, 1976.

———. *The Restoration of the Self*. New York: International Universities Press, 1977.

Livingston, Paisley. *Ingmar Bergman and the Ritual of Art*. Ithaca, N.Y.: Cornell University Press, 1982. Detailed examination of nine films, focusing on themes such as IB's fascination with "the patterns of violence, victimage, and humiliation," his oscillation between the values of the artist and the bourgeoisie, his theories of comedy vis-à-vis Henri Bergson's. Livingston's thesis is that the ritual of art functions to help IB manage his demonic urges.

Marion, Denis. *Ingmar Bergman*. Paris: Gallimard, 1979. Discusses the relationship between word and image in IB's films, then turns to themes: God and the problem of evil, contemporary crisis, eroticism, the tortured couple, art, and pessimism.

Marker, Lise-Lone, and Frederick J. Marker. *Ingmar Bergman: Four Decades in the Theatre*. Cambridge: Cambridge University Press, 1982. IB interviewed about his work in the theater. This is also a study of his stagings of Strindberg, Ibsen, and Molière.

————. *Ingmar Bergman: A Project for the Theatre*. New York: Frederick Ungar, 1983. The three plays that make up "the Bergman project"—IB's unified production of his adaptations of *A Doll's House, Miss Julie,* and *Scenes from a Marriage*—plus an interview with IB and commentary on the plays, the rehearsals, and the performances.

McIlroy, Brian. *2: Sweden*. World Cinema Series. London: Flicks Books, 1986. Treats IB at length as part of a history of Swedish cinema.

Oldrini, Guido. *La Solitudine di Ingmar Bergman*. Parma: Guanda Editore, 1965. Survey of IB's life and films through *Winter Light,* with emphasis on the importance of his Protestant background.

Petríc, Vlada, ed. *Film and Dreams: An Approach to Bergman*. South Salem, N.Y.: Redgrave, 1981. Focus is on dream research and theory and on IB's use of dreams in his filmmaking.

Simon, John. *Ingmar Bergman Directs*. New York: Harcourt Brace Jovanovich, 1972. Interview with IB is followed by a model of how, ideally, films should be treated in books. Relevant frame enlargements accompany sensitive and incisive close readings of four IB films: *The Naked Night (Sawdust and Tinsel), Smiles of a Summer Night, Winter Light,* and *Persona.*

Sjögren, Henrik. *Ingmar Bergman på teatern (IB in the Theater)*. Stockholm: Almqvist och Wiksell, 1968. Study of IB's career in the theater.

Sjöman, Vilgot. *L 136: Diary with Ingmar Bergman*. Translated from the Swedish by Alan Blair. Ann Arbor, Mich.: Karoma, 1978. Intimate account of interactions with IB just before, during, and after he was shooting *Winter Light.* Invaluable source.

Steene, Birgitta. *Ingmar Bergman*. New York: Twayne, 1968. Insightful study of Bergman's plays and his films through *Persona.*

————. *Focus on "The Seventh Seal."* Englewood Cliffs, N.J.: Prentice-Hall, 1972. Interview with IB, overviews of IB by Jean Béranger, Marianne Höök, and James Scott, the text of *Wood Painting,* and essays and reviews relating to *The Seventh Seal.*

Törnqvist, Egil. *Bergman and Strindberg*. Stockholm: Prisma, 1973. Focus is on IB's interpretation of Strindberg's plays.

Ullmann, Liv. *Changing.* New York: Knopf, 1977. Insights into IB and his films in which she acted.

Widerberg, Bo. *Visionen i Svensk Film (Vision in Swedish Cinema).* Stockholm: Bonniers, 1962. Rejects IB's introspective films for realistic films.

Wood, Robin. *Ingmar Bergman.* New York: Praeger, 1969. Wood, one of the most sensitive and illuminating of IB critics, analyzes his films through *Shame.*

Young, Vernon. *Cinema Borealis: Ingmar Bergman and the Swedish Ethos.* New York: David Lewis, 1971; reprint, New York: Avon, 1972. Addresses IB's social and cultural background and surveys his films through *The Touch.* Filled with errors, Young's lively style and perverse dislike of most of IB's films are all that make this interesting.

Articles and Parts of Books

Andersson, Bibi. "Dialogue on Film." *American Film Institute* 2, no. 5 (March 1977).

Archer, Eugene. "The Rack of Life." *Film Quarterly* (Berkeley) (Summer 1959).

Buntzen, Lynda, with Carla Craig. *"Hour of the Wolf:* The Case of Ingmar B." *Film Quarterly* (Winter 1976–77).

Kinder, Marsha. "From *The Life of the Marionettes* to *The Devil's Wanton." Film Quarterly* (Spring 1981).

Koskinen, Maaret. "The Typically Swedish in Ingmar Bergman." *Chaplin* (25th anniversary issue, 1984).

Nykvist, Sven. "Photographing the Films of Ingmar Bergman." *American Cinematographer* (October 1962).

———. "Sven Nykvist, ASC, Talks about Filming Ingmar Bergman's *The Magic Flute," American Cinematographer* (August 1975).

Rosen, Robert. "The Relationship of Ingmar Bergman to E. T. A. Hoffmann." *Film Comment* (Spring 1970).

Sarris, Andrew. *"The Seventh Seal." Film Culture* (New York), no. 19 (1959).

Steene, Birgitta. "Bergman's Portrait of Women. Sexism or Subjective Metaphor." In *Sexual Strategems: The World of Women in Film,* ed. Particia Erens. New York: Horizon Press, 1979.

Ullmann, Liv. "Dialogue on Film." *American Film Institute* 2, no. 3 (March 1973).

Ulrichsen, Erik. "Ingmar Bergman and the Devil." *Sight and Sound* (London) (Summer 1958).

Wexman, Virginia Wright. "An Interview with Liv Ullmann." *Cinema Journal* 20, no. 1 (Fall 1980).

FILMOGRAPHY

The film titles are given in order of (1) Swedish (or German) distribution title, (2) literal English title if the film was not originally distributed in the United States, (3) American distribution title, and (4) if different, the British distribution title.

Hets (Pressure/Frenzy/Torment). Swedish Premiere: 2 October 1944.

Screenplay: IB. Director: Alf Sjöberg. Photography: Martin Bodin. Music: Hilding Rosenberg. Art Direction: Arne Åkermark. Editing: Oscar Rosander. Production Company: Svensk Filmindustri (SFI). 101 minutes.

Cast: Stig Järrel (Caligula), Alf Kjellin (Jan-Erik Widgren), Mai Zetterling (Berta Olsson), Gösta Cederlund (Pippi), Olof Winnerstrand (the principal), Stig Olin (Sandman), Jan Molander (Pettersson), Olav Riego (Mr. Widgren, Jan-Erik's father), Märta Arbiin (Mrs. Widgren, Jan-Erik's mother), Anders Nyström (Jan-Erik's brother), Hugo Björne (the doctor), Gunnar Björnstrand (a teacher), Birger Malmsten (a student), Bertil Sohlberg (boy in opening scene).

Kris (Crisis). Swedish Premiere: 25 February 1946.

Screenplay: IB, from the radio play *Moderdyret* (The Mother Heart) (1944) by Leck Fischer. Director: IB. Photography: Gösta Roosling (assistant: Jarl Nylander). Sound: Lennart Svensson. Music: Erland von Koch. Art Direction: Arne Åkermark. Editing: Oscar Rosander. Artistic Adviser: Victor Sjöström. Production Manager: Harold Molander. Assistant Director: Lars-Eric Kjellgren. Production Company: SFI. 93 minutes.

Cast: Dagny Lind (Ingeborg Johnson), Inga Landgré (Nelly), Marianne Löfgren (Jenny), Stig Olin (Jack), Alla Bohlin (Ulf), Ernst Eklund (Uncle Edvard), Signe Wirff (Aunt Jessie), Svea Holst (Malin), Arne Lindblad (the mayor), Julia Caesar (his wife), Dagmar Olsson (singer at ball), Siv Thulin (assistant in beauty salon), Karl Erik Flens (Nelly's friend at the ball).

Det regnar på vår kärlek (It Rains on Our Love/The Man with an Umbrella). Swedish Premiere: 9 November 1946.

Screenplay: IB and Herbert Grevenius, from the play *Bra mennesker* (Decent People) (1930) by Oskar Braaten. Director: IB. Photography: Göran

478

Strindberg, Hilding Bladh. Sound: Lars Nordberg. Music: Erland von Koch, with extracts from Richard Wagner and Bernhard Flies. Art Direction: P. A. Lundgren. Editing: Tage Holmburg. Producer: Lorens Marmstedt. Production Company: Sveriges Folkbiografer, distributed through Nordisk Tonefilm. 95 minutes.

Cast: Barbro Kollberg (Maggi), Birger Malmsten (David Lindell), Gösta Cederlund (man with the umbrella), Ludde Gentzel (Håkansson), Douglas Håge (Mr. Andersson), Hjördis Pettersson (Mrs. Andersson), Julia Caesar (Hanna Ledin), Sture Ericsson, Ulf Johansson (peddlers), Gunnar Björnstrand (Mr. Purman), Torsten Hillberg (vicar), Åke Fridell (assistant vicar), Erland Josephson (clerk in vicar's office), Benkt-Åke Benktsson (prosecutor), Erik Rosén (judge), Magnus Kesster (bicycle repairman), Sif Ruud (Gerti, his wife).

Kvinna utan ansikte (Woman without a Face). Swedish Premiere: 16 September, 1947.

Screenplay: IB. Director: Gustav Molander. Photography: Åke Dahlqvist. Music: Erik Nordgren. Art Direction: Arne Åkermark. Editing: Oscar Rosander. Production Company: SFI. 100 minutes.

Cast: Gunn Wållgren (Rut Köhler), Alf Kjellin (Martin Grandé), Anita Björk (Frida Grandé), Stig Olin (Ragnar Ekberg), Olof Winnerstrand (Director Grandé), Marianne Löfgren (Charlotte, Rut's mother), Georg Funkquist (Victor), Åke Grönberg (Sam Svensson), Linnea Hillberg (Mrs. Grandé, Martin's mother), Calle Reinholdz, Sif Ruud.

Skepp till Indialand (Ship to India/The Land of Desire). Swedish Premiere: 22 September 1947.

Screenplay: IB, from the play *Skepp till Indialand* (1946) by Martin Söderhjelm. Director: IB. Photography: Göran Strindberg. Sound: Lars Norberg, Sven Josephson. Music: Erland von Koch. Art Direction: P.A. Lundgren. Editing: Tage Holmberg. Title Design: Alva Lundin. Production Manager: Allan Ekelund. Producer: Lorens Marmstedt. Production Company: Sveriges Folkbiografer, distributed through Nordisk Tonefilm. 102 minutes.

Cast: Holger Löwenadler (Capt. Alexander Blom), Anna Lindahl (Alice, his wife), Birger Malmsten (Johannes Blom), Gertrud Fridh (Sally), Lasse Krantz (Hans, crewman), Jan Molander (Bertil, crewman), Erik Hell (Pekka, crewman), Peter Lindgren (foreign crewman), Naemi Briese (Selma), Hjördis Pettersson (Sofie), Åke Fridell (director of music hall), Gustaf Hiort af Ornäs, Torsten Bergström (Blom's companions), Ingrid Borthen (girl in street), Amy Aaröe (young girl), Gunnar Nielsen, Torgny Anderberg (men), Svea Holst (woman), Kiki (the dwarf).

Musik i mörker (Music in Darkness/Night Is My Future). Swedish Premiere: 17 January 1948.

Screenplay: Dagmar Edqvist, from her novel (1946) by the same name. Director: IB. Photography: Göran Strindberg. Sound: Olle Jakobsson. Music: Erland von Koch, with extracts from Chopin, Beethoven, Badarczewska-Baranowska, Schumann, Handel, Wagner, and Tom Andy (pseudonym for Thomas Andersen). Art Direction: P.A. Lundgren. Editing: Lennart Wallén. Production Manager: Allan Ekelund. Producer: Lorens Marmstedt. Production Company: Terraproduktion, distributed through Terrafilm. 85 minutes.

Cast: Mai Zetterling (Ingred Olofsdotter), Birger Malmsten (Bengt Vyldeke), Bibi Skoglund (Agneta Vyldeke, his sister), Olof Winnerstrand (Kerrman, the vicar), Naima Wifstrand (Beatrice Schröder), Åke Claesson (Augustin Schröder), Hilda Borgström (Lovisa), Douglas Håge (Kruge, restaurant owner), Gunnar Björnstrand (Klasson, violinist), Bengt Eklund (Ebbe Larsson), Segol Mann (Anton Nord), Bengt Logardt (Einar Born), Marianne Gyllenhammar (Blanche), John Elfström (Otto Klemens, blind worker), Rune Andreasson (Evert), Barbro Flodquist (Hjördis, Evert's mother), Ulla Andreasson (Sylvia), Sven Lindberg (Hedström, music director), Svea Holst (post office lady), Georg Skarstedt (Jönsson, waiter), Reinhold Svensson (half-drunk man), Mona Geijer-Falkner (woman with garbage bin), Arne Lindblad (chef), Stig Johansson (man), Britta Brunius (woman).

Hamnstad (Port of Call). Swedish Premiere: 18 October 1948.

Screenplay: Olle Länsberg, IB. Director: IB. Photography: Gunnar Fischer. Sound: Sven Hansen. Music: Erland von Koch, Adolphe Adam, Sven Sjöholm. Art Direction: Nils Svenwall. Editing: Oscar Rosander. Production Manager: Harald Molander. Assistant Directors: Lars-Eric Kjellgren, Stig Ossian Ericson. Production Company: SFI. 99 minutes.

Cast: Nine-Christine Jönsson (Berit Holm), Bengt Eklund (Gösta Andersson), Erik Hell (Berit's father), Berta Hall (Berit's mother), Mimi Nelson (Gertrud), Sture Ericson (Gertrud's father), Birgitta Valberg (Agnes Vilander, social worker), Hans Strååt (Vilander, probation officer), Harry Ahlin (man from Skåne), Nils Hallberg (Gustav), Sven-Erik Gamble ("the Oak"), Sif Ruud (Mrs. Krona), Kolbjörn Knudsen (seaman), Yngve Nordwall (factory foreman), Torsten Lilliecrona, Hans Sundberg (his buddies), Bengt Blomgren (Gunnar), Helge Karlsson (Gunnar's father), Hanny Schedin (Gunnar's mother), Stig Olin (Thomas), Else-Merete Heiberg, Erna Groth (girls in reformatory), Britta Billsten (street girl), Nils Dahlgren (police commissioner), Bill Houston (Joe), Herman Greid (German captain),

Kate Elffors (Berit as a child), Gunnar Nielsen, Georg Skarstedt (two men), Britta Nordin (salvationist), Vanja Rudefeldt (girl on dance floor), Greta Blom (policewoman), Estrid Hesse (salvationist), Carl Deurell (priest), Edvard Danielsson (parish clerk), John Björling (stevedore), Rune Andreasson (Squirt), Siv Thulin (girl).

Eva. Swedish Premiere: 26 December 1948.

Screenplay: Gustav Molander, IB, from a synopsis by IB. Director: Gustav Molander. Photography: Åke Dahlqvist. Editing: Oscar Rosander. Art Direction: Nils Svenwall. Music: Erik Nordgren. Production Company: SFI. 97 minutes.

Cast: Birger Malmsten (Bo), Eva Stiberg (Eva), Eva Dahlbeck (Susanne), Stig Olin (Göran), Åke Claesson (Fredriksson), Wanda Rothgardt (Mrs. Fredriksson), Inga Landgré (Frida), Hilda Borgström (Maria), Axel Hogel (Johansson, a fisherman), Lasse Sarri (Bo at 12).

Fångelse (Prison/The Devil's Wanton). Swedish Premiere: 19 March 1949.

Screenplay: IB. Director: IB. Photography: Göran Strindberg. Sound: Olle Jakobsson. Music: Erland von Koch, Alice Tegnér, Oscar Ahnfelt. Art Direction: P. A. Lundgren. Editing: Lennart Wallén. Producer: Lorens Marmstedt. Production Company: Terraproduktion, distributed through Terrafilm. 80 minutes.

Cast: Doris Svelund (Birgitta Carolina Söderberg), Birger Malmsten (Tomas), Eva Henning (Sofi, his wife), Hasse Ekman (Martin Grandé, film director), Stig Olin (Peter), Irma Christenson (Linnéa, Birgitta Carolina's sister), Anders Henrikson (Paul, mathematics teacher), Marianne Löfgren (Mrs. Bohlin), Åke Fridell (Magnus), Birgit "Bibi" Lindqvist (Anna Bohlin), Arne Ragneborn (Anna's boyfriend, a postman), Curt Masreliez (Alf), Carl-Henrik Fant (Arne, actor), Inger Juel (Greta, actress), Torsten Lilliecrona (cinematographer), Segol Mann (lighting technician), Börje Mellvig, Åke Engfeld (policemen), Lasse Sarri (little boy), Britta Brunius (his mother), Gunilla Klosterberg (dark lady), Ulf Palme (man in dream).

Törst (Thirst/Three Strange Loves). Swedish Premiere: 17 October 1949.

Screenplay: Herbert Grevenius, from the collection of short stories *Törst* (1949–50) by Birgit Tengroth. Director: IB. Photography: Gunnar Fischer. Sound: Lennart Unnerstad. Music: Erik Nordgren. Choreography: Ellen Bergman. Art Direction: Nils Svenwall. Editing: Oscar Rosander. Production Company: SFI. 88 minutes.

Cast: Eva Henning (Rut), Birger Malmsten (Bertil, her husband), Birgit Tengroth (Viola), Mimi Nelson (Valborg), Hasse Ekman (Dr. Rosengren), Bengt Eklund (Raoul), Gaby Stenberg (Astrid, Raoul's wife), Naima Wifstrand (Miss Henriksson, ballet teacher), Sven-Erik Gamble (worker in glass factory), Gunnar Nielsen (Rosengren's assistant), Estrid Hesse (patient), Helge Hagerman (Swedish pastor on train), Calle Flygare (Danish pastor), Monica Weinzierl (small Norwegian girl on train), Else-Merete Heiberg (her mother), Verner Arpe (German conductor), Sif Ruud (widow in cemetery), Gerhard Beyer (newspaper boy), Herman Greid (customs official), Oscar Rosander (intruder in hotel), Inga Gill, Inga Norin-Welton, Ingeborg Bergius (ballerinas), Peter Winner (German policeman), Britta Brunius (nurse), Wiktor Andersson (doorman), Ingalill Åström (pianist), Gustaf A. Herzing (policeman), Ingmar Bergman (train passenger), Erik Arrhenius (man).

Till glädje (To Joy). Swedish Premiere: 20 February 1950.

Screenplay: IB. Director: IB. Photography: Gunnar Fischer. Editing: Oscar Rosander. Music: Beethoven (Egmont Overture, First and Ninth Symphonies), Mozart, Mendelssohn, Smetana, Sam Samson, Erik Johnsson. Art Direction: Nils Svenwall. Production Company: SFI. 98 minutes.

Cast: Maj-Britt Nilsson (Märta Ericsson), Stig Olin (Stig Ericsson), Berit Holmström, Björn Montin (their children), Dagny Lind (grandmother), Victor Sjöström (Sönderby), Birger Malmsten (Marcel), John Ekman (Michael Bro), Margit Carlqvist (Nelly Bro), Sif Ruud (Stina), Erland Josephson (Bertil), Rune Stylander (Persson), Ernst Brunman (doorman at concert house), Allan Ekelund (vicar at wedding), Maud Hyttenberg (toyshop salesgirl), George Skarstedt (Anker), Svea Holm, Carin Swensson (two housewives), Ingmar Bergman (expectant father), Svea Holst, Agda Helin (nurses).

Medan standen sover (While the City Sleeps). Swedish Premiere: 8 September 1950.

Screenplay: Lars-Eric Kjellgren, from a story by P. A. Fogelström based on a synopsis by IB. Director: Lars-Eric Kjellgren. Photography: Martin Bodin. Editing: Oscar Rosander. Music: Erik Nordgren. Art Direction: Nils Svenwall. Production Company: SFI. 101 minutes.

Cast: Sven-Erik Gamble (Jompa), Inga Landgré (Iris), Adolf Jahr (her father), Märta Dorff (her mother), Elof Ahrle (Basen), Ulf Palme (Kalle Lund), Hilding Gavle (Hälaren), John Elfström (Jompa's father), Barbro Hiort af Ornäs (Rut), Carl Strom (Portis), Harriet Andersson.

Sånt händer inte här (High Tension/This Doesn't Happen Here). Swedish Premiere: 23 October 1950.

Screenplay: Herbert Grevenius, from the novel *I Løpet Av Tolv Timer (Within Twelve Hours)* (1944) by Waldemar Brøgger. Director: IB.

Photography: Gunnar Fischer. Editing: Lennart Wallén. Music: Erik Nordgren (music in export version by Herbert Stéen-Östling). Art Direction: Nils Svenwall. Production Company: SFI. 84 minutes. Cast: Signe Hasso (Vera Irmelin), Alf Kjellin (Björn Almkvist), Ulf Palme (Atkä Natas), Gösta Cederlund (doctor), Yngve Nordwall (Lindell, a policeman), Hannu Kompus (pastor), Els Vaarman (woman in cinema), Hugo Bolander (hotel manager), Sylvia Tael (Vanja), Edmar Kuus (Leino), Helena Kuss (woman at wedding), Rudolf Lipp ("the Shadow"), Ragnar Klange (Filip Rundblom), Lillie Wästfeldt (Rundblom's wife), Segol Mann, Willy Koblanck, Gregor Dahlman, Gösta Holmström, Ivan Bousé (Liquidatzia agents), Stig Olin (young man), Magnus Kesster (house owner), Alexander von Baumgarten (ship's captain), Hanny Schedin (lady), Gunwer Bergkvist (radio operator), Mona Geijer-Falkner (woman in apartment building), Erik Forslund (porter), Akke Carlsson (young man in car), Helga Brofeldt (shocked elderly woman), Georg Skarstedt (worker with hangover), Tor Borong (lab supervisor and theater manager), Maud Hyttenberg (student), Wera Lindby (shocked woman), Mona Åstrand (young girl), Fritjof Hellberg (ship's mate), Viktor "Kulörten" Andersson (projectionist), Harald Björling (second projectionist), Sten Hansson (cook), Eddie Ploman (forensic official), Ingemar Jacobsson (policeman).

Bris soap commercials. 1951.

"Bris Soap," "The Film Shooting," "The Film Showing," "The Rebus," "The Inventor," "The Magic Theater," "The Magic Show," "King Gustavus III," and "The Princess and the Swineherd" (with 15-year-old Bibi Andersson).

Sommarlek (Summer Interlude/Illicit Interlude). Swedish Premiere: 1 October 1951.

Screenplay: IB, Herbert Grevenius, from the story "Marie" by IB. Director: IB. Photography: Gunnar Fischer. Editing: Oscar Rosander. Art Direction: Nils Svenwall. Music: Erik Nordgren, Delibes, Chopin, Tchaikovsky. Production Company: SFI. 96 minutes.
Cast: Maj-Britt Nilsson (Marie), Birger Malmsten (Henrik), Alf Kjellin (David), Georg Funkquist (Uncle Erland), Renée Björling (Aunt Elizabeth), Mimi Pollak (Henrik's aunt), Annalisa Ericson (Kaj, ballerina), Stig Olin (ballet master), Gunnar Olsson (pastor), John Botvid (Karl, workman at the opera), Carl Ström (Sandell, stage manager), Torsten Lilliecrona (lighting man), Marianne Schuler (Kerstin), Ernst Brunman (steamer captain), Olav Riego (doctor), Fylgia Zadig (nurse), Sten Mattsson (boathand), Carl-Axel Elfving (man with flowers), Gösta Ström (Carlsson), Gun Skogberg (Marie as

ballerina), Eskil Eckert-Lundin (orchestra conductor), and the ballet corps of the Royal Opera.

Frånskild (Divorced). Swedish Premiere: 26 December 1951.

Screenplay: IB, Herbert Grevenius, from a synopsis by IB. Director: Gustav Molander. Photography: Åke Dahlqvist. Editing: Oscar Rosander. Art Direction: Nils Svenwall. Music: Erik Nordgren. Production Company: SFI. 103 minutes.

Cast: Inga Tidblad (Gertrud Holmgren), Alf Kjellin (Dr. Bertil Nordelius), Doris Svedlund (Marianne Berg), Hjördis Pettersson (Mrs. Nordelius), Håkan Westergren (man on train), Holger Löwenadler (Tore Holmgren, engineer), Irma Christenson (Dr. Cecilia Lindeman, Tore's new wife), Marianne Löfgren (Ingeborg), Stig Olin (Hans), Sif Ruud, Yvonne Lombard.

Kvinnors väntan (Secrets of Women/Waiting Women). Swedish Premiere: 3 November 1952.

Screenplay: IB. Director: IB. Photography: Gunnar Fischer. Editing: Oscar Rosander. Art Direction: Nils Svenwall. Music: Erik Nordgren. Production Company: SFI. 107 minutes.

Cast: Anita Björk (Rakel Lobelius), Jarl Kulle (Kaj), Karl-Arne Holmsten (Eugen Lobelius, Rakel's husband), Maj-Britt Nilsson (Märta Lobelius), Birger Malmsten (Martin Lobelius, Märta's husband), Eva Dahlbeck (Karin Lobelius), Gunnar Björnstrand (Fredrik Lobelius, Karin's husband), Aino Taube (Anita Lobelius), Håkan Westergren (Paul Lobelius, Anita's husband), Naima Wifstrand (Mrs. Lobelius, mother of the four brothers), Gerd Andersson (Maj, Märta's younger sister), Björn Bjelvenstam (Henrik, Anita and Paul's son), Kjell Nordensköld (Bob, the American), Torsten Lilliecrona (host at nightclub), Douglas Håge (doorman), Lena Brogren (hospital worker), Wiktor Andersson (refuse man), Lil Yunkers (Compere), Marta Arbiin (Sister Rit), Carl Ström (anesthetist), Ingmar Bergman (man in lobby).

Sommaren med Monika (Monika/Summer with Monika). Swedish Premiere: 9 February 1953.

Screenplay: IB, P.A. Fogelström, from a novel of the same name (1951) by Fogelström. Director: IB. Photography: Gunnar Fischer. Editing: Tage Holmberg, Gösta Lewin, IB. Music: Erik Nordgren, with the waltz "Kärlekens Hamn" (Haven of Love) by Filip Olsson. Art Direction: P. A. Lundgren, Nils Svenwall. Production Company: SFI. 96 minutes.

Cast: Harriet Andersson (Monika), Lars Ekborg (Harry), John Harryson (Lelle), Georg Skarstedt (Harry's father), Dagmar Ebbesen (Harry's aunt), Naemi Briese (Monika's mother), Åke Fridell (Monika's father),

Gösta Eriksson (Harry's boss in the glass shop), Gösta Gustafsson, Sigge Fürst, Gösta Prüzelius (employees in glass shop), Arthur Fischer (Monika's boss in the greengrocery), Torsten Lilliecrona (driver), Bengt Eklund, Gustaf Färingborg (Monika's coworkers), Ivar Wahlgren (owner of country home), Renée Björling (his wife), Catrin Westerlund (their daughter), Harry Ahlin (villager), Wiktor "Kulörten" Andersson and Birger Sahlberg (two men in street), Hanny Schedin (Mrs. Bohman), Åke Grönberg (Harry's construction boss), Magnus Kesster and Carl-Axel Elfving (workers), Anders Andelius, Gordon Löwenadler (Monika's boyfriends), Kjell Nordensköld, Margaret Young (stars in movie), Astrid Bodin, Mona Geijer-Falkner (women in window), Ernst Brunman (tobacconist), Nils Hultgren (pastor), Nils Whitén, Tor Borong, Einar Söderback (beer drinkers).

Gycklarnas afton (Eve of the Jesters / The Naked Night/Sawdust and Tinsel). Swedish Premiere: 14 September 1953.

Screenplay: IB. Director: IB. Photography: Hilding Bladh, Göran Strindberg, Sven Nykvist. Editing: Carl-Olov Skeppstedt. Music: Karl-Birger Blomdahl. Art Direction: Bibi Lindström. Costumes: Mago (Max Goldstein). Producer: Rune Waldekranz. Production Company: Sandrews. 92 minutes.

Cast: Harriet Andersson (Anne), Åke Grönberg (Albert Johansson), Erik Strandmark (Jens), Anders Ek (Frost), Gudrun Brost (Alma), Hasse Ekman (Frans), Gunnar Björnstrand (Mr. Sjuberg), Lissi Ahland, Karl-Axel Forsberg, Olav Riego, John Starck, Erna Groth, Agda Hilin (theater actors), Annika Tretow (Agda, Albert's wife), Kiki (dwarf), Åke Fridell (officer), Curt Löwgren (Blom), Julie Bernby (tightrope walker).

En lektion i kärlek (A Lesson in Love). Swedish Premiere: 4 October 1954.

Screenplay: IB. Director: IB. Photography: Martin Bodin. Music: Dag Wirén. Art Direction: P. A. Lundgren. Editing: Oscar Rosander. Production Company: SFI. 94 minutes.

Cast: Eva Dahlbeck (Marianne Erneman), Gunnar Björnstrand (Dr. David Erneman, her husband), Yvonne Lombard (Suzanne), Harriet Andersson (Nix), Carl Ström (Uncle Axel), Åke Grönberg (Carl Adam), Olof Winnerstrand (Prof. Henrik Erneman, David's father), Renée Björling (Svea Erneman, David's mother), Birgitte Reimar (Lise), John Elfström (Sam), Dagmar Ebbesen (nurse), Helge Hagerman (traveling salesman), Sigge Fürst (pastor), Gösta Prüzelius (train conductor), Arne Lindblad (hotel manager), Torsten Lilliecrona (hotel clerk), Georg Adelly (bartender), Ingmar Bergman (man on train).

Kvinnodröm (Women's Dreams/Dreams/Journey into Autumn). Swedish
Premiere: 22 August 1955.

Screenplay: IB. Director: IB. Photography: Hilding Bladh. Sound: Olle
Jakobsson. Art Direction. Gittan Gustafsson. Editing: Carl-Olov
Skeppstedt. Production Company: Sandrews. 86 minutes.

Cast: Eva Dahlbeck (Susanne), Harriet Andersson (Doris), Sven Lindberg
(Palle, her boyfriend), Benkt-Åke Benktsson (Magnus, fashion
director), Git Gay, Gunhild Kjellqvist (women in studio), Jessie Flaws
(makeup artist), Marianne Nielsen (Fanny), Siv Ericks (Katja), Bengt
Schött (fashion designer), Axel Düberg (photographer in studio),
Ludde Gentzel (Sundström, photographer in Gothenburg), Gunnar
Björnstrand (Consul Sönderby), Kerstin Hedeby (Marianne, Sönderby's
daughter), Naima Wifstrand (Mrs. Arén), Ulf Palme (Henrik Lobelius),
Inga Landgré (Mrs. Lobelius, his wife), Renée Björling (Professor
Berger), Tord Ståhl (Mr. Barse), Richard Mattsson (Månsson), Inga Gill
(shop girl), Greta Stare, Millan Lyxell, Gerd Widestedt, Margareta
Bergström, Elsa Hovgren (women in café), Per-Erik Åström (driver),
Carl-Gustaf Linstedt (porter), Asta Beckman (waitress).

Sommarnattens leende (Smiles of a Summer Night). Swedish Premiere: 26
December 1955.

Screenplay: IB. Director: IB. Photography. Gunnar Fischer. Sound: P. O.
Pettersson. Music: Erik Nordgren. Art Direction: P. A. Lundgren.
Costumes: Mago (Max Goldstein). Makeup: Carl M. Lundh. Editing:
Oscar Rosander. Production Company: SFI. 108 minutes.

Cast: Eva Dahlbeck (Désirée Armfeldt), Gunnar Björnstrand (Fredrik
Egerman), Ulla Jacobsson (Anne Egerman, his wife), Björn
Bjelvenstam (Henrik Egerman, Fredrik's son), Harriet Andersson
(Petra, the maid), Jarl Kulle (Count Carl-Magnus Malcolm), Margit
Carlqvist (Charlotte Malcolm, his wife), Naima Wifstrand (Madame
Armfeldt), Åke Fridell (Frid, the groom), Jullan Kindahl (Beata, the
cook), Gull Natorp (Malla, Desirée's maid), Birgitta Valberg, Bibi
Andersson (actresses), Anders Wulff (Desirée's son), Gunnar Nielson
(Niklas, Malcolm's aide), Gösta Prüzelius (footman), Svea Holst
(dresser), Hans Strååt (Almgren, the photographer), Lisa Lundholm
(Mrs. Almgren), Sigge Fürst (policeman), Lena Söderblom, Mona
Malm (chambermaids to Mrs. Armfeldt), Börje Mellvig, Georg Adelly,
Carl-Gustaf Linstedt (lawyers).

Sista paret ut (The Last Couple Out). Swedish Premiere: 12 November 1956.

Screenplay: IB, Alf Sjöberg, from a story by IB. Director: Alf Sjöberg.
Photography: Martin Bodin. Editing: Oscar Rosander. Art Direction:

Harald Garmland. Music: Erik Nordgren, Charles Redland, Bengt Hallberg. Production Company: SFI. 98 minutes.

Cast: Björn Bjelvenstam (Bo Dahlin), Olof Widgren (Bo's father), Bibi Andersson (Kerstin), Aino Taube (Kerstin's mother), Harriet Andersson (Anita), Eva Dahlbeck (Bo's mother), Märta Arbiin (Bo's grandmother), Jullan Kindahl (Alma, the Dahlin's maid), Jarl Kulle (Dr. Fårell), Nancy Dalunde (Mrs. Fårell), Jan-Olof Strandberg (Claes Berg), Hugo Björne (lecturer), Göran Lundqvist (small boy), Johnny Johansson (Sven Dahlin, Bo's eight-year-old brother).

Det sjunde inseglet (The Seventh Seal). Swedish Premiere: 16 February 1957.

Screenplay: IB. Director: IB. Photography: Gunnar Fischer. Sound: Aaby Wedin. Special Sound Effects: Evald Andersson. Music: Erik Nordgren. Music Direction: Sixten Ehrling. Art Direction: P. A. Lundgren. Editing: Lennart Wallén. Choreography: Else Fisher. Costumes: Manne Lindholm. Makeup: Carl M. Lundh, Inc. (Nils Nittel). Production Company: SFI. 95 minutes.

Cast: Max von Sydow (Knight Antonius Block), Gunnar Björnstrand (Squire Jöns), Bengt Ekerot (Death), Nils Poppe (Jof), Bibi Andersson (Mia), Erik Strandmark (Skat), Åke Fridell (Plog, the blacksmith), Inga Gill (Lisa, Plog's wife), Maud Hansson (witch), Gunnel Lindblom (silent girl), Bertil Anderberg (Raval), Anders Ek (monk who leads flagellants), Inga Landgré (Block's wife), Gunnar Olsson (painter), Benkt-Åke Benktsson (merchant), Lars Lind (monk outside church), Gudrun Brost (tavern hostess), Ulf Johansson (leader of soldiers), Ove Svensson (corpse on hillside).

Smultronstället (Wild Strawberries). Swedish Premiere: 26 December 1957.

Screenplay: IB. Director: IB. Photography: Gunnar Fischer. Sound: Aaby Wedin, Lennart Wallén. Music: Erik Nordgren. Music Direction: E. Eckert-Lundin. Art Direction: Gittan Gustafsson. Editing: Oscar Rosander. Costumes: Millie Ström. Makeup: Nils Nittel. Production Company: SFI. 90 minutes.

Cast: Victor Sjöström (Prof. Isak Borg), Ingrid Thulin (Marianne, Isak's daughter-in-law), Bibi Andersson (the two Saras), Gunnar Björnstrand (Evald, Isak's son), Folke Sundquist (Anders), Björn Bjelvenstam (Viktor), Naima Wifstrand (Isak's mother), Jullan Kindahl (Agda, Isak's housekeeper), Gunnar Sjöberg (Alman), Gunnel Broström (Mrs. Alman), Gertrud Fridh (Karin, Isak's wife), Åke Fridell (Karin's lover), Max von Sydow (Åkerman), Anne-Marie Wiman (Mrs. Åkerman), Sif Ruud (Isak's aunt), Yngve Nordwall (Uncle Aron), Per Sjöstrand (Sigfrid, Isak's brother), Gio Petré (Sigbritt), Gunnel Lindblom (Charlotta), Maud Hansson (Angelica), Eva Norée (Anna), Lena

Bergman, Monica Ehrling (the twins), Per Skogsberg (Hagbart), Göran Lundquist (Benjamin), Prof. Sigge Wulff (rector, University of Lund), Gunnar Olsson (bishop), Josef Norman (Professor Tiger), Vendela Rönnbäck (Sister Elizabeth).

Nära livet (Brink of Life/So Close to Life). Swedish Premiere: 31 March 1958.
Screenplay: IB, Ulla Isaksson, based on the short story "Det vänliga, det värdiga" (The Kind, the Dignified) in her book *Dödens Faster* (Aunt of Death) (1954). Director: IB. Photography: Max Wilén. Sound: Lennart Svensson. Art Direction: Bibi Lindström. Editing: Carl-Olov Skeppstedt. Make-up: Nils Nittel. Production Company: Nordisk Tonefilm. 84 minutes.
Cast: Ingrid Thulin (Cecilia Ellius), Erland Josephson (Anders Ellius, her husband), Eva Dahlbeck (Christina "Stina" Andersson), Max von Sydow (Harry Andersson, her husband), Bibi Andersson (Hjördis Pettersson), Barbro Hiort af Ornäs (Sister Brita), Inga Landgré (Greta Ellius, Anders's sister), Monica Ekberg (Hjördis's friend), Gunnar Sjöberg (Dr. Nordlander), Anne-Marie Gyllenspetz (social worker), Sissi Kaiser (Sister Marit), Margareta Krook (Dr. Larsson), Lars Lind (Dr. Thylenius), Gun Jönsson (night nurse), Inga Gill (woman), Gunnar Nielsen (a doctor), Maud Elfsiö (trainee nurse), Kristina Adolphson (assistant), Nine-Christine Jönsson (a mother).

Ansiktet (The Magician/The Face). Swedish Premiere: 27 December 1958.
Screenplay: IB. Director: IB. Photography: Gunnar Fischer. Sound: Aaby Wedin, Åke Hansson. Music: Erik Nordgren. Music Direction: E. Eckert-Lundin. Art Direction: P. A. Lundgren. Editing: Oscar Rosander. Costumes: Manne Lindholm, Greta Johansson. Makeup: Börje Lundh, Nils Nittel. Production Company: SFI. 100 minutes.
Cast: Max von Sydow (Albert Emanuel Vogler), Ingred Thulin (Aman/Manda Vogler, his wife), Åke Fridell (Tubal), Naima Wifstrand (Albert's grandmother), Bengt Ekerot (Spegel), Gunnar Björnstrand (Dr. Vergérus), Erland Josephson (Consul Abraham Egerman), Gertrud Fridh (Ottilia Egerman, his wife), Toivo Pawlo (Police Chief Starbeck), Bibi Andersson (Sara Lindqvist), Lars Ekborg (Simson, the coachman), Sif Ruud (Sofia Garp), Ulla Sjöblom (Henrietta, Mrs. Starbeck), Oscar Ljung (Antonsson), Axel Düberg (Rustan, the butler), Birgitta Pettersson (Sanna, the maid), Tor Borong, Arne Mårtensson, Frithiof Bjärne (customs officer).

Jungfrukällan (The Virgin Spring). Swedish Premiere: 8 February 1960.
Screenplay: Ulla Isaksson, based on a fourteenth-century legend, "Töre's Daughter in Vänge." Director: IB. Photography: Sven Nykvist. Sound:

Aaby Wedin. Music: Erik Nordgren. Makeup: Börje Lundh. Editing: Oscar Rosander. Costumes: Marik Vos. Art Direction: P. A. Lundgren. Production Company: SFI. 88 minutes.

Cast: Max von Sydow (Töre), Birgitta Valberg (Märeta, his wife), Birgitta Pettersson (Karin, his daughter), Gunnel Lindblom (Ingeri), Axel Düberg (herdsman), Tor Isedal (his mute brother), Ove Porath (his small brother), Allan Edwall (beggar monk), Axel Slangus (bridge keeper), Gudrun Brost (Frida, housekeeper), Oscar Ljung (Simon), Tor Borong, Leif Forstenberg (farmhands).

Djävulens öga (The Devil's Eye). Swedish Premiere: 17 October 1960.

Screenplay: IB, based on the Danish play *Don Juan Vender Tilbage* (Don Juan Returns) by Oluf Bang. Director: IB. Photography: Gunnar Fischer. Sound: Stig Flodin. Music: Erik Nordgren, with extracts from Scarlatti played by Käbi Laretei. Art Direction: P. A. Lundgren. Editing: Oscar Rosander. Sound Effects: Evald Andersson. Costumes: Mago (Max Goldstein). Makeup: Börje Lundh. Production Company: SFI. 86 minutes.

Cast: Gunnar Björnstrand (lecturer), Stig Järrel (Satan), Jarl Kulle (Don Juan), Sture Lagerwall (Pablo, Don Juan's servant), Nils Poppe (vicar), Gertrud Fridh (Renata, his wife), Bibi Andersson (Britt-Marie, their daughter), Axel Düberg (Jonas, her fiancé), Inga Gill (housemaid), Georg Funkquist (Count Armand de Rochefoucauld), Gunnar Sjöberg (Marquis Giuseppe Maria de Maccopazza), Torsten Winge (old man), Kristina Adolphson (veiled woman), Allan Edwall (ear devil), Ragnar Arvedson (devil in attendance), John Melin (beauty doctor), Sten-Torsten Thuul (tailor), Arne Lindblad (tailor's assistant), Svend Bunch (quick-change expert), Börje Lundh (hairdresser), Lenn Hjortzberg (enema doctor), Tom Olsson (black masseur).

Såsom i en spegel (Through a Glass Darkly). Swedish Premiere: 17 October 1961.

Screenplay: IB. Director: IB. Photography: Sven Nykvist. Sound: Stig Flodin. Music: Erik Nordgren, with extracts from J. S. Bach's Suite No. 2 in D Minor for Violincello, played by Erling Bengtsson. Art Direction: P. A. Lundgren. Editing: Ulla Ryghe. Costumes: Mago (Max Goldstein). Props: Karl-Arne Bergman. Sound Effects: Evald Andersson. Production Company: SFI. 89 minutes.

Cast: Gunnar Björnstrand (David), Harriet Andersson (Karin, his daughter), Lars Passgård (Minus, his son), Max von Sydow (Martin, Karin's husband).

Lustgården (The Pleasure Garden). Swedish Premiere: 26 December 1961.
Screenplay: Buntel Eriksson (pseudonym for IB and Erland Josephson).
Director: Alf Kjellin. Photography: Gunnar Fischer (Eastmancolor). Art
Direction: P. A. Lundgren. Music: Erik Nordgren. Sound: Lars Lalin.
Editing: Ulla Ryghe. Production Company: SFI. 93 minutes.

Cast: Gunnar Björnstrand (David Franzén), Sickan Carlsson (Fanny), Bibi
Andersson (Anna, her daughter), Stig Järrel (Lundberg), Kristina
Adolphson (Astrid), Per Myrberg (young pastor).

Nattvardsgästerna (The Communicants/Winter Light). Swedish Premiere: 11
February 1963.
Screenplay: IB. Director: IB. Photography: Sven Nykvist. Sound: Stig
Flodin. Music: Extracts from Swedish psalms. Art Direction: P. A.
Lundgren. Editing: Ulla Ryghe. Costumes: Mago (Max Goldstein).
Makeup: Börje Lundh. Sound Effects: Evald Andersson. Production
Company: SFI. 80 minutes.

Cast: Gunnar Björnstrand (Rev. Tomas Ericsson), Ingrid Thulin (Märta
Lundberg), Gunnel Lindblom (Karin Persson), Max von Sydow (Jonas
Persson), Allan Edwall (Algot Frövik), Kolbjörn Knudsen (Aronsson,
sexton), Olof Thunberg (Fredrik Blom, organist), Elsa Ebbesen (old
woman in church), Bertha Sånnell, Helena Palmgren (mother and
daughter in church), Eddie Axberg (Johan Strand, schoolboy), Lars-
Owe Carlberg (local police officer), Tor Borong (Johan Åkerblom),
Ingmari Hjort, Stefan Larsson (Perssons' daughter and son), Lars-Olof
Andersson, Christer Öhman (boys who discover body).

Tystnaden (The Silence). Swedish Premiere: 23 September 1963.
Screenplay: IB. Director: IB. Photography: Sven Nykvist. Sound: Stig
Flodin. Music: Ivan Renliden, R. Mersey's "Mayfair Waltz," and
excerpts from J.S. Bach's Goldberg Variations. Art Direction: P. A.
Lundgren. Editing: Ulla Ryghe. Costumes: Marik Vos-Lundh, Bertha
Sånnell. Makeup: Gullan Westfelt. Production Company: SFI. 96
minutes.

Cast: Ingrid Thulin (Ester), Gunnel Lindblom (Anna, her sister), Jörgen
Lindström (Johan, Anna's son), Håkan Jahnberg (hotel hall porter),
Birger Malmsten (waiter in bar), the Eduardinis (dwarfs), Eduardo
Gutierrez (their impresario), Lissi Alandh, Leif Forstenberg (woman
and man in theater balcony), Nils Waldt (cinema cashier), Birger
Lensander (cinema doorman), Eskil Kalling (man in bar), Karl-Arne
Bergman (newspaper seller in bar), Kristina Olansson (Lindblom's
double for sex scenes).

För att inte tala om alla dessa kvinnor (Now about These Women). Swedish
Premiere: 15 June 1964.

Screenplay: Buntel Eriksson (IB, Erland Josephson). Director: IB.
Photography (Eastmancolor): Sven Nykvist. Sound: P. O. Pettersson.
Mixing: Olle Jakobsson. Music: Erik Nordgren, with extracts from J.
S. Bach's Suite No. 3 in C Major and Suite No. 3 in D Minor. Art
Direction: P. A. Lundgren. Editing: Ulla Ryghe. Costumes: Mago
(Max Goldstein). Makeup: Börje Lundh, Britt Falkemo, Cecilia Drott.
Sound Effects: Evald Andersson. Production Company: SFI. 80
minutes.
Cast: Jarl Kulle (Cornelius), Bibi Andersson (Bumble Bee), Harriet
Andersson (Isolde, chambermaid), Eva Dahlbeck (Adelaide, Felix's
wife), Karin Kavli (Madame Tussaud), Gertrud Fridh (Traviata), Mona
Malm (Cecilia), Barbro Hiort af Ornäs (Beatrice, Felix's accompanist),
Allan Edwall (Jillker, Felix's impresario), Georg Funkquist (Tristan),
Carl Billquist (young man), Jan Blomberg (English radio announcer),
Göran Graffman (French radio announcer), Jan-Olof Strandberg
(German radio announcer), Gösta Prüzelius (Swedish radio announcer),
Ulf Johansson, Axel Düberg, Lars-Erik Liedholm (men in black), Lars-
Owe Carlberg (chauffeur), Doris Funcke, Yvonne Igell (waitresses).

Persona. Swedish Premiere: 18 October 1966.

Screenplay: IB. Director: IB. Photography: Sven Nykvist. Sound: P. O.
Pettersson. Mixing: Olle Jakobsson. Music: Lars Johan Werle, with
extracts from J. S. Bach's Violin Concerto in E Major. Art Direction:
Bibi Lindström. Editing: Ulla Ryghe. Costumes: Mago (Max
Goldstein). Makeup: Börje Lundh, Tina Johansson. Sound Effects:
Evald Andersson. Production Company: SFI. 84 minutes.
Cast: Bibi Andersson (Sister Alma), Liv Ullmann (Elisabet Vogler),
Margaretha Krook (doctor), Gunnar Björnstrand (Mr. Vogler), Jörgen
Lindström (boy in morgue).

Stimulantia (Nine Swedish directors—Hans Abramson, IB, Jörn Donner,
Lars Görling, Arne Arnbom, Hans Alfredson and Tage Danielsson, Gustav
Molander, Vilgot Sjöman—contributed a short film on a common theme;
IB's segment, entitled "Daniel," is about his and Käbi's son, Daniel, from birth
to two years of age). Swedish Premiere: 28 March 1967.

Idea, Director, Photography (Eastmancolor 16mm): IB. Editing: Ulla
Ryghe. Music: Käbi Laretei plays Mozart's "Ah, vous dirai-je, Maman"
(piano). Production Company: SFI. 15 minutes.
Cast: Daniel Sebastian Bergman, Käbi Laretei.

Vargtimmen (Hour of the Wolf). Swedish Premiere: 19 February 1968.

Screenplay: IB. Director: IB. Photography: Sven Nykvist. Sound: P. O. Pettersson. Mixing: Olle Jakobsson. Music: Lars Johan Werle, with excerpts from J. S. Bach's "Saraband" in Partita No. 3 in A Minor and Mozart's *The Magic Flute*. Art Direction: Marik Vos-Lundh. Editing: Ulla Ryghe. Costumes: Mago (Max Goldstein), Eivor Kullberg. Makeup: Börje Lundh, Kjell Gustavsson, Tina Johansson. Sound Effects: Evald Andersson. Production Company: SFI. 89 minutes.

Cast: Max von Sydow (Johan Borg), Liv Ullmann (Alma, his wife), Ingrid Thulin (Veronica Vogler), Georg Rydeberg (Archivist Lindhorst), Erland Josephson (Baron von Merkens), Gertrud Fridh (Corinne, the baron's wife), Gudrun Brost (the baron's mother), Bertil Anderberg (Ernst, the baron's brother), Ulf Johansson (Curator Heerbrand), Naima Wifstrand (old woman with hat), Lenn Hjortzberg (Kapellmeister Kreisler), Mikael Rundqvist (boy in fishing scene), Agda Helin (m. at the von Merkenses), Folke Sundquist (Tamino), Mona Seilitz (corpse on bier).

Skammen (Shame/The Shame). Swedish Premiere: 29 September 1968.

Screenplay: IB. Director: IB. Photography: Sven Nykvist. Sound: Lennart Engholm. Mixing: Olle Jakobsson. Art Direction: P. A. Lundgren. Editing: Ulla Ryghe. Costumes: Mago (Max Goldstein). Sound Effects: Evald Andersson. Makeup: Cecilia Drott. Hairstyles: Börje Lundh. Military Adviser: Stig Lindberg. Production Company: SFI/ Cinematograph. 102 minutes.

Cast: Liv Ullmann (Eva Rosenberg), Max von Sydow (Jan, her husband), Gunnar Björnstrand (Mayor Jacobi), Birgitta Vahlberg (Mrs. Jacobi), Sigge Fürst (Filip), Hans Alfredson (Lobelius, antiques dealer), Ingvar Kjellson (Oswald, victim in schoolhouse), Ulf Palme (man with dislocated shoulder), Björn Thambert (Johan, young deserter), Vilgot Sjöman (TV interviewer), Frank Sundström (interrogator), Ulf Johansson (doctor), Bengt Eklund (orderly), Åke Jörnfalk (condemned man), Barbro Hiort af Ornäs (woman in boat), Gösta Prüzelius (pastor), Rune Lindström (stout gentleman), Willy Peters (older officer), Per Berglund, Karl-Axel Forsberg (secretary), Brita Oberg, Gregor Dahlman, Brian Wikström, Monica Lindberg, Nils Whitén, Georg Skarstedt, Lillian Carlsson, Börje Lundh, Eivor Kullberg, K. A. Bergman, Stig Lindberg, Agda Helin, Ellika Mann, Nils Fogelby, Jan Bergman.

Riten (The Ritual/The Rite). Swedish Television Premiere: 25 March 1969.

Screenplay: IB. Director: IB. Photography: Sven Nykvist. Sound Recording: Olle Jakobsson. Art Direction: Lennart Blomkvist. Editing:

Siv Kanälv. Costumes: Mago (Max Goldstein). Production Company: SFI/Sveriges TV/Cinematograph. 72 minutes.

Cast: Erik Hell (Judge Abramson), Ingrid Thulin (Thea Winkelmann), Gunnar Björnstrand (Hans Winkelmann, her husband), Anders Ek (Albert Emanuelle Sebastian Fisher), Ingmar Bergman (priest).

En passion (A Passion/The Passion of Anna). Swedish Premiere: 10 November 1969.

Screenplay: IB. Director: IB. Photography (Eastmancolor): Sven Nykvist. Sound: Lennart Engholm. Sound Effects: Ulf Nordholm. Mixing: Olle Jakobsson. Music: Excerpts from J. S. Bach's Partita No. 3 in A Minor, and Allan Gray's "Always Romantic." Art Direction: P. A. Lundgren. Editing: Siv Kanälv. Costumes: Mago (Max Goldstein). Makeup: Cecilia Drott. Hairstyles: Börje Lundh. Set Decoration: Lennart Blomkvist. Sound Effects: Ulf Nordholm. Production Company: SFI/ Cinematograph. 101 minutes.

Cast: Max von Sydow (Andreas Winkelmann), Liv Ullmann (Anna Fromm), Birger Malmsten (Andreas Fromm), Erland Josephson (Elis Vergérus), Bibi Andersson (Eva, his wife), Erik Hell (Johan Andersson), Sigge Fürst (Verner), Svea Holst (Verner's wife), Annika Kronberg (Katarina), Hjördis Pettersson (Johan's sister), Lars-Owe Carlberg, Brian Wikström (policemen), Barbro Hiort af Ornäs (Mary in Anna's nightmare), Malin Ek, Britta Öberg, Marianne Karlveck (other women in nightmare).

Fårö-dokument (The Fårö Document). Swedish Television Premiere: 1 January 1970.

Director: IB. Photography (part Eastmancolor): Sven Nykvist. Sound: Arne Carlsson. Editing: Siv Kanälv. Production Company: Cinematograph. 78 minutes.

Cast: IB (Interviewer/reporter), local people of Fårö.

The Touch/Beröringen. U.S. Premiere: 14 July 1971. Swedish Premiere: 30 August 1971.

Screenplay: IB. Director: IB. Photography (Eastmancolor): Sven Nykvist; Gunnar Fischer, title sequence. Sound: Lennart Engholm, Bernt Frithiof. Music: Jan Johansson. Art Direction: P. A. Lundgren. Editing: Siv Kanälv-Lundgren. Costumes: Mago (Max Goldstein). Production Company: ABC Pictures/Cinematograph. 114 minutes. Filmed in English.

Cast: Bibi Andersson (Karin Vergérus), Max von Sydow (Dr. Andreas Vergérus, her husband), Staffan Hallerstam (Anders, their son), Maria

Nolgård (Agnes, their daughter), Barbro Hiort af Ornäs (Karin's mother), Elliott Gould (David Kovac), Sheila Reid (Sara Kovac, his sister), Åke Lindström (doctor), Mimmi Wahlander (nurse), Carol Zavis (stewardess), Dennis Gotobed (passport official), Margareta Byström (Andreas's secretary), Aino Taube (woman on staircase), Erik Nyhlén (archeologist), Harry Schein, Stig Björkman (guests at party).

Viskningar och rop (Cries and Whispers). World Premiere: 21 December 1972.

Screenplay: IB. Director: IB. Photography (Eastmancolor): Sven Nykvist. Sound: Owe Svensson. Music: Chopin's Mazurka in A Minor, No. 4, Opus 17, played by Käbi Laretei; J. S. Bach's Sarabande No. 5 in D Minor, played by Pierre Fournier. Art Direction: Marik Vos. Costumes: Greta Johansson. Makeup: Börje Lundh, Cecilia Drott, Britt Falkemo. Editing: Siv Lundgren. Production Company: Cinematograph/SFI. 90 minutes.

Cast: Harriet Andersson (Agnes), Ingrid Thulin (Karin), Liv Ullmann (Maria), Kari Sylwan (Anna), Erland Josephson (the doctor), Henning Moritzen (Joakim, Maria's husband), Linn Ullmann (Maria's daughter), Georg Åhlin (Fredrik, Karin's husband), Anders Ek (pastor), Inga Gill (Aunt Olga), Rosanna Mariano (Agnes as a child), Lena Bergman (Maria as a child), Monika Priede (Karin as a child), Greta and Karin Johansson (women dressing Agnes's body).

Scener ur ett Äktenskap (Scenes from a Marriage). Swedish Television Premiere (in six weekly segments): 11 April—16 May 1973.

Screenplay: IB. Director: IB. Photography (Eastmancolor, 16mm): Sven Nykvist. Sound: Owe Svensson. Art Direction. Björn Thulin. Costumes: Inger Pehrsson. Makeup: Cecilia Drott. Editing: Siv Lundgren. Production Company: Cinematograph. TV Version: 282 minutes. American Film Version: 155 minutes.

Cast: Liv Ullmann (Marianne), Erland Josephson (Johan), Anita Wall (interviewer), Bibi Andersson (Katarina), Jan Malmsjö (Peter), Gunnel Lindblom (Eva), Barbro Hiort af Ornäs (Mrs. Jacobi), Bertil Norström (Arne, Johan's colleague), Wenche Foss (Marianne's mother in TV version).

Trollflöjten (The Magic Flute). Swedish Television Premiere: 1 January 1975. Swedish Film Premiere: 4 October 1975.

Screenplay: IB, based on Mozart's opera, libretto by Schikaneder. Director: IB. Photography (Eastmancolor): Sven Nykvist. Sound: Helmut Mühle, Peter Hennix. Musical Direction: Eric Ericson. Art Direction: Henny Noremark. Editing: Siv Lundgren. Costumes: Karin Erskine.

Choreography: Donya Feuer. Production Company: Sveriges TV 2/
Cinematograph. 135 minutes.
Cast: Helene Friberg (girl in audience), Josef Köstlinger (Tamino), Irma
Urrila (Pamina), Håkan Hagegård (Papageno), Elisabeth Eriksson
(Papagena), Ulrik Cold (Sarastro), Birgit Nordin (Queen of the Night),
Ragnar Ulfung (Monostatos), Erik Saedén (speaker), Gösta Prüzelius
(first priest), Ulf Johansson (second priest), Hans Johansson, Jerker
Arvidson (two guards), Urban Malmberg, Ansgar Krook, Erland von
Heijne (three boys), Lisbet Zachrisson, Nina Harte, Helena Högberg,
Elina Letho, Lena Wennergren, Jane Darling, Sonja Karlsson (seven
girls), Einar Larson, Siegfried Svensson, Sixten Falk, Sven-Eric
Jacobsson, Folke Johnsson, Gösta Backelin, Arne Hendriksen, Hans
Kyhle, Carl Henric Qvarfordt (nine priests).

Ansikte mot ansikte (Face to Face). Swedish Television Premiere (in four 50-
minute weekly segments: "The Breaking Up," "The Border," "The Twilight
Zone," "The Return"): 28 April–19 May 1976. U.S. Premiere: 5 April 1976.
Screenplay: IB. Director: IB. Photography (Eastmancolor): Sven Nykvist.
Sound: Owe Svensson. Music: Mozart's Fantasy in C Minor, K. 475,
played by Käbi Laretei. Art Direction: Anne Terselius-Hagegård, Anna
Asp, Maggie Strindberg. Set Decoration: Peter Krupenin. Costumes:
Maggie Strindberg. Makeup: Cecilia Drott. Editing: Siv Lundgren.
Producers: IB, Lars-Owe Carlberg. Production Company:
Cinematograph. English-language version: 135 minutes.
Cast: Liv Ullmann (Dr. Jenny Isaksson), Aino Taube (her grandmother),
Gunnar Björnstrand (her grandfather), Sven Lindberg (Erik, her
husband), Helene Friberg (Anna, Jenny and Erik's daughter), Marianne
Aminoff (Jenny's mother) Gösta Prüzelius (Jenny's father), Erland
Josephson (Dr. Tomas Jacobi), Kari Sylwan (Maria), Ulf Johansson (Dr.
Helmuth Wankel), Sif Ruud (Elisabeth Wankel, his wife), Tore Segelcke
(lady in black), Gösta Ekman (Mikael Strömberg), Kristina Adolphson
(nurse), Birger Malmsten (older friend of rapist), Göran Stangertz
(rapist), Rebecca Pawlo, Lena Olin (boutique girls), Käbi Laretei
(pianist), Daniel Bergman, Ingrid (von Rosen) Bergman (in concert
scene).

Das schlangenei (Ormens ägg/The Serpent's Egg). German Premiere: 26
October 1977. Swedish Premiere: 28 October 1977. U.S. Premiere: 26
January 1978.
Screenplay: IB. Director: IB. Photography (Eastmancolor): Sven Nykvist et
al. Sound: Karsten Ullrich. Music: Rolf Wilhelm. Production Designer:
Rolf Zehetbauer. Art Direction: Erner Achmann. Editing: Petra von
Oelffen, Jutta Hering. Scenic Artist: Friedrich Thaler. Special Effects:

Karl Baumgartner. Choreography: Heino Hallhuber. Costumes: Charlotte Flemming. Makeup, Wigs, Hairstyles: Raimund Stangl et al. Producer: Dino De Laurentiis. Production Company: Rialto Film/Dino De Laurentiis Corporation. 119 minutes. Filmed in English.

Cast: David Carradine (Abel Rosenberg), Hans Eichler (Max, his brother), Gert Froebe (Inspector Bauer), Liv Ullmann (Manuela Rosenberg), Heinz Bennent (Hans Vergérus), James Whitmore (American priest), Glynn Turman (Monroe), Georg Hartmann (Papa Hollinger), Edith Heerdegen (Frau Holle), Fritz Strassner (Dr. Soltermann), Hans Quest (Dr. Silbermann), Walter Schmidinger (Solomon), Lisi Mangold (Mikaela), Grischa Huber (Stella), Paul Bürks (cabaret comedian), Emil Feist (cupid in cabaret), Heino Hallhuber (bride in cabaret), Irene Steinbeisser (groom in cabaret), Toni Berger (Mr. Rosenberg), Erna Brunell (Mrs. Rosenberg), Christian Berkel (student), Paul Burian (person in experiment), Heida Picha (wife), Gunther Malzacher (husband), Richard Bohne (policeman), Kyra Mladeck (Miss Dorst).

Höstsonaten (Autumn Sonata). Swedish Premiere: 8 October 1978.

Screenplay: IB. Director: IB. Photography (Eastmancolor): Sven Nykvist. Sound: Owe Svensson. Music: Excerpts from Chopin's Prelude No. 2 in A Minor, performed by Käbi Laretei; J. S. Bach's Suite No. 4 in E Flat Major, performed by Claude Genetay; and Händel's Sonata in F Major, Opus 1, performed by Frans Brüggen, Gustav Leonhardt, Anne Bylsmå. Set Design: Anna Asp. Editing: Sylvia Ingemarsdotter. Costumes: Inger Pehrsson. Makeup: Cecilia Drott. Production Manager: Katinka Faragó. Production Company: Personafilm. 93 minutes.

Cast: Liv Ullmann (Eva), Lena Nyman (Helena), Ingrid Bergman (Charlotte, their mother), Halvar Björk (Viktor, Eva's husband), Gunnar Björnstrand (Paul, Charlotte's agent), Erland Josephson (Josef), Arne Bang-Hansen (Uncle Otto), Georg Løkkeberg (Leonardo), Linn Ullmann (Eva as a child), Eva von Hanno (nurse).

Fårö-dokument 1979 (Fårö 1979). Swedish Television Premiere: 25 December 1979.

Screenplay: IB. Director: IB. Photography (color, 16mm): Arne Carlsson. Sound: Thomas Samuelsson, Lars Persson. Sound Rerecording: Owe Svensson. Music: Svante Pettersson, Sigvard Huldt, Dag and Lena, Ingmar Nordströms, Strix Q, Rock de Luxe, Ola and the Janglers. Narrator: IB. Editing: Sylvia Ingemarsson. Production Company: Cinematograph. 103 minutes.

Cast: IB (interviewer), various people from Fårö.

Aus dem leben der marionetten (From the Life of the Marionettes). Paris Premiere: 8 October 1980. U.S. Premiere: 7 November 1980. Swedish Premiere: 24 January 1981.

Screenplay: IB. Director: IB. Photography (B/W; Eastmancolor): Sven Nykvist. Sound: Peter Beil. Sound Rerecording: Milan Bor. Music: Rolf Wilhelm, including the song, in English, "Touch Me, Take Me" (singer uncredited). Production Design: Rolf Zehetbauer. Art Direction: Herbert Strabel. Editing: Petra von Oelffen (English-language version: Geri Ashur). Costumes: Charlotte Flemming, Egon Strasser. Fashion Show: Heinz A. Schulze-Varell Couture. Makeup: Mathilde Basedow. Production Company. Personafilm/Bayerische Staatsschauspiel. 104 minutes.

Cast: Robert Atzorn (Peter Egerman), Christine Buchegger (Katarina Egerman, his wife), Lola Müthel (Cordelia Egerman, his mother), Martin Benrath (Dr. Mogens Jensen), Rita Russek (Katerina "Ka" Krafft), Walter Schmidinger (Tomas Isidor "Tim" Mandelbaum), Heinz Bennent (Arthur Brenner), Ruth Olafs (nurse), Karl-Heinz Pelser (police investigator), Gaby Dohm (Peter's secretary), Toni Berger (peepshow doorman).

Fanny och Alexander (Fanny and Alexander). Swedish Premiere: 19 December 1982. Swedish Television Premiere (in four segments): 26 December 1982. U.S. Premiere: 16 June 1983.

Screenplay: IB. Director: IB. Photography (Eastmancolor): Sven Nykvist. Music: Daniel Bell. Sound: Owe Svensson. Sync: Sylvia Ingemarsson. Art Direction: Ann Asp. Set Decoration: Kaj Larsen. Editing: Sylvia Ingemarsson. Costumes: Marik Vos-Lundh. Makeup: Leif Qviström. Production Manager: Katinka Faragó. Executive Producer: Jörn Donner. Production Company: SFI/Sveriges TV 1/Personafilm/ Gaumont. 197 minutes. TV version: 300 minutes.

Cast: Gunn Wållgren (Helena Ekdahl), Allan Edwall (Oscar Ekdahl, her son), Ewa Fröling (Emilie, Oscar's wife), Bertil Guve (Alexander, their son), Pernilla Allwin (Fanny, their daughter), Börje Ahlstedt (Carl Ekdahl, Helena's son), Christina Schollin (Lydia, Carl's wife), Jarl Kulle (Gustav Adolf Ekdahl, Helena's son), Mona Malm (Alma, Gustav's wife), Maria Granlund (Petra, their daughter), Christian Almgren (Putte, their son), Angelica Wållgren (Eva), Emilie Werkö (Jenny), Siv Ericks (Alida), Inga Alenius (Lisen), Kristina Adolphson (Siri), Eva von Hanno (Berta), Majlis Granlund (Miss Vega, Helena's cook), Svea Holst-Widén (Miss Ester, Helena's parlor maid), Pernillo Wållgren (Maj), Käbi Laretei (Aunt Anna), Sonya Hedenbratt (Aunt Emma), Erland Josephson (Isak Jacobi), Mats Bergman (Aron Retzinsky), Stina Ekblad (Ismael Retzinsky), Jan Malmsjö (Bishop Edvard Vergerus),

Kerstin Tidelius (Henrietta, the bishop's sister), Marianne Aminoff
(Blenda, the bishop's mother), Marrit Olsson (Malla Tander, cook),
Brita Billsten (Karna, maid), Harriet Andersson (Justina, maid), Gunnar
Björnstrand (Filip Landahl, actor), Anna Bergman (Hanna Schwartz),
Gösta Prüzelius (Dr. Fürstenberg), Georg Årlin (colonel), Ernst
Günther (dean of university), Carl Billquist (police inspector), Lena
Olin (Rosa).

Karins ansikte (Karin's Face). 1983.

Screenplay: IB. Director: IB. Photography (B/W and Sepia): Arne Carlsson.
Editing: Sylvia Ingemarsson. Music: Käbi Laretei. Sound: Owe
Svensson. Production Company: Cinematograph. 14 minutes.
Screened at Cannes Festival: May 1984.

Efter repetitionen (After the Researsal). Swedish Television Premiere: 1984.

Screenplay: IB. Director: IB. Photography (color): Sven Nykvist. Art
Direction: Anna Asp. Costumes: Inger Pehrsson. Editing: Sylvia
Ingemarsson. Executive Producer: Jörn Donner. Production Company:
Released by Triumph Films. 72 minutes.
Cast: Erland Josephson (Henrik Vogler), Lena Olin (Anna Egerman), Ingrid
Thulin (Rakel, her mother), Bertil Guve (Henrik as a young boy),
Nadja Palmstjerna-Weiss (Anna as a young girl).

Den god viljan (The Best Intentions). Swedish Television Premiere (four 90-
minute episodes) (also released as a feature film): 1992.

Screenplay: IB. Director: Billie August. Photography (color): Jörgen
Persson. Art Direction: Anna Asp. Costume Design: Ann-Mari Anttila.
Editing: Janus B. Jansen. Music: Stefan Nilsson. Producer: Lars
Bjälkeskog. Production Company: Channel 1 (Sweden), ZDF
(Germany), Channel 4 (England), RAI 2 (Italy), La Sept (France), DR
(Denmark), NRK (Norway), YLE (Finland); distributed by Film Four
International, London. 181 minutes.
Cast: Samuel Fröler (Henrik Bergman), Mona Malm (Alma Bergman,
Henrik's mother), Pernilla August (Anna Bergman), Max von Sydow
(Johan Åkerblom, Anna's father), Ghita Nørby (Karin Åkerblom,
Anna's mother), Börje Ahlstedt (Uncle Carl Åkerblom), Lennart
Hjulström (Managing Director Nordenson), Lena Endre (Frida
Strandberg), Keve Hjelm (Fredrik Bergman), Hans Alfredson (Rev.
Gransjö), Lena T. Hansson (Magda Såll), Anita Björk (Queen
Viktoria), Elias Ringquist (Petrus Farg), Ernst Günther (Freddy Paulin),
Maria Göranzon (Elin Nordenson), Björn Kjellman (Ernst Åkerblom),
Björn Granath (Oscar Åkerblom), Gunilla Nyroos (Svea Åkerblom),
Mikael Segerström (Gustav Åkerblom), Eva Gröndahl (Martha

Åkerblom), Sara Arnia (Mrs. Johansson), Inga Landgré (Magna Flink), Emy Storm (Tekla Kronström), Barbro Kollberg (Gertrud Tallrot), Marie Rikardson (Märta Werkelin), Inga Alenius (Alva Nykvist), Roland Hedlund (Manager Nagel), Lena Brogren (Miss Lisen), Björn Gustafson (Jesper Jakobsson), Tomas Bolme (Jansson), Kåre Santesson (Måns Lagergren), Ingalill Ellung (Mejan), Gösta Prüzelius (Count Sheriff), Åke Lagergren (Chamberlain Segerswärd).

Söndagsbarn (Sunday's Children). 1992. Reviewed at Sandrews, Stockholm, 22 July 1992; competed in Montreal and Venice film festivals.

Screenplay: IB. Director: Daniel Bergman. Photography (color): Tony Forsberg. Music: Rune Gustafsson. Production Design: Sven Wichmann. Editing: Darek Hodor. Sound: Klas Engström. Costumes: Mona Theresia Forsén. Producer: Katinka Faragó. Production Company: Sandrews/Svenska Filminstitutet/Sweetland Films/Sveriges Television Kanal 1/Metronome Prods./Finlands Filmstiftelse/Islands Film Fond & Norsk Film with support of Nordic Film and TV fund and Eurimages/Europarâdet. Executive Producer: Klas Olofsson. 120 minutes.

Cast: Thommy Berggren (Pu's father), Henrik Linnros (Pu), Lena Endre (Pu's mother), Börje Ahlstedt (Uncle Carl), Jakob Leygraf, Anna Linnros, Malin Ek, Birgitta Valberg.

INDEX

THE AUTHOR

Professor Hubert I. Cohen earned his M.A. and Ph.D. degrees in English and American literature at the University of Michigan and has been teaching film and literature there for over 25 years. In 1975 he was awarded the university's Distinguished Service Award for Excellence in Teaching. He currently holds a joint appointment in the university's Film and Video Program and its Residential College. His courses include film history and criticism, the Western, and such major directors as Woody Allen, Frank Capra, Stanley Kubrick, Federico Fellini, and Ingmar Bergman.

He has published articles on literary topics—on Nathaniel Hawthorne and J. D. Salinger, for example—but most of his writing has been devoted to film: "The Serious Business of Being Funny," in Harold Lloyd's *An American Comedy* (1971); *"The Heart of Darkness* in *Citizen Kane,"* *Cinema Journal* (1972); articles on Werner Herzog and Wim Wenders in *Lightworks* (1979, 1980); and in *Magill's Cinema Annual,* studies of several of Bergman's films as well as Lawrence Kasdan's *The Big Chill,* Robert Bresson's *A Man Escaped,* Martin Ritt's *The Front,* and Oliver Stone's *Platoon.*